The Agreement on the European Economic Area (EEA)

A Guide to the Free Movement of Goods and Competition Rules

The Agreement on the European Economic Area (EEA)

A Guide to the Free Movement of Goods and Competition Rules

THÉRÈSE BLANCHET

Legal Officer
EFTA Secretariat

RISTO PIIPPONEN

Legal Officer
EFTA Secretariat

MARIA WESTMAN-CLÉMENT

Legal Officer
EFTA Court

CLARENDON PRESS · OXFORD
1994

Oxford University Press, Walton Street, Oxford OX2 6DP
Oxford New York Toronto
Delhi Bombay Calcutta Madras Karachi
Kuala Lumpur Singapore Hong Kong Tokyo
Nairobi Dar es Salaam Cape Town
Melbourne Auckland Madrid
and associated companies in
Berlin Ibadan

Oxford is a trade mark of Oxford University Press

Published in the United States
by Oxford University Press Inc., New York

British Library Publication Data
Data available

Library of Congress Cataloging in Publication Data
Blanchet, Thérèse.
The agreement on the European economic area (EEA): a guide to the free movement of goods and competition rules/Thérèse Blanchet, Risto Piipponen, Maria Westman-Clément.
p. cm.
Includes bibliographical references.
1. Free trade—European Economic Community countries. 2. Antitrust law—European Economic Community countries. 3. Free trade—European Free Trade Association countries. 4. Antitrust law—European Free Trade Association countries. 5. European Economic Area. I. Piipponen, Risto. II. Westman-Clément, Maria. III. Title.
KJC6456.B53 1994
341.7'543—dc20 94-7304
ISBN 0-19-825892-5
ISBN 0-19-825884-4

Typeset by Cotswold Typesetting Ltd, Gloucester

Printed in Great Britain
on acid-free paper by
Biddles Ltd, Guildford and King's Lynn

FOREWORD

by Mr Jacques Delors,
President of the European Commission

The coming into force of the Oporto Treaty setting up a European Economic Area (EEA) on 1 January 1994 marks a new stage in the process of European integration.

It is a symbol for the ever greater attraction the European Union is exerting on the whole of the continent, which is also reflected in the agreements it recently concluded with Central and East European countries.

It marks a further step in the longstanding process of rapprochement between the Union and EFTA countries. In this sense, the system set up under the EEA Treaty represents the most sophisticated category of linkage between the Union and Third Countries, short of accession to the Union. Under this agreement, the already close ties between EFTA economies and the Union will become even closer.

There is no doubt that the implementation of the agreement will have positive effects on the economy of the continent as a whole. This is likely to produce new economies of scale and to boost competitiveness, as did the completion of the Single Market amongst the twelve Member States of the European Union.

The EEA Treaty will as a result benefit companies in both the Union and the relevant EFTA countries. This book should help them take advantage of the new opportunities which will be opened up by the Treaty, and I congratulate the authors, all of whom have hands-on experience of the subject matter, for their most timely initiative.

However, the EEA Treaty also shows a willingness on the part of the relevant EFTA countries to associate themselves with the Union as a whole. In that sense it can be regarded as a sort of 'learning process' which will ease the way towards the full membership of the Union that some of them have applied for.

Nevertheless, this should not lead us into thinking that the EEA will only be a short-lived arrangement; first, one of the EFTA members of the EEA has no intention of joining the Union. Second, and more importantly, I still believe that EEA membership could constitute an adequate stepping stone to becoming full members of the Union for countries which, while politically committed to its ultimate objective, could not consider it, for economic reasons, in the immediate future. It would help them to prepare for joining the Union at a later stage in the best possible conditions.

Lastly, the EEA reflects the Union's openness to third countries and its ability to adapt itself to new challenges and circumstances. Far from shutting itself from the outside world in its own routine, the Union is ready to go beyond traditional partnership links and to devise tailor-made solutions to the specific problems faced by its partners, while at the same time preserving the integrity of its own decision-making process.

A good grasp of the EEA system is thus essential for understanding how the process of European integration is evolving, and I have no doubt that this book will make an important contribution to that understanding.

Brussels,
December 1993

PREFACE

COMPANIES and other economic agents active in the European market are increasingly confronted with a 'legislative jungle' developing not only in the European Community and in the twelve EC Member States, but also within certain decentralized countries, in *Länder* and other regions. The recently signed Agreement on the European Economic Area (EEA) which entered into force on 1 January 1994 will add not only some trees and thick bushes to this already overgrown jungle, but also five new countries.

Regardless of how long the EEA Agreement stays in force and given the unpredictability of the outcome of the ongoing membership process with four of the five EFTA countries which are part of the EEA, its entry into force will have a certain number of immediate effects on the legal framework in which undertakings operate in Europe; all the more so since the number and length of transitional periods granted to EFTA States are rather limited.

This book is not intended to be a remake, *à la sauce* EEA, of the numerous excellent books on EC law which have already been published (and to which we refer in our Bibliography) but rather to provide the reader with a sort of 'survival kit', concentrating on the areas of primary interest for business and industry, that is, the free movement of goods in a wide context, also comprising rules on competition, State aid, and public procurement.

The three authors participated in the EEA negotiations as officials in the EFTA Secretariat. Being lawyers, and thus sometimes drafters, we, together with our colleagues and the EFTA and EC experts, happily contributed here and there to the plantation of some trees and bushes. We have been enthusiastic in helping to extend, through the EEA, the four magic freedoms of the EC (goods, persons, services, and capital) to the EFTA States. However, we realized, perhaps with a little feeling of guilt, that the EEA Agreement, its structure, the legislative technique used, the 'two pillar' system, the taking over of a great deal of *acquis communautaire* while at the same time leaving aside certain aspects, make it quite difficult to read and to understand for laymen.

We hope that this book will help these, and even perhaps some of the initiated, to find their way in the EEA jungle. Some wicked tongues, undoubtedly jealous, say that lawyers are very good at making things complicated. We here modestly try to prove the contrary, while remembering the words of the philosopher Pascal: '*Ce qui se conçoit bien s'énonce clairement.*'

T.B.
R.P.
M.W.-C.
January 1994

The views expressed in this book are entirely those of the authors and do not necessarily reflect those of the European Free Trade Association or its member States.

ACKNOWLEDGEMENTS

We would like to thank Ambassador Bruno Spinner, Mr Harold Carter, Mr Gerard Kingham, Mr Sten-Göte Lindström, and Mr Wolfgang Mederer, who have provided us with information, commented on certain chapters, or otherwise contributed to the realization of this book.

CONTENTS

ABBREVIATIONS

CCT	Common Customs Tariff
CEECs	Central and Eastern European countries
CEN	European Committee for Normalization
CENELEC	European Committee for Electrotechnical Normalization
CPA	Community Patent Agreement
EC	European Community
ECJ	Court of Justice of the European Communities
ECR	European Court Reports
ECSC	European Coal and Steel Community
ECU	European Currency Unit
EDIFACT	Electronic Data Interchange for Administration
EEA	European Economic Area
EEC	European Economic Community[1]
EFTA	European Free Trade Association
EIB	European Investment Bank
EOTA	European Organization for Technical Approvals
EPC	European Patent Convention
EPO	European Patent Office
ERDF	European Regional Development Fund
ESA	EFTA Surveillance Authority
ESF	European Social Fund
ETSI	European Telecommunications Standardization Institute
EURATOM	European Atomic Energy Community
FTA	Free Trade Agreement
GATT	General Agreement on Tariffs and Trade
GDP	Gross Domestic Product
HS	Harmonized System
IPR	Intellectual Property Rights
JV	Joint Venture
MFN	Most Favoured Nation
NAFTA	North American Free Trade Agreement
OECD	Organization for Economic Co-operation and Development
OJ	*Official Journal of the European Communities*
PCT	Patent Co-operation Treaty
QR	Quantitative Restrictions

[1] The Treaty on the European Union (EU Treaty, which entered into force on 1 Nov. 1993) amended the EEC Treaty by changing the name of the European Economic Community (EEC) to European Community (EC) and by changing the contents and numbering of certain articles. Due to the late entry into force of the EU Treaty, the references in this book are still made, for technical reasons, to the former version of the EEC Treaty, upon which also the EEA Agreement was actually based.

SAD	Single Administrative Document
SC	Standing Committee (of the EFTA States)
SME	Small and Medium-sized Enterprises
TBT	Technical Barriers to Trade
TEDIS	Trade Electronic Data Interchange System
TRIPs	Trade-Related Intellectual Property Rights
UPOV	Union for the Protection of New Varieties of Plants
VAT	Value Added Tax
WIPO	World Intellectual Property Organization

I

INTRODUCTION

1. GENERAL

1.1 Why the EEA Agreement?

The Agreement on the European Economic Area (EEA Agreement), signed in Oporto, Portugal, on 2 May 1992 between the European Community (EC), its twelve Member States,[1] and the seven States[2] of the European Free Trade Association (EFTA), finds its roots in the very creation of EFTA and can be seen as the result of a long maturation in the relationships between the EC and the EFTA States.

EFTA was established in 1960 between those States[3] who, because they basically disagreed with its integrative aim, did not wish to become members of the EC. They opted rather for the creation of a free trade zone limited both as to its scope, mostly free trade in industrial goods, and as to its institutional framework, classical intergovernmental bodies without legislative powers or supranational elements. When Denmark and the United Kingdom joined the EC in 1973, each of the remaining EFTA countries concluded bilateral Free Trade Agreements with the Community[4] (referred to hereinafter as '1972 FTAs'), their scope being very similar to that of the Stockholm Convention. These Agreements were essentially aimed at guaranteeing the maintenance of free trade between the two new EC Member States and their ex-EFTA colleagues.

A further rapprochement of the EC–EFTA relations came in April 1984, in Luxembourg, where for the first time ever a joint meeting at ministerial level was held between the Community, its Member States, and the EFTA countries.[5] The

[1] Belgium, Denmark, France, Germany, Greece, Ireland, Italy, Luxembourg, the Netherlands, Portugal, Spain, and the United Kingdom.

[2] Austria, Finland, Iceland, Liechtenstein, Norway, Sweden, and Switzerland.

[3] Convention establishing the European Free Trade Association (so-called Stockholm Convention) signed on 4 Jan. 1960, entered into force on 3 May 1960. Its founding members were Austria, Denmark, Norway, Portugal, Sweden, Switzerland, and the United Kingdom. Thereafter Iceland (1 Mar. 1970), Finland (1 Jan. 1986), and Liechtenstein (1 Sept. 1992) acceded to the Convention. Denmark and the United Kingdom (1 Jan. 1973) and Portugal (1 Jan. 1986) withdrew from the Convention as they acceded to the EC.

[4] The EC–Austria, EC–Sweden, and EC–Switzerland FTAs have been published in *OJ* L 300 (31 Dec. 1972), 1 *et seq.*, the EC–Iceland FTA in *OJ* L 301 (31 Dec. 1972), 1, the EC–Norway FTA in *OJ* L 171 (27 June 1973), 1, and the EC–Finland FTA in *OJ* L 328 (28 Nov. 1973), 1.

[5] For further details, see 1984: *Twenty-fourth Annual Report of the European Free Trade Association* (Geneva, Mar. 1985).

Ministers acknowledged the fact that the remaining tariff barriers and quantitative restrictions affecting their bilateral trade in industrial products had been abolished in early 1984. They then started what was later on called the 'Luxembourg process' or 'Luxembourg follow-up', whose purpose was to extend co-operation beyond the framework of the Free Trade Agreements in the different fields considered as being of mutual interest. Expert work therefore began on issues such a reduction of technical barriers to trade, in particular through European standardization (joint work in CEN and CENELEC[6]), simplification of trade documentation (Single Administrative Document (SAD)), research and development, mobility of qualified workers, intellectual property, social and consumer matters, and increased contacts in economic and monetary policy. Things went fairly smoothly but this was still a step-by-step strategy, somewhat lacking a wider underpinning project.[7]

As the EC launched its programme for further integration through the completion of the internal market[8] and the symbolic target date of 31 December 1992, the EFTA States increasingly felt the need for a closer relationship with their main trading partner.[9] They therefore welcomed the proposal made in January 1989[10] by Mr Jacques Delors, President of the EC Commission, to strengthen the relations between the EC and the EFTA States through a new form of association. This would be more institutionally structured, with common decision-making and management bodies, the co-operation being based on two pillars consisting of both organizations, the EC and EFTA.

1.2 EEA negotiations

The Delors invitation was the starting-point of the negotiations leading to the signature of the EEA Agreement. The EC Commission obtained its negotiation mandate from the EC Council on 18 June 1990 and the EEA negotiations formally started on 20 June 1990. On several occasions the Ministers or the chief negotiators of both sides stated their strong willingness to conclude the negotiations before the winter, before the summer, or before a given date or month. Several times 'historical breakthroughs' were proudly announced, followed by inevitable 'crisis'.

The EFTA countries, although a bit puzzled in the beginning, were very quick in learning the sinusoidal curves EC negotiations usually follow, where noisy celebrations alternate with deep dramas, in a *tragediente comediente* atmosphere.

[6] Abbreviations for European Committee for Normalization and European Committee for Electrotechnical Normalization.

[7] For further details, see *EFTA: The European Free Trade Association* (Geneva, Mar. 1985).

[8] Commission Communication on the completion of the internal market, COM (85) 310 final, the so-called White Paper.

[9] In 1992 61.8% of EFTA imports came from the EC and 60.1% of their exports went to the EC. The EFTA States absorbed 24.2% of EC exports to third countries, i.e. more than the USA and Japan together, and imports from the EFTA States accounted for 22.8% of third countries' imports to the EC (figures excluding intra-EC trade: see *EFTA Trade in 1992* (EFTA, Economic Affairs Dept., Apr. 1994)).

[10] Speech in the European Parliament of 17 Jan. 1989, Europe Docs. 1542/1543, 26 Jan. 1989.

The partners, including the different EC institutions, conscientiously fulfilled their role in the play.

In August 1991, in accordance with Article 228 of the EEC Treaty, the EC Commission asked the EC Court of Justice (ECJ) for its opinion on the compatibility with the EEC Treaty of the judicial mechanism planned in the EEA Agreement (i.e. the creation of an EEA Court). In the meantime the partners, who had forgotten this detail, concluded the negotiations on 22 October 1991 in Luxembourg. Some bottles of champagne were even opened. EC and EFTA officials had started to make frantic preparations for the signature of the Agreement when the ECJ decreed that, 'Au vu des problèmes graves et complexes que soulève la demande d'avis dont la Commission l'a saisie', a hearing would be held on 26 November 1991. This evident warning from the Court was followed by a very severe Opinion,[11] under which the EEA judicial system was said to conflict with the very foundations of the Community and thus to be incompatible with the EEC Treaty.

The three problem areas in the Court's eyes being competition (the percentage system for attributing the cases between the EC and EFTA pillars), dispute settlement, and safeguarding of homogeneity (uniform interpretation of common rules), there was no choice for the negotiators but to reconvene and try to find a solution. The renegotiations were concluded on 14 February 1992 after which the EC Commission, on 25 February 1992, again asked the ECJ for its opinion on the newly agreed texts.[12] Even the European Parliament claimed the right to submit observations to the EC Court, which it did in a letter to the ECJ President on 25 March 1992. In Opinion 1/92, delivered on 10 April 1992,[13] the Court stated that the new texts were compatible with the EEC Treaty.

1.3 Ratification process

The EEA Agreement was ready to be officially signed in Oporto on 2 May 1992. The ratification process began thereafter. It progressed smoothly until 6 December 1992, when Switzerland, in a referendum, refused to ratify the Agreement. This triggered another renegotiation between the EC side and the remaining EFTA States[14] in order to make the necessary adaptations to the Agreement, that is, to delete all references to Switzerland, and in particular to solve the question of the now missing Swiss 27 per cent share in the Cohesion Fund. The Protocol adjusting the EEA Agreement was signed between the remaining Contracting Parties on 17 March 1993 and should in principle have been ratified before 1 July 1993.[15]

[11] Opinion 1/91 of 14 Dec. 1991 [1991] ECR I-6079.

[12] i.e. on the amended Art. 56 on attribution of competition cases between the EC and EFTA pillars, the creation of an EFTA Court (Art. 108 (2)), the follow-up of case-law and exchange of information (Arts. 105 and 106), and the dispute settlement mechanism (Art. 111).

[13] [1992] ECR I-282.

[14] i.e. without Switzerland.

[15] The EEA Agreement and its Adjusting Protocol, having been ratified by the five EFTA States, the

1.4 The EEA Agreement in perspective

When considered in a historical perspective and in the wider context of the build-up of closer links in Europe, the EEA Agreement is the final stage of EC–EFTA relations which started to develop more than thirty years ago. The EFTA States were always hesitant about the very idea of the European Community. Three of their former partners joined the EC club and one, Norway, failed to do so. The remaining EFTA countries felt uncomfortable, which became even more apparent after the fall of the Berlin Wall, as it encouraged the Central and Eastern European countries to approach the Community. However, at that time both the EC and EFTA still considered the traditional free trade approach to be safer. For EFTA, it had the advantage of being politically more saleable at home, while it would permit the EC to keep potential applicants busy, thus allowing the Community first to deepen before enlarging.

Although five EFTA States[16] have lodged their accession applications, the EEA Agreement will have a special role in the European architecture, the difficulties encountered at its birth being proportionate to the revolution it brought in the mentalities of the governments and public opinions of the EFTA countries. Furthermore, it is interesting to note that Mr Delors, in a speech on 10 September 1993 referring to a plan of action for stabilizing the situation in Central and Eastern Europe, proposed to link these countries to the EC 'beginning with association, then accession to the European Economic Area, and finally Community membership, the ultimate goal'.[17]

Finally, the EEA, as it will account for 43.2 per cent of international trade,[18] may without any doubt be seen as part of the trend in world economy towards the creation of big regional trading blocks between neighbours, such as the NAFTA, for instance (which was also due to enter into force on 1 January 1994).[19]

2. EEA INSTITUTIONS

In accordance with what was already foreseen by Mr Delors in his speech of 17 January 1989, the institutional framework of the EEA lies on two pillars: the EC, with its institutions, and EFTA, which had to set up its own institutions.

twelve EC Member States, and the competent Community institutions (the Council for the EEC and the Commission for the ECSC after approval of the European Parliament), entered into force on 1 Jan. 1994 (published in *OJ* L 1 (3 Jan. 1994), 1). As regards Liechtenstein, see further Ch. XI s. 4.

[16] Austria (in July 1989), Sweden (in July 1991), Finland (in Mar. 1992), Switzerland (in May 1992), and Norway (in Nov. 1992). Official membership negotiations started on 1 Feb. 1993 with Austria, Finland, and Sweden and on 5 Apr. 1993 with Norway. The Swiss application has been 'frozen' for the time being.

[17] Speech delivered at annual meeting of the International Institute for Strategic Studies in Brussels.

[18] See *EFTA Trade in 1992*, op. cit. n. 9. The population of the EEA is 371.5 million people.

[19] North American Free Trade Agreement, approved on 17 Nov. 1993 by the US House of Representatives, which creates a free trade zone between the USA, Canada, and Mexico. See 'The trade winds shift', *The Economist* (20 Nov. 1993).

Therefore, under two Agreements also signed on 2 May 1992 in Oporto,[20] the EFTA States established three new institutions: the EFTA Standing Committee, a sort of EFTA Council for the purposes of the EEA composed of representatives of the EFTA countries; the EFTA Surveillance Authority (ESA), an independent body for ensuring that the EFTA States fulfil their EEA obligations and for applying the competition rules; and the EFTA Court, with competences comparable to those of the ECJ (e.g. infringement proceedings, actions for annulment, etc.).

There will also be a forum for the EC and EFTA to consult each other and to take common decisions: the EEA Council, the highest political body, meeting at ministerial level, and the EEA Joint Committee, which will be in charge of taking decisions and administering the Agreement. Joint discussions will also be held between parliamentarians and social partners of the two pillars.

3. SUBSTANTIVE RULES OF THE EEA AGREEMENT

3.1 General

The Agreement extends the internal market with its four freedoms, i.e. free movement of goods, persons, services, and capital, as well as some horizontal and flanking policies (e.g. environment or social policy), to the EFTA countries. In these areas, whether Community rules or EEA rules are applied, the legal result should in substance be the same. The Agreement does not, however, include agriculture, fiscal harmonization (directives on VAT and excise duties), and EC common policies, notably towards third countries.

The relevant Community secondary legislation (regulations, directives, and decisions) taken over in the EEA context is listed in the annexes[21] to the Agreement. These legal acts are referred to by their title and publication data in the *Official Journal of the EC*. Any specific adaptations relevant for the application of the act in the EEA context (e.g. transitional periods) are spelled out in connection hereto. Protocol 1 on horizontal adaptations is of the greatest importance. It should be taken as a 'key' or 'decoder' for understanding the EC secondary legislation for EEA purposes. It clarifies how to read, in the EEA context, the preambles, the provisions relating to EC committees, references to territories, use of language, etc.

In order to ensure the uniform application of these common rules, each provision in the Agreement which, in substance, is identical to a corresponding EC rule shall be interpreted in conformity with the relevant rulings of the ECJ given prior to the signature of the Agreement (2 May 1992). Specific procedures are foreseen for the

[20] i.e. Agreement on a Standing Committee of the EFTA States (SC Agreement) and Agreement between the EFTA States on the Establishment of a Surveillance Authority and a Court of Justice (ESA/Court Agreement).

[21] There are however also some protocols referring to secondary legislation.

subsequent case-law. Thus, ECJ case-law is of substantial importance in the understanding of the EEA Agreement.

A homogeneous EEA also requires that relevant new Community legislation be integrated into the Agreement. The Agreement currently contains the relevant EC acts adopted by 31 July 1991, a cut-off date decided upon at a time when the parties thought the Agreement would enter into force much sooner. Due to the delaying of the entry into force, the back-log of *acquis* adopted between that cut-off date and the actual entry into force of the Agreement is quite important. Those EC acts adopted after 31 July 1991 will be scrutinized in the EEA Joint Committee right after the entry into force for a decision on whether they are relevant for the EEA and thus to be included in the Agreement (this is often called the 'Additional Package'). Any such decision will be published in a special EEA section of the *Official Journal of the EC*, as well as, regarding Nordic languages, in a special EEA Supplement.

3.2 Product coverage and rules of origin

Compared to the EEC Treaty, the EEA Agreement has a more limited product coverage.[22] This limitation has certain consequences for the different parts of the Agreement involving goods, all the more so since there are exceptions to the rule. For instance, in contrast to the competition or State aid provisions, intellectual property rules apply to 'all products and services', i.e. also to basic agricultural products.

Moreover, the inclusion of a certain number of processed agricultural products within the scope of the Agreement involves price compensation measures which are needed as a result of differing domestic regimes for the production and sale of agricultural commodities incorporated in the products.

Furthermore, since it does not create a customs union but merely a free trade zone, the EEA Agreement had to contain origin rules defining those products having an EEA origin and which thus qualify for the preferential treatment granted under the EEA regime. These rules are designed to avoid circumvention of duties, in the sense that third country products might enter the EEA market through the country with the lowest third country customs tariff. Such rules also mean in practice that border controls, although simplified, cannot be abolished. The Agreement provides as well for full cumulation, general tolerance rules, and simplification of evidence of origin.

3.3 Technical barriers to trade

In the area of technical regulations, standards, testing, and certification, the EEA Agreement provides for harmonization of national laws. In fact, Annex II to the

[22] It covers industrial goods and certain processed agricultural products which are referred to by using the Harmonized Commodity Description and Coding System (HS).

Agreement contains some 600 Community acts, mainly directives, in areas as divergent as motor vehicles, measuring instruments, electrical material, foodstuffs, medicinal products, chemicals, telecommunications, construction products, toys, machinery, etc.

The directives are either of a full harmonization or of an optional character. A subject-matter regulated by an optional directive assures the manufacturer of market access if his product conforms to the requirements of the directive. However, it does not rule out the possibility of parallel national legislation covering the same subject-matter. The manufacturer is therefore free to choose whether to benefit, through the directive, from the market access or only to comply with a national law. On the other hand, in areas regulated by means of full harmonization, only those products that conform to the requirements of such directives can be lawfully put on the market. In the latter case the manufacturer is thus confronted with one law to which his products will have to conform.

In non-harmonized fields, or in areas where the harmonization is only optional, the principle of mutual recognition will apply. That principle emanates from the ECJ *Cassis de Dijon* rulings and implies, in the EEA context, that a product lawfully produced and put on the market in an EFTA State can also be sold on the Community market and vice versa. This main rule is however subject to exceptions relating, *inter alia*, to the protection of public health and environment.

Another important aspect relates to conformity assessment. The EC and EFTA countries will employ the same conformity mark, the CE mark. Test laboratories, so-called 'notified bodies', and/or manufacturers within the whole EEA will have the right to affix such a mark, and no distinction will be made between tests carried out in an EFTA State or within the Community.

3.4 Intellectual property

In the EC the traditionally limited territorial application of national intellectual property laws rapidly caused concern, as it emerged that the differences between laws constituted barriers to trade and a means to distort competition. Intellectual property rights have been tackled from three angles: free movement of goods (Articles 30 and 36 EEC, case-law of the ECJ on EC-wide exhaustion of rights), competition rules (group exemptions on patent licensing and know-how licensing agreements), and harmonization of national laws (on the basis of Article 100*a*), including the planned creation of EC-wide intellectual property rights (Community patent, Community trade mark, etc.). In view of the completion of the Single Market in 1992, the Community put more emphasis on harmonization of intellectual property laws and on the creation of EC-wide intellectual property rights.

The EEA Agreement takes over the three dimensions of EC intellectual property law, including some third country aspects. One of the main novelties the EEA brings to the EFTA States is the application of the regional exhaustion principle, under which intellectual property right holders can no longer use their right to impede parallel imports of products which have been put on the EEA market by them or with their consent.

The extension of EC intellectual property legislation and concepts to seventeen countries in Europe as well as the inclusion of intellectual property provisions in the different agreements with Central and Eastern European countries will certainly have an impact in the intellectual property discussions held in international settings such as WIPO or GATT.

3.5 Product liability

The EEA Agreement will impose the same obligations on producers and/or importers throughout the EEA for the risks created by their products for consumers. In fact, the question of product liability was solved by integrating the Council Directive 85/374/EEC into the Agreement (Annex III) and therefore giving EEA-wide application to the concept of liability disregarding fault ('strict liability').

As concerns the very important question of the importer's liability, the main rule will be that any person who imports from a third country into the EEA shall, without prejudice to the liability of the producer, be responsible as a producer. However, concerning imports from an EFTA State into the Community or vice versa or between EFTA countries, the importer's liability will only be waived between those States having ratified the Lugano Convention on jurisdiction and the enforcement of judgments in civil and commercial matters.

3.6 Public procurement

One of the central elements of the EEA Agreement for many businesses is the opening up of the procurement market. Public procurement in the EEA will be a large and lucrative market for potential bidders, as the Community places some 600 billion ECU/year in procurement orders and the EFTA countries some 50 to 60 billion. In this area too the EEA rules are based on the Community *acquis*, comprising directives on supplies, works, utilities, and legal remedies.

The rules provide for EEA-wide advertising of contracts, enabling manufacturers throughout the whole EEA to have an equal bidding opportunity. Technical specifications must be included in the contractual documents put out by the purchaser and, in order not to create barriers to trade, European standards or national standards implementing such standards should be used as far as possible. Furthermore, the purchaser should use only one of two criteria in determining the successful bid: 'lowest price' or 'most economically advantageous tender'.

Finally, the availability of rapid legal remedies will mean that purchasers risk a legal action if they infringe the rules.

3.7 Competition rules

It was obvious from the outset that strict competition rules would be needed in the EEA to avoid the companies involved nullifying, through the establishment of private trade barriers, the benefits expected from the introduction of free movement of goods and services. It was also clearly realized that it would be impractical and even impossible to create new competition rules for the EEA. The easiest solution was to base the EEA system on the existing EC rules. This applied both to the substance and to the procedural rules.

The EEA competition rules will, for the EFTA States, constitute a major advance when compared with the legal situation prevailing under both the Stockholm Convention (Article 15) and the Free Trade Agreements (FTAs) with the EC (Article 23). These two Agreements only provide for classical intergovernmental discussions, resulting in possible recommendations or reports, but without any direct power over the undertakings themselves or direct right for the companies to complain. The provisions have never been significantly used and can certainly not be compared with the active enforcement which has existed in the EC for thirty years.

The introduction of common competition rules will, *inter alia*, mean that undertakings operating in Europe will find themselves in the same legal framework in the seventeen countries of the EEA and that, thus, the well-known extra-territorial effects of EC competition rules will no longer apply to undertakings in EFTA States. Identical competition rules will also mean that, in principle, the use of anti-dumping measures within the EEA will not be possible. There are, however, some exceptions due to the different product coverage of the EEA and the EC.

Another new element is that, thanks to the 'one-stop shop' principle and a system of attribution of cases, only one of the pillars will be in charge of a given case. In order to ensure a smooth functioning of the competition procedures and to avoid delays in the handling of cases, a system of co-operation between the Commission and ESA is provided for. It concerns not only exchange of notifications and other information, but also participation in hearings and advisory committee meetings. A particular element, having a direct effect on undertakings, is the administrative assistance the two pillars will have to grant each other. For instance, the EC Commission may request ESA to carry out inspections on its behalf in undertakings operating within the EFTA territory and ESA will have the same right as regards the Community.

Finally, the EEA negotiations have already provoked some side-effects in the EFTA States such as a de facto harmonization of the national competition rules. Furthermore, the EEA competition rules will, without any doubt, bring about a new dimension to the EC type of competition rules, as opposed to different approaches followed in other parts of the world. The fact that the same competition rules apply to seventeen European countries can certainly not be disregarded in the future discussions within international fora such as OECD or GATT.

3.8 State monopolies and public undertakings

The EEA Agreement takes over two important provisions of the Rome Treaty relating to the behaviour of States in certain commercial activities, namely Article 37 on State monopolies of a commercial character (the substance of which is reproduced in Article 16 EEA) and Article 90 on public undertakings (reproduced in Article 59 EEA).

Article 16 EEA will oblige the Contracting Parties (notably the EFTA States) to adjust their State monopolies better to fit the principle of free movement of goods. This should in particular have an impact on the various alcohol monopolies in the Nordic countries.

Article 59 EEA makes the EEA competition rules applicable to public undertakings and enables the Commission (regarding EC Member States) and ESA (regarding EFTA States) to take individual legally binding decisions, addressed to a State, declaring incompatible with the EEA Agreement a given State measure and indicating the measures to be taken to remedy the situation. These decisions may be directly relied upon by individuals in national proceedings. The Commission is increasingly making use of this particular power, notably in the fields of postal and telecommunications services or assistance during stop-overs in airports and ports.

3.9 State aid

The EFTA State aid regime has been based on Article 13 of the Stockholm Convention, which prohibits certain export aid and other forms of aid undermining the benefits expected from the removal of duties and quantitative restrictions in trade between the EFTA States. The EFTA Council at a later period agreed on some guidelines on the interpretation of this provision. As an additional transparency element EFTA has had in place since 1987 a notification system for new State aid measures. The whole system has perhaps not, however, functioned in a satisfactory way. As a sign of that, aid measures have not normally been contested by other EFTA States.

It would certainly have been possible to create an adequate system for control of State aid in EFTA, if an efficient enforcement mechanism had existed. However, EFTA never has had the same means as the EC Commission to control its Member States in the area of subsidies.

The EEA Agreement will drastically change the control of State aid in the EFTA countries. The novelties are twofold. First, the substantive EC rules, including secondary legislation, will apply in the whole territory covered by the EEA Agreement. Secondly, the EFTA States will be submitted to the control exercised by ESA, a body with supranational powers. This will, inter alia, mean an obligation for the States to notify ESA of all their new aid measures; ESA has to clear them before they can be implemented. ESA will also have a duty to scrutinize existing aid. Already, in preparing for the entry into force of the EEA, the EFTA States, when examining their existing aid schemes, have had to introduce important changes in order to make them compatible with the new system. Finally, the transparency will be improved, as ESA will have an obligation to publish information concerning aid cases it is handling. Competing undertakings will be given the opportunity to submit their comments on proposed aid measures when ESA opens detailed investigations.

It is likely that the control of State aid will be one of the most important tasks of ESA. The EC side has underlined on many occasions the significance of efficient surveillance in this field. Perhaps not being fully convinced that the EFTA side would implement the new rules in a satisfactory way, the Community obtained, at the last moment in the negotiations, a specific provision on safeguard measures for cases where State aid rules were not properly applied by one of the two authorities. Although it is an open question whether this provision will ever be invoked, it is clear that its existence as such will put certain pressures on ESA and the EFTA countries.

3.10 The situation of Switzerland

Following the rejection of the EEA by the Swiss voters on 6 December 1992, the Swiss Government launched a programme to liberalize the economy (involving notably the amendment of the Swiss Cartel Law). It also decided nevertheless to take over some of the implementation measures planned in the EEA context (so-called 'Eurolex', which became 'Swisslex'). The Government furthermore decided to go for the so-called 'bilateral approach' with the EC and presented a list of sixteen issues for which it seeks an agreement with the Community. The Commission has submitted to the EC Council a communication on future relations with Switzerland and negotiation mandates should be adopted by the Council in the first half of 1994 for opening bilateral talks notably in the fields of transport and free movement of persons. Finally, both the EEA option and possible membership of the Community are still open. The situation of Liechtenstein is also briefly explained.

II

STRUCTURE, OBJECTIVES, AND FUNCTIONING OF THE EEA AGREEMENT

The very purpose of the EEA being to extend to the EFTA States the application of the EC Single Market, the Agreement had to be based on the so-called *acquis communautaire*, in particular the one concerning the four freedoms (goods, persons, services, and capital). As compared with the scope of the 1972 FTAs, which only concerned trade in industrial goods, the EEA without any doubt constituted a major qualitative step. However, unlike the objectives of the Community, those of the EEA are of an economic nature only and the Agreement is neither a customs union, nor does it cover all products or fields of EC activities. Furthermore, an institutional structure was created to manage and monitor the whole system, based notably on the so-called 'two pillar' approach, which is certainly not, however, the simplest solution one could have conceived.

This chapter first presents the structure of the Agreement (Section 1), then describes its objectives and the means to achieve them (Section 2), and discusses some other general provisions of the EEA (Section 3). The following sections give an overview of the legislative technique used (Section 4), the institutional framework (Section 5), and the decision-making and surveillance questions (Sections 6 and 7). Finally, Section 8 briefly describes how the implementation of the EEA Agreement is to be achieved.

1. STRUCTURE OF THE EEA AGREEMENT

The main part of the EEA Agreement contains 129 articles, divided into nine parts. Most of the articles correspond closely to the substantive provisions of the EEC Treaty.

The nine parts of the Agreement relate to the four freedoms (part II covers free movement of goods and part III free movement of persons, services, and capital), competition and other common rules (part IV),[1] horizontal provisions relevant to the four freedoms (part V),[2] as well as to co-operation in some other fields (part VI).[3] Part

[1] The rules governing competition and State aid and a reference article to intellectual property and public procurement.

[2] Social policy, consumer protection, environment, statistics, and company law.

[3] e.g. research and development, education.

VII contains the institutional provisions, including the decision-making procedure, measures safeguarding homogeneity, surveillance mechanism, settlement of disputes, and safeguard measures. Part VIII deals with the so-called 'cohesion fund', i.e. the financial mechanism established to contribute to the reduction of regional disparities in the EEA, and part IX contains some general and final provisions.

The main Agreement is followed by forty-nine protocols and twenty-two annexes. As a general rule, the protocols contain rules on particular matters, such as product coverage, rules of origin, customs matters, trade in specific products (fish, coal, and steel), and co-operation between the parties in various fields. The annexes are the instrument through which some 1,700 EC acts of secondary legislation (the *acquis communautaire*) are integrated in the EEA.

Each annex deals with a particular field, such as veterinary and phytosanitary matters, technical regulations, standards, testing and certification, product liability, energy, free movement of workers, social security, etc. Under Article 119, the annexes and the protocols form an integral part of the Agreement.

In addition, the Agreement contains several unilateral and joint declarations as well as agreed minutes, relating to the interpretation and future implementation of certain provisions.

2. OBJECTIVES OF THE AGREEMENT AND MEANS TO ACHIEVE THEM

2.1 Objectives of the EEA Agreement (Article 1 (1))

The general objective of the EEA Agreement, as stated in its Article 1 (1), is to 'promote a continuous and balanced strengthening of trade and economic relations between the Contracting Parties with equal conditions of competition, and the respect of the same rules, with a view to creating a homogeneous European Economic Area'.

The two basic objectives are thus the strengthening of trade and economic relations between the partners and the creation of a homogeneous EEA. The economic objective very much resembles the more classical free trade approach. The other objective, homogeneity, is a novelty as compared with the objectives of the 1972 FTAs. It reflects the new approach adopted in the EEA, which is to follow closely the *acquis communautaire* and its monitoring system.

Article 1 (1) of the EEA Agreement had already received an early interpretation by the Court of Justice when the latter scrutinized the compatibility of the judicial mechanism of the Agreement with the Rome Treaty.[4] The Court first recalled that an international treaty is to be interpreted in the light of its objectives. It then

[4] See Opinion 1/91, cited above in Ch. I n. 11.

compared the EEA and EEC objectives and stated, as regards the economic objective:

the [EEA] agreement is concerned with the application of rules on free trade and competition in economic and commercial relations between the Contracting Parties. In contrast, as far as the Community is concerned, the rules on free trade and competition . . . have developed and form part of the Community legal order, the objectives of which go beyond that of the agreement.

The Court continued with a description of the aims of the EEC to achieve economic integration leading to an internal market and economic and monetary union and finally added: 'It follows from the foregoing that the provisions of the EEC Treaty on free movement and competition, far from being an end in themselves, are only means for attaining those objectives.'

As regards the objective of homogeneity, the Court first recalled[5] that the fact that the EEA and EEC provisions 'are identically worded does not mean that they must necessarily be interpreted identically', and then concluded that 'the homogeneity of the rules of law throughout the EEA is not secured by the fact that the provisions of Community law and those of the corresponding provisions of the agreement are identical in their content or wording'.

The Court of Justice rejected the compatibility with the Rome Treaty of creating a joint EEA Court (which was designed to guarantee homogeneity). It is against this background that the EEA negotiators worked out a certain number of amendments to the first draft Agreement in order to secure as far as possible the homogeneity which was considered as the cornerstone of the EEA. This was made through different provisions which are further discussed below in Section 7.1.

2.2 Means to attain the objectives of the EEA Agreement (Article 1 (2))

Article 1 (2) lists six means to attain the objectives of the EEA Agreement: the four freedoms (goods, persons, services, and capital), the competition rules, and co-operation in certain 'flanking' areas.

The economic objective is thus to be attained through the extention of the EC

[5] On the interpretation of the 1972 FTAs' objectives and provisions as compared to the Rome Treaty, see Case 270/80 *Polydor* [1982] ECR 329 concerning the 1972 EEC–Portugal FTA (Portugal was at that time still an EFTA member): 'The considerations which led to that interpretation of Articles 30 and 36 of the treaty do not apply in the context of the relations between the Community and Portugal as defined by the Agreement. It is apparent from an examination of the Agreement that although it makes provisions for the unconditional abolition of certain restrictions on trade between the Community and Portugal, such as quantitative restrictions and measures having equivalent effect, it does not have the same purpose as the EEC Treaty, inasmuch as the latter, as has been stated above, seeks to create a single market reproducing as closely as possible the conditions of a domestic market.' However, in two recent cases (not yet reported) concerning the 1972 FTAs with Norway and with Austria, the ECJ interpreted the FTA provision on the prohibition of measures of equivalent effect to quantitative restrictions in the same way as Art. 30 EEC (see Case C-228/91 of 25 May 1993 on imports of Norwegian fish to Italy, OJ C 173 (24 June 1993), 16, and Case C-207/91 of 1 July 1993 on parallel imports of pharmaceuticals from Austria to Germany, OJ C 204 (28 July 1993), 6 (summarized in *Europe*, 6029, of 26–7 July 1993)). In

common market rules to the EFTA States. The homogeneity objective is to be attained through the application of common rules and the permanent updating of these rules following the evolution of the EC rules.

Clearly visible here is one of the originalities of the EEA Agreement, compared with ordinary international agreements: its dynamism. Since the EEA rules are all based on the *acquis communautaire* elaborated in the EC over more than thirty years and which is being continuously developed and amended, the Agreement is a sort of 'living animal' which, in parallel with the developments in the Community, will constantly evolve through integrating the new relevant EC legislation.

2.2.1 The four freedoms

Besides free movement of goods, the EEA Agreement extends the EC rules on *free movement of persons* (Articles 28 *et seq.* EEA) to the whole EEA territory.[6] No discrimination will be allowed on the basis of nationality between EC or EFTA workers as regards employment, pay, and other working or employment conditions, except for employment in the public sector. An important factor for increased mobility will be the mutual recognition of diplomas.[7] The free mobility will be further facilitated by the provisions on social security,[8] which, although each country maintains its own social security system, allow the employees to aggregate insurance periods and receive social security benefits, without discrimination on the basis of nationality, when working abroad and to have them exported when moving from one EEA country to another.

With *freedom of establishment* (Articles 31 *et seq.* EEA) both self-employed persons and undertakings will have the right to non-discriminatory treatment when taking up or pursuing activities in other EEA countries, with the only exceptions based on public policy, public security, or public health. Freedom of establishment covers not only the creation of new businesses but also the setting up of agencies, branches, or subsidiaries by undertakings already established in other EEA countries.

Services contribute to more than 60 per cent of the gross domestic product of the countries participating in the EEA. The trade in services has, however, a much smaller importance than the traditional exports and imports of goods. This is naturally mainly due to the very nature of the services, and makes them less tradable.[9] On the other hand, services have not really been dealt with in existing international trade agreements so far, although they are now on the agenda in the

another case, concerning provisions on internal discriminatory taxation, the ECJ did maintain a different interpretation of Art. 18 of the EC–Austria FTA as compared with Art. 95 EEC (see Case C-312/91 of 1 July 1993, OJ C 204 (28 July 1993), 6 (summarized in *Europe*, 6030, of 28 July 1993)).

[6] The EEA provisions on free movement of persons do not, following Art. 121, affect the even further-reaching free mobility of persons existing between the Nordic Countries.

[7] See Annex VII EEA.

[8] See Annex VI EEA.

[9] *European Economy*, 5 (May 1993), Supplement A, published by the Directorate-General for Economic and Financial Affairs of the EC Commission.

GATT Uruguay Round negotiations. The free movement of services was also already provided for in the original Rome Treaty but only the Single Market programme meant a breakthrough in this respect in the Community, bringing forth real liberalization.

In the EEA context, there will be no restrictions on the *provision of services* by nationals of EC Member States and EFTA States (Articles 36 *et seq.*, 47 *et seq.* EEA). The following examples illustrate the functioning of the system pertaining to some of the most important service sectors:

1. The principles of single licensing and home country control will apply to banks and other credit institutions. This means that a bank authorized to operate in its home country can provide cross-border services, through subsidiaries and branches also, without any prior approval of the host country. The control of all operations of the institution concerned will be the responsibility of the home country. This has necessitated harmonization of legislation concerning, *inter alia*, such issues as prudential requirements and accounting.[10]

2. Similar principles will cover the insurance sector, both life and non-life insurance. The liberalization in this field will introduce free cross-border market access to all EC and EFTA insurance companies throughout the EEA.[11]

3. For stock exchanges and securities strict rules on admission of securities to official stock-exchange listing, information to be published on listed undertakings or on acquisitions of major holdings of such companies, and insider dealing have been included in the EEA Agreement.[12]

4. In the field of so-called 'new technology services', whose economic importance is quickly growing, the EEA takes over the liberalization and harmonization measures adopted in the EC regarding telecommunications (withdrawal of certain exclusive rights entrusted to public monopolies and opening up of the public network to service providers), information services (transfrontier transmission of data), and audio-visual services (free flow of television programmes across Europe).[13]

5. The field of transport has given rise to a great number of acts liberalizing the markets and harmonizing various technical regulations. The markets will be opened to competition and there will be mutual access to them, for example through extended possibilities of cabotage. This will be facilitated through harmonized rules concerning such issues as technical characteristics of vehicles or other means of transportation, their maximum authorized weights and dimensions, etc.[14]

Free movement of capital (Articles 40 *et seq.* EEA) is a significant step towards

[10] See Annex IX EEA.

[11] Ibid.

[12] Ibid.

[13] See Annexes X and XI EEA.

[14] See Arts. 47 *et seq.* EEA and Annex XIII EEA. Furthermore, an important issue in the EEA context, although dealt with separately through a bilateral agreement with Austria, was the question of Alpine transit.

greater economic integration. It is also related to free movement of services, as the latter could not be fully realized without the right to direct investment. The EEA Agreement provides for a system based on non-discrimination for cross-border investments, capital transfers, and credits. There are only some derogations concerning ownership in the fisheries sector in Norway and Iceland. In addition, there are transitional periods mainly concerning direct investment and real estate investments in some of the EFTA States.[15]

The EEA Agreement also contains certain common rules to complement the functioning of the four freedoms: these are the rules on intellectual property, public procurement, competition, and State aid. As all these areas have a special importance, in particular, with regard to the free movement of goods, they will be dealt with in detail in Chapters V, VII, VIII, and X, respectively.

2.2.2 Horizontal provisions relevant to the four freedoms and co-operation outside the four freedoms

In addition to the establishment of the four freedoms, the Contracting Parties will co-operate in a wide range of other areas.

Part V of the Agreement contains provisions which are horizontally relevant to the four freedoms and constitute a sort of cement between the freedoms. The EFTA States thus take over the EC secondary legislation in the fields of social policy (Annex XVIII EEA), consumer protection (Annex XIX EEA), environment (Annex XX EEA), statistics (Annex XXI EEA), and company law (Annex XXII EEA).

Part VI of the Agreement concerns co-operation outside the four freedoms, known as 'flanking policies'. This part essentially aims at enabling the EFTA States to participate in EC programmes and other common actions in a number of areas indirectly related to the four freedoms. Details on the programmes concerned and the modalities of EFTA participation are contained in Protocol 31 EEA.

The legislation and co-operation belonging to these so-called 'horizontal and flanking policies' cover such issues as:

- social policy, where horizontal EC legislation regarding work safety, equal treatment for women and men, and labour law (notably through the introduction of binding minimum standards) is taken over. It covers in addition flanking actions such as assistance to the long-term unemployed or employment of disabled people.
- consumer protection, where common legislation will apply on, for instance, misleading advertising, consumer credits, health and safety of consumers, and price labelling. In this case, too, the legislation sets minimum levels, and stricter rules may be applied at a national level (to the extent that the free movement of goods is not impeded). The EEA covers also flanking actions related to consumer protection policy in general;
- environment, where the existing Community legislation in the field of

[15] See Annex XII EEA.

environment (i.e. relating to water, air, chemicals, industrial risk, biotechnology, and waste) will apply in the EEA context; however, individual States will be allowed to maintain stricter national standards (to the extent that the free movement of goods is not impeded). In addition, in the flanking areas, co-operation will be strengthened as regards policy and action programmes on the environment, integration of environmental protection requirements into other policies, economic and fiscal instruments, environmental questions with transboundary implications, as well as major regional and global issues under discussion within international organizations;

- company law, where, two years after the entry into force of the EEA, the EFTA States shall apply the horizontal legislation contained in the twelve EC directives regarding public and private limited companies (e.g. disclosure, nullity, formation, capital, mergers, accounts, groups, or branches), auditing, and European Economic Interest Groupings (EEIG);
- research and technological development, where the EFTA States will be granted participation in the various programmes and projects set up by the Community (flanking policy);
- education, training, and youth, where EFTA participation, if not already taking place, in different training and exchange programmes will be granted in general as from the beginning of 1995 (flanking policy);[16]
- small and medium-sized enterprises (SMEs), where the co-operation aims at removing undue administrative, financial, and legal constraints on business, encouraging subcontracting, business development, and co-operation between SMEs from different regions of the EEA (flanking policy);
- the audio-visual field, where the rules ensure EFTA participation in the programmes established under the EC MEDIA programme, aiming at promotion of the European audio-visual industry (flanking policy).

2.3 Reduction of economic and social disparities between regions

One of the demands of the less-developed EC Member States in the EEA negotiations was that EFTA should assist in the development and structural adjustment of the poorest Community regions. This was partly achieved through improved market access for certain agricultural products particularly important to the economies of those countries.[17] The main solution was, however, a system of financial assistance provided by EFTA States.[18]

[16] It can be noted that the EFTA States already participate in perhaps the two most important programmes, ERASMUS and COMETT.

[17] Austria, Finland, Iceland, Norway, and Sweden concluded, in parallel to the EEA Agreement, bilateral agreements with the EC granting tariff and other concessions in the field of agriculture. When the Adjustment Protocol (following the Swiss withdrawal) was agreed upon, it was also agreed provisionally to apply these bilateral agreements already as from 15 Apr. 1993.

[18] The provisions concerning the financial mechanism are contained in Arts. 115–117 and Protocol 38 EEA.

The financial mechanism is based on two different elements: grants and interest subsidies provided in connection with loans granted by the European Investment Bank (EIB). Priority will be given to projects putting particular emphasis on the environment (including urban development), transport (including transport infrastructure), or education and training. Among projects submitted by private undertakings, special consideration will be given to small and medium-sized enterprises.

The total amount of grants to be provided will be 500 million ECU, to be committed over a period of five years from the entry into force of the EEA Agreement. The grants will be disbursed by the EIB on the basis of proposals from the beneficiary EC Member States[19] and after the opinion of the EC Commission and the approval of the EFTA Financial Mechanism Committee.

The interest rebate will be fixed at two percentage points per annum, by reference to EIB interest rates, and it will be available for ten years for each loan subject to the programme. The total volume of loans benefiting from the interest rebate will be 1,500 million ECU, to be committed in equal tranches over a period of five years. The subsidized loans will, in the same way as the grants, be subject to the opinion of the EC Commission and approval of the EFTA Financial Mechanism Committee.

3. GENERAL PROVISIONS OF THE EEA

Without entering into all the details of the interpretation of these particular rules it is nevertheless useful to describe a certain number of general provisions which form part of the basics of the EEA legal framework. From the point of view of the Community, the EEA Agreement is an 'association agreement', i.e. falling within the category of those foreseen under Article 238 EEC.

3.1 Notion of 'Contracting Parties' and territorial scope of the Agreement (Articles 2 (*c*) and 126)

Article 2 (*c*) defines the notion of 'Contracting Parties'. While it clearly includes each EFTA State,[20] the notion, when applicable to the EC, is multifunctional as it may, depending on the subject-matter, mean the Community alone, both the Community and its Member States, or solely the Member States. This is owing to the fact that the EEA covers a wide scope of matters for which the distribution of competences within the EC is sometimes controversial. There are thus matters where the Community has exclusive external competence (for instance issues

[19] Assistance is limited to Greece, the island of Ireland, Portugal, and specific regions of Spain.

[20] That is to say, under Art. 2(*b*) EEA, as amended by Art. 2(2) of the Adjustment Protocol, Austria, Finland, Iceland, Norway, and Sweden. As regards Liechtenstein, see Ch. XI, s. 4.

relating to common commercial policy) and others where EC Member States have retained certain national competences (for instance certain intellectual property rights). In the Community jargon, the EEA Agreement is thus a 'mixed agreement', i.e. an agreement which covers areas under Community external competences and national competences.

Article 126 defines the territorial scope of application of the EEA Agreement. This is done, as regards the EC, through a reference to the territories to which the EEC and ECSC Treaties apply.[21] As regards the EFTA States concerned, the provision refers to their respective territories (with the exception of the Åland Islands (Finland); see Article 126 (2)).

3.2 Scope and limitations (Articles 118, 120, 121, and 123)

Article 118, without defining the scope of the Agreement, contains an evolutionary clause under which a Contracting Party can suggest that relations be extended to fields not covered by the Agreement. In this context, it is recalled that the EEA Agreement is not a customs union (no common external tariff) and does not apply to basic agricultural products, harmonization of taxes (e.g. VAT directives), or common policies (such as the common agricultural policy or common commercial policy). Each Contracting Party also keeps its full freedom *vis-à-vis* third countries.

Article 120 says that, unless otherwise specified and to the extent that the same subject-matter is governed by the EEA Agreement, the latter prevails over provisions in existing bilateral or multilateral agreements between the EC and one or more EFTA States.

Article 121 is the corresponding provision in the EEA Agreement to the so-called 'Benelux clause' of the EEC Treaty (Article 233). It reserves the possibility, to the extent that such agreements do not impair the smooth functioning of the EEA, of maintaining more ambitious co-operation agreements such as the Nordic co-operation.

Article 123 corresponds to the 'security clause' of Article 223 of the EEC Treaty, providing for exceptions regarding for instance trade in arms and serious international tension entailing a threat of war.

3.3 Principle of loyalty and general non-discrimination provision (Articles 3 and 4)

Article 3, which corresponds to Article 5 of the EEC Treaty, contains a loyalty clause which has been used extensively by the EC Court of Justice, usually in conjunction with another basic provision of the Treaty (such as Article 30) to

[21] See Art. 227 of the EEC Treaty and Art. 79 of the ECSC Treaty. However, in connection with the Adjustment Protocol of 17 Mar. 1993 (following Swiss withdrawal from the EEA), France made a declaration under which the EEA Agreement 'does not apply to overseas countries and territories associated to the [EEC] pursuant to the [EEC] Treaty'.

condemn a national law or administrative practice as contrary to Community law. This provision has been said to contain both a positive obligation (i.e. in addition to implementing measures, the Member States are to ensure that the *acquis* is effectively applied in reality and not only on paper) and a negative obligation (the Member States shall refrain from any measure which would undermine the *effet utile* of EC law).[22]

Article 4, which reproduces Article 7 (1) of the EEC Treaty, contains a general non-discrimination clause which also gave rise to an extensive case-law from the Court of Justice. This provision forbids any direct or indirect discrimination based on nationality criteria. This would be the case if, in comparable situations, a State should, on the basis of nationality, apply different solutions.[23] This provision benefits natural or legal persons and does not impede 'reverse discrimination' (discrimination against own nationals).

3.4 Legal effects of EC acts listed in the annexes to the Agreement (Article 7)

Article 7, which was partly modelled on Article 189 of the EEC Treaty, defines the legal effects, in the EEA, of the regulations and directives listed in the annexes to the Agreement and the way in which they should be implemented by the Contracting Parties. Although some of the features of Article 189 have been kept in Article 7, certain essential aspects such as direct applicability of a regulation have voluntarily been left out. This is owing to an intensive debate in the so-called dualist EFTA countries, in which international agreements do not directly form part of the national legal order (as in the 'monist' countries) but need first to be transposed into national legislation. This debate will certainly also have an impact on the well-known doctrines of direct effect (the right of individuals to invoke directly a Treaty or secondary legislation provision in the national courts) and primacy (the EC law takes precedence over conflicting national laws and measures). Some EFTA States seem to be of the opinion that Article 6 EEA (on ECJ case-law) does not entail the taking over in the EEA of the ECJ jurisprudence concerning the legal effects of the Treaty provisions and the EC acts integrated in the EEA (i.e. direct effect, primacy, State liability in the case of non-implementation of the directives)[24] but only the

[22] Leading cases on Art. 5 EEC are Cases 39/72 *Commission* v. *Italy* [1973] ECR 101, 33/76 *Rewe* [1976] ECR 1989, C-213/89 *Factortame* [1990] ECR I-2433, 804/79 *Commission* v. *UK* [1981] ECR 1045, and 311/85 *Vlaamse Reisbureaus* [1987] ECR 3801. For more detailed developments on this question, see J.-E. de Cockborne *et al.*, *Commentaire Mégret*, i (1992), 25 *et seq.*, and P. J. G. Kapteyn, *Introduction to the Law of the European Communities* (1990), 85 *et seq.* (referred to in the Bibliography).

[23] Leading cases in that respect are Cases 13/63 *Commission* v. *Italy* [1963] ECR 337, 61/77 *Commission* v. *Ireland* [1978] ECR 417, and 293/83 *Gravier* [1985] ECR 593. For more complete developments on this question, see *Commentaire Mégret*, op. cit. n. 22, p. 45 *et seq.*

[24] On direct effects of Treaty provisions, see Cases 26/62 *Van Gend & Loos* [1963] ECR 1, 57/65 *Lütticke* [1966] ECR 205, and 36/74 *Walrave* [1974] ECR 1405; on direct effects of regulations, see Cases 43/71 *Politi* [1971] ECR 1039 and 93/71 *Leonesio* [1972] ECR 287; on direct effects of directives, see Cases 11/70 *SACE* [1970] ECR 1213, 41/74 *Van Duyn* [1974] ECR 1337, 148/78 *Ratti* [1979] ECR 1629,

jurisprudence interpreting the substance of the provisions. This can however be questioned.

Furthermore, Protocol 35 EEA, while acknowledging that the EEA Agreement does not entail a transfer of legislative powers to the EEA institutions, obliges the EFTA States, in case of conflict between implemented EEA rules and other national rules, to introduce a statutory provision to the effect that the EEA rules prevail. Finally, it is interesting to note that Article 7 does not say anything about the legal effects of decisions.[25]

4. INTEGRATION OF THE *ACQUIS COMMUNAUTAIRE* IN THE AGREEMENT

4.1 The legislative technique used

One of the first practical challenges for the negotiators was to find a method for incorporating the important volume of EC secondary legislation which was to be taken over. As recopying the approximately 1,700 EC legal acts would have resulted in an agreement of more than 10,000 pages, it was decided that the second best solution would be to use the so-called 'reference technique', which was inspired by a system used earlier by the EC for the accession treaties with the new Member States.[26] The result was that the EC acts considered as relevant for the purposes of the EEA were listed in the twenty-two annexes to the Agreement through a reference to their title and publication data in the *Official Journal of the EC*.

The acts in the annexes have been divided into two categories. The first category is the regulations, directives, and decisions, all listed under the heading 'Acts referred to'. Those are what the negotiating jargon called 'binding acts'. The second category comprises acts such as recommendations, notices, communications, guidelines, resolutions, etc. Those, called 'non-binding acts', have been listed under the heading 'Acts of which the Contracting Parties shall take note'.[27]

Therefore, if one wishes to find out how a given issue is regulated in the EEA, it is

and 152/84 *Marshall* [1986] ECR 723. On primacy of EC law, see Cases 6/64 *Costa* v. *ENEL* [1964] ECR 585, 106/77 *Simmenthal* [1978] ECR 629, and 11/70 *Internationale Handelsgesellschaft* [1970] ECR 1125. On state liability for non-implementation, see Joined Cases 6 & 9/90 *Francovich* [1991] ECR I-5357. For detailed developments on these questions, see J.-V. Louis, *L'Ordre juridique communautaire* (1993), 129 *et seq.* Finally, regarding the possible direct effects and primacy of EEA rules, see Advocate General W. van Gerven, 'The genesis of EEA law and the principles of primacy and direct effect', *Fordham International Law Journal*, 16: 955.

[25] Compare with para. 4 of Art. 189 EEC.

[26] With the difference that, in the accession treaties, only those legislative acts where derogations or transitional periods were foreseen were listed in the annexes, while in the EEA Agreement, each and every act taken over had to be listed.

[27] However, when the non-binding acts concern the policy to be followed by the Commission and ESA, the acts have been put under the heading 'Acts of which the EC Commission and the EFTA Surveillance Authority shall take due account'.

not sufficient only to go to the annex concerned. In addition, the text of the original EC act is needed (which may sometimes have been amended several times). The reader has then to examine it in the light of the adaptations made for the EEA purposes (see explanations below). Furthermore, it is advisable to check whether some additional interpretative guidance on the application of the act concerned can be found elsewhere in the Agreement, in some agreed minute or declaration.

4.2 Protocol 1 and other adaptations to EC acts

The texts of the EC acts contain different references to EC institutions and internal procedures, EC Member States, nationals, languages, and other typical EC vocabulary. As such they would not have been transposable in the EEA context, so numerous adaptations were needed to make them fit the new environment. Moreover, there was a need to provide for some particular adaptations as regards the EFTA States (such as to complement lists of diplomas or competent national bodies, add derogations or transitional periods, etc.).

In theory, it would of course have been possible to make very detailed adaptations to each and every EC act, but, mainly due to the Herculean task and the lengthy annexes this would have entailed, it was hardly feasible.

The drafters therefore went through the different EC directives and regulations and attempted, as far as possible, to categorize the different Community procedures and terms to be adapted for the purposes of the EEA. This categorization work resulted in general adaptations which could cover words such as 'Member States', 'Community', 'common market', or specific internal EC procedures (involving a committee, notifications from Member States to the Commission, publication and reporting obligations, etc.). In other instances, it was appropriate to make such categorizations for a given annex only, while sometimes only an adaptation of a specific article of a directive was possible.

This is the reason why it was finally decided to make the adaptations needed for EEA purposes on three levels:

- the *horizontal adaptations*, i.e. those relevant for all the acts listed in the annexes, can be found in Protocol 1 to the Agreement (with a reminder to it at the beginning of each annex);
- the *sectoral adaptations*, i.e. those which are relevant for a whole annex, can be found at the beginning of each such annex, below the reminder concerning Protocol 1;[28]
- the *specific adaptations*, i.e. those that are relevant solely for a given provision of a particular EC act, are listed below the title of this act, usually with a reference to the specific article to which they apply.

[28] In voluminous annexes some sectoral adaptations have been made in the beginning of chapters under the annex concerned.

These three stages of adaptations should always be kept in mind when reading a piece of *acquis communautaire* in the EEA context, and in particular the fact that they work *en cascade*, meaning that a more specific adaptation may always derogate a more general one.

4.2.1 Protocol 1 on horizontal adaptations

Protocol 1 on horizontal adaptations contains twelve paragraphs which provide the overall key on how to understand the relevant EC secondary legislation in the EEA environment. The main principles laid down in Protocol 1 can be summarized as follows.[29]

Preambles and final provisions of EC acts (paragraphs 1, 11, and 12):

- the preambles and 'whereas' clauses of the EC acts have been taken over in the EEA due to their value as interpretative guidance. However, as they do not belong to the operative part of the act, no adaptations have been made to them;
- the classical final provisions of the EC acts on their entry into force,[30] implementation date,[31] or the fact that it is addressed to the Member States[32] are declared not applicable in the EEA context. This is due to the fact that the moment of entry into force of an act in the EEA is separately regulated in Article 129 EEA on the entry into force of the EEA Agreement (as adapted by the Adjusting Protocol) or decided by the EEA Contracting Parties (e.g. in cases where a transitional period has been granted). In practice, this means that the EC and the EFTA States were to implement all the *acquis* listed in the EEA annexes by the date of entry into force of the Agreement, unless a specific transitional period was provided for. Furthermore, it was the understanding of the Parties that, if the implementation date in the EC act itself is set later than the date of entry into force of the EEA Agreement, the EC date will also be applicable in the EEA and benefit the EFTA countries in the same way as the EC Member States. Finally, the legal effects of the acts integrated in the EEA are defined in Article 7 of the Agreement.[33]

EC vocabulary (paragraphs 7, 8, 9, and 10):

- the term 'Member State(s)', when used to refer to the State (or its public authorities, undertakings, or individuals) as the subject of rights and obligations under the *acquis*, is said to confer the same rights or impose the

[29] This Protocol is reproduced in Annex A at the end of this book.

[30] Such as 'This Regulation shall enter into force on 3 April 1992' or 'This Decision shall apply from 3 April 1992.'

[31] Such as 'Member States shall bring into force the laws, regulations and administrative provisions necessary to comply with this Directive no later than 3 April 1992.'

[32] Such as 'This Decision/Directive is addressed to the Member States.'

[33] Which covers ending provisions such as 'This Regulation shall be binding in its entirety and directly applicable in all Member States.' See remarks above in s. 3.4.

same obligations upon the EEA Contracting Parties (or their public authorities, undertakings, or individuals);[34]

- the terms 'Community' or 'common market' in their geographical sense are to be understood as referring to the territories to which the EEA applies (defined in Article 126 EEA[35]);
- the references to nationals of EC Member States also comprise nationals of the EFTA States;
- the references to the right or obligation for EC Member States (or their public authorities, undertakings, or individuals) to use an official language of the Community are to be understood as conferring the same right or imposing the same obligation upon the EEA Contracting Parties (or their public authorities, undertakings, or individuals) regarding the use of EEA languages;
- general references to Community law, such as 'Community law', 'Community provisions', 'Community rules', 'Community requirements', have not been adapted. This vocabulary should be interpreted in its context;[36]
- cross-references to other specific regulations, directives, or decisions are valid in the EEA context, unless expressly provided otherwise.

Internal EC decision-making or administrative procedures (paragraphs 2 to 6):

- where the EC act provides for internal EC procedures on its amendment, improvement, or the like, the EEA decision-making procedure will apply in the EEA context (i.e. Articles 97 *et seq.*). The same goes for procedures and other provisions concerning EC committees for which the EEA rules on participation of the EFTA States in the work of the committees will apply (i.e. Articles 81, 100, and 101, as well as Protocol 31);
- where the EC act provides for information to be forwarded by the EC Member States to the EC Commission or to other Member States, corresponding information will be forwarded by EFTA States to the competent EFTA body or to the other EFTA States. The EC Commission and the competent EFTA body will then exchange this information ('two pillar' approach);
- where the EC Commission is entrusted with management or surveillance tasks (verification, approval, consultation, etc.[37]), the competent EFTA body shall carry out the same task within its 'pillar' and the EC and EFTA sides shall keep each other informed. Any issue arising in this context may be referred to the EEA Joint Committee;

[34] The term 'Member State(s)' in its geographical sense has not been given a horizontal adaptation as the negotiators felt that the coverage of the EFTA States is self-evident.

[35] As regards the territorial scope of application of the EEA Agreement see s. 3.1 above.

[36] During the EEA negotiations, in order to fill in any possible remaining gaps, the drafters invented the notion of 'intelligent reader' (lecteur avisé), meaning that, when an adaptation is lacking, the 'intelligent reader' will anyhow understand it properly in the EEA context.

[37] This concerns for instance cases where EC acts provide for Commission approval of safeguard measures by Member States, dispute settlement procedure involving the Commission, Commission requests for information, etc.

– where a report or the like is to be prepared by an EC body, the competent EFTA body shall prepare a corresponding report. The two sides shall co-operate in making their reports and forward copies thereof to the EEA Joint Committee;
– where the act obliges the EC Member States to make an official publication, the EFTA States shall make a corresponding publication. The same goes where a publication is to be made in the EC *Official Journal*; the corresponding publication regarding EFTA States shall be made in a special EEA Section of the EC *Official Journal*.[38]

As regards the question of how the different procedural and administrative tasks are distributed within the EFTA pillar between the two EFTA bodies (i.e. the EFTA Surveillance Authority and the EFTA Standing Committee; see Section 5.2 below), only paragraph 4 (*a*) and (*b*) (on exchange of information) of Protocol 1 expressly attributes the task in question to one or the other of these EFTA bodies. The distribution of tasks in other situations is dealt with in the two internal EFTA Agreements which set up ESA and the Standing Committee (notably their main parts and respective Protocols 1).

Finally, it should be noted that Protocol 39 EEA explains that the terms 'ECU' or 'European unit of account' which appear throughout the EC acts shall mean ECU as defined by the competent Community authorities

4.2.2 Sectoral adaptations

As indicated above, the sectoral adaptations only apply to a specific annex or a chapter of such an annex. A good example of this type of adaptation is to be found at the beginning of Annex XIV on competition,[39] where for instance the term 'trade between Member States' is said to mean 'trade between Contracting Parties' or 'Article 85 (EEC)' to correspond to 'Article 53 (EEA)'.

4.2.3 Specific adaptations

The specific adaptations made to particular EC acts within a given annex always appear under a standard 'chapeau' provision which reads 'The provisions of this [Directive/Regulation/Decision] shall, for the purposes of the present Agreement be read with the following adaptation[s].' The adaptations are usually listed under a lower case letter within brackets, for instance: '(a) The following shall be added to Article . . .'

To facilitate the understanding of the EEA legislative technique, some examples illustrating the use of the reference technique are contained in Annex C to this book. It shows, by combining the text of the act as embodied in the EEA Agreement, the

[38] It is in fact intended to create both an 'EEA Section' of the EC *Official Journal* where publication will be made in EC languages and an 'EEA Supplement' for the four Nordic languages.

[39] This Annex is reproduced in Annex A.

provisions of Protocol 1, and the original EC text of the act, how this act would look if it had been reproduced in full in the Agreement.

5. INSTITUTIONAL SOLUTIONS

Given the particular characteristics of the EEA Agreement (its wide scope and dynamism), it was not sufficient to rely only on token institutional solutions for its implementation and future development. An important aspect which also had to be taken into account, when deciding on the institutional structures, was the maintenance of the Parties' independence.

This is the reason why it was decided to adopt a two pillar system, which in short means that the Community and the EFTA side will take care of their own internal matters. This necessitated that each had its own institutions for internal decision-making, surveillance, and judicial review. Some common institutions were, however, needed, in particular for joint decision-making and dispute settlement.

5.1 Common EEA institutions

The common EC-EFTA bodies are the EEA Council, the EEA Joint Committee, the EEA Parliamentary Committee, and the EEA Consultative Committee.

5.1.1 EEA Council (Articles 89 *et seq.*)

An EEA Council, consisting of members of the EC Council, EC Commission, and one member of the government of each EFTA State, will be responsible for giving the political impetus in the implementation of the EEA Agreement and laying down general guidelines for the work of the EEA Joint Committee, which is the body responsible for the day-to-day management of the Agreement.

The EEA Council will normally have its meetings twice a year, but it may also be convened more often if circumstances so require.

The presidency of the Council will be held alternately, for a period of six months, by a member of the EC Council and a member of the government of an EFTA State. The Council is to adopt its own rules of procedure.

Decisions by the EEA Council are taken by agreement between the Community, on the one hand, and the EFTA States, on the other. This means that, before a decision is made by the Council, both pillars have to agree, internally, on a common position.

5.1.2 EEA Joint Committee (Articles 92 *et seq.*)

In practice, the most important role in the development of the EEA Agreement will be that of the EEA Joint Committee, which has the task of ensuring the effective implementation and operation of the Agreement. To this end, the Joint Committee will take decisions on the introduction of new legislation into the EEA Agreement and constitute a forum for the exchange of views and information, as well as for dispute settlement.

The Joint Committee will consist of representatives of the Contracting Parties, which means in practice that it meets at the level of high officials. The meetings will normally be organized once a month.

The same principles as for the EEA Council apply as to the decision-making procedures, that is, the decisions will be taken by agreement between the Community, on the one hand, and the EFTA States speaking with one voice, on the other.

The presidency will, here again, be held alternately, for a period of six months, by a representative of the Community, i.e. the Commission, and a representative of an EFTA State. The EEA Joint Committee has the option of establishing subcommittees or working groups to assist it in carrying out its tasks.

The role of the Joint Committee in the decision-making and dispute settlement procedures will be discussed further under Sections 6.2 and 7.3, respectively.

5.1.3 EEA Joint Parliamentary Committee and co-operation between economic and social partners (Articles 95 and 96)

Parliamentary co-operation under the EEA Agreement will be carried out by an EEA Parliamentary Committee which is composed of an equal number, thirty-three representatives, from the European Parliament and from the parliaments of EFTA States.

The Parliamentary Committee will not have any powers concerning EEA decision-making, but it will contribute, through dialogue and debate, to a better understanding between the EC and EFTA parliamentarians in the fields covered by the Agreement. The Committee will express its views in the form of reports and resolutions.

The EEA Agreement also provides for co-operation between social and economic partners in order to enhance awareness about the economic and social aspects of the growing interdependence of the Contracting Parties' economies and of their interests in the EEA context. The co-operation will take place through an EEA Consultative Committee composed of members of the Economic and Social Committee of the Community and the EFTA Consultative Committee. Like the EEA Parliamentary Committee, the EEA Consultative Committee will express its views in the form of reports and resolutions.

5.2 New EFTA institutions

For internal procedures, surveillance, and judicial review the EC side already has its own institutions and these will have the responsibility of carrying out the same tasks in the context of the EEA Agreement. The EFTA pillar, however, had only the institutions laid down in the Stockholm Convention. As the latter would definitely have been insufficient for EEA purposes, new institutions had to be created. This is the reason why the Agreement between the EFTA States on the Establishment of a Surveillance Authority and a Court of Justice (ESA/Court Agreement) as well as the Agreement on a Standing Committee of the EFTA States (Standing Committee Agreement) were prepared in parallel with the EEA Agreement and also signed on 2 May 1992 in Oporto and are both due to enter into force on the same day as the EEA Agreement.

Under the *ESA/Court Agreement*, the EFTA States undertake to set up:

1. an EFTA Surveillance Authority (ESA) whose primary task will be to ensure the fulfilment by the EFTA States of their obligations under the EEA Agreement; and
2. an EFTA Court having jurisdiction notably in infringement actions brought by ESA against an EFTA State, appeals lodged by EFTA States or persons against decisions taken by ESA, or delivering advisory opinions on the interpretation of the EEA Agreement upon request by national courts in the EFTA States.

Under the *Standing Committee Agreement*, a Standing Committee of the EFTA States is set up as a co-ordination and consultation body in order to facilitate the elaboration of decisions to be taken on the EEA level.

5.2.1 EFTA Surveillance Authority

The EEA Agreement itself lays down the obligation for the EFTA States to establish the EFTA Surveillance Authority, which shall be independent and follow procedures similar to those existing in the Community[40] The establishment of the EFTA Surveillance Authority, which submits the EFTA States to the same discipline as the EC Member States, is essential to the balance of the rights and obligations of the Contracting Parties and was a prerequisite for the far-reaching opening up of the EC Single Market to the EFTA side.

As mentioned above, ESA was established through an internal EFTA agreement, the ESA/Court Agreement. In general terms ESA will have the task of ensuring the fulfilment by the EFTA States of their obligations under the EEA Agreement, applying the EEA competition rules, and monitoring the application of the EEA Agreement by the other Contracting Parties (which in fact is a reference to the Community). It can act upon complaints received from a Contracting Party, economic operators, or individuals, or on its own initiative.

To this end, ESA can take decisions in the same way as the EC Commission concerning infringements by States or in application of the competition rules. ESA also has powers to formulate recommendations, deliver opinions, and issue non-

[40] See Arts. 108 *et seq*. Although ESA will have equivalent powers and similar functions to those of the EC Commission as regards the surveillance tasks, it will not have the same legislative powers. This means that ESA will not have a similar role to the EC Commission as an initiator of legislation.

binding acts.[41] Furthermore, in order to maintain uniform surveillance within the EEA, ESA will co-operate with the EC Commission. Finally, ESA has certain management and surveillance-related tasks, similar to those of the Commission, in cases where such tasks fall under its responsibility through the application of Protocol 1 EEA and Protocol 1 ESA/Court Agreement. Decisions taken by ESA which impose pecuniary obligations are enforceable (Article 110 (1) EEA).

When carrying out its duties, ESA has powers to get all the necessary information from the governments and competent authorities of EFTA States and from undertakings and their associations.

ESA consists of five members,[42] in practice, one member coming from each EFTA country. All EFTA States have to approve the nominations made by the governments. The members shall be fully independent in the performance of their duties and are not allowed to seek any instructions or advice from the governments or other outside bodies. Their term of office lasts four years. The ESA College acts by a majority of its members and, in the event of an equal number of votes, the vote of the President is decisive.

ESA has been organized in the following way. There are five substance directorates, each of them responsible for a specific area, i.e. free movement of goods, competition (anti-trust), State aid (including State monopolies and public undertakings), free movement of services (transport excluded) and capital, and, finally, the directorate responsible for free movement of persons, horizontal and flanking policies, as well as transport services. Each directorate is led by a director and, following the example of the Commission, each member of the ESA College will have a special field of responsibility.[43]

5.2.2 EFTA Court

Several different options were discussed during the negotiations with regard to the judicial review mechanism. The issue was not an easy one to solve, mainly for political and constitutional reasons.

It was initially proposed to establish an EEA Court composed of judges from the ECJ and from EFTA countries. This solution was not, however, acceptable to the ECJ, which considered it incompatible with the EEC Treaty. In its Opinion 1/91 the ECJ stated in substance that, as the objectives of the Community and the EEA were different, despite various identical provisions, the interpretation given by the EEA Court to the identical provisions in the EEA context could have a 'polluting effect' for the interpretation of the similar EC provisions given by the ECJ (see Section 2.1 above).

[41] The adoption of non-binding acts in the fields of competition and State aid (such as notices and guidelines, frameworks, and communications) is the sole quasi-legislative power of ESA.

[42] This number will be increased by one if Liechtenstein becomes part of the EEA.

[43] An organigram of ESA is at Annex D.

The judicial mechanism had, therefore, to be renegotiated in early 1992. The solution found then was based on a clear distinction between the two pillars, the Court of First Instance and the ECJ having competence on the EC side and the EFTA Court for the cases concerning the EFTA pillar. The result of the renegotiations was approved by the ECJ in its new Opinion 1/92.[44]

The rules governing the EFTA Court of Justice are laid down in Article 108 (2) of the EEA Agreement and in more detail in the ESA/Court Agreement. The EFTA Court will consist of five judges[45] and it sits in plenary session.

As regards the EFTA States, the Court will have the following competences:

- to decide on infringement actions lodged by ESA against an EFTA State (Article 31 ESA/Court Agreement, which provides for a procedure similar to that of Article 169 EEC[46]);
- to decide on actions for annulment brought by an EFTA State against a decision of ESA on grounds of lack of competence, infringement of an essential procedural requirement, infringement of the EEA Agreement or ESA/Court Agreement or any rule of law relating to their application, or misuse of powers (Article 36 ESA/Court Agreement, which corresponds to Article 173 EEC);
- to decide on an action for failure to act brought by an EFTA State against ESA, after the latter has been called upon to act and has not done so within a two-month period (Article 37 ESA/Court Agreement, which corresponds to Article 175 EEC);
- to decide on disputes between EFTA States on issues related to the EEA Agreement, the ESA/Court Agreement, or the Standing Committee Agreement (Article 32 ESA/Court Agreement).

As concerns the right of natural and legal persons to bring actions for annulment of decisions by ESA,[47] such a right exists if the decision is addressed to that person or if, even if addressed to another person, it is of direct or individual concern to the former (Article 36 (2) and (3) ESA/Court Agreement). In addition, any natural or legal person may, after a two-month period, bring an action for failure to act against ESA (Article 37 ESA/Court Agreement).

The judgments of the EFTA Court are binding upon EFTA States. In the case of actions against ESA decisions, the decision is declared void if the action is well founded. If it has been established that ESA, in infringement of the EEA

[44] Opinion given on 10 Apr. 1992, *OJ* C 255 (2 Oct. 1992), 4; see also s. 1.2. of Ch. I above.

[45] This number will be increased by one if Liechtenstein becomes part of the EEA.

[46] Under Art. 31, if ESA considers that an EFTA State has failed to fulfil an obligation under the EEA Agreement or the ESA/Court Agreement, it shall deliver a reasoned opinion on the matter after giving the State concerned the opportunity to submit its observations. If the State concerned does not comply with the opinion within the period laid down by ESA, the latter may bring the matter before the EFTA Court.

[47] On grounds of lack of competence, infringement of an essential procedural requirement, or infringement of the ESA/Court Agreement, of the EEA Agreement, or of any rule of law relating to their application, or misuse of powers.

Agreement or the ESA/Court Agreement, has failed to act, it has to take the necessary measures to comply with the judgment (Article 38 ESA/Court Agreement).

Finally, the EFTA Court is competent to issue advisory opinions on the interpretation of the EEA Agreement at the request of courts or tribunals of EFTA States (Article 34 ESA/Court Agreement).[48] This is a somewhat watered down version of the famous Article 177 EEC on preliminary rulings, which has been one of the most original and useful instruments at the disposal of the ECJ. For various constitutional reasons, the EFTA States were unable to put the same instrument at the disposal of their national courts and of the EFTA Court. Under Article 34 ESA/Court Agreement the EFTA Court will not deliver rulings but only advisory opinions.

Actions brought before the EFTA Court do not have any suspensory effect. However, if the circumstances so require, the Court can give an order to that effect. On the other hand, the Court may, in any case before it, prescribe necessary interim measures (Articles 40 and 41 ESA/Court Agreement).

5.2.3 Standing Committee of the EFTA States

The EFTA side also needed a body responsible for decision-making procedures, administration, and management of the Agreement as well as for State consultations within the EFTA pillar. For these purposes a new institution, the Standing Committee of the EFTA States, was created.

One of the tasks of the Standing Committee is to prepare, on the EFTA side, decisions to be taken in the EEA Council and Joint Committee. It should be recalled that the EFTA States have to speak with one voice and the Standing Committee gives them an appropriate forum for internal consultations and preparation of common positions for the joint EC-EFTA decision-making procedures.

The Standing Committee has also an obligation to undertake various administrative and management tasks which are listed in the Agreement establishing it and which result from Protocol 1 to the EEA Agreement (procedures for the exchange of information, etc.). A more detailed listing of tasks can also be found in Protocol 1 to the Standing Committee Agreement.

Each EFTA State is represented in the Standing Committee and has one vote. The Committee normally meets at the level of high officials but can also meet at ministerial level. It may have subcommittees and other committees to assist it in carrying out the tasks.

The decisions and recommendations of the Committee are, in principle, made by unanimous vote, although a majority vote is permitted in a number of cases (listed in the annex to the Standing Committee Agreement).

[48] The right to request such an advisory opinion may be limited by an EFTA State to the last instance courts only. Only Austria has introduced such a limitation.

6. DECISION-SHAPING AND DECISION-MAKING PROCEDURES

6.1 Decision-shaping

Although it accepted the creation of an EEA, based on existing and future EC legislation, the Community was nevertheless not prepared to weaken its own decision-making powers and complicate its internal legislative process. The condition in the negotiations was that the Community would decide independently, and in accordance with its internal procedures, on new EC legislation and the amendment of existing legislation, and, where these pieces of legislation were relevant to the EEA, a separate decision on their inclusion in the EEA would be made with the EFTA partners. This did not, however, exclude the possibility of EFTA States participating in the preparatory stages of the EC legislative process, called 'decision-shaping'.

According to Article 99 EEA, as soon as new legislation is being drawn up by the Commission in a field relevant to the EEA Agreement, the Commission shall informally consult the EFTA side as it consults EC Member States. When the proposal for a new act is transmitted to the EC Council, a copy will be transmitted to the EFTA States. At this stage, if so wished by a Contracting Party, a preliminary exchange of views may take place in the EEA Joint Committee. During the phase preceding the decision of the EC Council, the Contracting Parties shall, upon request, consult each other in the Joint Committee at the significant stages.

Following the provisions of Article 100 EEA, the EC Commission shall ensure experts of the EFTA States as wide a participation as possible according to the areas concerned, in the preparatory stage of draft measures to be submitted subsequently to the committees which assist the EC Commission in the exercise of its executive powers (i.e. the so-called 'comitology committees'). If the EC Council is seized according to the procedures applicable, the Commission shall transmit to it also the views of the experts of the EFTA States.

As regards the committees which are not covered by Article 100 EEA, i.e. those cases where a committee has to be otherwise consulted, or where such consultation is based on practice or other arrangements, the EFTA participation will be granted if it is called for by the proper functioning of the Agreement (Article 101 EEA). Such committees are listed in Protocol 37. The modalities of participation in each committee listed in Protocol 37, which may be amended to add other committees, are set out in the relevant protocols and annexes dealing with the sector concerned.

6.2 Decision-making

As soon as a relevant EC legal act has been formally adopted by the Council or the Commission, the EEA Joint Committee shall take a decision concerning the appropriate amendment of the EEA Agreement. Such an amendment is naturally needed in order to guarantee the legal security and the homogeneity of the EEA. The EEA Joint Committee shall take its decision as closely as possible, in time, to the adoption by the Community of the corresponding new act with the view of permitting a simultaneous application in the EC and the EEA (Article 102 (1) EEA).

It is intended that for the amendment of the annexes of the EEA Agreement the Joint Committee will take a separate decision for each individual EC act. Pursuant to Article 103 EEA, these decisions will then be ratified by each Contracting Party following its constitutional requirements. If ratification has not been completed within six months after the decision it shall be applied provisionally unless a Party disagrees with such a provisional application. In that case, or in the case of non-ratification by a Party, the rules on suspension of the Agreement will apply. Therefore, the application might not in practice be completely simultaneous.[49]

As far as the *acquis* adopted between the cut-off date (31 July 1991) and the entry into force of the Agreement is concerned, this has been put in a so-called 'Additional Package' which will be adopted by the EEA Joint Committee as soon as the Agreement enters into force. It can be presumed that the entry into force of such EEA Joint Committee package decision will be approximately six months after the decision.

Another important aspect concerning the introduction of new acts into the EEA Agreement is transparency. For this purpose special arrangements have been agreed upon. A decision extending Community legislation to the whole of the EEA will be published in the Community languages, in a special EEA Section of the *Official Journal*. Translations into the Nordic languages will be published in an special EEA Supplement issued by the EFTA pillar.

Just as the Community was reluctant to surrender its autonomy in decision-making, the EFTA States were reluctant to restrict their own autonomy as regards the future additions to the EEA Agreement. Therefore, each new EC act has to be examined to find out whether it is EEA relevant and, if so, whether it is possible to take it over as such, amended only by the necessary technical adaptations, or whether there are some substantive problems which call for transitional periods or derogations.

If, notwithstanding the efforts made to find appropriate solutions, agreement on

[49] In some cases the non-simultaneous application may cause problems, at least in theory. This could happen when an act grants certain benefits to or lays obligations upon individuals or undertakings. An example could be the non-simultaneous entry into force of a group exemption in the field of competition, where undertakings in EFTA countries would not be in a position to include certain conditions in their agreements unless they had obtained an individual exemption, while the EC companies would be free to do so thanks to the new group exemption. The matter could certainly be solved through a mutual understanding by the two surveillance authorities to the effect that, *de facto*, both of them would act as if the group exemption were already in force EEA-wide from the date when it entered into force in the Community (i.e. a kind of provisional application). Another or a supplementary solution would be to give, in the EEA context, retroactive effect to the act in question as from the date of its entry into force in the EC.

the integration of a new EC act in the EEA context cannot be achieved, the EEA Joint Committee shall examine other possibilities which could guarantee the good functioning of the Agreement and take necessary decisions to that effect. A solution, expressly mentioned in the Agreement, could be to take note that the existing laws in EFTA countries are equivalent to the new EC legislation.

A decision by the Joint Committee shall be taken within six months from the referral to it or, if that date is later, on the date of entry into force of the corresponding Community legislation. If the Joint Committee has not been able to take a decision within this time-limit, the part of the EEA Annex directly affected by the new legislation shall be considered as provisionally suspended, unless otherwise decided by the Joint Committee. The Joint Committee will have in this kind of case an obligation to try to find a mutually acceptable solution in order for the suspension to be terminated as soon as possible. The suspension will also be without prejudice to the rights and obligations which individuals and economic operators have acquired under the Agreement.[50]

7. UNIFORM SURVEILLANCE, JUDICIAL MECHANISM, AND DISPUTE SETTLEMENT

7.1 Uniform interpretation

As seen above, homogeneity is one of the key objectives of the EEA Agreement. This objective was reinforced in different parts of the Agreement during the renegotiation phase after the first ECJ Opinion (1/91). In the preamble of the EEA Agreement it is stated:

> in full deference to the independence of the courts, the objective of the Contracting Parties is to arrive at, and maintain, a uniform interpretation and application of this Agreement and those provisions of the Community legislation which are substantially reproduced in this Agreement and to arrive at an equal treatment of individuals and economic operators as regards the four freedoms and the conditions of competition.

The EEA legal system is based on EC law. Although these two legal systems are, in principle, separate, it is necessary that the EEA provisions which are identical in substance to the corresponding provisions of the EEC and ECSC Treaties be interpreted in the same way as previously in the Community, otherwise no homogeneity would exist, even at the point of departure. This principle has been confirmed in Article 6 of the EEA Agreement, where it is stated:

> Without prejudice to future developments of case-law, the provisions of this Agreement, in so far as they are identical in substance to corresponding rules of the Treaty establishing the European Economic Community and the Treaty establishing the European Coal and Steel

[50] e.g. rights acquired under the provisions on free movement of persons and social security.

Community and the acts adopted in application of these two Treaties, shall, in their implementation and application, be interpreted in conformity with the relevant rulings of the Court of Justice of the European Communities given prior to the date of signature of this Agreement.

This does not, however, solve the problem of how to maintain homogeneity as regards future interpretation. It became obvious, following Court Opinion 1/91 rejecting the idea of an EEA Court, that extending the two pillar approach to the judicial review system required some balancing elements so that homogeneity could also be safeguarded in the future. This issue was addressed in other provisions of the EEA Agreement as well as in the ESA/Court Agreement. Without going into details, the different means to guarantee homogeneity and uniform interpretation can be described as follows:

1. According to Article 105 EEA, in order to achieve the objective of arriving at as uniform an interpretation as possible of the EEA Agreement and those provisions of the Community legislation which are substantially reproduced in it, the Joint Committee shall keep under constant review the developments of the case-law of the European Court of Justice and the EFTA Court and, when necessary, act so as to preserve the homogeneous interpretation of the Agreement. This is without prejudice to the independence of the Courts; that is, the Joint Committee cannot change the decisions of the courts but it has rather to take the situation into account and change the legislation. The EEA Joint Committee shall also set up a system of exchange of information concerning judgments by the EFTA Court, the ECJ, the EC Court of First Instance and the last instance courts of the EFTA States.

2. The EEA Agreement also gives the EFTA States the chance to allow their national courts to ask for a preliminary ruling from the European Court of Justice. This is provided for in Article 107 of and Protocol 34 to the Agreement. It seems, however, very unlikely that EFTA countries will make use of this possibility.[51]

3. The dispute settlement mechanism laid down in Article 111 EEA also contains provisions to safeguard homogeneity. If the dispute in question concerns interpretation of provisions of the EEA Agreement which are identical in substance to the corresponding EC rules and if agreed upon by the Contracting Parties to the dispute, it will be possible to ask the European Court of Justice to give a ruling on the interpretation of the relevant rules. The word 'ruling' implies that the interpretation given by the Court is of a binding nature.

4. Finally, Article 3 (2) of the ESA/Court Agreement provides that:

In the interpretation and application of the EEA Agreement and this Agreement, the EFTA Surveillance Authority and the EFTA Court shall pay due account to the principles laid down by the relevant rulings by the Court of Justice of the European Communities given after the date of signature of the EEA Agreement and which concern the interpretation of that Agreement or of such rules of the Treaty establishing the European Economic

[51] It is recalled that the national EFTA courts may also ask the EFTA Court to give an advisory opinion on the interpretation of the EEA Agreement (see s. 5.2.2. above).

Community and the Treaty establishing the European Coal and Steel Community in so far as they are identical in substance to the provisions of the EEA Agreement or to the provisions of Protocols 1 to 4 and the provisions of the acts corresponding to those listed in Annexes I and II to the present Agreement.

It seems that this unilateral commitment will be the most significant element as regards homogeneity. It should be recalled that there was reluctance among some of the EFTA countries to accept that the ECJ alone would have a decisive role as to the future interpretation of the EEA Agreement, which was also one of the reasons why Article 6 EEA refers to a 'cut-off date'. Although it can be argued that the wording in Article 3 (2) of the ESA/Court Agreement is somewhat less binding ('take due account of') and that the provision is contained in an internal EFTA Agreement, not creating obligations towards the EC side, there seems to be no doubt that the final result will be the same as if Article 6 EEA had been left without any reference to a particular date.

7.2 Uniform surveillance

The manner in which surveillance is carried out will certainly play an important role in safeguarding the uniformity of implementation and application of EEA rules. According to Article 109 (2) of the EEA Agreement, the two surveillance authorities, ESA and the EC Commission, shall co-operate, exchange information, and consult each other on surveillance policy issues and on individual cases. It is likely that effective co-operation will be one of the best guarantees of avoiding future problems.

Article 109 contains specific provisions on the handling of complaints from individuals. The EC Commission and ESA will examine complaints falling under one another's competence and inform each other on complaints received. If there is disagreement between the two bodies with regard to action to be taken in relation to a complaint or with regard to the result of the examination, either of them can refer the matter to the EEA Joint Committee, which shall deal with it in accordance with the provisions concerning the settlement of disputes to be discussed under Section 7.3. For the general exchange of information, reference can be made to Protocol 1 to the EEA Agreement.

In addition, there are specific provisions concerning co-operation between the two surveillance authorities in some protocols (see for instance Protocols 23 and 24 (competition) and Protocol 27 (State aid), to be discussed in Chapters VIII and X, respectively).

As can be seen from these different provisions, the question of homogeneity, whether achieved through uniform surveillance or uniform interpretation by the Courts, has not been an easy one to resolve. At the same time, another prerequisite was to safeguard the independence of the two surveillance authorities and the Courts. It is, however, to be expected that there should be enough willingness to resolve possible problems directly between the Commission and ESA, in the first place, and, if needed, by the Joint Committee at a sufficiently early stage. It is clear that, although the possibility exists for the Contracting Parties to use some rather drastic measures in cases of disputes, using those measures would, in the long term, not necessarily serve the interests of any of the Parties.

7.3 Dispute settlement

A procedure for settlement of disputes between the Contracting Parties is set out in Article 111 EEA. The EEA Joint Committee is competent to settle disputes and shall in doing so examine all possibilities for maintaining the good functioning of the Agreement. Certain 'cooling-off' periods are to be respected, after which, depending on the issue of the disputes, various retaliation actions such as safeguard measures or partial suspension of the Agreement might be used. A matter under dispute may be brought up by the Community or an EFTA State.

If the dispute concerns the interpretation of the provisions of the Agreement, which are identical in substance to corresponding provisions in the EEC or ECSC Treaties and to acts adopted in application of those two Treaties, and the Joint Committee has not been able to find a solution within three months, the Contracting Parties to the dispute may request the European Court of Justice to deliver a ruling on the interpretation of the rules in question.

If, within six months after the Joint Committee procedure has been initiated, there is no solution or if, by then, the parties have not decided to ask for a ruling by the ECJ, a Contracting Party may, in order to remedy possible imbalances, take safeguard measures governed by Articles 112 and 113 EEA or provisionally suspend the application of the Agreement in the field concerned by applying Article 102.

If, after a safeguard measure has been taken, there is a dispute concerning its scope or duration and if the EEA Joint Committee has not been able to solve it within three months after the dispute was brought before it, it is open to any of the Contracting Parties to refer the matter to arbitration.[52] This also applies to disputes concerning the proportionality of rebalancing measures taken to remedy imbalances created by safeguard measures.

7.4 General safeguard measures

If a Contracting Party is planning to take safeguard measures, it has, under Article 113 EEA, to notify the other Contracting Parties through the EEA Joint Committee. After the notification a consultation procedure is provided. Safeguard measures may not be taken until one month has elapsed since the date of notification unless the consultation procedure has been concluded. In exceptional situations the stage of prior examination can be excluded.

[52] The arbitration procedure is governed by Protocol 33 EEA.

The safeguard measures shall be restricted with regard to their scope and duration to what is strictly necessary in order to remedy the situation. Priority should be given to measures least disturbing the functioning of the Agreement. Although the dispute may concern only some of the Contracting Parties, the safeguard measures will apply to all of them.

When the Contracting Party concerned has taken safeguard measures, the EEA Joint Committee has to be notified of these too. They will be subject to consultations every three months with a view to their abolition or to the limitation of their scope of application.

If a safeguard measure taken by a Contracting Party creates an imbalance between the rights and obligations under the Agreement, Article 114 EEA enables any other Contracting Party to take rebalancing measures towards that Contracting Party. They have, however, to be proportionate, i.e. strictly necessary to remedy the imbalance.

These provisions of general safeguard measure are to be distinguished from more specific safeguard provisions contained either in the different EC directives or regulations listed in the annexes to the Agreement (so-called '*acquis* safeguards', notably in the TBT field; see Chapter IV below) or in special provisions elsewhere in the Agreement, such as Article 64 concerning State aid (see Chapter X below).

8. IMPLEMENTATION OF THE EEA AGREEMENT

The first paragraph of Article 3 EEA states that: 'The Contracting Parties shall take all appropriate measures, whether general or particular, to ensure fulfilment of the obligations arising out of this Agreement.'

The EFTA States have implemented their EEA obligations in two ways: first by adopting the two EFTA Agreements establishing the EFTA institutions which will function within the EFTA pillar (described above in Section 5.2); secondly by adopting the national legislation and measures necessary to put their domestic legal order in conformity with their EEA obligations.

Unless a specific transitional period has been granted in the EEA Agreement, the implementation work was to be completed by the entry into force of the Agreement (see paragraph 11 of Protocol 1 EEA, explained in Section 4.2.1 above). Furthermore, it should be noted that, as a result of the delay in the coming into force of the EEA, those specific transitional periods expressed in dates (e.g. 30 June 1993), and not in months (e.g. six months as from the entry into force), and which have already elapsed because of the delay, will in principle not be recovered by the EFTA States concerned. The latter are thus supposed to have complied with the EEA obligation in question by the date of entry into force of the Agreement. There are however certain cases where the Adjustment Protocol has set new dates for transitional periods (mainly in the field of veterinary and phytosanitary matters, Annex I EEA). This is to be checked in each instance.

The Community did not need specifically to amend the *acquis communautaire* to comply with its EEA obligations since, as the ECJ itself has declared in its Opinion 1/91:

> international agreements concluded by means of the procedure set out in Article 228 of the Treaty are binding on the institutions of the Community and its Member States and . . . the provisions of such agreements and the measures adopted by the institutions set up by such agreements become an integral part of the Community legal order when they enter into force.[53]

The Commission has, however, submitted to the Council a proposal for a Council Regulation concerning the arrangements for implementing the Agreement on the European Economic Area.[54] The purpose of the draft Regulation is to determine certain internal modalities, in particular through enabling the Commission to implement certain administrative measures on behalf of the Community. The proposal deals with the practical implementation of the EEA safeguard measures, the application of the competition rules, the determination of the share that certain EC regions are eligible to receive from the EEA Cohesion Fund, and the participation of the EFTA States in the meetings of the EC Banking and Insurance Advisory Committees. Finally, Article 8 of the draft Regulation obliges the EC Member States 'to take any measures necessary to ensure that obligations deriving from the EEA Agreement for the Community are fulfilled'. In its opinion of 28 April 1993, the Institutional Affairs Committee of the European Parliament suggested the addition of provisions concerning the decision-making process so that there is no 'erosion of the rights of Parliament on matters of political importance'.[55]

[53] Op. cit. Ch. I n. 11.

[54] See COM (92) 495 final, amended in COM (93) 466 final, of 5 Oct. 1993.

[55] See Opinion of the Committee on Institutional Affairs for the Committee of Foreign Affairs and Security (20 Apr. 1993, PE 204.533/fin, DOC EN\AD\226\226451).

III

PRODUCT COVERAGE AND RULES OF ORIGIN

(ARTICLES 8, 9, 17–20, 27, AND PROTOCOLS 2, 3, 4, 9, 14, AND 42)

With regard to circulation of goods, one of the main differences between the EEC and the EEA is that the latter does not apply to all products (i.e. agricultural products are excluded).

In that respect, the EEA is not radically different from what prevailed under the Free Trade Agreements of 1972 between the EC and each EFTA State and the Stockholm Convention of 1960 between the EFTA States, which also provided for a limited product coverage and had a free trade character. The same is true as regards the prohibition of customs duties and import quotas for industrial products which, under the FTAs regime, had already been suppressed between EFTA and the EC in early 1984.[1] Likewise, the EEA system of price compensation for certain processed agricultural products and the EEA origin rules are very much inspired by both the 1972 FTAs and the Stockholm Convention.

However, thanks in particular to its institutional structure and enforcement mechanisms, which created the necessary mutual confidence between the Parties, and therefore allowed for closer relations notably through the taking over of the *acquis communautaire*, the EEA Agreement entails several important qualitative steps:

- a somewhat extended product coverage as regards processed agricultural products, including simplification of the price compensation system for these products (see Section 2 below);
- prohibition of charges having equivalent effect to customs duties (including those of a fiscal nature), measures having equivalent effect to quotas, and internal discriminatory taxation. These were, with nuances, already prohibited on paper under the old regime but lacked the real enforcement means (regarding measures having equivalent effect, see Chapter IV);
- improved and simplified origin rules (introduction of full cumulation, relaxation of the territorial principle, simplification of evidences of origin, etc.). The EEA origin rules are explained below in Section 3;
- simplification of border formalities (inspired by the provisions of the agreement between the EC and Switzerland), mutual assistance in customs

[1] A supplementary Protocol to the FTAs in 1989 obliged the Parties also to abolish quantitative restrictions on exports by 1 Jan. 1990, and, for certain sensitive products, by 1 Jan. 1993 at the latest.

matters, and trade facilitation (co-operation to facilitate trade procedure such as the TEDIS[2] programme);

- removal of technical barriers to trade (including, for EFTA manufacturers, the right to affix the CE mark, the 'sesame' which opens the whole EEA market). These issues are developed in Chapter IV.

The sections below develop three of these issues which are of particular importance when trading goods within the EEA. They concern the product coverage of the Agreement (Section 1), the treatment of certain processed agricultural products (Section 2), and the EEA origin rules (Section 3).

1. PRODUCT COVERAGE

Article 8, on the product coverage of the EEA Agreement, reads:

> 1. Free movement of goods between the Contracting Parties shall be established in conformity with the provisions of this Agreement.
>
> 2. Unless otherwise specified, Articles 10 to 15, 19, 20 and 25 to 27 shall apply only to products originating in the Contracting Parties.
>
> 3. Unless otherwise specified, the provisions of this Agreement shall apply only to:
>
> (a) products falling within Chapters 25 to 97 of the Harmonized Commodity Description and Coding System, excluding the products listed in Protocol 2;
>
> (b) products specified in Protocol 3, subject to the specific arrangements set out in that Protocol.

When looking for whether a particular product falls within the coverage of the EEA, or specific provisions thereof, it should be checked against both paragraphs 2 and 3 of Article 8. Paragraph 2 lists the provisions which apply only to originating products and paragraph 3 lists the categories of products to which the EEA Agreement applies.

1.1 Paragraph 2: originating products

Like Article 2 of the 1972 FTAs, which limits the scope of application of the FTAs to products originating in the Contracting Parties, Article 8 (2) of the EEA Agreement reserves the benefit of the basic provisions on free movement of goods to products originating in the EEA Contracting Parties.[3]

This limitation in favour of solely EEA-origin products is legitimate as there

[2] TEDIS is the abbreviation of the EC programme Trade Electronic Data Interchange System, in which EFTA States have participated since 1989. The EC and EFTA also co-operate in EDIFACT (Electronic Data Interchange For Administration, Commerce and Transport), set up within the UN framework.

[3] For the notion of 'originating products' in the EEA context see s. 3 below.

would otherwise be little point in making an agreement under which the Contracting Parties grant each other preferential treatment.

Therefore, the following provisions will benefit the EEA-originating products alone:

- prohibition of customs duties, quantitative restrictions, and charges or measures of equivalent effect on imports and exports (Articles 10, 11, and 12) and derogations from the prohibition of quantitative restrictions (Article 13);
- prohibition of internal discriminatory taxation (Article 14) and conditions regarding the repayment of internal taxation for products exported to other EEA partners (Article 15);
- a settlement procedure for difficulties arising in trade of agricultural products and evolutionary clause regarding such trade (Article 19);
- arrangements for fish and other marine products (Article 20 and Protocol 9),[4] coal and steel products (Article 27 and Protocols 14 and 25),[5] and wine (Article 23 (*b*) and Protocol 47);
- a trade-related safeguard clause in relation to exports to prevent circumvention of trade measures taken towards third countries or serious shortage of an essential product (Article 25) and prohibition of intra-EEA anti-dumping duties (Article 26).

The other provisions will apply to all products falling within the scope of the Agreement regardless of their origin. This is the case notably for the provisions on State monopolies (Article 16), TBTs (Article 23 (*a*)), veterinary and phytosanitary measures (Article 17), product liability (Article 23 (*c*)), energy (Article 24), simplification of border formalities, mutual assistance in customs matters, and trade simplification (Article 21), competition (Articles 53–60), State aid (Articles 61–4), public procurement (Article 65 (1)), and intellectual property (Article 65 (2)).

Although it was discussed during the negotiations whether in particular the rules pertaining to technical barriers to trade (TBTs) or on exhaustion of intellectual property rights, should be limited to originating products, the negotiators voluntarily made them applicable to both originating and non-originating goods. The same applies for State monopolies, competition, or State aid rules.

1.2 Paragraph 3: categories of products

Like Article 2 of the 1972 FTAs, Article 8 (3) of the EEA Agreement limits its coverage to industrial products and a certain number of processed agricultural products (i.e. commodities obtained by the industrial processing of agricultural raw materials). This is achieved through an exhaustive listing of categories of products using the nomenclature of the so-called 'Harmonized System' (HS) established in

[4] See developments in s. 1.3.2 below.

[5] See developments in s. 1.4 below.

the International Convention on the Harmonized Commodity Description and Coding System of 1983.[6]

The Harmonized System is an international nomenclature which, essentially for customs purposes, lists and categorizes the different goods traded in world markets. It groups together goods related to the same industry, through listing in a given chapter, and, in a progressive way (from the raw material to the more processed products), all products obtained from the raw material in question. The HS nomenclature contains 1,011 headings, divided into twenty-one sections and ninety-nine chapters. Each heading is composed of four digits, the first two indicating the chapter to which the heading belongs and the last two the position of the heading in the chapter. Thus, for instance, heading 25.04 is the fourth heading ('Natural graphite') of chapter 25 ('Mineral products'). A heading may then be divided into subheadings by adding two digits (e.g. subheading 2504.10 is natural graphite 'in powder or in flaxes').

To help the users in classifying their products under the right heading and achieve as uniform an interpretation as possible, the HS nomenclature also contains interpretative rules and notes which form an integral part of the nomenclature. Furthermore, the Customs Co-operation Council (a body established by a Convention parallel to the HS Convention) may issue explanatory notes and classification opinions which contribute to harmonizing the interpretation of the nomenclature. Finally, in the EC context, the ECJ has produced a voluminous case-law notably on how to classify certain products in the different headings of the Common Customs Tariff (CCT), which is based on the HS nomenclature.

Instead of reproducing the HS list in the EEA Agreement, paragraph 3 of Article 8 simply refers to the relevant HS chapters and to a certain number of specific products listed in Protocols 2 and 3 to the Agreement. Subparagraph (*a*) concerns industrial products and subparagraph (*b*) processed agricultural products.

1.2.1 Subparagraph (*a*): industrial products

According to Article 8 (3) (*a*), the Agreement applies to products falling within HS chapters 25–95, with the exclusion of the products listed in Protocol 2 EEA.

Chapters 25–95 of the Harmonized System concern industrial products such as minerals, chemicals, plastics, leather, wood, paper, textiles, footwear, cement, glass, jewellery, metals, machinery, vehicles, optical, medical, or musical instruments, clocks, arms, etc.

However, some industrial products, although falling within these HS chapters, are nevertheless expressly excluded from the scope of the EEA. These products are limitatively listed in Protocol 2 and concern substances such as casein, albumins, and dextrins (within HS chapter 35).[7]

[6] This Convention replaced the 1950 Brussels Convention nomenclature formerly used for the Common Customs Tariff of the EEC.

[7] With regard to price compensation concerning these particular products, see below, at the end of s. 2.

The reference to chapters 25–97 alone means *a contrario* that HS chapters 1–24 (apart from the goods listed in Protocol 3; see Section 1.2.2 below) are excluded from the coverage of the EEA Agreement. These chapters concern agricultural and processed agricultural products belonging to the following HS sections:[8]

I. live animals; animal products (chapters 1–5);
II. vegetable products (chapters 6–14);
III. animal or vegetable fats and oils and their cleavage products; prepared edible fats; animal or vegetable waxes (chapter 15);
IV. prepared foodstuffs; beverages, spirits, and vinegar; tobacco and manufactured tobacco substitutes (chapters 16–24);

Unlike paragraph 2, which expressly quotes certain provisions which are said to apply only to originating products, paragraph 3 uses the more general terms 'the provisions of this Agreement'. This clearly implies that the exclusion of agricultural products from the coverage of the EEA does not relate only to part I of the Agreement on free movement of goods, but also to other provisions concerned with trade in goods, such as for instance part IV on 'Competition and other common rules' (which concern anti-trust, State aid, public procurement, and intellectual property, subject-matter of other chapters of this book).

This exclusion applies, however, only if it is not 'otherwise specified' in other provisions. There are four instances where it is expressly specified otherwise than in Article 8 (3):

- Article 21 on co-operation in customs-related matters and trade facilitation specifies in its paragraph 4 that 'Notwithstanding Article 8 (3), this Article applies to all products';
- Article 23, which is a reference point to Protocol 12 and Annex II (TBTs), Protocol 47 (on TBTs in wine), and Annex III (on product liability), specifies that 'They [the provisions in these three fields] shall apply to all products unless otherwise specified';
- Article 65 (1), which is a reference to Annex XVI (on public procurement), specifies that the provisions on procurement 'unless otherwise specified, shall apply to all products and to services as specified';
- Article 65 (2), which is a reference to Annex XVII (on intellectual property), specifies that the provisions on intellectual property 'unless otherwise specified, shall apply to all products and services';

1.2.2 Subparagraph (*b*): processed agricultural products

According to Article 8 (3) (*b*), the EEA Agreement shall also apply to a certain number of processed agricultural products (e.g. foodstuffs) which are listed in Protocol 3. However, such application shall be 'subject to the specific arrangements set out in that Protocol', that is, to the price compensation measures and other

[8] For a list of the HS chapters excluded from the application of the EEA Agreement see Annex E.

measures provided for in chapters II and III of Protocol 3, as well as in its seven appendices.

Annexed to Protocol 3 are two tables listing a number of headings taken from HS chapters below chapter 25 (i.e. 4, 7, 9, 13–15, and 17–22) as well as some headings from HS chapters above chapter 25 (i.e. chapters 29, 35, and 38); the latter are normally already covered under Article 8 (3) (*a*) as industrial products, but are submitted to special provisions.

Tables I and II of Protocol 3 concern products such as flavoured yoghurt, coffee, tea, cocoa, vegetable thickener, certain fats, malt extract, pasta, tapioca, prepared cereals, bread and pastry, tomato sauces, mustard, vinegar, mineral waters, beer, vermouth, spirits (whiskies, rum, gin, vodka, aquavit).

Furthermore, there are provisions in the Agreement which set out special arrangements regarding particular types of products and which thus, by virtue of their *lex specialis*[9] effects as to Article 8 (3), result in these products, which would not normally have been within the scope of the Agreement, being nevertheless submitted to certain EEA rules. This is the case notably for agricultural products (Article 18) and for fish and other marine products (Article 20), whose treatment in the EEA context is further discussed in Section 1.3 below.

Therefore, while keeping in mind the above-mentioned provisions, the following fall outside the EEA scope: products such as live animals, meat, fish, milk, eggs, cheese, butter, coral, live plants, cut flowers, vegetables (potatoes, tomatoes, lettuce, carrots, etc.), fruits and nuts (coconuts, bananas, citrus fruits, melons, apples, apricots, etc.), spices (pepper, vanilla, anise, ginger, etc.), cereals (wheat, maize, rice, etc.), cereal flours or groats, oil seeds (soya beans, sunflower seeds, etc.), animal or vegetable fats or oils, sausages, prepared and preserved fish, vegetable or fruit preparations (preserved in vinegar, marmalades, fruit juices), ice creams, flavoured water, wine, cider, residues from food industries, tobacco, or cigarettes.

1.3 Special arrangements as regards agricultural products and fish and other marine products

When traded, products face different sorts of obstacles which may be imposed either by States (customs duties, import or export licences (quotas), technical requirements (such as labelling or maximum levels of pesticides), veterinary inspections at the border, etc.), or by private persons (e.g. a cartel between distributors which obliges producers to market the product only through them).

For those products which fall within the scope of the EEA, all these barriers should be removed. In addition, the negotiators wanted to make certain agricultural or fisheries products, though they normally do not fall within the EEA scope, benefit from some of these trade liberalization measures. This is the reason why

[9] Under the classical law principle *lex specialis derogat generali*, meaning that a more specific provision takes precedence over a more general one.

Articles 18 and 20 refer to specific arrangements in these sectors. Given the sensitivity of the matter, notably the fisheries which are particularly important for Iceland (about 75 per cent of Icelandic exports) and Norway, the negotiations of these arrangements were among the last of all the issues on the table.

1.3.1 Agricultural products

With regard to agricultural products, in addition to the liberalization provided for in relation to the processed agricultural products listed in Protocol 3, the Agreement takes over the TBT *acquis communautaire* (Article 23 (*a*) and (*b*), Annex II, and Protocol 47), as well as the *acquis* concerning veterinary and phytosanitary issues.

Thus, in Chapter XII of Annex II (TBT) concerning foodstuffs fifty-four EC directives on harmonization are taken over, relating to issues such as colouring matters, preservatives, antioxidants, or additives for foodstuffs, maximum level of pesticide residues in fruits and vegetables or in cereals, labelling of foodstuffs, methods of analysis for testing different foodstuffs, or qualities of different materials intended to come in contact with foodstuffs.

The same goes for Protocol 47 on the abolition of technical barriers to trade in wine,[10] which refers to twenty-eight EC regulations relating to product definition, oenological practices, composition of products, and modalities for circulation and marketing.

Annex I on veterinary and phytosanitary matters, which contains about 190 EC regulations, directives, and decisions, takes over the *acquis communautaire* on veterinary issues (rules on trade in animals, control measures, notification of disease),[11] feedingstuffs for animals, and phytosanitary issues (marketing and labelling of seeds, names of varieties of certain vegetable species).[12]

The majority of the EC acts referred to above deal with products which, according to Article 8 of the Agreement, do not fall within the product coverage of the EEA (this is the case for instance of fruits, vegetables, cereals, wine, live animals, or meat). However, as already stated, the EEA Contracting Parties, though not giving up their respective agricultural policies, wanted to facilitate trade in these products. This is made clear in Article 18,[13] which in addition, by referring to 'other technical barriers to trade', intends to make sure that the '*Cassis de Dijon* principle'

[10] This Protocol only applies to 'originating wine products', which are defined as being 'wine products in which all the grapes or any materials derived from grapes used therein must be wholly obtained'.

[11] As the EC veterinary legislation is closely linked to the common agricultural policy, only those provisions relevant for trade between EEA States have been included in the annex, not the EC acts relating to relations with third countries, border controls, animal welfare, and financial arrangements.

[12] The EC legislation concerning plant health is not included in the version of the EEA Agreement as signed on 2 May 1992 because it was supposed to be substantially amended in the EC. It is intended that, once adopted, the new EC legislation should be included in the Agreement.

[13] Art. 18 EEA reads: 'Without prejudice to the specific arrangements governing trade in agricultural products, the Contracting Parties shall ensure that the arrangements provided for in Articles 17 and 23 (a) and (b), as they apply to products other than those covered by Article 8 (3), are not compromised by other technical barriers to trade. Article 13 shall apply.'

should also apply to those products which are not covered by Article 8 (3). This application of the *Cassis de Dijon* jurisprudence to these products is further developed below in Chapter IV.

Furthermore, each EFTA State has concluded with the EC, in parallel with the EEA Agreement, bilateral agreements in the field of agriculture[14] concerning so-called 'cohesion products' (certain fruits and vegetables) in order to contribute to the development of southern regions of the EC (Greece, Italy, Spain, and Portugal). These agreements are referred to in Protocol 42 EEA as forming part (together with the Cohesion Fund set up under the EEA) of the measures taken to reduce social and economic disparities between EEA regions. They basically contain a certain number of tariff concessions in favour of these cohesion products.

Finally, Article 19 EEA provides for an examination procedure should difficulties arise between the Contracting Parties in their trade in agricultural products. It also provides for an evolutionary clause with a view to achieving more liberalization of agricultural trade, which among-other things embraces the results of the GATT negotiations.

1.3.2 Fish and other marine products

With regard to fish and other marine products, which in principle fall outside the scope of the EEA, Protocol 9 EEA contains, in favour of the sole 'originating products', a certain number of measures concerning:

- the abolition of customs duties and charges of equivalent effects for the products listed in Tables I (for EFTA) and II (for the EC) of Appendix 2 to the Protocol;
- the abolition, by the EFTA States, of import quotas or measures of equivalent effect for the products listed in Table I of Appendix 2;
- the progressive reduction of customs duties, by the EC, on products listed in Table III of Appendix 2.

Furthermore, Article 4 of Protocol 9 contains provisions relating to State aid and market organization together with competition rules and anti-dumping measures. The Contracting Parties have agreed, in a joint declaration, on the interpretation to be given to paragraphs 1 and 2 of Article 4. As they relate to competition and State aid, these provisions are further discussed below in Chapters VIII and X, respectively.

Finally, in Protocol 46 EEA the Contracting Parties agree to develop their co-operation in the fisheries sector, 'on a harmonious, mutual beneficial basis and within the framework of their respective fisheries policies'. A matter which was left open at the time of the signature of the EEA Agreement was the question of transit

[14] These agreements are called 'Arrangement between the European Economic Community and [Austria, Finland, Iceland, Norway, and Sweden] in the field of agriculture'. On the occasion of the Adjustment Protocol signed on 17 Mar. 1993, it was agreed that these agreements would be provisionally applied as from 15 Apr. 1993.

of fish and fishery products. This bilateral issue between the EC and Norway still remained open in autumn 1993.

1.4 Coal and steel products

Although steel products are listed in HS chapters 72 and 73, and thus would normally fall within the scope of the EEA Agreement, as defined in Article 8 (3) (*a*), Article 27 of the Agreement, as a *lex specialis*, refers to Protocols 14 and 25, which concern coal and steel products.

Protocol 14 EEA, which applies only to originating products as defined in Protocol 4 EEA, may be summarized as follows:

- as concerns product coverage, the Protocol applies to products covered by the bilateral Coal and Steel FTAs[15] concluded between the ECSC, or its Member States, and each EFTA State (Article 1);
- as a general rule, the Coal and Steel FTA substantive provisions remain unaffected by the EEA Agreement, including the related FTAs' institutional provisions. However, where the FTA substantive provisions do not apply (e.g. in the field of competition or State aid), the EEA rules (substantive and institutional) apply (Article 2 (1));
- quantitative restrictions on exports, measures of equivalent effect, customs duties, and charges of equivalent effect are abolished (Article 2 (2)). The Contracting Parties shall not introduce any restrictions or administrative and technical regulation impeding free movement (Article 3);
- the competition rules applicable in this field are contained in Protocol 25 (Article 4) (see Chapter VIII). Article 5 concerns State aid rules with regard solely to the steel industry (see Chapter X).

2. PRICE COMPENSATION ARRANGEMENTS

The use of Protocol 3 is twofold: the lists contained in its two tables (I and II), which are in addition to be used for defining the product coverage of the Agreement (see Section 1.2.2), are also used, as regards Table I, to designate those goods which are submitted to a price compensation mechanism. This system aims at facilitating trade in those particular goods whose price is composed of two elements:

- the costs of the agricultural raw material (which remains submitted to differing domestic agricultural policies involving subsidies and protective customs duties and quotas);

[15] In parallel with the 1972 FTAs concluded between the EEC and each EFTA State, Free Trade Agreements for coal and steel products were also negotiated between the ECSC and each EFTA State (these entered into force about one year later than the 1972 FTAs).

– the value added by industrial processing (the protective duties or quotas on this industrial element have been removed).

The purpose of price compensation is thus, through making up for the differences in prices of agricultural raw materials, to try to ensure that competition is as little distorted as possible within the EEA and that producers of processed foodstuffs can, despite differing agricultural regimes, compete on an equal footing. Such a system was already applied in the 1972 FTAs (Protocol 2) as well as in the Stockholm Convention (Article 21).

Protocol 3 first contains certain rules as regards application of customs duties and other measures to the products listed in Tables I and II (Article 1 and chapter III of Protocol 3):

1. Products listed in both Tables I and II are, as a general rule, not subject to customs duties or charges of equivalent effect, nor to quantitative restrictions or measures of equivalent effect (Article 1).

2. However, for some of the products listed in Tables I and II, there are timetables for progressive abolition or reduction of customs duties and other fixed amounts (Articles 1 and 2 of Appendix 1). For some products listed in Table I there are in addition exceptions allowing certain customs duties or fixed amounts to be kept (Article 1 of Appendix 1);

The characteristics of the EEA price compensation mechanism are the following (chapter II of Protocol 3):

1. Price compensation measures are not permitted for products listed in Table II (Article 10 (1)).[16] Such measures may only be applied for products listed in Table I (Article 2 (1)).

2. As a general rule, price compensation consists in the levying of variable components upon import and the granting of refunds upon export (Article 2 (1)).

3. On import, only variable levies may be applied as compensation measures;[17] on export, only refunds may be granted (Article 2 (1)).[18]

4. The EEA price compensation mechanism is optional. It applies only if, in connection with the importation, a declaration of raw materials contained in the processed product is submitted to the authorities of the importing State (Article 4 (1)). If such a declaration is not made, Protocol 2 to the 1972 FTAs will apply (Article 11, first indent). Such a declaration shall also be made to the authorities of the exporting country when claiming refunds upon export.

5. The Contracting Parties are to establish a list of raw materials for which price compensation may be applied (Article 3 (3)); they are also to work out reference

[16] This table lists those processed agricultural products for which, already under the 1972 FTAs regime, the EC and the EFTA States did not in practice apply price compensation measures. Table II is thus a codification of a *de facto* situation.

[17] The FTA regime in addition authorizes the application of fixed levies or internal price compensation measures.

[18] The FTAs use the less precise wording 'measures upon export'.

prices for these raw materials (i.e. prices normally paid at the wholesale or the manufacturing stage by processing industries) (Article 6), as well as coefficients for converting amounts (value in the price) of raw materials into quantities of raw materials (Article 7).[19]

6. In the declaration submitted to the competent authorities, the amount (money value) of raw materials shall be indicated. On this basis, the authority will, using the agreed coefficient, convert this amount into a quantity, apply to it the reference price its government had notified, and then decide on the variable component to be applied to the product in question, in proportion to its net weight.

7. As a rule, the price compensation amount shall not exceed the difference between the domestic reference price and the lowest of the reference prices in any of the Contracting Parties (Article 8). Furthermore, if internal measures are applied so as to reduce the price of raw materials in favour of processing industries, these measures shall be taken into account in the calculation of price compensation amounts (Articles 2 (2) and 6 (1)).[20]

Since the Contracting Parties did not manage, before the signature of the EEA Agreement on 2 May 1992, to prepare six of the seven appendices to Protocol 3,[21] they agreed to work out these missing six appendices before the entry into force of the Agreement and at the latest by 1 July 1992. However, at the entry into force of the EEA, these appendices had not yet been finalized. Although it was expected that the missing appendices would be ready for adoption by the EEA Joint Committee soon after the entry into force of the Agreement, this will mean that, until the entry into force of the EEA Joint Committee decision on the appendices, the EEA price compensation rules (chapter II of Protocol 3) will not apply. It is foreseen that, in the meantime, the Parties will continue to apply the price compensation measures contained in the different Protocols 2 to the 1972 FTAs. The other provisions of Protocol 3 EEA whose application is not dependent upon the finalization of the missing appendices (e.g. Articles 1, 11, 13, 14, and Appendix 1) should thus be applicable already from the entry into force of the EEA Agreement.[22]

Furthermore, even after the EEA Protocol 3 has entered into force, FTAs

[19] These three lists, to be contained in Appendices 2, 6 and 7 to the Protocol were not yet finalized at the date of entry into force of the EEA Agreement.

[20] Under Art. 12 (3) the Contracting Parties shall inform the EEA Joint Committee of such internal measures.

[21] These missing appendices are the following: (2) list of raw materials subject to price compensation; (3) procedure for the amendment of the list of raw materials; (4) rules concerning the declarations to be used and procedures for their submission; (5) details of the verification procedure of the declaration; (6) details of the reference prices, the notification system, and the procedures for the confirmation of the reference prices and; (7) list of coefficients to be applied.

[22] This means in particular that the delay should not affect the application of Protocol 3 EEA for product coverage purposes (i.e. in the context of Art. 8 (3) (*b*) EEA). If that were not the case, the products listed in Tables I and II would fall totally outside the scope of the EEA until Protocol 3 is fully operational or, if one used Protocols 2 to the 1972 FTAs, on an interim basis, also for product coverage purposes in the EEA, the slight variations in the lists of products of these different bilateral agreements would make the EEA coverage 'variable' from one EFTA State to another.

Protocols 2 (price compensation arrangements) and 3 (origin rules) will still continue to apply in three alternative cases (Article 11):[23]

- if, concerning a Table I product, the conditions for the application of the price compensation system under Articles 3–9 of Protocol 3 EEA are not fulfilled;
- if the product falls within HS chapters 1–24 (thus outside the EEA scope) but is not listed in Tables I and II to EEA Protocol 3; or
- if the product is listed in Protocol 2 EEA (which refers to casein and certain albumins and dextrins; see Section 1.2.1).

Finally, the Contracting Parties will review at two-yearly intervals the development of their trade in processed agricultural products, the aim being a possible extension of the product coverage and the abolition of remaining customs duties (Article 14).

3. RULES OF ORIGIN

As already said above, the EEA does not entail a customs union. The EFTA countries may all maintain their own commercial policies, including customs tariffs with third (non-EEA) countries. In order to avoid circumvention of trade, rules of origin are therefore a necessity.

In the case of a *customs union*, the circulation of imported goods or their use in the manufacture of other products does not normally cause any problems. As the customs union implies common external tariffs for imports to all the countries belonging to the union, once the duty is paid for the imported goods, this allows them, and the end products manufactured by using the imported goods, to circulate freely within the area of the customs union (principle of free circulation stated in Article 10 EEC).

The situation is not necessarily so simple within a *free trade area*, as all the countries belonging to it have their own customs tariffs for goods imported from countries outside the area. For instance, imported goods cannot be allowed to enter into the free trade area through the country with the lowest tariff level and then circulate freely within the whole area. In principle, only goods which have been manufactured wholly or undergone sufficient processing within the free trade area or which do not contain materials imported from outside exceeding a certain value of the product, can get this benefit. The rules of origin are needed in this context to lay down the conditions a product has to fulfil in order to have the so-called 'originating status'.

The conditions to be applied for granting a product this preferential treatment within the EEA are contained in Protocol 4 to the EEA Agreement. The approach in

[23] In this context, according to an agreed minute, the Contracting Parties endeavour, with a view to facilitating the application of the FTA Protocol 2, to 'upgrade' as much as possible the FTA origin rules to the level of the EEA origin rules of Protocol 4.

the EEA negotiations was to improve and to simplify the complicated rules contained in the 1972 FTAs. These improvements concern some technical issues but also certain substantive changes.

3.1 Definition of originating products and full cumulation

The main principle is that a product can be considered to be originating in the EEA if it has been either wholly obtained or sufficiently worked or processed within the territory covered by the EEA Agreement.

A novelty as compared to the 1972 FTAs is the introduction of *full cumulation* in the EEA. This means that originating status can be conferred on goods by adding together production processes carried out in various EC or EFTA countries, even if each single process taken alone would be insufficient to confer originating status on the intermediate product.

3.1.1 Wholly obtained products

Article 3 of Protocol 4 EEA lists the cases where a product can be considered as wholly obtained in the EEA. Such are, for example, mineral products extracted from its soil or seabed, vegetable products harvested therein, live animals born and raised therein, products from live animals raised therein, products of sea fishing and other products taken from the sea outside the territorial waters of the Contracting Parties by their vessels, waste and scrap resulting from the manufacturing operations conducted therein, as well as goods produced there exclusively from these products.

3.1.2 Sufficiently worked or processed products

Detailed conditions are set out in Appendix II to Protocol 4 EEA for defining the sufficiently worked or processed products which comprise the other group of products benefiting from the originating status. Appendix II lists for all products covered by the Agreement the working or processing to be carried out on non-originating materials in order to grant the product manufactured an originating status. The listing is done by using the classification of the Harmonized System (HS).[24] Some excerpts from Appendix II are given in Table 1.

For reading the tables the following instructions are to be taken into consideration:[25]

1. The first two columns in the list describe the product obtained, the first one giving the heading or chapter number used in the Harmonized System and the second one the description of the goods used in that system. The word 'ex' indicates that the conditions do not apply to the whole heading or chapter but only to the products specified in column 2.

[24] For some other explanations concerning this System see s. 1.2 above.

[25] Appendix I to Protocol 4 contains guidance on the interpretation of the list contained in Appendix II.

TABLE 1. *Extracts from Appendix II to Protocol 4 EEA*

HS heading No	Description of product	Working or processing carried out on non-originating materials that confers originating status	
(1)	(2)	(3) or (4)	
[. . .]			
2203	Beer made from malt	Manufacture in which all the materials used are classified within the heading other than that of the product	
2205	Vermouth and other wine of fresh grapes flavoured with plants or aromatic substances	Manufacture in which all the grapes or any other materials derived from grapes used must be wholly obtained	
ex 2208	Undenatured ethyl alcohol of an alcoholic strength by volume of less than 80% volume; spirits, liqueurs and other spirituous beverages		
	– Ouzo	Manufacture from: – materials not classified within heading Nos 2207 or 2208, and – in which all the grapes or any material derived from grapes used must be wholly obtained	
[. . .]			
8418	Refrigerators, freezers and other refrigerating or freezing equipment, electric or other; heat pumps other than air-conditioning machines of heading No 8415	Manufacture in which: – all the materials used are classified within a heading other than that of the product, and – the value of all the materials used does not exceed 40% of the ex-works price of the product, and – where the value of all the non-originating materials used does not exceed the value of the originating materials used	Manufacture in which the value of all the materials used does not exceed 25% of the ex-works price of the product
ex 8419	Machines for the wood, paper pulp, and paperboard industries	Manufacture: – in which the value of all the materials used does not exceed 40% of the ex-works price of the product, and – where, within the above limit, the materials classified within the same heading as the product are only used up to a value of 25% of the ex-works price of the product	Manufacture in which the value of all the materials used does not exceed 30% of the ex-works price of the product
[. . .]			

2. Where there are different rules applied to different products within a heading, each indent contains the description of that part of the heading covered by the adjacent rules in columns 3 or 4.

3. If there is a rule provided in both columns 3 and 4, the exporter may choose to apply either of them.[26] If no rule is provided in column 4, there is no choice but to apply the conditions under column 3.

4. If a product has already obtained an originating status within the EEA and is used in the manufacture of other products, no account is taken of the non-originating materials which may have been used in its manufacture when assessing the originating status of the further processed goods. This means that, for example, in the value calculation to determine the origin status of a machine, the non-originating elements contained in the products used for the manufacture of the machine are not taken into consideration if those products themselves have obtained an EEA originating status.

5. The rules in the list represent the minimum amount of working or processing required, which means that the carrying out of more working or processing also confers originating status. This implies, in addition, that if it is possible to use non-originating material at a certain level of manufacture, the use of such material at an earlier stage is also allowed but not at a later stage.

6. Where a rule specifies that a product must be manufactured from a particular material, the condition does not prevent the use of other materials which, because of their inherent nature, cannot satisfy the rule. For instance, the use of additives for the manufacture of prepared foods is possible, although they would not be referred to expressly.

7. If a product cannot be manufactured from the particular material specified in the list, the starting material taken into consideration is normally the one of the same nature at an earlier stage of manufacture.

It has to be noted that not all working and processing can be considered sufficient for granting a product originating status even if they would, in principle, fulfil the conditions set out in Appendix II. Those operations which are considered as insufficient working or processing are listed in Article 5 of Protocol 4 and contain, *inter alia*:

- operations to ensure the preservation;
- simple operations consisting of sorting, classifying, matching, washing, painting, etc.;
- changes of packaging and breaking up and assembly of packages; simple placing in bottles, cases, boxes, etc.;
- affixing marks, labels, and other distinguishing signs;
- simple mixing of products where one or more components do not meet the conditions to enable them to be considered as originating in the EEA;

[26] Alternative percentages apply to certain chemicals and chemical industry products which fall under HS chapters 28–9 and 31–9 as well as some manufactures related to machines, electronic equipment, and instruments under HS Chapters 84–91.

– simple assembly of parts to constitute a complete product; or
– a combination of some of these operations.

In this respect all the operations carried out in the EEA on a given product are considered together when determining whether the working or processing undergone by that product is to be regarded as insufficient.

With regard to the accessories, spare parts, and tools dispatched with a piece of equipment or similar, they are considered as one with the product in question if they normally form part of it and are included in its price (Article 7).

Finally, there are certain neutral elements which need not be taken into consideration when determining whether a product originates in the EEA or not. Such are the energy, plant, and equipment, as well as machines and tools used to obtain the product. Therefore, their originating status does not affect the originating status of the product concerned. In the same way, other goods used in the course of production which do not enter or were not intended to enter into the final composition of the product do not affect its originating status, whether or not originating themselves (Article 9).

3.2 General tolerance rule

In addition to the product-specific rules concerning origin status, the EEA Agreement contains a so-called general tolerance rule (Article 4 (2) of Protocol 4). It allows the use of non-originating materials under certain circumstances even if, according to the conditions set out in the list for a given product, they could not normally be used in the manufacture of this product.

According to the general tolerance rule, such materials can be used up to 10 per cent of the value of the ex-works price[27] of the product. In addition, where, in the list of Appendix II, one or several percentages are given for the maximum value of non-originating materials, the materials used under the general tolerance rule have to be calculated together with other non-originating materials. Therefore, the value of the materials used under the general tolerance rule and the other non-originating materials, put together, cannot exceed the maximum percentage specified for the product concerned.

3.3 Specific tolerance rules for textiles

The general tolerance rule does not apply to textiles falling under HS chapters 50–63. However, specific tolerance rules apply to part of these products.

[27] 'Ex-works price' means the price paid for the product, delivered at the production plant, to the manufacturer in the EEA in whose undertaking the last working or processing is carried out or to the person in the EEA who arranged for the last working or processing to be carried out outside the EEA, provided the price includes the value of all the materials used, minus any taxes which are, or may be, repaid when the product obtained is exported.

First, if so specified in Appendix II, concerning a particular product, it is possible to use any basic textile materials which, according to the conditions set out in the list would not normally be permitted, if they, taken together, represent 10 per cent or less of the total weight of all the basic textile materials used. This tolerance may only be applied to mixed products which have been made from two or more basic textile materials listed in Appendix I to Protocol 4.[28]

Secondly, if so specified concerning a particular product, it may be possible to use any textile materials which do not satisfy the specific conditions concerning the particular end product if they are classified in another heading than the end product and their value does not exceed 8 per cent of its ex-works price. Materials which are not classified within chapters 50–63 may, in addition, be used freely.

3.4 Territorial requirements

Under the 1972 FTAs, a product normally lost the right to preferential treatment if it had been outside the EC and the EFTA countries during the production process. This is also the main principle in the EEA Agreement. It is stated in Article 12 of Protocol 4 that the acquisition of originating status is interrupted when goods which have undergone working or processing in the EEA have left the EEA. This principle is not, however, absolute; there are important exceptions allowing even working or processing to be carried out to a limited extent in non-EEA countries.

For the relaxation of territorial requirements concerning working or processing outside the EEA, the following cumulative conditions apply (Article 11):

- the materials used are wholly obtained in the EEA or they have undergone there working or processing which goes beyond the insufficient operations listed in Article 5 (see Section 2.1) prior to their exportation outside the EEA;
- the reimported goods result from working or processing of the exported materials; and
- the total added value[29] acquired outside the EEA does not exceed 10 per cent of the ex-works price of the final product for which the originating status is claimed.

In addition, if the list setting out the conditions for originating status in Appendix II gives the maximum value of all the non-originating materials which may be used for a certain product, the total value of non-originating materials used in the EEA and the total added value acquired outside the EEA have to be calculated together and may not exceed the percentage given.

The relaxation of the principle of territoriality does not apply to products which

[28] Example: a yarn of heading No 5205 made from cotton fibres of heading No 5203 and synthetic staple fibres of heading No 5506 is a mixed yarn. Therefore, non-originating synthetic staple fibres that do not satisfy the origin rules may be used up to a weight of 10% of the yarn. For further examples see Appendix I to Protocol 4.

[29] The term 'total added value' means all the costs accumulated outside the EEA, including the value of the materials added there.

do not fulfil the conditions set out in Appendix II but need the benefit of the general tolerance rule to achieve originating status. Again, as is the case for the general tolerance rule, the textile products within HS chapters 50–63 fall outside the territorial relaxation rule.

Finally, there are some additional exceptions from the territorial requirements concerning reimportation of goods, direct transport, and exhibitions:

1. Reimportation of goods, without them losing originating status, is permissible if the goods returned are the same as those exported and they have not undergone any operation beyond that necessary to preserve them in good condition (Article 12).

2. In principle, the preferential treatment provided for in the EEA Agreement applies only to products which are transported within the EEA. However, products constituting one single consignment may be transported through third countries with a possible trans-shipment or warehousing in those countries. The condition for maintaining originating status is that the goods have remained under the surveillance of customs authorities and that they have not undergone operations other than unloading, reloading, or those designed to preserve them in good condition (Article 13).

3. Goods which are sent from one Contracting Party for exhibition in a third country and sold by the exporter to a person in another Contracting Party may be imported to the latter without losing originating status (Article 14).

3.5 Prohibition of drawback and exemption

Article 15 of Protocol 4 lays down a prohibition concerning drawback. Drawback means repayment of duties to exporters on imported materials used in making their products. In the same way it is not possible, at an earlier stage, to grant exemption of the customs duties on such imported components. These prohibitions are necessary in a free trade area because it would otherwise be possible to distort competition: if a product has been manufactured from both originating and non-originating materials but in such a way that it has obtained an originating status and then been exported, inside the free trade area, to another EEA country, the use of drawback would put this particular product in a better position as compared with similar products manufactured in the importing country for the domestic market, where the local industries have had to pay a duty on the non-originating materials used.

The prohibition of drawback applies to all arrangements for refund, remission, or non-payment of customs duties or charges having an equivalent effect applicable to materials used in the production of goods which are exported within the free trade area if the same products retained for home use do not get the same benefit.

The exporter of products which are covered by a proof of origin has an obligation to prove, upon request of the customs authorities, that no drawback has been obtained in respect of the non-originating materials and that all the customs duties applicable to such materials have actually been paid.

The prohibition, however, applies only to materials covered by the Agreement. Neither does it preclude the use by the Contracting Parties of price compensation measures for agricultural products in accordance with the relevant provisions of the Agreement (see chapters II and III of Protocol 3 EEA as well as explanations in Section 2 above).

3.6 Simplification of evidence of origin

The EEA Agreement lays down a simplification of the evidence of origin. The previous means used under the 1972 FTAs for proving originating status were the movement certificate EUR.1, issued by the customs authorities, the same document used as a long-term certificate by approved exporters (see Section 3.6.2), the invoice declaration for exporting goods with a low value, and the invoice declaration used by approved exporters. In the EEA the use of EUR.1 as a long-term certificate disappears and will be replaced by a more flexible use of invoice declarations. In addition, some other simplifications are proposed.

As mentioned, the proof of origin will, in the EEA, be based on either

- the movement certificate EUR.1, a specimen of which is provided in Appendix III to Protocol 4; or
- the invoice declaration which, under certain conditions, may be used by the exporter as a proof of origin and which has to contain the text provided in Appendix IV to Protocol 4.

3.6.1 EUR.1 movement certificate

The EUR.1 movement certificates are issued by the customs authorities of the exporting country on application by the exporter or his representative. The customs authorities have an obligation to issue the movement certificate if the products concerned fulfil the conditions for obtaining originating status. The exporter has to provide the authorities with all the documentation necessary for assessing the status of the products. In addition, the customs authorities may request supplementary evidence and carry out any inspection of the exporter's accounts, or any other check which they consider appropriate.

3.6.2 Invoice declaration

The invoice declaration can be used for consignments of originating products the value of which does not exceed 6,000 ECU. In this case, also, the customs authorities may request additional information and documentation proving originating status.

The invoice declaration may also be used, irrespective of the value of the goods exported, by 'approved exporters'. This means that the customs authorities of the exporting country may authorize exporters who make frequent shipments and who can offer all necessary guarantees for the verification of the originating status of the products concerned to issue invoice declarations. The authorities may put conditions to the authorization granted to the approved exporter, which can also be withdrawn at any time.

3.6.3 Supplier's declaration

Finally, a supplier's declaration may be necessary in some cases where a movement certificate is issued or an invoice declaration is made out. This is the case concerning products in the manufacture of which goods have been used which have undergone working or processing in another EEA country, but this working or processing has not been sufficient to give them the preferential origin status. In other words, the supplier's declaration serves as evidence of the preceding manufacturing stages undertaken in other EEA countries, which may be important for the application of the full cumulation rule. It is recalled that the full cumulation makes it possible to grant originating status to a product which has been sufficiently worked or processed within the EEA. Therefore, it does not make any difference whether the various components come from several EEA countries or the different stages of production take place in more than one country, as long as the conditions for preferential treatment are fulfilled as regards the final product.

The supplier's declaration is made out, in principle, for each consignment by the supplier in the form which is prescribed in Appendix V to Protocol 4. However, if the supplier delivers to a particular customer on a regular basis, it is possible to provide a so-called long-term supplier's declaration to cover several subsequent consignments. The long-term declaration will normally be valid for up to one year.

As is the case with the movement certificate and the invoice declaration, the person issuing the supplier's declaration has an obligation to submit at any time, upon request of the customs authorities, any necessary documentation proving that the information given in the declaration is correct.

The simplified procedures concerning evidence of origin could, however, lead to increased attempts to misuse the system. To prevent this, the customs authorities will provide each other with wide mutual assistance and co-operate in matters related to the verification of the proofs of origin and supplier's declarations.

3.7 Issues related to third countries

The discussion on rules of origin has not been limited to Western Europe. There have been various initiatives for creating a so-called pan-European Free Trade Area and a system of pan-European cumulation, which would cover some of the Central and Eastern European countries in addition to the EC and EFTA States. This is a relevant question as there is already a significant number of different agreements in the wider European context: in addition to the EEA Agreement, the Stockholm Convention, and the 1972 FTAs between the EFTA States and the Community, one has to take into consideration the Association Agreements between the EC and the Central and Eastern European Countries, as well as the free trade agreements these countries have concluded with the EFTA States and between themselves.[30] It would certainly facilitate wider European co-operation and decrease the administrative burden related to trade if it were possible to find a broader solution for these issues. On the other hand, the possible decisions, related for example to improved market access for East European goods to Western Europe, are politically and economically very sensitive. Therefore, it remains to be seen whether such solutions are at all possible and if so, how soon they can be realized. Furthermore, the particular situation of Switzerland has had to be taken into account by the EEA Contracting Parties since many Swiss products are incorporated in EEA products (see Chapter XI, Section 3.1).

[30] See, for instance, the Central European Free Trade Agreement (CEFTA) concluded on 21 Dec. 1992, between Poland, Hungary, and the Czech and Slovak republics.

IV

TECHNICAL BARRIERS TO TRADE
(ARTICLES 11–13, 18, 23 (*a*) AND (*b*), PROTOCOLS 12 AND 47, ANNEX II)

By technical barriers to trade is understood barriers *de jure* or *de facto* to the free movement of goods resulting from differences in national laws, regulations, and administrative practices relating, *inter alia*, to the production and marketing (composition, weight, price, packaging, denomination, advertisement, labelling, energy consumption, etc.) of products.

The elimination of such technical barriers to trade is a major condition for the realization of the internal market. The White Paper[1] had already in 1985 set out to remove technical barriers to trade on the basis of a combination of harmonization of national legislation and mutual recognition. As far as harmonization is concerned, the legislative programme put forward in the White Paper is now virtually complete.

The relevant provisions in the EEA Agreement are to be found in Articles 11–13 (measures having equivalent effect to quantitative restrictions); 18 (technical barriers to trade in certain types of products not covered by the Agreement); 23 (*a*), Annex II, and Protocol 12 (technical regulations, standards, testing, and certification); 23 (*b*) and Protocol 47 (technical barriers to trade in wine), as well as joint and unilateral declarations and agreed minutes.

1. HARMONIZATION OF NATIONAL LAWS

1.1 Technical regulations, standards, testing, and certification

Annex II EEA on technical regulations, standards, testing, and certification contains some 600 Community acts that the EFTA countries undertake to implement in their national legislation. That represents an almost complete taking over of the EC secondary legislation in this area and therefore guarantees the same degree of harmonization throughout the whole EEA. The following subject-matters are covered (each one under a separate chapter of the annex):

I. motor vehicles (e.g. type approvals, sound levels, exhaust systems,

[1] See Commission Communication on the completion of the internal market COM (85) 310 final ('White Paper'), point 2 of ch. XX of Annex II EEA.

steering equipment, doors, braking devices, interior fittings, speedometer equipment, safety belts, lamps);

II. agricultural and forestry tractors (e.g. type approvals, steering equipment, braking devices);

III. lifting and mechanical handling appliances (e.g. electrically operated lifts, self-propelled industrial trucks);

IV. household appliances (e.g. energy consumption, labelling, noise);

V. gas appliances (e.g. appliances burning gaseous fuels);

VI. construction plant and equipment (e.g. noise emission, sound power levels);

VII. other machines (sound power level of lawn-mowers);

VIII. pressure vessels (e.g. aerosol dispensers, simple pressure vessels);

IX. measuring instruments (e.g. methods of meteorological control, gas volume meters, non-automatic weighing instruments, bottle sizes);

X. electrical material (e.g. low-voltage equipment, equipment for use in potentially explosive atmospheres, electro-medical equipment, electromagnetic compatibility, active implantable medical devices);

XI. textiles (e.g. textile names);

XII. foodstuffs (e.g. colouring matters, preservatives, antioxidants, emulsifiers, stabilizers, thickeners and gelling agents, maximum levels for pesticide residues, labelling, presentation, and advertising);

XIII. medicinal products (e.g. analytical, pharmacotoxicological, and clinical standards, veterinary medicinal products, protection of experimental animals);

XIV. fertilizers (e.g. methods of sampling and analysis, calcium, magnesium, sodium, and sulphur content);

XV. dangerous substances (chemicals) (e.g. classification, packaging, and labelling of substances and preparations, detergents, restrictions on marketing and use, plant protection products, good laboratory practice, batteries and accumulators, ozone-depleting substances);

XVI. cosmetics (e.g. methods of analysis);

XVII. environment protection (e.g. sulphur content of certain liquid fuels, lead content of petrol);

XVIII. information technology, telecommunication and data processing (e.g. high-definition television, telecommunications terminal equipment, and mutual recognition of conformity);

XIX. general provisions in the field of technical barriers to trade (e.g. information procedure, rapid exchange system, modules for conformity assessment procedures);

XX. general provisions on the free movement of goods (*Cassis de Dijon* communication and the White Paper);

XXI. construction products;

XXII. personal protective equipment;

XXIII. toys;
XXIV. machinery;
XXV. tobacco (e.g. labelling, maximum tar yield);
XXVI. energy (substitute fuel components in petrol);
XXVII. spirit drinks (definitions, descriptions, and presentation).

Pursuant to Article 8 (2) of the EEA Agreement, Annex II is applicable to the relevant products irrespective of their origin. It is further stated in Article 23 that the annex should be applied to all products, i.e. the product coverage provision in Article 8 (3) does not apply.

The acts referred to in Annex II are applicable with the relevant adaptations and derogations put forward in Protocol 1 and in the Annex itself. The main parts of the acts are directives, leaving the choice of form and method of implementation to the respective countries (Article 7 (*b*) EEA, which, in that respect, mirrors Article 189 EEC). Directives are of two different types: optional or full harmonization directives.

1.1.1 Optional or full harmonization directives

A subject-matter regulated by an optional directive (sometimes also described as a 'partial' or 'minimum' directive) assures the manufacturer market access if his product conforms to the requirements of the directive. However, it does not rule out the possibility of parallel national legislation covering the same subject-matter. In such a case, the manufacturer is thus free to choose whether to benefit, through the directive, from the market access or to comply with a national law. In combination with the principle of mutual recognition (as expressed in the *Cassis de Dijon* case-law, discussed under Section 2 below), a manufacturer in country A wanting to export a product to country B could in principle therefore rely on the directive, or on the law in country B, or on any other national legislation within the EEA fulfilling in a satisfactory manner the same aims, i.e. also the law in country A.[2]

In areas regulated by means of full harmonization, only those products that conform to the requirements of the directives can be lawfully put on the market. The manufacturer is therefore confronted with one common law, the same within the whole EEA, to which his products will have to conform. A total harmonization thus rules out any parallel national legislation on the same subject-matter. For some directives in the foodstuffs area, and for the directives relating to textiles, cosmetics, dangerous substances, and to measuring instruments, this approach has been chosen.

[2] For the non-initiated reader, it is not always easy to distinguish an optional directive from a full harmonization directive. Generally speaking, however, an optional directive would contain a free circulation clause phrased for example as follows: 'No Member State may either prohibit or restrict the marketing of the household appliances listed in Article 1, on grounds relating to the indication by labelling of their energy consumption, where the provisions of this Directive and of the implementing Directives are satisfied' (Dir. 79/530/EEC of 14 May 1979 on the indication by labelling of the energy consumption of household appliances, Art. 4 (1)). The national implementation would need to mirror this obligation.

The so-called 'new approach directives' (see Section 4 below) also provide for total harmonization.[3]

1.2 Derogations, transitional periods, and other special solutions for the EFTA countries[4]

In the course of the negotiations, the EFTA countries introduced some requests for derogations from the *acquis communautaire*. The Community made clear at quite an early stage that such derogations could not be unlimited in time. The derogations agreed upon in the area covered by Annex II are written out in connection with the acts to which they relate. Unfortunately, partly as a result of late-night mangling sessions, the texts are not always crystal clear.

1.2.1 Motor vehicles/motorcycles

The EFTA countries may, until 1 January 1995, apply their national legislation relating to emission of gaseous pollutants for all engines, particulates of diesel engines, and noise of motor vehicles (for motorcycles, relating to sound level and exhaust system). The directives concerned are 70/157/EEC, 70/220/EEC, 72/306/EEC, 88/77/EEC, 70/156/EEC, and 78/1015/EEC. Even after 1 January 1995 the EFTA countries may continue to apply their national legislation, but they must allow free circulation according to the Community *acquis*.[5] After 1 January 1995 the EFTA countries will be entitled to grant EEC type approval according to the requirements of Directive 70/156/EEC.

Regarding safety belts, the Contracting Parties may refuse, within the period expiring 1 July 1997, the placing on the market of vehicles of category M1, M2, and M3 whose safety belts or restraint systems do not satisfy the requirements of Directive 77/541/EEC.

1.2.2 Measuring instruments

Regarding Directive 75/106/EEC relating to the making-up by volume of certain prepackaged liquids, Sweden, Norway, and Austria[6] have certain specific arrangements in order to make use of their returnable bottles of various sizes until 31 December 1996. The EFTA countries, however, ensure the free circulation of products according to the Directive as from the entry into force of the EEA.

[3] The full harmonization directive usually contains a clause phrased for example in the following way: 'Member States shall take all necessary measures to ensure that only cosmetic products which conform to the provisions of this Directive and its Annexes may be put on the market' (Dir. 76/768/EEC of 27 July 1976 on the approximation of the laws of the Member States relating to cosmetic products, Art. 3).

[4] Transitional periods not going beyond 1 Jan. 1994 have not been taken into account.

[5] According to a declaration by the Governments of the EFTA States, the free circulation of light duty commercial vehicles from 1 January 1995 is accepted by the EFTA States on the understanding that new legislation will be applicable, by that date, in line with the other vehicles categories.

[6] This transitional period is also valid for Liechtenstein if it becomes part of the EEA.

1.2.3 Foodstuffs

On the basis of Article 101 (1) EEA, a specific solution has been found as to EFTA participation in the EC Scientific Committee for Food. The EC Commission shall nominate at least one highly qualified scientific person from the EFTA States to be present in the deliberations of the Committee.

Regarding Directive 79/112/EEC relating to the labelling, presentation, and advertising of foodstuffs, the EFTA countries may place foodstuffs, labelled in accordance with the relevant national legislation before the entry into force of the Agreement, on their own national markets until 1 January 1995. This arrangement was agreed upon in order to allow for the selling out of stocks.

1.2.4 Medicinal products

Participation from the EFTA side has been explicitly provided for in the Pharmaceutical Committee, where ESA may designate two observers when the Committee deals with tasks relating to questions of implementation.

The more important issue of EFTA participation in the Committees for Proprietary Medical Products (CPMP) and Veterinary Medicinal Products (CVMP) was not, however, solved during the negotiations. These committees play an important role, for instance in the 'Multi-State procedure', where they are to issue opinions in case of disagreements between national authorities arising during examinations relating to the market authorization of a product already registered in one EC Member State. The lack of a joint EEA forum for this kind of evaluation would seem to threaten seriously the free movement of pharmaceuticals in the EEA. The new Community system establishing, *inter alia*, a centralized procedure leading to Community authorization directly valid in all EC Member States for the most innovative medicines is at present subject to negotiations between the EC and the EFTA side. Whether to extend the system to the EEA, and under which conditions, will therefore be subject to a decision by the EEA Joint Committee.[7].

1.2.5 Fertilizers

The EFTA countries are free to limit access to their national markets, according to the requirements of their legislation existing at the date of entry into force of the EEA, of fertilizers containing cadmium (Directive 76/116/EEC). The Contracting Parties will however review the situation in 1995.

1.2.6 Dangerous substances (chemicals)

Finland is the only EFTA country taking over the *acquis* in the area of classification, packaging, and labelling of dangerous substances and preparations

[7] For the new Community system, see Reg. 2309/93, Dir. 93/39, 93/40, 93/41 (*OJ* L 214 (24 Aug. 1993)). For a concise description of Community policy regarding pharmaceuticals, in the past, present, and for the future, see P. Deboyser 'Le marché unique des produits pharmaceutiques', *Revue du Marché Unique Européen*, 3 (1991), 101–76.

(Directives 67/548/EEC and 88/379/EEC). The aim is that the other EFTA countries should join in by 1 January 1995.[8] An important implication of this is that only Finland will participate in the notification scheme for new chemicals to be placed on the market. Finland will therefore appoint competent authorities for receiving notifications and carry out assessments in accordance with the general principles laid down in the directives, including, for example, requirements on confidentiality. A decision by any appointed competent authority, to the extent that the notified substance or preparation is in conformity with the Directives and therefore can be placed on the market, will be valid throughout the EEA.

Regarding restrictions on the marketing and use of certain dangerous substances and preparations (Directive 76/769/EEC), the EFTA countries are free to limit access to their markets according to the requirements of their legislation existing at the date of entry into force of the Agreement concerning chlorinated organic solvents, asbestos fibres, mercury compounds, arsenic compounds, organostannic compounds, pentachlorophenol, cadmium, and batteries (concerning batteries, also Directive 91/157/EEC). The Contracting Parties have agreed to review the situation in 1995.

The EFTA countries are also free to limit access to their markets, according to requirements of their legislation existing at the date of entry into force of the EEA Agreement, of pesticides (Directive 78/631/EEC relating to the classification, packaging, and labelling hereof), plant protection products (Directive 79/117/EEC), as well as of substances that deplete the ozone layer (Regulation EEC 594/91). For the latter, the Contracting Parties have further undertaken to organize practical ways of co-operation and to review the situation in 1995.

1.2.7 Toys

Norway has a transitional period until 1 January 1995 to comply with the Toys Directive (88/378/EEC). The derogations applicable for dangerous substances and preparations (see Section 1.2.6 above) are also valid for toys containing such substances and preparations (e.g. chemistry experiment boxes).

1.2.8 Construction products

The EFTA States' participation in the work of the European Organization of Technical Approval (EOTA) is based on the comitology solution laid down in

[8] The exact wording of the first part of the derogation text is as follows: 'The Contracting Parties agree on the objective that the provisions of the Community acts on dangerous substances and preparations should apply by 1 January 1995. Finland shall comply with the provisions of the acts as from the entry into force of the seventh amendment to Council Directive 67/548/EEC. Pursuant to cooperation to be initiated from the signature of this Agreement in order to solve remaining problems, a review of the situation will take place during 1994, including matters not covered by Community legislation. If an EFTA State concludes that it will need any derogation to the Community acts relating to classification and labelling, the latter shall not apply to it unless the EEA Joint Committee agrees on another solution.' Points 1 and 10 of chapter XV of Annex II EEA. The above-mentioned seventh amendment was adopted by the Council on 30 April 1992 (92/32 EEC, *OJ* L 154 (5 June 1992), 1) and entered into force on 31 Oct. 1993.

Article 100 EEA. The EOTA consists of a number of approval bodies from all the EC Member States. It issues European Technical Approvals, a parallel, but speedier, route to an assessment procedure, recognized by the Construction Products Directive. How the practical participation of EFTA approval bodies in this organization is to function remains unclear.

2. MUTUAL RECOGNITION

2.1 Measures having equivalent effect to quantitative restrictions[9]

According to Articles 11 and 12 of the EEA Agreement, all quantitative restrictions on import and export and all measures having equivalent effect shall be prohibited between the Contracting Parties.[10] This wording corresponds to that of Articles 30 and 34 EEC.[11] A quantitative restriction, or a quota, is a measure restricting the import or export of a given product by amount or by value. As such, the notion of a quantitative restriction poses very little difficulty. As the ECJ explained in *Geddo* v. *Ente Nazionale Risi*, 'The prohibition of quantitative restrictions covers measures which amount to a total or partial restraint of, according to the circumstances, imports, exports, or goods in transit.'[12]

Between the EFTA States and the Community, quantitative restrictions on imports were already prohibited under the 1972 FTAs. A supplementary Protocol to the FTAs (1989) obliged the Contracting Parties in addition to abolish quantitative export restrictions by 1 January 1990, and for some sensitive products by at the latest 1 January 1993. Even though measures having equivalent effect to quantitative restrictions were also prohibited under the FTAs, that prohibition remained more or less a dead letter. The ECJ has explicitly stated that the notion 'measures having equivalent effect' could not be given the same interpretation in the context of a Free Trade Agreement as the one given under Articles 30 and 36 EEC.[13]

Articles 30 to 36 EEC and 11 to 13 EEA cannot be applied in areas subject to a total harmonization. The lack of harmonizing measures on an EC/EEA level, or the existence of only optional harmonization, is therefore a prerequisite for applying those Articles.[14]

[9] The literature on this subject is quite abundant. It is not our aim to rewrite what has already been explained in a clear manner by various experts on Community law, but to put it in an EEA perspective. Readers wanting to deepen their knowledge on this issue should see the Bibliography relating to technical barriers to trade.

[10] In derogation of Art. 11, Iceland may according to Protocol 7 maintain quantitative restrictions with regard to some products of minor general importance.

[11] See table of correspondence in Annex B.

[12] Case 2/73 [1973] ECR 865, at 879.

[13] e.g Case 270/80 *Polydor* op. cit. Ch. II n. 5 and the other cases referred to where the ECJ recently became more flexible in that respect.

[14] See e.g Case 227/82 *van Bennekom*: 'It is only when Community directives, in pursuance of Article 100 of the Treaty, make provision for the full harmonization of all measures needed to ensure the protection of human and animal life and institute Community procedures to monitor compliance therewith that recourse to Article 36 ceases to be justified' (ground 35).

2.1.1 What are 'measures having equivalent effect'?

The novelty brought by the EEA Agreement is that, by the combined reading of Articles 11 and 12 with Article 6 EEA, the ECJ interpretation of 'measures having equivalent effect' will also be valid for the EFTA countries.[15] In the *Dassonville* case the ECJ defined such measures to be: 'All trading rules enacted by Member States which are capable of hindering, directly or indirectly, actually or potentially, intra-Community trade.'[16]. Consequently, in the EEA context, a measure having equivalent effect to a quantitative restriction would be defined as a trading rule capable of hindering, directly or indirectly, actually or potentially, intra-EEA trade.

As seen from this definition, and the very abundant case-law of the ECJ, the concept of 'measures having equivalent effect' has been given a very wide interpretation. However, in a recent judgment rendered by the ECJ on 24 November 1993 (Joined Cases 267 & 268/91 *Keck & Mithouard*) an indication was given that changes might be under way to alter the definition (or at least to narrow the interpretation thereof). The Court held:

> In view of the increasing tendency of traders to invoke Article 30 of the Treaty as a means of challenging any rules whose effect is to limit their commercial freedom even where such rules are not aimed at products from other Member States, the Court considers it necessary to re-examine and clarify its case-law on this matter. . . . contrary to what has previously been decided, the application to products from other Member States of national provisions restricting or prohibiting certain selling arrangements is not such as to hinder directly or indirectly actually or potentially, trade between Member States within the meaning of the *Dassonville* judgment . . . provided that those provisions apply to all affected traders operating within the national territory and provided that they affect in the same manner, in law and in fact, the marketing of domestic products and of those from other Member States. (grounds 14 and 16)

The particular selling arrangement at stake in this case was a French law imposing a general prohibition on resale at a loss, which the Court, consequently, considered to be compatible with Article 30 EEC.

It is not the intention here to enter into polemics. Readers having an interest in this matter, however, are advised to keep an eye on the development of the case-law. Some types of measures which have, in the past, been considered to fall under the prohibition of Article 30 EEC are presented below.

The ECJ case-law is here particularly abundant. In order to make things easier for the reader, some 270 cases with short descriptions and references have been listed in Annex F. Some of those cases will be referred to in the sections below.[17]

2.1.1.1 Price controls

The ECJ has on several occasions scrutinized the compatibility of national

[15] For Article 6 see Ch. II, s. 7.1.

[16] Case 8/74, ground 5.

[17] Annex F further contains the precise references as to, for example, publication data for the cases quoted in the sections below.

price-fixing measures with Article 30 EEC. Generally, the ECJ has considered that although a maximum or minimum price-regulatory measure, applicable without distinction to domestic and imported products, does not in itself constitute a measure having an effect equivalent to a quantitative restriction, it may have such an effect when it is fixed at a level where the sale of the imported products becomes, if not impossible, more difficult than that of domestic products.[18] This would be the case in particular:

- where fixed minimum prices prevent the lower cost price of the imported products from being reflected in the retail selling price, therefore cancelling out the competitive advantage conferred by lower cost prices;[19]
- where fixed maximum prices have the effect that importers of more highly priced goods might have to cut their profit margins or be forced to sell at a loss;[20]
- where national price freeze rules, by preventing increases in the prices of imported products from being passed on in selling prices, freeze prices at such a low level that, having regard to the general situation of imported products compared to that of domestic products, dealers wishing to import the product in question can only do so at a loss or, in the light of the level of the frozen prices of national products, are induced to give preference to the latter.[21]

Selective price measures taken by national authorities to restrict importation of products from other Member States have been declared clearly incompatible with Article 30.[22]

2.1.1.2 Rules concerning the production, designation, and marketing of products

A wide range of national measures relating to the composition of products, production methods, designation, origin marking, packaging requirements, advertisement, etc. have been considered by the ECJ to be measures having an equivalent effect to quantitative restrictions. For example, such measures are in particular:

- national legislation requiring products imported from other Member States to bear an indication of origin or the word 'foreign';[23]

[18] Case 13/77 *GB-INNO-BM* v. *ATAB* at ground 52. Also Case 65/75 *Tasca*, Case 82/77 *Van Tiggele*, and Joined Cases 177 and 178/82 *Van de Haar and Kaveka de Meern*.

[19] Case 82/77 *Van Tiggele*, grounds 10–21. Also Case 231/83 *Cullet*. In the first case, the Court suggested however that a prohibition on selling below cost price, or a minimum profit margin, would be acceptable, since it would have no adverse effect on trade between Member States (principle applied in Case 78/82 *Commission* v. *Italy*).

[20] Case 65/75 *Tasca*.

[21] Case 5/79 *Buys*, ground 26. Also Cases 16–20/79 *Danis*, ground 7.

[22] Case 90/82 *Commission* v. *France*, ground 27.

[23] Case 113/80 *Commission* v. *Ireland*, regarding souvenirs and articles of jewellery. Also Case 207/83 *Commission* v. *UK*, regarding origin marking of certain retail goods (clothing, textiles).

- national legislation making the marketing conditional upon the product being packed in a wrapping of a certain shape;[24]
- requirements that the whole or part of the production process should take place on national territory;[25]
- national legislation making the use of a trade name for a foodstuff subject to the observance of minimum fat contents;[26]
- national provisions banning the import of alcoholic beverages with an alcohol content lower than the minimum prescribed in the exporting Member State for its domestic market when no such minimum is prescribed for marketing the beverage produced in the importing Member State;[27]
- national rules prohibiting without prior authorization the marketing of foodstuffs to which vitamins have been added;[28]
- national rules prohibiting the marketing of foodstuffs not fulfilling certain purity requirements where, in view of the findings of international scientific research, the additive in question does not present a risk to public health;[29]
- national rules reserving a certain designation only to fresh and not to identical frozen products;[30]
- obligation to use exclusively a specific language for the labelling of foodstuffs, without allowing for the possibility of using another language easily understood by purchasers or of ensuring that the purchaser is informed by other measures.[31]

2.1.1.3 Buy-national policies

In *Commission* v. *Ireland* the ECJ considered the implementation of a programme 'defined by the government which affects the national economy as a whole and which is intended to check the flow of trade between Member States by encouraging the purchase of domestic products, by means of an advertising campaign on a national scale and the organization of special procedures applicable solely to domestic products, and where those activities are attributable as a whole to the government and are pursued in an organized fashion throughout the national territory'[32] to be a measure having an effect equivalent to quantitative restrictions. The ECJ further stated in *Apple and Pear Development Council*[33] that it would be

[24] Case 261/81 *Rau*, where margarine had to be packed in cube-shaped boxes. Also Case 16/83 *Prantl*, where national legislation allowed only certain national producers to use a specific shape of wine bottle.

[25] Case 13/78 *Eggers*.

[26] Case 286/86 *Deserbais* (use of the name 'Edam' restricted to cheese having a certain minimum fat content).

[27] Case 59/82 *Schutzverband* (vermouth).

[28] Case 174/82 *Sandoz*.

[29] Case 178/84 *Commission* v. *Germany* (purity of beer).

[30] Case 298/87 *Smanor* (the name 'yoghurt' was reserved solely to fresh, and not frozen, yoghurt).

[31] Case 369/89 *Peeters*. See further 'Interpretative Commission communication concerning the use of languages in the marketing of foodstuffs in the light of the judgment in the Peeters case' (COM (93) 532 final).

[32] Case 249/81 *Buy Irish Campaign*, ground 29.

[33] Case 222/82 *Apple and Pear Development Council.*

contrary to Article 30 EEC for a national development organization to engage in publicity intended to discourage the purchase of products from other Member States or to disparage those products in the eyes of consumers or to advise consumers to purchase domestic products solely by reason of their national origin.

2.1.1.4 Duplication of tests, inspections, and administrative practices

National measures amounting to duplication of tests and inspections already carried out in another Member State have been considered to be contrary to Article 30 EEC when such procedures entail unreasonable costs or delays. In *Biologische Producten*, a case where a Member State required approval for imported plant protection products already approved in another Member State, the ECJ ruled that checks should not exceed what is necessary to achieve the intended purpose or subject the importer to excessive obligations or unnecessary expenses.[34]

In the matter of approval procedures for registration of imported vehicles already approved or authorized for use in a Member State, the ECJ has stated that such procedures are compatible with the EEC Treaty only on condition that:

(a) the checking procedure does not entail unreasonable cost or delay and the public authorities ensure that these conditions are fully met where the manufacturer or his authorized representative is called on to carry out the necessary checks;
(b) the importer may, as an alternative to the checking procedure, produce documents issued in the exporting Member State in so far as those documents provide the necessary information based on checks already carried out.[35]

The concept of measures having an effect equivalent to quantitative restrictions further applies to systematic veterinary and public health inspections.[36]

2.1.2 The *Cassis de Dijon* case-law

By *Cassis de Dijon* case-law is understood a wide range of cases aimed at further clarifying the notion of measures having equivalent effect. Its importance stems from the fact that, on the one hand, it introduced the principle of *mutual recognition*, and, on the other, it recognized the existence of so-called *mandatory requirements*.

2.1.2.1 Case 120/78: Cassis de Dijon

The German company Rewe-Zentral AG requested authorization from the

[34] Case 272/80 *Frans-Nederlandse Maatschappij voor Biologische Producten*. Also Case 188/84 *Commission* v. *France*, regarding requirement that imported woodworking machines comply with technical standards and undergo a type-approval procedure.

[35] Case 406/85 *Gofette & Gilliard*, ground 12. Also Case 154/85 *Commission* v. *Italy*, where an increase by a Member State in the number of administrative requirements involving the production of documents necessary for parallel imports of vehicles, whether new or already registered, from other Member States was considered to be a prohibited measure. Also Case 50/83 *Commission* v. *Italy*, on non-admission to registration procedures for buses older than seven years imported from another Member State as well as roadworthiness tests. On inspections and charging of fees regarding parallel imports of pharmaceutical products see Case 32/80 *Kortmann*.

[36] Cases 251/78 *Denkavit* and 132/80 *United Foods & Van den Abeele*.

Bundesmonopolverwaltung für Branntwein (Federal Monopoly Administration for Spirits) to import from France, for the purposes of marketing in Germany, certain potable spirits, including the liqueur Cassis de Dijon, containing 15 to 20 per cent by volume of alcohol. The Bundesmonopolverwaltung informed Rewe-Zentral AG that authorization to import was not necessary. However, it informed Rewe-Zentral AG that the Cassis de Dijon which it intended to import could not be sold in Germany since a national law provided that the wine-spirit content of potable spirits should be at least 32 per cent. Rewe-Zentrale AG brought the case before the Verwaltungsgericht Darmstadt, which referred the case to the Hessisches Finanzgericht. The Finanzgericht decided to stay the proceedings until the ECJ had given a preliminary ruling on the question whether the fixing of a minimum wine-spirit content for potable spirits came within the concept of measures having an effect equivalent to quantitative restrictions on import.

The Court commenced by stating that, in the absence of common rules relating to the production and marketing of alcohol, it is for the Member States to regulate all matters relating to the production and marketing of alcohol and alcoholic beverages on their own territory. The Court continued:

> Obstacles to movement within the Community resulting from disparities between the national laws relating to the marketing of the products in question must be accepted in so far as those provisions may be recognized as being necessary in order to satisfy mandatory requirements relating in particular to the effectiveness of fiscal supervision, the protection of public health, the fairness of commercial transactions and the defence of the consumer.[37]

The Government of Germany put forward various arguments which, in its view, justified the application of the disputed provision, adducing considerations relating, on the one hand, to the protection of public health and, on the other, to the protection of the consumer against unfair commercial practices.

As regards the protection of public health the German Government stated that the purpose of the fixing of minimum alcohol contents by national legislation was to avoid the proliferation of alcoholic beverages on the national market, in particular alcoholic beverages with a low alcohol content, since, in its view, such products may more easily induce a tolerance towards alcohol than more highly alcoholic beverages. The Court considered that argument not to be decisive since the consumer can obtain on the market an extremely wide range of weakly or moderated alcoholic products and furthermore a large proportion of alcoholic beverages with a high alcohol content freely sold on the German market generally is consumed in a diluted form.

The German Government based its second argument, the protection of the consumer against unfair commercial practices, on the consideration that the lowering of the alcohol content secures a competitive advantage in relation to beverages with a higher alcohol content, since alcohol constitutes by far the most

[37] Ground 8, 2nd para.

expensive constituent of beverages by reason of the high rate of tax to which it is subject. Furthermore, according to the German Government, to allow alcoholic products into free circulation wherever, as regards their alcohol content, they comply with the rules laid down in the country of production would have the effect of imposing as a common standard within the Community the lowest alcohol content permitted in any of the Member States, and even of rendering any requirements in this field inoperative, since a lower limit of this nature is foreign to the rules of several Member States. According to the Court, that argument was not valid, since it is a simple matter to ensure that suitable information is conveyed to the purchaser by requiring the display of an indication of origin and of the alcohol content on the packaging of products.

The Court further considered it clear that the requirement relating to the minimum alcohol content of alcoholic beverages did not serve a purpose which was in the general interest and such as to take precedence over the requirements of the free movement of goods, constituting one of the fundamental rules of the Community.

The Court concluded that:

> There is therefore no valid reason why, provided that they have been lawfully produced and marketed in one of the Member States, alcoholic beverages should not be introduced into any other Member State; the sale of such products may not be subject to a legal prohibition on the marketing of beverages with an alcohol content lower than the limit set by the national rules.[38]

Consequently, in answer to the question referred to it by the Hessisches Finanzgericht, the Court ruled:

> The concept of 'measures having an effect equivalent to quantitative restrictions on imports' contained in Article 30 of the EEC Treaty is to be understood to mean that the fixing of a minimum alcohol content for alcoholic beverages intended for human consumption by the legislation of a Member State also falls within the prohibition laid down in that provision where the importation of alcoholic beverages lawfully produced and marketed in another Member State is concerned.

2.1.2.2 Communication from the Commission concerning the consequences of the Cassis de Dijon judgment

After the *Cassis de Dijon* judgment, the Commission sent a letter to the Member States containing some policy conclusions it had drawn from the ruling. It was issued as a 'Communication from the Commission concerning the consequences of the judgment given by the Court of Justice on 20 February 1979 in Case 120/78 ("*Cassis de Dijon*")'.[39] That Communication is included as a so-called 'non-binding act' in the EEA Agreement.[40] The Commission concluded:

[38] Ground 14, 4th para.

[39] OJ C 256 (3 Oct. 80), 2.

[40] Point 1 of ch. XX of Annex II EEA. The notion of 'non-binding act' is explained in Ch. II, s. 4.1.

Any product imported from another Member State must in principle be admitted to the territory of the importing Member State if it has been lawfully produced, that is, conforms to rules and processes of manufacture that are customarily and traditionally accepted in the exporting country, and is marketed in the territory of the latter . . . Only under very strict conditions does the Court accept exceptions to this principle; barriers to trade resulting from differences between commercial and technical rules are only admissible:

- if the rules are necessary, that is appropriate and not excessive, in order to satisfy mandatory requirements (public health, protection of consumers or the environment, the fairness of commercial transactions, etc.);
- if the rules serve a purpose in the general interest which is compelling enough to justify an exception to a fundamental rule of the Treaty such as the free movement of goods;
- if the rules are essential for such a purpose to be attained, i.e. are the means which are the most appropriate and at the same time least hinder trade.

Therefore, in the light of Article 6 EEA[41] and due to the fact that this Communication is taken note of in the Agreement, it can be deduced that the following main principle will apply within the EEA: any product imported from another EEA country must in principle be admitted to the territory of the importing EEA country if it has been lawfully produced, that is, conforms to rules and processes of manufacture that are customarily and traditionally accepted in the exporting country and is marketed in the territory of the latter.

2.1.2.3 *Mandatory requirements*

As has been stated above, barriers to trade resulting from differences between commercial and technical rules are only admissible if the rules are necessary, that is appropriate and not excessive, in order to satisfy so-called 'mandatory requirements'. These mandatory requirements are a creation of case-law and are applicable only to the extent that the measures in question apply to domestic and imported products alike (indistinctly applicable measures).

So far the ECJ has indicated that national measures justified in the interest of consumer protection,[42] the prevention of unfair commercial practices,[43] the effectiveness of fiscal supervision,[44] environmental protection,[45] improvement of working conditions,[46] the protection of public health,[47] or the promotion of culture in general[48] may be accepted, even though they are capable of affecting trade between Member States. To be justified the measures must however be reasonable and must not restrict trade between Member States any more than is absolutely

[41] Regarding Art. 6 of the EEA Agreement, see Ch. II, s. 7.

[42] Cases 120/78, 113/80, 130/80, 193/80, 94/82, 51/83, 177/83, 178/84, 216/84, 76/86, 274/87, 382/87, 67/88, 362/88, 369/88, 210/89, 238/89, 39/90, and 239/90.

[43] Cases 58/80, 113/80, 130/80, 193/80, and 6/81.

[44] Case 120/78.

[45] Cases 3, 4, and 6/76 and 302/86.

[46] Case 155/80.

[47] On the issue of protection of human health see s. 2.3.3 below.

[48] Case 95/84.

necessary for the attainment of the legitimate purpose. If a Member State has a choice between various measures to attain the same objective, it should choose the means which least restrict the free movement of goods.

2.2 Measures having equivalent effect to quantitative restrictions justified under Article 13 EEA

Article 13 EEA, reproducing the wording of Article 36 EEC, permits a derogation from the prohibition in Articles 11 and 12 EEA. It states that prohibitions or restrictions on imports, exports, or goods in transit can be justified on grounds of public morality, public policy, or public security; the protection of health and life of humans, animals, or plants; the protection of national treasures possessing artistic, historical, or archaeological value; or the protection of industrial and commercial property. However, such prohibitions or restrictions shall not constitute a means of arbitrary discrimination or a disguised restriction on trade between the Contracting Parties.

This was expressed for example in the *Dassonville* case:

> In the absence of a Community system guaranteeing for consumers the authenticity of a product's designation of origin, if a Member State takes measures to prevent unfair practices in this connection, it is however subject to the condition that these measures should be reasonable and that the means of proof required should not act as a hindrance to trade between Member States and should, in consequence, be accessible to all Community nationals. Even without having to examine whether or not such measures are covered by Article 36, they must not, in any case, by virtue of the principle expressed in the second sentence of that Article, constitute a means of arbitrary discrimination or a disguised restriction on trade between Member States.[49]

The ECJ has on several occasions repeated that Article 36, as it constitutes a derogation from the basic rule that all obstacles to the free movement of goods between Member States shall be eliminated, must be interpreted strictly.[50]

The various grounds for justification are examined below, with the exception of the protection of national treasures (which has not had any considerable practical impact). Regarding industrial and commercial property rights, see Chapter V.

2.2.1 The notion of public morality

In *Henn and Darby* the ECJ stated that, under the first sentence of Article 36:

> it is for each Member State to determine in accordance with its own scale of values and in the form selected by it the requirements of public morality in its territory . . . the first sentence of Article 36 upon its true construction means that a Member State may, in principle, lawfully impose prohibitions on the importation from any other Member State of articles which are of an indecent or obscene character as understood by its domestic laws and that such

[49] Case 8/74, grounds 6 and 7.
[50] Cases 46/76, 95/81, and 103/84.

prohibitions may lawfully be applied to the whole of its national territory even if, in regard to the field in question, variations exist between the laws in force in the different constituent parts of the Member State concerned.[51]

2.2.2 The notion of public policy and public security

The scope of public policy and public security is difficult to define. In the *Campus Oil* case, the ECJ recognized the aim of ensuring a minimum supply of petroleum products at all times to be capable of constituting an objective covered by the concept of public security.[52] In the *Regina* v. *Thompson* case the ECJ examined a prohibition on the export from a Member State of silver alloy coins which had been but were no longer legal tender in that State. The melting down or destruction of the coins was forbidden on national territory, and the prohibition on export had been adopted with a view to preventing melting down or destruction in another Member State. The ECJ considered the prohibition justified on grounds of public policy within the meaning of Article 36, 'because it stems from the need to protect the right to mint coinage which is traditionally regarded as involving the fundamental interests of the State'.[53]

2.2.3 The protection of health and life of humans, animals, or plants[54]

Member States have often invoked the protection of health and life of humans, animals, or plants as justification for applying measures coming within the scope of Article 30 EEC. Such measures have been, for example:

- prohibition of certain additives in foodstuffs;[55]
- prohibition of certain residues of pesticides on foodstuffs;[56]
- national rules on microbiological requirements affecting the production and marketing of foodstuffs;[57]
- requirement of health inspections and technical or chemical analyses on the importation of goods irrespective of whether or not the goods have already undergone equivalent inspections or analyses in the country of dispatch;[58]
- requirement of roadworthiness test of imported vehicles;[59]
- restriction in advertisement in respect of, for example, alcoholic drinks;[60]

[51] Case 34/79, grounds 15 and 17. On public morality see also Case 121/85.

[52] Case 72/83.

[53] Case 7/78, ground 34. On public policy see also Cases 177/83, 34/84, 114 and 115/84, 149/84, 201/84, 202/84, and 239/90.

[54] Relating to the protection of public health see Cases 120/78, 788/79, 152/78, 53/80, 130/80, 247/81, 174/82, 227/82, 94/83, 97/83, 35/84, 176/84, 178/84, 87 and 88/85, 261/85, 190/87, 215/87, 266 and 267/87, 125/88, 42/90, 62/90, and 271/92.

[55] Cases 53/80, 174/82, 227/82, 97/83, 176/84, 178/84, 247/84, 304/84, and 42/90.

[56] Case 94/83.

[57] Case 97/83.

[58] Cases 251/78, 132/80, 272/80, 42/82, and 35/84.

[59] Case 50/85.

[60] Case 152/78.

– restrictions in marketing authorizations for parallel imports of pharmaceuticals.[61]

No general conclusions can be drawn as to what measures qualify for an exception, the ECJ always making the examinations on a case-by-case basis, applying a test of proportionality and reasonableness. The Court is, however, searching for genuine aims of health policy. In *Kaasfabriek Eyssen*, it stated:

> There can be no dispute that the issue of the addition of preservatives to foodstuffs is embraced by the more general issue of health protection which calls for the adoption of national measures designed to regulate the use of such additives in the interest of the protection of human health. In the particular case of the addition of nisin to products intended for human consumption, such as processed cheese, it is indeed accepted that the increasingly widespread use of that substance, not only in milk but also in numerous preserved products, has revealed the need, both at national level in certain countries and at international level, to study the problem of the risk which the consumption of products containing the substance presents, or may present, to human health and has led certain international organizations, such as the Food and Agriculture Organization of the United Nations and the World Health Organization, to undertake research into the critical threshold for the intake of that additive. Although those studies have not as yet enabled absolutely certain conclusions to be drawn regarding the maximum quantity of nisin which a person may consume daily without serious risk to his health, this is essentially due to the fact that the assessment of the risk connected with the consumption of the additive depends upon several factors of a variable nature, including, in particular, the dietary habits of each country.[62]

Serious doubts or divergencies in scientific opinions as to the harmfulness of the product could therefore prove enough for an exception under Article 36 EEC or 13 EEA.

2.3 Articles 11–13 in relation to other provisions of the EEA Agreement

Other provisions of the EEA Agreement that are of importance for the application of Articles 11–13 are related to the questions of originating products (Article 8 (2)) and product coverage (Articles 8 (3) and 18).[63]

According to Article 8 (2), the prohibition of quantitative restrictions and all measures having equivalent effect shall apply only to products originating in the Contracting Parties. As concerns quantitative restrictions (quotas), this is indispensable in order to avoid circumvention of trade. The limitation however seems unnecessary, and even contradictory, as concerns measures having equivalent effect to quantitative restrictions: contradictory to the principle of mutual recognition expressed by case-law, since a situation could arise where non-EEA products, lawfully put on the market in an EC or EFTA country could be

[61] Cases 87 and 88/85, 266 and 267/87. On importation of pharmaceuticals by a private individual for personal needs see Cases 215/87 and 62/90.

[62] Case 53/80, ground 13.

[63] For the general aspects of origin rules and product coverage see Ch. III.

hindered from further access to EEA markets.[64] Indirectly, this would imply that the national rules of the EC or EFTA country where the non-EEA product was initially marketed would not be recognized in the sense expressed, for example, in the *Cassis de Dijon* ruling.[65]

As far as the product coverage (Article 8 (3)) is concerned, mention should be made of Article 18. It imposes upon the Contracting Parties the obligation of ensuring that the arrangements provided for in Articles 17 (veterinary and phytosanitary matters), 23 (*a*) (technical regulations, standards, testing and certification), and 23 (*b*) (trade in wine) are not compromised by 'other technical barriers to trade'. That article was felt necessary as these areas contained harmonizing measures applying to products other than those referred to in Article 8 (3), for which, as a consequence, measures having an equivalent effect to quantitative restrictions would not be prohibited. Although the notion of 'other technical barriers to trade' might perhaps not as such be interpreted as being identical to the notion of 'measures having equivalent effect', the link to Article 11 seems clear, especially as it is explicitly stated in Article 18 that Article 13 shall apply.

3. THE INFORMATION PROCEDURE ON DRAFT TECHNICAL REGULATIONS

Above have been examined the instruments for the elimination of technical barriers to trade, namely the harmonization of national provisions and mutual recognition. Just as important, however, is the *prevention of new barriers to trade*. In the Community this is carried out by means of Directive 83/189/EEC, whereby the Member States are obliged to notify the Commission of any new draft national technical regulation[66] that could cause barriers to trade.

The EFTA countries have had, between themselves, a corresponding system laid down in Annex H of the Stockholm Convention. On 19 December 1989 an agreement was signed between the Community and the EFTA countries so as to

[64] The ECJ has, on several occasions, ruled that products in free circulation (in the sense of Art. 9 (2) EEC) which have been lawfully marketed in one EC Member State can move freely within the EC irrespective of their origin (e.g. Case 41/76 *Donckerwolcke*). The notion of 'free circulation', as it relates to EC provisions on customs union, cannot however be applied as such in the EEA.

[65] Another contradictory aspect is that Art. 23 (*a*), referring to Annex II containing the acts harmonizing technical legislation, is applicable to products irrespective of origin.

[66] By technical regulations are understood specifications laying down the characteristics required of a product, such as levels of quality, performance, safety, or dimensions as well as the requirements applicable to the products as regards terminology, symbols, testing and test methods, packaging, marketing, or labelling. They include relevant administrative provisions, the observance of which is compulsory, *de jure* or *de facto*, in the case of marketing or use in a Member State or a major part thereof, except those laid down by local authorities.

form a 'bridge', allowing for the exchange of information, between the two systems.[67] It entered into force on 1 November 1990.[68]

The entry into force of the EEA Agreement will allow for one common system built on two pillars. This has been achieved by including Directive 83/189/EEC in the EEA Agreement[69] with specific adaptations. To the extent that a matter is not regulated in Directive 83/189 as adapted for EEA purposes, Annex H to the Stockholm Convention will continue to apply to notifications within EFTA.

The EC Commission has proposed amendments to Directive 83/189,[70] planning, for example, to include within the procedure such national measures as fiscal incentives or disincentives intended to promote or discourage the use of a particular product, so-called 'voluntary' agreements to which the authorities are a party, or rules affecting the life-cycle of a product after it has been placed on the market. The proposed amendments will have to be negotiated in the EEA Joint Committee before being extended to the whole EEA (see Chapter II, Section 6.2).

3.1 Notifications

The EFTA countries shall immediately communicate to ESA any draft technical regulation that they are aiming at enacting. They shall also let ESA have a brief statement of the grounds which make the enactment of such a technical regulation necessary. The Community countries do the same to the Commission. ESA and the Commission exchange the information received and forward it to the other EFTA countries and the EC Member States respectively. The Community, on one side, and ESA or the EFTA countries, on the other side, may ask for further information on the draft technical regulation notified.

3.2 Comments, detailed opinions, and triggering of standstills

ESA, the EFTA countries, the Commission, and the EC Member States may, within three months after the notification, make comments to the country which has

[67] See e.g. Dec. 90/518/EEC of 24 Sept. 1990 concerning the conclusions of an Agreement between the European Economic Community, on the one hand, and the Republic of Austria, the Republic of Finland, the Republic of Iceland, the Kingdom of Norway, the Kingdom of Sweden and the Swiss Confederation, on the other, laying down a procedure for the exchange of information in the field of technical regulations (*OJ* L 291 (23 Oct. 1990), 1).

[68] In 1991 there were 435 Community notifications and 120 EFTA notifications. On the EFTA side, thirty-seven of these notifications were made by Austria, twenty-seven by Finland, twenty by Norway, twenty by Sweden, and sixteen by Switzerland.

[69] Point 1 of ch. XIX of Annex II EEA.

[70] Proposal for a Council directive amending for the second time Dir. 83/189/EEC, laying down a procedure for the provision of information in the field of technical standards and regulations (*OJ* C 340 (23 Dec. 1992), 7). These proposals for amendments arose from a number of national regulations which were seen as 'borderline cases'. The first dispute on this subject was triggered in 1991 by tax incentives for 'environmentally clean' vehicles introduced in several EC Member States (Germany, the Netherlands, Luxembourg). The initiatives by Germany and the Netherlands on packaging and packaging waste on the basis of voluntary agreements or on approaches for recycling or for the reuse of

forwarded a draft technical regulation. The comments of the EFTA countries shall be forwarded by ESA to the Commission in one single co-ordinated communication and the comments of the Community shall be forwarded by the Commission to ESA. The notifying country shall take such comments into account as far as possible in the subsequent preparation of the technical regulation.

A system for triggering of standstills is set out, if any Party should consider that the measure envisaged must be amended in order to eliminate or reduce any barriers which it might create to the free movement of goods. That system is also based on two pillars.

For the Community countries, the notifying Member State shall postpone the adoption of the draft technical regulation for six months from the date of notification, if the Commission or another Member State delivers a detailed opinion to that effect within three months of that date.[71] The standstill shall however be twelve months, counted from the date of notification, if the Commission gives notice of its intention of proposing or adopting a directive on the subject.[72]

Within EFTA, a corresponding six-month standstill shall apply to the notifying EFTA country, if any other EFTA country delivers a detailed opinion.[73] It should be noted that ESA does not, as is the case for the Commission, have the power to deliver a detailed opinion in order to trigger off the standstill period. This does not of course prejudge ESA's general obligation with regard to surveillance, that is, the possibility of initiating an infringement procedure under Article 31 of the ESA/Court Agreement once the national regulation in question is adopted.

A standstill is also possible between the pillars; the EC and EFTA countries' competent authorities shall postpone the adoption of the draft technical regulation notified for three months from the date of receipt of the text by the Commission, in the case of drafts notified by a Community country, or by ESA, for drafts notified by an EFTA country. This standstill period of three months shall not, however, apply in those cases where, for urgent reasons relating to the protection of public health or safety, or the protection of life and health of animals or plants, the competent authorities are obliged to prepare technical regulations in a very short period of time.[74]

3.3 Questions of non-validity of national regulations not notified

The Commission has issued two communications related to Directive 83/189, of both of which the Contracting Parties to the EEA Agreement shall take note.[75] In

certain products were also the subject of discussion. More recent examples of national regulations concerning the shipment of waste between EC Member States and proposals on 'eco-taxes' highlight the potential economic importance of such measures.

[71] Dir. 83/189/EEC, Art. 9. In the view of the Commission, a detailed opinion in this context is equivalent to a reasoned opinion in the sense of Art. 169 EEC.

[72] Ibid.

[73] Art. 8 of Annex H to the Stockholm Convention.

[74] Adaptation (*f*) of point 1 of ch. XIX of Annex II EEA.

[75] Commission Communication concerning the non-respect of certain provisions of Council Dir.

the first communication, the Commission considers that 'when a Member State enacts a technical regulation falling within the scope of Directive 83/189/EEC without notifying the draft to the Commission and respecting the standstill obligation, the regulation thus adopted is unenforceable against third parties in the legal system of the Member State in question'.[76] In the second communication the Commission announced its intention to publish regular lists of notifications received, in order to bring draft technical regulations to the notice of European industry.

Under the EEA Agreement, and as far as EFTA notifications are concerned, there seems to be no actual obligation to publish these notifications also. Protocol 1 on horizontal adaptations and point 6 (*b*) regarding publication are only applicable to acts referred to in the annexes of the Agreement, and not to these so-called 'non-binding acts'. It is however not excluded that the EFTA side could, on a voluntary basis, publish EFTA notifications in the EEA section of the *Official Journal*. It can further be presumed that ESA will take the same viewpoint as the Commission as to the question of non-validity of national regulations not notified.

4. THE NEW APPROACH TO TECHNICAL HARMONIZATION AND STANDARDS

In the Council Resolution of 7 May 1985 on a new approach to technical harmonization and standards (a 'non-binding act' in the EEA Agreement)[77] four fundamental principles on which the new approach is based are enumerated:

- legislative harmonization is limited to the adoption of the essential safety requirements (or other requirements in the general interest) with which products put on the market must conform;
- the task of drawing up the technical specifications needed for the production and placing on the market of products conforming to the essential requirements established by the directives is entrusted to organizations competent in the standardization area;
- these technical specifications are not mandatory and maintain their status of voluntary standards;
- but at the same time national authorities are obliged to recognize that products manufactured in conformity with harmonized standards (or, provisionally, with national standards) are presumed to conform to the 'essential

83/189/EEC, laying down a procedure for the provision of information in the field of technical standards and regulations (*OJ* C 245 (1 Oct. 1986), 4), and Commission communication concerning the publication in the *Official Journal of the European Communities* of the titles of draft technical regulations notified by the Member States pursuant to Council Dir. 83/189/EEC, as amended by Council Dir. 88/182/EEC (*OJ* C 67 (17 Mar. 1989), 3). Points 6 and 7 of ch. XIX of Annex II EEA.

[76] Communication published 1 Oct. 1986, last paragraph.

[77] Point 5 of ch. XIX of Annex II EEA.

requirements' established by the directive. (This signifies, on the other hand, that the producer has the choice of not manufacturing in conformity with the standards but that in this event he has an obligation to prove that his products conform to the essential requirements of the directive.)[78]

4.1 The new approach directives

Since 1987 and up to the EEA cut-off date, ten Community directives have been adopted on the basis of the provisions relating to the new approach. All of those directives are included in the EEA Agreement and are therefore to be implemented by the EFTA countries.[79] They concern:

- simple pressure vessels (87/404/EEC; point 6 of chapter VIII of Annex II EEA);
- toy safety (88/378/EEC; point 1 of chapter XXIII of Annex II EEA);
- construction products (89/106/EEC; point 1 of chapter XXI of Annex II EEA);
- electromagnetic compatibility (89/336/EEC; point 6 of chapter X of Annex II EEA);
- safety of machinery (89/392/EEC; point 1 of chapter XXIV of Annex II EEA);
- personal protective equipment (89/686/EEC; point 1 of chapter XXII of Annex II EEA);
- gas appliances (90/396/EEC; point 2 of chapter V of Annex II EEA);
- non-automatic weighing instruments (90/384/EEC; point 27 of chapter IX of Annex II EEA);
- active implantable medical devices (90/385/EEC; point 7 of chapter X of Annex II EEA);
- telecommunications terminal equipment, including the mutual recognition of their conformity (91/263/EEC; point 4 of chapter XVIII of Annex II EEA).

4.1.1 The concept of 'placing on the market'

The new approach directives provide for total harmonization.[80] Generally, the directives contain a clause worded along the following lines: 'Member States shall take all steps to ensure that instruments may not be placed on the market unless they meet the requirements of this Directive which apply to them.' By 'placing on the market' one should understand the moment when the product first passes from the stage of manufacture to the stage of distribution and/or use on the EEA market. Since placing on the market refers only to the first time that the product is made available for distribution or use within the EEA, the directives apply only to new

[78] Annex II of the said Resolution (*OJ* C 136 (4 June 1985), 1).

[79] For an explanation of how the Community acts referred to in the EEA Agreement are to be applied, see Ch. II, s. 5, on the integration of the *acquis communautaire*: Protocol 1.

[80] See s. 1.1.1 above.

products manufactured within the EEA and to new or used products imported from a non-EEA country.

The following actions would however not be considered as 'placing on the market': transfer of the product from the manufacturer to his authorized representative, import into the EEA with a view to re-export (e.g. under processing arrangements), manufacture of the product within the EEA with a view to export to a non-EEA country, and display of the product at fairs and exhibitions. Furthermore, the storage of a product by the manufacturer or importer would not constitute placing on the market, unless the directive provides otherwise.

With effect from the date set for implementation by the directive (or, for the EFTA countries, if that date is prior to the entry into force of the EEA Agreement, from the date of entry into force of the latter), only products which comply with the provisions of the directive may be placed on the EEA market. From then on, the EC and EFTA countries are also under an obligation not to create obstacles to, prohibit, restrict, or hamper the placing on the market of such products, and to take any measures necessary to ensure that they are placed on the market only if they meet the requirements of the directive (full harmonization).

The directives may provide for a transitional period during which products complying with the national rules in force on the date when the directive took effect may still be manufactured, placed on the market, and/or put into service.[81] For the EFTA countries, such a transitional period is to be counted from the date of the entry into force of the EEA Agreement. It is important to note that the free movement of products, manufactured in line with national regulations, is assured during such a transitional period on the basis of Article 30 EEC and Article 11 EEA (see Section 2 above). Consequently, such products could be blocked by rules laid down by other EC or EFTA countries on the basis of one or more of the objectives mentioned in Articles 36 EEC and 13 EEA. They will qualify for mutual recognition on the basis of Article 30 EEC and Article 11 EEA, if they conform to regulations or specifications ensuring an equivalent level of protection.

Finally, 'placing on the market' would refer to each individual product which is covered by the directive in question and which exists physically and in finished form, regardless of when and where it was manufactured, and whether it was produced individually or as part of a batch.

4.1.2 The concept of 'putting into service'

By 'putting into service' should be understood the first use, by the end user, of a

[81] e.g. Council Dir. 90/384/EEC of 20 June 1990 on the harmonization of the laws of the Member States relating to non-automatic weighing instruments (point 27 of ch. IX of Annex II EEA): 'However, by way of derogation from paragraph 2, Member States shall permit during a period of 10 years from the date on which they apply the provisions referred to in paragraph 1 the placing on the market and/or putting into service of instruments which conform to the rules in force before that date' (Art. 15.3).

product covered by a directive.[82] If a product has already been placed on the market before the date set by the directive for implementation by the EC Member States (or, for the EFTA States, the date of entry into force of the EEA Agreement), but has not yet been put into service by that date, it may be put into service only if it meets the requirements of the directive. This holds true unless express provisions have been made to the contrary in the directive. However, products for mass consumption which are ready for use as soon as they are placed on the market and where the distribution conditions (storage, transport, etc.) make no difference to the safety of the product are considered to have been put into service as soon as they are placed on the market if it is impossible to determine when they were first used.

4.1.3 The concept of 'manufacturer' and 'authorized representative'

By 'manufacturer' should be understood the person responsible for designing and manufacturing a product covered by the directive, with a view to placing it on the market on his own behalf. An authorized representative is a person appointed by the manufacturer to act on his behalf in carrying out certain tasks required by the directive.

The new approach directives contain various provisions referring to manufacturers and representatives that have to be established in the Community, such as: 'The manufacturer or his authorized representative established within the Community shall keep the following information available for inspection . . .',[83] or 'The manufacturer, or his authorized representative established in the Community, shall, in order to certify the conformity of machinery with the provisions of this Directive, draw up an EC declaration of conformity . . .'.[84] The territorial reference ('established within the Community') is under the EEA regime to be understood as a reference to the territories of the Contracting Parties to the EEA Agreement.[85] Therefore, and this is an important point, all manufacturers within the EEA will have the same rights and obligations as 'EEA manufacturers'. This also implies that a manufacturer established in an EFTA country will not need to have a representative in the Community and that a non-EEA manufacturer can have his authorized representative established in an EFTA country.

4.2 Standardization work

Standards are technical specifications, intended for continuous and wide use, which may cover a range of subjects: products, procedures, installations, and services. As

[82] Example of the typical phrasing of such an article: 'Member States shall take all steps to ensure that instruments may not be put into service for the uses referred to in Article . . . unless they meet the requirements of this Directive which apply to them.'

[83] Dir. 89/686/EEC of 21 Dec. 1989 on the approximation of the laws of the Member States relating to personal protective equipment, Art. 8 (*b*).

[84] Dir. 89/392/EEC of 14 June 1989 on the approximation of the laws of the Member States relating to machinery, Art. 8.

[85] By the horizontal effect of para. 8 of Protocol 1 EEA. See Ch. II, s. 4.

pointed out above, they are adopted by independent bodies and are therefore, unlike regulations, not mandatory. However, standards, as adopted by European standards organizations such as CEN,[86] CENELEC,[87] or ETSI,[88] nevertheless play an important role, indispensable for the functioning of the EEA market. The Commission has issued a communication ('green paper') on the development of European standardization, a communication which is part of the EEA Agreement as a 'non-binding act'. This was later followed up by a communication on standardization in the European economy.[89]

Membership of the three European standardization bodies is mainly confined to the member countries of the Community and EFTA. In January 1986 EFTA concluded an agreement with CEN/CENELEC in which EFTA undertakes to share the costs of standardization work resulting from standardization mandates of the EC Commission.

4.2.1 Presumption of conformity

According to new approach directives, conformity with national standards transposing harmonized standards (adopted by CEN/CENELEC/ETSI) confers a presumption of conformity with the essential requirements covered by the harmonized standards. This presumption of conformity is however dependent upon publication in the EC *Official Journal* and, as stated, transposition of the European standard into a national standard.

Regarding the publication, EEA relevant standards elaborated under parallel mandates from the Community and EFTA must be published in the EEA section of the EC *Official Journal*.[90] Without such a publication, use of standards will not legally speaking give rise to the presumption of conformity.

It results from the provisions in the new approach directives mentioned above that presumption of conformity is, in addition to publication, also dependent on transposition of the European standard into a national standard. This means that no such presumption will exist if European standards have not been transposed, even if the reference has been published in the *Official Journal*. For reasons of transparency and legal certainty, EC Member States have further to publish nationally references to the national standards in question. This obligation to publish is also valid for the EFTA countries.[91]

[86] European Committee for Normalization.

[87] European Committee for Electrotechnical Normalization.

[88] European Telecommunications Standardization Institute.

[89] Commission communication on the development of European Standardization: action for faster technological integration in Europe (*OJ* C 20 (28 Jan. 1991), 1). Point 9 of ch. XIX of Annex II EEA. Commission Communication—Standardization in the European Economy (follow-up to the Commission Green Paper of October 1990) (COM (91) 521) (*OJ* C 96 (15 Apr. 1992), 2).

[90] By the horizontal effect of para. 6 (*b*) of Protocol 1 EEA. See Ch. II, s. 4 above.

[91] By the horizontal effect of para. 6 (*a*) of Protocol 1 EEA. See Ch. II, s. 4 above.

4.2.2 Voting rules: a threat to a homogeneous EEA?

Although not obligatory, common standards are indispensable for the functioning of the EEA, especially as they, after their publication and transposition, benefit from a presumption of conformity with the essential requirements under the new approach. The present voting rules in the European standards organizations might however give some contradictory results in that respect.

Under CEN/CENELEC rules a draft European standard which receives a favourable vote from a qualified majority of member bodies (EC and EFTA) is deemed to be adopted and is implemented by all. In the event that a standard does not receive a favourable vote from a majority of the entire CEN/CENELEC membership, the votes of members from the EC Member States are counted separately and a qualified majority in favour requires the adoption of those standards by all EC member bodies and those EFTA member bodies which have voted in favour.[92]

As a result of this, cases might arise where standards related to directives which are part of the EEA Agreement are not recognized in all EFTA countries. Such a situation would, however, be a serious threat to homogeneity in the EEA, and would bring uncertainty for the economic operators. If a practical problem should arise, it would seem to be an issue for the EEA Joint Committee.

5. CONFORMITY ASSESSMENT AND THE CE MARK

5.1 Global approach

Intrinsically linked to the new approach is the global approach. In the Council Resolution of 21 December 1989 on a global approach to conformity assessment,[93] part of the EEA Agreement as a 'non-binding act',[94] some guiding principles were announced, for example:

1. A consistent approach in Community legislation should be ensured by devising modules for the various phases of conformity assessment procedures and by laying down criteria for the use of those procedures, for the designation and notification of bodies under those procedures, and for the use of the CE mark.

2. Generalized use of the European standards relating to quality assurance (standard EN 29 000) and to the requirements to be fulfilled by the above-mentioned bodies (standard EN 45 000), the setting-up of accreditation systems, and the use of techniques of intercomparison should be promoted in all Community Member States as well as at Community level.

This Resolution was followed by a Council Decision (90/683/EEC) concerning

[92] A similar procedure is also provided for in the rules of ETSI.

[93] *OJ* C 10 (16 Jan. 1990), 1.

[94] Point 8 of ch. XIX of Annex II EEA.

the modules for the various phases of the conformity assessment procedures which are intended to be used in the technical harmonization directives.[95] That Decision is part of the EEA Agreement.[96]

5.2 Notified bodies

One important result of the EEA Agreement is that the EFTA countries will have the same right as EC Member States to designate bodies to carry out the conformity assessment requirements as set out in the directives. The notified bodies are free to offer the conformity assessment services for which they are notified to any economic operator and shall do so in a competent, neutral, independent, and non-discriminatory manner. Notified bodies are third parties. As such they should remain independent of their clients and other interested parties.

EC Member States and EFTA States are free to notify any number of bodies they consider necessary, as long as the qualitative conditions are fulfilled (e.g. conformity to the EN 45 000 series of standards). Each body notified will be assigned an identification number and this information will be published in the *Official Journal*, for the EFTA countries in the EEA section thereof.[97]

It is the responsibility of the notifying country to ensure that notified bodies implement fully the conditions under which they are notified. Should a body cease to fulfil these conditions, an EC Member State shall immediately inform the Commission and the other EC Member States, and an EFTA State shall accordingly inform ESA and the other EFTA States. If doubts arise as to the competence of a notified body, and the notifying country refuses to provide appropriate documented evidence, it is the Commission's or, in the case of an EFTA country, ESA's responsibility to act. They may initiate the infringement procedure in Article 169 EEC and Article 31 ESA/Court Agreement respectively.

5.3 CE mark

The CE mark shows conformity with Community legislation. It will, as such, be used within the whole EEA, and it can also be affixed by manufacturers and notified bodies in the EFTA countries. The principal guidelines for the affixing and use of the CE marking are as follows:

- the CE marking symbolizes conformity to all the obligations incumbent on manufacturers for the product by virtue of the Community directives providing for its affixing. Thus, such conformity is not limited to the essential requirements relating to safety, public health, consumer protection, etc., as certain directives may impose specific obligations not necessary forming part of the essential requirements;

[95] *OJ* L 380 (21 Dec. 1990), 13.
[96] Point 3 of ch. XIX of Annex II EEA. See, however, s. 5.3 and note 99 below.
[97] See n. 90 above.

– the CE marking affixed to industrial products symbolizes the fact that the natural or legal person having affixed or been responsible for the affixing has verified that the product conforms to all the Community total harmonization provisions which apply to it and has been the subject of the appropriate conformity evaluation procedures;
– where the industrial products are subject to other directives concerning other aspects and which also provide for the affixing of the CE marking, the latter must indicate that the products are also presumed to conform to the provisions of those directives;
– the CE marking must be affixed to the product or to its data plate. However, where this is not possible, it must be affixed to the packaging, if any, and to the accompanying document;
– the CE marking must be followed by the identification number of the notified body where the said body is involved in the production control;
– a product may bear different marks, for example marks indicating conformity to national or European standards or with traditional optional directives, provided such marks are not liable to cause confusion with the CE marking.

Reference to the use of the CE mark is made in the ten directives based on the new approach (see Section 4.1 above). Examination of these directives shows that there are differences as regards the affixing of the CE mark. In order to clear up some of the confusion on this issue and enable economic operators to know exactly what their marking obligations are under the various Community acts, the Commission presented, on 17 May 1991, a proposal for a regulation harmonizing the provisions regarding the affixing and use of the CE mark in the various new approach directives.[98] In its Opinion of April 1992 at first reading, the European Parliament approved the Commission's initiative while at the same time proposing a number of amendments. The Commission adopted most of these amendments and on 10 July 1992, by virtue of Article 149 (3) EEC, sent the Council a new proposal amended on that basis. The Council examined these proposals, but finally preferred a directive amending existing new approach directives as well as a decision to establish marking rules to apply to future directives.[99] The decision constitutes an amendment of the Council Decision 90/683/EEC concerning the certification modules for use in future technical directives (see Section 5.1 above).

As the new approach directives as well as the Council Decision 90/683/EEC concerning the certification modules are part of the EEA Agreement, it can be expected that the Council directive and decision will, by decision of the EEA Joint Committee, become applicable within the EEA.

[98] Proposal for a Council regulation (EEC) concerning the affixing and use of the CE mark of conformity on industrial products (COM (91) 145 final).

[99] Council Dir. 93/68/EEC of 22 July 1993 and Council Dec. 93/465/EEC of 22 July 1993 (both published in *OJ* L 220 (30 Aug. 1993)).

5.3.1 Use of the CE mark by non-EEA countries

In its Resolution of 21 December 1989 (see Section 5.1 above) the Council also gave guidance as to the Community's relations to third countries in the area of conformity assessment. The Community will endeavour to promote international trade in regulated products, in particular by concluding mutual recognition agreements on the basis of Article 113 EEC in accordance with Community law and with the Community's international obligations, while ensuring in the latter case that:

- the competence of the third country bodies is and remains on a par with that required of their Community counterparts,
- the mutual recognition arrangements are confined to reports, certificates and marks drawn up and issued directly by the bodies designated in the agreements,
- in cases where the Community wishes to have its own bodies recognized, the agreements establish a balanced situation with regard to the advantages derived by the parties in all matters relating to conformity assessment for the products concerned.

As the CE mark certifies conformity with 'new approach' criteria common, through the EEA Agreement, to both the EC and the EFTA countries, the Contracting Parties had to agree on a specific solution in cases where such third country mutual recognition agreements were negotiated by the Community. The solution was spelled out in Protocol 12 to the EEA Agreement:

Mutual recognition agreements with third countries concerning conformity assessment for products where the use of a mark is provided for in EC legislation will be negotiated on the initiative of the Community. The Community will negotiate on the basis that the third countries concerned will conclude with the EFTA States parallel mutual recognition agreements equivalent to those to be concluded with the Community. The Contracting Parties shall cooperate in accordance with the general information and consultation procedures set out in the EEA Agreement. Should a difference arise in relations with third countries, it will be dealt with in accordance with the relevant provisions of the EEA Agreement.

The conclusion is therefore that negotiations leading to authorizations allowing institutions in non-EEA countries to grant the CE mark to producers in these countries will remain the prerogative of the 'owner' of the mark, i.e. the Community. In order to respect the EFTA countries' treaty-making power (although, in this case, more of a theoretical nature), parallel identical agreements are thereafter to be concluded between the non-EEA country in question and the EFTA countries.

6. MARKET CONTROL AND GENERAL PRODUCT SAFETY

6.1 Market control

Market control refers to surveillance carried out on products already available on the market. In theory, the primary control carried out by means of conformity assessment procedures should ensure that only safe products are placed on the market. It is nevertheless possible that already marketed products may prove unsafe due to, for example, previously unknown safety risks, risks not detected until after a certain period of use or simply because no safety standards exist for some, especially new, products.

Market control is primarily carried out by national public authorities which shall be entitled to act when necessary, e.g. in the form of a ban on sales or recall of a product. The principles that apply to such interventions vary from product to product and with the degree of potential danger. However, a study of the Community secondary legislation taken over in the EEA Agreement reveals that common rules relating to market control are relatively scarce, with the exception of the possibility, as a last resort, of taking safeguard measures.

6.1.1 Safeguard measures

Specific safeguard clauses in the *acquis* enable the EC Member States and through the EEA Agreement, the EFTA States to withdraw dangerous products from the market or to prohibit them from being placed on the market. As to the new approach directives, the inclusion of such provisions is foreseen in Article 100a (5) EEC.[100]

Whereas the grounds on which EC Member States may resort to safeguard measures are more or less similar under the old and new approach directives (e.g. safety, health), divergencies exist with regard to the procedure to be applied. However, these safeguard procedures have in common the following main elements:

- an EC Member State may resort to safeguard measures without prior notification to the Commision; no prior agreement of the Commission is thus required. Assessment of the risk to persons, animals, or goods remains the full responsibility of the Member State;
- the safeguard measures are subject to a review under the authority of the Commission; however, it should be noted that the Commission does not take binding decisions on the appropriateness of safeguard measures;
- EC Member States which do not follow the recommendation of the Commission might be subject to an infringement procedure under Article 169 EEC;
- the resort to safeguard measures may lead to the amendment of existing legislation in order to remedy difficulties (e.g. adaptation to technical progress), and, as far as the new approach directives are concerned, revision of standards.

Under the EEA Agreement, the safeguard clauses contained in the *acquis* will be applicable with the adaptations following from Protocol 1 on horizontal adaptations

[100] Art. 100a (5): 'The harmonization measures referred to above shall, in appropriate cases, include a safeguard clause authorizing the Member States to take, for one or more of the non-economic reasons referred to in Article 36, provisional measures subject to a Community control procedure.'

unless otherwise stated. The EC and EFTA countries will have the same rights and obligations as regards the triggering of safeguard measures. EFTA States having invoked such a clause shall inform ESA, which will exchange this information with the Commission. The review carried out by the Commission on the EC side will, for the EFTA countries, be the competence of ESA.[101] In evaluating the measures taken, ESA will have to consult with a committee of experts to the extent the Commission is required to do so under the directive in question.[102] No binding decision can be taken by ESA, but recourse to the infringement procedure put forward in Article 31 of the ESA/Court Agreement is of course possible.

As mentioned above, the last step of the procedure may lead to the amendment of existing legislation and/or revised standards. Such measures (at least as far as amendment of directives is concerned)[103] are solely in the power of the Community, taking however the decision-making provisions of the EEA Agreement into account.[104] It goes without saying that co-operation and consultation between the Commission, ESA, and the respective national administrations are of the utmost importance in order to achieve a homogeneous EEA if a safeguard measure should be triggered by any EC or EFTA country.

6.1.2 The rapid exchange of information system

The Community system for the rapid exchange of information on dangers arising from the use of consumer products is through the EEA extended to the EFTA countries.[105]

The objective of the system laid down in Decision 89/45/EEC is an exchange of information between the EC Member States on market control measures taken at a national level. In the EEA this will function through the two pillar system. A Community country having taken market control measures notifies the Commission, which forwards the information to the other Member States. An EFTA country notifies ESA, which informs the other EFTA countries. The Commission and ESA shall immediately inform each other when they have received notifications.[106]

Article 8 of the Decision clearly makes the link to the General Product Safety Directive: 'This Decision shall remain in force until the date by which Member States will have to comply with the Directive on the approximation of the laws,

[101] ESA/Court Agreement, Protocol 1, Art. 1 (1) (*a*).

[102] ESA/Court Agreement, Protocol 1, Art. 3.

[103] Revision of common standards in the form of the issuing of mandates could also hardly be done unilaterally by one of the 'pillars'.

[104] By the horizontal effect of para. 3 of Protocol 1 EEA.

[105] Council Dec. (89/45/EEC) of 21 Dec. 1988 (*OJ* L 17 (21 Jan. 1989), 51); point 2 of ch. XIX of Annex II EEA.

[106] See the specific adaptation laid down in connection to Dec. 89/45/EEC, point 2 of ch. XIX of Annex II EEA. The text refers to the 'entity designated by the EFTA States', as it was not clear from the outset whether this task would be assigned to the Standing Committee or to ESA. The EFTA countries decided, however, to let ESA run the system.

regulations and administrative provisions of the Member States concerning general product safety.'

6.2 General product safety

Council Directive 92/59/EEC on general product safety was adopted on 29 June 1992.[107] As such, it is too recent to be part of the EEA Agreement. It can however be expected that it will be included in the Agreement by a decision in the EEA Joint Committee soon after the entry into force. According to Article 17 of the Directive, it will for the EC countries enter into force on 29 June 1994.

6.2.1 Objectives and scope of the Directive

The primary objective of the Directive is to introduce a general safety requirement, which applies to all economic operators in the marketing chain, to ensure that products placed on the market are safe. By introducing such a provision of a general nature, applicable in all cases whenever specific Community rules or national rules are lacking, the Directive can best be described as filling the gaps in the existing regulatory structure.

The Directive is applicable to products intended for consumers or likely to be used by consumers, whether new, used, or reconditioned. However, second-hand products supplied as antiques, or products to be repaired or reconditioned prior to being used, are excluded from the scope of the Directive, provided that the supplier clearly informs the person to whom he supplies the product to that effect.

As to the notion of 'safe product', the Directive defines it as 'any product which, under normal or reasonably foreseeable conditions of use, including duration, does not present any risk or only the minimum risks compatible with the product's use, considered as acceptable and consistent with a high level of protection for the safety and health of persons'.[108]

In order to ensure that only safe products will be found on the market, Article 6 states that Member States shall have the necessary power to adopt appropriate measures with a view, *inter alia*, to:

- organizing appropriate checks, at all stages of marketing, even after sale to the consumer;
- requiring all necessary information from the parties concerned;
- taking samples;
- subjecting product marketing to prior conditions and requiring that suitable warnings be affixed regarding the risks which the product may present;
- making arrangements to ensure that persons who might be exposed to a risk

[107] *OJ* L 228 (11 Aug. 1992), 24.
[108] Art. 2 (*b*) of the Directive.

from a product are informed in good time and in a suitable manner of the said risk;

- temporarily prohibiting anyone from supplying, offering to supply, or exhibiting a product whenever there are precise and consistent indications that it is dangerous;
- prohibiting the placing on the market of a product which has proved dangerous and establishing the accompanying measures needed to ensure that the ban is complied with;
- organizing the effective and immediate withdrawal of a dangerous product already on the market and, if necessary, its destruction under appropriate conditions.

Once the Directive has been made part of the EEA Agreement, the EFTA countries will have the same obligations and powers as the EC Member States. Only at that stage can one therefore talk about a common general product safety regime.

6.2.2 Notification procedures and emergency situations

Article 7 of the Directive establishes a new notification procedure for products that fail to conform with Community or national provisions applicable to them and which constitute a risk to the health and safety of consumers, even if they do not constitute a serious and immediate danger. For emergency situations, the rapid exchange of information system (see Section 6.1.2 above) has been integrated into the Directive together with some new features to enhance its effectiveness. The procedure is triggered when a Member State notifies the Commission of the fact that it has adopted or intends to adopt emergency measures to prevent, restrict, or impose specific conditions on the possible marketing or use on its territory of a product because of the serious and immediate risk presented by that product to the health and safety of consumers. On receiving this information, the Commission checks its conformity with the Directive and forwards it to the other Member States. The latter must in turn immediately communicate the measures they have taken to tackle the problem. If the Member States are not in a position to take appropriate measures and/or there is a divergence between the Member States as regards the measures to be taken, the Commission may, after consulting the Member States and at the request of at least one of them, adopt a decision whose validity is limited to three months (with the possibility of extension). A condition for such a decision is, however, that it is in accordance with the opinion of the Emergencies Committee.[109]

When the Directive also becomes applicable to the EFTA countries, it will have to be decided which entity on the EFTA side (the Standing Committee or the

[109] The Committee on product safety emergencies is set up under Art. 10 of the Directive. The procedure to be followed is that of a 'regulatory committee procedure' in its variant III (*b*) of Council Dec. 87/373/EEC (i.e. the so-called 'Comitology Decision').

EFTA Surveillance Authority) will fulfil the procedural functions corresponding to those given to the Commission in the Directive. The character of the tasks to be fulfilled, especially in the case of divergencies in measures taken or omissions to take measures, makes it probable that ESA would be that entity.

V

INTELLECTUAL PROPERTY
(ARTICLE 65 (2), PROTOCOL 28, ANNEX XVII)

When the EEA negotiations started in 1990, intellectual property was in the spotlight as the EC Commission was, in the framework of its '1992 programme', working on a number of proposals in this field. Moreover, intellectual property had been under discussion for some time between EC and EFTA in the context of the so-called 'Luxembourg follow-up' and the experts already knew each other rather well thanks to the numerous international settings, such as WIPO or GATT (TRIPs[1]), in which they could meet.

Intellectual property was, without any doubt, an important chapter of the *acquis communautaire*, where it had been tackled from three angles:

- free movement of goods (Articles 30 and 36 EEC and the case-law of the EC Court of Justice on EC-wide exhaustion of intellectual property rights);
- competition rules (Articles 85 and 86 EEC and the group exemptions on patent licensing, know-how licensing, and franchising agreements); and
- harmonization of national laws (on the basis of Articles 100 or 100a EEC) as well as creation of Community-wide intellectual property rights (Community patent, Community trade mark, etc.).

As the field of intellectual property is rather complicated, is developing fast in the European context, and its European aspect has only to a limited extent been specifically covered in literature, it was considered appropriate first to recall some general aspects of intellectual property (Section 1), then describe the jurisprudence of the ECJ regarding intellectual property (in particular the case-law on Community-wide exhaustion) (Section 2), before turning to the EEA provisions concerning intellectual property (Section 3).

1. GENERAL ASPECTS OF INTELLECTUAL PROPERTY RIGHTS

The intention here is not to give a comprehensive and detailed description of intellectual property law (which naturally differs from country to another) but rather to recall some basic principles which could then be useful when explaining the EC and EEA rules on intellectual property.

[1] 'Trade-related aspects of intellectual property rights' in the framework of the GATT Uruguay Round.

1.1 The concept

The concept of intellectual property rights (hereafter abbreviated 'IPRs') is rather recent in the history of law as compared with the classical notion of property rights on goods or real estate. It started to develop during the nineteenth century in parallel to the growth of industrialization and international trade.

IPRs are rights of property, but the subject-matter of the property is immaterial: it concerns an idea, an invention, a creation, or a designation. Being a property right, the IPR is an exclusive right which can be asserted against anybody and whose owner may dispose of it (e.g. through assignment or licensing).

However, the two main differences between classical property rights on goods and IPRs are, first, the strict territoriality principle and, second, the limitation in time:

- each national law autonomously defines the content of IPRs and the conditions and procedures under which protection is granted; their validity is territorially limited to the country in which they are granted, the right not being automatically recognized abroad;
- IPRs are generally limited to a certain period of time after which they fall into the 'public domain' and can freely be used by anyone.

IPRs are therefore rather fragile when compared with ordinary property rights. Their respect very much depends on their owners' action as well as on the level of protection and the enforcement possibilities granted in the law of each country.

1.2 The branches

Without entering into the debate as to whether such a distinction really exists or is worth pursuing, it is generally acknowledged that intellectual property has two branches: industrial property and copyright (or author's right).

1.2.1 Industrial and commercial property

Industrial and commercial property includes the protection of inventions (through patents), trade marks, and industrial designs. One can also put in this branch the protection of plant variety:

1. An invention is a new idea which permits in practice the solution of a specific problem in the field of technology. To be protectable, the idea must be new, non-obvious, and immediately applicable to industry. The duration of protection in Europe is twenty years from the filing of the patent applications.[2] In spite of ethical controversy, patents have recently extended, in several countries, to include also inventions in the field of biotechnology (living matter).

[2] See e.g. Art. 63 of the European Patent Convention. However, in the particular case of medicinal products which are very costly to develop, a system for prolonging the patent protection was found necessary in order to compensate for the loss of exclusivity time due to the need to get from each country

2. A trade mark is a sign which is used to distinguish the goods from an industrial or commercial enterprise. The duration of protection is generally not limited in time provided the registration is periodically renewed.

3. An industrial design is the ornamental aspect (two- or three-dimensional) of a useful article. The duration of protection in Europe is between fifteen and twenty-five years.[3]

4. A plant variety right (also known as plant breeder's right) protects botanical varieties where they are distinct and new. The duration of protection is between fifteen and eighteen years under the UPOV Convention,[4] from the moment when the protection is granted, and twenty to twenty-five years under the current Commission proposal for Community plant variety rights.[5]

1.2.2 Copyright

Copyright (or author's right) includes the protection of original creations in the field of literature, music, and the arts (including choreography, photography, and audio-visual works). The duration of protection in Europe is from fifty to seventy years after the death of the author.[6] Copyright has recently been extended to new fields such as computer programs and databases.

Copyright also comprises the so-called neighbouring rights (or 'related rights') such as rights of performers, producers, and broadcasting organizations. The duration of protection is usually from twenty to fifty years.[7]

a separate market authorization before being able to commercialize the pharmaceutical products. It was estimated that an average of twelve years is necessary between the filing of the patent application and the granting of the market authorizations, thus leaving the producer with only eight years of exclusivity to cover its costs. See in this respect the recent Council Reg. 1768/92 concerning the creation of a supplementary protection certificate for medicinal products (so-called 'SPC' Regulation), which grants fifteen years of protection as from the market authorization. This Regulation is part of the 'Additional Package' of new acquis to be included in the EEA Agreement. It should also be noted that the EC Council adopted a Regulation instituting a European Agency, with a centralized procedure leading to Community authorization of medicines. This should contribute to diminishing the problems described above (see Council Reg. 2309/93 of 22 July 1993 laying down Community procedures for the authorization and supervision of medicinal products for human and veterinary use and establishing a European Agency for the Evaluation of Medicinal Products, *OJ* L 214 (24 Aug. 1993), 1). Under a Decision by the EC Governments (*OJ* C 323 (30 Nov. 1993), 1), this Agency will be established in London. On medicinal products, see further Ch. IV, s. 1.2.4.

[3] It varies very much from one country to another; the Commission proposal for a Community design proposes a protection up to twenty-five years as from the date of filing of the application (see Art. 13). For full reference see n. 82.

[4] For a short description of this Convention, see Annex G.

[5] Art. 18 of the amended proposal; for full reference, see in s. 3.2.3 below, n. 81.

[6] However, under the recent Council Directive harmonizing the term of protection of copyright and certain related rights (93/98/EEC, of 29 Oct. 1993, *OJ* L 290 (24 Nov. 1993), 9), the duration of protection for copyright is harmonized at seventy years.

[7] Under the above-mentioned Directive, the term of protection in the EC is now harmonized at fifty years.

1.2.3 Other rights

In addition, there are rights which, although generally considered as belonging to intellectual property in a wide sense, cannot really be put in one of its two branches. This is due to the fact that they have either been tailor made to suit the particularities of the protected item (e.g. semiconductors) or are provided for in laws (such as protection of business secrets or consumer protection) which do not really belong to classical intellectual property legislation:

- protection of topographies of semiconductors (or 'chips'), which are a series of images representing the three-dimensional pattern of the layers composing a semiconductor and which result from the creator's intellectual effort. The duration of the protection in Europe is ten years from the first commercial exploitation or from the filing of the application;[8]
- geographical indications, including appellations of origin, which protect the use of the name of a region or a country in relation to a specific product giving it a particular quality or reputation;
- know-how and undisclosed information, which comprise secret and substantial technical information and which are usually protected by rules on the protection of business secrets;
- repression of unfair competition, which, although not an exclusive right in the classical sense, is directed against acts of competition contrary to honest practices in industrial or commercial matters (acts which create confusion, false or misleading allegations or indications, etc.).

1.3 Rights granted, enforcement, and registration systems

1.3.1 Exclusive rights

The person holding an IPR is granted different exclusive rights (or monopoly rights), which constitute the valuable part of the property, the part of which the owner can dispose notably through assignment or licensing to a third party. Moral rights are however considered as inalienable, although their exercise may be waived by the author.

For patented invention, industrial design, or plant variety right, owners are granted the exclusive right to exploit, that is to say to manufacture, use, sell, or import/export, the protected item (which may be the product itself, the process, the product directly obtained by the process, the product to which the design has been applied, etc.).

For trade mark, owners are granted the right to use the protected sign, at least for connected goods or services, that is to say to affix the sign on goods or use it on business papers and in advertising and to sell or import/export goods bearing that sign or offer services under the mark.

[8] See Art. 7 (3) of the Semiconductor Directive (87/54/EEC).

For copyright (including neighbouring rights), the authors are granted, as economic rights, the exclusive right to copy or reproduce, record, communicate to the public (including right to sell, rent, and lend products incorporating the protected work), broadcast, translate, and adapt works protected by copyright. As a so-called 'moral right', they in addition have the right to ask that their authorship be indicated and can oppose mutilation or deformation of their works;

For semiconductors, the owners are granted the right to reproduce and commercially exploit the topography or the product incorporating such topography.

For geographical indications, owners are granted the exclusive right to the direct or indirect commercial use of the registered name in respect of the products or comparable products.

1.3.2 Enforcement

The best way to test the real effectiveness of a right is to look at the enforcement means which are put at the disposal of the right owners. Intellectual property laws generally give the right holders different means to deter or prohibit third parties from infringing their IPRs:

- civil remedies, both preventive (seizures and injunctions) and compensatory (damages and delivery up of the infringing material);
- criminal remedies (fines and imprisonment);
- administrative remedies (such as measures against piracy and counterfeit products, seizure of infringing material at the border by custom authorities).

1.3.3 Registration

In order to be protected, industrial and commercial property rights generally require registration and publication in each country where protection is sought. This registration has constitutive effects and forms the basis for the protection. It also allows the registering authority to check that at least the basic conditions for protection under the national law in question are fulfilled (such as for instance the novelty condition for inventions).

Copyright, however, does not need, at least in Europe, any registration. The protection automatically starts as soon as the work is created.

1.4 Purpose of IPRs

The very reason for a State to enact intellectual property law is to encourage innovation, quality, and creation and thus to contribute to economic development. IPRs are the award granted by States for the use of imagination and knowledge.

No enterprise would invest the high amount of money necessary to discover for instance a new pharmaceutical product nor make the effort to develop and maintain the quality of its products or services under a given trade mark if it was not protected, at least for a certain time, against free riders and counterfeiters. The same goes for authors, who would otherwise have little chance to live from their art and who in addition, should be protected against any injury, as they put into their work part of their personality.

The effect of IPRs is to bring about products, services, or artistic works which otherwise would not have been worth creating and putting on the market. As they reward the efforts of their owners, IPRs stimulate scientific and economic progress, as well as artistic creation, and therefore contribute to increasing efficiency and consumer choice.

1.5 Limitations to IPRs

In order to balance private and public interests, to balance the interests of the IPR owners with those of the other operators and users and prevent IPR holders abusing their monopoly right, the scope of the rights has been limited either in the intellectual property legislation itself or in the jurisprudence of the courts.

1.5.1 Statutory limitations

The limitations of IPRs contained in intellectual property laws are generally of three types:

- as seen above, IPRs have a limited duration, after which they fall in the public domain;[9]
- under certain conditions, a limited number of uses of the protected objects or ideas is free (such as private and non-commercial acts, acts done for experimental or teaching purposes);
- notably in the field of patents, the right may be partially expropriated by the State in the form of a compulsory licence because of 'failure to work', that is, because the patent holder does not exploit his right on the patented invention and thus deprives the public from benefiting from the invention (for instance does not produce and sell a new pharmaceutical product or only allows very limited imports so as to maintain a high price). There are in principle strict conditions to compulsory licensing (such as the existence of a public interest and the fact that the licence should be non-exclusive, non-discriminatory, limited in duration and in scope, and subject to equitable remuneration and to judicial review). However, compulsory licensing may sometimes be used as a protectionist measure to favour domestic operators or as a tool for price policy in certain sectors (for instance to limit health cost).[10]

[9] With the exception of moral rights of authors and of trade marks (unless their registration is not renewed or they become a generic name like, for instance, 'aspirin').

[10] For further development on the issue of compulsory licensing in the EC context see s. 2.4.2.5 below.

1.5.2 Case-law limitations

The limitations developed in the jurisprudence of the courts (sometimes codified later on in the law) could also be seen as an attempt to avoid IPRs being exercised in a way which could constitute a sort of abuse. This is particularly so in the context of the so-called *exhaustion rule*, that is, the exhaustion, under certain conditions, of the exclusive right to market the protected products. Under this rule, once the protected product has been put on a given market by the right holder himself or with his consent (e.g. by his licensee), the right holder can no longer oppose the resale of such product by others; that is, his IPR is exhausted as concerns the marketing rights (but not as regards the other rights such as the exclusive right to manufacture or to reproduce).

This exhaustion rule may apply:

- nationally (i.e. only the sale of the product on the national territory exhausts the exclusive right to sell);
- regionally (i.e. exhaustion of the marketing right once the product has been sold within the territory of one of the States party to a given agreement, as within the EC);
- internationally (i.e. exhaustion once the product has been put on the market anywhere in the world).

The question of exhaustion of IPRs in the context of the EC and its extension to the EEA is developed further in Sections 2 and 3.2.2 below.

1.6 International conventions in the field of IPRs

As a consequence of the territoriality principle, the different national laws are concerned only with what happens in the country itself. An IPR registration is effective only in the country where it was made. If the right holder wants protection in several countries, he must register his right at the same time in each of those countries. This usually means, in each case, appointing a local specialist (e.g. patent agent), preparing the necessary translations of the applications, fulfilling the particular formal and substantial conditions of the local law, and, last but not least, paying the fees and other related costs.

With a view to softening this rather chaotic situation, a number of countries, more than a century ago, started to conclude international agreements which primarily aimed at guaranteeing the right of their own citizens to obtain protection in other countries, but also containing some common substantive rules to secure a certain level of protection in the member countries as well as to facilitate registration procedures. International organizations have been established to administer these conventions.

1.6.1 Industrial property

In the field of industrial property, there are mainly two international instruments:

the Paris Union (administered by WIPO[11]) and the European Patent Convention (administered by the EPO[12]).

The Paris Union[13] covers patents, trade marks, and industrial designs (as well as some provisions on trade names, indications of source, and unfair competition). Its main substantive rules provide for:

- national treatment (i.e. each contracting State shall grant to citizens of the other Parties and to nationals of non-contracting States domiciled or established in a contracting State the same treatment as to its own nationals);
- right of priority for patents, trade marks, and industrial designs (i.e. on the basis of a regular first application filed in one of the contracting States, the applicant benefits for one year for patents and six months for trade marks and industrial designs, during which period he can apply for protection in any of the other contracting States, these later applications being then regarded as if they had been filed on the same day as the first one);
- common rules concerning for instance certain grounds for refusal, compulsory licensing, well-known trade marks, minimum protection, industrial property offices, publication.

There are in addition twelve other agreements concluded under the aegis of the Paris Union,[14] the best known being:

- the Patent Co-operation Treaty ('PCT'), which enables the applicant to file, with the national patent office of a contracting State (or with the EPO), an 'international' patent application and to designate those States in which he wishes his application to have effect. The application is then subject to an 'international search' (list of prior patents which might affect the patentability) and is published. The advantages are that the applicant is granted an additional eight or eighteen months as compared with the normal Paris Convention priority right system to reflect on whether he still wants to register and in which countries (where he will then have to follow the ordinary national procedure and pay the different fees);
- the Madrid Agreement concerning the International Registration of Marks and its Protocol, which enables the applicant, after he has first registered with the trade mark office of the country of origin (which must be a contracting State), to make a true international registration (one fee and one language) at

[11] The World Intellectual Property Organization (WIPO), whose seat is in Geneva, is one of the specialized agencies of the United Nations. Established in 1967, it is responsible for promoting the protection of IPRs and for administering various 'Unions' based on multilateral treaties. In Oct. 1993 it had 140 member countries.

[12] The European Patent Office (EPO), whose seat is in Munich, was created by the European Patent Convention of 1973.

[13] The International Union for the Protection of Industrial Property (Paris Union) was created by eleven countries which concluded on 20 Mar. 1883 the Paris Convention for the Protection of Industrial Property. The Convention had, in Oct. 1993, 113 member countries. It has been revised or amended eight times, the last version being the Stockholm Act of 1967.

[14] See Annex G.

the International Bureau of WIPO. WIPO then publishes the registration and notifies the States in which the applicant seeks protection. If, within one year, the States concerned have not declared that protection cannot be granted, the international registration has the effect of a national registration in those States. The Madrid Protocol gives the opportunity to base an international application not only on the first national registration but also on a national application. It gives eighteen months (instead of one year) to the notified countries for reacting and establishes a link with the future Community trade mark system.

The European Patent Convention (EPC[15]) provides for a comprehensive system of both common substantive rules (definition of what is patentable, maximum duration of protection, common interpretation of granted patents) and procedure (single application leading to the grant of a package of national patents contained in a single document issued by the EPO). Only the questions of infringement and revocation are still dealt with nationally, it being understood that revocation grounds can only be those listed in the EPC and that the effects of such proceedings are limited to the country concerned. There is also an opposition procedure in the EPO which is open for nine months after the EPO publication on the granting of the package of patents.

1.6.2 Copyright

In the field of copyright, there are two main international conventions,[16] both administered by WIPO:

- the Berne Convention of 9 September 1886 (last revised in Paris in 1971[17]) for the Protection of Literary and Artistic Works. The Convention rests on three basic principles (national treatment for works originating in one of the contracting States, automatic protection of copyright without any formality, and independence of the protection, i.e. the protection in other countries is independent from the existence of a protection in the country of origin), and it furthermore provides for minimum standards of protection (as to the works and rights to be protected and the duration of such protection);
- the Rome Convention of 26 October 1961 for the Protection of Performers, Producers of Phonograms, and Broadcasting Organizations, which, for

[15] The European Patent Convention was concluded on 5 Oct. 1973. In July 1993 seventeen European countries were parties to the EPC, i.e. the twelve EC Member States (plus Monaco) and four EFTA countries (i.e. Austria, Liechtenstein, Sweden and Switzerland). Finland is negotiating participation in the EPC.

[16] For a list of international conventions in the field of copyright see Annex G.

[17] A protocol to the Berne Convention has been under negotiation since autumn 1991 (see Memorandum prepared by the International Bureau of WIPO entitled *Questions Concerning a Possible Protocol to the Berne Convention* (document BCP/CE/III/2), see also document BCB/CE/III/2-III). Another Committee is studying the question of rights of performers and producers of phonograms (see document *Questions Concerning a Possible Instrument on the Protection of the Rights of Perfomers and Producers of Phonograms*, INR/CE/I2).

performers and broadcasting organizations, secures protection against unauthorized broadcasting (or rebroadcasting), communications to the public, fixation of their work, and reproduction of such fixation, and for phonogram producers secure protection against unauthorized reproduction.

2. THE JURISPRUDENCE OF THE EUROPEAN COURT OF JUSTICE CONCERNING IPRS

In order to provide the reader with a complete picture on the jurisprudence concerning IPRs, and in particular on the so-called 'EC-wide exhaustion principle', which, in the hands of the European Court of Justice, became an important tool for economic integration and is nowadays being further and further codified in the emerging EC legislation on intellectual property, this section first presents the issue, then describes how the case-law on IPRs started (Article 222 EEC and existence/exercise principle) as well as how the competition provisions of the Treaty (Articles 85 and 86 EEC) have been applied to IPRs,[18] and then comes to the Community exhaustion doctrine (Articles 30 to 36 EEC), to end with some considerations on compulsory licensing.

2.1 The issue: IPRs versus EEC Treaty objectives

Under Article 2 EEC the creation of a common market is referred to, besides the approximation of national economic policies, as the main tool for realizing the Community's objectives (i.e. promotion of economic development, expansion, stability, etc.). Article 3 EEC then lists eleven Community activities, among which are free movement of goods and undistorted competition, which also aim at realizing these objectives.[19] The establishment of a common market became a priority target, so much so that it has increasingly become regarded as, in itself, one of the Treaty objectives.

IPRs have two characteristics which could only make them opposed to the EC objectives of free movement of goods and services and the creation of an integrated internal market:

- they are national exclusive rights whose scope of application is territorially limited (their validity stops at the border);
- they are invisibly incorporated in most of the products and services circulating on the market.

IPRs were therefore a good candidate for re-creating private trade barriers along

[18] It is recalled that this particular jurisprudence is taken over in the EEA context through the application of Art. 6 EEA (Art. 222 EEC is reproduced in Art. 125 EEA and Arts. 85 and 86 EEC are reproduced in Arts. 53 and 54 EEA).

[19] For a comparison between the EEC Treaty objectives and the EEA Agreement objectives see developments relating to ECJ Opinion 1/91 in s. 2.1 of Ch. II.

the national borders and thus contributing to the partitioning of markets which, on the other hand, the EEC was desperately trying to unify.

As an IPR gives its owner an exclusive right to exploit (i.e. to manufacture, use, or put on the market) the protected object on his territory, some companies soon found out that they did not even need to draft complicated agreements with export bans and similar clauses for insulating the national markets from each other. It was enough to register 'parallel' patents or trade marks (i.e. to register for a single product a right in each State), assign or license them to a company or a subsidiary in each State, and then rely on the mere exercise of the monopoly right protected by the national law to block the 'infringing' product (i.e. usually mere parallel imports of the same product coming from other States).

This is the reason why IPRs quickly came under the eye of one of the Common Market's protectors, the Court of Justice, which during the 1960s based itself on the competition rules (Articles 85 and 86 EEC) to try to limit the insulating use of IPRs and then turned, in 1971, to rely on the rules on free movement of goods (Articles 30–36 EEC).[20]

2.2 The Court case-law on Article 222 EEC and on the existence and exercise of IPRs

The first question to be solved was whether the Court had jurisdiction to address a matter related to intellectual property, since Article 222 EEC states that 'This Treaty shall in no way prejudice the rules in Member States governing the system of property ownership.'[21] In answering this question, the Court drew a distinction between the existence and the exercise of IPRs. It said that, while the existence of the rights remains unaffected by the Treaty (i.e. the property itself is not touched[22]), their exercise by the right holders may sometimes infringe the provisions of the Treaty, for instance Articles 85, 86, or 30–36 EEC.[23]

This distinction between existence and exercise of IPRs, confirmed on several occasions by the Court thereafter, gave rise to a lot of criticism due to its artificial character. The very nature of a right consists in the way in which it can be exercised.

[20] Annex H contains the precise references and relevant excerpts of the most important cases quoted in the sections below.

[21] The corresponding provision in the EEA Agreement, Art. 125, reads: 'This Agreement shall in no way prejudice the rules of the Contracting Parties governing the system of property ownership.'

[22] The same goes for the conditions and procedures under which IPRs are granted which are a matter for national law. See in this respect *Nancy Kean Gift's* and 37/87 *Thetford* v. *Fiamma* [1988] ECR 3585. They may however be caught by the Treaty provisions if they are discriminatory (contrary to Art. 7 EEC), see the recent Joined Cases C-92/92 and C-326/92 *Phil Collins* of 20 Oct. 1993 (not yet reported) forbidding to make the grant of a right subject to the condition of being a national of the State granting that right. Or if they constitute measures of equivalent effect to quantitative restrictions to trade (Art. 30 EEC) or are otherwise liable to jeopardize the attainment of the Treaty objectives (Art. 5 EEC applied in connection with one of the basic four freedom provisions). For an application of Art. 30 to conditions under which a compulsory licence is granted see s. 2.4.2.5 below.

[23] On Art. 222 EEC and the existence/exercise theory, see in particular *Consten and Grundig*, *Parke Davis*, *Deutsche Grammophon*, and *Coditel II*.

Therefore, if the range of possible ways to exercise the right is diminished, this also diminishes the value of the right itself. In the view of many commentators, the refined existence/exercise distinction is considered as leaving the IPR actually rather naked.

2.3 The Court case-law applying the competition rules to IPRs (Articles 85 and 86 EEC)

The first Court cases in the field of intellectual property, before the exhaustion rule was elaborated in 1971, were delivered in the field of competition (Articles 85 and 86 EEC[24]). The point of departure of the reasoning developed by the Court of Justice was, in line with the existence/exercise dogma, that the existence of the IPRs granted in the Member States is not affected by the prohibitions contained in Articles 85 (1) and 86 EEC and that the exercise of the IPRs cannot in itself fall under the prohibitions contained in Articles 85 (1) and 86.[25]

2.3.1 Application of Article 85 (1) EEC

To fall under Article 85 (1), the exercise of an IPR should manifest itself as the subject, the means, or the result of an agreement or a concerted practice, as defined in the Article, which, by preventing imports from other Member States of products lawfully distributed there, has as its effect the partitioning of the market.[26] Thus, the mere unilateral enforcement of an IPR in the absence of a restrictive agreement does not infringe Article 85 (1).[27]

The situations referred to above were mainly concerned with vertical agreements (i.e. agreements between a supplier and his customer or a licensor and a licensee) where the IPR was used as one of the means for organizing the manufacturing and/or distribution within the Community of the same protected product, trying to give each licensee or distributor as much territorial protection as possible, in particular against parallel imports from others' territories. The Court even went quite far in detecting possible restrictive agreements behind the enforcement of IPRs. It considered for instance that the combination of assignment to different users of trade marks protecting the same product[28] or the use of one or more patents in concert between undertakings[29] may very well be caught by the prohibition of Article 85 (1).

Some cases also concerned a particular type of horizontal agreement (i.e. between competitors at the same level of manufacturing or trade) which is quite common in

[24] To which correspond Arts. 53 and 54 EEA.

[25] See *Parke Davis* case.

[26] See *Deutsche Grammophon* case.

[27] According to the Court of Justice, it is however up to the national judge to check that the right owner enforces his rights with the same strictness regardless of the nationality of the infringer (see *Terrapin* v. *Terranova*). See also s. 2.4.2.2 below, last para.

[28] See *Sirena* case.

[29] See *Parke Davis* case.

the field of intellectual property: the so-called 'delimitation' or settlement agreement. This, particularly for trade marks, aims at avoiding or settling disputes about prior or confusing rights. It often happens that, when trying to register a trade mark in different countries, a company faces opposition from a right holder who has already registered, in one or the other country, the same or a similar trade mark in the same class of products or services. This is one of the classical conflicts in the field of intellectual property.[30]

Rather than embarking on long, costly, and uncertain court proceedings, the parties sometimes prefer an amicable solution.[31] Being horizontal, these agreements were likely to be considered severely by the Commission, especially when they resulted in the sharing of the markets between the right holders.[32] However, provided that they fulfil certain conditions, the Commission recognized the benefit of such agreements as they could result in keeping on the market conflicting products which otherwise, if the national opposition proceedings had succeeded, could have been totally excluded. The conditions set out by the Commission are that the companies should seek the least restrictive solution possible, such as differentiating measures (distinguishing shapes or colours, addition of the trade name, etc.), limitations as to the classes of products, or obligation to assign or waive the trade mark but only if it does not entail too costly a re-establishment of goodwill for the one giving up his right.[33]

2.3.2 Application of Article 86 EEC

To fall under Article 86, the company exercising its IPR should satisfy the three conditions for the Article to apply, that is, the company must have a dominant position, this dominant position must be abused, and that abuse must be liable to affect trade between Member States. As regards IPRs in the context of Article 86, the following elements should be borne in mind:

- dominance: the mere fact that someone is holding an IPR, with all the exclusive rights it entails, does not automatically give him a dominant

[30] In *Terrapin* v. *Terranova* the Court recognized the legitimacy of an enforcement action against a confusing trade mark, as the specific objective of the IPR in question would otherwise be undermined. It added however that such legitimacy would fall in cases where there was a restrictive agreement or legal or economic ties between the undertakings and where the respective IPRs would not have arisen independently from each other.

[31] Which may take different forms, such as assignment of the already registered right, an undertaking to keep away from the other's market, an obligation to register another trade mark or to limit the registration to certain classes of products, non-challenge clauses, the introduction of differentiating elements in the appearance of the trade marks so as to make them look more different in the eyes of consumers, etc.

[32] Such as reciprocal exclusion from each other's markets (see Commission Dec. 75/297/EEC *Sirdar-Phildar* of 5 Mar. 1975, *OJ* L125 (16 Apr. 1975), 27), assignment or waiver used as a means of market sharing (see hint by the Commission in Dec. *Penneys*), or heavy limitations on entry imposed upon a small manufacturer by a big one on the basis of a confusing (but 'sleeping') trade mark (see Commission Dec. *Toltecs/Dorcet*).

[33] See Commission press release on informal settlement in *Persil* case as well as Commission Decs. *Penneys* and *Toltecs/Dorcet*.

position.[34] However, IPRs are one of the factors which, besides market share, may contribute to the dominance (other factors are e.g. highly developed sales networks, financial power, access to raw materials);

– abuse: the exercise of IPRs may be one of the means through which a company abuses its dominant position (for instance the charging of high prices for the protected products[35] or the registration of a 'blocking' trade mark knowing that a competitor holds the same or a similar one in another country but did not have the time or the money to register it in several countries[36]).

2.3.3 Limits on the use of the competition rules

The *Parke Davis* case showed the limits of the use of Articles 85 and 86, in particular in instances where a company simply holds parallel IPRs in the different Member States and assigns them to its subsidiaries,[37] who merely enforce them, without those rights being the subject, the means, or the result of an agreement or a concerted practice (Article 85 (1)), or fulfilling the three conditions of Article 86.

Evidently, something else was needed to catch those situations where the competition rules could not apply. The first time the Court took this step was in its 1971 *Deutsche Grammophon* case, from which the whole story of the 'EC-wide exhaustion rule' started.

2.4 The Court case-law applying the rules on free movement of goods to IPRs (Articles 30 to 36 EEC, the EC-wide exhaustion principle)

Article 30 EEC prohibits quantitative restrictions on imports and equivalent measures. Article 34 EEC prohibits the same as regards exports. Article 36 EEC provides, in its first sentence, for possible exceptions to these two provisions, on condition that they do not constitute 'a means of arbitrary discrimination or a disguised restriction on trade between Member States' (second sentence).[38] The use of IPRs being without any doubt capable of hindering the free movement of goods,

[34] Although the wording used by the Court in *Parke Davis* was not crystal clear on this particular point, this was affirmed in *Sirena* and in *Deutsche Grammophon*. As to the definition of dominance, see in particular Case 27/76 *United Brands* [1978] ECR 1391, which defines a dominant position as being 'a position of economic strength enjoyed by an undertaking which enables it to prevent effective competition being maintained on the relevant market by giving it the power to behave to an appreciable extent independently of its competitors, customers and ultimately of its consumers'.

[35] The Court said, however, that the mere fact that a protected product is sold at a higher price does not in itself constitute an abuse but is only one of the factors to be taken into account when assessing whether there is abuse of a dominant position (see *Sirena* and *Deutsche Grammophon*).

[36] See informal settlement of the *Osram/Airam* case, reported in *XIth Report on Competition Policy* (1981), 97.

[37] In this context, it is recalled that an agreement between a parent company and its subsidiaries (i.e. 'intra-enterprise' agreement, where the subsidiary has no freedom to determine its course of action on the market and which is merely an internal allocation of tasks within the same economic entity) is not considered as an 'agreement between undertakings' in the sense of Art. 85 (1) EEC (see *Sterling Drug* case).

[38] Arts. 30, 34, and 36 EEC are reproduced in Arts. 11, 12, and 13 EEA. For a full picture of the

it remained to be seen whether and to what extent the IPR holder could benefit from the mention in Article 36 of 'the protection of industrial and commercial property' as one of the possible derogations from the free movement of goods provided for in Articles 30 and 34.

2.4.1 The *Deutsche Grammophon* case

The company Deutsche Grammophon distributed its records either directly (in Germany) or through its subsidiaries established in several countries (among them Polydor in France), to which it assigned the exclusive right to exploit the recordings in their respective territories. The Metro company bought records put on the market by Polydor in France and resold them in Germany at a lower price than the one adopted by Deutsche Grammophon. This was a typical case of parallel imports at lower prices and the competition rules could hardly apply since the licensing and assignment agreements were 'intra-enterprise' between the parent Deutsche Grammophon and its different subsidiaries.

After recalling the existence/exercise principle and before stating the EC-wide exhaustion rule, the Court introduced a new notion, the *specific subject-matter of IPRs*, about which it said: 'Article 36 only admits derogations from that freedom [i.e. free movement of goods] to the extent to which they are justified for the purpose of safeguarding rights which constitute the specific subject-matter of such property.'

It follows from the way the notion of 'specific subject-matter' has later been applied to the different types of IPRs that this concept is a mixture of the definition of the very nature of the right and a description of its rationale.[39] In any case, the elaboration of this notion shows that the Court was concerned not to empty IPRs of their substance and to find the right balance between conflicting interests (i.e. those of the right holder, of the free flow of goods within the EC, and also of the States to encourage innovation and quality). Defining in each case what is the specific subject-matter of the respective IPR has since then become a standard element in the Court jurisprudence on exhaustion.

Having safeguarded the core of IPRs, the Court went on to introduce for the first time the *principle of EC-wide exhaustion*:

> It is in conflict with the provisions prescribing the free movement of products within the common market for a manufacturer of sound recordings to exercise the exclusive right to distribute the protected articles, conferred upon him by the legislation of a Member State, in such a way as to prohibit the sale in that State of products placed on the market by him or with his consent in another Member State solely because such distribution did not occur within the territory of the first Member State.

interpretation of these provisions as well as the abundant case-law on the notion of measure of equivalent effect to a quantitative restriction and on Art. 36 EEC see Ch. IV.

[39] For an overview of how the specific subject-matter of the different IPRs has been defined by the Court see relevant excerpts of case-law in Annex H.

2.4.2 The EC-wide exhaustion principle: contents and limits

2.4.2.1 Contents

The Community exhaustion doctrine could be expressed in the following way: the holder of an IPR granted under the national intellectual property law of a Member State cannot exercise his exclusive right to prevent the importation and sale in that Member State of a protected product which has been lawfully put on the market in another Member State by the right owner himself or with his consent.

The main elements to be underlined are the following:

- the EC-wide exhaustion principle applies to all types of IPRs (i.e. patents, trade marks, designs, copyright,[40] and neighbouring rights, etc.[41]);
- the exhaustion rule only affects exclusive rights related to trade (i.e. right to import, export, or sell). The other exclusive rights (e.g. right to manufacture, to use, to reproduce) remain so far unaffected by the exhaustion rule;[42]
- the IPR holder keeps the exclusive right to be the first one to put the protected product on the market,[43] either himself or through someone he has authorized to do so (i.e. with whom he has legal or commercial links, such as through a sale licence, regardless of whether they belong to the same business group[44]). But once he has exercised this right, the exhaustion applies and he cannot prevent the protected product moving freely within the EC.

In addition, the Court held in *Merck* v. *Stephar* that the exhaustion of the marketing right also applies for a product imported from a Member State where it could not be patented.[45] According to the Court, it is up to the right holder to decide where he wants to sell his products and, if he chooses also to sell them in a country which does not grant patent protection, he must bear the consequences of his choice (i.e. the fact that the products can then move freely within the EC thanks to the exhaustion rule).

Likewise, it was held in *Winthrop* that the fact that a government of a given Member State imposes price control or other measures which make the prices of the protected products lower in that State than in the importing State cannot be invoked against the application of the exhaustion rule.

Similarly, in the *GEMA* case it was decided that it is up to the author to choose the place in which to put his work into circulation and then to bear the consequences

[40] See *GEMA* case and n. 67 below.

[41] See in Annex H the relevant excerpts of case-law where the exhaustion was applied to these different IPRs. For a general description of the different types of IPRs see s. 1.2 above.

[42] As regards performing, lending, and manufacturing rights and the limitations of the right to affix a trade mark see paragraphs under s. 2.4.2.2 below.

[43] In *Merck* v. *Stephar*, the Court said that 'the substance of a patent right lies essentially in according the inventor an exclusive right of first placing the product on the market'.

[44] See n. 37 above on intra-enterprise agreements.

[45] The case concerned a drug which was marketed in Italy by Merck, holder of the patent in several Member States but not in Italy, where, at that time, drugs were not patentable. Such a case could very well happen again, concerning for instance products incorporating biotechnological inventions, which, given the ethical debate going on in several countries in Europe, are far from being uniformly protected in the different States.

of this choice, including results such as lower royalties in one country than in another. The case was concerned with the UK copyright legislation under which the reproduction right of sound recordings was in a sense exhausted once the author had reproduced the sound recordings in the UK for the purpose of retail sale. Pursuant to that law, it was then sufficient for a sound recordings manufacturer to notify the copyright owner of his intention to reproduce the recordings and to pay him a royalty fixed at 6.25 per cent of the retail selling price of the records. The Court said that the German copyright management society GEMA could not, when the British product was imported into Germany, claim the difference between the lower royalty paid in the UK and the higher one granted in Germany. The Court rejected at that time the argument under which the UK law amounted to granting compulsory licences to any manufacturer as long as he was ready to pay the fixed royalty of 6.25 per cent.

2.4.2.2 Limits

In *Pharmon*, the Court stated that a right holder cannot be said to have consented to the marketing of the protected product when the patent has been the subject of a *compulsory licence* granted by the government of a Member State to a third party which has, under this licence, manufactured and marketed the protected product. The exclusive right of the patent holder to import and sell the protected product in other Member States was therefore not exhausted and could still be relied upon to block the infringing imports.

The Court has recently applied a similar approach concerning the trade mark Hag (for coffee), which initially used to have a single owner ('common origin of the trade mark') but which after the Second World War had been *subdivided and expropriated* in Belgium in favour of a third party, while in Germany it remained with its original holder. After having held in a first very controversial case known as *Hag I*[46] that, despite the expropriation, the identical trademark, because of its 'common origin', could not be relied upon by the German holder to prevent import of the coffee manufactured and sold by the Belgian owner, the Court totally reversed this first jurisprudence in the Case *Hag II*, where it said that the German holder could not be said to have consented to the marketing in Belgium of the coffee bearing the mark Hag, since it was expropriated. Therefore, to the relief of many commentators, the Court abandoned its 'common origin' dogma, at least for cases where there has been an expropriation, and admitted that the German owner of the identical trade mark Hag in Germany could rely on his right to prevent imports from Belgium since the consumers would be misled as to the production origin of the coffee (i.e. whether it had been produced by the Belgian or German manufacturer) and that avoiding such confusion as to the origin of the product was

[46] This case was confirmed in *Terrapin* v. *Terranova*, where the Court nevertheless stated that the first sentence of Art. 36 EEC may be used to prevent the import of products bearing a name giving rise to confusion where the right in question has been acquired by different and independent owners under different national laws.

indeed the essential function of the trade mark. It is believed, however, that the 'common origin' doctrine would still be fully applicable in a case where, for instance, a trade mark belonged originally to a single owner and had then been split between two different owners, both having the mark registered in the EC (though not in the same countries).[47]

In *EMI* v. *CBS*, concerning *third country products*, the Court held that, since the free movement of goods between EC Member States was not affected and that thus the exercise of the IPR would not jeopardize the Common Market's unity, EMI (UK) could rely on its trade mark right to the name Columbia, registered in different EC countries, to prevent the import and sale in those countries of products bearing an identical mark and imported into the EC by CBS (holder of the trademark Columbia in North and South America). The Court added in particular that the rules on free circulation of third country products (Articles 10 (1) and 9 (2) EEC, related to customs union provisions[48]) only refer to compliance with customs formalities and duties, but that such compliance does not allow the contravention of trade mark rights owned in the EC.

In the *Polydor* case (see Chapter II n. 5) the Court stated that the fact that the product comes from a third country with which the Community has concluded a Free Trade Agreement which contains a clause similar to Article 36 EEC does not mean that the exhaustion rule applies. The similarity in the terms used is not a sufficient reason for transposing in the Free Trade Agreement context the exhaustion jurisprudence developed in the EC. This is due to the fact that the objectives of a Free Trade Agreement (facilitation of trade) and of the Rome Treaty (merging of the national markets into a Single Market) are different. The EC right holder can consequently rely on his exclusive right to prevent imports of infringing products from the third country in question.

The Court also addressed the particular issue of *repackaging* of trademarked products (drugs) or *reaffixing of marks* by parallel importers and thus the question of whether the exclusive right to affix the mark on the product may be exhausted. For a given product, the right holder may hold, in the EC Member States, either the same trade mark or different marks. In addition, although the product is the same, the way it is packaged (e.g. number of tablets per box) may differ from one country to another. Different packages or different trade marks of course complicate the task of parallel importers and some managed to overcome these problems by reaffixing the local trade mark on the box of imported drugs or by repackaging it so as to put the number of tablets per box required in the local market and then reaffixing the mark.

[47] The Court hinted at this possibility in Case 51/75 *EMI* v. *CBS* [1976] ECR 811 (discussed in the next paragraph), but did not examine the question further as the trade mark which belonged to CBS was not registered in the EC but in a third country (USA).

[48] Due to the fact that the EEA Agreement is not a customs union but a free trade area (although 'substantially improved'), there are no rules in the EEA similar to the EC ones on free circulation of third country products once customs formalities, duties, and other related obligations have been complied with in the first EC Member State.

In the two cases *Hoffmann-La Roche* and *American Home Products*, the Court considered that the right to affix the trade mark, as it is part of the specific subject-matter of the trade mark, remained exclusively in the hands of the right holder and was therefore not touched by the exhaustion rule (i.e. the first sentence of Article 36 could apply).

The Court nevertheless hinted at the fact that putting on the market in various Member States an identical product in different packages or bearing different trade marks could, under certain circumstances, be considered as contrary to the second sentence of Article 36 (which prohibits 'disguised restriction on trade between Member States'). According to the Court, the main question as regards repackaging is whether it is capable of affecting the original condition of the product and would thus hinder the essential function of the trade mark, which is to guarantee for the consumer the unaffected origin of the product. As regards the use of different trade marks for the same product, the Court said that it was lawful but that it is possible for such a practice to be followed by the right holder 'as part of a system of marketing intended to partition the market artificially'.[49]

The Court then formulated four cumulative conditions which make the second sentence of Article 36 ('disguised restriction') apply to, and thus restrict, the exercise of the right to affix a trade mark:

- It is established that the use of the trade-mark right by the proprietor, having regard to the marketing system which he has adopted, will contribute to the artificial partitioning of the markets between Member States;
- It is shown that the repackaging cannot adversely affect the original condition of the product;
- The proprietor of the mark receives prior notice of the marketing of the repackaged product; and
- It is stated on the new packaging by whom the product has been repackaged.

The second sentence of Article 36 was applied later on in a repackaging case, *Pfizer* (same trade mark but different number of tablets per box), where the importer, who had certainly carefully read the Court case-law, repackaged a drug so as to change only the external wrapping without touching the internal packaging, with a window through which one could see the original trade mark (so that the mark did not need to be reaffixed), and with an indication, on the external package, that the product had been manufactured by the subsidiary of the right holder and repackaged by the importer. The latter even informed the right holder of his plans. The Court supported the importer's point of view.

As regards the *exclusive right to manufacture*, the Court clearly held, in *Maxicar* v. *Renault* (related to design rights on body panels of cars), that this right cannot be exhausted by the application of Articles 30 and 36, as it forms part of the specific subject-matter of the design.[50]

[49] See ground 21 of *American Home Products* and Case 1/81 *Pfizer* [1981] ECR 2913.

[50] See Case 53/87 [1988] ECR 6039.

As regards *copyright*, the Court first made a difference between those literary or artistic works which are put at the disposal of the public through circulation in a material form (e.g. books or records sold in shops whose retail price already includes the royalty, paid once for all) and those works, such as cinematographic films or recorded musical works, which in addition can be made available to the public through public performances or rental, each time giving rise to a separate royalty. While the first putting of the protected product on the market exhausts the exclusive right to import, export, and sell it in its material form, it does not exhaust the performing right (for films or recorded musical works[51]) or the rental right (for videotapes[52]).

As regards *confusing trade marks or designs*, it was held in *Terrapin* v. *Terranova* and in *Nancy Kean Gifts* that legally registered IPRs may be exercised to prevent the importation of products from another Member State which are identical or confusing with the protected product provided the IPRs have been acquired by different and independent proprietors under different national laws, that the imported products have not been put on the market in the other Member State by the right owner or with his consent, and that there is no kind of agreement or concerted practice contrary to the competition rules.

Finally, one should always keep in mind the *second sentence of Article 36*, which is a sort of general and last condition under which, even if the exercise of the IPR in question has successfully passed all the previous stages of the analysis, such exercise can still be barred if it would constitute a 'means of arbitrary discrimination or a disguised restriction of trade between Member States'. For a right holder not to exercise his right with the same strictness whatever the national origin of the infringer would constitute an arbitrary discrimination (*Terrapin* v. *Terranova*). Likewise, the use of a trade mark in such a way as artificially to partition the markets between the Member States would constitute a disguised restriction of trade (as in the case of registration of different marks for a given product or a packaging method tailor made to insulate the different markets[53])

2.4.2.3 Structure of the Court's reasoning

From the reading of its case-law on exhaustion, the Court's reasoning can be summarized as follows:

1. The principle is the free movement of goods (Articles 30 and 34 EEC).
2. Exceptions to this principle are possible (first sentence of Article 36 EEC), notably on the basis of intellectual property law, but they are interpreted restrictively.
3. The principle of free movement of goods does not affect the existence of IPRs but may nevertheless affect their exercise.

[51] See *Coditel I* and 402/85 *SACEM* [1987] ECR 1747.
[52] See Case 158/86 *Warner* [1988] ECR 2605.
[53] See *American Home Products* and *Hoffmann-La Roche* cases.

4. As regards IPRs, an exception on the basis of Article 36 EEC can be admitted only to the extent that such an exception is justified for the purpose of safeguarding the exclusive rights which constitute the specific subject-matter of the intellectual property.
5. Even in cases where the exclusive right in question belongs to the specific subject-matter of the intellectual property, its exercise may still be prohibited as being contrary to the principle of free movement of goods if it constitutes a 'means of arbitrary discrimination or a disguised restriction of trade between Member States' (second sentence of Article 36 EEC).

2.4.2.4 Codification of the Community exhaustion rule in the EC secondary legislation

Although the case-law of the Court will without any doubt remain an important element, it should be noted that the Community exhaustion principle is being increasingly codified in the EC secondary legislation on intellectual property, either in directives which harmonize the national laws,[54] or in legislative measures creating separate genuine EC-wide systems of intellectual property protection in addition to the existing national systems.[55]

This development has the advantage of bringing better legal certainty for the economic agents, as it diminishes the inherent risk of any jurisprudence which is to change, the problem being not that jurisprudence changes but the time it takes to change (for instance, sixteen years between *Hag I* and *Hag II*). There is, however, as yet no ECJ jurisprudence interpreting exhaustion provisions contained in the secondary legislation.[56]

2.4.2.5 The particular issue of compulsory licensing

It took a long time before the issue of compulsory licensing could really be addressed at Community level. This is due to the fact that it is basically a question related to the protection of public interest, which, in principle, remains in the hands of the States. However, it became evident that certain conditions provided for in national law for the grant of compulsory licences were discriminatory or contrary to the principle of free movement of goods.

The issue was first addressed in *Pharmon* (discussed above in Section 2.4.2.2), which however limited itself to the question, in the context of exhaustion, of whether a right holder can be said to have consented or not to the marketing of products manufactured and sold by a third party who has been granted a compulsory licence.

The first case which looked at the compatibility with Articles 30 and 36 EEC of

[54] Such as the Trade Mark, the Semiconductor, or the Computer Programs Directives.

[55] Such as the Community patent, Community trade mark, Community plant variety, Community design, etc.

[56] Annex I reproduces the relevant provisions of the adopted and pending EC legislation which have codified the exhaustion rule.

the national legal conditions under which a compulsory licence (or the like) is granted was *Allen and Handburrys* v. *Generics*,[57] where the Court held that the principle of free movement of goods prohibits administrative authorities from imposing on a licensee different terms depending on whether he imports the protected products from other Member States or manufactures them in the domestic territory and markets them there.

In a recent case, *Commission* v. *UK*,[58] the Court stated clearly that a national legislation on compulsory licensing which lists as one of the possible grounds for granting a compulsory licence the fact that the needs of the domestic market as regards the protected product are mostly met through imports constitutes, as it results in reducing imports, a measure of equivalent effect to a quantitative restriction and is thus contrary to Article 30 EEC. The Court concluded that there is no reason to discriminate between a patent which is exploited through manufacturing within the country concerned and a patent exploited through importation of the protected product from other Member States.

This case-law is in line with the provisions on compulsory licensing contained in the Community Patent Agreement (CPA), which reads, as regards Community patents (Article 46 CPA):

> A compulsory licence may not be granted in respect of a Community patent on the ground of lack or insufficiency of exploitation if the product covered by the patent, which is manufactured in a Contracting State, is put on the market in the territory of any other Contracting State, for which such a licence has been requested, in sufficient quantity to satisfy needs in the territory of that other Contracting State. This provision shall not apply to compulsory licences granted in the public interest.

As regards national patents (Article 77 CPA):

> Article 46 shall apply mutatis mutandis to the grant of compulsory licences for lack or insufficiency of exploitation of a national patent.

3. INTELLECTUAL PROPERTY PROVISIONS IN THE EEA

As explained at the beginning of this chapter, intellectual property was from the outset considered as belonging to the *acquis communautaire* which would qualify for becoming part of the EEA Agreement. However, the negotiators quickly realized that the general principles to be followed when drafting the EEA provisions[59] would

[57] Case 434/85 [1988] ECR 1245.

[58] Case C-30/90 [1992] ECR I-858. See also Case C-235/90 *Commission* v. *Italy* [1992] ECR I-818 on the same subject-matter.

[59] Among which are to reproduce as closely as possible the wording of the EC original text when integrated in the EEA Agreement and to put provisions corresponding to EC primary law in the main part of the Agreement and those corresponding to EC secondary legislation in the annexes and protocols thereto.

not fit in this particular case as most of the acquis to be taken over was either in the form of jurisprudence of the Court of Justice or still at a preparatory stage in the EC legislative process.[60] The only express reference to intellectual property in the Rome Treaty was contained in Article 36, which lists 'the protection of industrial and commercial property' as one of the possible exceptions to the principle of free movement of goods and on the basis of which, as explained above, the Court developed its case-law on EC-wide exhaustion of IPRs.

The EC and EFTA experts were nevertheless very keen on putting genuine intellectual property provisions in the EEA Agreement, as these are one of the essential elements of the proper functioning of the free movement of goods. Furthermore, it would reflect the fact that the EEA was a 'fundamentally improved free trade area', a 'second generation' free trade agreement, thus in line with the general mood of what was being negotiated elsewhere (TRIPs in GATT Uruguay Round, Free Trade and Association Agreements with the Central and Eastern European countries, NAFTA,[61] etc.)

It was first envisaged to include intellectual property provisions as primary law in the main part of the Agreement itself, while putting the secondary EC legislation in an annex. At the end, however, in order not to break the parallel between the structure of the main part of the Agreement and that of the Rome Treaty, it was decided that the basic intellectual property provisions would go in a protocol (Protocol 28) and the secondary law in an annex (Annex XVII), the main part of the Agreement containing only a reference point (Article 65 (2)) to those two. There remains nevertheless a trace of this first intention in the fact that Protocol 28 is not listed in Article 98 of the Agreement ('light' amendment procedure for annexes and certain protocols by an EEA Joint Committee decision), which results in the fact that Protocol 28 can only be amended through the more heavy procedure to be followed for the main part of the Agreement (i.e. through diplomatic conference between the Contracting Parties).

3.1 Article 65 (2) EEA

Article 65 (2) reads: 'Protocol 28 and Annex XVII contain specific provisions and arrangements concerning intellectual, industrial and commercial property, which, unless otherwise specified, shall apply to all products and services.'

Article 65 (2) is placed in chapter 3 ('Other common rules') of part IV ('Competition and other common rules') of the Agreement. As part IV comes after the parts containing the four basic freedoms rules (goods, persons, services, and

[60] When the first legal texts were drafted at the beginning of 1991, there were only two directives adopted in the field of intellectual property, i.e. the 1986 Directive on topographies of semiconductors and the 1988 Directive on trade marks. All the other EC legislative measures were still in what the negotiating jargon called the 'pipeline *acquis*', i.e. still in the form of Commission proposals to the EC Council or provisions not yet in force.

[61] i.e. North American Free Trade Agreement signed between the USA, Canada, and Mexico on 17 Dec. 1992, which is due to enter into force on 1 Jan. 1994.

capital), this indicates that its provisions apply, as appropriate, to the subject-matters of the preceding parts.

Furthermore, Article 65 (2) EEA, on purpose, uses more modern language than Article 36 EEC (reproduced in Article 13 EEA) as it refers to 'intellectual, industrial and commercial property', and not only to 'industrial and commercial property', thus covering all types of IPRs. This is in line with the definition of intellectual property given in Article 1 of Protocol 28 and with the Court case-law, which, in *GEMA*, said that copyright also falls within the scope of Article 36 EEC.[62]

Finally, Article 65 (2) EEA states that, 'unless otherwise specified' (in the different specific intellectual property provisions), the EEA intellectual property rules apply to 'all products and services', meaning that the limitations as to the product coverage of the Agreement contained in Article 8 EEA (see Chapter III) do not apply in the context of intellectual property. Should, for instance, the inclusion in the EEA of the proposed regulations on Community plant variety rights or on geographical indications be envisaged, the wording of Article 65 (2) EEA would prevent them from being considered as falling outside the scope of the EEA because they concern agricultural products.[63]

3.2 Protocol 28 EEA

Protocol 28[64] contains nine articles which address three types of issues: level of protection (Articles 1 and 2, discussed in Sections 3.2.1 and 3.2.2), commitment to participate in or adhere to different Community measures or international conventions (Articles 3, 5, 6, and 8, discussed in Sections 3.2.3 and 3.2.4), and matters related to third countries or to international activities (Articles 4 and 7, discussed in Section 3.2.5). In addition, there is a general reserve as regards the distribution of competence between the EC Member States and the Community in intellectual property matters (Article 9).[65]

The inclusion was also envisaged during the negotiations of a provision similar to the text of the GATT-TRIPs prohibiting EEA States from granting compulsory licences for non-working of a patent when the protected product has been put on the market in another EEA State and the imports of such product satisfy the needs of the market of the State concerned. The idea was however abandoned.[66] In any case,

[62] See *GEMA* case and the comments in s. 3.2.1 below regarding Art. 1 of Protocol 28.

[63] It is recalled that basic agricultural products do not fall within the scope of the EEA Agreement; for further details see s. 1 of Ch. III above. The question of product coverage of the EEA in the context of IPRs has already given rise to some doctrinal debate (see article by M. Abbey in [1992] 6 ECLR 231 and the interesting answer by F. Prändl in [1993] 2 ECLR 43).

[64] Protocol 28 is reproduced in Annex A.

[65] Intellectual property is one of the matters in the EC where there is disagreement as to whether external competences remain with the Member States or have been transferred to Community level. Intellectual property therefore became one of the EEA chapters which made it being a 'mixed agreement' (see Ch. II, s. 3.1).

[66] For further developments on compulsory licensing in the EC context see s. 2.4.2.5 above.

the recent jurisprudence of the ECJ (referred to above in Section 2.4.2.5) relating to compulsory licensing should contribute to solve the issue.

Likewise, it was envisaged that the regional exhaustion rule developed by the Court of Justice might be codified. However, the idea was also left aside, as the application of Article 6 of the Agreement (interpretation in conformity with the EC case-law) together with Article 13 EEA (exceptions to free movement of goods, which reproduces Article 36 EEC) was already having the effect of bringing into the EEA context the jurisprudence on exhaustion. It was nevertheless agreed, as an indication of the importance of the principle, and in a spirit of transparency and legal certainty, to include in Protocol 28 a specific reference to the exhaustion rule. For further developments on this matter, see Section 3.2.2 below.

3.2.1 Substance of the protection (Article 1)

Article 1 of Protocol 28 contains three paragraphs, the first giving a definition and the two other dealing with protection levels to be attained.

Paragraph 1 defines 'intellectual property' as a generic term which includes, as does Article 65 (2) EEA, all types of IPRs. The purpose was to avoid any debate on whether the wording 'industrial and commercial property' also comprises copyright or not, as occurred once in the Community.[67]

Paragraphs 2 and 3 provide a sort of framework, the purpose of which is better to tie the parties together and to fill in the possible gaps. They are however general provisions to which the principle *lex specialis derogat generali* should apply, meaning that the more specific provisions contained in the Protocol or in Annex XVII take precedence over these general rules. Furthermore, these provisions, as they resemble similar clauses in the Agreements with Central and Eastern European countries, contribute to the creation of a common platform of intellectual property protection on the whole Continent.

Paragraph 2[68] aims at equalizing the general level of protection and enforcement of IPRs in the EEA. It has partly been modelled on the first paragraph of Protocol 8 to the Act of Accession of Spain and Portugal. Its different elements are the following:

[67] See the Court case *GEMA*. The main reason for this debate was that copyright comprises both economic and non-economic rights (i.e. the moral rights of authors), the latter element putting them, according to some, in a special category 'above' mere mercantile considerations. This debate in fact reflected the differences between two main legal traditions in this respect, the Anglo-Saxon one putting emphasis on the commercial aspect (as indicated by the use of the word 'copyright') and the 'Continental' one insisting more on the protection of artists and authors (as the use of the wording 'author's right' shows). This old divergence recently emerged again in the GATT negotiations, where the US delegation wanted the audio-visual and cinematographic sector to be liberalized like any other product where the European side favoured a more culture-oriented approach.

[68] Para. 2 reads: 'Without prejudice to the provisions of this Protocol and of Annex XVII, the Contracting Parties shall upon the entry into force of this Agreement adjust their legislation on intellectual property so as to make it compatible with the principle of free circulation of goods and services and with the level of protection of intellectual property attained in Community law, including the level of enforcement of those rights.'

- the use of the term 'Contracting Parties' means that both the EC (and its Member States) and the EFTA sides undertake to make the adjustments in question;
- the phrase 'so as to make it compatible with the principle of free circulation of goods and services', in addition to relating indirectly to the exhaustion rule, also concerns the way national intellectual property laws are drafted, in particular provisions on compulsory licences (discrimination based on nationality, barriers to imports, etc.);[69]
- the word 'attained' indicates an equalization towards the top (i.e. the lower levels should be brought up);
- the term 'Community law' was meant to include both the EC legislation in force (in a wide sense, i.e. also the international conventions to which the Community would be party) and the case-law of the Court of Justice.

Paragraph 3[70] also aims at equalizing the level of protection but only after a certain procedure has been followed (i.e. no automatism). It contains the following elements:

- the adjustment obligation is imposed on the EFTA States only (one-sided clause);
- such adjustment will take place only 'upon request', 'after consultation between the Contracting Parties', and 'subject to the procedural provisions of the Agreement', the latter implying a reference to the EEA decision-making procedure (Articles 97 *et seq.*). This means that the adjustment should be an ad hoc procedure targeting a specific situation;
- the level of protection referred to is the one 'prevailing' (the average of the majority) 'in the Community', which is meant to refer also to national intellectual property laws of the EC Member States;
- the term 'reach at least' means that this average level should be a bottom line and that, should an EFTA State have a higher level of protection in a given field, it would not be obliged to lower it to the average level;
- the wording 'upon signature of the Agreement' freezes the reference level of protection on 2 May 1992 and thus avoids the obligation becoming a moving target.

3.2.2 Exhaustion of rights (Article 2)

Given the importance of the exhaustion rule, the developments below, in addition to comments on the text of the provision, also address some of the consequences

[69] This application of free movement of goods provisions to the national rules on compulsory licences is in line with the recent Court case *Commission* v. *UK*. For further developments see s. 2.4.2.5 above.

[70] Para. 3 reads: 'Subject to the procedural provisions of this Agreement and without prejudice to the provisions of this Protocol and of Annex XVII, the EFTA States will adjust, upon request and after consultation between the Contracting Parties, their legislation on intellectual property in order to reach at least the level of protection of intellectual property prevailing in the Community upon signature of this Agreement.'

which might occur as a result of the extension of the exhaustion principle to the EFTA States. The jurisprudence of the Court of Justice on IPRs, and in particular the Community exhaustion rule, is described in Section 2 above.

3.2.2.1 The drafting of Article 2

As said above, it was first envisaged that the regional exhaustion rule developed by the Court of Justice should be codified in Protocol 28. From this idea a provision remains, paragraph 1 of Article 2, which expressly takes over in the EEA the 'Community measures or jurisprudence' on exhaustion and puts an obligation on the Contracting Parties to 'provide for such exhaustion of intellectual property rights'. The reference to Community measures, in addition to the case-law, concerns the different provisions in the EC secondary legislation which deal with exhaustion of IPRs.[71]

The second sentence of the provision reproduces, in a shorter form, the wording of Article 6 EEA (on the case-law of the Court of Justice given prior to the signature of the EEA, 2 May 1992). This was the only way to be precise enough while at the same time avoiding the difficult exercise of codification. As regards future case-law of the European Court of Justice, it is recalled that Article 3 (2) of the ESA/Court Agreement obliges ESA and the EFTA Court to pay due acount to the ECJ jurisprudence given after 2 May 1992.[72]

Paragraph 2 gives the right holders a one-year transitional period concerning the exhaustion of patent rights. This aspect is commented further on below.

3.2.2.2 Consequences of the introduction of an EEA-wide exhaustion rule in the EFTA States

The two main effects of the introduction of the EEA-wide exhaustion rule in the EFTA States will be, as regards patents, the 'upgrading' of the exhaustion of exclusive marketing rights from a national exhaustion to a regional (EEA) exhaustion. As regards trade marks and, at least for some countries, copyright, it is debatable whether the introduction of the EEA-wide exhaustion principle will oblige the EFTA States concerned to 'downgrade' from international exhaustion to regional exhaustion or whether they can keep international exhaustion (in other words, whether the EEA-wide exhaustion rule is a minimum standard or is a mandatory rule). These two issues are discussed below.

With regard to *patents*, before the introduction of regional exhaustion (EEA-wide), only national exhaustion was applied in the different EFTA States, with the result that the patent holder could use his exclusive right to market the patented product for opposing in particular cheap parallel imports. Switching from national to EEA-wide exhaustion in the EFTA countries will thus mean that the patent

[71] For a description of the EC case-law on exhaustion see s. 2 above. See also Annex I, where these provisions are reproduced.

[72] For further details see s. 7.1 of Ch. II above.

owners will lose the marketing-right weapon and will have to reassess their commercialization arrangements in light of the new EEA provisions on free movement of goods, intellectual property, and also competition.

This is the reason why, to provide the patent holders with some kind of 'soft landing', the negotiators agreed to grant them, as from the entry into force of the Agreement, a transitional period of one year before regional exhaustion starts to apply to patent rights (Article 2 (2) of Protocol 28).

In addition, it should be noted that the competition rules allow, to a limited extent, some control over parallel imports, at least concerning the first level of trade (between the licensor and his licensees or between licensees) but not at the users' or resellers' level (second-level trade). The Patent Licensing Regulation[73] permits the following provisions in a licence contract:

- ban on the licensor to exploit (i.e. manufacture, use, and market) the licensed invention in the licensee's territory (Article 1 (1) (2));
- ban on the licensee to exploit the licensed invention in the territories reserved for the licensor (Article 1 (1)(3));
- ban on the licensee actively pursuing commercial activity in another licensee's territory (active sales, Article 1 (1)(5));
- ban for up to five years, on the licensee accepting orders from outside his territory (passive sales, Article 1 (1)(6)).[74]

The licensee must be free to accept orders from users or resellers established within his territory, even if they intend to resell the product in another territory (protection of the second-level trade, Article 3 (11) (*a*)). Other means of impeding parallel imports at this second level, such as price restrictions or customer restrictions, are forbidden (Article 3 (6) and (7)).

With regard to *trade marks and copyright*, the situation is the opposite from that of patents as most of the EFTA countries apply international exhaustion,[75] the question being whether EFTA will have to give up international exhaustion for regional exhaustion, thus recreating trade barriers.

This question could actually be asked in the same terms within the EC, as most of the EC Member States also apply international exhaustion. The issue was however never addressed by the Court of Justice.[76] It was nevertheless raised when the Commission made its first draft for the Community Trade Mark Regulation in

[73] Commission Reg. (EEC) 2349/84 of 23 July 1984 on the application of Art. 85 (3) of the Treaty to certain categories of patent licensing agreements (*OJ* L 219 (16 Aug. 1984), 15, taken over in the EEA under point 5 of Annex XIV).

[74] This possibility is available only during the first five years from the moment the protected goods are first marketed within the Community (after which the ban is no longer permitted, see Art. 3 (10)).

[75] i.e. the commercialization right is exhausted once the protected product has been put on the market anywhere in the world by the right holder himself or with his consent. For an indicative chart on international exhaustion in EC and EFTA States see Annex J.

[76] The case *EMI* v. *CBS* involved an identical trade mark owned by two unrelated companies. For the international v. regional exhaustion issue to be addressed, one would have needed a case where the trade mark was held by the same company or related companies.

1978. The Commission was then of the opinion that, in order to remain consistent with the function of the trade mark (which is to indicate the production origin) and the relevant national case-law, international exhaustion should apply to the Community trade mark.[77] However, the idea met fierce opposition from both government experts and interested circles and was therefore replaced by a mere regional exhaustion provision in the draft Community Trade Mark Regulation (as well as in the Trade Mark Directive).[78]

The present, very unclear, situation in the EC seems therefore to be that the codification of regional exhaustion in the EC secondary legislation would oblige those States which used to apply international exhaustion to reduce it to EC-wide exhaustion. It could however be argued that, since the introduction of Community exhaustion by the EC Court in 1971 (*Deutsche Grammophon* case) did not prevent national judges from continuing to apply international exhaustion, the subsequent codification of the exhaustion rule in EC legislation did not fundamentally change the legal environment in that respect. As both the Court jurisprudence and EC legislation are constitutive parts of the Community law body which, under the primacy principle, takes precedence over conflicting national law (including national case-law), it would seem rather strange that a national rule which for twenty years was never expressly considered as contrary to EC jurisprudence should, all of a sudden, become an infringement of Community law merely because the said EC jurisprudence has been codified in a directive. It is also true that some EC Member States could take this opportunity to put an end to international exhaustion, which, in times of recession and fierce world competition, might seem to be too generous.

3.2.3 Participation of EFTA States in EC-wide measures for the protection of IPRs (Articles 3 and 8)

Although, apart from the Regulation on geographical indications, none of them has yet entered into force, one of the tools to eliminate trade distortions resulting from the differences between the various national laws is to create EC-wide protection systems of IPRs such as:

[77] See draft Council regulation on the Community trade mark, Working Document 11, July 1978, III/S/753/78 (published in GRUR Int. (1978), 452), whose Art. 14 (1) reads: 'A Community trade mark shall not confer on its proprietor the right to prohibit the use of the trade mark in respect of goods which have been put on the market under that trade mark by the proprietor or with his consent' (for the revised, and latest, version of the exhaustion provision, see Annex I).

[78] For a comprehensive study on this issue, see F.-K. Beier and A. Mühlendal (from the Max-Planck Institute), 'Study on the Principle of Exhaustion in Trade Mark Laws of Member States of the EEC and of Some Other Countries', EC document II/0/1427/79. See also G. Aschenbrenner, 'How far should the Exhaustion of Intellectual Property Rights Rules Developed in the Case Law of the EEC Court of Justice be Introduced into EC–EFTA Relations', in *Creating a European Economic Space: Legal Aspects of EC–EFTA Relations* (Dublin Conference, Irish Centre for European Law, Oct. 1989), 207). For an analysis of the regional exhaustion rule in the context of the future new GATT-TRIPs rules, see A. A. Yusof and A. Moncayo van Hase, 'Intellectual Property Protection and International Trade: Exhaustion of Rights revisited', *World Competition*, 16 (1992–3), 115).

– Community patents;[79]
– Community trade mark;[80]
– Community plant variety rights;[81]
– Community design;[82]
– Community geographical indications;[83]

These EC-wide systems are characterized notably by the fact that they come in addition to the different national intellectual property laws without replacing them. They create a genuine central registration system and the rights granted are valid throughout the Community. Economic agents will therefore have the choice between protecting their rights only through national laws (possibly using some of the simplified registration procedures provided for in international conventions) or registering a Community IPR, which, once extended to the EEA, will provide them at once with protection for a fair share of the European continent. There are also rules linking these Community IPRs to international conventions (such as Paris Union agreements or the European Patent Convention).

Articles 3 and 8 of Protocol 28 aim at guaranteeing EFTA participation in these Community systems, Article 3 providing for more precise conditions as regards the Community Patent Agreement. These Articles are discussed below.

[79] Council Agreement 89/695/EEC of 15 Dec. 1989 relating to Community patents (*OJ* L 401 (30 Dec. 1989), 1) which includes the Community Patent Convention, implementation regulations, as well as a Protocol on Litigation. In Sept. 1993 it had been ratified by eleven EC Member States and was still waiting for ratification by Spain.

[80] Amended proposal of 9 Aug. 1984 for a Council regulation on the Community trade mark (*OJ* C 230 (31 Aug. 1984), 1), as well as related proposals concerning implementing rules (COM (85) 844 final, 23 Jan. 1986), fees (*OJ* C 67 (14 Mar. 1987), 5), and rules of procedure for the Boards of Appeal of the Community Trade Mark Office (COM (86) 731 final, 23 Dec. 1986). The Community Trade Mark Regulation was finally adopted by the Council on 20 Dec. 1993. This decision was made easier after the European Council cleared the issue of location of the future Trade Mark Office, which will be in Alicante (Spain), within the 'Office for Harmonization of the Internal Market' (also due to host Community designs and models, see Decision op. cit. n. 2). The Trade Mark Regulation was published in *OJ* L 11 (14 Jan. 1994), 1.

[81] Amended proposal of 29 Mar. 1993 for a Council regulation (EEC) on Community plant variety rights (COM (93) 104 final), which, in Nov. 1993, was still blocked due to divergences on the farmer's privilege.

[82] Preliminary draft proposal for a regulation on the Community design contained in the Green Paper of June 1991 on the legal protection of industrial design (see annex 1 of Working Document of the EC Commission, III/F/5131/91-EN). After having held two hearings with interested circles in 1992, the Commission adopted on 28 July 1993 two proposals for a Council regulation on the Community design and a Council directive on the legal protection of designs (see COM (93) final–COD 463 and COM (93) 344 final–COD 464, both of 3 Dec. 1993).

[83] Council Reg. (EEC) 2081/92 of 14 July 1992 on the protection of geographical indications and designations of origin for agricultural products and foodstuffs (*OJ* L 208 (24 July 1992), 1), to be read together with Council Reg. (EEC) 2082/92 of 14 July 1992 on certificates of specific character for agricultural products and foodstuffs (and its implementing Commission Reg. (EEC) 1848/93 of 9 July 1993 laying down detailed rules for the application of Council Reg. (EEC) 2082/92 on certificates of specific character for agricultural products and foodstuffs). See also Commission Dec. 93/53/EEC of 21 Dec. 1992 setting up a scientific committee for designations of origin, geographical indications, and certificates of specific character (*OJ* L 13 (21 Jan. 1993), 16) and Commission Reg. (EEC) 2037/93 of 27 July 1993 laying down detailed rules of application of Council Reg. (EEC) 2081/92 (*OJ* L 185 (28 July 1993), 5).

3.2.3.1 Community Patent Agreement (Article 3)

Article 3 contains six paragraphs, the first three dealing with the conditions and procedure under which EFTA countries will adhere to the Community Patent Agreement (CPA), the fourth with compliance of the EFTA States with the substantive provisions of the European Patent Convention (EPC), and the last two with patentability of pharmaceutical products and foodstuffs in Finland and Iceland.

Paragraph 1 contains a best endeavour clause pursuant to which the Community and the EFTA States should, within three years of its entry into force, conclude adherence negotiations to the CPA. Iceland is however granted a transitional period until 1 January 1998.

Paragraph 2 makes it clear that the first paragraph is not a blank cheque but that the specific situation (such as for instance particular ethical conditions regarding biotechnology) of each applicant should be subject to negotiations. This is one example where the *lex specialis* effect should outrule the general level-of-protection Article 1 (2).

Paragraph 3 is designed to simplify, for EFTA States, the procedural conditions foreseen in Article 8[84] of the CPA as regards accession of third countries. The wording 'The Community undertakes . . . to invite' puts an obligation on the Community and thus already takes care of the unanimity requirement provided for when the EC Council invites the EFTA State in question to participate in the CPA. The term 'those EFTA States who so request' could be seen as meaning that not necessarily all EFTA countries should adhere to the CPA, while the wording of paragraph 1 ('the participation of the EFTA States to that Agreement') implies participation of all EFTA countries. Furthermore, the Community invitation shall not be addressed to Finland before 1 January 1995 nor to Iceland before 1 January 1997 (see last sentence of paragraph 5).

Paragraph 4 alleviates the second condition set out in Article 8 of the CPA (which requires that the candidate third State be already party to the EPC), as it only obliges the EFTA States to comply in their national patent laws with the substantive provisions of the EPC, regardless of whether they are formally party to the EPC. This obligation particularly concerns Iceland, Finland, and Norway, which have not yet adhered to the EPC.

Paragraphs 5 and 6 deal with the particular situation of Finland and Iceland, where certain products (pharmaceuticals and foodstuffs for Finland and pharmaceuticals for Iceland) are not yet patentable. Paragraph 5 grants them until 1 January 1995 (Finland) and 1 January 1997 (Iceland) to introduce into their

[84] Art. 8 of the CPA reads: 'The Council of the [EC] may, acting by a unanimous decision, invite a State party to the [EPC] which forms a customs union or a free trade area with the [EEC] to enter into negotiations with a view to enabling that third State to participate in this Agreement on the basis of a special agreement, to be concluded between Contracting States to this Agreement and the third State concerned, determining the conditions and details for applying this Agreement to that State.'

national patent law a protection substantially similar to the one provided for in the EPC. Furthermore, and for two years following the date when patentability is introduced, paragraph 6 renders the regional exhaustion rule inapplicable as regards products coming from Finland and Iceland, thus avoiding the effect of the *Merck* v. *Stephar* case (importation of a product from a country where it could not be patented, see Section 2.4.2.1 above). This paragraph was modelled on Article 47 of the Act of Accession of Spain and Portugal.

3.2.3.2 Other EC-wide measures (Article 8)

Article 8 concerns the participation of EFTA countries in the other EC-wide systems of intellectual property protection. There are two elements to be particularly noted in this Article:

- the term 'full participation' is designed to ensure that a proper solution will be found not only concerning compliance with the substantive rules but also as to the administrative system which is to be set up (central registration procedure, Community Office, appeal bodies, etc.);
- the term 'interested EFTA States' implies that not necessarily all EFTA countries will participate in these EC-wide systems.

As indicated above, so far only the Regulations on geographical indications and on Community trade mark have been adopted in the EC. Their inclusion in the EEA context is being discussed between the EC and EFTA sides.

3.2.4 Adherence to different international conventions and reference to the results of the GATT-TRIPs negotiations (Articles 5 and 6)

Again with a view to creating in Europe a common platform of intellectual property protection (see above in Section 3.2.1 remarks concerning Article 1 (2) and (3)), Article 5 obliges the EEA Contracting Parties (both the EC and the EFTA States) to adhere, by 1 January 1995, to seven multilateral intellectual property conventions.[85] However, the obligation in fact concerns only some of the EC and EFTA States as most of the others are already parties to these agreements:[86]

- the Paris Convention (Stockholm Act of 1967);
- the Berne Convention (Paris Act of 1971);
- the Rome Convention (1961);

[85] For further details on these conventions see s. 1.6 above, as well as Annex G. Note also Council Res. 92/C 138/01 of 14 May 1992 on increased protection for copyright and neighbouring rights (*OJ* C 138 (28 May 1992), 1), which notes the undertaking of the EC Member States concerned to adhere to the Berne and Rome Conventions by 1 Jan. 1995 and encourages the Commission to include, as far as possible, the ratification of these Conventions as part of agreements which it negotiates with third countries.

[86] This obligation in fact concerns only the following States: Paris Convention: Iceland (Arts. 1 to 12); Berne Convention (Paris Act 1971): Belgium, Iceland, Ireland, Liechtenstein, and Norway; Rome Convention: Belgium, Iceland, Liechtenstein, Portugal, and Spain; Madrid Protocol: all EC and EFTA countries, apart from Iceland, have signed the Protocol but only Spain has so far ratified; Nice Agreement: Greece and Iceland; Budapest Treaty: Iceland, Ireland, Luxembourg, and Portugal; PCT: Iceland.

– the Protocol to the Madrid Agreement (1989);
– the Nice Agreement (Geneva Act of 1977);
– the Budapest Treaty (1977, modified in 1980);
– the Patent Co-operation Treaty (1970, modified in 1984).

Paragraph 3 obliges the EEA Contracting Parties concerned, as from the entry into force of the EEA Agreement[87] and pending their formal adherence in 1995, to align in substance their national legislation with the first three conventions (Paris, Berne, and Rome). Paragraph 2 gives, as regards adherence to the Protocol to the Madrid Agreement, a one-year delay for Finland, Ireland, and Norway (1 January 1996 instead of 1995) and a two-year delay for Iceland (1 January 1997).

Article 6 provides that, as far as this would constitute an improvement, the EEA intellectual property regime should be amended in light of the results of the GATT-TRIPs agreement. One could imagine that such an improvement might for instance concern compulsory licensing[88] or even, depending on the outcome of the EC–EFTA discussion, geographical indications.[89]

3.2.5 Relations with third countries and activities in international fora (Articles 4 and 7)

On principle, the EEA Agreement does not cover relations with third countries and thus leaves the EEA Contracting Parties full freedom of action in this respect. However, the negotiators admitted that, to the extent this would be required for the good functioning of the Agreement, pragmatism was desirable and a case-by-case co-ordination of action towards third countries should be possible. In the field of intellectual property, especially in cases where there is harmonization, the parties felt that at least a certain co-operation as regards third countries and within international organizations would be useful. This was the case in particular for the Semiconductor Directive, whose Article 3 (6) to (8) provides for a possible extension of the benefit of the protection to persons from third countries.

3.2.5.1 Extension of the semiconductor protection to persons from third countries (Article 4)

Article 4 concerns the procedure for extending the benefit of semiconductor protection to persons from third countries. This provision finds its origin in the fact that Article 3 (6) to (8) of the Semiconductor Directive is declared not to apply in the EEA context (see adaptation (*b*) under point 1 of Annex XVII). A provision was therefore needed which, though acknowledging that the EEA Contracting Parties

87 With the exception of Ireland, which, as regards the Berne Convention, shall comply with its provisions only as from 1 Jan. 1995 (this date being in any case the deadline set down in para. 1 for acceding to the Berne Convention as revised in the Paris Act of 1971).

88 See Art. 31 (compulsory licensing) of the draft TRIPs agreement ('Dunkel text', MJN.TNC/W/FA, Dec. 1991).

89 Ibid., Arts. 22–4 (geographical indications).

remain free to extend the protection independently to third countries (paragraph 1), would organize this freedom to avoid possible trade distortions. Paragraph 2 thus provides that, when extending the benefits of the protection to a third country, the EEA Contracting Party concerned should see to it that the country in question accords reciprocal protection also to the other EEA Contracting Parties. Under paragraph 3, a decision of extension 'shall be respected and recognized by all the Contracting Parties'. Paragraphs 4 and 5 refer to the ordinary EEA procedure concerning mutual information, consultation, dispute settlement, and safeguard (in particular Articles 92 and 111 *et seq.*).

There are already two EC Council decisions extending semiconductor protection to persons from certain third countries, either on a permanent basis (because the country in question has an appropriate legislation and grants reciprocity to the EC[90]) or on an interim basis only (pending proper legislation being passed in the country concerned[91]). These decisions have been taken over in the EEA context (listed in points 2 and 3 of Annex XVII), together with specific adaptations to the effect that reciprocity should, within a year from the entry into force of the EEA, be granted to the EFTA States by countries which are listed in the First Decision (see adaptation (*b*) under point 2 of Annex XVII) and that the EFTA States should take over the present and amending or replacing Decisions adopted in the context of the Second Decision (see adaptation under point 3[92]).

3.2.5.2 International fora and agreements (Article 7)

Article 7 provides for a general mutual information obligation regarding activities within international organizations and intellectual property agreements (including bilateral ones). It furthermore provides for prior consultations when the issue in question belongs to a harmonized field in the EEA. This could for instance apply in the current negotiations in WIPO concerning a Protocol to the Berne Convention (see n. 17 above).

[90] First Council Dec. 90/510/EEC of 9 Oct. 1990 on the extension of the legal protection of topographies of semiconductor products to persons from certain countries and territories (*OJ* L 285 (17 Oct. 1990), 29, amended by Council Dec. 93/17/EEC of 21 Dec. 1992 (*OJ* L 11 (19 Jan. 1993), 22)), which extends the protection, as regards both natural and legal persons, to Australia, Japan, Switzerland, and a certain number of French overseas territories (the other EFTA States listed will be covered by the EEA Agreement).

[91] Second Council Dec. 90/511/EEC of 9 Oct. 1990 on the extension of the legal protection of topographies of semiconductor products to persons from certain countries and territories (*OJ* L 285 (17 Oct. 1990), 31, prolonged by Council Dec. 93/16/EEC (*OJ* L 11 (19 Jan. 1993), 20)), together with Commission Dec. 90/541/EEC of 26 Oct. 1990 (*OJ* L 307 (7 Nov. 1990), 21), which lapsed on 31 Dec. 1992. The new Commission Dec. 93/217/EEC of 19 Mar. 1993 (*OJ* L 94 (20 Apr. 1993), 30) extended the protection to a certain number of British overseas territories until 31 Dec. 1994 (as regards natural persons only) and to the USA until 31 Dec. 1993 (as regards both natural and legal persons). Furthermore, Council Dec. 93/520/EEC of 27 Sept. 1993 (*OJ* L 246 (2 Oct. 1993), 31) adds to the list of the Second Council Decision certain Dutch overseas territories.

[92] This obligation thus concerns the amendments and prolongations quoted above (Decs. 93/17, 93/16, 93/217, and 93/520).

3.3 Annex XVII

3.3.1 *Acquis communautaire* included in the original Annex XVII

There were, in the field of intellectual property, only three pieces of *acquis* in force at the time of the cut-off date of 31 July 1991 (when the annexes to the Agreement listing the EEA relevant *acquis communautaire* were 'closed'). These three acts are listed in Annex XVII on intellectual property:[93]

- the Semiconductor Directive (87/54/EEC),[94] which obliges the Member States to introduce protection of topographies of semiconductors, or align their law in accordance with the terms of the Directive;
- the Trade Mark Directive (89/104/EEC), which harmonizes existing national laws;
- the Software Directive (91/250/EEC), which obliges the Member States to introduce protection of computer programs, or align their laws in accordance with the terms of the Directive.

The purpose here is not to give a detailed description of the substantive rules of these different directives but merely to indicate how they will apply in the EEA context. The following elements should be pointed out:

- the inclusion of these EC acts in Annex XVII has the effect of extending their application to the EFTA States;
- the main specific adaptations made in this Annex, better to suit the EEA context and to avoid any uncertainty, are those concerning the regional exhaustion provisions, which have been recopied in full, using the term 'Contracting Party' instead of 'Member State' or 'Community';
- the other specific adaptations concern the extension decisions in the field of semiconductors (see developments above in Section 3.2.5.1) and the references in the Trade Mark Directive to the Community trade mark (references which are declared not to apply to EFTA States as long as the Community Trade Mark Regulation has not been extended to (interested) EFTA States).

The experts also envisaged, during the negotiations, the inclusion in Annex XVII of the Regulation on counterfeit goods,[95] which lays down the conditions under which the customs authorities shall intervene as to goods imported from third countries when it is suspected, or indeed established, that the goods are counterfeit.[96] The Commission has proposed to extend the scope of this Regulation

[93] Annex XVII is reproduced in Annex A.

[94] Together with the extension Decs. 90/510, 90/511, and 90/541 referred to in nn. 91 and 92 above.

[95] Council Reg. (EEC) 3842/86 of 1 Dec. 1986 laying down measures to prohibit the release for free circulation of counterfeit goods (*OJ* L 357 (18 Dec. 1986), 1), implemented by Commission Reg. 3077/87 (*OJ* L 291 (15 Oct. 1987), 19).

[96] i.e. goods bearing without authorization a trade mark which is identical to a trade mark validly registered in a Member State, or which is confusing, and thereby infringes the registered trade mark right.

(to include also goods protected by copyright) and to strengthen the powers of the customs authorities.[97] In the EEA context, the idea to include the Counterfeit Regulation was however left aside as it belongs to the EC Customs Union *acquis* and therefore fell outside the scope of the EEA. The experts nevertheless underlined that the EEA rules on mutual assistance in customs matters (see Protocol 11 to the EEA Agreement) should as far as possible be used so as to arrive in practice at a result similar to the one provided for in the Regulation.

3.3.2 Subsequent and pending *acquis communautaire*

As explained above in Chapter II (Section 2.2), it results from the very nature of the EEA Agreement that it is a 'living animal' which will continually be amended so as to follow closely the evolution of the *acquis communautaire*. This follow-up exercise started immediately after the cut-off date of 31 July 1991 in a process which the negotiation jargon called the 'Additional Package' (composed of EC acts adopted between 31 July 1991 and the entry into force of the EEA). In the field of intellectual property, eight pieces of *acquis* have been adopted in the Community and have been since then under discussion between EC and EFTA experts in the context of the Additional Package:

- four new extending decisions in the field of semiconductors (Decisions 93/17, 93/16, 93/217, and 93/520);[98]
- Council Regulation (1768/92) concerning the creation of a supplementary protection certificate for medicinal products (so-called 'SPC Regulation');[99]
- Council Directive (92/100/EEC) on rental right and lending right and on certain rights related to copyright in the field of intellectual property;[100]
- Council Regulation (2081/92) on the protection of geographical indications and designations of origin for agricultural products and foodstuffs;[101]
- Council Directive 93/98/EEC of 29 October 1993 harmonizing the term of protection of copyright and certain related rights (see n. 6);
- Council Regulation on Community trade mark and its implementing regulations (the former was adopted on 20 December 1993, see n. 80);
- Commission Communication of 22 Oct. 1992 on intellectual property rights and standardization;[102]
- Council Directive 93/83/EEC of 27 September 1993 on the co-ordination of certain rules concerning copyright and rights related to copyright applicable to satellite broadcasting and cable retransmission.[103]

[97] COM (93) 329 final, of 13 July 1993.

[98] For full *OJ* references and some explanations see s. 3.2.5.1 and nn. 91 and 92 above).

[99] *OJ* L 182 (2 July 1992), 1. The purpose of this Regulation is briefly explained in s. 1.2.1 above, n. 2.

[100] *OJ* L 346 (27 Nov. 1992), 61.

[101] For full *OJ* references see s. 3.2.3 above, n. 83. Its inclusion in Annex XVII EEA is not at all certain due to some divergences of opinion between the Parties.

[102] COM (92) 445 final.

[103] *OJ* L 248 (6 Oct. 1993), 15.

Once the negotiations on their inclusion in the EEA will have been concluded, their addition to the list in Annex XVII should be made through a decision of the EEA Joint Committee at the entry into force of the EEA (see Chapter II, Section 6.2).

There are in addition a number of planned or pending Commission proposals (the so-called 'pipeline *acquis*') which are still being discussed within the EC and whose inclusion in the EEA should be negotiated (in accordance with the decision-making procedure) once the Community adopts them:

- Community Patents: already adopted on 15 December 1989 but waiting for ratification by Spain (see n. 79 above);
- Community design: the Commission adopted, on 28 July 1993, two proposals to be submitted to the Council: a draft regulation establishing 'Community design' and a draft harmonization directive (see n. 82 above);
- Community plant variety rights: Commission proposal amended after first reading in European Parliament (see n. 81 above);
- biotechnology: Commission proposal of 16 December 1992 amended after first reading in European Parliament (COM (92) 589 final); political agreement reached in EC Council on 16 Dec. 1993;
- Extension of SPC to plant health products: planned Commission proposal for autumn 1993;
- databases: Amended Commission proposal issued on 4 October 1993 following first reading in European Parliament (forty amendments suggested) (COM (93) 464 final);
- author's moral rights: planned in follow-up of Copyright Green Paper;
- reprography: planned in follow-up of Copyright Green Paper;
- resale rights: planned in follow-up of Copyright Green Paper;
- collective management of copyright and neighbouring rights: planned in follow-up of Copyright Green Paper. A study is being conducted to compare the different national systems;
- home copying: a first Commission proposal was withdrawn but the submission of a new proposal is envisaged (a questionnaire has been sent to interested circles).

4. INTELLECTUAL PROPERTY PROVISIONS OF THE EC AND EFTA AGREEMENTS WITH CENTRAL AND EASTERN EUROPEAN COUNTRIES

The Community, as well as the EFTA States, has concluded a number of agreements with the Central and Eastern European Countries (CEECs). The EC has in particular concluded five so-called 'Association Agreements'.[104] The EFTA

[104] With the Czech and Slovak republics, Hungary, Poland, Bulgaria, and Romania.

States have, in parallel, concluded five Free Trade Agreements with the same CEECs.

All these agreements contain provisions on intellectual property which usually follow a similar line, although the provisions in the EFTA agreements are more detailed and sometimes go further than the EC ones.[105] The essential content of these provisions may be summarized as follows; for the EC agreements:

- a basic general provision on the level of protection of intellectual property to be ensured;
- a list of international conventions to be complied with or adhered to;
- guarantees concerning enforcement means.

The EFTA agreements contain:

- a basic general provision on the level of protection of intellectual property to be ensured and definition of the notion of intellectual property;
- an MFN clause,[106] with possible exception regarding existing bilateral agreements and existing or future multilateral or regional agreements;
- particular standards of protection to be ensured concerning specific branches or fields of intellectual property, including a clause concerning the conditions under which compulsory licences may be granted;
- a list of international conventions to be complied with or adhered to;
- particular standards to be ensured as regards the procedures for acquiring, maintaining, and enforcing intellectual property rights.

As regards the MFN clause contained in the EFTA agreements, it should be noted that the use of this clause is not very common in international agreements dealing with intellectual property. The latter are usually based on 'national treatment', meaning that a State cannot treat third country nationals less favourably than its own nationals. The MFN clause of the EFTA agreements is however designed to avoid any misuse of the 'national treatment' principle.[107] Furthermore, with a view to avoiding the need for the better treatment granted in the context of the EEA (regional agreement) to be extended to the other partner in the context of the FTA agreement, the MFN clause contains an exception. This means that, for instance, the EEA-wide exhaustion rule will not have to be extended to the FTA context.

[105] In particular thanks to the fact that there was, on the EFTA side, no such problem as the transfer of external competence from EC Member States to the Community (for instance as regards provisions on compulsory licensing).

[106] 'most favoured nation' clause, which means that a State shall automatically extend to the other States the favourable treatment it has granted to one of these States.

[107] As has notably been the case with South Korea, which concluded an agreement with the USA under which it would grant US nationals better treatment than its own nationals, meaning that the other third country nationals would, thanks to the 'national treatment' principle, continue to be as 'badly' treated as South Korean nationals. After more than two years of negotiations, the EC finally secured equal treatment with the USA (see *Europe* 6107 of 15 Nov. 1993). This does not however improve the situation of other countries, notably the EFTA States.

The intellectual property provisions contained in the EC and EFTA agreements with the CEECs are very similar to the ones contained in the EEA Agreement. The intended effect was to put together in the whole European continent a common platform of intellectual property protection which would contribute to stimulating investments and trade.

It should finally be noted that the EFTA States have also concluded free trade agreements with Israel and Turkey which contain intellectual property provisions similar to those of the agreements with the CEECs.[108]

[108] The intellectual property provisions of the EFTA–Turkey agreement are however less far reaching than the ones agreed upon with the CEECs. There is nevertheless a common understanding under which these provisions should be reviewed in light of the results of the ongoing negotiations between the EC and Turkey to revise their Association Agreement.

VI

PRODUCT LIABILITY
(ARTICLE 23 (*c*) AND ANNEX III)

Product liability can be defined as the liability of a professional producer or supplier of a product for damage caused by that product. As such, it can be considered a key area of law for economic operators throughout Europe. In the EEA Agreement rules on product liability are dealt with in Article 23 (*c*), and, in particular, in Annex III. That annex refers to Council Directive 85/374/EEC on the approximation of the laws, regulations, and administrative provisions of the Member States concerning liability for defective products. In other words, the product liability regime of the Community has been extended to the EFTA countries. Some specific solutions, of great practical importance, have however been negotiated in relation to the importer's liability.

I. COUNCIL DIRECTIVE 85/374/EEC

As put forward in the preamble to the Directive, the approximation of national laws concerning the liability of the producer for damage caused by the defectiveness of his products is 'necessary because the existing divergences may distort competition and affect the movement of goods within the common market and entail a differing degree of protection of the consumer against damage caused by a defective product to his health or property'. It is clear that liability rules imposed on producers of defective products which vary in strictness lead to differences in costs, and therefore may result in unequal conditions of competition. Different national laws also constitute a threat to the free movement of goods, as a producer's decision as to the country in which to sell could be influenced by the existence of more or less strict liability laws. The Directive can further be said to be a brick in the consumer protection wall, another brick being constituted by the General Product Safety Directive (see Chapter IV, Section 6.2). The broad purpose of the Directive is thus to ensure that consumers have the same high degree of protection (in form of strict liability, see below), and that every producer has the same burden in maintaining this standard.

Taking all these aspects into consideration, the Directive clearly has its place within the EEA Agreement as a necessary complement to the rules safeguarding the free movement of goods, competition, and consumer protection.

1.1 Strict liability

The more traditional concept of fault has in the Directive given way to liability disregarding fault, or so-called 'strict liability'. The liability of the producer is based simply on the fact that the damage has been caused by a defect although no fault on his part is involved. The injured person must prove three essential elements: first, that damage occurred;[1] secondly that the product was defective;[2] and thirdly the causal link between the two. The producer's liability to an injured person cannot be limited or excluded by contract or any other form of agreement.[3]

Article 23 EEA explicitly states that the arrangements concerning product liability shall apply to all products, that is, irrespective of the product coverage of the Agreement. The definition of 'product' in Article 2 of the Directive is therefore also applicable to the EFTA countries.[4] However, liability for injury or damage arising from nuclear accidents, to the extent covered by an international convention ratified by EC and EFTA States, falls, according to a specific adaptation to Article 14, outside the scope of the Directive.[5]

1.2 Defences for the producer

Article 6 of the Directive provides the producer with six defences. The producer shall not be liable if he can prove:

- that he did not put the product into circulation; or
- that, having regard to the circumstances, it is probable that the defect which caused the damage did not exist at the time when the product was put into circulation by him or that this defect came into being afterwards; or
- that the product was neither manufactured by him for sale or any form of distribution for economic purpose nor manufactured or distributed by him in the course of his business; or
- that the defect is due to compliance of the product with mandatory regulations issued by the public authorities; or
- that the state of scientific and technical knowledge at the time when he put the

[1] By damage is understood: damage caused by death or by personal injuries, damage to, or destruction of, any item of property other than the defective product itself, with a lower threshold of 500 ECU, provided that the item of property is of a type ordinarily intended for private use or consumption, and was used by the injured person mainly for his own private use or consumption (Art. 9 of the Directive).

[2] A product is defective when it does not provide the safety which a person is entitled to expect, taking all circumstances into account, including: the presentation of the product; the use to which it could reasonably be expected that the product would be put; the time when the product was put into circulation (Art. 6 of the Directive).

[3] Art. 12 of the Directive.

[4] Art. 2: 'For the purpose of this Directive "product" means all movables, with the exception of primary agricultural products and game, even though incorporated into another movable or into an immovable. "Primary agricultural products" means the product of the soil, of stock-farming and of fisheries, excluding products which have undergone initial processing. "Product" includes electricity.'

[5] Adaptation (*b*) to Annex III EEA.

product into circulation was not such as to enable the existence of the defect to be discovered; or

– in the case of a manufacturer of a component, that the defect is attributable to the design of the product in which the component has been fitted or to the instructions given by the manufacturer of the product.

2. THE IMPORTER'S LIABILITY

According to Article 3 (1) of the Directive, a producer is defined as 'the manufacturer of a finished product, the producer of any raw material or the manufacturer of a component part and any person who, by putting his name, trade mark or other distinguishing feature on the product presents himself as its producer'.

Without prejudice to the liability of the producer, Article 3 (2) contains a fundamentally important rule: any person who imports into the Community a product for sale, hire, lease, or any form of distribution in the course of his business shall be responsible as if he was its producer. The liability of the importer therefore ensures the consumer a right of action where the actual producer is not within the Community.

2.1 Imports into the EEA

The question of the liability of the importer has been clarified in the context of the EEA Agreement by means of a specific adaptation to the Product Liability Directive laid down in Annex III: '(i) Without prejudice to the liability of the producer any person who imports into the EEA a product for sale, hire, leasing or any form of distribution in the course of his business shall be responsible as a producer.'[6] The main rule is therefore that the notion of 'importer' shall be understood on an EEA-wide basis.

2.2 Intra-EEA trade

The main rule, as expressed above, however, raised problems of jurisdiction and enforcement of judgments on the one hand between the EC Member States and the EFTA States and, on the other, between the EFTA States themselves. The waiving of the importer's liability in trade within the EEA was therefore linked to the ratification of the Lugano Convention on jurisdiction and the enforcement of

[6] Adaptation (*a*) (i) of Annex III EEA. In fact, this is only putting into words what would anyhow follow from the horizontal adaptation laid down in para. 8 of Protocol 1 EEA.

judgments in civil and commercial matters.[7] The solution was put forward in the following wording:

(ii) the same [i.e. as in (i) above] applies as concerns imports from an EFTA State into the Community or from the Community into an EFTA State or from an EFTA State into another EFTA State. From the date of entry into force for any EC Member State or EFTA State of the Lugano Convention on jurisdiction and the enforcement of judgments in civil and commercial matters of 16 September 1988, this paragraph shall no longer apply between those States which have ratified the Convention to the extent a national judgment in favour of the injured person is, by the fact of those ratifications, enforceable against the producer or the importer within the meaning of subparagraph (i).

The Lugano Convention entered into force on 1 January 1992. By December 1993 it had been ratified and entered into force between eleven EC and EFTA countries. It concerns:

- France (ratified 3 Aug. 1990, in force 1 Jan. 1992);
- Great Britain (ratified 5 Feb. 1992, in force 1 May 1992);
- Italy (ratified 22 Sept. 1992, in force 1 Dec. 1992);
- Ireland (ratified 27 Sept. 1993, in force 1 Dec. 1993);
- Luxembourg (ratified 5 Nov. 1991, in force 1 Feb. 1992);
- the Netherlands (ratified 23 Jan. 1990, in force 1 Jan. 1992);
- Portugal (ratified 14 Apr. 1992, in force 1 July 1992);
- Switzerland (ratified 18 Jan. 1991, in force 1 Jan. 1992);
- Norway (ratified 2 Feb. 1993, in force 1 May 1993);
- Sweden (ratified 9 Oct. 1992, in force 1 Jan. 1993); and
- Finland (ratified 27 Apr. 1993, in force 1 July 1993).

It can therefore be concluded that, in trade between the Community and EFTA countries and between the EFTA countries themselves, the importer's liability will be waived between the countries (above) having ratified and for which the Lugano Convention has entered into force.[8]

[7] 'Convention on Jurisdiction and the Enforcement of Judgments in Civil and Commercial Matters' (Lugano, 18 Sept. 1988). The Convention was concluded between the twelve EC Member States, Austria, Finland, Iceland, Norway, Sweden, and Switzerland.

[8] At the date of the EEA entering into force, Belgium, Denmark, Germany, Greece, Spain, Austria, and Iceland had not ratified the Convention. It should be noted, however, that Switzerland could not, on this basis, benefit from the waiver as it did not ratify the EEA Agreement. See Chapter XI on Switzerland.

VII

PUBLIC PROCUREMENT
(ARTICLE 65 (1) AND ANNEX XVI)

The public procurement market in the EEA is a large and lucrative market for potential bidders. The financial stakes are considerable. It is estimated that the public sector in the Community places some 600 billion ECU and the EFTA States some fifty to sixty billion ECU a year in public procurement orders.

The opening-up of the procurement market will also constitute a major change to the situation prevailing before the entry into force of the EEA Agreement. In fact, access to public procurement was not dealt with under the 1972 FTAs. The relations between the Community and EFTA countries were therefore based on GATT rules. Community legislation having gone further, the inclusion of procurement rules in the EEA was a prerequisite for the free movement of goods under equal conditions of competition.

1. THE SUBSTANTIVE RULES

Article 65 (1) of and Annex XVI to the EEA Agreement contain the entirety of the Community procurement *acquis* as of the cut-off date of 31 July 1991.[1] As stated in Article 65 (1) EEA, the rules are applicable to all products and to services as specified, that is, the specific provisions on product coverage laid down in Article 8 (3) EEA are not applicable.

The directives referred to in Annex XVI EEA,[2] and which the EFTA countries are to implement in their national legislation, cover the following fields:

- public works contracts (Directive 71/305/EEC, amended by Directive 89/440/EEC, updated by Decision 90/380/EEC, hereinafter referred to as 'the Works Directive');[3]
- public supply contracts (Directive 77/62/EEC supplemented by Directive

[1] With the exception of Dir. 70/32/EEC of 17 Dec. 1969 (*OJ* L 13 (19 Jan. 1970), 1). This Directive was issued to secure the abolition of measures having an effect equivalent to quantitative restrictions in government procurement that were in operation when the EEC Treaty came into force. Since the end of the transitional period, the ban on such measures in public sector purchasing has been directly applicable on the base of Art. 30 EEC, and the Directive would therefore, today, only have an explanatory value.

[2] Annex XVI is reproduced (without its appendices) in Annex A to this book.

[3] Point 2 of Annex XVI EEA. Transitional period provided for Liechtenstein until 1 Jan. 1995.

80/767/EEC, amended by Directive 88/295/EEC, hereinafter referred to as 'the Supplies Directive');[4]

- procurement procedures of entities operating in the water, energy, transport, and telecommunications sectors (Directive 90/531/EEC, hereinafter referred to as 'the Utilities Directive').[5] For this Directive, Norway has been granted a transitional period until 1 January 1995 at the latest. The Directive may however enter into force earlier upon notification by Norway. During the transitional period the application of the Directive will be reciprocally suspended between Norway and the other EEA partners;
- legal remedies to the award of public supply and public works contracts (Directive 89/665/EEC, hereinafter referred to as 'the first remedies Directive').[6]

Since the cut-off date (31 July 1991) for legislation to be included in the Agreement, this body of law has been consolidated and amended by the following three new directives adopted on 14 June 1993:

- Directive 93/36/EEC co-ordinating procedures for the award of public supply contracts (consolidating and amending the original Supplies Directives 77/62, 80/767, and 88/295), to be implemented by 14 June 1994;
- Directive 93/37/EEC concerning the co-ordination of procedures for the award of public works contracts (mainly consolidating the Works Directives 71/305, 89/440, and 90/380). The implementation dates remain those of the Works Directive;
- Directive 93/38/EEC co-ordinating the procurement procedures of entities in the water, energy, transport, and telecommunications sectors (amending the Utilities Directive 90/531), to be implemented by 1 July 1994, but with transitional periods for Greece, Portugal, and Spain.[7]

Further, two completely new and very important directives were adopted after the cut-off date. They are:

- Directive 92/13/EEC co-ordinating the laws, regulations, and administrative provisions relating to the application of Community rules on the procurement procedures of entities operating in the water, energy, transport, and telecommunications sectors (*OJ* L 76 (23 Mar. 1992), 14). This is the so-called 'second remedies Directive', to be implemented by 1 January 1993 but with transitional periods for Greece, Portugal, and Spain.
- Directive 92/50/EEC relating to the co-ordination of procedures for the award of public service contracts (*OJ* L 209 (14 July 1992), 1), to be implemented by 1 July 1993.

[4] Point 3 of Annex XVI EEA. Transitional period provided for Liechtenstein until 1 Jan. 1995.

[5] Point 4 of Annex XVI EEA. Transitional period for Liechtenstein until 1 Jan. 1995.

[6] Point 5 of Annex XVI EEA. Transitional period for Liechtenstein until 1 Jan. 1995.

[7] All these directives were published in *OJ* L 199 (9 Aug. 1993).

Although these directives are not part of the EEA from the outset, it can be expected that they will be integrated into Annex XVI EEA through a decision by the EEA Joint Committee once the Agreement has entered into force (see Chapter II, Section 6.2). Pending such a decision, and eventual special solutions or transitional periods, this chapter deals mainly with the *acquis* as contained in the Agreement by its entry into force.[8]

The works, supplies, and utilities sectors will, since they present similarities as to the tender award procedures, definition of technical specifications, publication requirements, etc., be dealt with under common headings, starting with their scope of application.[9]

1.1 Scope of application

The Supplies Directive (77/62) applies to 'public supply contracts'. These are defined in Article 1 (*a*) of the Directive as 'contracts for pecuniary interest concluded in writing involving the purchase, lease, rental or hire purchase, with or without option to buy, of products between a supplier (a natural or legal person) and one of the contracting authorities'. In addition, the delivery of such products may include siting and installation operations, that is, services necessary to make the products supplied operational. However, the contract is to be qualified as a public works contract, if the value of the services exceeds that of the goods and if the services are in the nature of construction or civil engineering work coming within the scope of application of the Works Directive. In the Utilities Directive, the definition of 'supply contract' in addition covers software services (Article 1 (3)(*a*) of Directive 90/531).

The definition of 'public works contracts', set out in Article 1 (*a*) of the Works Directive (71/305 as amended), covers contracts for pecuniary interest between a contractor and a contracting authority which have as their object either the execution, or both the execution and design, of works related to building and civil engineering activities,[10] or the execution by whatever means of a work corresponding to the requirements specified by the contracting authority. The definition is also valid in the utilities sectors, with the addition, however, that these

[8] For a comprehensive description of the new set of rules on procurement in the EC, see P.-A. Trepte, *Public Procurement in the EC* (Bicester, 1993). It can, however, in this context, be noted that the substantive changes brought by the new Supplies and Works Directives are, to a great extent, very limited. The major importance of the new directives is that they provide consolidated versions of the previous texts. If substantive changes of importance have occurred, they are briefly referred to in this chapter. A reference can also be made to correlation tables contained in Dir. 93/36 and 93/37 establishing the links between the articles contained in them and those of the old directives. As regards the new Utilities Dir. 93/38, the main novelty is the inclusion of services within its scope, in addition to the previous supplies and works.

[9] On legal remedies see s. 2 below.

[10] A more detailed description of these activities (class 50 of the general industrial classification of economic activities within the European Communities) is in Annex II of Dir. 71/305 as amended.

contracts may cover supplies and services necessary for their execution (Article 1 (3) (*b*) of Directive 90/531).

Concerning the definition of 'contracting authorities', the Supplies Directive refers to them as being 'the State, regional or local authorities and the legal persons governed by public law or, in Member States where the latter are unknown, bodies corresponding thereto as specified in Annex I' (Article 1 (*b*) of Directive 77/62). Annex I to the Directive has, for the purpose of the EEA Agreement, been supplemented by Appendix 3 (lists of bodies and categories of bodies governed by public law) to Annex XVI EEA, and, as concerns Annex I to Directive 80/767, by Appendix 2 (list of central purchasing entities) to Annex XVI EEA.

In the Works Directive, the corresponding definition is almost identical.[11] The additional list of bodies and categories of bodies governed by public law concerning the EFTA States is set out in Appendix 1 to Annex XVI EEA. The ECJ has confirmed that it is imperative that a wide interpretation is given to the concept of State, region, or local authority.[12]

The new Supplies Directive (93/36) and Works Directive (93/37) adopted on 14 June 1993 aim at clarifying this somewhat confusing situation. The new Supplies Directive adopts the terminology of the new Works Directive, even to the extent of referring to the annex of the new Works Directive in order to indicate the list of bodies or of categories of such bodies which fulfil the appropriate criteria.

In the Utilities Directive, the entities operating in the water, energy, transport, and telecommunications sectors are denominated 'contracting entities'. This concept includes:

- public authorities[13] or public undertakings[14] to the extent that these authorities or undertakings exercise a relevant activity, among which are the supply of drinking water, electricity, gas, or heat to networks as well as the provision or operation of networks intended to provide a service to the public in connection with the production, transport, or distribution of drinking water, electricity, gas, or heat, or the provision or operation of networks in the field of transport or public telecommunications; or
- entities which are not public authorities or public undertakings but have as one of their activities those referred to above and which operate on the basis of a special or exclusive right granted by a competent authority of a Member State.

[11] The words 'legal persons governed by public law' have, however, as a result of the amending Dir. 89/440, been replaced by 'bodies governed by public law'. Art. 1 (*b*) of Dir. 71/305 as amended by Dir. 89/440 further contains a list of specific criteria to help define the notion of 'body governed by public law'.

[12] Case 3/87 *Beentjes* [1988] ECR 4635.

[13] i.e. the State, regional, or local authorities, bodies governed by public law, or associations of such authorities or bodies (Art. 1 (1) of Dir. 90/531).

[14] i.e undertakings under the dominant influence of public authorities by virtue of majority ownership, control of the majority of the voting rights, or power to appoint more than half of the members of the undertaking's administrative, managerial, or supervisory body (Art. 1 (2) of Dir. 90/531).

1.2 Thresholds

The rules will only apply to procurement contracts above a specified threshold (threshold values are expressed in ECU net of VAT). The Supplies Directive covers contracts awarded by local and regional authorities, as well as those contracts awarded by central government authorities which do not fall under the GATT Agreement, exceeding 200,000 ECU. For contracts awarded by central government authorities which are covered by the GATT Agreement, a lower threshold (approximately 130,000 ECU), as defined by that Agreement, is applicable.[15] The Works Directive covers contracts of a value of five million ECU or more.[16] In the utilities sector, the threshold for supplies is 400,000 ECU and 600,000 ECU in the telecommunications sector. The five million ECU threshold in the case of works contracts is also applicable.[17]

1.3 Tender award procedures

The tender award procedures are more or less the same in the Supplies, Works, and Utilities Directives. Three types of procedures can be distinguished:

- 'open procedures' are those national procedures whereby all interested suppliers or contractors can present an offer;
- 'restricted procedures' are those national procedures whereby only those suppliers or contractors invited by the contracting authorities may submit tenders; and
- 'negotiated procedures' are those national procedures whereby contracting authorities consult suppliers or contractors of their choice and negotiate the terms of the contract with one or several of them.[18]

The open procedure is stated to be the normal procedure in the Supplies Directive. Recourse to restricted or negotiated procedures requires a special justification.[19] The corresponding provision concerning work contracts also requires justification when recourse is made to negotiated tendering, while, however, use of the restricted procedure does not.[20] The Utilities Directive gives the contracting entities the freedom to choose any of the three types of tendering procedure.[21]

The new Supplies Directive (93/36) has been brought into line with the Works Directive, so that there is a choice between open or restricted procedures.

The question of publication of notices will be dealt with in Section 1.5 below.

[15] Art. 5 (1) (*a*) of Dir. 77/62 as amended.

[16] Art. 4a (1) of Dir. 71/305 as amended.

[17] Art. 12 of Dir. 90/531.

[18] Art. 1 (*d*) to (*f*) of the Supplies Directive (77/62 as amended), Art. 1 (*e*) to (*g*) of the Works Directive (71/305 as amended), and Art. 1 (6) of the Utilities Directive (90/531).

[19] Art. 6 of the Supplies Directive (77/62 as amended).

[20] Art. 5 of the Works Directive (71/305 as amended).

[21] Arts. 15 and 16 of the Utilities Directive (90/351).

1.4 Technical specifications

The use of different sorts of technical specifications constitutes one of the main obstacles in the opening-up of public procurement. Therefore, the Supplies and Works Directives provide that 'without prejudice to the legally binding national technical rules in so far as these are compatible with Community law, such technical specifications shall be defined by the contracting authorities by reference to national standards implementing European standards, or by reference to European technical approvals or by reference to common technical specifications'.[22]

The general rule is therefore that contracting authorities have to define the technical specifications of the goods to be supplied by reference to national standards transposing European standards where they exist, except in certain exceptional circumstances. In the absence of European standards or common technical specifications, purchasers may refer to other specifications. EC and EFTA States shall however prohibit the introduction into the contractual clauses relating to a given contract of technical specifications which mention goods of a specific make or source or of a particular process and which have the effect of favouring or eliminating certain undertakings or products. This is particularly the case with the indication of trade marks, patents, types, or specific origin or production, which are prohibited unless the subject of the contract cannot otherwise be described. In such a case the indication must however be accompanied by the words 'or equivalent'. In this context, it is important to note that the principle of mutual recognition, stemming from Article 30 EEC (and, for the EFTA countries, Article 11 EEA), must be respected.[23]

1.5 Publication and advertising

In order to ensure equal conditions of competition between economic operators, EEA-wide advertising of contracts is laid down. EC and EFTA purchasers shall publish notices in the Community languages in the S-series of the *Official Journal of the European Communities* and in the Tenders Electronic Daily, to the extent required by the directives.[24]

[22] Art. 7 of Dir. 77/62 as amended and Art. 10 of Dir. 71/305 as amended.

[23] See further in Ch. IV, s. 2 (mutual recognition), s. 4.2 (standardization), as well as Annex F (case-law).

[24] In Annex XVI EEA sectoral adaptation 2 reads: 'When the acts referred to in this Annex require the publication of notices or documents the following shall apply:

(a) The publication of notices and other documents as required by the acts referred to in this Annex in the *Official Journal of the European Communities* and in the Tenders Electronic Daily shall be carried out by the Office for Official Publications of the European Communities.

(b) Notices from the EFTA States shall be sent in at least one of the Community languages to the Office for Official Publications of the [EC]. They shall be published in the Community languages in the S-series of the [*OJ* of the EC] and in the Tenders Electronic Daily. EC notices need not be translated into the languages of the EFTA States.'

The Supplies Directive requires contracts to be advertised in three stages:

- indicative notice: an advance notice, sent as soon as possible at the beginning of each budgetary year. For the time being, this requirement applies only to the list of entities laid down in Annex I to Directive 80/767 as supplemented, concerning the EFTA countries, by Appendix 2 to Annex XVI EEA. Indicative notice further need only be given if the total amount of the contracts projected is for a value equal to or greater than 750,000 ECU.[25]
- notice calling for tenders: a second notice required in all but the most exceptional cases giving more specific details of the project and calling for tenders.[26]
- post-award notice: obligation for the contracting authorities who have awarded a contract to make known the result. The notice shall be sent at the latest forty-eight days after the award of the contract in question.[27]

The information to be given in the notices is set out in detail in Annex III to Directive 77/62 (as amended by Directive 88/295). Notices shall be sent as rapidly as possible to the Office for Official Publications of the European Communities, which is responsible for the publication.[28]

The provisions on publication and advertisement in the Works Directive correspond more or less to those of the Supply Directive, the main difference being that all the authorities covered by the Works Directive have to publish indicative notices.

A significant waiver from the obligation to publish notice for tenders can however be found in the Utilities Directive. A separate call for competition for a specific project can be considered published by use of the periodic indicative notice (given at least once a year) or by means of publishing the existence of a qualification system (see Section 1.6 below *in fine*). When a call for competition is made by means of a periodic indicative notice, the notice must:

- refer specifically to the supplies or works which will be the subject of the contract to be awarded;
- indicate that the contract will be awarded by restricted or negotiated procedure without further publication of a notice of a call for competition and invite interested undertakings to express their interest in writing.

Contracting entities shall subsequently invite all candidates to confirm their interest on the basis of detailed information on the contract concerned before beginning the selection of tenderers or participants in negotiations.[29] Article 15 (2)

[25] Art. 9 (1) of Dir. 77/62 as amended.

[26] Art. 9 (2) of Dir. 77/62 as amended.

[27] Art. 9 (3) and (4*b*) of Dir. 77/62 as amended.

[28] Art. 9 (4)–(9) of Dir. 77/62 as amended. As set out in a sectoral adaptation to Annex XVI EEA, the EC Publication Office is also responsible for carrying out publications of EFTA notices (see n. 24 above). The final act to the EEA Agreement further contains, in the form of an exchange of letters, an arrangement regarding the publication of EFTA notices on procurement.

[29] Art. 16 of Dir. 90/531.

enumerates a number of cases where contracting entities may use a tender award procedure without a prior call for competition.

1.6 Criteria for the selection of candidates or tenderers

The criteria for selection laid down in the Supplies and Works Directives can be divided into three categories:

- the criteria that authorities may rely on for the exclusion of certain candidates or tenderers: these are, *inter alia*, if the supplier is bankrupt or is being wound up, has been convicted of an offence concerning his professional conduct, has not fulfilled obligations relating to the payment of social security contributions or taxes, etc.;[30]
- the type of information that can be requested to prove that a candidate has a registered business: a supplier may be requested to prove enrolment in the professional or trade register;[31]
- the type of information that may be requested to prove that a tenderer has sufficient financial, economic, and technical capacity to fulfil the contract: such as appropriate statements from bankers, submission of the undertaking's balance-sheets, etc. and, as far as evidence of the supplier's technical capacities is concerned, lists of principal deliveries, descriptions of the undertaking's technical facilities, certificates drawn up by official quality control institutes, etc.[32]

In the Utilities Directive a wider margin of discretion is given to contracting entities. They are entitled to make their own rules for selection (so-called 'qualification systems') provided they are objective and that they are made available to interested suppliers or contractors.[33]

1.7 Criteria for the award of contracts

Supply and works contracts must be awarded on the basis of either:

- the lowest price only; or
- the most economically advantageous tender, taking into consideration various criteria, such as price, delivery date, running cost, cost-effectiveness, quality,

[30] Art. 20 of Dir. 77/62 and Art. 23 of Dir. 71/305.

[31] Art. 21 of Dir. 77/62 and Art. 24 of Dir. 71/305 as amended. By specific adaptations to Annex XVI EEA, point 3 (adaptation (*h*)) and point 2 (adaptation (*e*)), the names of the relevant trade registers in the EFTA countries have been added.

[32] Arts. 22 and 23 of Dir. 77/62 and Arts. 25 and 26 of Dir. 71/305. On the financial and economic standing of contractors see Joined Cases 27, 28, and 29/85 *CEI* and *Bellini* [1987] ECR 3347, where the ECJ ruled that the list of references mentioned in Art. 25 of Dir. 71/305 was not exhaustive. On the contrary, the ECJ ruled, in Case 76/81 *Transporoute* [1982] ECR 417, that the list of references that authorities may require in order to check the contractor's technical suitability is of an exhaustive nature. See also Case *Beentjes*, *op. cit.* n. 12.

[33] Arts. 24 and 25 of Dir. 90/531.

aesthetic and functional characteristics, technical merits, after-sales service, and technical assistance.

The contracting authority must state, in the contracts document or the notice, the criteria of the award which it intends to apply. If not, it will be assumed to be awarded on the basis of the lowest tender. Tenders which appear to be abnormally low may be rejected after the tenderer has been given the opportunity to furnish the necessary explanation.[34]

There is one exception to the above rules. It is laid down in Article 25 (4) of the Supplies Directive and in Article 29 (4) of the Works Directive and provides that the EC Member States are free to use different criteria within the framework of their rules existing at the time the directives were adopted. As Annex XVI EEA does not contain any specific adaptation in this respect, this would also be valid for the EFTA countries, the time of adoption of the legal act being the entry into force of the EEA Agreement. A condition is however that the rules are compatible with the EEC Treaty (and in particular Article 7, non-discrimination, and Articles 30–6, measures having an effect equivalent to quantitative restrictions), and the EEA Agreement (in particular Articles 4 and 11–13). The above-mentioned exception is, however, no longer valid under the new Supplies Directive 93/37.

The above-mentioned criteria for the award of contracts also hold true for the Utilities sectors (Articles 27 and 28 of the Utilities Directive). The controversial Community preference rule expressed in Article 29 of the Utilities Directive, applying to the award of supply contracts under this Directive, has been taken over in the EEA Agreement with the understanding that the term 'third countries' is, throughout Article 29, to be understood as meaning 'countries other than the Contracting Parties to the EEA Agreement'. By way of specific adaptations (see point 4 of Annex XVI EEA), the article shall therefore apply to tenders comprising products originating in countries other than the Contracting Parties to the EEA Agreement with which the Community, as regards Community entities, or the EFTA States, as regards their entities, have not concluded, multilaterally or bilaterally, an agreement ensuring comparable and effective access for their respective undertakings, to the markets of those non-EEA countries. The application of the article shall be without prejudice to the obligation of either the Community or its Member States in respect of third countries or the EFTA States in respect of third countries. In order to enable the contracting entities in the EEA to apply Article 29 (2) and (3) the origin of the products in the tenders for supply contracts is determined in conformity with Regulation 802/68 on the common definition of the concept of the origin of goods (*OJ* L 148 (28 June 1968), 1). In order to obtain maximum convergence, Article 29 will be applied in the EEA context on the understanding that the operation of Article 29 (3) is without prejudice to the existing degree of liberalization towards non-EEA countries and that the Contracting Parties are to consult closely in their negotiations with

[34] Art. 25 of Dir. 77/62 and Art. 29 of Dir. 71/305 as partly amended.

non-EEA counties. The application of the regime is to be jointly reviewed during 1996, and annual reports shall be submitted on the progress made in multilateral or bilateral negotiations regarding access for Community and EFTA undertakings to the markets of non-EEA countries (see Article 29 (6) as adapted).

2. PROCEDURAL RULES

In order to attain the goal of a liberalized procurement market, the substantial rules will have to be effectively enforced. The enforcement is mainly done nationally. The EC and EFTA States must make arrangements to ensure that public supplies and works contracts can be rapidly and effectively reviewed if a supplier or contractor has been injured, or risks an injury, by an alleged infringement of EEA obligations. In clear and manifest infringements the Commission and ESA will, however, have a role to play. For the division of competences between the Commission and ESA, a sectoral adaptation to Annex XVI EEA stipulates that the competence for surveillance of alleged infringements lies with the EC Commission, if it is committed by a contracting entity in the Community, and with ESA, if it is committed by a contracting entity in an EFTA State.

Directive 89/665/EEC relates to the application of review procedures to the award of public supply and public works contract ('first remedies Directive') and forms part of the EEA Agreement.[35] It can be recalled that Directive 92/13/EEC, which relates to the application of Community rules on the procurement procedures of entities operating in the water, energy, transport, and telecommunications sectors (the so-called 'second remedies Directive'), was adopted after the cut-off date of 31 July 1991, and is intended to be integrated into Annex XVI EEA through a decision of the EEA Joint Committee upon the entry into force of the Agreement. Correspondingly, revision will have to be made in Protocol 2 of the ESA/Court Agreement.

2.1 Enforcement at national level

The purpose of the first remedies Directive is to co-ordinate review procedures and to ensure that, on the national level, there is the possibility of

- taking interim measures with the aim of correcting the alleged infringement or preventing further damage to the interests concerned, including measures to suspend or to ensure the suspension of the procedure for the award of a public contract or the implementation of any decision taken by the contracting authority;

[35] Point 5 of Annex XVI EEA. The substance of Arts. 3 and 4 of that Directive has also been reproduced in Protocol 2 to the ESA/Court Agreement in order to clarify the functions and powers of ESA in the field of procurement.

- either setting aside or ensuring the setting aside of decisions taken unlawfully, including the removal of discriminatory technical, economic, or financial specifications in the invitation to tender, the contract documents, or in any other document relating to the contract award procedure;
- awarding damages to persons harmed by an infringement.[36]

These powers may be conferred to special review bodies. If these are not judicial in character, they must allow a right of appeal to another body which is a court or tribunal within the meaning of Article 177 EEC[37] and which is independent of both the awarding authority and the review body.

2.2 Enforcement at EEA level

The Commission's power of intervention is laid down in Articles 3 and 4 of the first remedies Directive. The corresponding powers of ESA regarding the EFTA States are set out in Protocol 2 to the ESA/Court Agreement, which is, in substance, near to a copy of the above-mentioned articles.[38]

If confronted with a clear and manifest infringement, the Commission and ESA may, respectively, prior to a contract being concluded, notify the EC or EFTA State and the contracting authority concerned of the reasons which it believes constitute the clear and manifest infringement. Within twenty-one days of receipt of the notification, the State concerned shall communicate to the Commission (for EC Member States) or ESA (for EFTA States):

1. its confirmation that the infringement has been corrected; or
2. a reasoned submission as to why no correction has been made; or
3. a notice to the effect that the contract award procedure has been suspended either by the contracting authority on its own initiative or on the basis of the powers in the Directive.

If the reasoned submission in (2) claims that the matter is already the subject of a review pursuant to the Directive, the State must also inform the Commission or ESA of the results of those proceedings as soon as they become known. If the State notifies the Commission or ESA that the procedure has been suspended, then it must also make known when the suspension is lifted or another contract procedure relating in whole or in part to the same subject-matter is begun. That

[36] Art. 2 (1) of Dir. 89/665.

[37] For the purpose of the EEA Agreement, adaption (*b*) of point 5 of Annex XVI EEA contains the following precision: 'the reference to "Article 177 of the EEC Treaty" shall be read as a reference to the "criteria laid down by the Court of Justice in its interpretation of Article 177 of the EEC Treaty"'. As examples are given Case 61/65 *Vaassen* v. *Beambtenfonds Mijnbedrijf* [1966] ECR 261, Case 36/73 *Nederlandse Spoorwegen* v. *Minister van Verkeer en Waterstraat* [1973] ECR 1299, and Case 246/80 *Broekmeulen* v. *Huisarts Registratie Commissie* [1981] ECR 2311.

[38] For the basic provision concerning the powers of ESA in the field of public procurement, see Art. 23 ESA/Court Agreement (reproduced in Annex A).

notification shall confirm that the alleged infringement has been corrected or include a reasoned submission as to why no correction has been made.

ESA may bring an EFTA State to the EFTA Court under Article 31 ESA/Court Agreement in case of breach of the above-mentioned obligations. ESA can also apply to the EFTA Court for interim measures including suspension of the award procedure.

The review and reporting obligations in Article 4 of the first remedies Directive have, for the EFTA countries, been set out in Article 2 of Protocol 2 to the ESA/Court Agreement. According thereto, ESA shall, not later than 1 January 1996, together with an advisory committee composed of representatives of the EFTA States, review the manner in which the provisions of the Protocol and Directive 89/665 have been implemented. By 1 March each year the EFTA States shall communicate to ESA information on the operation of their national review procedures during the preceding calendar year.

VIII

COMPETITION
(ARTICLES 53–59, PROTOCOLS 21–25, AND ANNEX XIV)

Both the 1972 FTAs (their Articles 23) and the Stockholm Convention (Article 15) contain competition rules with wording inspired by Articles 85 and 86 EEC. However, the fundamental difference is that the former were far from having any direct effect and lacked the necessary 'mailed fist' to be genuinely enforced. Should a competition case arise between the Community and an EFTA State or within EFTA, it could only be channelled through representatives of the Parties in the relevant FTA Joint Committee or in the EFTA Council, the consequences being limited to the making of a report, a recommendation, or, as a last resort, the triggering of a safeguard or withdrawal of tariff concessions.

It is against this background that, in its 1990 negotiation mandate to the Commission, the EC Council referred to the taking over of the *acquis communautaire* in the field of competition and, in particular, the establishment on the EFTA side of an authority with powers equivalent to those of the Commission, as being essential prerequisites for realizing the EEA.

Indeed the EC would never have opened the 'holy' Single Market to its EFTA counterparts without being sure that they would submit to the same tight competition rules, with regard to both substance and enforcement. The EC negotiators were therefore very concerned to set up 'a system ensuring that competition is not distorted and that the rules thereon are equally respected' (Article 1 (2) (*e*) EEA).

Competition quickly proved to be a complicated chapter of the negotiations, especially for certain EFTA countries whose domestic law was, at that time, somewhat underdeveloped or who were particularly sensitive to any idea of supranationality. In addition, both sides were very attentive to safeguarding their autonomy.

Having agreed that the EEA competition rules should, in substance, be a blueprint of the EC provisions, the main difficulty was how to apply and enforce them. Two questions were at the centre of the negotiators' discussions for more than a year: who should be in charge of applying and enforcing the rules and how should the competences be divided between the competition authorities?

This chapter first explains where to find the competition rules in the EEA Agreement and in the ESA/Court Agreement (Section 1). It then discusses the objectives of the EEA competition rules and their interpretation notably under Article 6 EEA (Section 2). Section 3 presents the substantive competition rules and recalls the basic principles and conditions of Articles 85 and 86 EEC, which are also valid for Articles 53 and 54 EEA, as well as those concerning the Merger Regulation and the coal and steel sector. Section 4 underlines certain particularities of the substantive EEA rules. Section 5 explains the surveillance system (so-called 'two pillar' system) and the attribution of cases between the Commission and ESA. Section 6 concentrates on the procedural rules, Section 7 on the administrative co-operation between the surveillance bodies, and Section 8 contains some final remarks.

For obvious reasons of length, it is impossible to enter into all details of the EC competition system. This chapter attempts rather to concentrate on the peculiarities of the EEA rules and their differences as compared with the EC rules.

The EEA provisions concerning competition, as well as some relevant parts of the ESA/Court Agreement, are reproduced in Annex A to this book. Furthermore, Annex B contains a table of correspondence between the EEA and EC provisions.

1. WHERE TO FIND THE EEA COMPETITION RULES

In accordance with the overall structure of the EEA Agreement, the EEA competition rules may be found in several places in the Agreement, i.e. in its main part, five protocols, one annex, as well as in the ESA/Court Agreement.

In order better to map the situation, one could divide the rules into three categories: the substantive rules, the competence and co-operation rules, and the procedural rules.

The substantive rules, which mirror the EC rules, are to be found in chapter 1 of part IV of the EEA Agreement, i.e. Articles 53 (restrictive agreements), 54 (dominant position), 57 (1) (mergers), and 59 (public undertakings),[1] in Protocol 25 (coal and steel), and in Annex XIV EEA (substantive secondary legislation).

The competence and co-operation rules, which are a consequence of the two pillar system and were therefore created solely for the EEA, are to be found in the above-mentioned part IV, i.e. Articles 56 (attribution of Article 53 and 54 cases), 57 (2) (attribution of merger cases), and 58 (co-operation), as well as in Protocols 22 (definition of 'undertaking' and 'turnover'), 23 (co-operation in general) and 24 (co-operation in merger cases).

Finally, the procedural rules, which mirror the EC rules, are to be found in Article 55 EEA (grant of application powers), in Protocol 21 EEA (procedural (merely listed) and transition rules), and in Protocol 4 to the ESA/Court Agreement (procedural (reproduced in full) and transition rules).

There are also several declarations and agreed minutes which clarify the meaning of certain provisions or the intention of the Contracting Parties.

[1] Art. 59 EEA is addressed in Ch. IX below.

2. OBJECTIVE AND INTERPRETATION OF THE EEA COMPETITION RULES

2.1 Objective of the EEA competition rules

As in the EC, the EEA competition rules should be construed in the light of the objectives of the EEA Agreement. Articles 85 and 86 EEC as well as Articles 53 and 54 EEA are a specific application of the EEC/EEA objective under which shall be set up 'a system ensuring that competition . . . is not distorted,'[2] and seek to achieve the same aim, i.e. the maintenance of effective competition within the area concerned (EC or EEA).[3]

In that respect, the differences between the objectives of the EEA Agreement and those of the Rome Treaty[4] should not have any influence on the way EEA competition rules will be interpreted. The use of the same wording in Article 1 (2) (*e*) EEA as in Article 3 (*f*) EEC and the objective to realize the four freedoms (goods, persons, services, and capital), together with the taking over in the EEA of the Single Market *acquis*, mean that the EEA competition provisions basically serve the same purpose as the Community ones.

As in the EC, the primary goal of the EEA competition rules is to promote the integration of national markets through the elimination of private practices which interfere with that integration. Furthermore the EEA takes over the EC *acquis* in such a comprehensive manner that it also embraces all the underlying philosophy of the EC competition rules, influenced by the far-reaching objectives of the EEC Treaty. These include, for instance, besides competition-related criteria, encouraging certain forms of co-operation between small and medium-sized enterprises, taking into account favourable effects on industrial development, technological progress, employment or other social conditions, etc.

The idea is that, the more one integrates national markets through abolition of government barriers and harmonization of law, the more one needs to prevent these barriers being replaced by cartels or other practices which re-partition the market along national borders or otherwise jeopardize the realization of a single market.

2.2 Interpretation of the EEA competition rules

In the competition field, the negotiators were particularly concerned to guarantee that the common rules would receive uniform interpretation. Since the EEA rules are substantially identical to the EC ones, Article 6 EEA (relating to the ECJ case-

[2] See Art. 3 (*f*) EEC and Art. 1 (2) (*e*) EEA.

[3] See Case 6/72 *Continental Can* [1973] ECR 215, in which the ECJ analyses the objectives of the EEC Treaty underlining the importance of the competition policy.

[4] Which the ECJ pointed out in its Opinion 1/91; see Ch. II, s. 2.

law) will be fully relevant as concerns the jurisprudence given prior to the signature of the EEA Agreement (2 May 1992).[5]

With regard to the case-law delivered after the signature of the Agreement, the uniform interpretation should be taken care of by Articles 105 and 106 EEA (constant review of developments in case-law of EC and EFTA Courts, action in case of difference, and system of exchange of information on judgments) and by Article 3 (2) of the ESA/Court Agreement (under which ESA and the EFTA Court shall pay due account to the ECJ rulings given after 2 May 1992).

In addition, the preamble of the ESA/Court Agreement states that in the application of Protocol 4 ESA/Court (which reproduces all the EC procedural rules such as Regulations 17, 27, or 99) 'due account shall be paid to the legal and administrative practices of the Commission of the [EC] prior to the entry into force of this Agreement' (i.e. the same day as the EEA Agreement). This is designed to enlarge the scope of uniform interpretation to cover also the interpretation given by the Commission in its decisions on individual competition cases and make sure that ESA will follow the same administrative practice as the Commission when assessing the cases.

3. SUBSTANTIVE COMPETITION RULES

Except for the necessary vocabulary adaptations, the substantive EEA competition rules, primary or secondary, are the same as the EC ones. These different provisions are analysed below, indicating first what adaptations have been made in the EEA context and then the conditions for the competition provisions to apply.

3.1 Primary rules

The primary competition provisions are contained in Articles 53, 54, 57 (1), 59, and in Protocol 25 EEA.

3.1.1 Article 53 EEA (restrictive practices)

Article 53 EEA reproduces Article 85 EEC. Paragraph 1 prohibits agreements and practices between undertakings which may affect cross-border trade and which have as their object or effect to restrict competition. Paragraph 2 declares these agreements void. Paragraph 3 provides for possible exemptions from the prohibition if the agreement in question meets certain conditions.

3.1.1.1 Adaptations for EEA purposes

In paragraph 1, three expressions have been adapted to the EEA context:

– the term 'incompatible with the common market' of the EEC version has been

[5] See further Ch. II, s. 7.1.

replaced by the term 'incompatible with the functioning of this [EEA] Agreement';
- the term 'trade between Member States' has been replaced by 'trade between the Contracting Parties';
- the term 'within the common market' has been replaced by 'within the territory covered by this Agreement'.

In the first case, the expression 'common market' refers to the objective of creating a common market within the EC and the evolutive body of law which goes with it. The negotiators felt that, in the EEA context, the best way to translate this wide and evolutive notion was to refer to the functioning of the EEA Agreement. In the latter case, 'common market' has a geographical meaning, i.e. the market located within the borders of the Community. This is the reason why it was replaced by an expression relating to the EEA territory.

The term 'trade between Member States' refers to the States as geographic entities. In the EEA Agreement 'Member States' has usually been replaced by 'Contracting Parties' which, as indicated in Chapter II (Section 3.1) above, may, regarding the EC side have several meanings. However, it is clear that in Article 53 EEA 'Contracting Party' refers to the Community as such and not to the EC Member States.

3.1.1.2 Prohibition under Article 85 (1) EEC/53 (1) EEA

For the prohibition of Article 85 (1)/53 (1) to apply, three conditions must be met:[6]

- an agreement, decision, or concerted practice between undertakings;
- which may affect trade between EC Member States/EEA Contracting Parties; and
- which has as its object or effect to prevent, restrict, or distort competition within the EC/EEA.

'*Undertaking*' is a very broad concept which 'encompasses every entity engaged in an economic activity, regardless of the legal status of the entity and the way in which it is financed'.[7] In Article 1 of Protocol 22 EEA the word 'undertaking' is defined (for the purposes of Article 56 EEA on attribution of cases) as being 'any entity carrying out activities of a commercial or economic nature'.[8] The important criteria are economic activity and autonomy of action.

[6] The explanations given below, for each of the three conditions of Art. 85 (1) EEC, essentially reflect interpretations given in ECJ case-law and Commission decisions. In order not to overburden the text, only some leading cases will be quoted. For more detailed references and a thorough analysis see the books listed in the Bibliography, notably C. Bellamy and G. Child, *Common Market Law of Competition* (1987; supplement 1991), and V. Korah, *An Introductory Guide to EEC Competition Law and Practice* (1990).

[7] See Case C-41/90 *Höfner and Elser* [1991] ECR I-1979 and Joint Cases C-159/91 and C-160/91 *AGF* of 17 Feb. 1993 (not yet reported).

[8] In its Decision *Film Purchases* (89/356/EEC, OJ L 284 (3 Oct. 1989), 36) the Commission adopts a somewhat wider definition: 'The functional concept of undertaking in Art. 85 (1) covers any activity

Regardless of their nationality, location, or size, the following have been considered as undertakings in the context of Article 85 (1) EEC: companies (whatever their corporate form); State-owned companies, in so far as they carry on commercial activities (but not if they act as public authorities); partnerships; trade associations; and individuals engaged in economic activities in their own right (e.g. sole traders, IPR holders, consultants, controlling shareholders, etc.).

However, the definition of undertaking in principle excludes: employees (as they normally act on behalf of their employer, unless they pursue their own economic interests and thus become 'individuals engaged in economic activities'); agents (which are considered as auxiliaries of the principal and are therefore not independent traders); workers' organizations; branches; Member States (and their regional and local authorities);[9] and social security institutions.[10]

The same goes for a subsidiary which, as it forms part of an economic unit, has thus no real freedom to determine its course of action and whose conduct will therefore be imputed to its parent.[11] The economic unit itself, the group of companies, will be treated as a single undertaking.[12] Consequently, an agreement between a parent company and its subsidiaries (i.e. 'intra-enterprise' agreement), which constitutes a mere internal allocation of tasks within the same economic entity, is not considered as an 'agreement between undertakings' in the sense of Article 85 (1) EEC.[13]

The notions of 'agreements, decisions by associations of undertakings and concerted practices' are also very broad and often overlap or complement each other.

'*Agreements*' have been considered to comprise all sorts of contracts (e.g. signed or not, oral or written, express or tacit, legally or only morally binding, separate but connected, in force or lapsed but still applied in practice), as well as standard conditions of sale, invoices bearing the words 'export prohibited' tacitly accepted by dealers, or acquiescence under pressure.

In principle, a unilateral action is not an agreement, which, as shown by the use of the plural in 'undertakings', requires at least two parties. However, the concept of

directed at trade in goods or services irrespective of the legal form of the undertaking and regardless of whether or not it is intended to earn profits.'

[9] However, the behaviour of Member States regarding competition is looked at from the angle of Art. 5 EEC, which, applied in connection with Arts. 85 and 86 EEC, prohibits States from taking measures liable to deprive the competition provisions of their *effet utile* (see Cases 13/77 *GB-INNO-BM* v. *ATAB* [1977] ECR 2115 and 229/83 *Leclerc* [1985] ECR 1). As regards practices of public undertakings for which the State is responsible, see Ch. IX below.

[10] In *AGF* (see n. 7) the ECJ denied the quality of 'undertaking' to sickness funds as they fulfil a function of an exclusively social character, based on the principle of solidarity, and have no lucrative aim. Their activity is therefore not an economic activity.

[11] See Joint Cases 6 and 7/73 *Commercial Solvents* [1975] ECR 223.

[12] According to the Complementary Note to Form A/B, a group relationship is deemed to exist where a firm, alternatively, owns more than half the capital of business assets, has the power to exercise more than half the voting rights, has the power to appoint more than half the members of the board, or has the right to manage the affairs of another.

[13] See Case 15/74 *Centrafarm* v. *Sterling Drug* [1974] ECR 1147.

collusion has been interpreted so widely that, in the context of a long-term contract, the tacit acceptance by dealers of the supplier's policy to exclude from the distribution network the low margin dealers was considered as an agreement.[14] Agreements required by national legislative measures are not 'agreements' within the meaning of Article 85 (1) EEC.[15] However, if these agreements are only encouraged or approved by the authorities, but not actually required, they may be caught by Article 85 (1).

'*Decisions by associations of undertakings*' have been considered to comprise, in addition to decisions proper, non-binding recommendations, rules of the association, or implementation of agreements during the association meetings.

In the case of doubts about whether there is an agreement or a decision, the behaviour often constitutes a '*concerted practice*'.[16] In *Dyestuffs*, the ECJ has defined such a practice as being 'a form of coordination between undertakings which, without having reached the stage where an agreement properly called has been concluded, knowingly substitutes practical co-operation between them for the risks of competition'.

The principle is that each economic operator must determine its policy on the market independently, including the choice of its suppliers and customers. What is forbidden is to replace this independent action by a co-ordinated action. A strong indication of the existence of such co-ordination is the fact that the undertakings have been in communication about their market behaviour (meetings, oral or written exchange of detailed and strategic information such as amount, subject-matter, date and place of price increases, price lists, supply sources, quantities produced and sold, etc.), with a view to removing in advance doubts about the future competitive conduct of the others and influencing each other's commercial policy. The same goes for 'parallel behaviour' (e.g. increase of prices by the same percentage and at the same moment, refusal to export to a given country, etc.), which leads to competition conditions different from normal market conditions.

However, parallel behaviour does not amount per se to a concerted practice. Such behaviour may be due to the structure of a given market (e.g. very few producers of the product concerned, provoking what is called 'oligopolistic interdependence') or to sudden changes in economic conditions (e.g. sudden increase of the price of a commodity on world markets) or other plausible economic justifications. In *Sugar* the ECJ acknowledged that the requirement of independence 'does not deprive economic operators of the right to adapt themselves intelligently to the existing and anticipated conduct of their competitors'.

Once it is established that there is an agreement or practice between undertakings, the next test is whether it '*may affect trade between EC Member*

[14] See Case 107/82 *AEG* [1983] ECR 3151.

[15] Regarding the responsibility of the States when they oblige companies to make agreements in breach of Art. 85 see above n. 9.

[16] In this respect Cases 48/69 *Dyestuffs* [1972] ECR 619 and 40/73 etc. *Sugar* [1975] ECR 1663 are considered as leading cases.

States/EEA Contracting Parties'.[17] The concept of 'affecting trade' is first of all a rule of jurisdiction: within the Community, it divides jurisdiction between the EC Member States and the Commission;[18] within the EEA 'affect trade between Contracting Parties' (Article 53 (1) EEA) divides jurisdiction between the States and the surveillance authorities (Commission and ESA).

Secondly, the reference to 'trade between Member States' in Article 85 EEC brings in the whole issue of free movement of goods and services across the borders. The concept of 'trade' has a very wide scope. It covers any economic activity related to goods and services,[19] including the free establishment of traders in another country. As to the notion of 'Contracting Parties' used in Article 53 (1), it designates, as explained above in Section 3.1.1.1, the Community and each EFTA State.

Inter-State trade may be affected by an agreement which is 'capable of constituting a threat, either direct or indirect, actual or potential, to freedom of trade between Member States in a manner which might harm the attainment of the objectives of a single market'.[20] There is no need to establish that the agreement in question actually affects trade. It is enough to demonstrate that it is capable of doing so; that is, mere potential effect is sufficient.

This is the case for agreements which partition the common market (such as import or export restrictions, obstruction of parallel imports, sharing of markets or of supply sources, etc.) and thus hold up the interpenetration of national economies. This is also the case for agreements which alter the competitive structure within the common market (i.e. even when the anti-competitive behaviour injures a competitor all of whose products are exported outside the EC, since to eliminate this competitor would modify the competitive structure within the EC).

It is normally assumed that international agreements (i.e. relating to cross-border transactions, applying to several States, and/or whose parties are situated or operate in different States) affect inter-State trade. However, agreements covering only one Member State may also affect inter-State trade as they have, by their very nature, the effect of reinforcing the compartmentalization of the markets along national borders. The same is true for agreements whose parties are located in one Member State, as well as for agreements which, taken alone, would be insignificant, but which form part of a network of similar agreements within the country. Finally, agreements between EC undertakings and their third country competitors which

[17] The leading cases are Joint Cases 56 and 58/64 *Consten and Grundig* [1966] ECR 299; Case 56/65 *La Technique Minière* [1966] ECR 235 (partitioning of markets); Joint Cases and *Commercial Solvents* op. cit. n. 11 (alteration of competitive structure); Case 19/77 *Miller* [1978] ECR 131 (potential effect); and Case 8/72 *Cementhandelaren* [1972] ECR 977 (agreement covering the whole territory of a Member State).

[18] See Case *Consten and Grundig* (op. cit. n. 17), under which the concept 'affecting trade' is used to define 'the boundary between the areas respectively covered by Community law and national law'.

[19] e.g. banking and money transmission, foreign exchange brokerage, insurance, copyrights management, message forwarding services, TV broadcasting, services of public utilities, etc.

[20] See *Consten and Grundig*, op. cit. n. 17.

reduce the supply, within the EC, of third country products or otherwise relate to imports into the Community also affect trade between Member States. The same reasoning applies to agreements which, although relating to exports from the Community to outside markets, are likely to or actually impede the reimportation of the goods in question into the EC.

Agreements do not affect trade if their effects are exclusively confined within a single State without perceptible repercussions outside or if they relate solely to trade outside the EC (save the above-mentioned proviso concerning restriction on supplies or reimports to the EC).

The last condition is that the agreement 'has as its *object or effect to prevent, restrict or distort competition* within the EC/EEA'.[21] Article 85 (1) EEC/53 (1) EEA provides five examples of provisions restricting competition (i.e. price fixing; limits or controls of production, markets, etc.; market sharing; discriminatory conditions; and abusive supplementary obligations). However, the great bulk of principles and interpretation is to be found in the ECJ case-law, in Commission decisions and notices, and in the lists of black and white clauses contained in the various so-called 'group exemptions' issued by the Commission.[22]

In its case *La Technique Minière*, the ECJ stated the essential elements of the definition of 'restriction of competition' and the analysis to be made. In the examination, one should first 'consider the precise purpose of the agreement, in the economic context in which it is to be applied', that is, look at the object of the agreement. If at this stage the object is already found to be obviously restrictive of competition, there is no need to go further in the analysis and to look at its concrete effects. Several types of agreement have been held to have, by nature, the object of restricting competition: horizontal agreements to fix prices, share markets, deal through agreed channels or vertical agreements imposing export bans, prohibiting sales between authorized dealers, etc.

In instances where the object is not obviously restrictive, 'the consequences of the agreement should then be considered and for it to be caught by the prohibition it is then necessary to find that those factors are present which show that competition has in fact been prevented or restricted or distorted to an appreciable extent. The competition in question must be understood within the actual context in which it would occur in the absence of the agreement.'[23] Thus the effects, both actual

[21] The leading cases are *La Technique Minière* (op. cit. n. 17); Case 23/67 *Brasserie de Haecht (I)* [1967] ECR 407; Case 161/84 *Pronuptia* [1986] ECR 353; and Case 5/69 *Völk* [1969] ECR 295.

[22] About 'group' exemptions, see further in s. 3.1.1.4 below. Black clauses are provisions which, if contained in an agreement, impede it to benefit from the group exemption. White clauses are those which benefit from the group exemption. In general, horizontal agreements (i.e. between undertakings at the same level of trade) are forbidden as they restrict competition between competing products of different brands ('inter-brand' competition, though e.g. certain JVs between SMEs for entering a new market may be acceptable). Vertical agreements (i.e. between undertakings at different levels of trade) usually involve exclusivity clauses which restrict competition between products of the same brand ('intra-brand'). Some of these clauses in favour of distributors or licensees may be acceptable if limited in time and scope (no absolute territorial protection, i.e. against parallel imports).

[23] See *La Technique Minière* (op. cit. n. 17).

(competition in fact prevented) and potential (competition which would occur without the agreement), should be examined. Regarding the parties, this means looking at the way they are likely to behave and whether they are at least potential competitors. The effect on third parties should also be considered (e.g. prevention of parallel imports by third parties, reduction of their access to supplies or technology, reduction of the number of independent suppliers, discrimination, etc.). Finally, the whole economic context should be taken into consideration, for which a certain number of relevant factors should be examined.

In *La Technique Minière*, the Court refers to competition being distorted to an 'appreciable extent'. In *Völk*, the Court held that an agreement 'falls outside the prohibition in Article 85 when it has only an insignificant effect on the markets'. This jurisprudence formed the basis for the famous Commission Notice on agreements of minor importance (the '*de minimis* Notice')[24] under which agreements which fulfil certain cumulative conditions do not fall under Article 85 (1) EEC, i.e.:

- the undertakings concerned do not have a market share of more than 5 per cent in the relevant product and geographical market; and
- the combined turnover of the parties and connected undertakings does not exceed 200 million ECU.

The application of the criterion 'appreciable effect' requires evaluation of the size of the parties and their market shares, that is to say the identification of the so-called 'relevant market' (i.e. the product and geographical market in which the product competes). Other important aspects are the characteristics of the market (whether it is concentrated, oligopolistic, fragmented, competitive, or declining), the effects on related markets, the share of export trade, the cumulative effect of parallel networks of similar agreements, or the gravity of the restrictions.

In the EEA context, ESA will issue, with the necessary adaptations, a similar notice to the *de minimis* Notice of the Commission. When assigned a case, ESA will thus follow the same policy as the Commission with regard to *de minimis* cases. In this adapted Notice, the reference market is the EEA territory, instead of 'the Community' or 'the common market' (paragraph 13 of the Notice). The Commission will not adapt its present Notice to the EEA context, but apply it *mutatis mutandis* to EEA competition cases.[25]

There are three other Notices which allow certain agreements to escape the prohibition of Article 85 (1) EEC: the Commercial Agents Notice[26] concerning agreements between a principal and commercial agent; the Subcontracting Notice concerning certain legitimate restrictions in a subcontract (i.e. restrictions on the use of the technology and equipment transferred and on the goods or services

[24] See *OJ* C 231 (12 Sept. 1986), 2 (point 24 of Annex XIV EEA).

[25] See Art. 7 (1) of the amended Commission proposal for a Council regulation concerning the arrangements for implementing the Agreement on the European Economic Area (COM (93) 466 final).

[26] See *OJ* C 139 (24 Dec. 1962), 2921 (point 20 of Annex XIV EEA).

resulting thereof);[27] and the Notice on co-operative joint ventures (JVs) (concerning e.g. intra-group JVs, 'neutral' JVs i.e. between non-competitors or not affecting third parties, etc.).[28]

Likewise, there are individual cases where agreements have been considered to fall outside the scope of Article 85 (1) EEC: 'open'[29] exclusive licence of IPRs involving dissemination of new technology; exclusive licence to exhibit a film; restriction on resale of technically complex goods based on objective and non-discriminatory criteria; prohibition on a wholesaler supplying consumers; non-competition clause in connection with the sale of a business if reasonable in time and in scope.

3.1.1.3 Nullity under Article 85 (2) EEC/53 (2) EEA

If an agreement falls within the prohibition of Article 85 (1)/53 (1), the first sanction is that, pursuant to Article 85 (2)/53 (2), that agreement is automatically void *ab initio* and cannot be enforced.

However, the nullity applies only to those provisions of the agreement which are contrary to Article 85 (1)/53 (1), provided that those elements are severable from the agreement as a whole. The effect of the nullity on the rest of the agreement and the extent to which it can, or cannot, be divided into pieces while still remaining viable is a matter for national law to determine.[30]

In addition, other consequences may arise both at EC/EEA level and at national level: fines imposed by the Commission or ESA, interim or final orders from the Commission or ESA requiring the infringement to cease, damages awarded by national courts, and/or injunctions. The national remedies may be used between the parties to the agreement (e.g. recovery of money paid or goods transferred under an illegal agreement) or by third parties (e.g. defence against an action for infringement of IPRs, claim for damages for loss of business caused by an export ban, or injunction to restrain predatory pricing or exclusion from a distribution network).[31]

3.1.1.4 Exemptions under Article 85 (3) EEC/53 (3) EEA

The prohibition in Article 85 (1)/53 (1) may be declared inapplicable to agreements or categories of agreements which, though containing provisions which restrict competition, nevertheless have beneficial effects (improvement of production or

[27] See *OJ* C 139 (24 Dec. 1962), 2921 (point 23 of Annex XIV EEA).

[28] See *OJ* C 43 (16 Feb. 1993), 2 (not listed in Annex XIV EEA because adopted after the cut-off date of 31 July 1991, but to be issued by ESA in due time).

[29] i.e. the exclusivity relates solely to licensor/licensee relations, while competition from third parties (e.g. from parallel importers or licensees from other territories) remains open (see Case 258/78 *Nungesser* [1982] ECR 2015).

[30] See *La Technique Minière* (op. cit. n. 17) and Case 319/82 *Ciments et Bétons* [1983] ECR 4173.

[31] By virtue of the direct effects of the EC competition rules, which create rights the individuals may invoke in national courts (see Case 127/73 *BRT* v. *SABAM* [974] ECR 51). The situation should be the same in the EEA context (however, see Ch. III, s. 3.4, above).

distribution, promotion of technical or economic progress, and fair share of the benefits to consumers), while keeping within certain proportions (i.e. do not impose non-indispensable restrictions and do not afford the possibility of eliminating competition).

Such an exemption may be granted:

- through a decision by the Commission or ESA concerning an agreement which the parties have notified ('individual exemptions'); on
- by 'group exemptions' (also called 'block exemptions' or 'exemptions by categories'), which are regulations through which the Commission, after having been empowered to do so by the Council, exempts certain classes of agreements. To date, there are thirteen group exemptions.[32]

The advantage of an individual exemption is that it gives the parties legal certainty and makes their agreement enforceable. However, the main disadvantage is the length of the procedure which follows the notification of the agreement to the Commission (two to three years, sometimes more).[33]

In contrast, the obvious advantage of the group exemptions is that they automatically exempt agreements which comply with their provisions, thus avoiding all the troubles of the above-mentioned procedure.

Individual exemptions, therefore, enter into play only in cases where the agreement is not covered by a group exemption.

Article 85 (3)/53 (3) provides for *four cumulative conditions* which must be satisfied for an exemption to be granted:

- improvements in production or distribution or promotion of technical or economic progress;
- benefits to consumers;
- restrictions are indispensable; and
- no elimination of competition.

As to the *first two conditions*, the following have been considered as improving production: agreements enabling the production of a new high technology product or of a wider range of products, strengthening a weaker competitor or encouraging a new competitor, improving the quality of products, achieving standardization of types or interchangeability, bringing capacity more in line with demand, ensuring regularity of supply, and even maintaining employment. Likewise, it has been said that distribution is improved by certain exclusive distribution or purchasing agreements and franchising agreements (on which there are group exemptions), as well as by certain selective distribution agreements (more likely to be permitted in

[32] Ten of which are listed in Annex XIV EEA (points 2–11) and three of which (the most recently adopted in the fields of insurance and air transport) will form part of the 'Additional Package' to be included in the EEA through an EEA Joint Committee decision after the entry into force of the Agreement.

[33] In order to remedy these delays, the Commission launched an internal reform of its administrative practice, including informal time-limits (see s. 6.1.4.6 below).

respect of technically complex or high quality goods[34]). Technical or economic progress has often been held to result from agreements on joint R. & D. and specialization (on which there are group exemptions), joint manufacture, or licensing of new technology. As to the benefits for consumers, there should be a reasonable probability that the benefits of the agreements will be passed on to the final consumers. These benefits may be, for instance, an improved supply, the introduction of new or improved products, or lower prices.

As to the *third condition* (necessity of the restrictions), guidance may be sought in the various group exemptions which indicate which provisions are acceptable and which are not acceptable. The following have been held unnecessary: absolute territorial protection, restriction on the customers to be supplied, or resale price restrictions. The *fourth condition* (non-elimination of competition) requires that sufficient competition from competing products should remain. It entails an analysis of the relevant product and geographical markets.

According to the policy followed by the Commission to date the following are most unlikely to be exempted: horizontal agreements (between competitors) aimed at restricting price competition, exchanging confidential market information, limiting production, limiting or controlling markets, dealing only through agreed distribution channels, or co-operating in joint selling. The same goes for vertical agreements which provide for resale price maintenance, export bans, restrictions on resale, or other measures intended to bar parallel imports. The Commission is particularly attentive to safeguarding parallel imports. It has therefore developed the notion of 'active' sales (i.e. actively seeking customers and promoting sales outside the reserved area) and 'passive' sales (i.e. responding to unsolicited orders from outside the reserved area), only restrictions on the former being possible (notably in exclusive distribution agreements and patent licences), while restrictions on the latter are admitted only under certain conditions (such as limitation in time).

3.1.2 Article 54 EEA (abuse of dominant position)

Article 54 EEA reproduces Article 86 EEC, which prohibits abuse on dominant position by one or more undertakings in so far as it may affect cross-border trade.

3.1.2.1 Adaptations for EEA purposes

The same adaptations as in Article 53 EEA have been made to Article 54 EEA: the term 'territory covered by this Agreement' is used instead of 'common market'; the

[34] This form of distribution (under which a brand owner sets up a network of authorized retailers which comply with certain requirements as to premises, stocks of spare parts, and skills, and may limit the number of outlets in a given area) is the main one left for individual exemptions. There is a group exemption for selective distribution of motor vehicles. Leading cases on selective distribution are Cases 26/76 *Metro (I)* [1977] ECR 1875, 75/84 *Metro (II)* [1986] ECR 3021, and *AEG* op. cit. n. 14, as well as Commission Decisions *Yves Saint Laurent Parfums* (*OJ* L 12 (18 Jan. 1992), 24) and *Parfums Givenchy* (*OJ* L 236 (19 Aug. 1992), 1).

term 'incompatible with the functioning of this Agreement' instead of 'incompatible with the common market'; and the term 'trade between Contracting Parties' instead of 'trade between Member States'.

3.1.2.2 Prohibition under Article 86 EEC/54 EEA

For the prohibition of Article 86 EEC/54 EEA to apply, three conditions must be met:[35]

- one or more undertakings hold a dominant position within the common market/EEA or a substantial part thereof;
- this or these undertakings abuse their dominant position; and
- trade between EC Member States/EEA Contracting Parties may thereby be affected.

Thus Article 86/54 does not prohibit the dominance in itself, but the abuse of such dominance. In *Michelin*, the ECJ even said that the dominant undertaking 'has a special responsibility not to allow its conduct to impair genuine undistorted competition on the common market'.

The notion of *dominant position* has been defined by the Court, in *United Brands*, as being 'a position of economic strength enjoyed by an undertaking which enables it to prevent effective competition being maintained on the relevant market by giving it the power to behave to an appreciable extent independently of its competitors, customers and ultimately of its consumers'.

Two steps are usually followed for establishing that a firm holds a dominant position:

- definition of the relevant market (product and geographic); and
- assessment of the dominance of the undertaking therein.

Defining the *relevant market* could be described as setting the scene in which the market power of the dominant firm and the competition conditions will be evaluated. The relevant product market consists in the products which the (allegedly) dominant firm supplies (or buys), together with the interchangeable products. The relevant geographical market is the area (i.e. the EC/EEA or a substantial part thereof) in which these particular products are marketed and where the competition conditions are sufficiently homogeneous. Furthermore, the level of trade concerned (production, wholesale, retail) should also be identified.

The relevant product market is established with the help of two tests: the first one concerns the demand side, that is, what are the products which, in the eyes of their users/buyers, have a sufficient degree of interchangeability with those of the dominant firm (so-called 'demand substitutability')? It is necessary to take into consideration the nature of the goods, their prices and use, the buyer's preferences

[35] The leading cases concerning abuse of dominant position are Cases *Continental Can* op. cit. n. 3, 27/76 *United Brands* [1978] ECR 207, 85/76 *Hoffmann-La Roche* [1979] ECR 461, and 322/81 *Michelin* [1983] ECR 3461.

and needs, the competitive conditions, the structure of the supply and demand, as well as the so-called 'cross-elasticity of demand' (i.e. whether a mere change in the price of the product in question would make buyers switch to other products, thus proving their interchangeability). For a given product to be regarded as forming a sufficiently differentiated market, one should be able to single out the product by such 'special features distinguishing it from other [products] that it is only to a limited extend interchangeable with them and is only exposed to their competition in a way which is hardly perceptible'.[36] Separate product markets have been found for a specific use of the same product (i.e. a product used for different applications may fall in different markets[37]), for groups of products,[38] for raw materials (as compared with products processed out of them[39]), for spare or replacement parts,[40] or for ancillary services (such as issuance of conformity certificates[41]).

The second test concerns the supply side, that is, how easy or difficult is it for other suppliers to switch to producing interchangeable products (so-called 'supply substitutability')? For a product market to be sufficiently separated one should prove that 'competitors from other sectors of the market . . . are not in a position to enter this market, by a simple adaptation, with sufficient strength to create a serious counterweight'.[42] Thus, if the production techniques, plants, and tools needed are too different, if it would cost too much and/or take too long for a competing manufacturer to switch and produce interchangeable products, there is no 'elasticity of supply'.

The relevant geographical market is established by examining whether the competition conditions applying to the product concerned are the same for all traders, i.e. are sufficiently homogeneous. Factors to be looked at include the nature and characteristics of the products concerned, transport costs, tariff provisions and other government regulations, minimum efficient scale of operation, etc. The geographical market may be the whole of the EC/EEA territory or a substantial part thereof, i.e. the territory of a State or even only a region within a State. In the latter cases, the Court stated that:

> For the purpose of determining whether a specific territory is large enough to amount to 'a substantial part of the common market' within the meaning of Article 86 of the Treaty the pattern and volume of the production and consumption of the said product as well as the habits and economic opportunities of vendors and purchasers must be considered.[43]

Assessing dominance consists in evaluating the economic strength of the firm in question and how much this enables it to behave independently from its

[36] See *United Brands*, op. cit. n. 35.

[37] e.g. vitamins for bio-nutritive use and vitamins for industrial use (see *Hoffmann-La Roche*, op. cit. n. 35).

[38] e.g. replacement tyres for trucks and buses (see *Michelin*, op. cit. n. 35).

[39] See *Commercial Solvents*, op. cit. n. 11.

[40] See Cases 22/78 *Hugin* [1979] ECR 1869 and *Michelin*, op. cit. n. 35.

[41] See Case 26/75 *General Motors* [1975] ECR 1367.

[42] See *Continental Can* and also *Michelin*, op. cit. n. 35.

[43] See Case *Sugar* op. cit. n. 16.

competitors, customers, and consumers. This is assessed by looking at what the undertaking has so far achieved (and for how long) and what are its potentials (as well as those of its competitors). Achievement is evaluated by looking at the market share held by the firm. A very large market share, held for some time (three years or more), which makes the dominant firm an 'unavoidable trading partner', may in itself be sufficient to prove dominance without further evidence being required. This was held to be the case in general for market shares above 50 per cent over a three-year period, in particular if there is an important gap before the shares of the largest competitors or if it is a narrow oligopolistic market.[44]

Market shares between 30 and 50 per cent usually need further evidence, notably related to the potentials of the undertaking in question. These other factors usually concern the organization of the firm (e.g. strong vertical integration, strict quality control, highly developed sales networks), technical and technological resources (e.g. technological lead over competitors, ownership of IPRs), financial situation (e.g. strong financial basis, easy access to capital, ability to make large investments), access to raw materials, extensive range of products, strong reputation thanks to large-scale advertising, dependency of customers, overall size and strength, barriers to entry for actual or potential competitors, etc. More than one undertaking may be held to have a dominant position (i.e. so-called 'collective dominance'), for instance where two or more independent economic entities are united by such economic links as a joint technological lead over their competitors.[45] However, as already said above in relation to concerted practices, a dominant position must be distinguished from 'parallel courses of conduct which are peculiar to oligopolies', as in oligopolies the courses of conduct interact, while in cases of dominance the conduct is to a great extent determined unilaterally.[46]

The *concept of abuse* is, according to the ECJ,

> an objective concept relating to the behaviour of an undertaking in a dominant position which is such as to influence the structure of a market where, as a result of the very presence of the undertaking in question, the degree of competition is weakened and which, through recourse to methods different from those which condition normal competition in products or services on the basis of the transactions of commercial operators, has the effect of hindering the maintenance of the degree of competition still existing in the market or the growth of that competition.[47]

Article 86 EEC/54 EEA gives four examples of prohibited abuses: unfair prices or trading conditions; limitation measures; discrimination; and tying.

As regards pricing practices, it is abusive for a dominant firm to charge an excessive price, i.e. a price not having reasonable relation to the economic value of

[44] See *Hoffmann-La Roche*, op. cit. n. 35, where the market shares were ranging between 75 and 87% or 63 and 66% over three years or 47% in a narrow oligopolistic market. See also Case C-62/86 *AKZO* [1991] ECR I-3359.

[45] See Joint Cases T-68, 77 and 78/89 *Flat Glass* [1991] ECR II-1405.

[46] See *Hoffmann-La Roche*, op. cit. n. 35.

[47] Ibid.

the product.[48] Likewise, it is abusive to charge an excessive price, or discriminatory price with a view to detering parallel imports[49] or resales of the products in other territories.[50] In general, price discrimination (not treating like cases alike) without objective justification for the difference is abusive, as is price discrimination based on the maintenance of national boundaries (e.g. dependent upon buyer's nationality or location); so-called 'predatory pricing', that is, pricing essentially aimed at eliminating or seriously weakening a competitor, is also forbidden.[51]

As regards discounts or rebates, only so-called 'quantity rebates' based on objective criteria are acceptable, that is, exclusively linked with the volume purchased from the producer and cost based (i.e. based on the differences in costs borne by the supplier depending on whether he supplies a larger or smaller quantity).[52] In contrast, so-called 'fidelity rebates', though not putting a formal exclusive purchasing obligation on the customer, may amount to the same, as they reward the customer for his loyalty and are thus designed to prevent him obtaining his supplies from competing producers. These rebates are conditional on the customer's obtaining all or a high percentage of his requirements (regardless of the actual quantity) from the dominant undertaking.[53] They result in making the customers dependent upon the dominant firm and treating differently customers who buy the same quantity, thus putting them at a competitive disadvantage. The same goes for 'across-the-board' rebates which enable the aggregation of purchases of different products from the same supplier. A so-called 'English clause'[54] does not help, and may even worsen the situation, as such a clause may in addition help the dominant undertaking to carry out its market strategy. So-called 'target rebates', the percentage of which varies according to the dealer's turnover in the firm's products in the previous year, have been held to be calculated over an excessively long period, induce customers to buy higher quantities, discourage them from switching to another supplier, and put them under considerable pressure to reach the target at the end of the reference period.[55]

Although there is no duty to supply, in some cases refusal to supply may amount to an abuse contrary to Article 86/54. For instance, 'an undertaking dominant as regards the production of raw material and therefore able to control the supply to manufacturers of derivatives, cannot just because it decides to start manufacturing

[48] Ibid. The excess should be determined objectively, by making a comparison between the selling price and the production costs.

[49] e.g. excessive price charged by a firm holding a monopoly when issuing conformity certificates for imported cars (*General Motors*, op. cit. n. 41).

[50] See *United Brands*, op. cit. n. 35.

[51] See *AKZO*, op. cit. n. 44; e.g. through selective price cuttings, systematically offering to the competitor's customers lower prices, or unprofitable or barely profitable price levels.

[52] See *Sugar*, op. cit. n. 16.

[53] See *Hoffmann-La Roche*, op. cit. n. 35.

[54] An 'English clause' allows the customer to inform its supplier about more favourable offers, request the supplier to adjust its prices accordingly, and, in the case of refusal, accept the competing offer without losing the benefit of the rebates (see *Hoffmann-La Roche*, op. cit. n. 35).

[55] See *Michelin*, op. cit. n. 35.

these derivatives (in competition with a former customer)' refuse to supply its now customer/competitor.[56] The same was applied in *United Brands*, where the dominant firm refused to supply a long-standing customer because he had participated in an advertising campaign for one of the firm's competitors. The unreasonable refusal by a copyright association to supply its services was also held to be an abuse.[57] However, dominant undertakings may protect their interests as long as the measures taken are proportionate to the threat and their actual purpose is not to strengthen the dominance and the abuse.[58]

Other restrictions or obligations have been considered as abuses, such as abusive registration of a trade mark, when knowing that a similar trade mark is already used by a competitor in other States,[59] imposition of restrictions on resales, tie-in clauses (i.e. making a sale of a product conditional upon the sale of another product), or exclusive agreements such as an exclusive patent licence (in spite of it falling within the provision of the patent licensing group exemption[60]).

As to the condition of '*affecting trade*', the developments and explanations given above in Section 3.1.1.2. concerning Article 85 EEC/53 EEA are also valid for Article 86 EEC/54 EEA.

As to the relationship between Articles 85/53 and 86/54, the Court acknowledged in *Tetrapak*[61] that the applicability of Article 85 to an agreement does not rule out the application of Article 86, the two provisions being complementary, though legally independent. It also confirmed that an abuse of dominant position could never be exempted.

Finally, before the adoption of the Merger Regulation,[62] the ECJ accepted, in its famous *Continental Can* case,[63] that Article 86 could apply to a merger through which an undertaking in a dominant position strengthens that position in such a way that the degree of dominance reached substantially fetters competition. However, since the adoption of the Merger Regulation, Articles 85 and 86 are normally no longer applicable to concentrations as defined by the Regulation (see developments below in Section 3.1.3.2).[64]

3.1.3 Article 57 EEA (merger control)

Article 57 EEA contains both a substantive rule (on incompatible mergers) and a

[56] See *Commercial Solvents*, op. cit. n. 11.

[57] See *BRT* v. *SABAM*, op. cit. n. 31.

[58] See *United Brands*, op. cit. n. 35.

[59] See informal settlement in *Osram/Airam*, op. cit. in Ch. V, n. 36.

[60] See Case T-51/89 *Tetrapak* [1990] ECR II-347. See *XXth Report of Competition Policy* (1990), 115 *et seq.*

[61] Ibid.

[62] Council Reg. (EEC) 4064/89 of 21 Dec. 1989 on the control of concentrations between undertakings (point 1 of Annex XIV EEA).

[63] Op. cit. n. 3.

[64] On the application of Art. 85 EEC to the acquisition of a minority shareholding giving control over the undertaking in question, while still remaining independent firms, see Joined Cases 142 and 156/84 *Philip Morris* [1987] ECR 4487.

procedural rule (attribution of merger cases between the Commission and ESA). The originality of Article 57 EEA is that it makes primary in the EEA a provision which in the EC is contained in a secondary source (a Council regulation).[65]

Article 57 (1) EEA reproduces paragraph 3 of Article 2 of the EC Merger Regulation. It reads:

Concentrations the control of which is provided for in paragraph 2 and which create or strengthen a dominant position as a result of which effective competition would be significantly impeded within the territory covered by this Agreement or a substantial part of it, shall be declared incompatible with this Agreement.[66]

3.1.3.1 Adaptations for EEA purposes

The same adaptations as in Article 53 EEA have been made to Article 57 (1) EEA, that is, the term 'territory covered by this Agreement' is used instead of 'common market' and the term 'incompatible with the functioning of this Agreement' instead of 'incompatible with the common market'. The reasons for doing so and the explanations given above, in Section 3.1.1.1, as regards Article 53 EEA are also valid concerning Article 57 (1) EEA.

In addition, a reference to paragraph 2, on attribution of competence, has been added at the beginning of Article 57 (1) EEA and the term 'within' the EEA is used instead of 'in'.

3.1.3.2 The Merger Regulation in general

The whole body of EC merger control legislation, comprising the Merger Regulation itself, the implementing Regulation,[67] the Notice on concentrative and co-operative JVs,[68] and the Notice on ancillary restrictions,[69] has been taken over in the EEA Agreement.

The Merger Regulation sets up a system of prior control of concentrations having 'Community dimension', based on the principle of a mandatory notification by the undertakings concerned, which shall be processed by the Commission within very tight deadlines.

Under Article 1 of the Regulation, a concentration has a Community dimension, and thus falls within the scope of the Merger Regulation, where the combined

[65] The Merger Regulation was adopted on the basis of Arts. 87 and 235 EEC, as the EEC Treaty 'contains no provisions making specific reference to the prior control of concentrations' (see Council Minutes, 'Community Merger Control Law', *Bulletin of the EC*, Supplement 2/90: 23 *et seq.*).

[66] Op. cit. n. 62. This Article in fact appears twice in the EEA since the Regulation is also referred to in Annex XIV EEA (point 1).

[67] Commission Reg. (EEC) 2367/90 of 23 July 1990 on the notifications, time-limits, and hearings provided for in Council Reg. (EEC) 4064/89 (*OJ* L 219 (14 Aug. 1990), 5), referred to in Art. 3, point 2, of Protocol 21 EEA and reproduced in ch. XIV of Protocol 4 ESA/Court Agreement.

[68] Commission Notice on the concentrative and co-operative operations under Council Reg. (EEC) 4064/89 (*OJ* C 203 (14 Aug. 1990), 5) (point 16 of Annex XIV EEA).

[69] Commission Notice on restrictions ancillary to concentrations (*OJ* C 203 (14 Aug. 1990), 10) (point 17 of Annex XIV EEA).

aggregate world-wide turnover of the undertakings concerned is five billion ECU or more and the Community-wide aggregate turnover of each of at least two undertakings concerned is at least 250 million ECU, unless each of the undertakings concerned achieves two-thirds of its turnover within one and the same Member State. It was envisaged that these thresholds should be lowered to two billion ECU (world-wide) and 100 million ECU (EC-wide). However, the Commission decided to postpone the proposal until 1996.[70]

In the EEA context, the specific adaptations made, in Annex XIV EEA, to Article 1 of the Merger Regulation have replaced 'Community dimension' by 'Community or EFTA dimension' (and not by 'EEA dimension'). Likewise, the term 'Community-wide turnover' in Article 1 (2) (*b*) of the Regulation has been replaced by 'Community-wide or EFTA-wide turnover' (and not by 'EEA-wide turnover'). This is due to the strict two pillar system which applies for allocating the merger cases between the Commission and ESA and aims at safeguarding the Commission competencies.

Article 3 of the Regulation defines a concentration as being either a merger or independent undertakings coming under common control. Article 3 excludes co-operative JVs but includes concentrative JVs.

The basic concept was to establish a clear allocation of competence (known as a 'one-stop shop') between the Commission (solely competent for Community dimension mergers, Article 21 Merger Regulation) and the EC Member States (competent for mergers whose main impact is in a State territory). Instead of using the 'affecting trade' criterion of Articles 85 and 86 EEC, the Regulation uses a turnover criterion which is better from a legal certainty point of view. The 'one-stop shop' rule is also relevant to the scope of application of the Merger Regulation *vis-à-vis* that of Articles 85 and 86 EEC.[71]

However, there are two cases where the Member States may still have a say concerning a Community dimension merger: referral to a Member State in the case of dominance on a 'distinct market' within a State territory (Article 9) and invocation by a State of legitimate interests which enable it to take appropriate measures (Article 22 (3)). Likewise, although Regulation 17 no longer applies to concentrations (above or below the turnover thresholds), the Commission still retains some residual powers to take action under Articles 85 and 86 EEC as regards concentrations below the thresholds.[72] Furthermore, the national courts still have

[70] See 'Community Merger Control', Report from the Commission to the Council on the implementation of the Merger Regulation (COM (93) 385 final).

[71] See Art. 22 (2): 'Regulations No 17 [procedure for applying Arts. 85 and 86 EEC] . . . shall not apply to concentrations as defined in Article 3.'

[72] The Commission stated in the Council Minutes: 'it reserves its right to take action in accordance with the procedures laid down in Article 89 of the Treaty [on Commission powers to apply Arts. 85 and 86] for concentrations as defined in Article 3 [of the Merger Regulation], but which do not have a Community dimension within the meaning of Article 1, in hypotheses not provided for by Article 22. . . . it does not intend to take action in respect of concentrations with a worldwide turnover of less than 2,000 million ECUs or below a minimum Community turnover level of 100 million ECUs.'

power to apply Article 86 EEC to mergers. Finally, the Commission retains its powers as regards agreements which are not a concentration within the meaning of Article 3 of the Regulation (e.g. co-operative JVs).

3.1.3.3 Mergers incompatible under Article 2 (3) of Regulation 4064/89 and Article 57 (1) EEA

Contrary to Article 85 EEC/53 EEA, Article 2 (3)/57 (1) does not contain a prohibition rule, nor an automatic sanction, but obliges the Commission/ESA to declare incompatible with the common market/EEA a concentration falling within the terms of Article 2 (3)/57 (1).

The examination of compatibility involves two tests:

- the creation or strengthening of a dominant position;
- as a result of which effective competition would be significantly impeded within the common market/EEA or a substantial part of it.

As regards the *first test* (dominance), although it is very similar to the wording used in Article 86 EEC/54 EEA, the novelty is that a concentration may also be attacked if it creates a dominant position, and not only if it strengthens such dominance (which was caught in *Continental Can*[73]). For the rest, the concept of dominance in itself is not really different from the one contained in Article 86/54, apart from the fact that it is assessed in the perspective of its results on 'effective competition' rather than that of how it is abused. As regards the definition of the relevant market (product and geographic) and the market share element, the explanations above in Section 3.1.2.2 are to a great extent valid here. In addition, useful indications are contained in Sections 5 and 6 of the notification Form CO.[74] Concerning the market share, recital 15 of the Merger Regulation states that a limited share is presumed not to impede competition, an indication being a share not exceeding 25 per cent.

As regards the *second test* (significant impediment of effective competition), the wording is new as compared with Article 86/54, though not really different from the words used by the Court in *Continental Can*: 'the degree of dominance reached substantially fetters competition'. However the main point is that Article 2 (3) Regulation/57 (1) EEA, as it concerns prior control (and not *ex post* as in Article 86/54), entails a predictive analysis about what 'would' happen if the concentration did take place. Moreover, Article 2 (3)/57 (1), like other competition provisions, is to be considered in the light of the objectives of the EEC Treaty/EEA Agreement.

Article 2 (1) (*a*) and (*b*) of the Merger Regulation enumerates appraisal criteria to be followed by the Commission/ESA when ascertaining whether the concentration is liable significantly to affect competition. *Littera* (*a*) concerns the maintenance and development of effective competition and is of a general policy nature, while (*b*)

[73] Op. cit. n. 3.

[74] This Form is annexed to the implementing Reg. 2367/90.

contains several more specific criteria, ranging from market shares and barriers to entry to consumer interests. These criteria to a large extent codify the Court case-law developed under Article 86 EEC (as well as Article 85 (3) EEC when it comes to 'technical or economic progress'[75] and consumer interest).

As a result of the need to look into the future, it emerges from the practice followed so far that the Commission analysis has been more dynamic and economically oriented than under Article 86 EEC, putting more emphasis on the structure of the market concerned, potential competition, barriers to entry, etc. This has resulted in the fact that, despite high market shares, potential pressure from imports and from substitutable product may permit a denial that dominance would be created. The same goes for a concentration leading only to a temporary dominance which will rapidly be eroded by the likely entry of new competitors. According to the Commission, 'only a dominant position that is likely to persist in the future represents a real danger to the competitive structure of the market'.[76] Finally, in the famous *Perrier/Nestlé* case the Commission for the first time interpreted Article 2 (3) of the Merger Regulation as also covering 'joint oligopolistic dominance' (i.e. between the two biggest actors (duopoly) on the French water market, Nestlé and BSN).[77]

3.1.4 Protocol 25 EEA (coal and steel)

As seen above in Section 1.4 of Chapter III, apart from a short reference in Article 27 EEA, the basic rules on coal and steel are not contained in the main part of the EEA Agreement itself, but in two Protocols, namely Protocols 14 (general) and 25 (competition). According to Article 1 of Protocol 14 EEA, these two Protocols apply to the products listed in the bilateral FTAs concluded between the ECSC and each EFTA State in 1973.[78] The provisions of these ECSC–EFTA FTAs remain applicable, including the related institutional provisions, unless otherwise provided (Article 2 (1) of Protocol 14 EEA).

As regards competition, Article 4 of Protocol 14 EEA indicates that the rules are to be found in Protocol 25 (basic substantive rules), Annex XIV (secondary substantive rules), and Protocol 21 (procedures).

Protocol 25 EEA contains seven articles. Article 1, on restrictive agreements, reproduces the substantive paragraphs of Article 65 ECSC Treaty. Article 2, on concentrations and abuse of dominant position, reproduces the substantive paragraphs of Article 66 ECSC. Article 3, on the definition of 'undertaking', reproduces Article 80 ECSC. The other four articles refer to Annex XIV EEA

[75] In the Council Minutes the Commission stated that 'the concept of technical and economic progress must be understood in the light of the principles enshrined in Article 85 (3) of the Treaty, as interpreted by the case law of the Court of Justice.'

[76] See *XXIst Report on Competition Policy* (1991), which in its Annex II.7 contains a useful outline of the interpretation given so far by the Commission to the Regulation provisions (p. 351).

[77] See *OJ* L 356 (5 Dec. 1992), 1, and comments in *XXIInd Report on Competition Policy* (1992).

[78] For the EFTA States, the coverage in practice mainly concerns steel.

(Article 4), empower the Commission and ESA to apply the rules as set out in Protocol 21 EEA (Article 5), and refer to the attribution of cases provision (Article 6) and to the co-operation rules of Protocol 23 EEA (Article 7).

3.1.4.1 Adaptations for EEA purposes

The first particularity of Articles 1 and 2 of Protocol 25 EEA is that they result from a splitting of the original ECSC provisions (Articles 65 and 66 ECSC). Protocol 25 EEA only contains the substance paragraphs of the original ECSC provisions,[79] while Protocol 21 EEA (Article 3 (2)) refers to the procedural paragraphs of the original ECSC rules, which have been reproduced in full in Protocol 4 to the ESA/Court Agreement.[80]

The second particularity of Articles 1 and 2 of Protocol 25 EEA is that the condition 'affecting trade' has been added in the three instances (restrictive agreements, concentrations, and abuse of dominant position), while this condition does not appear in the original Articles 65 and 66 ECSC. The idea was to bring the analysis of coal and steel cases more in line with that under Articles 85 and 86 EEC (53 and 54 EEA).

A third difference from the original ECSC text may be found in Article 2 (3) of Protocol 25 EEA (which corresponds to Article 66 (3) ECSC) (regarding the possibility of exemption from the requirement of prior authorization for concentrations). Article 2 (3) only takes over the substance of Article 66 (3) ECSC without referring to the possibility of making regulations on this issue. This is due to the fact that such implementing regulations have been adopted in the EC and are taken over in the EEA Agreement through a reference in point 15 of Annex XIV EEA.[81] Likewise, Article 2 (4) of Protocol 25 EEA (which corresponds to Article 66 (7) ECSC), regarding abuse of dominant position, reproduces only the first sentence of Article 66 (7) ECSC and not the second one concerning the possibility for the Commission to determine prices and conditions of sale or to draw up production and delivery programmes.

As regards the 'vocabulary adaptations' made to the original ECSC text, they are of the same type as for the other competition provisions seen in the subsections above, that is, the term 'territory of this Agreement' replaces the term 'common market'. In addition, where the original ECSC text refers to the 'High Authority', the EEA text refers to the 'competent surveillance authority, as provided for in Article 56 of the Agreement', i.e. the Commission or ESA, depending on which of them is given the competence under the rules on attribution of cases. Finally, in Article 1 (3) of Protocol 25 EEA (which corresponds to Article 65 (4), subparagraph

[79] i.e. Art. 65 (1), (2) subparas. 1 and 2, and (4) subpara. 1; Art. 66 (1), (2) subpara. 1, (3), and (7), 1st sentence.

[80] Part IV, Section 1 of Protocol 4 to the ESA/Court Agreement reproduces, *inter alia*, the text of Art. 65 (2) subparas. 3–5, (3), (4) subpara. 2, and (5) ECSC, as well as the text of Art. 66 (2) subparas. 2–4, and (4)–(6) ECSC.

[81] i.e. Dec. 25/67, as amended, which contains a sort of *de minimis* rule.

1, ECSC), the reference to 'court or tribunal in the Member States' has been replaced by 'court or tribunal in the EC Member States or the EFTA States'.

Thus, apart from the addition of the 'affecting trade' criterion, the adaptations made for EEA purposes to the original text of Articles 65 and 66 ECSC should not have any substantial impact in practice.

3.1.4.2 Conditions of application of Articles 65 and 66 ECSC/1 and 2 Protocol 25 EEA

The coal and steel competition rules apply, within the EC, to the particular products listed in Annex 1 to the ECSC Treaty, and, within the EEA, to the particular products covered by the relevant ECSC–EFTA FTAs. Furthermore, these specific rules apply to undertakings as defined in Article 80 ECSC/3 Protocol 25 EEA, that is, undertakings engaged in the production of coal and steel and undertakings regularly engaged in distribution of those products, other than to domestic consumers or small craft industries.

As regards *restrictive agreements* (Article 65 (1) ECSC/1 (1) Protocol 25 EEA), the ECJ has stated that Articles 85 (1) EEC and 65 (1) ECSC were drafted on the basis of the same common intention.[82] It therefore seems that the principles described above, in Section 3.1.1.2, are also valid in the context of Article 65 (1)/1 (1). Agreements contrary to the latter are automatically void and may not be relied upon in national courts. In addition, Article 65 (2) ECSC/1 (2) Protocol 25 EEA states that certain types of agreement shall be authorized if they fulfil three conditions.[83]

As regards *concentrations* (Article 66 (1) ECSC/2 (1) Protocol 25 EEA), the principle of prior authorization is similar to the one provided for in the Merger Regulation. The ECSC provision, though far less sophisticated than the rules of the Merger Regulation, in fact gives more powers to the surveillance authorities. Any transaction which has the direct or indirect effect of bringing about a concentration between undertakings, of which at least one is covered by Article 80 ECSC/3 Protocol 25 EEA, whether it concerns a single product or a number of different products, and whether it is made by way of merger, acquisition of shares, parts, or assets, loan, contract, or other means of control, must have prior authorization. The concept of 'control' is defined in Decision 24/54 (listed in point 14 of Annex XIV EEA). Furthermore, as seen above, Article 66 (3) ECSC/2 (3) Protocol 25 EEA (implemented by Decision 25/67) exempts certain concentrations from the prior authorization requirement.

As regards *abuse of dominant position* (Article 66 (7) ECSC/2 (4) Protocol 25

[82] Case 13/60 *Geitling* [1962] ECR 83.

[83] Specialization, joint-buying, and joint-selling agreements shall be authorized: if they make substantial improvements in production or distribution; if they are essential to achieve those results and are not more restrictive than necessary; and if they are not liable to give the parties power to determine prices, or control or restrict the production or marketing, of a substantial part of the products, or to shield them from effective competition.

EEA), though worded in a slightly different manner from Article 86 EEC/54 EEA, gives rise in practice to the same analysis as under the EEC Treaty. Therefore, the principles described above, in subsection 3.1.2.2, should also be valid in the context of Article 66 (7) ECSC/2 (4) Protocol 25 EEA.

3.2 Secondary legislation

The secondary competition legislation is listed in Annex XIV EEA. The Annex is divided, by matters, into nine chapters (A to I), within which the Community acts are arranged in a chronological order. These chapters are the following:

A. merger control;
B. exclusive dealing agreements;
C. patent licensing agreements;
D. specialization and research and development agreements;
E. franchising agreements;
F. know-how licensing agreements;
G. transport;
H. public undertakings;
I. coal and steel.

Annex XIV EEA enumerates the Merger Regulation, all the group exemptions, the competition regulations in the field of transport, the two Telecommunications Directives (terminal equipment and telecommunications services), and the decisions in the coal and steel sector.

In addition, the Annex also lists, at the end, the so-called 'non-binding *acquis*',[84] that is, the different notices issued by the Commission such as the *de minimis* Notice and the Notices on commercial agents, on subcontracting, on restrictions ancillary to mergers, etc.

3.2.1 Adaptations for EEA purposes

As in the other annexes to the EEA Agreement, Annex XIV applies the so-called 'reference technique' explained in Section 4 of Chapter II above. However, with a view to safeguarding the legal certainty which is particularly important in the competition sector, the negotiators felt it necessary not to rely upon the automatic system of horizontal adaptations provided for in Protocol 1 EEA, but rather to make detailed sectoral and specific adaptations so that the readers of the regulations could easily 'consolidate' the texts.

The sectoral adaptations, at the beginning of the annex, concern a certain

[84] See explanations on this term in Ch. II, s. 4.1.

number of standard terms which appear throughout the EC acts and which could not be used as such in an EEA context, such as 'Commission', 'common market', or 'trade between Member States'. The same goes for references to the articles of the EEC or ECSC Treaty.

Those terms not covered by sectoral adaptations are adapted specifically within each EC act, following the method described in Section 4.2.3 of Chapter II above. The purpose here is not to describe all these adaptations, which actually, though detailed, have been drafted in a relatively clear manner. Four issues, however, merit being pointed out.

A first particularity is that, due to the two pillar system and the rules of Protocol 21 EEA which specifically empower the surveillance authorities to enforce the EEA competition rules, some of the regulations listed in Annex XIV EEA have been split between substantive rules (which remain in Annex XIV EEA) and procedural rules, which are referred to in Protocol 21 EEA and then reproduced in Protocol 4 to the ESA/Court Agreement. This splitting takes the form of a reference, in the 'chapeau' sentence above the specific adaptations, to certain articles only e.g.: 'The provisions of Articles 1 to 5 of the Regulation shall, for the purposes of the present Agreement, be read with the following adaptations:' instead of using the standard sentence 'The provisions of the Regulation shall . . .'.

Such splitting has occurred in the following three instances:

- the Merger Regulation 4064/89 (splitting between substance Articles 1–5, which remain in Annex XIV EEA, and procedural Articles 6–25, which are referred to in Protocol 21 EEA);
- the Inland Transport Regulation 1017/68 (splitting between substance Articles 1–5 and 7–9, in Annex XIV, and procedural Articles 6 and 10–31, in Protocol 21 EEA); and
- the Maritime Transport Regulation 4056/86 (splitting between substance section I, in Annex XIV EEA, and procedural section II, in Protocol 21 EEA).

A second particularity is that the transitional provisions, concerning existing or already notified agreements, contained in the different group exemptions have been declared not applicable in the EEA context.[85] This is due to the fact that these instances are taken care of by the transitional rules of Protocol 21 EEA (notably Articles 7, 11, and 12). There are also, in the transport field, in the Telecommunications Directives, and in the coal and steel decisions, provisions which are declared not applicable, but this is due to other reasons involving the non-applicability in the EEA context of typically internal EC provisions (e.g. decision-making or provisions on entry into force).

A third particularity is that Annex XIV EEA does not list the so-called 'enabling Regulations' whereby the EC Council enables the Commission to adopt group

[85] This concerns Arts. 7 of Reg. 1983/83, 15 of Reg. 1984/83, 7–9 of Reg. 123/85, 4 (4) and 6–8 of Reg. 2349/84, 4 (4) of Reg. 417/85, 7 (4) of Reg. 418/85, 6 (4) of Reg. 4087/88, and 4 (5) and 8–10 of Reg. 556/89.

exemptions.[86] This is due to the fact that these regulations have been considered by the negotiators as belonging to internal Community decision-making procedure and being therefore irrelevant for the EEA.

A fourth particularity is that Annex XIV EEA, as it stands at the entry into force of the EEA Agreement, does not list any of the three group exemptions in the field of air transport which were in force at the time when Annex XIV was drafted (i.e. Regulations 82/91, 83/92, and 84/91). There is a merely technical reason for this: as these regulations were due to expire on 31 December 1992, i.e. before the expected date of entry into force of the EEA Agreement, and be replaced by new group exemptions, the negotiators felt that it would be more logical simply to take over the new regulations. The best evidence of this intention is that they listed in Protocol 21 EEA the connected procedural regulations in the air transport sector.[87] However, this was counting without the slight problems which emerged on the way concerning both the ratification of the Agreement (one year's delay) and the adoption on time of the new replacing regulations.[88]

This combination of negotiators' over-confidence and the uncertainties of life resulted in a situation where, at the entry into force of the EEA, the surveillance authorities will formally have the powers to apply the competition rules to the air transport sector (Protocol 21 EEA), but there will be no group exemptions available for the economic operators concerned (Annex XIV EEA is empty in that respect). This will be so until the new air transport regulations, listed in the Additional Package of new *acquis*, finally enter into force in the EEA. However, in practice, it is likely that in the mean time the Commission and ESA will not apply Article 53 (1) and (3) EEA too strictly to agreements in the field of air transport which would otherwise have been covered by the new group exemptions. This should be all the more true since there is, in the regulations, a retroactivity clause in favour of existing agreements already complying with the provisions of the group exemption.[89]

Another interesting issue is the coexistence of the EEA competition rules (notably the powers of the Commission and ESA in the field of air transport) and the specific competition rules provided for in the air transport Agreement concluded in 1992 between the Community, Norway, and Sweden (so-called 'Trilateral Agreement').[90] This Agreement, which extends the 'open skies' *acquis* to Norway and Sweden, contains, contrary to the EEA Agreement, the most recently adopted group exemptions, but also contains a 'self-destruction' clause under which, once a

[86] e.g. Reg. 19/65 (exclusive dealing agreements) and Reg. 2821/71 (specialization and R. & D.).

[87] See Regs. 3975/87 and 4261/88, listed respectively in points 13 and 14 of Art. 3 (1) of Protocol 21 EEA.

[88] In fact, two of the three group exemptions were prolonged until the end of June 1993; one was then replaced by Reg. 1617/93, while the other one (Reg. 83/91) was again prolonged until the end of 1993 (see Reg. 1618/93) and was then replaced by Reg. 3652/93.

[89] See Art. 7 (2) of Reg. 1617/93 and Art. 15 (2) of Reg. 3652/93.

[90] The original Trilateral Agreement entered into force on 4 July 1992 (see *OJ* L 200 (18 July 1992), 20) and was amended in 1993 so as to incorporate the 'third liberalization package' on civil aviation (see *OJ* L 212 (23 Aug. 1993), 17; the amended Agreement entered into force on 16 Aug. 1993).

matter of the Trilateral Agreement becomes fully covered by the EEA Agreement, the latter takes precedence. The question could therefore arise whether the procedural regulations of the Trilateral Agreement will be superseded by those of the EEA at its entry into force or whether they will 'survive' until the EEA fully integrates the whole competition *acquis* (i.e. the two new group exemptions also).

3.2.2 The new EC legislation (adopted after 31 July 1991)

Annex XIV EEA only integrates the *acquis communautaire* adopted until the cut-off date agreed upon during the negotiations, i.e. 31 July 1991. The relevant *acquis* adopted in between that date and the entry into force of the EEA Agreement has been put in an Additional Package to be adopted by the EEA Joint Committee after the EEA comes into effect. In the field of competition, six regulations or decisions and four 'non-binding' acts have been adopted in the EC since 31 July 1991, namely:

- the insurance group exemption (Regulation 3932/92);[91]
- the regulation extending the scope of four existing group exemptions to cover also certain types of JVs (Regulation 151/93);[92]
- the two air transport group exemptions (Regulations 1617/93 and 3652/93) and the extension of the procedural regulation to cover national transport also (Regulation 2410/92);[93]
- the coal and steel decision increasing the *de minimis* provisions concerning the exemption of prior authorization of concentrations (Decision 3654/91/ECSC);[94]
- the clarification concerning motor vehicle intermediaries, the so-called 'beer Notice', the national courts Notice, and the Notice on co-operative JVs.[95]

As regards the last item, 'non-binding' acts, it is envisaged that these acts should no longer formally be listed in Annex XIV. Since it is up to ESA to issue corresponding notices, it must simply be relied upon to issue the relevant notices each time the Commission does so. This solution should be indicated in an explanatory text to be inserted at the end of Annex XIV EEA. Furthermore, as explained above, the enabling regulations adopted after the cut-off date have been left out as being irrelevant for EEA purposes.[96]

[91] *OJ* L 398 (31 Dec. 1992), 7.

[92] *OJ* L 21 (29 Jan. 1993), 8.

[93] *OJ* l 155 (26 June 1992), 18, *OJ* L 333 (31 Dec. 1993), 37, and *OJ* L 240 (24 Aug. 1992), 18.

[94] *OJ* L 348 (17 Dec. 1991), 12.

[95] Respectively, *OJ* C 329 (18 Dec. 1991), 20, *OJ* C 121 (13 May 1992), 2, *OJ* C 39 (13 Feb. 1993), 6, and *OJ* C 43 (16 Feb. 1993), 2.

[96] This is the case notably concerning Reg. 479/92 authorizing the Commission to make group exemptions in the field of liner shipping companies (*OJ* L 55 (29 Feb. 1992), 3). The Commission has already prepared a draft proposal for a group exemption and begun consultations with interested circles preceding the adoption which is foreseen in early 1994.

4. PARTICULAR ASPECTS OF THE EEA SUBSTANTIVE COMPETITION RULES

4.1 Consequences in the field of competition of the limited product coverage of the EEA Agreement

As explained in Section 1 of Chapter III above, as a result of Article 8 (3) EEA, combined with the fact that there is no express specification to the contrary in the field of competition, the EEA competition rules do not apply to products not falling within the product coverage of the EEA Agreement as defined in Article 8 (3), regardless of their origin. Therefore, the EEA competition provisions do not apply to the products belonging to HS chapters 1–24, save for a certain number of processed agricultural products enumerated in Tables I and II of Protocol 3 EEA.[97] In practice, all basic agricultural products are excluded from the coverage (e.g. meat, vegetables, sugar, tobacco, but also a number of processed products such as fruit juice, ice cream, or cigarettes).

Within the EC, agricultural products (i.e. those listed in Annex II to the EEC Treaty) benefit from a treatment apart. Article 42 of the EEC Treaty tries to reconcile the aims of the common agricultural policy (involving market organization) with those of the competition policy. Therefore, under Regulation 26/62,[98] the competition rules (Articles 85 and 86 EEC) apply to production and trade in agricultural products, in so far as their application does not impede the functioning of national market organizations or does not jeopardize the attainment of the objectives of the common agricultural policy. However, Regulation 26/62 has voluntarily not been integrated in the EEA Agreement.

The conclusion is that, as regards these particular products, the EEA competition rules will not apply and the surveillance authorities will have no competence in that respect. The legal situation will therefore continue to be the same as before the entry into force of the EEA Agreement, that is, application only of the national rules of the EFTA countries and possible extraterritorial application of the Community rules on competition where a restrictive agreement or practice has effects, even if only potential, within the common market. Moreover, the Community will still be in a position to rely on its trade remedies, such as anti-dumping measures. Finally, it should be noted that Protocol 25 (coal and steel) only applies to originating goods (see Article 8(2) EEA which refers to Article 27).

[97] For more detailed indications of the kind of products falling outside the scope of the Agreement, see Ch. III, s. 1.2.2, as well as Annex E to this book. Moreover, it should be noted that, due to problems in finalizing certain appendices to Protocol 3 EEA, the Parties have agreed instead to continue to apply Protocols 2 to the different bilateral 1972 FTAs. Should this solution also materialize for product coverage purposes, this would mean that the coverage of the EEA would, until Protocol 3 EEA is finalized, slightly differ from one EFTA country to another, since the lists of products in the Protocols 2 FTAs are not totally identical. It is however believed that, pending the finalization of these appendices, Protocol 3 EEA (notably its Article 1 and Tables I and II) will nevertheless apply from the entry into force of the EEA as far as product coverage is concerned.

[98] *OJ* 30 (20 Apr. 1962), 62 (Special Edition 1959–62: 129).

4.2 The particular case of fisheries (Protocol 9 EEA)

As explained in Chapter III, the sector of fish and other marine products is submitted to a special regime within the EEA (Protocol 9 and a joint declaration). Article 4 (2) deals, to a limited extent, with competition in the field of fisheries. It states that: 'Legislation relating to the market organization in the fisheries sector shall be adjusted so as not to distort competition.' The addressees of this provision are clearly the Contracting Parties themselves, i.e. the legislation makers, not the private parties submitted to such legislation. Private practices or agreements are therefore not directly caught by this provision.

The fact that the responsibility of avoiding distortions of competition lies with the Contracting Parties themselves is confirmed by Article 4 (3) of Protocol 9 EEA, which reads: 'The Contracting Parties shall endeavour to ensure conditions of competition which enable the other Contracting Parties to refrain from the application of anti-dumping measures and countervailing duties.' It is therefore up to the Parties to take the necessary measures internally; both legislative measures and, pursuant to the wider wording of Article 4 (3), perhaps through enforcement of national competition rules, so as to ensure that competition is not distorted.

Regarding market organizations, a joint declaration states the principles to be followed by the EFTA States in their legislation, i.e. the principles laid down in the *acquis communautaire* on common organization of market. The next paragraph of the Declaration introduces a presumption of compatibility with the *acquis* in favour of a national legislation which would contain at least the three following elements:

- the legislation on producers' organizations reflects the principles of the *acquis* on establishment on the producers' initiative, freedom to become and cease to be a member, and absence of dominant position, unless necessary to attain objectives similar to those of Article 39 EEC;
- compliance with the principles of Article 7 of Regulation 3687/91 in case of extension of the rules of the producers' organizations to non-members; and
- compliance with title III of Regulation 3687/91 as regards rules on interventions to support prices.

The EEA competition rules in the fishery sector look more like a classical intergovernmental arrangement. The remedy in case of distortion of competition is clearly indicated as being the classical trade measures (such as anti-dumping and countervailing duties), as well as, under Article 6 of Protocol 9 EEA, raising the issue in the EEA Joint Committee and the possible recourse to Article 114 EEA on rebalancing measures.

4.3 Anti-dumping measures in the EEA (Article 26 EEA)

The reward for introducing strict competition rules in the EEA is Article 26, which forbids intra-EEA anti-dumping measures, countervailing duties, and other trade measures, 'unless otherwise specified'.

Protocol 13 EEA states what 'otherwise specified' means; that is, the interdiction of intra-EEA anti-dumping 'is limited to areas covered by the provisions of this [EEA] Agreement and in which the Community acquis is fully integrated'. In addition to cases where the *acquis* is not 'fully integrated' (e.g. because of specific transitional arrangements or failure to implement the Agreement properly), there are at least three instances where anti-dumping or other trade measures would still be possible between EEA partners:

- in general, due to the absence of common commercial policy in the EEA, measures to avoid circumvention in the EEA of trade measures adopted against third countries (like anti-dumping measures, countervailing duties, or measures against illicit commercial practices attributable to third countries) (see Protocol 13 EEA);
- measures concerning products falling outside the scope of the EEA Agreement (such as agricultural products; see Article 8 (3) EEA and explanations in Chapter III);
- measures in the fisheries sector towards a Contracting Party which would not ensure competition conditions which enable the others to refrain from anti-dumping (see Article 4 (3) of Protocol 9 EEA). In this context, it should be noted that there are agreed minutes stating that, before the EEA entry into force, interested Parties shall examine whether, irrespective of Protocol 13 EEA, the conditions of Article 26 EEA (prohibition of intra-EEA anti-dumping measure) apply in the fisheries sector, in other words whether the competition conditions are satisfactory enough that the Parties are already at that stage of the opinion that they will refrain from taking anti-dumping measures.

4.4 Jurisdiction over undertakings located outside the EC/EEA

Known also under the misleading title of 'extraterritorial' application of competition rules, the jurisdiction of the Commission over undertakings located outside EC territory has given rise to a lot of discussion, in particular after the famous *Woodpulp* Commission Decision and Court judgment.[99]

This question of jurisdiction was nothing new in the field of anti-trust as it had already been addressed first in the USA. As early as in 1945, in the *Alcoa* case,[100] the so-called 'effects doctrine' was admitted. The case concerned an international cartel of non-American producers which met abroad and agreed to limit production and stabilize prices notably in their exportations to US territory (i.e. facts very similar to those of the *Woodpulp* case). The Court stated: 'any state may impose liabilities, even upon persons not within its allegiance, for conduct outside the borders which

[99] Commission Decision in *OJ* L 85 (26 Mar. 1985), 1; ECJ Joint Cases 89/85 and others *Woodpulp I* [1988] ECR 5193.

[100] *Alcoa* 148 F. 3d 416 (2d Cir. 1945).

the state reprehends . . . the agreements were unlawful, though made abroad, if they were intended to affect imports (in the United States) and did affect them.' The 'effects doctrine' was later on also adopted in other countries, such as in Article 98.2 of the German Antitrust Law,[101] or in the jurisprudence of certain European countries.

In its *Woodpulp* Decision, the Commission said that Article 85 EEC applies to 'restrictive practices which may affect trade between Member States even if the undertakings . . . are established or have their headquarters outside the Community, and even if the restrictive practices in question also affect markets outside the EEC. . . . The effect of the agreements . . . within the EEC was . . . not only substantial but intended, and was the primary and direct result of the agreements and practices.'

In the *Woodpulp* judgment the ECJ first noted that the direct sale by foreign woodpulp producers to EC purchasers and the price competition between those producers for winning orders from EC customers constitutes 'competition within the common market' and that concerted decisions on prices to be charged within the EC and the putting into effect of such decisions was 'restricting competition within the common market'. The Court then stated that:

> The decisive factor is therefore the place where it [the agreement] is implemented. The producers in this case implemented their pricing agreement within the common market. It is immaterial in that respect whether or not they had recourse to subsidiaries, agents, sub-agents, or branches within the Community in order to make their contracts with purchasers within the Community. Accordingly the Community's jurisdiction to apply its competition rules to such conduct is covered by the territoriality principle as universally recognized in public international law.

The ECJ did not fully apply the 'effects doctrine' but still referred to the fact that the agreement had been 'implemented' within the EC. As regards the ancillary question of whether the EC–Finland FTA applied, the Court said that, since it was not just EC–Finland trade which was affected, the FTA Joint Committee could not have adopted 'appropriate measures' to remedy the situation and thus that the Commission had rightly applied Article 85 EEC also regarding EC–Finland trade.

The entry into force of the EEA competition rules will in fact supersede the use of the 'effects doctrine' towards companies established in EFTA countries since the EEA provisions will give both the Commission and ESA, within their respective fields of competence under Article 56 EEA, jurisdiction over companies located outside their strictly limited EC or EFTA territory. In addition, the EEA rules will empower the surveillance authorities to conduct inquiries and enforce pecuniary obligations imposed on companies located within the EEA.

However, the use of the 'effects doctrine' by the Community should still be

[101] Art. 98.2 GWB says in substance that the German anti-trust law applies to all competition restrictions having effect within Germany, even where these restrictions result from acts accomplished outside German territory.

possible in areas falling outside the scope of the EEA (for instance regarding agricultural products). The reasoning could here be similar to that followed above as concerns the remaining possibilities of adopting intra-EEA anti-dumping and other trade measures.

Another question is whether the 'effects doctrine' could be used when applying the EEA competition rules. This should in principle be possible, since Article 6 EEA (on interpretation of EEA rules in conformity with ECJ jurisprudence) makes applicable to Article 53 EEA the *Woodpulp* jurisprudence attached to Article 85 EEC. This interpretation could be confirmed by the fact that the so-called 'Japanese Notice' has been listed in Annex XIV (point 22). In this Notice, the Commission points out to those concerned (e.g. producers established outside the Community) that Article 85 EEC prohibits restrictive practices or agreements regardless of where the seat of the companies involved is situated as long as they have an effect within EC territory. A similar notice will be issued by ESA after the EEA comes into force which should target not only 'Japanese goods' but more widely 'third country goods'.

5. ENFORCEMENT BODIES AND ATTRIBUTION OF CASES

The real effectiveness of a law may best be evaluated by looking at the means it has been given to attain its aims, in other words how strictly and efficiently the law in question can be and actually is enforced. A developed and courageous way to deal with the matter in the international context is to entrust the enforcement task to an independent supranational authority, with judicial control. This is the model developed in the Community over more than thirty years and this is what was agreed upon for the EEA through the so-called 'two pillar' system and the creation of ESA and the EFTA Court on the EFTA side.[102] The classical possibility of using threat and safeguards is not absent from the EEA but it really comes as a last resort.

In the field of competition, the importance of a genuine enforcement mechanism is underlined in the objectives of the EEA Agreement; Article 1 (2) (*e*) requires the setting up of a system ensuring that the competition rules 'are equally respected'.

5.1 The 'two pillar' system

5.1.1 Two enforcement bodies and the 'one-stop shop' principle

As briefly explained at the beginning of this chapter, the Parties wanted the competition rules to be properly applied and enforced, while at the same time

[102] The judicial system of the EEA is also based on two pillars, the ECJ being one (final review of the Commission decisions after the EC Court of First Instance) and the EFTA Court being the other (review of ESA decisions) (see Art. 108 (2) EEA and part IV of the EFTA/Court Agreement). For further explanations of the role of the EFTA Court, see Ch. II, s. 5.2.2, above.

safeguarding their respective autonomy. The two questions which kept the negotiators busy for more than a year were who should enforce the EEA competition and how to divide the competencies.

Different models could be imagined: to ask each EFTA State to entrust the task to its national surveillance body; to create a joint EC–EFTA surveillance body; to have two different bodies, i.e. the Commission and an EFTA body ('two pillar' model); perhaps to add a 'joint linking body' between the pillars.

The negotiators finally opted for the so-called 'two pillar' solution, i.e. two surveillance authorities, the Commission and ESA, with equivalent enforcement powers. The uniform interpretation of the EEA rules would ultimately be guaranteed by the two Courts (ECJ and EFTA Court), combined with a system to safeguard EEA homogeneity (Articles 105 *et seq.* EEA).

Having two enforcement bodies would inevitably bring the risk of double competence. This question already existed in the Community (division of competence between EC Member States and Commission) and was solved in Articles 85 and 86 EEA through the 'affecting trade' criterion and in the Merger Regulation through the use of a turnover criterion. The EEA negotiators agreed that, on principle, an individual competition case should be allocated to only one of the two surveillance authorities and that the decision on the case should be valid throughout the EEA. These principles are combined in a concept already used in the context of the Merger Regulation, the so-called 'one-stop shop' principle.

5.1.2 Attribution of cases

For allocating individual competition cases to the right authority, what was needed was a clear-cut criterion which would give the Commission and ESA, the EC and EFTA States, and the economic operators enough legal certainty, while not being too arbitrary.

The solution normally used in the EEA context for the surveillance of States (the Commission deals with matters related to EC Member States and ESA with those related to EFTA States) could obviously not be used for competition cases which concern the behaviour of economic operators and, by definition, suppose that inter-State trade is affected, i.e. that not only one State is concerned. Moreover, the playing-field of the EEA competition rules is the entire EEA market, the very purpose of the rules being to safeguard effective competition there, and not within EC or EFTA markets taken separately.

Different criteria for allocating the competition cases were envisaged: the formal seat of the company (but there are cases where there is no such seat within the EEA and, even if there were a seat, there would have been a risk of 'shopping', whereby the firms would actually choose the jurisdiction under which they prefer to fall); the effective place of business (but it is sometimes difficult to determine, and, again, it might be located outside the EEA); the market share (but defining a market, especially if used as a jurisdiction rule, may be problematic); the turnover (but what definition of turnover, and what amount should be used?).

The rules on attribution of cases can be found in Article 56 EEA concerning restrictive practices and abuse of dominant position and in Article 57 (2) EEA concerning merger control. As regards cases falling under Articles 53 and 54 EEA, it was finally decided to use an 'affecting trade' criterion combined with a turnover-related criterion, expressed in percentage of turnover achieved in the EFTA territory. In addition, the notion of 'appreciable' effect on trade or competition as understood in the *de minimis* Notice of the Commission has been linked to the 'affecting trade' criterion. As regards merger cases, the rules are more clear-cut, as they refer to the present turnover thresholds of the Merger Regulation.

The original solution agreed upon by the negotiators in November 1991 was simpler[103] than the revised version now contained in the EEA Agreement. This first version was amended after the ECJ made it understood in its Opinion 1/91 that the rules concerning the attribution of cases would not be compatible with the EEC Treaty.

Therefore, Article 56 EEA was renegotiated in early 1992, the whole question being how to leave totally untouched the existing competences of the Commission under Articles 85 and 86 EEC. The problem with the original version was that, although to a very limited extent, the Commission was giving up some of its powers to deal with cases which affect trade between EC Member States (Articles 85 and 86 EEC). In cases falling under the EEA rules, the Commission, when assigned a case, intended always to make a 'double-check', meaning that it would always have checked that neither the Community nor the EEA competition rules were infringed.[104] However, when ESA had been assigned a case under the turnover percentage rules, it would have assessed the case under the EEA rules only (i.e. no 'double-check') and could have cleared EEA-wide an agreement possibly infringing the EEC or ECSC rules.

The outcome of the renegotiations was that, while keeping the turnover percentage criterion (although it is more or less emptied from its substance), in paragraph 1 (*c*) of Article 56 a reference was added to cases affecting trade between EC Member States, and instead of the review clause originally planned concerning the turnover percentage, the cases which are *de minimis* within the EC were assigned to ESA.

The ECJ accepted this solution in its Opinion 1/92 and stated that, under the

[103] Under this original solution, Art. 53 EEA cases (restrictive practices) would have been attributed according to the following principles: '(a) individual cases where only trade between EFTA State is affected shall be decided upon by [ESA]; (b) [ESA] decides, as provided for [in Art. 58, Protocols 21 and 23, and Annex XIV] on cases where the turnover of the undertakings concerned in the territory of the EFTA States equals 33% or more of their turnover in the territory covered by this Agreement; (c) the EC Commission decides on the other cases, taking into account [Art. 58, Protocols 21 and 23, and Annex XIV].' The position for Art. 54 cases (dominant position) was the same as the present version. Finally, there was a review clause under which, 'In order to ensure that [ESA] has an adequate number of individual cases to handle, the Contracting Parties agree to review the percentages referred to in paragraph 1.'

[104] The Commission will still make this 'double-check' under the present rules, as it results from a joint declaration under which 'the implementation of EEA competition rules, in cases falling within the

EEC competition rules and its implementing measures, the Community is empowered to conclude international agreements in the competition field, this necessarily implying that the EC may accept rules as to the sharing of the respective competences, 'provided that those rules do not change the nature of the powers of the Community and its institutions as conceived in the Treaty'.

These modified rules on attribution of cases are explained in detail in the sections below. It should be noted that, in the awareness that these rules might no longer be that clear-cut, it was agreed that, even if the undertakings are in principle requested to notify the right surveillance authority, there will be no negative consequences if they choose wrongly. In such situations, the case will be automatically transmitted to the responsible authority. This issue is further discussed in Sections 7.2.2 and 7.3.2.

Furthermore, in order to facilitate the reading of the explanations given below, it is useful briefly to define some terms used during the negotiations:

- 'pure cases' are the competition cases where only trade within the EC or within the EFTA territory is affected;
- 'mixed cases' are the competition cases where trade between the Community and one or more EFTA States is affected (regardless whether trade between EC Member States is affected or not);
- '1+1 cases' are a subcategory of 'mixed cases' where trade between EC Member States is not affected, but only trade between the Community and one or more EFTA States;
- '*de minimis* cases' are the competition cases which, within the Community, are covered by the *de minimis* Notice of the Commission.

5.1.2.1 Article 53 EEA cases

The rules for attributing the individual cases falling under Article 53 EEA are the following.

Pure cases:

- 'EFTA pure cases', where only trade between EFTA States is affected will be dealt with by ESA (Article 56 (1) (*a*) EEA);
- 'EC pure cases', i.e. those where only trade between EC Member States is affected, do not fall under the EEA Agreement, but will be dealt with by the EC Commission solely on the basis of Articles 85 and 86 of the EEC Treaty.

Mixed cases:

- 'mixed cases' where both trade between EC Member States and trade between the EC and one or more EFTA States is affected will be dealt with by the Commission (Article 56 (1) (*c*) EEA);
- those mixed cases which are '*de minimis* cases' from the EC point of view, i.e.

responsibility of the EC Commission, is based on the existing Community competences, supplemented by the provisions contained in the [EEA] Agreement'.

whose effects on trade and competition within the Community are not appreciable,[105] will be dealt with by ESA (Article 56 (3) EEA);

- '1 + 1 cases' (i.e. trade between EC Member States not affected) will be handled by ESA, if at least 33 per cent of the turnover of the undertakings[106] concerned is coming from EFTA territory, regardless of whether the effects on competition within the EC are or are not appreciable (Article 56 (1) (*b*) EEA);
- ESA should also deal with '1 + 1 cases' where less than 33 per cent of the turnover comes from EFTA territory, but where the effects on competition within the EC are not appreciable (Article 56 (1) (*b*) combined with 56 (3) EEA).

With regard to agreements or practices which concern both products covered by the EEA agreement and products falling outside its scope (Article 8 (3) EEA), it would seem obvious that, in the context of attribution of cases, the calculation of market share for defining the appreciable effects on Community trade or competition should take into account also those products which do not fall within the EEA scope. The reason for this is that the EEA Agreement cannot affect the competence of the EC institutions as regards the application of the EEC and ECSC competition rules.

5.1.2.2 Article 54 EEA cases

The rules for attributing the individual cases falling under Article 54 EEA are the following:

- cases where the dominance exists only within the EFTA territory will be dealt with by ESA (Article 56 (2), first sentence, EEA);
- cases where the dominance exists only within the Community will be dealt with by the Commission (Article 56 (2), first sentence, EEA);
- cases where dominance exists within both EC and EFTA territories, the rules concerning mixed cases stated above apply (Article 56 (2), last sentence, EEA)

The latter rule has the original effect of bringing into the context of dominant position, for the purposes of attribution of EEA cases, the *de minimis* rule, which, in the EC, applies only to Article 85 EEC, not to Article 86 EEC.

5.1.2.3 Merger cases

The mergers falling under paragraph 1 of Article 57 EEA, that is, where a dominant position would be created or strengthened in the EEA territory or in a substantial

[105] Under Agreed Minutes ad Art. 56 (3), 'the word "appreciable" . . . is understood to have the meaning it has in the Commission Notice of 3 September 1986 on agreements of minor importance' (op. cit. in s. 3.1.1.2 n. 24; see also the explanations given on the substantive conditions for its application).

[106] The terms 'turnover' and 'undertaking' are, for the purposes of Art. 56, defined in Protocol 22 EEA. The definition of 'turnover' is inspired by the definition contained in Art. 5 (1) and (3) of the Merger Regulation (4064/89).

part of it, as a result of which effective competition would be significantly impeded, will be attributed under the following rules:

- the Commission will be responsible for merger cases where the thresholds of the EC Merger Regulation are met (Article 57 (2) (*a*) EEA);[107]
- ESA will be responsible for other cases where thresholds identical to those of the Merger Regulation (point 1 of Annex XIV EEA) are met in EFTA territory (Article 57 (2) (*b*) EEA). Moreover, the ESA competence is without prejudice to the concurrent competence of the EC Member States (Article 57 (2) (*b*) EEA).

Article 57 (2) EEA means that even if some 'EFTA undertakings' (undertakings which mainly operate from an EFTA State), reaching the total combined turnover of five billion ECU, are merging, the Commission will be competent to decide on the compatibility of the merger if at least two of these 'EFTA undertakings' reach the 250 million ECU threshold in the Community. Even if such a merger results in a dominant position within EFTA territory alone, the Commission will still be competent (contrary to what would have happened under Article 56 (2) EEA). Therefore, in practice, the great majority of the mergers falling under the EEA Agreement will be decided upon by the Commission, at least until the thresholds are lowered.[108]

In addition, the 'one-stop shop' principle does not apply between ESA and the EC Member States, meaning that the latter fully retain their respective national competences, concurrently with those of ESA.

6. PROCEDURAL RULES

When assessing individual competition cases, the two pillars (Commission and ESA) will follow the same procedural rules. In the EEA, undertakings will have the same opportunities as in the EC to notify their agreements for getting an individual exemption, to complain about anti-competitive behaviour, etc. The pillars will also have the same investigating and decision-making powers.

The basis for this is Protocol 21 EEA, which states, in its Article 1, that, on the

[107] i.e. the combined aggregate world-wide turnover of all the undertakings concerned is more than five billion ECU, each of at least two of the undertakings concerned has an aggregate Community-wide turnover of more than 250 million ECU, and the impact of the merger is not mainly national (i.e. the undertakings concerned do not each achieve more than two-thirds of their aggregate Community-wide turnover within one and the same EC Member State).

[108] Art. 1 (3) of the Merger Regulation provides for a review of the thresholds by the end of 1994. This amendment has been postponed by the Commission until 1996 (see n. 70 above). The specific adaptation in Annex XIV EEA which declares this Article not applicable was made because the Article refers to an internal EC decision-making procedure not relevant in the EEA. It does not mean that the possible modification of the threshold resulting from such a review should not also be reflected in the EEA context. Such modification should certainly be considered as 'relevant *acquis*' and be integrated in the Agreement following the EEA decision-making procedure.

one hand, the Community shall ensure that the Commission will follow, when applying the EEA competition rules, the same procedures as when it applies the EEC and ECSC Treaties, and, on the other hand, the EFTA States shall, in an agreement between themselves, entrust ESA 'with equivalent powers and similar functions to those of the EC Commission . . . for the application of the competition rules of the [EEC] Treaty and the [ECSC] Treaty'. Protocol 21 also lists, in Article 3, the specific EC procedural acts reflecting the powers and functions of the EC Commission which ESA also needs to have, and obliges the Contracting Parties, each time these EC acts are amended, to amend the list of Article 3 accordingly so that ESA 'will be entrusted simultaneously with equivalent powers' (Article 2).[109]

The obligation put on the EFTA States in Protocol 21 EEA has been implemented through Protocol 4 to the ESA/Court Agreement. This Protocol contains the procedural rules which ESA will have to follow when applying the EEA competition rules. It reproduces in full, but adapted to the EEA context, the relevant EC procedural regulations of a general nature, the particular rules in the fields of transport, merger control, and coal and steel, as well as the transitional rules. In general, to each EC regulation corresponds one chapter of Protocol 4. The following have thus been reproduced in Protocol 4 to the ESA/Court Agreement:

- Regulation 17/62 on the general procedural rules implementing Articles 85 and 86 (chapter II of the Protocol) (hereafter 'Regulation 17');
- Regulation 27/62 on the form, content, and other details concerning applications and notifications (chapter III) (hereafter 'Regulation 27');
- Regulation 99/63 on hearings provided for in Article 19 (1) and (2) of Regulation 17/62 (chapter IV) (hereafter 'Regulation 99); and
- Regulation 2988/74 on limitation periods in proceedings and the enforcement of sanctions under the rules relating to transport and competition (chapter V).

Chapters VI to XII of the Protocol contain the relevant procedural rules in the field of transport (Regulations 1017/68 (Articles 6 and 10–31), 1629/69, 1630/69, 4056/86 (section II), 4260/88, 3975/87, and 4261/88, respectively).[110] Chapters XIII and XIV of the Protocol contain the procedural rules concerning merger control (Regulations 4064/89 (Articles 6–25) and 2367/90, chapter XV the procedural rules in the field of coal and steel (the procedural parts of Articles 65 and 66 ECSC and Decisions 26/54, 715/78, and 379/84), and chapter XVI the different transitional provisions.

The obligation put on the Community in Protocol 21 EEA has been put into practice through Article 7 (1) of the draft Regulation implementing the EEA under which 'the Community rules giving effect to the principles covered by Articles 85 and 86 of the EEC Treaty and Council Regulation (EEC) No 4064/89 . . . shall

[109] However, given the rules on EEA decision-making, such simultaneity could be difficult to achieve in practice (on this question, see Ch. II, s. 6.2, above, in particular n. 49).

[110] On the splitting of certain regulations and articles between procedural and substance provisions see explanations in s. 3.2.1 above. Furthermore, in order to facilitate the comparison of Protocol 4 with the original EC acts, the substantive articles have been quoted but left without text, so that the numbering of articles in the Protocol's chapters follows that of the original regulations.

apply mutatis mutandis,'[111] meaning that the Commission, when applying the EEA competition rules, will follow the procedural rules it already follows within the EC context. Thus, none of the EC procedural regulations will be amended as a consequence of the EEA. The only amendment being made concerns the forms provided for by some of the regulations adopted by the Commission (which are thus easier to amend, see explanations in Section 6.1.3 below).

The competition procedures to be followed by the surveillance authorities when applying the EEA Agreement are described in general terms below. Again, a number of good books, referred to in the Bibliography, explain in detail the EC procedures. Finally, one should always remember that, as explained above in Section 5.1.2, the Commission will for each 'EEA case' make a 'double-check', i.e. assess the case against both Articles 85/86 EEC and 53/54 EEA.

6.1 Procedures for cases falling under Articles 53 and 54 EEA

There are basically four ways for an Article 53/54 procedure to start:

- an application for negative clearance under which undertakings wish to get formal assurance that their agreements or practices do not fall under the prohibition contained in Articles 53 (1) or 54 EEA (Article 2 Regulation 17);[112]
- a notification for obtaining an individual exemption under Article 53 (3) EEA, that is, to get a decision by the surveillance authority that the notified agreement or practice, although containing elements which, in principle, would be prohibited, leads also to such benefits that it can be exempted from the prohibition of Article 53 (1) EEA (Article 4 Regulation 17). Certain group exemptions provide for a so-called 'opposition procedure' which also supposes a notification;
- a complaint about an infringement of Articles 53 or 54 EEA brought by a State or any natural or legal person claiming a legitimate interest (Article 3 (2) Regulation 17);
- an ex officio procedure launched by a surveillance authority which suspects that there is an infringement of Article 53 or 54 EEA (Article 3 (1) Regulation 17). The authority may also make an inquiry into a particular economic sector (Article 12 Regulation 17).

6.1.1 Applications and notifications

Undertakings wishing to obtain a negative clearance or an individual exemption or benefit from the 'opposition procedure' under certain group exemptions have to

[111] Op. cit. n. 25.

[112] For practical purposes, the procedural provisions quoted will be those of the EC regulations (Regs. 17, 27, etc.) and not of the chapters of Protocol 4 to the ESA/Court Agreement, keeping in mind that the article numbers of the regulations are the same in the corresponding Protocol's chapters.

notify their agreements to the competent surveillance authority under Article 56 EEA, the Commission or ESA (Article 10 (1) of Protocol 23 EEA).[113]

The undertakings may, at the same time ask for both a negative clearance and, if this should not be granted, an individual exemption. It is not necessary that all the undertakings which are parties to an agreement or a practice submit a notification jointly. It is sufficient for one of them to notify and inform the other parties. If the notification is submitted jointly, the parties have to appoint a joint representative (Article 1 Regulation 27).

Exemptions are granted for a limited period and conditions and obligations may be attached thereto (Article 8 (1) Regulation 17). If an undertaking wants to have an exemption renewed, it shall, before the end of the period of validity of the exemption, apply for its renewal (a simple letter is sufficient) (Article 8 (2) Regulation 17). If, however, the agreement has been amended so that its substance is no longer the same as the one originally exempted, this 'new' agreement should be notified formally.

It is up to the undertakings concerned to decide whether to notify their agreements or practices. Before asking for an individual exemption, it is advisable to check whether the agreement or practice in question could fall under one of the cases listed in Article 4 (2) Regulation 17,[114] could be automatically exempted by the effect of a group exemption, or could benefit from one of the notices giving interpretative guidance for the application of competition rules.[115]

The main advantage of notifying is that, apart from the possibility of getting an exemption, it gives immunity from fines as from the notification date (Article 15 (5) Regulation 17), under the condition, however, that the notification contains all the relevant information concerning the agreement or practice.[116] It should be noted that this benefit concerns only agreements or practices notified in order to obtain an exemption, not those where the undertakings only apply for a negative clearance. Such immunity may, however, be revoked (see Section 6.1.4.6 below).

Five group exemptions[117] set out a so-called 'opposition procedure' under which an agreement which contains 'grey clauses' (i.e. neither expressly prohibited nor permitted by the group exemption in question) may be notified to obtain, after a quick procedure of six months, an exemption. If the surveillance authority does not

[113] However, in cases of error about which authority is competent to deal with the case, see remarks in s. 7.2.2 below.

[114] This Article lists cases where a notification is considered unnecessary, such as agreements between undertakings from one country only and not relating to imports or exports between the Contracting Parties, agreements having as their sole object the development or uniform application of standards or types, or joint R. & D., etc.

[115] See for instance the *de minimis* Notice, the Notices on commercial agents, on subcontracting, etc. (listed at the end of Annex XIV EEA).

[116] See e.g. Commission Decision in *Papiers peints de Belgique* (*OJ* L 237 (29 Aug. 1974), 3), and *AEG* (*OJ* L 117 (30 Apr. 1982), 15).

[117] i.e. the Regulations on specialization (417/85), R. & D. (418/85), patent licensing (2349/84), franchising (4087/88), and know-how licensing (556/89).

react within this period, the agreement is deemed to be exempted under the regulation.

The surveillance authority may revoke or amend its exemption decision in the case of change of the basic facts, breach of a condition or obligation attached to the decision, incorrect information or deceit, or abuse of the exemption (Article 8 (3) Regulation 17). Likewise, the benefit of the group exemption may be withdrawn concerning a particular agreement if it has effects incompatible with the conditions of Article 53 (3) EEA. Such revocation or withdrawal may happen ex officio or under complaint.

6.1.2 Complaints and ex officio procedures

Under Article 3 (2) of Regulation 17, a State or any natural or legal person claiming legitimate interests may lodge a complaint. The natural or legal persons should provide sufficient information supporting the application in order to enable the surveillance authority to assess, *inter alia*, whether the applicant has 'legitimate interests'. Such information includes the identification of the complainant and of his interest in the case, the subject-matter of the complaint, and as much information as possible on the agreement or practice complained about. The complaint should also contain a request for initiation of procedure by the surveillance authority, to establish the existence of an infringement of the rules. If these conditions have been fulfilled, the case should normally be considered as a formal complaint which guarantees certain rights to the applicant, such as participation in the subsequent procedure.[118]

In contrast to notifications, a complaint may be addressed to either of the authorities (Article 10 (1) of Protocol 23 EEA), which shall transmit it to the competent surveillance authority (Article 10 (2)).

Anonymous or otherwise incomplete or informal complaints may lead to the opening of an ex officio procedure. The initiator of the procedure is then formally the surveillance authority itself. The complainant does not, therefore, benefit from the same procedural rights as he would in the case of a formal complaint. The surveillance authority may, in addition, use other means to detect possible infringements, such as information arising from the media, the analysis of a particular economic sector, national authorities, etc.

6.1.3 Forms and language to be used

The use of a particular form is compulsory concerning applications for negative clearance, notifications for individual exemptions, and notification in the context of an 'opposition procedure' provided for in a group exemption.

[118] Apart from the documents containing business secrets, the complainant will in principle receive information concerning the most important steps of procedure, such as requests for information and replies, statement of objections and replies. The complainant may also be heard in writing or orally. If the authority decides to reject the complaint, this can be done either informally or in a more formal way through a letter under Art. 6 of Reg. 99 (so-called 'Article 6 letters'), or even through a decision.

Form A/B is to be used for notifications and applications in Article 53/54 cases, while there are specific forms for land transport, maritime transport (Form MAR) and air transport (Form AER).[119]

For complaints, the use of a particular form is not compulsory, although there exists a Form C (general) and one for complaint in the field of land transport.[120] The use of these forms may be useful as they provide the complainant with a good check-list of what information to give to the surveillance authority.

In the EEA context, as there are two surveillance authorities, there will also be two sets of forms, one issued by each pillar.[121] The old EC forms have been amended in order to add the relevant references and questions concerning the EEA.[122] There will thus be one form for notifications both under the EEC rules and under the EEA rules. The EFTA forms will be identical in substance to the EC forms, with the difference that they do not refer to Articles 85/86 EEC, but only to EEA and ESA/Court Agreement provisions. As they are identical in substance, the forms themselves declare that notifications made using the form of the other pillar are equally valid; however, for 'EC pure cases' the companies are advised to use the EC Form A/B.

As regards the language regime, Article 12 of Protocol 23 EEA gives undertakings the right to choose any official EC or EFTA language when addressing the Commission or ESA. For practical reasons it is, however, advisable to use one of the languages of the authority concerned (and it should be noted that English is the working language of ESA).

The forms are available in the thirteen languages of the EEA. The language the undertaking uses for submitting its application, notification, or complaint to the surveillance authority will govern the subsequent procedure. The supporting documents are to be submitted in their original language, and if that language is not an official language in the Community or EFTA, a translation into such a language is to be attached.

6.1.4 The different procedural steps

Once an Article 53/54 procedure has started following one of the ways indicated

[119] See annexes to Regs. 1629/69, 4260/89, and 4261/89, respectively.

[120] See annex to Reg. 1629/69.

[121] Copies of these forms may be obtained from the Commission, ESA, the national competition authorities of each EC and EFTA State, and the Commission Information Offices in the different countries.

[122] The main amendments have consisted in adding the references to the relevant provisions of the EEA Agreement, protocols, and annex. In the complementary note a text has been added on the purpose of the EEA competition rules and on the Commission and ESA competences to apply the rules, as well as questions concerning the turnover, market shares, effect on trade in relation to EEA as a whole, and EFTA territory. For the purposes of establishing whether the products concerned fall within the EEA scope, the undertakings are also requested to indicate the HS number of the products affected by their agreement. Finally, the number of copies to be supplied has increased to fifteen in the case of Form A/B and twenty-one in the case of Form CO (nine copies shall be supplied when notifying ESA).

above, there may be several steps before it ends, either formally or informally. The authority is under no obligation to close the procedure through a formal decision.

6.1.4.1 Fact-finding procedures

Before deciding on whether the procedure should be formally opened under Article 9 (3) Regulation 17, the surveillance authority will usually need sufficient information to assess whether the case is worth pursuing or not. This information is collected during a so-called 'fact-finding' phase. In certain circumstances, notably when there is a need to avoid a situation of double competence between the surveillance authority and a State, the procedure may be formally initiated before the fact-finding phase (on the initiation of the procedure, see Section 6.1.4.2 below).

The two formal fact-finding means at the disposal of the surveillance authority are requests for information and investigations (or inspections). In both cases the powers of the Commission and ESA are rather extensive.

The *requests for information* are governed by Article 11 Regulation 17, under which the surveillance authority 'may obtain all necessary information from Governments and competent authorities . . . and from undertakings'. There are two ways to request information, the first having to be used before the second (two-stage procedure):

– requests made by a simple letter (Article 11 (2) Regulation 17) (to States and undertakings); and
– requests by decision (Article 11 (5) Regulation 17) (only to undertakings).

If the undertaking, because the simple request does not put a legal obligation on it, does not supply the information within the time-limit fixed[123] in the letter or supplies incomplete information, it may be necessary to go for a formal decision which obliges the undertaking to provide the information requested. Both requests may give rise to the imposition of fines under Article 15 (1) (*b*) Regulation 17 if incorrect information is supplied and the requests by decision may, in addition, result in the imposition of periodic penalty payments (Article 16 (1) (*c*) Regulation 17). The requests for information are made in the language of the country where the addressee is located.

The other way to obtain the necessary information is to make an *inspection* on the premises of an undertaking. According to Article 14 (1) Regulation 17, the surveillance authority 'may undertake all the necessary investigations into undertakings or associations of undertakings'. As it is the case with the requests for information, there are also two types of inspection between which the authority can choose (this is not a two-stage procedure as under Article 11 Regulation 17):[124]

– simple inspections, to which the undertaking is under no obligation to submit

[123] The time-limits for replying to a letter are usually from three to six weeks and those for replying to a decision are shorter (two to three weeks).

[124] See Joined Cases 46/87 and 227/88 *Hoechst* [1989] 2859.

and which are thus normally made in agreement with the firm concerned (Article 14 (2) Regulation 17); or

- inspections by decision, where the Commission or ESA officials may come without warning to the undertaking's premises, the latter being under legal obligation to submit to the investigation (Article 14 (3) Regulation 17).

The officials of the surveillance authority shall exercise their powers upon production of a written mandate (and, in the case of Article 14 (3), a decision). This should specify the subject-matter and purpose of the investigation. In *Hoechst* (op. cit.) the Court held that this requirement aims at demonstrating that the inspection is justified and enables the undertaking 'to assess the scope of its duty to cooperate while at the same time safeguarding the rights of defense'.

Under Article 14 (1) Regulation 17 the officials of the surveillance authority have the powers to examine books and business records, take copies thereof, ask for oral explanations on the spot, and enter the professional premises. The Commission in its Decision *Fabbrica Pisana* stated that the obligation on the undertaking to supply all documents required means not merely giving access to all files in general 'but actually producing the specific documents required'.[125] In *Hoechst* the Court stated that the right of access to premises 'implies the powers to search for various items of information which are not already known or fully identified'. It is up to the officials conducting the investigation to determine, if a document is necessary in the framework of the inspection, whether it must be produced, whether it is of a professional character, or is covered by legal privilege.[126]

However, it is commonly agreed that the Commission officials cannot 'fish' for information (i.e. look for information outside the scope of the inspection mandate and/or decision), nor 'obtain access to premises or furniture by force or oblige the staff of the undertaking to give them such access, or carry out searches without the permission of the management of the undertaking',[127] nor seize documents. If an undertaking opposes the Commission's inspection (ordered by decision), the Commission may request the help of the national authorities.

The inspections are made in co-operation with the national authorities of the country concerned. Under Article 14 (5) and (6) Regulation 17 (and the corresponding provision in the ESA/Court Agreement), the EC and EFTA national authorities have an obligation to assist the Commission and ESA officials in carrying out inspections. Article 10 of Protocol 21 gives the Contracting Parties six

[125] See Commission Decision in *OJ* L 75 (21 Mar. 1980), 35.

[126] See Cases 155/79 *AM & S.* [1982] ECR 1575 and *Hoechst*, op. cit n. 124. The protection of legal privilege concerns correspondence with a lawyer registered at an EC Member State's bar, not in-house lawyers (see also Commission Dec. *Deere OJ* L 35 (7 Feb. 1985), 58). According to the Commission documents which are not linked to the exercise of the undertaking's defence rights are not covered by legal privilege. As concerns the legal privilege of lawyers registered at an EFTA State bar, there is in the EEA context a Community Declaration under which the EC will 'take the necessary measures in order to ensure lawyers of the EFTA States the same rights as to legal privilege under Community law as lawyers of EC Member States'.

[127] See *Hoechst*, op. cit. n. 124.

months as from the entry into force of the EEA Agreement for taking the necessary measures to comply with this obligation. Under the *Hoechst* case such assistance concerns in particular the cases where the undertaking opposes an inspection, but may also cover precautionary measures, such as a search warrant given in advance by the national court in order to overcome any opposition on the part of the undertaking.

In addition, should an undertaking produce incomplete documents or refuse to submit to an inspection, fines and periodic penalties may be imposed (Articles 15 (1) (*c*) and 16 (1) (*c*) Regulation 17).

6.1.4.2 Formal initiation of procedure

Following the fact-finding phase, the surveillance authority may decide[128] to open a formal procedure. However, the Commission has not in practice been very keen to do so except in cases of serious infringement or when a formal decision of exemption could be used to develop further its competition policy. Good examples of this are two exemption decisions granted to selective distribution agreements in the perfume sector which the Commission considers as covering the pertinent legal issues and defining the EC competition principles applying to companies in this sector.[129]

If the matter concerns a less important case, an issue already solved, or an issue covered by a notice or a group exemption, the Commission has developed a practice of closing the file through informal means. The Commission may thus issue, in cases of applications or notifications, a so-called 'comfort letter', which is a sort of 'quasi-exemption' or quasi-negative clearance. In such a letter the undertaking is informed that there is no reason to take further action and that the file is closed, the reasons being that the agreement either does not appear to infringe Article 85 (1) EEC, or falls within the scope of a notice or a group exemption, or would merit an individual exemption under Article 85 (3) EEC. This practice has given rise to many comments and sometimes dissatisfaction on the part of companies, which criticize the lack of legal certainty.[130]

If the agreement notified clearly contains restrictive elements which could not give rise to an exemption but the case is of so little importance that there is no use in opening a formal procedure, the Commission may simply send a letter indicating

[128] This is not a decision and thus not a challengeable act within the meaning of Art. 173 EEC or Art. 36 ESA/Court Agreement.

[129] See Decisions in *Yves Saint Laurent* and *Givenchy*, op. cit. n. 34. The Commission considers these exemptions as a sort of 'soft group exemption' under which firms notifying agreements which conform with the principles laid down in these decisions will be sent a comfort letter expressly referring to the exemptions decisions (see *XXIst Report on Competition Policy* (1991), 99).

[130] These letters are administrative acts and not decisions (as the Commission itself stated in a Notice in *OJ* C 295 (2 Nov. 1983), 6). They do not bind national courts or authorities, or third parties, but may however be taken into account by the local courts and authorities when assessing the compatibility of the agreement with Art. 85 EEC (see Cases 253/78 and 1–3/79 *Guerlain* [1980] ECR 2327).

which elements are not satisfactory so that the undertakings may adjust their agreement accordingly (such a letter is sometimes called a 'discomfort letter').

In cases of procedure for a not too serious infringement (under complaint or ex officio), it may also happen that the case is informally settled through allowing the companies concerned voluntarily to adjust their agreement instead of bringing the matter to a final decision with possible sanctions.

Finally, taking the opportunity of the debate on 'subsidiarity', the Commission has indicated that, when a complaint lacks 'Community interest' (i.e. it concerns exclusively or mostly a single State), and where adequate redress is available at national level, the Commission will reject the complaint and refer the complainant to the local authorities. This approach was admitted by the ECJ in *Automec II.*[131]

In cases where there is an interest in continuing the procedure, the authority formally initiates the procedure under Article 9 (3) Regulation 17. One of the main consequences of doing so is that the national authorities (but not the courts), as well as the other surveillance authority (however for transmission of cases, see Section 7.2.2), lose their concurrent competence to deal with the matter under the EEC/EEA competition rules. Before such a decision is made, either of the surveillance authorities as well as the national authorities concerned have parallel jurisdiction. The other important consequence is that it interrupts the limitation periods for imposing fines provided for in Regulation 2988/74 and starts them running afresh.[132]

The subsequent procedural steps vary depending on whether an exemption or negative clearance is sought (i.e. a 'positive decision') or a decision establishing an infringement, imposing, during the procedure, fines or periodic penalty payments, revoking the immunity from fines, or imposing interim measures (i.e. a 'negative decision'). There are, however, certain standard steps, such as hearing of the parties and consultation of Member States, which are in any case to be followed.

6.1.4.3 Hearing of the parties and third persons

The general obligation put on the surveillance authority to give the parties the opportunity to be heard before a decision (positive or negative) is taken is contained in Article 19 (1) Regulation 17. Article 19 (2) says that, upon request, other natural or legal persons may also be heard. This right to be heard is further developed in Regulation 99. If a negative decision is expected, the parties' right to be heard becomes consequential. The same goes for the opportunity given to interested third parties to express their views as it allows the authority to get a full picture of the case.

If a negative decision is expected, the first step in the process of hearing the defendants is the sending of the *statement of objections* (Article 2 Regulation 99), in

[131] Case T-24/90 [1992] ECR II-2250. See also speech by Sir Leon Brittan on 'The Future of EC Competition Policy', Centre for European Policy Studies (Brussels, 7 Dec. 1992).

[132] Other acts also interrupt the limitation period, such a written requests for information, written authorizations to carry out inspections, or the statement of objections (see Art. 2 of Reg. 2988/74).

which the surveillance authority informs the undertakings of its objections as regards the agreement or practice concerned, in order to allow the latter to express their views on the matter. All the relevant facts related to the case and its legal assessment are to be contained in the statement, as, under Article 4 Regulation 99, the final decision can only deal with those objections in respect of which the parties have been afforded the opportunity to express their views.[133] The defendant is given the right to submit his comments in writing on the objections within the set time-limit.[134] In addition, the defendant may ask to be heard orally (such hearing usually takes place two months after the deadline for written comments).

Access to the file is also part of the parties' right to be heard and is considered as an important element of their defence. Such access was not initially provided for in the procedural regulations but developed later on through the practices of the Commission and the jurisprudence of the ECJ.[135] The access to the file means that the undertaking targeted in a statement of objections has the right to examine the documents *à charge* and *à décharge* contained in the Commission's file.[136]

In addition to the right to be heard in writing, the surveillance authority may, upon request, organize an *oral hearing*, if the undertaking concerned shows a sufficient interest or if the surveillance authority proposes to impose on it a fine or a periodic penalty payment (Article 7 Regulation 99). Third parties may also be heard if they so request and can show a sufficient interest (e.g. complainant) or if they may corroborate facts or proofs. The hearing is conducted by the Hearing Officer who is a Commission high official specifically mandated for that purpose, independent from those in charge of handling the cases and having direct access to the Commissioner in charge of competition matters.[137]

In a case where a positive decision is expected, an important step from the third

[133] In practice, the Commission attaches to the statement of objections a copy of the documents quoted in the objections as evidence. The Court stated in *AEG* op. cit. n. 14 that what is important is not the documents in themselves, but the conclusions drawn from them by the Commission. On the purpose of the statement of objections, see Cases 60/81 *IBM* [1981] ECR 2639 and T-11/89 *Shell* [1992] ECR II-757.

[134] With a view to meeting some of the concerns expressed by the companies and their lawyers, DG IV has decided internally to normalize these time-limits in the following way: two months (for normal cases), three months (for complicated cases), and an extra two weeks (if it comprises Christmas or Easter) or an extra one month (if it comprises part or the whole of August), i.e. a maximum four- month period, without further prolongations. In interim measure proceedings, the two-week time-limit will still apply, without possible extension.

[135] In *Hoffmann-La Roche* (op. cit. n. 35) and in *Dutch Books* (Cases 43 and 63/82 [1984] ECR 19) the ECJ pointed out the need for the parties to have access to the documents used by the Commission to support its claim (i.e. the evidence actually used), but stated that there is no rule obliging the Commission to divulge the content of its files. The Commission itself decided, in its *XIIth Report on Competition Policy* (1982), that a list of the documents contained in the file would be annexed to the statement of objections and the parties would be allowed to consult the file on the Commission premises, except for documents containing business secrets or classified as confidential or internal documents. On confidentiality and business secrets see Cases 53/85 *Akzo* [1986] ECR 1965, 142 and 156/84 *Philip Morris* (op. cit. n. 64), and T-7/89 *Hercules* [1992] ECR II-1715.

[136] See *Hercules*, op. cit. n. 135. See also T-10/92 *Cement* [1992] ECR 11-2667.

[137] For a description of the tasks of the Hearing Officer see *XIIth Report on Competition Policy* (1982).

parties' point of view is the so-called '*Article 19 (3) publication*' (Article 19 (3) Regulation 17), that is, the publication of a summary of the case inviting third parties to submit their observations on the envisaged exemption or negative clearance within a set time-limit before the surveillance authority takes its decision. This gives the third parties the opportunity to express their views and defend their interests, and enables the surveillance authority to get information which it otherwise would not necessarily have received.

6.1.4.4 Liaison with the States

Under Article 10 Regulation 17, the handling of cases by the surveillance authority has to be carried out in close and constant liaison with the competent authorities of the States. This applies from the notification stage until the final decision is made.

After having received a notification or application the surveillance authority has to submit a copy of it to the States under its competence. During the procedure the national authorities have the right to express their views. This kind of co-operation is certainly important having regard, in particular, to the fact that the national authorities have concurrent competences until the opening of the formal procedure by the surveillance authority. The national authorities may also, thanks to their knowledge of the national markets, provide the surveillance authority with valuable information concerning the case.

Before a final decision is made, an Advisory Committee composed of States' representatives has to be consulted.[138] The opinion of the Committee on the draft proposed decision is not binding on the surveillance authority, but it is attached to the final draft decision which is submitted for adoption to the EC Commissioners or ESA College members. The opinion of the Advisory Committee is however not made public.

6.1.4.5 Decision

Experience has shown that, in practice, the number of competition cases ending up with a formal decision is very limited as compared with the overall number of cases handled in the Commission services. This is in fact mainly due to a heavy workload, combined with lack of resources and the time-consuming character of the proceedings leading to a formal decision.

In an attempt to speed-up the procedures, DG IV has indicated that, in the treatment of structural JVs, it would, within two months of the notification, send either a comfort letter or a 'warning letter' to which is attached a timetable indicating when the Commission intended to reach a final decision).[139] A similar

[138] There are four different Advisory Committees for Art. 85/86 cases: a general one under Reg. 17 and three specific ones in the field of transport (Reg. 1017/68, 4056/86, and 3975/87).

[139] See speech by Sir Leon Brittan on 7 Dec. 1992, op. cit. n. 131, and *XXIInd Report on Competition Policy* (1992), 81–2. The new internal deadlines should apply, as regards structural JVs, for notifications made as from 1 Jan. 1993. Furthermore, companies planning JVs were encouraged to have pre-notification talks with DG IV (as in the merger cases).

system should apply as from 1 April 1993 for other cases, under which DG IV should indicate the time in which the first stage of its inquiries will be completed.

There are basically *two groups of decisions*: those taken during the course of the procedure and those ending the procedure.

During the course of the procedure, four types of decisions may be taken: under the ECJ interpretation of Article 3 (1) Regulation 17,[140] the surveillance authority may, upon request of the complainant or ex officio, take interim measures which are indispensable for the effective exercise of its functions, the purpose being to avoid irreparable damage being caused before the final decision in cases of urgency where there is prima facie an infringement of competition rules; under Article 15 (6) Regulation 17, the surveillance authority may provisionally revoke immunity from fines when, after a preliminary examination, it is of the opinion that an agreement infringes Article 53 (1) EEA in such a manner that an exemption is not justified. The Commission is apparently willing to make more use of this particular procedure; as seen above, the surveillance authority may take decisions requesting information from the undertakings or ordering an inspection (Articles 11 and 14 Regulation 17) and it may also, under Articles 15 and 16 Regulation 17, impose fines or periodic penalty payments for procedural infringements.

At the end of the procedure, basically three types of decisions may be taken: in the case of infringement of Articles 85/86 EEC or 53/54 EEA, the surveillance authority may take a decision establishing the infringement and, if the infringement has not ceased to exist, requiring the undertakings concerned to bring it to an end (Article 3 Regulation 17). The surveillance authority may also, in the same decision, impose a fine of up to 10 per cent of the turnover in the preceding year of each of the participating undertakings (Article 15 (2) Regulation 17).[141] In the case of application or notification, the surveillance authority may grant a negative clearance or an individual exemption (Articles 2 and 6 Regulation 17). An individual exemption is granted for a limited duration (usually five to ten years, sometimes fifteen years) and may have conditions and obligations attached.[142] It may be renewed, if the conditions of Article 85 (3)/53 (3) are still fulfilled, or revoked if there has been a fundamental change of the facts, if a stipulation attached has been infringed, or if the parties have given false information or abused the exemption.

Under Articles 190 EEC and 16 ESA/Court Agreement, decisions of the Commission and ESA have to state the reasons on which they are based. The Court stated that 'Article 190 is not taking mere formal considerations into account but seeks to give an opportunity to the parties of defending their rights, to the Court of

[140] See Case 792/79R *Camera Care* [1980] 119. See also Case T-44/90 *La Cinq* [1992] ECR 3.

[141] In fixing the amount of the fine, the surveillance authority shall take into account the gravity of the infringement (intention or negligence, nature of the restrictions and their actual effects, number and size of the undertakings, nature and value of the products, behaviour of the parties, etc.).

[142] Such as an obligation for the parties to submit periodic and detailed reports (on how the agreement operates, on amendments thereto, on cases of refusal to supply, on further acquisitions), or to inform about licences granted, staff exchanges, shareholding links, etc.

exercising its supervisory functions and to Member States and to all interested nationals of ascertaining the circumstances in which the Commission has applied the Treaty.' The decision should thus set out 'in a concise but clear and relevant manner, the principal issues of law and of fact upon which it is based and which are necessary in order that the reasoning which has led the Commission to its Decision may be understood'.[143]

6.2 Merger control

It is recalled that the procedural rules applicable in merger cases can be found in the Merger Regulation (Articles 6–25) and in Regulation 2367/89, which have been reproduced, respectively, in chapters XIII and XIV of Protocol 4 ESA/Court Agreement. It is also recalled that, following the splitting between procedural and substantive provisions, the latter (Articles 1–5 of the Merger Regulation) are to be found in Annex XIV EEA.

The main differences between the Articles 53/54 EEA procedure and the merger procedure are the following:

- the undertakings are obliged to notify their concentration operations before their realization;
- the surveillance authority is obliged to take a formal decision in all cases (there are no possibilities of closing the file through informal means, such as comfort letters, etc.);
- if the surveillance authority fails to take a decision within the deadlines, the notified concentration is deemed to be compatible with the EEA.

6.2.1 Notifications, forms, and language

The procedure officially starts with a notification. However, the Commission has developed an extensive practice of pre-notification meetings with the undertakings which are of great help, as they allow the Commission to give advice to the companies, to discuss a possible draft of the notification, and to check that the project falls within the scope of the Regulation.

The notifications have to be submitted to the competent authority under Article 57 (2) EEA.[144] It is recalled that the last sentence of Article 57 (2) (*b*) EEA provides that the competence of ESA to decide a case is without prejudice to the rights of EC Member States. Therefore, the economic operators who notify ESA of a merger case may also have to notify the authorities of an EC Member State.

If a case is notified as a concentration but the surveillance authority considers that the case falls within the scope of Article 53 or 54 EEA (e.g. a co-operative JV instead of a concentrative JV), it can, after consultations with the undertakings concerned, 'convert' the notification into an application or notification under Regulation 17 and

[143] Case 24/62 *Germany* v. *Commission* [1963] ECR 63.

[144] On the transmission of cases wrongly addressed see remarks in s. 7.3.2 below.

the case will be treated following procedures described in Section 6.1 above (see Article 5 of Regulation 2367/90).

The parties cannot put a concentration into effect before it has been notified or within the first three weeks following the notification (Article 7 Merger Regulation).

The notifications shall be made by using Form CO (Article 2 Regulation 2367/90). Again, both the Commission and ESA have their own forms, which are identical in substance and also include questions relating to the 'EFTA dimension' of the operation, in the same way as for Article 53/54 cases. Either form may, in principle, be used for notifications to each surveillance authority.

The notification form is available in the thirteen official languages of the Community and EFTA States and the notification can be submitted using any one of them. If, however, a notification is made using a language which is not one of the official languages of the notified authority or a working language of that authority, all the documentation has to be supplemented by a translation into such a language. In these cases the language of the translation becomes the one which the surveillance authority uses when addressing the notifying undertakings (see Article 12 of Protocol 24 EEA).

6.2.2 The different procedural steps

The procedure in merger cases comprises two phases: the first phase ('Phase I'), whose duration is one month, may give rise to the following decisions (Article 6 (1) Merger Regulation):[145]

- decision stating that the concentration notified does not fall within the scope of the Merger Regulation;
- decision of 'non-opposition' if the concentration falls within the scope of the Regulation but does not raise serious doubts as to its compatibility with the EEA;
- decision to initiate the proceeding if the concentration raises serious doubts as to its compatibility with the EEA.

In the latter case, the second phase of the procedure starts ('Phase II'), whose duration is four months, and which shall necessarily be closed by one of the following decisions (Article 8 Merger Regulation):

- clearance decision, if the surveillance authority finds, following an eventual modification by the undertakings, that the concentration is not likely to create or strengthen a dominant position as a result of which effective competition would be significantly impeded in the EEA or in a substantial part thereof;
- clearance decision with conditions and obligations, if the concentration falls under the case above but the authority needs to ensure that the commitments

[145] For practical purposes references below are simply made to the Merger Regulation (4064/89) rather than, using the formal EEA jargon, to 'the act referred to in point 1 of Annex XIV EEA' (when it concerns Arts. 1–5 of the Regulation) or to 'chapter XIII of Protocol 4 to the ESA/Court Agreement' (when it concerns Arts. 6–25 of the Regulation).

undertaken by the parties with a view to modifying the original concentration plan will be complied with;

- prohibition decision, if the concentration creates or strengthens a dominant position as a result of which effective competition would be significantly impeded in the EEA or in a substantial part thereof;
- divestiture decision, if the concentration has already been implemented (i.e. separation of undertakings or assets, cessation of joint control, or any other action needed for restoring conditions of effective competition). Such a decision may be made separately or be part of a prohibition decision;
- revocation of a clearance decision, if the latter was made on the basis of incorrect information from the undertakings or information obtained by deceit, or if the undertakings concerned commit a breach of an obligation attached to the decision. Such a decision can be made even after the four-month deadline.

The surveillance authority may also take provisional or interim measures, such as, during Phase I, continuation of the suspension of the concentration. It may also grant a derogation from such suspension (see Article 7 Merger Regulation). The decisions will then have to follow different procedural steps (e.g. hearing of the parties) before becoming final.

As to the fact-finding procedure preceding the decision, the same possibilities as under Regulation 17 are afforded to the surveillance authorities (requests for information and inspections) and the principles explained above should also be valid here (see Section 6.1.4.1 above). However, it should be noted that, for obvious reasons related to the tight deadlines to which it is bound, the Commission has mainly in practice used letters requesting information (not even decisions).

As regards the hearing of parties, the surveillance authority shall, as concerns 'negative decisions',[146] give the undertakings concerned the opportunity, at every stage of the procedure up to the consultation of the Advisory Committee, of making known their views on the objections against them. A decision can only be made on the basis of objections on which the parties have been able to submit their observations. Specific reference is made to respect for the defence's rights and access to the file. Third parties may also be heard if necessary (see Article 18 Merger Regulation).[147]

Before one of the Phase II decisions is made, the Advisory Committee on Concentrations has to be consulted (Article 19 (3) Merger Regulation). The same

[146] i.e. clearance with conditions and obligations, prohibition, divestiture, revocation of clearance, as well as, with possible exceptions, continuation of suspension or derogation from suspension, and imposition of fines or periodic penalty payments.

[147] Any person showing a sufficient interest, and especially members of the administrative or management bodies of the undertakings concerned or the recognized representatives of their employees, shall have this right, upon request. The Commission intends to improve transparency towards third parties before accepting commitments from the parties in both Phases I and II (see Report referred to in n. 70 above).

principles as explained above apply in the merger field (see Section 6.1.4.5), the main difference being that the Committee's opinions may be published, if it so decides (Article 19 (4)–(7) Merger Regulation). In practice, there are already in Phase I many informal contacts with the Member States, in particular those concerned by the case in question.

6.2.3 Rights of individual States

There are two ways for the States still to deal with a case falling within the scope of the Merger Regulation: so-called 'Article 9 referral' and the invocation of legitimate interests.

Under Article 9 Merger Regulation a State may, within three weeks of the date of receipt of its copy of the notification, request that the case be referred to it, because the concentration threatens to create or to strengthen a dominant position on a 'distinct market' within that State. It is however up to the surveillance authority to decide whether to refer the case or not.[148] If the case is referred, the national authorities will apply to it their national competition law.

In the EEA context, an EFTA State may request a referral from the Commission[149] or ESA.[150] The EC Member States have the right to request referral from the Commission (Article 9 Merger Regulation). However, as regards their relations with ESA, the EC Member States do not need to ask for such referral from ESA since they in any case can apply their national law concurrently with ESA applying the EEA rules (Article 57 (2) (*b*) last sentence EEA).

Under Article 21 (3) Merger Regulation, notwithstanding the sole competence of the EC Commission to deal with concentrations of a Community dimension, EC Member States may take appropriate measures to protect legitimate interests concerning public security, plurality of media, and prudential rules, or any other interest communicated to and recognized by the Commission. The EFTA States have the same right *vis-à-vis* the Commission under Article 7 of Protocol 24 EEA. Again, the EC Member States do not need to have recourse to this procedure as they may apply their national law concurrently with ESA applying the EEA rules.

Finally, the States (notably small ones) may also, through a form of delegation of powers, ask the surveillance authority, which is presumably better equipped than them, to decide on a merger which has no Community dimension but creates or strengthens a dominant position in their territory and affects inter-State trade (Article 22 (3) Merger Regulation). In the EEA the States will make such a request to their respective surveillance authority (EC States to Commission and EFTA States to ESA).

[148] The triggering of the referral procedure by a State automatically prolongs the one-month period of Phase I to six weeks (to be counted in days as from the notification and not by adding two weeks to the one-month period of Phase I!).

[149] Art. 6 of Protocol 24 EEA.

[150] Art. 9 of ch. XIII of Protocol 4 ESA/Court Agreement.

6.3 Coal and steel

As indicated above at the beginning of this section, the procedural rules in the field of coal and steel have been listed in Protocol 21 EEA and reproduced, in an adapted form, for the purposes of the EFTA pillar in chapter XV of Protocol 4 to the ESA/Court Agreement.

Without going into any specificities of the procedures in this sector, as the powers of the surveillance authorities and the rights of parties correspond roughly to what has been described above, it should be pointed out that the notifications are to be made using the appropriate ECSC notification form for mergers and agreements or the corresponding EFTA form. The ECSC form has been amended for this purpose and the use of ECSC or EFTA forms is equally valid. For notifications concerning both EEC and ECSC products, Form CO, or the corresponding EFTA form, is also acceptable.

6.4 Transitional rules

Some transitional arrangements have been provided for in Protocol 21 EEA and in Article 14 of Protocol 24 EEA to enable the undertakings to adapt to the new legal situation. These arrangements are very similar to those contained in Regulation 17, notably those introduced under the Accession Acts when new Member States entered the EC. There is also a transitional period of six months for the States to introduce the administrative assistance they are to grant to Commission and ESA officials in inspections (Article 10 of Protocol 21 EEA). Furthermore, similar transitional provisions to those of Articles 5 *et seq.* of Protocol 21 EEA are contained in chapter XIV of Protocol 4 ESA/Court Agreement. The explanations given below concerning Protocol 21 EEA are thus also valid for the corresponding provisions in the ESA/Court Agreement.

6.4.1 Article 53 cases

6.4.1.1 New agreements

All the agreements which are concluded after the entry into force of the EEA and for which the parties seek a negative clearance or an individual exemption, have to be notified in accordance with the normal procedures to the Commission or ESA. The transitional periods do not concern them (Article 4 of Protocol 21 EEA).

6.4.1.2 Existing agreements

For agreements in existence when the EEA comes into force which fall under the prohibition contained in Article 53 (1) EEA, and of which the EC Commission has not earlier been notified, there is an adaptation period of six months as from the EEA entry into force. Within that period the undertakings should either modify their agreement, so that it no longer falls under Article 53 (1) EEA or complies with existing group exemptions, or they should notify it in order to obtain an individual exemption.[151] Agreements notified within the six-month period after the entry into force of the EEA Agreement will also be granted immunity from fines for the time preceding the notification[152] and they should in principle benefit from provisional validity.

As regards the particular question of provisional validity, the following ECJ jurisprudence[153] should also be valid in the EEA context, by effect of Article 6 EEA (on the taking over of the ECJ case-law delivered before 2 May 1992). The Court has ruled that, for reasons of contractual certainty, the principle of provisional validity applies to agreements which were already in existence before the entry into force of Regulation 17 and of which the Commission has been notified. The Court later on also extended this provisional validity to agreements which do not need to be notified under Article 4 (2) Regulation 17 (corresponding to Article 4 (2) of Protocol 21 EEA). The provisional validity is secured until such time as the Commission intervenes and by decision declares the agreement contrary to Article 85 (1), non-exemptable under Article 85 (3) EEC. Such 'intervention' by the Commission may also take the form of a comfort letter stating that the agreement does not infringe Article 85 (1) due to its small effects. The Commission applied these principles by analogy to so-called 'accession agreements' (i.e. agreements in existence at the time of accession of a new Member State) notified within the six-month period.

The notifications submitted to the EC Commission prior to the entry into force of the EEA Agreement but not yet decided upon will be considered as complying with the EEA provisions on notifications. Their contents will, however, be examined in the light of the EEA rules and the competent surveillance authority may request the undertaking to complete its notification with EEA-relevant information (Article 8 of Protocol 21 EEA).

Agreements which have already been granted an individual exemption within the Community will continue to benefit from it under the EEA rules for the duration of the Commission decision, unless the Commission withdraws the exemption (Article 13 of Protocol 21 EEA). However, agreements which have been granted a negative clearance or which have been subject to an administrative letter (e.g. a comfort letter) before the entry into force of the EEA Agreement should be reviewed by the undertakings concerned, in order to bring them into line with the EEA rules.

[151] Arts. 5, 11, and 12 of Protocol 21 EEA.

[152] Art. 9 of Protocol 21 EEA.

[153] The relevant cases on this issue are Case 48/72 *Brasserie de Haecht II* [1973] ECR 77; Case 59/77 *De Bloos* [1977] ECR 2359; and Case 99/79 *Lancôme* [1980] ECR 2511. See also *IIIrd Report on Competition Policy* (1973), 19, point 5 (*a*).

6.4.2 Merger cases

The EEA provisions will apply to concentrations as from the entry into force of the Agreement. The EEA provisions will not apply to any concentration which was the subject of an agreement or announcement or where control was acquired before the EEA entry into force or a concentration in respect of which proceedings were initiated by a national authority with responsibility for competition before the entry into force (Article 14 of Protocol 24 EEA). This transitional provision should be understood in the same way as Article 25 (2) Merger Regulation, whose wording is similar.

6.4.3 Coal and steel

There are no particular transitional rules for the coal and steel sector but the general transitional rules contained in Protocol 21 EEA apply.

7. CO-OPERATION BETWEEN THE TWO SURVEILLANCE AUTHORITIES

7.1. General principles of co-operation

Article 58 EEA states that, with a view to developing and maintaining a uniform surveillance throughout the EEA in the field of competition and to promoting a homogeneous implementation, application, and interpretation of the competition rules, the two authorities shall co-operate closely. More detailed provisions on co-operation are contained in Protocols 23 and 24 EEA.

The close co-operation applies both to handling of individual cases and to general policy issues. The two surveillance authorities should follow the same policies, same procedural rules, and, to a great extent, similar practices, as the decisions to be adopted in individual cases cannot differ depending on whether they are taken by ESA or by the Commission.

It is clear that strict rules of professional secrecy will need to apply with regard to the information received in the context of the co-operation and the administrative assistance. The information can only be used for the purpose of procedures under the relevant rules. On the other hand, the rules of the EEA Agreement itself or in the legislation of the Contracting Parties cannot prevent exchanges of information provided for in the two co-operation Protocols.[154]

[154] See Arts. 9 of Protocol 23 and 9 of Protocol 24 EEA. See also Agreed Minutes ad Article 123 EEA (security clause), under which the Contracting Parties agree that 'they would not make improper use of provisions in Article 123 to prevent the disclosure of information in the field of competition'.

7.2 Co-operation in Article 53/54 cases[155]

7.2.1 Mutual information and consultation during the different stages of the procedure

Under Protocol 23 EEA, the co-operation concerning individual cases falling under Articles 53 and 54 EEA will take place at different stages of the proceedings:[156]

- the two surveillance authorities shall, for example, forward to each other copies of notifications and complaints, as well as copies of 'comfort letters' or letters rejecting a complaint ('Article 6 letter');
- the other surveillance authority shall be consulted when the competent authority is publishing its intention to grant a negative clearance or an individual exemption ('Article 19 (3) publication') or addressing a statement of objections to undertakings;
- the surveillance authorities shall invite each other to be represented at hearings and Advisory Committee meetings. The invitation extends also to the States falling within the competence of the other surveillance authority. As regards the Advisory Committee meetings, the States of the other pillar do not, however, have the right to vote.

In addition, the other surveillance authority may request at all stages of the proceedings copies of the most important documents lodged with the competent surveillance authority for the purpose of establishing the existence of infringements of Articles 53 and 54, or of obtaining negative clearance or exemption, and may, furthermore, before a final decision is taken, make any observations.

7.2.2 Transmission of cases

As mentioned earlier, the fact of misinterpreting Article 56 EEA and addressing a notification to the wrong surveillance authority does not have any negative effects on the undertakings concerned. It may even sometimes be only after the initial phases of proceedings, for example after the fact-finding procedures, that the surveillance authorities are able to determine which one will deal with the matter.

Under Article 10 (2) of Protocol 23 EEA, the notifications or complaints which are not submitted to the right surveillance authority are to be transmitted, without delay, to the competent authority. The date of submission of a notification will in such a situation be the date on which it was originally received. In the same way, if, in the preparation or initiation of ex officio proceedings, it becomes apparent that the other surveillance authority is competent to decide on a case, the case shall be transferred to the latter (Article 10 (3)).

Once a case is transmitted to the other surveillance authority, a retransmission

[155] Under Art. 7 of Protocol 25 EEA, the co-operation concerning coal and steel cases shall follow the rules of Protocol 23 EEA.

[156] It is recalled that the co-operation does not apply to 'pure cases', but only to 'mixed cases', i.e. where trade between the EC and EFTA is affected.

cannot take place. Neither can it take place after certain late stages of the proceedings, i.e. after the 'Article 19 (3) publication', the addressing of a statement of objections, or the sending of an 'Article 6 letter'.

7.2.3 Mutual administrative assistance in fact-finding

Under Article 8 of Protocol 23 EEA, the surveillance authorities will have to provide each other with administrative assistance in fact-finding procedures. With regard to requests for information, both surveillance authorities may request information (by letter or by decision) from any company located within the EEA. If the request is made to an enterprise located in the territory of the other surveillance authority, the latter shall receive a copy of it. A copy shall also be forwarded to the competent authorities of the State in which the company is situated.

The most important implication of this co-operation, however, concerns the inspections. The EC Commission may request ESA to carry out inspections on its behalf in EFTA territory and ESA will have the same right as regards the EC. The competent surveillance authority has the right to be represented and to take an active part in investigations carried out by the other surveillance authority.

As regards 'mixed cases' where the competent authority carries out inspections within its own territory, it has an obligation to inform the other authority of the fact that such investigations have taken place and shall, on request, transmit to that authority the relevant results of the investigations.

7.3 Co-operation in merger cases

7.3.1 Information and consultation

Co-operation between the pillars concerning merger cases is governed by Protocol 24 EEA. This Protocol is drafted in a unilateral way, that is, it only concerns the co-operation to be granted to ESA where the Commission has been allocated a case under Article 57 (2) (*a*) EEA. In addition, such co-operation only takes place if one of the following conditions is met (Article 2 of Protocol 24):

- the combined turnover of the undertakings concerned in the EFTA States is at least 25 per cent of their EEA-wide turnover; or
- each of at least two of the undertakings concerned has a turnover exceeding 250 million ECU in the EFTA territory; or
- the concentration is liable to create or strengthen a dominant position significantly impeding competition in the EFTA territory or a substantial part thereof.

The same applies where the concentration threatens to create or strengthen a dominant position impeding effective competition within an EFTA State which presents all the characteristics of a distinct market, even if it is not a substantial part of the EEA, or if an EFTA State wishes to adopt measures to protect legitimate interests, such as public security, plurality of media, or prudential rules.

The co-operation then covers the same aspects as explained above concerning Protocol 23 EEA (though within shorter deadlines), such as transmission of copies of notifications to ESA, right of ESA and EFTA States to express their views at different stages of proceedings, and opportunity for ESA and EFTA States to attend hearings and Advisory Committee meetings.

7.3.2 Transmission of cases

The notifications received by the wrong surveillance authority are to be transmitted without delay to the competent authority. The date of submission of a notification will in such a situation be the date on which it is received by the competent authority (not by the original authority) (Articles 10 (2) and 11 (1) of Protocol 24).

If the case is notified as a concentration but falls under Article 53 EEA, the date of submission will be the one when it was received by the original authority (Article 11 (2)).

7.3.3 Administrative assistance in fact-finding

When carrying out the duties assigned to it for the implementation of Article 57 EEA the Commission may obtain all necessary information from ESA and EFTA States. For the rest (requests for information and inspections), the rules are the same as under Protocol 23 EEA described above.

7.4 Enforcement of decisions of the surveillance authorities

Thanks to the 'one-stop shop' principle, the decisions taken by the Commission and ESA in application of the EEA competition rules will be valid for the whole EEA and will have to be respected by the other pillar. These decisions may be directly addressed to the undertakings concerned wherever located in the EEA.[157] Decisions which impose pecuniary obligations shall be enforceable in accordance with Article 110 EEA (which corresponds to Article 192 EEC), under which enforcement shall be governed by the relevant national rules of civil procedure, the only formality for the enforcement order being the verification of its authenticity.

Austria has made, in the EEA context, a unilateral declaration under which it states that its obligation to enforce on its territory decisions by the EC institutions imposing pecuniary obligations shall only refer to such decisions as are fully covered by the provisions of the EEA Agreement. The EC has made a 'counter-declaration' stating that it understands the Austrian declaration as meaning that enforcement will be guaranteed to the extent that the decisions imposing such obligations are based, even if not exclusively, on provisions contained in the EEA Agreement.

Norway has also made a unilateral declaration under which it states that its present Constitution does not provide for direct enforceability of decisions of EC

[157] However, in the case of inspections to be made on the territory of the other pillar, it is for the latter to undertake on its own territory the inspections requested by its partner (see Art. 8 of Protocol 23 EEA).

institutions regarding pecuniary obligations addressed to companies located in Norway, but that it acknowledges that such decisions should continue to be sent directly to the companies in question and that they should fulfil their obligations 'in accordance with the present practice'. Norway adds that, should difficulties arise, it is ready to enter into consultation and work towards a mutually satisfactory solution. The EC replied that it will keep the situation under review and enter into consultations as appropriate.

8. HARMONIZING EFFECTS OF THE EEA COMPETITION RULES AND POSSIBLE FUTURE DEVELOPMENTS IN A WIDER CONTEXT

The EEA competition rules will create the same legal framework for all the undertakings operating in Western Europe. This will also contribute to helping the EFTA undertakings to get accustomed to the system of Europe-wide competition rules which they will be confronted with when their respective countries become members of the EC.

It is a fact that, until recently, not very much attention had been paid to these issues on the EFTA side. On paper, the competition rules provided for in the Stockholm Convention or in the 1972 FTAs between the individual EFTA States and the EC looked fine, but their application had not been remarkably efficient.[158] The same was in general true on a national level: in the majority of EFTA States the national competition legislation and its enforcement was to a large extent insufficient. In that respect, the introduction of the EC traditional competition rules in the EEA had a sort of 'spill-over effect' in the different EFTA States: although the EEA rules do not oblige the States to amend their national competition rules, each of them either amended its existing competition law or introduced a new one.[159]

Therefore, with the EEA coming into force, many EFTA economic operators will be facing completely new challenges. On the other hand, those EFTA undertakings which have already been submitted to the Community competition rules, in particular through the application of the 'effects doctrine', and have already experienced a procedure with the EC Commission, should not have any difficulty in understanding and complying with the EEA competition rules, as the resemblance of the two systems is so striking.

[158] This relative weakness of the 1972 FTAs system was indirectly underlined in the *Woodpulp* case (op. cit. n. 99) where the ECJ stated that it would have been of little use to trigger the competition rules of the EC–Finland FTA since the effects of the woodpulp cartel reached so much further than merely EC–Finland trade that referring the matter to the FTA Joint Committee could not possibly have led to the adoption of appropriate measures to remedy the situation.

[159] Austria adopted a new law in Feb. 1993; Finland had a new law enter into effect on 1 Sept. 1992; Iceland passed a new law on 25 Feb. 1993 which entered into force on 1 Mar. 1993; Norway is due to adopt a new law by 1994; and Sweden adopted a 'blueprint' of the EC competition rules which entered into force on 1 July 1993.

It should be underlined that the new EEA competition rules do not only mean prohibitions. The numerous group exemptions and the interpretative guidance given in the notices and guidelines will make it possible, in particular, for the small and medium-sized enterprises to co-operate widely. Moreover, undertakings suffering from the pressure of a competitor or supplier abusing its dominant position, or whose entrance into a new market is complicated by restrictive practices, may lodge a complaint with the Commission or ESA, or bring the matter before their national court or authorities.

In this context it can be recalled that the EC competition rules will also play an important role more widely in Europe. They will, in a way, become an all-European standard of conduct for economic operators participating in cross-border trade and operations. This is due to the fact that the association agreements the Community has concluded with the Central and Eastern European countries contain a reference to the interpretation given to Articles 85 and 86 EEC in the Community as the basis for the interpretation and application to be given to the competition rules provided for in these agreements, thus again making the *acquis communautaire* applicable in this context also.

Finally, there is an ongoing debate in GATT-related circles concerning the possible introduction in the next round of negotiations of a competition chapter. There are convergent views in the EC and in the USA that, as the classical tariff and non-tariff barriers are going down, what is left is mainly entry barriers and other distortions based on restrictive business practices.[160] It will be interesting to see how the idea launched in the 1992 Davos World Economic Forum, by Sir Leon Brittan, at the time competition Commissioner, of drawing up world competition rules covering subsidies, cartels, merger policy, and public monopolies in the context of the next round of GATT negotiations, will develop. The point was again made by the new Commissioner responsible for competition matters, Mr Karel Van Miert, who, in October 1993, referred to the Japanese and Korean markets being closed not so much by tariffs, but by exclusionary behaviour based on distribution systems or other private practices.[161] In the positive case, the principles of the Community competition rules, including their use as a tool for deepening economic integration when trade barriers are being otherwise abolished, might have effects in an even wider context.

[160] It is recalled that the Commission and the US Government signed on 23 Sept. 1991 an administrative agreement providing for consultation procedures and dispute avoidance mechanism in competition matters, which is being challenged in the ECJ (Case C-327/91).

[161] Reported by the *Financial Times* of 9–10 Oct. 1993.

IX

STATE MONOPOLIES AND PUBLIC UNDERTAKINGS
(ARTICLES 16 AND 56, PROTOCOL 8)

This chapter gives a description of the EEA rules on State monopolies of a commercial character (Article 16 EEA) and on public undertakings (Article 59 EEA), as well as describing how the corresponding EEC rules (Articles 37 and 90 EEC) have so far been interpreted and applied by the Commission and the ECJ. These provisions have recently been given a new impulse by the Commission, in particular in the field of services, as part of its policy to introduce more competition in the so-called 'regulated industries'.

This concerns notably telecommunications, postal services, and energy, which for many years have been under the responsibility of monopolies operating under public service obligations, but usually organized within the limits of national borders, thus incompatible with the idea of single market. However, a balance needs to be found between, on the one hand, the needs of the single market and, on the other hand, justifications such as security of supply and maintenance of a universal public service.[1] However, 'universal' could also be seen in the wider perspective of the EC or EEA territory. In sectors such as energy and telecommunications the Commission has put a particular emphasis on free access to networks by outsiders and transparency of the structure of the operator's costs.

The EC side has therefore already reached a sort of second stage in its tackling of monopolies and public undertakings, where a number of EFTA States have not even passed the first stage of adjustment of their old monopolies (such as for instance the famous alcohol monopolies in certain Nordic countries). On the other hand, the telecommunication sector, for example, is already more liberalized in certain EFTA States than in most of the EC countries.

1. STATE MONOPOLIES OF A COMMERCIAL CHARACTER

1.1 The EEA obligations (Article 16 EEA)

Article 16 EEA reproduces the text of Article 37 (1) EEC on adjustment of State monopolies of a commercial character. As compared with Article 37 EEC, the substance obligation is exactly the same, with the consequence that, under Article 6

[1] For an overview of the intentions of the Commission concerning regulated industries, see *XXIst Report on Competition Policy* (1991), 25 *et seq*. See also *XXIInd Report on Competition Policy* (1992), 29 *et seq*.

EEA, Article 16 should be implemented and applied 'in conformity with the relevant rulings of the Court of Justice'.

There are certain differences in the drafting of Article 16 EEA as compared with Article 37 EEC, but they are essentially of a procedural nature:

- there is no general transitional period (no reference to a 'progressive' adjustment);[2]
- there is no specific provision on possible 'protective measures' by other States, as this is superseded by the general safeguard system in the EEA;
- there is no reference to agricultural products or to international agreements, as agriculture and third country relations fall outside the scope of the EEA Agreement;
- there is no reference to the possibility of making recommendations to the States during the transitional period (since there is no such transitional period in the EEA).

Under Protocol 8 EEA, however, a specific transitional period of two years has been granted for Austria (salt monopoly) and Iceland (fertilizers monopoly). The Protocol also states that Article 16 EEA applies to wine (HS heading 22.04). This was specifically mentioned due to the fact that otherwise wine, and thus a great part of the Nordic alcohol monopolies would, as a consequence of Article 8 (3) EEA on product coverage, have been excluded from the scope of Article 16. As regards other alcoholic beverages, as a result of Article 8 (3) (*b*) EEA those beverages which are listed in Tables I and II of Protocol 3 EEA are covered by the EEA Agreement (and thus also by Article 16 EEA). Agricultural products (notably tobacco) are, however, not covered.[3]

1.2 Interpretation given to Article 37 EEC by the ECJ and the Commission

After thirty years of experience in the EC, during which monopolies on products such as tobacco, oil, matches, alcohol, fertilizers, salt, cigarettes, or newspaper paper have been tackled, it is possible to draw a synthetic description of the interpretation and the practice developed by the Commission and the ECJ. As mentioned above, in 1988 the Commission started a new wave of application of Article 37 EEC in the sector of telecommunications terminals[4] and transport of electricity and gas.[5]

[2] This particular point is underlined by the Commission in its *XXIInd Report on Competition Policy*, where it says: 'monopolies must in principle be fully adjusted not later than the date of entry into force of the Agreement.' (p. 237).

[3] For more details on the product coverage of the EEA, see Ch. III, s. 1, above.

[4] See Dir. 88/301/EEC on competition in the markets in telecommunications terminal equipment which is formally based on Art. 90 (3) but expressly refers to Art. 37 EEC in its preamble (see n. 53 below).

[5] It is recalled that electricity and gas are considered as goods (see Case 6/64 *Costa* v. *ENEL* [1964] ECR 585). The Commission has launched six infringement proceedings in this field (see *XXIInd Report*, op. cit. n. 1, p. 280).

1.2.1 Objective of Article 37 EEC

Article 37 EEC is aimed at ensuring compliance with the rule of the free movement of goods.[6] It is designed to prevent the Member States from using their commercial monopolies for protectionist purposes.

Thus, the main concern in Article 37 EEC is non-discrimination[7] regarding the conditions under which goods are procured and marketed between Community nationals. Its application is not limited to import or export of products which are directly subject to the monopoly but covers all measures which are connected with its existence and affect inter-State trade in certain products, whether or not subject to the monopoly.[8] Even if the rules apply without distinction to domestic and imported products, one has to examine whether the monopoly is nevertheless liable to have discriminatory effects or to distort competition by restricting imports and thereby impeding inter-State trade.[9]

Article 37 EEC does not, however, entail the total abolition of State monopolies, but requires that they are adjusted in such a way as to ensure that there is no discrimination between nationals of Member States and between imported and domestic products. This may nevertheless necessitate the elimination of certain exclusive rights.[10]

1.2.2 Definition and scope of Article 37 EEC

A monopoly is a set of exclusive rights which a State either exercises itself or delegates to another body or undertaking. Article 37 applies only to:

- legal monopolies (i.e. monopolies originating in an act of sovereignty of the State and whose exclusivity is guaranteed by law). Under Article 37 (2) the notion extends to cases where the State, by using the legal provisions which enable it to do so, indirectly or de facto influences[11] inter-State trade.[12] This should not be mixed up with *de facto* monopolies, which are to be considered under the usual rules such as Article 90 EEC in connection with Article 86 EEC or other relevant Treaty provisions (see Section 2 below);
- national monopolies, it being understood that a set of regional monopolies may constitute a national monopoly;[13]
- monopolies on goods, as Article 37 EEC is placed in the goods chapter of the

[6] See Case 59/75 *Manghera* ECR [1976] 91.

[7] However, so-called 'reverse discrimination' (i.e. treating national production less favourably than the foreign) is of course always possible.

[8] See Cases 13/70 *Cinzano* [1970] ECR 1089 and 86/78 *Peureux I* [1979] ECR 897).

[9] See Case 78/82 *Commission* v. *Italy* [1983] ECR 1955.

[10] Ibid.

[11] In order to exercise an influence for instance on imports, it is not necessary for the State to control all the imports directly or indirectly. It is enough that it controls e.g. 65% of the needs of the domestic market (see Case C-347/88 *Commission* v. *Greece* [1990] ECR I-4747).

[12] See *Cinzano*, op. cit. n. 8.

[13] See Case 30/87 *Bodson* v. *Pompes funèbres* [1988] ECR 2479.

EEC Treaty.[14] The monopoly must concern commercial products capable of being subject to competition rules and inter-State trade.[15] Article 37 thus does not apply to service monopolies except in cases where such monopolies are liable to have an effect on inter-State trade in goods.[16] Furthermore, the obligation of adjustment applies only as regards products imported from other EC Member States (products in 'free circulation'[17] within the EC) and not *vis-à-vis* products imported into the State in question from third countries (for which e.g. import monopolies may be maintained).[18]

1.2.3 Exclusive rights and adjustments required

A monopoly is usually constituted by the sum of all or some of the following exclusive rights:

- prospecting (petroleum and gas);
- production, extraction (petroleum and gas), refining (petroleum), distillation;
- importation;
- exportation;
- wholesale trade;
- retail trade.

As regards *prospecting* (petroleum and gas), the practice of the Commission is to request that the Member States at least guarantee that the licences they grant for prospecting are offered also to foreign undertakings and that the conditions are objective and non-discriminatory. There are plans to make a directive on that subject,[19] but the Commission has not so far initiated very firm actions on these sensitive issues.

As regards *production*, the maintenance of production monopolies (i.e. in the wide sense, which includes extraction (petroleum and gas), refining (petroleum), and distillation monopolies) has been accepted. Such monopolies should however

[14] See Case 155/73 *Sacchi* [1974] ECR 409.

[15] See Case 6/64 *Costa* v. *ENEL*, op. cit. n. 5.

[16] See Case 271/81 *Mialocq* [1983] ECR 2057.

[17] The notion of products in 'free circulation' (*libre pratique*) is linked to the customs union provisions of the EEC Treaty. It means that a third country product can circulate freely in the Community once it has paid the relevant customs duties at the EC border. This notion is thus not directly transposable as such in the EEA context, which is not a customs union. However, the result in practice should be the same as in the EC since Art. 16 EEA applies regardless of the origin of the product.

[18] For instance, France has maintained, *vis-à-vis* third countries, its monopolies on potassic fertilizers, manufactured tobacco, and matches and had to adjust them *vis-à-vis* the new EC Member States. This means that some of the EC States will, due to the EEA, also have to adjust parts of monopolies which they have continued to apply towards EFTA States. This is the reason why the Commission has sent a questionnaire on this issue to all the EC Member States (see *XXIInd Report on Competition Policy*, 287).

[19] i.e. the 'Oil Directive' proposal, which covers prospecting, exploration, and extraction, and has caused great concern in Norway (*OJ* C 139 (2 June 1992), 12).

comply with the conditions that they are established in the public interest[20] and for non-economic reasons, respect the principle of proportionality, and are exercised in a non-discriminatory manner. The following discriminations have for instance been forbidden:

- interdiction, for the production monopoly, to distil raw material which is imported;[21]
- marketing of a product by the monopoly at an abnormally low price, before taxation, with the help of State subsidies;[22]
- fixing by the government of the prices of imported products when they are competing with those produced by the production monopoly;[23]

The production monopoly may be combined with a marketing monopoly (wholesale and retailing), but only for selling its own product.[24] The marketing of imported products (which compete with those of the production monopoly) should in principle be free, in accordance with the rules described below.

As regards *importation, exportation, and wholesale*, the following exclusive rights have been forbidden, and thus abolished, in the EC:

- exclusive right to import, which, as it constitutes a prohibited discrimination *vis-à-vis* the Community exporters, has been declared incompatible *per se* with Article 37 EEC,[25] this is also the case where import licences are automatically delivered or where a prior declaration of import is required;[26]
- exclusive right to export, which, as it is the corollary of the import right (Articles 30 and 34 EEC), has also been considered to be incompatible with Article 37 EEC;[27]
- exclusive right on wholesale, which, as its maintenance would deprive the abolition of exclusive right to import of its effects, is also contrary to Article 37 EEC.[28]

The following discriminations have for instance been forbidden:

- a stock obligation which is not obligatory when the products are procured from the national refinery (Greek oil monopoly);

[20] It would not, for instance, be possible to have a monopoly on the production of such items as cars or tables.

[21] See Case 119/78 *Peureux II* [1979] ECR 975.

[22] See Case 91/78 *Hansen II* [1979] ECR 935.

[23] See Case 90/82 *Commission* v. *France* [1983] ECR 2011. However, that the Italian Government should fix an 8% retail margin for tobacco products was accepted; see below.

[24] See for instance the case of the oil monopoly in Spain, where, for imported products, exclusive wholesale and retail rights have been abolished but the production monopoly still benefited from its exclusive service-station network (which was however abolished in Dec. 1992, see *XXIInd Report*, op. cit. n. 1, p. 280).

[25] See *Manghera*, op. cit. n. 6.

[26] However, a simple obligation to declare the operations of import or export is compatible with Art. 37 (see *Commission* v. *Greece*, op. cit. n. 11).

[27] See for instance Art. 14 (2) of the Greek Accession Act or Art. 48 (2) of the Spanish Accession Act.

[28] See for instance Arts. 48 (2) and 208 (2) of the Spanish and Portuguese Accession Act.

- an obligation for the wholesalers selling foreign products to be established in France and to furnish, as the production monopoly does, all the outlets of the national territory (French tobacco monopoly).

The only case where an import monopoly has been accepted by the ECJ was a situation where the State had the exclusive right to import crude oil intended for refining, an activity for which it also had an exclusive right. The Court said that the fact that the imports of crude oil are effected exclusively by the State, or under its control, is inherent in the existence of the State refining monopoly, the legality of which was not contested by the Commission.[29] However, the maintenance of exclusive import and marketing rights for other petroleum products was said to be incompatible with Community law.

As regards *retail trade*, the basic principle is that the conditions under which imported goods may be marketed (wholesale or retail) are by nature linked with potential barriers to entry. A monopoly on marketing, as it obliges importers to sell their products to the monopoly, makes it very difficult for newcomers to enter a market and to commercialize their goods therein. This usually results in a discrimination between national and foreign production.

The Commission often intervened with regard to 'marketing exclusive rights' (without distinguishing between wholesale and retail trade, see e.g. Article 208 (2) of the Portuguese Accession Act). Directive 88/301/EEC on telecommunications terminals[30] requires, *inter alia*, the abolition of all exclusive rights on the marketing of telecom terminals, regardless of whether they concern wholesale and/or retail trade.

Furthermore, the Court has ruled that, by having an exclusive right to market petroleum products, the Greek State had the power appreciably to influence imports.[31] Likewise, it has stated that the existence of import and marketing exclusive rights deprives EC economic operators of the possibility of having their products bought by the consumers in the country where the monopoly is granted such rights.[32]

The maintenance of a monopoly on retail trade also for imported products, has however, under certain strict conditions, been accepted. This has been the case for the Italian monopoly on manufactured tobacco.[33] The retail trade monopoly consisted in restricting retail trade to tobacconists (about 80,000) approved by the fiscal authorities, who are required to sell tobacco products at public resale prices indicated by a scale of charges fixed by law. The scale comprised a wide range of retail prices (more than 500 prices), each price being composed of the remuneration of the manufacturer and the wholesaler, the share taken by the exchequer, and the

[29] See *Commission* v. *Greece*, op. cit. n. 11.

[30] Op. cit. n. 4. This Directive is listed in Annex XIV EEA (competition), point 12. The Directive was partly annulled by the ECJ in its Case C-202/88 *Telecom I* [1991] ECR I-1223 (see explanations below in s. 2.3).

[31] See *Commission* v. *Greece*, op. cit. n. 11.

[32] See Case *Telecom I*, op. cit. n. 30.

[33] See *Commission* v. *Italy*, op. cit. n. 9. A preliminary ruling concerning this monopoly has recently been introduced which it could be interesting to follow (Case C-387/93).

margin of the retailer (fixed at 8 per cent). The production monopoly and the importers of foreign products were free to choose for each of their products one of the public resale prices or even a price not shown which was then incorporated in the scale.

The Court, without ruling on the legality of the retail trade monopoly, limited itself to declaring that the fixed margin of 8 per cent for the retailers, as it did not prevent foreign producers and importers freely determining their prices and thus prevent competition between the different brands, was not discriminatory and therefore not contrary to Article 37 EEC.

The Commission policy towards retail trade monopolies for imported products is thus the following:

1. Such a monopoly can be maintained in cases where it concerns heterogeneous products and may be analysed as an objective and non-discriminatory legislation regulating commerce. The monopoly should not be capable of hindering, directly or indirectly, actually or potentially, intra-Community trade[34] and should safeguard equality of chances between the different economic operators.

2. However, if it coexists with a production monopoly, appropriate measures should be taken to ensure a complete separation between the activities of the State as a producer and its activities as a retailer.

3. If the monopoly concerns homogeneous products where competition only exists as regards prices and the level of services offered by the retailer (such as petroleum products), a retail trade monopoly for imported products cannot be accepted (see above concerning the Spanish oil monopoly).

When discussing the necessary adjustments to retail trade monopoly with the Member States, the Commission has often requested that amendments be made to enable the laws to be analysed as or replaced by non-discriminatory commerce regulations which the Member States have the right to maintain, since, under certain conditions related to public interest, the disparities between national laws concerning the marketing of products are acceptable.[35] The following principles emerge from the practice followed by the Commission:

1. If the exercise of the distribution activity is submitted to the granting of an authorization, such authorization should be delivered according to objective criteria, for instance relating to the legal form of the undertakings, the sufficient technical means (e.g. stock capacities) compatible with the usual market conditions.

2. The conditions for the exercise of the distribution activity should be non-discriminatory as to the nationality of distributors, the quantities and the origin of the products procured, the credit facilities, the free choice of the products' prices,

[34] i.e. Wording used in the famous *Dassonville* case for defining the notion of measures of equivalent effect to quantitative restrictions (Case 8/74 [1974] ECR 837).

[35] See the well-known *Cassis de Dijon* case. It should be noted in this context that, formally, Art. 36 EEC (on possible derogations to the interdiction of quantitative restrictions) is not applicable to Art. 37 EEC. This is also the case in the EEA concerning Art. 13 EEA.

the fiscal regime, the sanctions in case of non-respect of the conditions for authorization, the opportunities for foreign producers to make themselves known to the distributors, the rules on publicity, etc.

3. The government may, for instance, as long as it does not do so in a discriminatory way, fix minimum distances between outlets, regulate the maximum number of outlets in a certain area, forbid advertising or exhibition in the shop windows, fix retail margins, etc.

There are also examples of other forbidden discriminations (related to the taxation of imported products). As said above, certain rules, although in appearance non-discriminatory, are nevertheless liable to have discriminatory effects. The following discriminations have been forbidden:

- imposition of a charge on the imported product to compensate for the difference in prices between such a product and the price paid by the monopoly to national producers;[36]
- imposition on the sole imported product of a charge for contributing to the costs of the monopoly;[37]
- imposition on the imported products of a charge attributed to the general budget and on the national products of a 'price complement' financing the monopoly and indirectly benefiting the national producers who sell their product to the monopoly (French alcohol monopoly).

As regards electricity and gas the Commission, although it acknowledges the special features of electricity, has recently initiated infringement proceedings against six Member States to force them to abolish their exclusive rights to import and export gas and electricity. As to exclusive rights on transmission, distribution, and production, the Commission has taken steps to liberalize the markets.[38] In this context, one of the important aspects is that vertically integrated monopolies should have production, transport, and distribution handled by separate divisions, with separate accounts (known as 'unbundling').

1.2.4 The procedure applicable for enforcing Article 37 EEC

Article 37 (1) and (2) has direct effect[39] and may thus be relied upon by individuals in national courts. The basic procedure at the disposal of the Commission for forcing a State to adjust its monopoly is the one laid down in Article 169 EEC (infringement procedure). Another procedure which may be used is that of Article

[36] See Case 91/75 *Miritz* [1976] ECR 217.

[37] See Case 45/75 *Rewe I* [1976] ECR 91.

[38] See proposal for a Council directive concerning common rules for the internal market in electricity and proposal for a Council directive concerning common rules for the internal market in natural gas (*OJ* C 65 (14 Mar. 1992), 4 and 14). Some EFTA States, such as Finland, Norway, and Sweden, have however already taken liberalization initiatives which to a certain extent anticipate the EC plans. On 8 Dec. 1993 the Commission adopted two amended proposals which were to be presented to the Energy Council on 10 Dec. 1993 (see *Europe*, 6124 (9 Dec. 1993), 13).

[39] See *Manghera*, op. cit. n. 6, and *Costa* v. *ENEL*, op. cit. n. 5.

90 (3) EEC, applied in connection with Article 37 or other provisions of the EEC Treaty (such as for instance the rules on free movement of goods or competition). This procedure is described in Section 2.5 below.[40]

However, in practice the Commission tries hard to solve the problems informally with the State concerned and uses its enforcement weapons mainly as a means of pressure (as the Member States usually 'spontaneously' amend their legislation or practices once the Commission starts a formal procedure).[41]

1.2.5 The monitoring of adjusted monopolies

According to the Court, Article 37 remains applicable wherever, even after the adjustment prescribed, the exercise by a State monopoly of its exclusive rights entails a discrimination or restriction prohibited by that article.[42]

Once a State monopoly has been adjusted, the products in 'free circulation' in the EC should be allowed non-discriminatory access to the market of the country where the monopoly in question operates. The monopoly's behaviour on the market will thus be closely monitored, and in particular from the competition point of view. This is due to the fact that the monopolies, although adjusted, are vertically integrated undertakings often having a dominant position and thus a strong bargaining power. For instance, in the case of a tobacco monopoly, foreign producers, having for years been used to licensing the manufacturing and distribution of their brand to the local monopoly, may still find it easier, even after the exclusive importing and distribution rights of the said monopoly have been abolished, to continue to have the whole process performed by the 'adjusted' monopoly (i.e. the production monopoly), instead of taking the trouble to set up an import and distribution network for the product they have manufactured themselves abroad.

Therefore, as regards an adjusted production monopoly, the following should be particularly examined:

1. If the foreign producers choose, instead of producing abroad and then importing, to give a production licence to the production monopoly, such a licence should not be too long or, if long, there should be an opportunity to end it at short notice (e.g. two months) and without penalties.

2. If the foreign producers choose to license the production monopoly for the distribution as well (i.e. to use the network of wholesale and retailers which the monopoly maintained for its own products), it should be ensured that the

[40] If there has been privatization or if the undertaking otherwise acts independently from the State, the behaviour is judged solely under Arts. 85 and 86 EEC.

[41] It is recalled that ESA may also, under Art. 31 of the ESA/Court Agreement, initiate infringement procedures in the EFTA Court against EFTA States which do not fulfil their EEA obligations. Likewise it may, under Art. 59(3) EEA (corresponding to Art. 90 (3) EEC), address appropriate measures to the EFTA States.

[42] See *Rewe I*, op. cit. n. 37.

distribution contracts or licences are non-exclusive and easily cancellable (e.g. at four months' notice).

As regards adjusted retail trade monopolies, the following require close attention:

1. Concerning the distribution of imported products and in cases where the exclusive retail rights have been abolished for imported products, the foreign producers or the importers should be given real opportunities to set up an independent distribution network, in parallel to the one tied or belonging to the monopoly.

2. If the exclusive retail rights have also been maintained concerning imported products, the supply contracts passed by the retailers operating within the monopoly with the production monopoly should be non-exclusive (so as to enable them also to distribute the imported products) and either concluded for a fairly short duration or easily cancellable.

The ECJ recently allowed, regarding service-station contracts concluded by the Spanish and Portuguese oil monopolies before EC accession, a duration of fifteen years (instead of ten years as provided for in Title III of Regulation 1984/83 on exclusive purchasing agreements) as long as the other conditions of the group exemption Regulation were respected (see Case C-39/92 of 19 November 1993, not yet reported).

2. PUBLIC UNDERTAKINGS

2.1 The EEA obligations (Article 59 EEA)

Article 59 EEA reproduces the text of Article 90 EEC on application of the competition rules to public undertakings. As compared with Article 90, the substance obligation is exactly the same and this implies the same remark as in Section 1 above regarding interpretation in conformity with the ECJ case-law. The only difference is that, in paragraph 3, the terms 'directives or decisions', as they partly reflected the legislative power of the Commission, have disappeared from the EEA text (which instead uses the word 'measures').

As regards the products to which Article 59 may apply, as a result of Article 8 (3) EEA, Article 59 EEA does not apply to products not falling under the EEA Agreement (e.g. agricultural products). Therefore, contrary to Article 16 EEA, Article 59 EEA as such does not apply to wine.

2.2 Interpretation given to Article 90 EEC by the ECJ and the Commission

The general features of Article 90 (1) EEC are the following:

– it is addressed to the Member States (and not to the undertakings);

- it constitutes a particular application of Article 5 (2) (loyalty clause);[43]
- it has direct effect when invoked in connection with another provision of the Treaty having itself direct effect;
- the 'measure' referred to is a measure taken by the State *vis-à-vis* the undertaking concerned (such as legislative acts, administrative directives, exercise of shareholders' rights, and even non-binding recommendations) and which thus forms the basis for the liability of the State. If the undertaking has acted independently, on its own initiative, the conduct should be judged solely under Articles 85 and 86 EEC;[44]
- the Commission may take general legislative measures (directives) on the basis of Article 90 (3) EEC (see Section 2.3 below);
- the Commission may also, on the basis of Article 90 (3), take individual decisions binding upon the Member State to which they are addressed. In these decisions, Article 90 (1) EEC is never applied alone, but always in connection with another provision of the EEC Treaty (such as Articles 7, 30, 34, 85, 86, 92, 93, or 95) (see Sections 2.4 and 2.5 below).

As to the notion of public undertaking, Article 2 of the Transparency Directive[45] gives a useful definition of a public undertaking: 'any undertaking over which the public authorities[46] may exercise directly or indirectly a dominant influence by virtue of their ownership of it, their financial participation therein, or the rules which govern it.'

According to the same Article, there is a presumption of dominant influence when the public authorities, directly or indirectly, in relation to an undertaking:

- hold the major part of the undertaking's subscribed capital;
- control the majority of the votes attaching to shares issues by the undertaking; or
- can appoint more than half of the members of the undertaking's administrative, managerial, or supervisory body.

There may however be cases where an undertaking could be 'public' for the purposes of Article 90 (1) EEC without meeting the criteria of Article 2 of the Transparency Directive.

Undertakings granted special or exclusive rights may be public or private undertakings. They usually form part of a 'closed class' (such as airlines granted particular routes or undertakings engaged in radio and television transmissions).[47]

The general features of the derogation under Article 90 (2) EEC are the following:

[43] To which corresponds Art. 3 (2) EEA. See Case 13/77 *GB-INNO-BM* v. *ATAB* [1977] ECR 2115.

[44] See *Telecom I*, op. cit. n. 32.

[45] Dir. 80/723 (*OJ* L 195 (29 July 1980), 35), point 1 of Annex xv EEA State aid; see Ch. X below.

[46] Being the State or regional or local authorities.

[47] See notably Cases 66/86 *Ahmed Saeed* [1989] ECR 803 (airlines), *Sacchi*, op. cit. n. 14 (TV broadcasting), and C/179/90 *Porto di Genova* [1991] I-5889 (port handling operations).

- it concerns both private and public undertakings;[48]
- it concerns undertakings 'entrusted with the operation of services of general economic interest', that is to say the provision and exploitation of a universal network (i.e. having general geographical coverage, and being provided to any service provider or user upon request within a reasonable period of time);[49]
- it also concerns undertakings which have 'the character of a revenue producing monopoly', i.e. undertakings which enjoy a fiscal monopoly by exploiting their exclusive rights to raise money for the State;
- such 'entrusting' must have been an act of public authority;[50]
- the burden of proof is on the State or the undertaking which invokes the provision.

The Commission examined the question of the application of Article 90 (2) in the preambles of the two Telecommunications Directives (referred to below in Section 2.3). In recital 18 of Directive 90/388, the Commission recognized that the conditions for applying the derogation of Article 90 (2) to voice telephony service were fulfilled. It admitted that voice telephony is one of 'the particular tasks' referred to in Article 90 (2). The Commission also admitted that the financial resources for the development of the network derive mainly from voice telephony and that its opening-up to competition could threaten the financial stability of the telecommunications organizations.

However, in recital 11 of Directive 88/301 (terminals) the Commission denied that the conditions for applying the derogation were fulfilled as the abolition of the special rights to import and market terminals would not obstruct the performance of the provision of the telecom network for the public (which is a service of general interest). The part on 'special rights' was however annulled by the ECJ (see in Section 2.3 below).

In two decisions taken on the basis of Article 90 (3) EEC[51] the Commission also examined whether the conditions of the derogation would apply, that is, whether reserving to the postal monopoly the express international delivery services was necessary for the performance of the operation services of general economic interest. The Commission rejected the arguments of the Dutch and Spanish authorities as they did not demonstrate that competition from private express mail undertakings would endanger the operation of the basic postal service.

The ECJ followed a similar line of reasoning in a recent case regarding the Belgian postal monopoly and the extent to which the EC competition rules should

[48] See Case 127/73 *BRT* v. *SABAM* [1974] ECR 313.

[49] e.g. a television undertaking operating under statutory powers, water authorities, basic postal services, voice telephony, or railways.

[50] See *BRT* v. *SABAM*, op. cit. n. 48.

[51] i.e. the so-called 'express delivery service' cases, Commission Decs. 90/16/EEC of 20 Dec. 1989 (Dutch case) (*OJ* L 10 (12 Jan. 1990), 47) and 90/456/EEC of 1 Aug. 1990 (Spanish case) (*OJ* L 233 (28 Aug. 1990), 19). Regarding the 'Dutch case', see also Joined Cases C-48 and C-66/90 *Express Delivery Service* [1992] ECR I-627, in which the ECJ annulled the Commission Decision for procedural reasons.

apply to it. The Court held that the competition rules were not applicable to the extent necessary for the achievement of the basic postal service operated in the general interest (which may presuppose a subsidy from the economically viable sectors of the postal service activity to less profitable sectors). The ECJ however recognized that services by private firms, such as collection of mail from the sender's premises and express delivery, do not belong to the basic postal service, and thus would not jeopardize the economic stability of the latter.[52]

2.3 Use by the Commission of the legislative powers granted to it by Article 90 (3) EEC

The Commission has so far issued three directives on the basis of Article 90 (3) EEC (ESA has not such a legislative power under Article 59 (3) EEA):

- Directive 88/301/EEC on competition in the markets in telecommunications terminal equipment (which requires, *inter alia*, the withdrawal of exclusive rights to import, market, connect, bring into service, and maintain telecom terminals);[53]
- Directive 90/388/EEC on competition in the markets for telecommunications services (which requires, *inter alia*, the withdrawal of exclusive rights to the supply of telecom services other than voice telephony and access to the telecom networks under objective and non-discriminatory conditions);[54]
- Directive 80/723 on the transparency of financial relations between Member States and public undertakings (op. cit. n. 45).

Annex XIV EEA gives the EFTA States a transitional period of six months as from the EEA entry into force for implementing the two Telecommunications Directives.

Furthermore, it should be noted that, in its cases *Telecom I* and *Telecom II*,[55] the Court, though recognizing the power of the Commission to adopt such general legislative directives, annulled certain provisions or parts of provisions due to insufficient motivation (the notion of 'special rights' was not precisely defined and the fact that the conclusion of certain contracts resulted from State measures was not demonstrated).[56]

[52] Case C-320/91 *Corbeau*, of 19 May 1993 (not yet reported).

[53] *OJ* L 131 (27 May 1988), 73, point 12 of Annex XIV EEA (competition).

[54] *OJ* L 192 (24 July 1990), 10, point 13 of Annex XIV EEA (competition).

[55] Respectively Case C-202/88, op. cit. n. 30, and Case C-271/90 *Telecom II* [1992] ECR I-5859.

[56] As to the consequences of these annulments by the ECJ in the EEA context, the situation is more than confused since one case was delivered on 19 Mar. 1991 (before the signature of the EEA) and the other one on 12 Nov. 1992 (after the EEA signature), meaning that even the possible application of Art. 6 EEA is complicated. However, this problem is mainly of a technical legal nature.

2.4 Examples of application of Article 90 (1) EEC to specific cases

The difficulty of applying Article 90 (1) EEC lies in the fact that one has first to determine whether the conduct of the public undertaking concerned is dictated by the State, or whether it results from an independent decision of the undertaking.

If the public undertaking has acted independently, on its own initiative, Article 90 (1) EEC is not applicable and the conduct in question should be evaluated, as for any private undertaking, under the normal competition rules. In cases where the public undertaking has acted in compliance with State 'measures' (as defined above), Article 90 (1) EEC applies.

The Commission has taken four individual decisions based on Article 90 (3) EEC in the field of insurance, special transport tariffs for Spanish nationals, and international express delivery service, under which the following State measures have been declared incompatible with Article 90 (1) EEC:[57]

- provisions obliging all public properties in Greece to be insured with a State-owned insurance company and obliging State banks to recommend customers seeking a loan to take out the insurance required in connection with it with a State-owned company;[58]
- provisions reserving tariff reductions for transport only for Spanish nationals residing in the Balearic and Canary Islands and excluding from such reductions EC nationals also residing in such islands;[59]
- Dutch provisions reserving to the PTT the express service of collecting, transport, and distribution of certain letters up to 500 grammes at a certain price as well as provisions requiring the prior registration of tariffs for such services by private undertakings;[60]
- Spanish provisions reserving to the PTT the service of express international couriers for the collecting, the transport, and the distribution of letters.[61]

Each time the Member States concerned are required to inform the Commission, within two months of the notification of the decision, of what measures they have taken to comply with the decision.

Furthermore, the Commission has taken action[62] as regards, for instance, the following exclusive rights: remailing services (Denmark); supply of modems to be connected with the telephone network (Belgium, Germany, Italy, and Spain);

[57] As to liberalization of postal services in general, the Commission issued a green paper on the matter (COM (91) 476) and guidelines on postal services (COM (93) 247).

[58] Dec. 85/276/EEC of 24 Apr. 1985 (*OJ* L 152 (11 June 1985), 25). Art. 90 (1) applied in connection with Arts. 52, 53, 5 (2), and 3 (*f*) EEC.

[59] Dec. 87/359/EEC of 22 June 1987 (*OJ* L 194 (15 July 1987), 28). Art. 90 (1) applied in connection with Art. 7 EEC.

[60] Dec. 90/16/EEC, op. cit. n. 51. Art. 90 (1) applied in connection with Art. 86 EEC. The Commission also convinced some other Member States to change their provisions on international express delivery service.

[61] Dec. 90/456/EEC, op. cit. n. 51. Art. 90 (1) applied in connection with Art. 86 EEC.

[62] Cases solved informally (without formal action) or still pending.

supply of the first telex terminals (Belgium and Italy); radiotelephony (Greece); retransmission of telex messages originating in the country concerned (Greece); exclusive right to provide job-placement services (Germany);[63] reduced or preferential fares for air and sea transport granted only to nationals of the country concerned residing in some islands (Italy, Portugal, and Spain); obligation for civil servants of the State concerned to fly with the national airline (Belgium and Germany); provision of assistance during stop-overs at national airports (reserved to the national airline company) (Spain); reduction in charges for assistance supplied during stop-overs by the national airline company to other national airline companies; handling services in maritime ports.

On some of these exclusive rights, the Commission has started a general inquiry in the EC (i.e. a questionnaire sent to all the Member States) to find out what the practices are in the other Member States. This is the case concerning assistance during stop-overs in airports; reduced or preferential fares for the transport of nationals residing, for example, in islands but not granted to EC nationals residing in these places; and betting, gaming, lotteries, and similar activities.

2.5 Features of Article 90 (3) decisions and the procedure applied by the Commission when taking such decisions

As seen above, Article 90 (3) EEC empowers the Commission to adopt directives as well as to take individual legally binding decisions.[64]

The Commission decisions based on Article 90 (3) EEC have the following features:

- they are addressed to a specific Member State;
- they declare incompatible with Article 90 (1) EEC, in connection with another Treaty provision, a given State measure and indicate the measures that the State should adopt in order to comply with its Community obligations;
- they may be directly relied upon by individuals in national proceedings.

The 'Dutch case' referred to above has however been annulled by the Court of Justice,[65] which, after having recognized the right of the Commission to adopt such decisions, stated that the Commission did not respect the right of defence of the parties involved, i.e. the Netherlands and the Dutch PTT.

The Court outlined what procedural steps the Commission should follow in a procedure leading to an Article 90 (3) decision in order to respect the elementary

[63] In its Case C-41/90 *Höfner and Elser*, op. cit. Ch. VIII n. 7, the Court stated that a public agency providing a job-placement service for executives was an 'undertaking' for the purposes of competition rules and that a Member State would be in breach of Art. 90 if the public agency having exclusive rights was manifestly incapable of satisfying demand for such services.

[64] See *Express Delivery Service*, op. cit. n. 51.

[65] Ibid.

rights of defence (right to be heard) and the Commission practice is nowadays the following:[66]

1. The Commission usually sends a written request for information to the State in question and has contact with the public undertaking concerned as well as with possible complainants.

2. The Commission then sends to the State concerned a complete and precise statement of objections, containing a description of the facts, the objections of the Commission, and a time-limit for reply (two months). The State should also be given an opportunity to make known its views on any comments submitted by interested third parties.

3. A copy of the statement of objections is forwarded to the public undertaking concerned which should be given the opportunity to be heard (i.e. to send written comments).

4. According to the Court, the public undertaking concerned should be given the right to be heard if:

- it is a direct beneficiary of the contested State measure;
- it is named in the State measure;
- it is expressly mentioned in the Commission decision;
- it directly bears the economic consequences of the decision;

5. The Commission adopts an Article 90 (3) decision.

As this procedure is much quicker and gives it more powers, the Commission clearly now has a tendency to apply it rather than the more cumbersome infringement procedure under Article 169 EEC. This procedure is also at the disposal of ESA regarding EFTA States (Article 59 (3)).

[66] See *XXIInd Report on Competition Policy*, 201. This procedure is a sort of mixture between Reg. 17 (competition) and Art. 93 EEC (State aid, i.e. resembling the infringement procedure under Art. 169 EEC).

X

STATE AID

(ARTICLES 61–64, PROTOCOLS 26 AND 27, AND ANNEX XV)

1. IMPORTANCE OF THE STATE AID RULES IN THE EEA CONTEXT

State aid rules, being part of the competition rules in the wide sense, are an essential element for securing that the benefits resulting from the liberalization of trade are not circumvented by aid measures taken by governments or State agencies at any level. The EEA Agreement will bring the EFTA States into a completely new era in this respect.

The former EFTA State aid regime was based on Article 13 of the Stockholm Convention, which lays down the prohibition of certain export aid and other forms of aid having as a purpose or effect to frustrate the benefits expected from the removal of duties and quantitative restrictions on trade between Contracting Parties. In addition, this provision has been supplemented by some guidelines on its interpretation, issued by the EFTA Council. These guidelines, being mainly of a general nature, are not, however, comparable to the quasi-legislative measures—frameworks, communications, and letters—adopted in the Community.

As regards enforcement, EFTA, being a traditional intergovernmental organization without supranational character, has never had sufficient means to control its Member States in the field of subsidies. Following the provisions of the Stockholm Convention, the control mechanism was based on the action taken by other countries when one of the Contracting Parties has granted unlawful aid; but this possibility has not been used actively.

Neither have the State aid provisions contained in the free trade agreements between the Community and the EFTA States been invoked very often. It is only very recently that the EC has brought up some cases of aid in Austria, stating that the aid in question was contrary to the EC–Austria FTA.

As compared with the situation described above, the EEA Agreement will mean a considerable change. As from now, not only EC Member States are submitted to a strict control of their subsidies, exercised by a supranational body; EFTA States also will find themselves under similar control. In principle, the competent surveillance authority will have to be notified of all aid measures, that is, either the

EC Commission or ESA, and they may not be implemented without prior approval. In addition, existing aid in the EFTA countries will be under constant scrutiny, as has been the case in the Community.

State aid may, if not used in a correct manner, be one of the most harmful ways to distort free trade. Therefore, the task of controlling subsidies will certainly be one of the most important ones for safeguarding that the equal conditions of competition in the EEA are not distorted by actions of States. The means for this, that is; rather detailed substantive rules and the powers to carry out the control, are put in place through the EEA and ESA/Court Agreements. In addition, the close co-operation between the surveillance authorities should ensure that diverging policies between the pillars will not exist.

The objective of this chapter is to clarify issues related to State aid which are specific to the EEA Agreement. Therefore, questions concerning the interpretation of the rules which are common to the EEC or ECSC Treaties, on the one hand, and the EEA Agreement, on the other, are only briefly described.

2. SUBSTANTIVE STATE AID RULES

2.1 Article 61 EEA

The EEA rules on State aid are, as is the case with so many other fields, based on the corresponding Community rules. This means, as regards the substantive rules, that the provisions contained in Article 92 EEC have been reproduced, with some technical adaptations, in Article 61 of the EEA Agreement.

Article 61 (1) contains a general prohibition on aid granted by EC Member States, EFTA States, or through State resources which distorts or threatens to distort competition by favouring certain undertakings or production of certain goods and affects trade between Contracting Parties.

On the other hand, Article 61 (2) lists categories of aid which are considered compatible with the functioning of the Agreement:[1]

- aid having a social character and granted to individual consumers, provided that it is granted on a non-discriminatory basis as to the origin of the goods concerned;
- aid to make good the damage caused by natural disasters or exceptional occurrences;
- aid granted to certain areas of Germany affected by the former division of the country, which aid has continued to be permissible to some extent even since the reunification.

Finally, Article 61 (3) contains a list of cases where aid may be exempted. The categories referred to are the following:

[1] The relevant provisions of the EEA Agreement relating to State aid are reproduced in Annex A.

- aid to promote economic development of areas where the standard of living is abnormally low or where there is serious underemployment;
- aid to promote important projects of common European interest or to remedy a serious economic disturbance in the economy of an EC Member State or an EFTA State;
- aid to facilitate the development of certain economic activities or of certain economic areas if the effects of the aid to trade are not contrary to the common interest.

Following the provisions concerning homogeneity (notably Article 6 EEA, see above in Chapter 2, Section 7.1), the interpretation to be given to Article 61 EEA is one which has already been developed in the Community regarding Article 92 EEC. Without going into any details, this means, *inter alia*, the following:

- the concept of aid has to be interpreted broadly, which means that the measures constituting State aid may take also forms other than direct subsidies, such as tax measures favouring certain undertakings, loan guarantees or interest subsidies, capital injections, differentiated prices for goods or services provided by public enterprises or authorities, etc.;[2]
- economic measures which are of a general nature and apply to all economic operators in a non-discriminatory way and without leaving discretionary powers to the authorities do not normally constitute State aid;
- State aid rules cover aid granted to all undertakings, whether private companies or public enterprises;[3]
- the legal basis of the measure (law, decree, ministerial decision, etc.) or how it is administered has no significance as regards the applicability of Article 61;[4]
- likewise aid granted by regional or local authorities has to be assessed under the State aid rules;[5]
- potential effects on trade between Contracting Parties also have to be taken into consideration.[6]

The use of the exemptions granted under subparagraphs (*a*) and (*c*) of Article 61 (3) is discussed later under Section 2.2.3. As to the use of Article 92 (3) (*b*) EEC (to which corresponds Article 61 (3) (*b*) EEA), which has been very limited, some remarks can be made concerning the concept of 'common European interest'. A derogation based on the common European interest has been applied in the EC, for

[2] For the concept of aid see e.g. the following judgments of the ECJ: Case 323/82 *Intermills* v. *Commission* [1984] ECR 3809, Case 18/84 *Commission* v. *France* [1985] ECR 1339, Case 234/84 *Belgium* v. *Commission* [1986] ECR 2263, Case 40/85 *Belgium* v. *Commission* [1986] ECR 2321, Joined Cases 67, 68, and 70/85 *Van der Kooy and Others* v. *Commission* [1988] ECR 219, Case 57/86 *Greece* v. Commission [1988] ECR 2855.

[3] See e.g. Case 40/85 *Belgium* v. *Commission*, op. cit. n. 2.

[4] See e.g. Case 78/76 *Steinike & Weinlig* [1977] ECR 595 and Case 290/83 *Commission* v. *France* [1985] ECR 439.

[5] See e.g. Case 248/84 *Germany* v. *Commission* [1987] ECR 4013.

[6] See e.g. Case 102/87 *France* v. *Commission* [1988] ECR 4067.

example to projects which are both qualitatively and quantitatively important, are transnational in character, and allow Community industry to benefit from all the advantages of the Single Market.[7] Naturally, it was important for the EFTA countries that the concept should also serve the interests of the whole EEA, or that it should not, at least, be detrimental to EFTA countries. Therefore, there was obviously a need to broaden the scope of the definition, in order to avoid conflicting interests in the EEA context. The problem was solved through a joint declaration on the matter,[8] stating that in establishing whether a derogation can be granted under Article 61 (3) (*b*) the EC Commission shall take the interests of the EFTA States into account and ESA the interests of the Community. It seems likely that the co-operation between the two surveillance authorities will also need to be close in this type of case.

2.2 Secondary legislation

2.2.1 General issues related to Annex XV EEA

The secondary legislation in the field of State aid is contained in Annex XV to the EEA Agreement.[9] The EC legislation in this area has developed almost entirely by means of so-called 'non-binding *acquis*'. This means that, with the exception of Commission Directive 80/723/EEC on transparency of financial relations between Member States and public undertakings,[10] the *acquis* taken over and listed in Annex XV comprises various frameworks, letters from the Commission to the Member States, Commission communications, and even extracts from the Commission Annual Reports on Competition Policy. These kinds of acts have in principle no binding effects as such *vis-à-vis* the State Parties to the Agreement.[11] On the other hand, the listing puts an obligation on both the EC Commission and ESA to take due account of them in the EEA context, which is important with regard to the uniform application of the provisions in the main Agreement. Furthermore, it clearly shows to the States and also to the undertakings what kind of interpretation can be expected from the surveillance authorities.

The substantive non-binding acts cover various issues, such as:

- frameworks on sectoral aid schemes (aid to textile, synthetic fibres, and motor vehicle industries);

[7] *XXIst Report on Competition Policy* by the Commission of the European communities (1991), 132. See also Judgments of the ECJ in Joined Cases 62 and 72/87, *Exécutif régional Wallon and SA Glaverbel* v. *Commission* [1988] ECR 1573.

[8] Joint Declaration on Art. 61 (3) (*b*) of the Agreement, reproduced in Annex A below.

[9] Annex XV is reproduced in Annex A below. The only State aid act listed elsewhere is Council Reg. (EEC) 1107/70 of 4 June 1970 on the granting of aid for transport by rail, road, and inland waterway, which, as last amended, can be found in Annex XIII on transport (in point 11).

[10] It has to be noted that there is also another binding act, the Seventh Shipbuilding Directive, which was not taken over. The issue is further discussed in s. 2.2.3 below.

[11] In the Community, the frameworks have been considered as non-binding policy statements or proposals for appropriate measures under Art. 93 (1) EEC. The latter may have a binding effect provided that the Member State concerned has agreed to it. See Case C-325/91, *France* v. *Commission* of 16 June 1993 (not yet reported).

- frameworks on general systems of regional aid, laying down the principles applicable for such aid;
- horizontal frameworks (such as those covering environmental aid and aid to research and development);
- rules applicable to general aid schemes (such as those covering aid related to rescue and restructuring);
- rules applicable to cases of cumulation of aid for different purposes;
- aid to employment; and
- control of aid to the steel industry.

As it is the case with the notices and guidelines in the field of competition, ESA had an obligation to issue acts corresponding to those included in Annex XV.[12] For this purpose, ESA has made a certain number of adaptations to the text of the non-binding acts which have been, in principle, only of a technical nature, as it could not, due to the homogeneity requirements, change the substance of the rules contained in the acts. The acts are to be issued in the form of a consolidated version.[13] This has made it possible to set together the original texts which have been developed over more than two decades, while at the same time leaving aside those parts of the original acts which were already outdated. Due to this, the ESA compilation is more readable than the Commission texts. The latter are, in many cases, difficult to understand for others than those who are real experts in the field.

The purpose here is not to discuss all the secondary State aid legislation, binding or non-binding. There are, however, certain issues concerning substantive rules which need to be brought up due to some specificities in the EEA. Such issues cover regional aid (Section 2.2.2), aid to shipbuilding (Section 2.2.3), and the steel sector (Section 2.2.4).

2.2.2 Regional aid

The granting of regional aid within the EEA is based on Article 61 (3) (*a*) and (*c*) EEA. Pursuant to Article 6 EEA, the interpretation given to these provisions is the one already applied in the Community. In addition, the different frameworks on regional aid developed by the EC Commission have been taken over.

Article 61 (3) (*a*) can be used as a basis for authorizing regional aid in cases where the standard of living is abnormally low or where there is serious underemployment. Article 61 (3) (*c*), on the other hand, is used for the development of certain economic areas, provided that such aid does not affect trading conditions to an extent contrary to the common interest. The aid granted on the basis of these two provisions is, therefore, aimed at different purposes, i.e. at areas with a different level of economic development.

[12] This obligation is contained in Art. 24 of the ESA/Court Agreement and concerns only those acts actually listed in Annex XV. As regards the future issuing of non-binding acts in the field of State aid, the same principles as concerning competition apply; see further Ch. VIII s. 3.2.2.

[13] The future non-binding acts will be reflected as amendments of this consolidated version.

The application of the two provisions also differs. For Article 61 (3) (*a*), the decisions are based on a method assessing the relative level of development by comparing the GDP figures of the area with the average figures of the EEA.[14] To get more accurate and comparable information the GDP figures are measured in purchasing power standards (GDP/PPP), that is, the differences in the cost of living are taken into account. The Commission (for the Community) and ESA (for the EFTA States) then decide on the maximum aid ceilings applicable for each region eligible for aid under Article 61 (3) (*a*). The highest permissible aid has been fixed at 75 per cent net grant equivalent (NGE)[15] of initial investment, the alternative ceiling being 13,000 ECU per job created by the investment. Normally the aid ceilings are, however, set lower. Even operating aid, which is normally not permissible, may under very strict conditions be authorized in the context of Article 61 (3) (*a*).

'Article 61 (3) (*c*) regions' are those with more general socio-economic problems in relation to the national level. For the application of this provision, a method has been established which takes into consideration the national regional problems, also placing them, however, in the EEA context. The method is divided into two stages. In the first stage, the surveillance authority concerned assesses the socio-economic situation of the region on the basis of two alternative criteria: the income measured by gross domestic product (GDP) or gross value added at factor cost (GVA, which is an indicator closely corresponding to GDP), as well as structural unemployment. The better the position of the State concerned is in relation to the whole EEA,[16] the wider the disparity of the region within that country has to be in order to make it possible to grant aid. The first stage is complemented by a second stage of analysis allowing other relevant factors to be taken into account, such as the trend and structure of unemployment, the development of employment, net migration, demographic pressure, population density, activity rates, productivity, the structure of economic activity, investment, geographic situation and topography, as well as infrastructure. Meeting the relevant threshold in the first stage does not automatically qualify the region to receive State aid if the second stage of analysis does not support the findings. On the other hand, regions which are at the margin of the thresholds applied may be eligible for aid if the second stage reveals an adequate justification.

As a novelty, the EEA Agreement introduced an additional element for the appreciation of regional aid. According to the Joint Declaration on Article 61 (3) (*c*) (reproduced in Annex A to this book), it is possible, in addition to the criteria developed earlier within the Community, to take into account also some exceptional situations, such as a very low population density, even if the eligibility of the regions has to be denied in the context of Article 61 (3) (*a*) and according to the criteria of

[14] This applies, in practice, only to EFTA countries, as for aid granted by EC Member States the average taken as a point of comparison will continue to be the EC average.

[15] i.e. the tax effects are taken into consideration in the calculation of the aid intensity.

[16] In the case of EC Member States, the comparison is made to EC averages.

the first stage of analysis under subparagraph (*c*). This is an important element especially for the Nordic EFTA countries, which are economically rather developed but which, due to some of their large but underpopulated regions, face problems the overcoming of which may necessitate the use of regional incentives. It remains, however, open how this principle will be applied in practice. It looks possible that it may have a certain importance with regard to some very remote regions as well as those which are close to fulfilling the thresholds although not quite achieving them.

Another aspect related to regional aid is the aid granted through the various Community financial instruments, the most important ones being the EC Structural Funds,[17] which aim at promoting economic and social cohesion in the Community. In addition, financial support for the same purpose is provided through the European Investment Bank and some other instruments. For the aid granted through these institutions or instruments, the general EC rules on State aid are not applicable as such. Therefore, it would obviously not have been possible to have either in the EEA Agreement provisions subjecting Community aid to the same rules as aid granted by States, although the funds are of enormous magnitude.

As the EFTA countries do not have any similar internal financial arrangements, the situations arising may in some cases look unbalanced, especially when more developed EC Member States may also be beneficiaries of this support. Although a clear majority of the EC assistance is directed to infrastructural investments, there are also measures which concern certain activities or types of enterprises and would normally be subject to notification under Article 93 (2) EEC if granted at Member State level. From the EFTA States' point of view, the latter cases might even sometimes have been considered as trade-distortive in the EEA context.

The compromise achieved on this issue is reflected in the text of a joint declaration,[18] where it is stated that financial support to undertakings by the EC Structural Funds, EIB, or other financial instruments shall be in keeping with the provisions of the Agreement. This principle concerning compatibility of the aid granted through the funds has already been applied within the Community and is now extended to cover the whole EEA. In addition, exchange of information and views on these forms of aid can be requested by either of the two surveillance authorities.

2.2.3 Aid to shipbuilding

The shipbuilding industry is considered to be of great importance for many Community regions. At the same time, the industry has been facing hard competition from foreign shipyards, encouraged in many cases by important subsidies granted to them. In order to allow the Community shipyards to respond to the competition, the EC Member States have been allowed to grant operating aid to

[17] The European Regional Development Fund (ERDF, known as 'Feder' in French), the European Social Fund (ESF), and the European Agricultural Guidance and Guarantee Fund (EAGGF, known as 'FEOGA' in French).

[18] Joint Declaration on aid granted through the EC structural funds and other financial instruments.

their shipyards, which is certainly a very exceptional situation, as normally such aid is considered as most distortive and, therefore, strictly prohibited. This operating aid has been made possible through application of Article 92 (3) (*d*) EEC, which allows the EC Council to exempt other categories of aid than those listed in the preceding subparagraphs (*a*)–(*c*). On basis of Article 92 (3) (*d*) the Council has adopted directives, the latest of which is the Seventh Shipbuilding Directive.[19] The Shipbuilding Directives have set the conditions for operating aid and laid down the principles for the ceilings to be applied.

The shipbuilding industry is also economically significant for some of the Nordic EFTA countries. Therefore, it would undoubtedly have been important for them to obtain equal conditions of competition in this area, especially as EC shipyards have also been able to obtain subsidies when competing with shipyards located in EFTA States. It was not, however, possible to find a solution for including the Seventh Shipbuilding Directive in the Agreement, and the only arrangement in this situation was to exclude the whole sector from the application of State aid provisions. Otherwise the EC shipyards would have continued to be subsidized while the EFTA shipyards would have been subjected to the normal rules applicable to State aid prohibiting the granting of operating aid.

The solution was realized through two declarations. A joint declaration on shipbuilding provides that the Contracting Parties shall refrain from the application of the general rules on State aid laid down in Article 61 EEA to the sector of shipbuilding 'until the expiry of the Seventh Shipbuilding Directive (i.e. at the end of 1993)'. In a unilateral declaration by the Community, it was stated that the Commission, while assessing the competitive situation in shipbuilding, in connection with the decision on a possible new directive, will do so taking into account the whole EEA and will also consult closely with the EFTA States.

In May 1993 the EC Council made a decision in principle to prolong the application of the Seventh Shipbuilding Directive. As this situation is something that was not foreseen in the EEA Agreement, it remains to be seen how it will be dealt with; that is, whether equal conditions of competition will be introduced by including the Seventh Shipbuilding Directive in the Agreement, whether the sector will still be excluded from the application of general rules through the prolongation of the Joint Declaration, or if the general rules will apply normally in the EEA context. The last option would materialize if the Directive is not taken over and the Joint Declaration is not prolonged, in which case the EC Member States could only grant operating aid to their shipyards if there were no EFTA shipyard competing for the same order with an EC shipyard.

2.2.4 Steel sector

Issues related to coal and steel products falling within the scope of the ECSC Treaty were earlier covered by the Free Trade Agreements between the European Coal and

[19] Council Dir. 90/684/EEC of 21 Dec. 1990 on aid to shipbuilding (*OJ* L 380 (31 Dec. 1990), 27).

Steel Community, its Member States, and the individual EFTA States. After the entry into force of the EEA, these agreements remain unaffected, unless otherwise provided in Protocol 14 EEA.[20]

Article 5 of Protocol 14 provides that the Contracting Parties shall comply with the rules for aid to the steel industry. In this context, reference is made in particular to Commission Decision 322/89/ECSC concerning State aid to the steel sector (aid to research and development, environmental investments, and closures). This decision expired at the end of 1991 but the Contracting Parties declared their commitment to integrate into the Agreement, by its entry into force, those new rules which replaced the said Decision.[21]

Those steel products which fall outside the scope of the ECSC Treaty are dealt with on the basis of the general EEA rules on State aid.

3. PROCEDURAL RULES

3.1 General issues

Article 62 EEA provides that all existing systems of State aid in the territory of the Contracting Parties, as well as any plans to grant or alter aid, shall be subject to constant review as to their compatibility with Article 61. This task will, as to the EC Member States, be carried out by the EC Commission according to the rules laid down in Article 93 EEC. With regard to the EFTA States, ESA will have this obligation according to the rules laid down in the ESA/Court Agreement.

In addition, Protocol 26 to the EEA Agreement obliges the EFTA States to entrust ESA with equivalent powers and similar functions to those of the EC Commission for the application of the competition rules applicable to State aid. This obligation concerns the application of both the EEC and ECSC provisions.

The EFTA States have fulfilled the obligation set out in Protocol 26 through Article 24 of and Protocol 3 to the ESA/Court Agreement. Article 1 of Protocol 3 reproduces Article 93 EEC and Article 2 lays down the principles concerning the establishment and functions of an EFTA Advisory Committee on aid granted for transport by rail, road, and inland waterway, a Committee which also exists on the EC side.

The main features of the procedural State aid rules are discussed below.

3.2 Notification of new aid measures

All State aid measures, whether aid schemes or individual cases, have to be notified to the EC Commission (for aid proposed by EC Member States) or ESA (for those

[20] Protocol 14 EEA, which covers trade in coal and steel products, is briefly described in Ch. III, s. 1.4.

[21] i.e. Commission Dec. 3855/91/ECSC of 27 Nov. 1991 establishing Community rules for aid to the steel industry, which can be expected to be included in the Additional Package to be adopted by the EEA Joint Committee after the entry into force of the Agreement.

by EFTA States) with the exception of individual awards under aid schemes already approved. As in the field of competition, there are also in the field of State aid certain cases, not exceeding the thresholds specified (*de minimis*),[22] which fall outside the scope of application of Article 61 (1) EEA.

The State aid rules apply, as mentioned earlier, also to aid granted on a regional or local level. In these cases too the notification has to be submitted by the central government authorities.

If the surveillance authority concerned finds, after having received a notification, that the information provided is not complete, it has the right to request further information. The time-limit[23] allowed for the assessment of the notification starts to run only after this additional information has been received.

3.3 Decisions following the notification of proposed aid measures

As provided for in Article 93 (3) EEC and Article 1 (3) of Protocol 3 to the ESA/Court Agreement, proposed aid measures cannot be implemented before an authorization has been granted by the Commission or ESA. The authorization can be given either through a clearance without opening a formal procedure, or, if such a procedure has been opened, after the proceedings have been completed.

3.3.1 Clearance of a proposed aid measure without opening a formal procedure

If the proposed aid measure does not fall under the prohibition contained in Article 92 (1) EEC or Article 61 (1) EEA, is covered by categories listed in Article 92 (2) EEC or Article 61 (2) EEA (aid considered compatible with the rules), or is eligible for exemption provided under Article 92 (3) EEC or Article 61 (3) EEA, the measure can be cleared without any further proceedings. Before such a decision not to raise an objection is made, the surveillance authority concerned is not obliged to provide information to or request comments from other States or interested parties.[24] Only after the decision is made is a short notice published in the *EC Official Journal* in order to give information to interested parties and to increase transparency on decision-making in the State aid field.[25] If the surveillance authorities fail to respect the time-limit of two months to make a decision, the State

[22] The conditions of the *de minimis* rule, in the State aid field, are specified in ch. 12 of the ESA guide to procedures and substantive rules in State aid cases, corresponding to the Community guidelines on State aid for small and medium-sized enterprises (*OJ* C 213 (19 Aug. 1992), 2) and Letter from the Commission to Member States IV.E.1 (93) D/06878 of 23 Mar. 1993. In short, payments up to the cash grant equivalent of 50,000 ECU within a three-year period, or up to 100,000 ECU if the aid is granted for different categories of expenditure, can be granted to an undertaking without prior notification and authorization. This does not, however, apply to export aid or aid to sectors subject to special rules, such as synthetic fibres, the motor vehicle industry, transport, and steel.

[23] Normally two months.

[24] See ECJ Cases 84/82 *Germany* v. *Commission* [1984] ECR 1451, and 91 and 127/83 *Heineken* v. *Inspecteurs der Vennootschapsbelasting* [1984] ECR 3435.

[25] The decisions of ESA will be published in the EEA section of the *EC Official Journal* and the EEA supplement (Nordic languages).

concerned can implement the notified measure, provided that it has given prior notice to the surveillance authority in question, and the aid is then treated as an existing aid.[26]

On the other hand, if there are any doubts on the compatibility of the proposed aid measure, a procedure under Article 93 (2) EEC or Article 1 (2) of Protocol 3 to the ESA/Court Agreement has to be opened.

3.3.2 Opening of a formal procedure

The opening of a formal investigation procedure gives the surveillance authorities a chance to examine more thoroughly cases where doubts on the compatibility of the aid exist. It also gives the parties concerned the right to be heard. It has to be noted that the opening of the procedure does not mean that the aid measure could not, at the end, be authorized.

The opening of a formal investigation procedure means that the State concerned is informed about the doubts the surveillance authority has with regard to the aid measure proposed and is given a short time to comment upon them. If the State does not reply to the opening of proceedings or does not provide information requested by the surveillance authority, a decision can be made on the basis of the information available.[27]

The other EEA States as well as interested third parties (such as natural persons, undertakings, or associations whose interests might be affected by the granting of aid, and in particular competing undertakings and trade associations[28]) may also submit their comments (which is not the case as regards an aid measure cleared without opening a formal procedure). This opportunity is granted through the publication of a notice in the *EC Official Journal*, inviting interested third parties to comment, normally within one month of the publication. The notice published contains the same information as the notice of proceedings addressed to the State concerned, with the exception that confidential information contained in the latter cannot be made public.

The State concerned is informed of all comments made by other States or interested third parties and is allowed to make remarks on them. If this opportunity is not offered, the information provided by other parties cannot, in principle, be used in the final decision.[29]

3.3.3 Final decision

At the end of the investigation procedure, the surveillance authority concerned has to take a decision which can be subject to a judicial review under Article 173 EEC or Article 36 ESA/Court Agreement.

[26] See ECJ Cases 120/73 *Lorenz* v. *Germany* [1973] ECR 1471 and C-312/90 *Spain* v. *Commission* [1992] ECR I-4117.

[27] See e.g. Case 40/85 *Belgium* v. *Commission*, op. cit. n. 2.

[28] See Case *Intermills* v. *Commission*, op. cit. n. 2.

[29] Case 234/84 *Belgium* v. *Commission*, op. cit. n. 2. See also Case C-301/87 *France* v. *Commission* [1990] ECR-307.

The decision can either authorize the aid measure proposed or prohibit it. It can also authorize the aid partially or put conditions on it, such as a reporting obligation.

The negative decisions and those laying down conditions are published in full in the *EC Official Journal*. In the case of a positive decision, only the letter informing the State concerned about the authorization of the aid is made public.

3.4 Unlawful aid

The procedure explained above in Section 3.2 applies, in principle, also to unlawful aid, by which is meant either aid which has not been notified or aid which, despite the fact that it has been notified, has been put into effect in a different way from that authorized or before an authorization has been granted.

In cases involving unlawful aid, the surveillance authorities first request information on the measure in question from the State concerned. After receiving a reply, the surveillance authority may either authorize the aid without opening a formal investigation procedure or decide to continue the examination of the case. If no or only insufficient information is received, the assessment of the situation is made on the basis of the information which is available.[30]

In the case of unlawful aid, the surveillance authority has the right to issue, after giving the State concerned the opportunity to submit its comments on the matter, an interim decision ordering the suspension of the payments pending the outcome of the examination and requesting the State to provide any information and documentation which are necessary for the assessment of the case. If the State fails to suspend payment of the aid, the surveillance authority in question is entitled, while carrying out the examination on the substance of the matter, to bring the matter before the competent Court by applying for a declaration that such payment amounts to an infringement of the EEC Treaty/EEA Agreement.[31]

A final negative decision concerning unlawfully granted aid may contain an order to the State concerned to reclaim the aid in question from the recipient.[32] It has, however, to be recalled that the decision ordering the reimbursement of the aid, if it is followed in the first place, is not, from the economic point of view, necessarily a sufficient sanction, as the aid may already have had effects which cannot be undone. Claiming damages before a national court would not necessarily, on the other hand, prove successful either.

3.5 Existing aid

In addition to the examination of aid notified prior to its implementation and examination of unlawfully granted aid, the surveillance authorities have, following

[30] Case *France* v. *Commission*, op. cit. n. 29.

[31] Ibid.

[32] Stated for the first time, in ECJ Case 70/72 *Commission* v. *Germany* [1973] ECR 813.

Article 93 (1) EEC or Article 1 (1) of Protocol 3 to the ESA/Court Agreement, the power to keep under constant review all systems of existing aid. This means that aid earlier duly authorized may, through a new assessment, be ordered to be altered or even abolished if, in the new situation, the effects of the aid become negative.

As regards EFTA countries, the notion of existing aid also covers 'pre-EEA' aid measures if they continue to be applied after the entry into force of the EEA Agreement.

3.6 Judicial review

A decision by the surveillance authorities, taken after the opening of a formal investigation procedure, is a decision in the meaning of Article 173 EEC or Article 36 ESA/Court Agreement and may, therefore, be subject to an appeal before the ECJ or EFTA Court.

This right belongs naturally to the States which have proposed or implemented the measure and also to undertakings recipient of the aid. In addition, third parties may have a position allowing them to institute proceedings. According to Article 173 (2) EEC and Article 36 (2) ESA/Court Agreement, any natural or legal person may, under the conditions set out in the first paragraphs of these articles,[33] institute proceedings against a decision addressed to another person, if that decision is of direct and individual concern to the former.

The ECJ has confirmed this right, for example in the case *COFAZ and Others* v. *Commission*.[34] The ECJ stated that, for the examination of admissibility, it is necessary to examine the role which the third parties have played in the preceding administrative procedure, that is, whether they have complied with the Commission's request to submit their comments under Article 93 (2) EEC. If this has been done but the comments have not been taken into account, and the parties can adduce pertinent reasons to show that the decision in question may adversely affect their position on the market, the application has to be considered admissible.

In addition, the ECJ has confirmed that cases where the Commission has failed to open proceedings or decided not to raise any objections can be subject to an appeal.[35] The same applies to decisions to open proceedings.[36]

It has to be noted that, in the case of unlawful aid, third parties can, subject to substantive and procedural limitations of the national law, also bring the matter up before a national court opposing the implementation of the aid measure in question,

[33] Lack of competence, infringement of an essential procedural requirement, infringement of the EEC Treaty/EEA Agreement or any rule of law relating to their application, or misuse of powers.

[34] Case 169/84 [1986] ECR 391. See also Joined Cases *Van der Kooy and Others* v. *Commission*, op. cit. n. 2.

[35] See Cases C-313/90 *Comité International de la Rayonne et des Fibres Synthétiques and Others* v. *Commission* of 24 Mar. 1993 (not yet reported), C-198/91 *W. Cook* v. *Commission* of 19 May 1993 (not yet reported), and C-225/91 *Matra* v. *Commission* of 15 June 1993 (not yet reported).

[36] See Cases *Spain* v. *Commission*, op. cit. n. 26, and *Italy* v. *Commission* C-47/91 [1992] ECR 4145.

as the ECJ has recognized the direct effect of the final sentence of Article 93 (3).[37] The conditions for such an action are that the national measures constitute State aid in the meaning of Article 92 EEC or Article 61 EEA and that the procedure laid down in Article 93 (3) EEC or Article 1 (3) of Protocol 3 EFTA/Court Agreement has not been respected. If the procedures provided have been followed, there is no right to bring the matter before a national court on substantive grounds.[38]

4. CO-OPERATION BETWEEN THE TWO SURVEILLANCE BODIES

The point of departure as regards the competences of the surveillance authorities, in the field of State aid, was that both sides should have their own decision-making autonomy. The attribution of cases depends on the State which is proposing the aid measure. Hence, the EC Commission is competent as regards aid granted by EC Member States, basing itself on Articles 92 and 93 EEC, also taking into account the wider EEA context, where necessary, and ESA examines the cases concerning EFTA States, basing itself on the corresponding provisions of the EEA and ESA/Court Agreements.

However, here again there is a need for wide co-operation in order to maintain homogeneous implementation, application, and interpretation of the rules. This co-operation is governed by Protocol 27 EEA. It is provided that the Commission and ESA have an obligation to exchange information and views on general policy issues and inform each other on all decisions as soon as they have been taken.

The surveillance authorities also have the right to submit comments on cases where the other one has opened an Article 93 (2) procedure or the corresponding procedure under the ESA/Court Agreement. No copies of notifications are distributed but the information in these cases is submitted by giving a notice to the other surveillance authority. Upon request of one of the surveillance authorities, exchange of information and views has to take place on a case-by-case basis on other State aid cases.

Due to its nature, all the information received during the co-operation procedures is treated as confidential.

5. SPECIFIC ISSUES

5.1 Product coverage

It is recalled that Article 8 (3) and Protocol 3 EEA define the products falling under the EEA Agreement. Article 8 (3) also indicates that, if a wider product coverage

[37] See e.g. Case 6/64 *Costa* v. *ENEL* [1964] ECR 585 and *France* v. *Commission*, op. cit. n. 29.

[38] See Joined Cases *Heineken* v. *Inspecteurs der Vennootschapsbelasting*, op. cit. n. 24.

should apply to a specific field, this should be expressly mentioned in the provisions covering the field in question. As this kind of reference is missing in the State aid provisions, it is clear that the scope of application follows the general rules laid down in Article 8 (3), with the sole exception of the fisheries sector, which is covered in accordance with the provisions of EEA Protocol 9.[39] In addition, it has to be borne in mind that the State aid rules also apply to the services sector.

The product coverage does not necessarily cause any particular problems in the field of State aid. It should, however, be noted that there will most likely be individual cases or schemes which will concern at the same time products both covered and not covered by the Agreement. In this case, ESA will examine only that part of the aid proposal which provides for subsidies for products covered by the Agreement. The dividing line is to be found in a case-by-case approach taking into consideration all specific elements related to the aid measure in question. This situation does not, in practice, apply to the EC pillar, as the EEA Agreement and its narrower product coverage do not limit the existing powers of the Commission under the EEC and ECSC Treaties.

The specific areas which should be examined somewhat more closely are the fisheries sector (see Section 5.1.1 below), processed agricultural products, and the forestry sector (see Section 5.1.2 below). The assessment of the situation concerning these areas applies, in practice, only to the EFTA pillar and ESA, as here again the Commission will continue to apply the EEC provisions in the EEA context also.

5.1.1 Fisheries sector

Protocol 9 EEA, related to the trade in fish, contains some references to State aid. According to its Article 4 (1), aid granted through State resources to the fisheries sector which distorts competition shall be abolished. In addition, Article 4 (2) provides that the Contracting Parties shall endeavour to ensure conditions of competition which will enable the other Contracting Parties to refrain from the application of anti-dumping measures and countervailing duties.

As no reference is made to the normal State aid procedural rules, it seems that aid to the fisheries sector under the EEA Agreement, although in principle covered by the State aid rules, does not necessitate any notifications or prior authorization. Therefore, the Contracting Parties have an obligation to refrain from granting trade-distorting aid, in addition to which ESA will have the right to obtain information on any aid granted by EFTA States to this sector and take appropriate action, where necessary. The EC Commission will continue to act on the basis of the EEC provisions.

5.1.2 Processed agricultural products and forestry

As to the forestry sector and food-processing, a distinction has to be made between

[39] See s. 5.5.1 below, as well as Ch. III, s. 1.3.2.

agricultural and industrial activities. Only the latter activity is covered by the EEA Agreement.

Therefore, subsidies to basic agriculture are not subject to the State aid rules, which only enter the picture at the processing phase. In this context reference can be made to the list of processed agricultural products in Protocol 3 EEA. Similarly, forestry only becomes an industrial activity after the wood has been harvested and, therefore, the preceding phases do not fall under Articles 61 and 62 EEA.

5.2 Article 64 (1) EEA

In addition to the general provisions on dispute settlement, Article 64 (1) EEA contains specific provisions concerning State aid. This article covers situations where one of the surveillance authorities considers that the implementation of the rules contained in Articles 61 and 62 EEA or Article 5 of Protocol 14 EEA (ECSC steel) is not in conformity with the maintenance of equal conditions of competition within the EEA. This kind of situation could arise, for instance, if the other surveillance authority makes decisions diverging from the previous policies or does not act in an efficient way as regards the control of existing aid.

Under these circumstances the surveillance authority questioning the action of the other surveillance authority may request an exchange of views, which shall be held within two weeks according to the procedure of Protocol 27, paragraph (*f*). If no commonly acceptable solution can be found by the end of this two-week period, the competent authority of the affected Contracting Party may immediately adopt appropriate interim measures in order to remedy the distortion of competition.

After this, consultations are held in the EEA Joint Committee with a view to finding a solution. If within three months no commonly acceptable solution has been found and the practice in question causes, or threatens to cause, distortion of competition affecting trade between the Contracting Parties, the interim measures may be replaced by definitive ones.

5.3 Importance of common State aid rules for the EC and EFTA as regards their relations with Central and Eastern European countries

The free trade agreements which the Central and Eastern European countries (CEECs) have concluded with EFTA States (EFTA–CEEC Agreements), their association agreements with the EC, and the EEA Agreement will most likely have, in the future, as a common reference point for the control of State aid, the existing EC rules on State aid.

The basic State aid provisions in the EFTA–CEEC Agreements are based on those of the Stockholm Convention and the later interpretations given to them. This differs, for the time being, from the association agreements concluded between CEECs and the Community, as, according to these agreements, the State aid provisions will be assessed on the basis of the criteria arising from the application of

Article 92 of the EEC Treaty, which means that all the secondary State aid legislation as well as the judgments of the ECJ will also be valid in this context.

The EFTA–CEEC agreements contain, however, a record of understanding stating that the criteria set out in the agreements for the interpretation of the State aid rules are to be complemented by the criteria arising from the EEA Agreement, after its entry into force.

As the EFTA States, with the exception of Switzerland, and the CEECs, after the transitional periods set out in their association agreements with the Community, will all be in a situation where they have to follow the substantive EC State aid rules as regards their relations with the Community, it would be natural that the same rules should also govern the free trade relations between EFTA and the CEECs. Even without any specific decisions to that end, the situation will most likely develop in that direction. The EC rules, including the secondary legislation and the jurisprudence of the ECJ, are more detailed and stricter than the 'EFTA *acquis*', and, if the parties have to respect these rules towards one partner, they would automatically also do so towards the others, which have similar links with the first partner.

If this kind of development materializes, there will actually be only one set of substantive State aid rules covering the whole Continent, which as such should be welcomed. In addition, it would most probably lead to more efficient enforcement of the rules, because the monitoring of the action of other parties, all under similar obligations, would actually be carried out by several partners. In the longer term, the effects could hopefully be seen as improved functioning of the network of European trade agreements and better competitiveness of European industries on the world market.

XI

THE SITUATION OF SWITZERLAND

1. SWITZERLAND AND EUROPEAN INTEGRATION

1.1 Brief history of EC–Switzerland relations

One of the essential *raisons d'être* of Switzerland is expressed at the beginning of Article 2 of its 1874 Constitution, which says that 'La Confédération a pour but d'assurer l'indépendance de la patrie contre l'étranger.'[1] Switzerland has thus always been jealously protecting what its Government calls 'its traditional policy of independence in matters of external relations', in particular its famous neutrality.[2] On the other hand, it is an unavoidable fact that 'Switzerland is part of Europe', as the recent Commission Communication of 14 September 1993 on the future of EC–Switzerland[3] relations noticed with perspicacity (a good example of what the French call a *lapalissade*). Unfortunately, however evident this fact may be, it seems that many Swiss citizens, while claiming that the Swiss Confederation is a sort of universal example of democracy, economic success, and peaceful cohabitation between different languages, are not yet sure whether their country really belongs to Europe.

After the turmoil of the Second World War, when the traumatized former enemies founded the three European Communities (ECSC, EEC, and EURATOM) in 1951 and 1957, Switzerland was among those countries which followed the United Kingdom in its attempt, in February 1957, to 'dissolve the common market like a piece of sugar in a cup of tea'[4] through the creation of a large free trade zone in Europe, which would have involved the six founders of the EC and some outsiders (UK, Austria, the Nordic countries, and Switzerland). Following the breaking off of these negotiations by France, Switzerland took part in 1960 with the UK and the others in the establishment of the much smaller free trade zone constituted by EFTA. When, one year later, the UK, Denmark, Ireland, and Norway made their first attempt to join the EC, Switzerland tried to avoid isolation by negotiating an association agreement with the Community. However, following

[1] Free translation: 'The Confederation shall have as its aim to ensure the independence of the fatherland against foreign forces.'

[2] See 'Rapport sur la position de la Suisse dans le processus d'intégration européenne', 24 Aug. 1988 (88.045, FF 1988 III 233).

[3] See COM (93) 486 final.

[4] Quoted by A. Prate in *Quelle Europe?* (Paris, 1991).

the refusal in 1963 by Mr de Gaulle to let the applicants enter the EC, the Swiss plans also failed.

Almost ten years later, thanks to the request of the UK and Denmark not to remove, as a consequence of their accession to the EC Common External Tariff, the tariff concessions already made to their now ex-EFTA partners, Switzerland and its EFTA colleagues concluded the 1972 FTAs with the EC. The latest significant event in the relations of Switzerland with the EC is the EEA negotiations, again conducted together with the EFTA partners, the urgency of these negotiations having been stimulated by both the 1992 Single Market Programme and the fall of the Berlin Wall. Finally, the Swiss Government, making a sudden courageous jump into the future, decided in May 1992 to apply for membership to the Community.

This brief description of the relations between Switzerland and the EC shows how much outside events have in fact always strongly determined what sorts of agreements 'independent Switzerland' was able to conclude with its big European neighbour. However, a certain majority of Swiss citizens decided on 6 December 1992 ('black Sunday' as it was called by Mr Delamuraz, Minister for External Economic Affairs) to show 'l'étranger' once for all just how independent the fatherland was. They thereby forgot the other aims of Article 2 of the Swiss Constitution, which are to preserve peace inside the country and increase common prosperity, objectives which strongly resemble those of the Rome Treaty, the founding Act of another would-be confederation of independent States.

1.2 Eurolex

With the perspective of the participation of Switzerland in the EEA, the Swiss Confederation and cantons prepared the necessary modifications of Swiss law. On the federal level, a report was presented to Parliament on 18 May 1992[5] comprising the modification of sixty-one laws and adoption of nine new ones. The package became known as 'Eurolex'. The proposals were examined by Parliament during a special session in August and further during the autumn. On 9 October 1992 Parliament approved the Eurolex package without any major modifications. However, Switzerland being, with Liechtenstein, one of the two EEA Contracting Parties having to submit the EEA Agreement to a referendum, the final verdict was in the hands of 'le souverain', the Swiss citizens.

1.3 The referendum of 6 December 1992 and its consequences for the EEA

In view of the importance of the issue, the Government had chosen to submit the issue to a constitutional type of referendum which requires a so-called 'double

[5] 'Message relatif à l'Accord EEE' (FF 1992 IV 1) of 18 May 1992, supplemented by additional reports on 27 May and 15 June 1992 (FF 1992 V 1 and V 520).

majority', i.e. both of the voters and of the twenty-three cantons. On 6 December 1992 the Swiss people were called to a poll to accept or reject the EEA Agreement. The outcome of the vote was negative, as the Agreement was rejected narrowly by the population (49.7 per cent 'yes' and 50.3 per cent 'no'), but clearly by the cantons: sixteen 'no' and seven 'yes'.[6]

The most conspicuous feature of the vote was the difference between the two main linguistic regions: while all French-speaking cantons approved the EEA, all Swiss-German cantons, except Basle, rejected it. The gap between the most Euro-friendly canton, Neuchâtel, with 80 per cent of positive votes, and the most Euro-sceptic canton, Uri, with only 25.5 per cent of positive votes, is an illustrative example. The outcome of the vote caused a general feeling of uneasiness in Switzerland, fuelling the theory of 'Röschtigraben'.[7] Political crises were looming on the Swiss doorstep.

The intense public debate preceding the poll did not, however, end on 7 December. During the winter and spring of 1993 several popular initiatives and petitions were launched, requesting everything from a re-vote on the EEA to an immediate withdrawal of the Swiss request for EC membership. Although the initiative requesting a second vote on the EEA, launched by the 'Born on 7 December' Committee, has collected a sufficient number of signatures (above 100,000) to request that a second referendum be organized, this does not seem probable before the year 1995.

In the EEA camp, the EC and EFTA partners (less Switzerland) had once again to renegotiate the EEA. Through an Adjustment Protocol, they removed all the references to Switzerland from the EEA Agreement and adapted the Cohesion Fund. In a Joint Declaration, they nevertheless said they would 'welcome Swiss participation in the EEA' and that such participation 'should be based on the results laid down in the original EEA Agreement and bilateral agreements negotiated at the same time as well as on possible subsequent changes in those agreements'. Though it remains a full party to EFTA, Switzerland has reduced its contribution to the EFTA budget to take into account the fact that it does not participate in the EEA exercise. Swiss observers are however allowed to attend the EFTA internal meetings, even when they relate to EEA matters (though under certain conditions).

In its latest report on foreign policy of 29 November 1993, presented on 3 December 1993, the Swiss Government stated that accession to the European Union constitutes the strategic objective of its integration policy, due to the fact that Switzerland finds its roots deeply in Europe and is closely linked to it. In the meantime, and until the next federal parliamentary elections in 1995, the Government will put the emphasis, in a pragmatic way, on the bilateral negotiations

[6] For precise figures as well as a very interesting analysis of the vote, see University of Geneva, 'Analyse des votations fédérales du 6 décembre 1992'.

[7] '*Röschti*': a potato dish from the German-speaking part of Switzerland; '*Graben*'; a ditch. This term, among others, is used to designate ironically the difference between the mentalities of the French-speaking and German-speaking parts of Switzerland.

with the EC, the results of which will be reassessed at the end of 1994. Participation in the EEA at a later stage remains a serious option, all the more so since the time limit for the Government to submit the popular initiative 'Born on 7 December' to a referendum expires on 3 September 1995. During the next legislature (1995–9), the Government will open the way towards the multilateral integration of Switzerland in Europe (it being accession either to the European Union or to the EEA).

1.4 Swisslex

On 24 February 1993 the Swiss Federal Council presented a report to Parliament on the follow-up to the vote, outlining Switzerland's integration policy.[8] The report rejects the option of an isolated Switzerland ('Alleingang'), and underlines the importance of 'keeping all doors open', including the formal maintenance of the request for EC membership. The Eurolex project is to some extent kept alive and has been rebaptized 'Swisslex', with the aim of increasing, to the highest extent possible, the Euro-compatibility of Swiss law. Of the initial Eurolex package, the Swiss Federal Council proposed, in the above-mentioned report, to take over twenty-seven laws. These were, *inter alia*, related to processed agricultural products, measuring instruments, machinery, and product liability. Out of these, twelve were adopted by Parliament in April 1993 and ten others in June. The five remaining projects are still being discussed.

Furthermore, a 'Swisslex II' is under preparation to take into account the evolution in the *acquis communautaire* since July 1991.

2. THE 'SWISS INTERNAL MARKET'

Switzerland being a confederation of twenty-three cantons with their own governments and parliaments, a certain number of competences are left to the cantons. Therefore problems similar to those within the EC also arise in Switzerland, that is, differences between the cantonal laws may cause distortions of competition and barriers to trade within the country. The fact of negotiating the EEA for almost three years and of understanding better some of the solutions found in the Community paradoxically helped the Swiss to figure out solutions which could also be valid for their own 'internal market'.

In an effort to revitalize the Swiss economy, a federal law on a Swiss internal market, that is, a sort of '1992 Single Market Programme' *à la suisse*, is currently under preparation. It aims at harmonizing certain laws between the cantons in the areas of goods, services, professional qualifications, public procurement, and subsidies granted by cantonal governments. To a large extent, however, the creation of this Swiss internal market is based on the principle of mutual recognition

[8] 'Message sur le programme consécutif au rejet de l'Accord EEE' (no. 93.100).

of the various cantonal laws. It seems to emerge from preliminary consultations that a number of cantons are of the opinion that some aspects of this draft federal law are encroaching upon their competences (e.g. in the field of public procurement notably) and should therefore not be included in the law but rather be solved through a so-called 'concordat intercantonal'. However, this sort of agreement would require unanimity of the cantons, which is usually far from easy to achieve.

Furthermore, another effect of the 'mental revolution' created by the EEA negotiations in Switzerland is the project to change the Cartel Law[9] in order to bring it more in line with the spirit of modern competition laws, in particular the EC rules. A new law on competition, containing provisions inspired by the EC rules, is therefore under preparation. The first draft (dated 3 September 1993) has been circulated to interested circles for comments by the end of February 1994. Since the 'abuse principle' stems from the Swiss Constitution (Article 31 *bis*), the Government preferred, instead of changing the Constitution, to amend the law so as, while formally keeping the abuse principle, to introduce a number of presumptions under which certain practices are considered *per se* as unlawful abuses. This concerns in particular practices such as horizontal agreements on prices, quantities, and markets, as well as certain vertical agreements. Abuses of dominant position and prior control of mergers are also dealt with. In this context, a new Federal Office for competition, having wider competences than the old Swiss Cartel Commission, will be set up.

These legislative steps are also in line with the strong criticisms of the current Swiss competition system made notably by OECD in its 1992 study on Switzerland, where it was underlined that 90 per cent of the seventy-two industrial branches were cartelized and that this was the main reason for the prices of goods and services for private consumption being 40 per cent higher in Switzerland than the average in the twenty-four OECD countries.[10]

3. CURRENT RELATIONS WITH THE COMMUNITY

Without the EEA, what is left between the EC and Switzerland is essentially the good old-fashioned 1972 FTA.[11] Within the framework of the FTA Joint Committee, a meeting was held on 28 June 1993 between EC and Swiss representatives. On that occasion Switzerland presented a list of sixteen areas where bilateral negotiations would be of interest, namely:

[9] Law of 20 Dec. 1985 (RO 1986 874).

[10] See OECD Economic Studies, *Switzerland 1991/1992* (Paris, 1992). See also report in the *Financial Times* of 13 Nov. 1992.

[11] Since the 1950s, Switzerland has concluded a number of bilateral agreements with the EC, ranging from trade in cheese or clocks and watches to non-life insurance, research and development (i.e. participation in EC programmes such as 'Science' and 'COMETT'), or training ('ERASMUS'). However, most of these are qualified by the Commission itself as being of 'minor importance' (see Communication, op. cit. s. 1.1, which contains in its annex 1 a list of those bilateral conventions).

1. rules of origin;
2. outward processing of textiles;
3. processed agricultural products;
4. technical barriers to trade;
5. public procurement;
6. product liability;
7. veterinary rules;
8. phytosanitary rules;
9. intellectual property (in particular, protection of geographical indications and designations of origin);
10. air transport;
11. road transport;
12. audio-visual program MEDIA;
13. statistics;
14. research (Fourth EC Framework Program);
15. education and training (ERASMUS, COMETT, etc.);
16. mutual recognition of diplomas and professional qualifications.

Of these points, the first nine areas mentioned could be linked to the already existing 1972 FTA, while the remaining seven would fall outside its scope.

As a response to the Swiss proposal, the Commission forwarded, on 14 September 1993, a communication to the Council and Parliament on the EC's future relations with Switzerland (referred to above in s. 1.1). The Commission Communication takes stock of the current situation and points out that a certain flexibility with Switzerland would be desirable, in particular due to the fact that the relations between Switzerland and the Community are 'mutually beneficial'.[12] The Community should therefore be ready to examine the requests put forward by Switzerland to the extent that liberalization is of mutual interest and advantage. Clearly, in the Commission's view, it is not possible for Switzerland to enjoy all the benefits of an EEA Agreement which it has rejected. In areas of no reciprocal interest, negotiations should be conducted on the basis of mutual give and take, if necessary by linking different agreements and making the entry into force of one dependent upon the ratification of the other.[13]

On 22 September 1993 the Commission adopted a first draft negotiation mandate for the conclusion of an EC–Switzerland bilateral agreement in the areas of road and air transport. The draft mandate was discussed at the EC Transport Council on

[12] Switzerland is one of the main trading partners of the EC as it is its second export market (after the USA) and its third import source (after the USA and Japan).

[13] This EC position is due to the fear that the Swiss voters could refuse a federal law implementing an agreement which is of interest to the EC while only accepting a law implementing the agreement which interests Switzerland. This clause could however prove difficult to put into practice in Switzerland, as a referendum can only ask a single question strictly limited within the same subject-matter ('unité de la matière'), therefore excluding the possibility that such a link between two matters could be expressed in the question to the voters.

28 September and its adoption was postponed to November. The Commission, supported by certain southern EC countries, would like to link this transport agreement to another one in the field of free movement of persons, including recognition of diplomas and social security. The Commission presented its Communication on 4 October 1993 to the General Affairs Council, which decided to postpone the discussion until November 1993.

At its meeting of 8 and 9 November, the EC Council concluded that EC–Switzerland relations could be developed, *inter alia*, in the fields of transport, free movement of persons, research, access to the market for agricultural products, technical barriers to trade, public procurement, veterinary and phytosanitary legislation, intellectual property, and geographical indications and indications of origin. In a first stage, negotiations should as soon as possible be started regarding the four first issues and, if possible, the next two, the Commission being invited to present the Council with draft negotiation mandates in these fields. The Council furthermore looked forward to a rapid solution, within the framework of the 1972 FTA, to the problem of origin rules and indicated it would ensure an appropriate parallelism where necessary between the different sector-based agreements concerned.[14]

On 30 November 1933, the Transport Council decided again to postpone the adoption of a negotiation mandate until its meeting in early April 1994.

Although the bilateral talks between Switzerland and the Community are still at a preparatory stage, it is worth examining in some more detail some of the subject-matters enumerated in the sixteen points above. The examination below concentrates on areas related directly to the fields covered in this book.

3.1 Rules of origin

The non-ratification of the EEA Agreement by Switzerland causes some important problems as regards the origin rules not only to the country itself but also to the other EFTA States and the Community.

So far, the provisions of the Stockholm Convention have been applied to trade between EFTA States, and the virtually identical provisions of the bilateral 1972 FTAs to the trade between each EFTA State and the Community. Under the FTAs and the Stockholm Convention, it was possible, thanks to a clause linking all these agreements together, to use (i.e. cumulate with), under certain conditions, materials originating in all EFTA and EC countries for obtaining the originating status for products, and thus the preferential treatment. The participation of all EFTA States (including Switzerland) in the EEA would have meant that these two sets of rules would have been replaced by the new more developed EEA rules.

Now, however, three different sets of rules will co-exist in the West European context:

[14] See press release 9622/93 (Presse 178-G) of 8/9 Nov. 1993 and *Europe*, 6104 (10 Nov. 1993), 10.

- the rules contained in the EEA Agreement (Protocol 4) will multilaterally apply to the EC and the EFTA countries participating in the EEA;
- for trade between Switzerland and each of the other EFTA States the provisions of the Stockholm Convention (annex B) will be applied; and
- the provisions of the bilateral 1972 FTA between Switzerland and the Community (Protocol 3) will continue to apply as to their trade.

Without any changes, this would have posed complicated problems in practice and in fact would have represented a major set-back in the current relations between EFTA and EC partners, as the above-mentioned linkage clause would no longer have been applicable (since the EEA Agreement partly replaces the FTAs and the Stockholm Convention). The consequence would have been that, for example, Swiss materials used in other EFTA countries would have had to be regarded as third country materials when used in products exported from such EFTA countries to the Community; EC materials used in Switzerland would have had to be considered as third country materials when integrated in a product exported to other EFTA countries; EFTA materials used in EC products exported to Switzerland would have been considered by the latter as third country products, as would have EC materials used in EFTA products exported to Switzerland. One has to add to the list the administrative burden caused for both the authorities and the undertakings by such a situation where three sets of rules are applied.

The problem was under discussion between the Community and Switzerland from spring 1993, both sides recognizing the need to find a solution. The optimal way to solve the problem would have been the following: first, to have, between the EEA countries, two parallel regimes: on the one hand, the EEA rules for trade where Swiss products are not involved and, on the other hand, the rules of the Stockholm Convention and the 1972 FTAs between the Community and the EFTA States for trade where Swiss products are involved. Secondly, to 'upgrade' the rules of origin contained in the Stockholm Convention and the 1972 FTAs to the level of the EEA as far as possible. Thirdly, to make a decision to grant Swiss materials EEA status and to create the necessary other links between the two parallel systems with a view to obtaining full cumulation.

This solution would actually have led, as far as origin rules are concerned, to the same situation as if Switzerland were participating in the EEA. It was not, however, possible to reach this kind of optimal solution. The future system foreseen will be asymmetric, meaning that Switzerland will not obtain all the benefits it would have achieved if it had been part of the EEA.

The exporters in the Community and the EEA EFTA countries will benefit from a preferential status as regards their products exported to Switzerland even if such products can be considered as originating in the EEA within the meaning of Protocol 4 to the EEA Agreement, i.e. full cumulation is foreseen to apply in this respect. For Swiss exporters the situation will, however, be different: full cumulation in the meaning of Protocol 4 EEA will not be introduced but originating status is granted only to products wholly obtained in Switzerland or to products obtained in Switzerland incorporating materials which have not been wholly obtained there, provided that such materials have either undergone sufficient working or processing there or the materials incorporated originate in the Community or the EEA EFTA countries. As an important element of the new rules it will be possible for Swiss materials to contribute towards conferring originating status on EEA products when incorporated into such products.

There are also other changes to the system foreseen, concerning such issues as a general tolerance rule, relaxation of territorial requirements, and review of currency values related to simplified administrative procedures, with the aim of having the rules in this respect harmonized with those of the EEA Agreement.

The whole system, due to enter into force in early 1994, will necessitate changes not only in the EC–Switzerland FTA but also in the Stockholm Convention, in FTAs between the EC and other EFTA States, as well as in the EEA Agreement.

3.2 Processed agricultural products

The Swiss food industry had a big interest in the new system of price compensation contained in Protocol 3 EEA. Switzerland is, on a unilateral basis, in the process of updating its law on the import and export of processed agricultural products to the level of Protocol 3 EEA (see Section 1.4 above). However, for trade with its EC and EFTA partners, amendments will also be necessary in Protocol 2 of the 1972 FTA and of the Stockholm Convention.

3.3 Technical barriers to trade

The elimination and prevention of technical barriers to trade have been pursued in EC–EFTA relations for the last thirty years or more. The EEA Agreement can be seen as the prime achievement of that co-operation. For Switzerland, however, the non-ratification of the EEA Agreement could entail a step backwards as compared to the situation prevailing before the EEA.

In the non-harmonized fields, the *Cassis de Dijon* principle will not, or at least not to the same extent, be applied between the EEA countries and Switzerland.[15] In the harmonized fields, even if Switzerland autonomously harmonizes its technical regulations with those of the EC, the Community will not automatically recognize the tests carried out in Switzerland on the conformity of the products to, for example, the essential requirements of the EC new approach directives. Reciprocally, Switzerland will not automatically recognize proofs of conformity issued in the EC.

In order to limit the consequences in this area of the rejection of the EEA

[15] See Ch. IV, s. 2.

Agreement by the Swiss electorate, Switzerland has expressed a wish to start negotiations on:

- the mutual recognition of test results and proofs of conformity of products;
- the continuation of Swiss participation in the procedure for the exchange of information in the field of technical regulations between the EC and the EFTA countries.[16]

It can be presumed that a unilateral harmonization and recognition of EEA products and tests by Switzerland would be dependent on reciprocal treatment in EC and EFTA countries, especially in areas where there are, by tradition, strong Swiss export interests.

As regards the exchange of information system, it is envisaged that Switzerland will continue to use the notification system which was set up under the Stockholm Convention (Article 12 *bis* and Annex H) and that the agreement with the EC side will be prolonged, together with informal solutions concerning the forwarding of comments on EC notifications.

3.4 Public procurement

The opening-up of public procurement is part of the Swiss internal market project (with the foreseeable reservations indicated above in Section 2 regarding the cantonal competences). The Swiss Federal Council however aims at the reciprocal opening-up of the procurement sector between Switzerland and the Community within the framework of the 1972 FTA. Swiss authorities find it desirable in particular to open to competition procurement in the water, energy, transport, and telecommunications sectors ('utilities').

3.5 Product liability

At present, no specific provisions regarding product liability are contained in Swiss law, where, so far, compensation for damages can be obtained under general rules of liability developed in the jurisprudence of Swiss courts. The Swisslex project, however, contains a proposal for a new law incorporating the substance of Directive 85/374. During the EEA negotiations, the main problem in this area was that of the importer's liability.[17] The EC side agreed that it would be possible to do away with the special responsibility on the part of the importer on the double condition that the EFTA countries would provide a level of protection equivalent to that applying in the EC, and would ratify the Lugano Convention of 16 September 1988 concerning the jurisdiction and the execution of judgments (on the state of ratification of the Lugano Convention, see Chapter VI, Section 2.2). Taking into account that Switzerland has ratified that Convention and is on the point of

[16] See Ch. IV, s. 3.

[17] See Ch. VI, s. 2.

adopting a national law on product liability corresponding to Directive 85/374, the Swiss authorities are of the opinion that the principle of the importer's liability is an obstacle to free trade which could be eliminated within the framework of the 1972 FTA.

3.6 Intellectual property

Similar to the area of technical barriers to trade, there is a long tradition of co-operation between EC and EFTA concerning matters of intellectual property. Switzerland has introduced new laws in the fields of trade marks, neighbouring rights, and topographies of semiconductor products, the purpose of which is to ensure substantial compatibility with Community law. Following the adoption of EC Regulation 1768/92 ('SPC' Regulation), Switzerland will submit a proposal to Parliament for a law relating to the creation of a supplementary protection certificate for medicinal products. Switzerland is further interested in becoming party to the Community Patent Agreement on the basis of its Article 8, and in co-operating in future Community regulations on the Community trade mark and Community design, as well as on plant varieties. The Swiss Government also wishes to enter into negotiation with the EC on issues relating, in particular, to the protection of geographical indications and designations of origin of agricultural products and foodstuffs, in order to:

- determine the precise conditions which will allow Switzerland to benefit from the third country regime set out in Article 12 of Regulation 2081/92 (on geographical indications);
- clarify the questions arising from the list of generic names of the Community which will be established pursuant to the said Regulation, as far as these designations relate to Switzerland;
- work out a system of protection for wines and spirit drinks based on reciprocity.

4. SOME WORDS ABOUT LIECHTENSTEIN

One week after the Swiss voters, the citizens of tiny Liechtenstein, to the surprise of everybody, voted 'yes' to the EEA by a majority of 55.81 per cent (87 per cent of the electorate took part in the poll). Paradoxically, this just created an additional problem to the realization of the EEA since Liechtenstein is in a customs union with Switzerland (as well as a monetary and postal union) and is formally represented by Switzerland in a number of international commercial negotiations.

In order to try to avoid another 'headache', the EEA partners decided that, as regards Liechtenstein, the EEA Agreement would enter into force only once the EEA Council had so decided, that is, only once Liechtenstein has amended its customs agreement, and other agreements, with Switzerland so that 'the good functioning of the EEA Agreement' will not be impaired (see Adjusting Protocol in *OJ* L 1 (3 January 1994), 572). The obvious fear of the other EEA partners, and particularly of the EC, was that Switzerland would use Liechtenstein as a sort of 'submarine' to benefit from certain EEA advantages without being a formal partner. The Swiss–Liechtenstein negotiations will apparently not be completed before the entry into force of the EEA Agreement, Liechtenstein being thus absent from the EEA until further notice.[18]

[18] Liechtenstein hopes to be able to join the EEA before the end of 1994. The renegotiated customs union treaty between Switzerland and Liechtenstein should be submitted to a referendum in Liechtenstein in spring 1994. If the outcome of this referendum should be negative, Liechtenstein could not ratify and participate in the EEA.

ANNEXE A

EXCERPTS OF RELEVANT PARTS OF THE EEA AGREEMENT AND OF THE ESA/COURT AGREEMENT[1]

Contents

[1] It is recalled that references to Switzerland have been deleted and some other related amendments made in the Adjusting Protocols (for the EEA Agreement: *OJ* L 1 (3 Jan. 1994) 572).

1. AGREEMENT ON THE EUROPEAN ECONOMIC AREA

THE EUROPEAN ECONOMIC COMMUNITY,

THE EUROPEAN COAL AND STEEL COMMUNITY,

THE KINGDOM OF BELGIUM,

THE KINGDOM OF DENMARK,

THE FEDERAL REPUBLIC OF GERMANY,

THE HELLENIC REPUBLIC,

THE KINGDOM OF SPAIN,

THE FRENCH REPUBLIC,

IRELAND,

THE ITALIAN REPUBLIC,

THE GRAND DUCHY OF LUXEMBOURG,

THE KINGDOM OF THE NETHERLANDS,

THE PORTUGUESE REPUBLIC,

THE UNITED KINGDOM OF GREAT BRITAIN AND NORTHERN IRELAND,

AND

THE REPUBLIC OF AUSTRIA,

THE REPUBLIC OF FINLAND,

THE REPUBLIC OF ICELAND,

THE PRINCIPALITY OF LIECHTENSTEIN,

THE KINGDOM OF NORWAY,

THE KINGDOM OF SWEDEN,

THE SWISS CONFEDERATION

hereinafter referred to as the CONTRACTING PARTIES;

CONVINCED of the contribution that a European Economic Area will bring to the construction of a Europe based on peace, democracy and human rights;

REAFFIRMING the high priority attached to the privileged relationship between the European Community, its Member States and the EFTA States, which is based on proximity, long-standing common values and European identity;

DETERMINED to contribute, on the basis of market economy, to world-wide trade liberalization and co-operation, in particular in accordance with the provisions of the General Agreement on Tariffs and Trade and the Convention on the Organisation for Economic Co-operation and Development;

CONSIDERING the objective of establishing a dynamic and homogeneous European Economic Area, based on common rules and equal conditions of competition and providing for the adequate means of enforcement including at the judicial level, and achieved on the basis of equality and reciprocity and of an overall balance of benefits, rights and obligations for the Contracting Parties;

DETERMINED to provide for the fullest possible realization of the free movement of goods, persons, services and capital within the whole European Economic Area, as well as for strengthened and broadened cooperation in flanking and horizontal policies;

AIMING to promote a harmonious development of the European Economic Area and convinced of the need to contribute through the application of this Agreement to the reduction of economic and social regional disparities;

DESIROUS of contributing to the strengthening of the co-operation between the members of the European Parliament and of the Parliaments of the EFTA States, as well as between the social partners in the European Community and in the EFTA States;

CONVINCED of the important role that individuals will play in the European Economic Area through the exercise of the rights conferred on them by this Agreement and through the judicial defence of these rights;

DETERMINED to preserve, protect and improve the quality of the environment and to ensure a prudent and rational utilization of natural resources on the basis, in particular, of the principle of sustainable development, as well as the principle that precautionary and preventive action should be taken;

DETERMINED to take, in the further development of rules, a high level of protection concerning health, safety and the environment as a basis;

NOTING the importance of the development of the social dimension, including equal treatment of men and women, in the European Economic Area and wishing to ensure economic and social progress and to promote conditions for full employment, an improved standard of living and improved working conditions within the European Economic Area;

DETERMINED to promote the interests of consumers and to strengthen their position in the market place, aiming at a high level of consumer protection;

ATTACHED to the common objectives of strengthening the scientific and technological basis of European industry and of encouraging it to become more competitive at the international level;

CONSIDERING that the conclusion of this Agreement shall not prejudge in any way the possibility of any EFTA State to accede to the European Communities;

WHEREAS, in full deference to the independence of the courts, the objective of the Contracting Parties is to arrive at, and maintain, a uniform interpretation and application of this Agreement and those provisions of Community legislation which are substantially reproduced in this Agreement and to arrive at an equal treatment of individuals and economic operators as regards the four freedoms and the conditions of competition;

WHEREAS this Agreement does not restrict the decision-making autonomy or the treaty-making power of the Contracting Parties, subject to the provisions of this Agreement and the limitations set by public international law;

HAVE DECIDED to conclude the following Agreement:

PART I
OBJECTIVES AND PRINCIPLES

Article 1

1. The aim of this Agreement of association is to promote a continuous and balanced strengthening of trade and economic relations between the Contracting Parties with equal conditions of competition, and the respect of the same rules, with a view to creating a homogeneous European Economic Area, hereinafter referred to as the EEA.

2. In order to attain the objectives set out in paragraph 1, the association shall entail, in accordance with the provisions of this Agreement:

(a) the free movement of goods;
(b) the free movement of persons;
(c) the free movement of services;
(d) the free movement of capital;
(e) the setting up of a system ensuring that competition is not distorted and that the rules thereon are equally respected; as well as
(f) closer co-operation in other fields, such as research and development, the environment, education and social policy.

Article 2

For the purposes of this Agreement:

(a) the term 'Agreement' means the main Agreement, its Protocols and Annexes as well as the acts referred to therein;
(b) the term 'EFTA States' means the Contracting Parties, which are members of the European Free Trade Association;
(c) the term 'Contracting Parties' means, concerning the Community and the EC Member States, the Community and the EC Member States, or the Community, or the EC Member States. The meaning to be attributed to this expression in each case is to be deduced from the relevant provisions of this Agreement and from the respective competences of the Community and the EC Member States as they follow from the Treaty establishing the European Economic Community and the Treaty establishing the European Coal and Steel Community.

Article 3

The Contracting Parties shall take all appropriate measures, whether general or particular, to ensure fulfilment of the obligations arising out of this Agreement.

They shall abstain from any measure which could jeopardize the attainment of the objectives of this Agreement.

Moreover, they shall facilitate co-operation within the framework of this Agreement.

Article 4

Within the scope of application of this Agreement, and without prejudice to any special provisions contained therein, any discrimination on grounds of nationality shall be prohibited.

Article 5

A Contracting Party may at any time raise a matter of concern at the level of the EEA Joint Committee or the EEA Council according to the modalities laid down in Articles 92 (2) and 89 (2), respectively.

Article 6

Without prejudice to future developments of case law, the provisions of this Agreement, in so far as they are identical in substance to corresponding rules of the Treaty establishing the European Economic Community and the Treaty establishing the European Coal and Steel Community and to acts adopted in application of these two Treaties, shall, in their implementation and application, be interpreted in conformity with the relevant rulings of the Court of Justice of the European Communities given prior to the date of signature of this Agreement.

Article 7

Acts referred to or contained in the Annexes to this Agreement or in decisions of the EEA Joint Committee shall be binding upon the Contracting Parties and be, or be made, part of their internal legal order as follows:

(a) an act corresponding to an EEC regulation shall as such be made part of the internal legal order of the Contracting Parties;

(b) an act corresponding to an EEC directive shall leave to the authorities of the Contracting Parties the choice of form and method of implementation.

PART II

FREE MOVEMENT OF GOODS

Chapter 1

Basic Principles

Article 8

1. Free movement of goods between the Contracting Parties shall be established in conformity with the provisions of this Agreement.

2. Unless otherwise specified, Articles 10 to 15, 19, 20 and 25 to 27 shall apply only to products originating in the Contracting Parties.

3. Unless otherwise specified, the provisions of this Agreement shall apply only to:

(a) products falling within Chapters 25 to 97 of the Harmonized Commodity Description and Coding System, excluding the products listed in Protocol 2;

(b) products specified in Protocol 3, subject to the specific arrangements set out in that Protocol.

Article 9

1. The rules of origin are set out in Protocol 4. They are without prejudice to any

international obligations which have been, or may be, subscribed to by the Contracting Parties under the General Agreement on Tariffs and Trade.

2. With a view to developing the results achieved in this Agreement, the Contracting Parties will continue their efforts in order further to improve and simplify all aspects of rules of origin and to increase co-operation in customs matters.

3. A first review will take place before the end of 1993. Subsequent reviews will take place at two-yearly intervals. On the basis of these reviews, the Contracting Parties undertake to decide on the appropriate measures to be included in this Agreement.

Article 10

Customs duties on imports and exports, and any charges having equivalent effect, shall be prohibited between the Contracting Parties. Without prejudice to the arrangements set out in Protocol 5, this shall also apply to customs duties of a fiscal nature.

Article 11

Quantitative restrictions on imports and all measures having equivalent effect shall be prohibited between the Contracting Parties.

Article 12

Quantitative restrictions on exports and all measures having equivalent effect shall be prohibited between the Contracting Parties.

Article 13

The provisions of Articles 11 and 12 shall not preclude prohibitions or restrictions on imports, exports or goods in transit justified on grounds of public morality, public policy or public security; the protection of health and life of humans, animals or plants; the protection of national treasures possessing artistic, historic or archaeological value; or the protection of industrial and commercial property. Such prohibitions or restrictions shall not, however, constitute a means of arbitrary discrimination or a disguised restriction on trade between the Contracting Parties.

Article 14

No Contracting Party shall impose, directly or indirectly, on the products of other Contracting Parties any internal taxation of any kind in excess of that imposed directly or indirectly on similar domestic products.

Furthermore, no Contracting Party shall impose on the products of other Contracting Parties any internal taxation of such a nature as to afford indirect protection to other products.

Article 15

Where products are exported to the territory of any Contracting Party, any repayment of internal taxation shall not exceed the internal taxation imposed on them whether directly or indirectly.

Article 16

1. The Contracting Parties shall ensure that any State monopoly of a commercial character be adjusted so that no discrimination regarding the conditions under which goods are procured and marketed will exist between nationals of EC Member States and EFTA States.

2. The provisions of this Article shall apply to any body through which the competent authorities of the Contracting Parties, in law or in fact, either directly or indirectly supervise, determine or appreciably influence imports or exports between Contracting Parties. These provisions shall likewise apply to monopolies delegated by the State to others.

Chapter 2
Agricultural and Fishery Products

Article 17
Annexe I contains specific provisions and arrangements concerning veterinary and phytosanitary matters.

Article 18
Without prejudice to the specific arrangements governing trade in agricultural products, the Contracting Parties shall ensure that the arrangements provided for in Articles 17 and 23 (a) and (b), as they apply to products other than those covered by Article 8 (3), are not compromised by other technical barriers to trade. Article 13 shall apply.

Article 19
1. The Contracting Parties shall examine any difficulties that might arise in their trade in agricultural products and shall endeavour to seek appropriate solutions.

2. The Contracting Parties undertake to continue their efforts with a view to achieving progressive liberalization of agricultural trade.

3. To this end, the Contracting Parties will carry out, before the end of 1993 and subsequently at two-yearly intervals, reviews of the conditions of trade in agricultural products.

4. In the light of the results of these reviews, within the framework of their respective agricultural policies and taking into account the results of the Uruguay Round, the Contracting Parties will decide, within the framework of this Agreement, on a preferential, bilateral or multilateral, reciprocal and mutually beneficial basis, on further reductions of any type of barriers to trade in the agricultural sector, including those resulting from State monopolies of a commercial character in the agricultural field.

Article 20
Provisions and arrangements that apply to fish and other marine products are set out in Protocol 9.

Chapter 3
Co-operation in Customs-Related Matters and Trade Facilitation

Article 21
1. In order to facilitate trade between them, the Contracting Parties shall simplify border controls and formalities. Arrangements for this purpose are set out in Protocol 10.

2. The Contracting Parties shall assist each other in customs matters in order to ensure that customs legislation is correctly applied. Arrangements for this purpose are set out in Protocol 11.

3. The Contracting Parties shall strengthen and broaden co-operation with the aim of simplifying the procedures for trade in goods, in particular in the context of Community programmes, projects and actions aimed at trade facilitation, in accordance with the rules set out in Part VI.

4. Notwithstanding Article 8 (3), this Article shall apply to all products.

Article 22

A Contracting Party which is considering the reduction of the effective level of its duties or charges having equivalent effect applicable to third countries benefiting from most-favoured-nation treatment, or which is considering the suspension of their application, shall, as far as may be practicable, notify the EEA Joint Committee not later than thirty days before such reduction or suspension comes into effect. It shall take note of any representations by other Contracting Parties regarding any distortions which might result therefrom.

Chapter 4
Other Rules Relating to the Free Movement of Goods

Article 23

Specific provisions and arrangements are laid down in:

(a) Protocol 12 and Annexe II in relation to technical regulations, standards, testing and certification;
(b) Protocol 47 in relation to the abolition of technical barriers to trade in wine;
(c) Annexe III in relation to product liability.

They shall apply to all products unless otherwise specified.

Article 24

Annexe IV contains specific provisions and arrangements concerning energy.

Article 25

Where compliance with the provisions of Articles 10 and 12 leads to:

(a) re-export towards a third country against which the exporting Contracting Party maintains, for the product concerned, quantitative export restrictions, export duties or measures or charges having equivalent effect; or
(b) a serious shortage, or threat thereof, of a product essential to the exporting Contracting Party;

and where the situations referred to above give rise, or are likely to give rise, to major difficulties for the exporting Contracting Party, that Contracting Party may take appropriate measures in accordance with the procedures set out in Article 113.

Article 26

Anti-dumping measures, countervailing duties and measures against illicit commercial practices attributable to third countries shall not be applied in relations between the Contracting Parties, unless otherwise specified in this Agreement.

Chapter 5
Coal and Steel Products

Article 27

Provisions and arrangements concerning coal and steel products are set out in Protocols 14 and 25.

[. . .]

Part IV
Competition and Other Common Rules

Chapter 1
Rules Applicable to Undertakings

Article 53

1. The following shall be prohibited as incompatible with the functioning of this Agreement: all agreements between undertakings, decisions by associations of undertakings and concerted practices which may affect trade between Contracting Parties and which have as their object or effect the prevention, restriction or distortion of competition within the territory covered by this Agreement, and in particular those which:

(a) directly or indirectly fix purchase or selling prices or any other trading conditions;
(b) limit or control production, markets, technical development, or investment;
(c) share markets or sources of supply;
(d) apply dissimilar conditions to equivalent transactions with other trading parties, thereby placing them at a competitive disadvantage;
(e) make the conclusion of contracts subject to acceptance by the other parties of supplementary obligations which, by their nature or according to commercial usage, have no connection with the subject of such contracts.

2. Any agreements or decisions prohibited pursuant to this Article shall be automatically void.

3. The provisions of paragraph 1 may, however, be declared inapplicable in the case of:

- any agreement or category of agreements between undertakings;
- any decision or category of decisions by associations of undertakings;
- any concerted practice or category of concerted practices;

which contributes to improving the production or distribution of goods or to promoting technical or economic progress, while allowing consumers a fair share of the resulting benefit, and which does not:

(a) impose on the undertakings concerned restrictions which are not indispensable to the attainment of these objectives;
(b) afford such undertakings the possibility of eliminating competition in respect of a substantial part of the products in question.

Article 54

Any abuse by one or more undertakings of a dominant position within the territory covered by this Agreement or in a substantial part of it shall be prohibited as incompatible with the functioning of this Agreement in so far as it may affect trade between Contracting Parties.

Such abuse may, in particular, consist in:

(a) directly or indirectly imposing unfair purchase or selling prices or other unfair trading conditions;
(b) limiting production, markets or technical development to the prejudice of consumers;
(c) applying dissimilar conditions to equivalent transactions with other trading parties, thereby placing them at a competitive disadvantage;
(d) making the conclusion of contracts subject to acceptance by the other parties of supplementary obligations which, by their nature or according to commercial usage, have no connection with the subject of such contracts.

Article 55

1. Without prejudice to the provisions giving effect to Articles 53 and 54 as contained in Protocol 21 and Annexe XIV of this Agreement, the EC Commission and the EFTA Surveillance Authority provided for in Article 108 (1) shall ensure the application of the principles laid down in Articles 53 and 54.

The competent surveillance authority, as provided for in Article 56, shall investigate cases of suspected infringement of these principles, on its own initiative, or on application by a State within the respective territory or by the other surveillance authority. The competent surveillance authority shall carry out these investigations in co-operation with the competent national authorities in the respective territory and in co-operation with the other surveillance authority, which shall give it its assistance in accordance with its internal rules.

If it finds that there has been an infringement, it shall propose appropriate measures to bring it to an end.

2. If the infringement is not brought to an end, the competent surveillance authority shall record such infringement of the principles in a reasoned decision.

The competent surveillance authority may publish its decision and authorize States within the respective territory to take the measures, the conditions and details of which it shall determine, needed to remedy the situation. It may also request the other surveillance authority to authorize States within the respective territory to take such measures.

Article 56

1. Individual cases falling under Article 53 shall be decided upon by the surveillance authorities in accordance with the following provisions:

(a) individual cases where only trade between EFTA States is affected shall be decided upon by the EFTA Surveillance Authority;
(b) without prejudice to subparagraph (c), the EFTA Surveillance Authority decides, as provided for in the provisions set out in Article 58, Protocol 21 and the rules adopted for its implementation, Protocol 23 and Annexe XIV, on cases where the turnover of the undertakings concerned in the territory of the EFTA States equals 33 per cent or more of their turnover in the territory covered by this Agreement;
(c) the EC Commission decides on the other cases as well as on cases under (b) where trade between EC Member States is affected, taking into account the provisions set out in Article 58, Protocol 21, Protocol 23 and Annexe XIV.

2. Individual cases falling under Article 54 shall be decided upon by the surveillance authority in the territory of which a dominant position is found to exist. The rules set out in paragraph 1 (b) and (c) shall apply only if dominance exists within the territories of both surveillance authorities.

3. Individual cases falling under subparagraph (c) of paragraph 1, whose effects on trade between EC Member States or on competition within the Community are not appreciable, shall be decided upon by the EFTA Surveillance Authority.

4. The terms 'undertaking' and 'turnover' are, for the purposes of this Article, defined in Protocol 22.

Article 57

1. Concentrations the control of which is provided for in paragraph 2 and which create or strengthen a dominant position as a result of which effective competition would be significantly impeded within the territory covered by this Agreement or a substantial part of it, shall be declared incompatible with this Agreement.

2. The control of concentrations falling under paragraph 1 shall be carried out by:

(a) the EC Commission in cases falling under Regulation (EEC) No 4064/89 in accordance with that Regulation and in accordance with Protocols 21 and 24 and Annexe XIV to this Agreement. The EC Commission shall, subject to the review of the EC Court of Justice, have sole competence to take decisions on these cases;

(b) the EFTA Surveillance Authority in cases not falling under subparagraph (a) where the relevant thresholds set out in Annexe XIV are fulfilled in the territory of the EFTA States in accordance with Protocols 21 and 24 and Annexe XIV. This is without prejudice to the competence of EC Member States.

Article 58

With a view to developing and maintaining a uniform surveillance throughout the European Economic Area in the field of competition and to promoting a homogeneous implementation, application and interpretation of the provisions of this Agreement to this end, the competent authorities shall cooperate in accordance with the provisions set out in Protocols 23 and 24.

Article 59

1. In the case of public undertakings and undertakings to which EC Member States or EFTA States grant special or exclusive rights, the Contracting Parties shall ensure that there is neither enacted nor maintained in force any measure contrary to the rules contained in this Agreement, in particular to those rules provided for in Articles 4 and 53 to 63.

2. Undertakings entrusted with the operation of services of general economic interest or having the character of a revenue-producing monopoly shall be subject to the rules contained in this Agreement, in particular to the rules on competition, in so far as the application of such rules does not obstruct the performance, in law or in fact, of the particular tasks assigned to them. The development of trade must not be affected to such an extent as would be contrary to the interests of the Contracting Parties.

3. The EC Commission as well as the EFTA Surveillance Authority shall ensure within their respective competence the application of the provisions of this Article and shall, where necessary, address appropriate measures to the States falling within their respective territory.

Article 60

Annexe XIV contains specific provisions giving effect to the principles set out in Articles 53, 54, 57 and 59.

Chapter 2
State Aid

Article 61

1. Save as otherwise provided in this Agreement, any aid granted by EC Member States, EFTA States or through State resources in any form whatsoever which distorts or threatens to distort competition by favouring certain undertakings or the production of certain goods shall, in so far as it affects trade between Contracting Parties, be incompatible with the functioning of this Agreement.

2. The following shall be compatible with the functioning of this Agreement:

(a) aid having a social character, granted to individual consumers, provided that such aid is granted without discrimination related to the origin of the products concerned;
(b) aid to make good the damage caused by natural disasters or exceptional occurrences;
(c) aid granted to the economy of certain areas of the Federal Republic of Germany affected by the division of Germany, in so far as such aid is required in order to compensate for the economic disadvantages caused by that division.

3. The following may be considered to be compatible with the functioning of this Agreement:

(a) aid to promote the economic development of areas where the standard of living is abnormally low or where there is serious underemployment;
(b) aid to promote the execution of an important project of common European interest or to remedy a serious disturbance in the economy of an EC Member State or an EFTA State;
(c) aid to facilitate the development of certain economic activities or of certain economic areas, where such aid does not adversely affect trading conditions to an extent contrary to the common interest;
(d) such other categories of aid as may be specified by the EEA Joint Committee in accordance with Part VII.

Article 62

1. All existing systems of State aid in the territory of the Contracting Parties, as well as any plans to grant or alter State aid, shall be subject to constant review as to their compatibility with Article 61. This review shall be carried out:

(a) as regards the EC Member States, by the EC Commission according to the rules laid down in Article 93 of the Treaty establishing the European Economic Community;
(b) as regards the EFTA States, by the EFTA Surveillance Authority according to the rules set out in an agreement between the EFTA States establishing the EFTA Surveillance Authority which is entrusted with the powers and functions laid down in Protocol 26.

2. With a view to ensuring a uniform surveillance in the field of State aid throughout the territory covered by this Agreement, the EC Commission and the EFTA Surveillance Authority shall co-operate in accordance with the provisions set out in Protocol 27.

Article 63

Annexe XV contains specific provisions on State aid.

Article 64

1. If one of the surveillance authorities considers that the implementation by the other surveillance authority of Articles 61 and 62 of this Agreement and Article 5 of Protocol 14 is not in conformity with the maintenance of equal conditions of competition within the territory covered by this Agreement, exchange of views shall be held within two weeks according to the procedure of Protocol 27, paragraph (f).

If a commonly agreed solution has not been found by the end of this two-week period, the competent authority of the affected Contracting Party may immediately adopt appropriate interim measures in order to remedy the resulting distortion of competition.

Consultations shall then be held in the EEA Joint Committee with a view to finding a commonly acceptable solution.

If within three months the EEA Joint Committee has not been able to find such a solution, and if the practice in question causes, or threatens to cause, distortion of competition affecting trade between the Contracting Parties, the interim measures may be replaced by definitive measures, strictly necessary to offset the effect of such distortion. Priority shall be given to such measures that will least disturb the functioning of the EEA.

2. The provisions of this Article will also apply to State monopolies, which are established after the date of signature of the Agreement.

Chapter 3
Other Common Rules

Article 65

1. Annexe XVI contains specific provisions and arrangements concerning procurement which, unless otherwise specified, shall apply to all products and to services as specified.

2. Protocol 28 and Annexe XVII contain specific provisions and arrangements concerning intellectual, industrial and commercial property, which, unless otherwise specified, shall apply to all products and services.

[. . .]

Part VII
Institutional Provisions

Chapter 1
The Structure of the Association

Section 1
The EEA Council

Article 89

1. An EEA Council is hereby established. It shall, in particular, be responsible for giving the political impetus in the implementation of this Agreement and laying down the general guidelines for the EEA Joint Committee.

To this end, the EEA Council shall assess the overall functioning and the development of the Agreement. It shall take the political decisions leading to amendments of the Agreement.

2. The Contracting Parties, as to the Community and the EC Member States in their respective fields of competence, may, after having discussed it in the EEA Joint Committee, or directly in exceptionally urgent cases, raise in the EEA Council any issue giving rise to a difficulty.

3. The EEA Council shall by decision adopt its rules of procedure.

Article 90

1. The EEA Council shall consist of the members of the Council of the European Communities and members of the EC Commission, and of one member of the Government of each of the EFTA States.

Members of the EEA Council may be represented in accordance with the conditions to be laid down in its rules of procedure.

2. Decisions by the EEA Council shall be taken by agreement between the Community, on the one hand, and the EFTA States, on the other.

Article 91

1. The office of President of the EEA Council shall be held alternately, for a period of six months, by a member of the Council of the European Communities and a member of the Government of an EFTA State.

2. The EEA Council shall be convened twice a year by its President. The EEA Council shall also meet whenever circumstances so require, in accordance with its rules of procedure.

SECTION 2
THE EEA JOINT COMMITTEE

Article 92

1. An EEA Joint Committee is hereby established. It shall ensure the effective implementation and operation of this Agreement. To this end, it shall carry out exchanges of views and information and take decisions in the cases provided for in this Agreement.

2. The Contracting Parties, as to the Community and the EC Member States in their respective fields of competence, shall hold consultations in the EEA Joint Committee on any point of relevance to the Agreement giving rise to a difficulty and raised by one of them.

3. The EEA Joint Committee shall by decision adopt its rules of procedure.

Article 93

1. The EEA Joint Committee shall consist of representatives of the Contracting Parties.

2. The EEA Joint Committee shall take decisions by agreement between the Community, on the one hand, and the EFTA States speaking with one voice, on the other.

Article 94

1. The office of President of the EEA Joint Committee shall be held alternately, for a period of six months, by the representative of the Community, i.e. the EC Commission, and the representative of one of the EFTA States.

2. In order to fulfil its functions, the EEA Joint Committee shall meet, in principle, at

least once a month. It shall also meet on the initiative of its President or at the request of one of the Contracting Parties in accordance with its rules of procedure.

3. The EEA Joint Committee may decide to establish any subcommittee or working group to assist it in carrying out its tasks. The EEA Joint Committee shall in its rules of procedure lay down the composition and mode of operation of such subcommittees and working groups. Their tasks shall be determined by the EEA Joint Committee in each individual case.

4. The EEA Joint Committee shall issue an annual report on the functioning and the development of this Agreement.

SECTION 3
PARLIAMENTARY CO-OPERATION

Article 95

1. An EEA Joint Parliamentary Committee is hereby established. It shall be composed of equal numbers of, on the one hand, members of the European Parliament and, on the other, members of Parliaments of the EFTA States. The total number of members of the Committee is laid down in the Statute in Protocol 36.

2. The EEA Joint Parliamentary Committee shall alternately hold sessions in the Community and in an EFTA State in accordance with the provisions laid down in Protocol 36.

3. The EEA Joint Parliamentary Committee shall contribute, through dialogue and debate, to a better understanding between the Community and the EFTA States in the fields covered by this Agreement.

4. The EEA Joint Parliamentary Committee may express its views in the form of reports or resolutions, as appropriate. It shall, in particular, examine the annual report of the EEA Joint Committee, issued in accordance with Article 94 (4), on the functioning and the development of this Agreement.

5. The President of the EEA Council may appear before the EEA Joint Parliamentary Committee in order to be heard by it.

6. The EEA Joint Parliamentary Committee shall adopt its rules of procedure.

SECTION 4
CO-OPERATION BETWEEN ECONOMIC AND SOCIAL PARTNERS

Article 96

1. Members of the Economic and Social Committee and other bodies representing the social partners in the Community and the corresponding bodies in the EFTA States shall work to strengthen contacts between them and to co-operate in an organized and regular manner in order to enhance the awareness of the economic and social aspects of the growing interdependence of the economies of the Contracting Parties and of their interests within the context of the EEA.

2. To this end, an EEA Consultative Committee is hereby established. It shall be composed of equal numbers of, on the one hand, members of the Economic and Social Committee of the Community and, on the other, members of the EFTA Consultative

Committee. The EEA Consultative Committee may express its views in the form of reports or resolutions, as appropriate.

3. The EEA Consultative Committee shall adopt its rules of procedure.

Chapter 2
The Decision-Making Procedure

Article 97

This Agreement does not prejudge the right for each Contracting Party to amend, without prejudice to the principle of non-discrimination and after having informed the other Contracting Parties, its internal legislation in the areas covered by this Agreement:

- if the EEA Joint Committee concludes that the legislation as amended does not affect the good functioning of this Agreement; or
- if the procedures referred to in Article 98 have been completed.

Article 98

The Annexes to this Agreement and Protocols 1 to 7, 9 to 11, 19 to 27, 30 to 32, 37, 39, 41 and 47, as appropriate, may be amended by a decision of the EEA Joint Committee in accordance with Articles 93 (2), 99, 100, 102 and 103.

Article 99

1. As soon as new legislation is being drawn up by the EC Commission in a field which is governed by this Agreement, the EC Commission shall informally seek advice from experts of the EFTA States in the same way as it seeks advice from experts of the EC Member States for the elaboration of its proposals.

2. When transmitting its proposal to the Council of the European Communities, the EC Commission shall transmit copies thereof to the EFTA States.

At the request of one of the Contracting Parties, a preliminary exchange of views takes place in the EEA Joint Committee.

3. During the phase preceding the decision of the Council of the European Communities, in a continuous information and consultation process, the Contracting Parties consult each other again in the EEA Joint Committee at the significant moments at the request of one of them.

4. The Contracting Parties shall cooperate in good faith during the information and consultation phase with a view to facilitating, at the end of the process, the decision-taking in the Joint Committee.

Article 100

The EC Commission shall ensure experts of the EFTA States as wide a participation as possible according to the areas concerned, in the preparatory stage of draft measures to be submitted subsequently to the committees which assist the EC Commission in the exercise of its executive powers. In this regard, when drawing up draft measures the EC Commission shall refer to experts of the EFTA States on the same basis as it refers to experts of the EC Member States.

In the cases where the Council of the European Communities is seized in accordance with the procedure applicable to the type of committee involved, the EC Commission shall transmit to the Council of the European Communities the views of the experts of the EFTA States.

Article 101

1. In respect of committees which are covered neither by Article 81 nor by Article 100 experts from EFTA States shall be associated with the work when this is called for by the good functioning of this Agreement.

These committees are listed in Protocol 37. The modalities of such an association are set out in the relevant sectoral Protocols and Annexes dealing with the matter concerned.

2. If it appears to the Contracting Parties that such an association should be extended to other committees which present similar characteristics, the EEA Joint Committee may amend Protocol 37.

Article 102

1. In order to guarantee the legal security and the homogeneity of the EEA, the EEA Joint Committee shall take a decision concerning an amendment of an Annexe to this Agreement as closely as possible to the adoption by the Community of the corresponding new Community legislation with a view to permitting a simultaneous application of the latter as well as of the amendments of the Annexes to the Agreement. To this end, the Community shall, whenever adopting a legislative act on an issue which is governed by this Agreement, as soon as possible inform the other Contracting Parties in the EEA Joint Committee.

2. The part of an Annexe to this Agreement which would be directly affected by the new legislation is assessed in the EEA Joint Committee.

3. The Contracting Parties shall make all efforts to arrive at an agreement on matters relevant to this Agreement.

The EEA Joint Committee shall, in particular, make every effort to find a mutually acceptable solution where a serious problem arises in any area which, in the EFTA States, falls within the competence of the legislator.

4. If, notwithstanding the application of the preceding paragraph, an agreement on an amendment of an Annexe to this Agreement cannot be reached, the EEA Joint Committee shall examine all further possibilities to maintain the good functioning of this Agreement and take any decision necessary to this effect, including the possibility to take notice of the equivalence of legislation. Such a decision shall be taken at the latest at the expiry of a period of six months from the date of referral to the EEA Joint Committee or, if that date is later, on the date of entry into force of the corresponding Community legislation.

5. If, at the end of the time limit set out in paragraph 4, the EEA Joint Committee has not taken a decision on an amendment of an Annexe to this Agreement, the affected part thereof, as determined in accordance with paragraph 2, is regarded as provisionally suspended, subject to a decision to the contrary by the EEA Joint Committee. Such a suspension shall take effect six months after the end of the period referred to in paragraph 4, but in no event earlier than the date on which the corresponding EC act is implemented in the Community. The EEA Joint Committee shall pursue its efforts to agree on a mutually acceptable solution in order for the suspension to be terminated as soon as possible.

6. The practical consequences of the suspension referred to in paragraph 5 shall be discussed in the EEA Joint Committee. The rights and obligations which individuals and economic operators have already acquired under this Agreement shall remain. The

Contracting Parties shall, as appropriate, decide on the adjustments necessary due to the suspension.

Article 103

1. If a decision of the EEA Joint Committee can be binding on a Contracting Party only after the fulfilment of constitutional requirements, the decision shall, if a date is contained therein, enter into force on that date, provided that the Contracting Party concerned has notified the other Contracting Parties by that date that the constitutional requirements have been fulfilled.

In the absence of such a notification by that date, the decision shall enter into force on the first day of the second month following the last notification.

2. If upon the expiry of a period of six months after the decision of the EEA Joint Committee such a notification has not taken place, the decision of the EEA Joint Committee shall be applied provisionally pending the fulfilment of the constitutional requirements unless a Contracting Party notifies that such a provisional application cannot take place. In the latter case, or if a Contracting Party notifies the non-ratification of a decision of the EEA Joint Committee, the suspension provided for in Article 102 (5) shall take effect one month after such a notification but in no event earlier than the date on which the corresponding EC act is implemented in the Community.

Article 104

Decisions taken by the EEA Joint Committee in the cases provided for in this Agreement shall, unless otherwise provided for therein, upon their entry into force be binding on the Contracting Parties which shall take the necessary steps to ensure their implementation and application.

Chapter 3
Homogeneity, Surveillance Procedure and Settlement of Disputes

SECTION I
HOMOGENEITY

Article 105

1. In order to achieve the objective of the Contracting Parties to arrive at as uniform an interpretation as possible of the provisions of the Agreement and those provisions of Community legislation which are substantially reproduced in the Agreement, the EEA Joint Committee shall act in accordance with this Article.

2. The EEA Joint Committee shall keep under constant review the development of the case law of the Court of Justice of the European Communities and the EFTA Court. To this end judgments of these Courts shall be transmitted to the EEA Joint Committee which shall act so as to preserve the homogeneous interpretation of the Agreement.

3. If the EEA Joint Committee within two months after a difference in the case law of the two Courts has been brought before it, has not succeeded to preserve the homogeneous interpretation of the Agreement, the procedures laid down in Article 111 may be applied.

Article 106

In order to ensure as uniform an interpretation as possible of this Agreement, in full deference to the independence of courts, a system of exchange of information concerning judgments by the EFTA Court, the Court of Justice of the European Communities and the Court of First Instance of the European Communities and the Courts of Last Instance of the EFTA States shall be set up by the EEA Joint Committee. This system shall comprise:

(a) transmission to the Registrar of the Court of Justice of the European Communities of judgments delivered by such courts on the interpretation and application of, on the one hand, this Agreement or, on the other hand, the Treaty establishing the European Economic Community and the Treaty establishing the European Coal and Steel Community, as amended or supplemented, as well as the acts adopted in pursuance thereof in so far as they concern provisions which are identical in substance to those of this Agreement;

(b) classification of these judgments by the Registrar of the Court of Justice of the European Communities including, as far as necessary, the drawing up and publication of translations and abstracts;

(c) communications by the Registrar of the Court of Justice of the European Communities of the relevant documents to the competent national authorities, to be designated by each Contracting Party.

Article 107

Provisions on the possibility for an EFTA State to allow a court or tribunal to ask the Court of Justice of the European Communities to decide on the interpretation of an EEA rule are laid down in Protocol 34.

SECTION 2
SURVEILLANCE PROCEDURE

Article 108

1. The EFTA States shall establish an independent surveillance authority (EFTA Surveillance Authority) as well as procedures similar to those existing in the Community including procedures for ensuring the fulfilment of obligations under this Agreement and for control of the legality of acts of the EFTA Surveillance Authority regarding competition.

2. The EFTA States shall establish a court of justice (EFTA Court).

The EFTA Court shall, in accordance with a separate agreement between the EFTA States, with regard to the application of this Agreement be competent, in particular, for:

(a) actions concerning the surveillance procedure regarding the EFTA States;

(b) appeals concerning decisions in the field of competition taken by the EFTA Surveillance Authority;

(c) the settlement of disputes between two or more EFTA States.

Article 109

1. The fulfilment of the obligations under this Agreement shall be monitored by, on the one hand, the EFTA Surveillance Authority and, on the other, the EC Commission acting in conformity with the Treaty establishing the European Economic Community, the Treaty establishing the European Coal and Steel Community and this Agreement.

2. In order to ensure a uniform surveillance throughout the EEA, the EFTA Surveillance Authority and the EC Commission shall cooperate, exchange information and consult each other on surveillance policy issues and individual cases.

3. The EC Commission and the EFTA Surveillance Authority shall receive any complaints concerning the application of this Agreement. They shall inform each other of complaints received.

4. Each of these bodies shall examine all complaints falling within its competence and shall pass to the other body any complaints which fall within the competence of that body.

5. In case of disagreement between these two bodies with regard to the action to be taken in relation to a complaint or with regard to the result of the examination, either of the bodies may refer the matter to the EEA Joint Committee which shall deal with it in accordance with Article 111.

Article 110

Decisions under this Agreement by the EFTA Surveillance Authority and the EC Commission which impose a pecuniary obligation on persons other than States, shall be enforceable. The same shall apply to such judgments under this Agreement by the Court of Justice of the European Communities, the Court of First Instance of the European Communities and the EFTA Court.

Enforcement shall be governed by the rules of civil procedure in force in the State in the territory of which it is carried out. The order for its enforcement shall be appended to the decision, without other formality than verification of the authenticity of the decision, by the authority which each Contracting Party shall designate for this purpose and shall make known to the other Contracting Parties, the EFTA Surveillance Authority, the EC Commission, the Court of Justice of the European Communities, the Court of First Instance of the European Communities and the EFTA Court.

When these formalities have been completed on application by the party concerned, the latter may proceed to enforcement, in accordance with the law of the State in the territory of which enforcement is to be carried out, by bringing the matter directly before the competent authority.

Enforcement may be suspended only by a decision of the Court of Justice of the European Communities, as far as decisions by the EC Commission, the Court of First Instance of the European Communities or the Court of Justice of the European Communities are concerned, or by a decision of the EFTA Court as far as decisions by the EFTA Surveillance Authority or the EFTA Court are concerned. However, the courts of the States concerned shall have jurisdiction over complaints that enforcement is being carried out in an irregular manner.

SECTION 3
SETTLEMENT OF DISPUTES

Article 111

1. The Community or an EFTA State may bring a matter under dispute which concerns the interpretation or application of this Agreement before the EEA Joint Committee in accordance with the following provisions.

2. The EEA Joint Committee may settle the dispute. It shall be provided with all information which might be of use in making possible an in-depth examination of the

situation, with a view to finding an acceptable solution. To this end, the EEA Joint Committee shall examine all possibilities to maintain the good functioning of the Agreement.

3. If a dispute concerns the interpretation of provisions of this Agreement, which are identical in substance to corresponding rules of the Treaty establishing the European Economic Community and the Treaty establishing the European Coal and Steel Community and to acts adopted in application of these two Treaties and if the dispute has not been settled within three months after it has been brought before the EEA Joint Committee, the Contracting Parties to the dispute may agree to request the Court of Justice of the European Communities to give a ruling on the interpretation of the relevant rules.

If the EEA Joint Committee in such a dispute has not reached an agreement on a solution within six months from the date on which this procedure was initiated or if, by then, the Contracting Parties to the dispute have not decided to ask for a ruling by the Court of Justice of the European Communities, a Contracting Party may, in order to remedy possible imbalances,

- either take a safeguard measure in accordance with Article 12 (2) and following the procedure of Article 113;
- or apply Article 102 *mutatis mutandis*.

4. If a dispute concerns the scope or duration of safeguard measures taken in accordance with Article 111 (3) or Article 112, or the proportionality of rebalancing measures taken in accordance with Article 114, and if the EEA Joint Committee after three months from the date when the matter has been brought before it has not succeeded to resolve the dispute, any Contracting Party may refer the dispute to arbitration under the procedures laid down in Protocol 33. No question of interpretation of the provisions of this Agreement referred to in paragraph 3 may be dealt with in such procedures. The arbitration award shall be binding on the parties to the dispute.

Chapter 4
Safeguard Measures

Article 112

1. If serious economic, societal or environmental difficulties of a sectorial or regional nature liable to persist are arising, a Contracting Party may unilaterally take appropriate measures under the conditions and procedures laid down in Article 113.

2. Such safeguard measures shall be restricted with regard to their scope and duration to what is strictly necessary in order to remedy the situation. Priority shall be given to such measures as will least disturb the functioning of this Agreement.

3. The safeguard measures shall apply with regard to all Contracting Parties.

Article 113

1. A Contracting Party which is considering taking safeguard measures under Article 112 shall, without delay, notify the other Contracting Parties through the EEA Joint Committee and shall provide all relevant information.

2. The Contracting Parties shall immediately enter into consultations in the EEA Joint Committee with a view to finding a commonly acceptable solution.

3. The Contracting Party concerned may not take safeguard measures until one month has elapsed after the date of notification under paragraph 1, unless the consultation

procedure under paragraph 2 has been concluded before the expiration of the stated time limit. When exceptional circumstances requiring immediate action exclude prior examination, the Contracting Party concerned may apply forthwith the protective measures strictly necessary to remedy the situation.

For the Community, the safeguard measures shall be taken by the EC Commission.

4. The Contracting Party concerned shall, without delay, notify the measures taken to the EEA Joint Committee and shall provide all relevant information.

5. The safeguard measures taken shall be the subject of consultations in the EEA Joint Committee every three months from the date of their adoption with a view to their abolition before the date of expiry envisaged, or to the limitation of their scope of application.

Each Contracting Party may at any time request the EEA Joint Committee to review such measures.

Article 114

1. If a safeguard measure taken by a Contracting Party creates an imbalance between the rights and obligations under this Agreement, any other Contracting Party may towards that Contracting Party take such proportionate rebalancing measures as are strictly necessary to remedy the imbalance. Priority shall be given to such measures as will least disturb the functioning of the EEA.

2. The procedure under Article 113 shall apply.

[. . .]

Part IX
General and Final Provisions

Article 118

1. Where a Contracting Party considers that it would be useful in the interests of all the Contracting Parties to develop the relations established by this Agreement by extending them to fields not covered thereby, it shall submit a reasoned request to the other Contracting Parties within the EEA Council. The latter may instruct the EEA Joint Committee to examine all the aspects of this request and to issue a report.

The EEA Council may, where appropriate, take the political decisions with a view to opening negotiations between the Contracting Parties.

2. The agreements resulting from the negotiations referred to in paragraph 1 will be subject to ratification or approval by the Contracting Parties in accordance with their own procedures.

Article 119

The Annexes and the acts referred to therein as adapted for the purposes of this Agreement as well as the Protocols shall form an integral part of this Agreement.

Article 120

Unless otherwise provided in this Agreement and in particular in Protocols 41, 43 and 44, the application of the provisions of this Agreement shall prevail over provisions in existing bilateral or multilateral agreements binding the European Economic Community, on the one hand, and one or more EFTA States, on the other, to the extent that the same subject matter is governed by this Agreement.

Article 121

The provisions of this Agreement shall not preclude co-operation:

(a) within the framework of the Nordic cooperation to the extent that such co-operation does not impair the good functioning of this Agreement;
(b) within the framework of the regional union between Switzerland and Liechtenstein to the extent that the objectives of this union are not attained by the application of this Agreement and the good functioning of this Agreement is not impaired;
(c) within the framework of cooperation between Austria and Italy concerning Tyrol, Vorarlberg and Trentino-South Tyrol/Alto Adige, to the extent that such co-operation does not impair the good functioning of this Agreement.

Article 122

The representatives, delegates and experts of the Contracting Parties, as well as officials and other servants acting under this Agreement shall be required, even after their duties have ceased, not to disclose information of the kind covered by the obligation of professional secrecy, in particular information about undertakings, their business relations or their cost components.

Article 123

Nothing in this Agreement shall prevent a Contracting Party from taking any measures:

(a) which it considers necessary to prevent the disclosure of information contrary to its essential security interests;
(b) which relate to the production of, or trade in, arms, munitions and war materials or other products indispensable for defence purposes or to research, development or production indispensable for defence purposes, provided that such measures do not impair the conditions of competition in respect of products not intended for specifically military purposes;
(c) which it considers essential to its own security in the event of serious internal disturbances affecting the maintenance of law and order, in time of war or serious international tension constituting threat of war or in order to carry out obligations it has accepted for the purpose of maintaining peace and international security.

Article 124

The Contracting Parties shall accord nationals of EC Member States and EFTA States the same treatment as their own nationals as regards participation in the capital of companies or firms within the meaning of Article 34, without prejudice to the application of the other provisions of this Agreement.

Article 125

This Agreement shall in no way prejudice the rules of the Contracting Parties governing the system of property ownership.

Article 126

1. The Agreement shall apply to the territories to which the Treaty establishing the

European Economic Community and the Treaty establishing the European Coal and Steel Community is applied and under the conditions laid down in those Treaties, and to the territories of the Republic of Austria, the Republic of Finland, the Republic of Iceland, the Principality of Liechtenstein, the Kingdom of Norway, the Kingdom of Sweden and the Swiss Confederation.

2. Notwithstanding paragraph 1, this Agreement shall not apply to the Åland Islands. The Government of Finland may, however, give notice, by a declaration deposited when ratifying this Agreement with the Depositary, which shall transmit a certified copy thereof to the Contracting Parties, that the Agreement shall apply to those Islands under the same conditions as it applies to other parts of Finland subject to the following provisions:

(a) The provisions of this Agreement shall not preclude the application of the provisions in force at any given time on the Åland Islands on:

  (i) restrictions on the right for natural persons who do not enjoy regional citizenship in Åland, and for legal persons, to acquire and hold real property on the Åland Islands without permission by the competent authorities of the Islands;

  (ii) restrictions on the right of establishment and the right to provide services by natural persons who do not enjoy regional citizenship in Åland, or by any legal person, without permission by the competent authorities of the Åland Islands.

(b) The rights enjoyed by Ålanders in Finland shall not be affected by this Agreement.

(c) The authorities of the Åland Islands shall apply the same treatment to all natural and legal persons of the Contracting Parties.

Article 127

Each Contracting Party may withdraw from this Agreement provided it gives at least twelve months' notice in writing to the other Contracting Parties.

Immediately after the notification of the intended withdrawal, the other Contracting Parties shall convene a diplomatic conference in order to envisage the necessary modifications to bring to the Agreement.

Article 128

1. Any European State becoming a member of the Community shall, or becoming a member of EFTA may, apply to become a Party to this Agreement. It shall address its application to the EEA Council.

2. The terms and conditions for such participation shall be the subject of an agreement between the Contracting Parties and the applicant State. That agreement shall be submitted for ratification or approval by all Contracting Parties in accordance with their own procedures.

Article 129

1. This Agreement is drawn up in a single original in the Danish, Dutch, English, Finnish, French, German, Greek, Icelandic, Italian, Norwegian, Portuguese, Spanish and Swedish languages, each of these texts being equally authentic.

The texts of the acts referred to in the Annexes are equally authentic in Danish, Dutch, English, French, German, Greek, Italian, Portuguese and Spanish as published in the Official Journal of the European Communities and shall for the authentication thereof be drawn up in the Finnish, Icelandic, Norwegian and Swedish languages.

2. This Agreement shall be ratified or approved by the Contracting Parties in accordance with their respective constitutional requirements.

It shall be deposited with the General Secretariat of the Council of the European Communities by which certified copies shall be transmitted to all other Contracting Parties.

The instruments of ratification or approval shall be deposited with the General Secretariat of the Council of the European Communities which shall notify all other Contracting Parties.

3. This Agreement shall enter into force on 1 January 1993, provided that all Contracting Parties have deposited their instruments of ratification or approval before that date. After that date this Agreement shall enter into force on the first day of the second month following the last notification. The final date for such a notification shall be 30 June 1993. After that date the Contracting Parties shall convene a diplomatic conference to appreciate the situation.

Protocol 1
On Horizontal Adaptations

The provisions of the acts referred to in the Annexes to the Agreement shall be applicable in accordance with the Agreement and this Protocol, unless otherwise provided in the respective Annex. The specific adaptations necessary for individual acts are set out in the Annex where the act concerned is listed.

1. Introductory Parts of the Acts

The preambles of the acts referred to are not adapted for the purposes of the Agreement. They are relevant to the extent necessary for the proper interpretation and application, within the framework of the Agreement, of the provisions contained in such acts.

2. Provisions on EC Committees

Procedures, institutional arrangements or other provisions concerning EC committees contained in the acts referred to are dealt with in Articles 81, 100 and 101 of the Agreement and in Protocol 31.

3. Provisions Setting up Procedures for Adapting/Amending Community Acts

Where an act referred to provides for EC procedures on its adaptation, extension or amendment or for the development of new Community policies, initiatives or acts, the relevant decision-making procedures provided for in the Agreement shall apply.

4. Exchange of Information and Notification Procedures

(a) Where an EC Member State is to submit information to the EC Commission, an EFTA State shall submit such information to the EFTA Surveillance Authority and to a Standing Committee of the EFTA States. The same shall apply when the transmission of information is to be carried out by the competent authorities. The EC Commission and the EFTA Surveillance Authority shall exchange information they have received from the EC Member States or from the EFTA States or from the competent authorities.

(b) Where an EC Member State is to submit information to one or more other EC Member States, it shall also submit that information to the EC Commission which shall pass it on to the Standing Committee for distribution to the EFTA States.

An EFTA State shall submit corresponding information to one or more other EFTA States and to the Standing Committee which shall pass it on to the EC Commission for distribution to the EC Member States. The same shall apply when the information is to be submitted by the competent authorities.

(c) In areas where, for reasons of urgency, rapid transfer of information is called for, appropriate sectoral solutions providing for direct exchange of information shall apply.

(d) Functions of the EC Commission in the context of procedures for verification or approval, information, notification or consultation and similar matters shall for the EFTA States be carried out according to procedures established among them. This is without prejudice to paragraphs 2, 3 and 7. The EC Commission and the EFTA Surveillance Authority or the Standing Committee, as the case may be, shall exchange all information regarding these matters. Any issue arising in this context may be referred to the EEA Joint Committee.

5. Review and Reporting Procedures

Where, according to an act referred to, the EC Commission or another EC body is to prepare a report or an assessment or the like, the EFTA Surveillance Authority or the Standing Committee, as the case may be, shall, unless otherwise agreed, concurrently prepare, as appropriate, a corresponding report or assessment or the like, with regard to the EFTA States. The EC Commission and the EFTA Surveillance Authority or the Standing Committee, as the case may be, shall consult each other and exchange information during the preparation of their respective reports, copies of which shall be sent to the EEA Joint Committee.

6. Publication of Information

(a) Where, according to an act referred to, an EC Member State is to publish certain information on facts, procedures and the like, also the EFTA States shall, under the Agreement, publish the relevant information in a corresponding manner.

(b) Where, according to an act referred to, facts, procedures, reports and the like are to be published in the Official Journal of the European Communities, the corresponding information regarding the EFTA States shall be published in a separate EEA section[1] thereof.

7. Rights and Obligations

Rights conferred and obligations imposed upon the EC Member States or their public entities, undertakings or individuals in relation to each other, shall be understood to be conferred or imposed upon Contracting Parties, the latter also being understood, as the case may be, as their competent authorities, public entities, undertakings or individuals.

8. References to Territories

Whenever the acts referred to contain references to the territory of the 'Community' or of the 'common market' the references shall for the purposes of the Agreement be understood to be

[1] The table of contents of the EEA section would also contain references to where the information in question concerning the EC and its Member States could be found.

references to the territories of the Contracting Parties as defined in Article 126 of the Agreement.

9. References to Nationals of EC Member States

Whenever the acts referred to contain references to nationals of EC Member States, the references shall for the purposes of the Agreement be understood to be references also to nationals of EFTA States.

10. References to Languages

Where an act referred to confers upon the EC Member States or their public entities, undertakings or individuals rights or imposes obligations regarding the use of any of the official languages of the European Communities, the corresponding rights and obligations regarding the use of any of the official languages of all Contracting Parties shall be understood to be conferred or imposed upon Contracting Parties, their competent authorities, public entities, undertakings or individuals.

11. Entry into Force and Implementation of Acts

Provisions on the entry into force or implementation of the acts referred to in the Annexes to the Agreement are not relevant for the purposes of the Agreement. The time limits and dates for the EFTA States for bringing into force and implementing acts referred to follow from Article 129 (3) of the Agreement, as well as from provisions on transitional arrangements.

12. Addressees of the Community Acts

Provisions indicating that a Community act is addressed to the Member States of the Community are not relevant for the purposes of the Agreement.

Protocol 2

On Products Excluded from the Scope of the Agreement in Accordance with Article 8 (3) (a)

The following products falling within HS, Chapters 25 to 97, are excluded from the scope of the Agreement:

HS Heading No	Product description
35.01	Casein, caseinates and other casein derivatives; Casein glues
35.02	Albumins, albuminates and other albumin derivatives:
10	– Egg albumin:
ex 10	– – Other than unfit, or to be rendered unfit, for human consumption
90	– Other
ex 90	– – Milk albumin (lactalbumin), other than unfit, or to be rendered unfit, for human consumption
35.05	Dextrins and other modified starches (for example, pregelatinised or esterified

	starches); glues based on starches, or on dextrins or other modified starches:
10	– Dextrins and other modified starches:
ex 10	– – Starches, esterified or etherified

[. . .]

PROTOCOL 8
ON STATE MONOPOLIES

1. Article 16 of the Agreement shall be applicable at the latest from 1 January 1995 in the case of the following State monopolies of a commercial character:

- Austrian monopoly on salt;
- Icelandic monopoly on fertilizers;
- Swiss and Liechtenstein monopolies on salt and gunpowder.

2. Article 16 shall also apply to wine (HS Heading No 22.04).

PROTOCOL 9
ON TRADE IN FISH AND OTHER MARINE PRODUCTS

Article 1

1. Without prejudice to the provisions referred to in Appendix 1, the EFTA States shall upon entry into force of the Agreement abolish customs duties on imports and charges having equivalent effect on the products listed in Table I of Appendix 2.

2. Without prejudice to the provisions referred to in Appendix 1, the EFTA States shall apply no quantitative restrictions on imports or measures having equivalent effect on the products listed in Table I of Appendix 2. In this context the provisions of Article 13 of the Agreement shall apply.

Article 2

1. The Community shall, upon the entry into force of the Agreement, abolish customs duties on imports and charges having equivalent effect on the products listed in Table II of Appendix 2.

2. The Community shall reduce customs duties on the products listed in Table III of Appendix 2 progressively in accordance with the following timetable:

(a) on 1 January 1993 each duty shall be reduced to 86% of the basic duty;
(b) four further reductions of 14% each of the basic duty shall be made on 1 January 1994, 1 January 1995, 1 January 1996 and 1 January 1997.

3. The basic duties to which the successive reductions provided for in paragraph 2 are to be applied shall, for each product, be the duties bound by the Community under the General Agreement on Tariffs and Trade, or, where the duty is not bound, the autonomous duty on 1 January 1992. Should, after 1 January 1992, any tariff reductions resulting from the multilateral trade negotiations of the Uruguay Round become applicable, such reduced duties shall be used as the basic duties.

Whenever in the context of bilateral agreements between the Community and individual

EFTA States reduced duties exist for certain products, those duties shall be considered as the basic duties for each of the EFTA States concerned.

4. The rates of duty calculated in accordance with paragraphs 2 and 3 shall be applied by rounding down to the first decimal place by deleting the second decimal.

5. The Community shall apply no quantitative restrictions on imports or measures having equivalent effect on the products listed in Appendix 2. In this context the provisions of Article 13 of the Agreement shall apply.

Article 3

The provisions of Articles 1 and 2 shall apply to products originating in the Contracting Parties. The rules of origin are set out in Protocol 4 of the Agreement.

Article 4

1. Aid granted through State resources to the fisheries sector which distorts competition shall be abolished.

2. Legislation relating to the market organization in the fisheries sector shall be adjusted so as not to distort competition.

3. The Contracting Parties shall endeavour to ensure conditions of competition which will enable the other Contracting Parties to refrain from the application of anti-dumping measures and countervailing duties.

Article 5

The Contracting Parties shall take the necessary measures to ensure that all fishing vessels flying the flag of other Contracting Parties enjoy access equal to that of their own vessels to ports and first-stage marketing installations together with all associated equipment and technical installations.

Notwithstanding the provisions of the preceding paragraph, a Contracting Party may refuse landings of fish from a fish stock of common interest over the management of which there is serious disagreement.

Article 6

Should the necessary legislative adaptations not have been effected to the satisfaction of the Contracting Parties at the time of entry into force of the Agreement, any points at issue may be put to the EEA Joint Committee. In the event of failure to reach agreement, the provisions of Article 114 of the Agreement shall apply *mutatis mutandis*.

Article 7

The provisions of the agreements listed in Appendix 3 shall prevail over provisions of this Protocol to the extent they grant to the EFTA States concerned more favourable trade regimes than this Protocol.

[. . .]

Protocol 13
On the Non-application of Anti-dumping and Countervailing Measures

The application of Article 26 of the Agreement is limited to the areas covered by the provisions of the Agreement and in which the Community *acquis* is fully integrated into the Agreement.

Moreover, unless other solutions are agreed upon by the Contracting Parties, its application is without prejudice to any measures which may be introduced by the Contracting Parties to avoid circumvention of the following measures aimed at third countries:

- anti-dumping measures;
- countervailing duties;
- measures against illicit commercial practices attributable to third countries.

Protocol 14
On Trade in Coal and Steel Products

Article 1
This Protocol applies to products covered by the bilateral Free Trade Agreements (hereinafter referred to as the 'Free Trade Agreements') concluded between, on the one hand, the European Coal and Steel Community and its Member States and the individual EFTA States, on the other hand, or, as the case may be, between the Member States of the European Coal and Steel Community and the respective EFTA States.

Article 2
1. The Free Trade Agreements shall remain unaffected unless otherwise provided in this Protocol. Where the Free Trade Agreements do not apply, the provisions of this Agreement are applicable. Where the substantive provisions of the Free Trade Agreements continue to be applied, the institutional provisions of those agreements will also be applicable.

2. Quantitative restrictions on exports, measures having equivalent effect and customs duties and charges having equivalent effect, applicable to trade within the European Economic Area, shall be abolished.

Article 3
The Contracting Parties shall not introduce any restrictions or administrative and technical regulations which would form, in trade between the Contracting Parties, an impediment to the free movement of products covered by this Protocol.

Article 4
The substantive competition rules applicable to undertakings concerning products covered by this Protocol are included in Protocol 25. Secondary legislation is set out in Protocol 21 and Annexe XIV.

Article 5
The Contracting Parties shall comply with the rules for aid to the steel industry. They

recognize in particular the relevance of, and accept, the Community rules for aid to the steel industry as laid down in Commission Decision 322/89/ECSC which expires on 31 December 1991. The Contracting Parties declare their commitment to integrate into the EEA Agreement new Community rules for aid to the steel industry by the entry into force of this Agreement, provided that they are substantially similar to those of the aforementioned act.

Article 6

1. The Contracting Parties shall exchange information on markets. The EFTA States shall use their best endeavours in order to ensure that steel producers, consumers and merchants provide such information.

2. The EFTA States shall use their best endeavours in order to ensure that the steel-producing undertakings established within their territories will participate in annual surveys concerning investment referred to in Article 15 of Commission Decision No 3302/81/ECSC of 18 November 1981. The Contracting Parties will exchange, without prejudice to the requirements of business confidentiality, information on significant investment or disinvestment projects.

3. All matters relating to the exchange of information between the Contracting Parties shall be covered by the general institutional provisions of this Agreement.

Article 7

The Contracting Parties note that the rules of origin laid down in Protocol 3 of the Free Trade Agreements concluded between the European Economic Community and individual EFTA States are replaced by Protocol 4 to this Agreement.

[. . .]

Protocol 21

On the Implementation of Competition Rules Applicable to Undertakings

Article 1

The EFTA Surveillance Authority shall, in an agreement between the EFTA States, be entrusted with equivalent powers and similar functions to those of the EC Commission, at the time of the signature of the Agreement, for the application of the competition rules of the Treaty establishing the European Economic Community and the Treaty establishing the European Coal and Steel Community, enabling the EFTA Surveillance Authority to give effect to the principles laid down in Articles 1 (2) (e) and 53 to 60 of the Agreement, and in Protocol 25.

The Community shall, where necessary, adopt the provisions giving effect to the principles laid down in Articles 1 (2) (e) and 53 to 60 of the Agreement, and in Protocol 25, in order to ensure that the EC Commission has equivalent powers and similar functions under this Agreement to those which it has, at the time of the signature of the Agreement, for the application of the competition rules of the Treaty establishing the European Economic Community and the Treaty establishing the European Coal and Steel Community.

Article 2

If, following the procedures set out in Part VII of the Agreement, new acts for the implementation of Articles 1 (2) (e) and 53 to 60 and of Protocol 25, or on amendments of the acts listed in Article 3 of this Protocol are adopted, corresponding amendments shall be made in the agreement setting up the EFTA Surveillance Authority so as to ensure that the EFTA Surveillance Authority will be entrusted simultaneously with equivalent powers and similar functions to those of the EC Commission.

Article 3

1. In addition to the acts listed in Annexe XIV, the following acts reflect the powers and functions of the EC Commission for the application of the competition rules of the Treaty establishing the European Economic Community:

Control of concentrations

1. **389 R 4064**: Articles 6 to 25 of Council Regulation (EEC) No 4064/89 of 21 December 1989 on the control of concentrations between undertakings (OJ No L 395, 30.12.1989, p. 1), as corrected by OJ No L 257, 21.9.1990, p. 13.

2. **390 R 2367**: Commission Regulation (EEC) No 2367/90 of 25 July 1990 on the notifications, time limits and hearings provided for in Council Regulation (EEC) No 4064/89 on the control of concentrations between undertakings (OJ No L 219, 14.8.1990, p. 5).

General procedural rules

3. **362 R 0017**: Council Regulation No 17/62 of 6 February 1962. First Regulation implementing Articles 85 and 86 of the Treaty (OJ No 13, 21.2.1962, p. 204/62), as amended by:

- **362 R 0059**: Regulation No 59/62 of 3 July 1962 (OJ No 58, 10.7.1962, p. 1655/62),
- **363 R 0118**: Regulation No 118/63 of 5 November 1963 (OJ No 162, 7.11.1963, p. 2696/63),
- **371 R 2822**: Regulation (EEC) No 2822/71 of 20 December 1971 (OJ No L 285, 29.12.1971, p. 49),
- **1 72 B**: Act concerning the conditions of Accession and Adjustments to the Treaties—Accession to the European Communities of the Kingdom of Denmark, Ireland and the United Kingdom of Great Britain and Northern Ireland (OJ No L 73, 27.03.1972, p. 92),
- **1 79 H**: Act concerning the conditions of Accession and Adjustments to the Treaties—Accession to the European Communities of the Hellenic Republic (OJ No L 291, 19.11.1979, p. 93),
- **1 85 I**: Act concerning the conditions of Accession and Adjustments to the Treaties—Accession to the European Communities of the Kingdom of Spain and the Portuguese Republic (OJ No L 302, 15.11.1985, p. 165).

4. **362 R 0027**: Commission Regulation No 27/62 of 3 May 1962. First Regulation implementing Council Regulation No 17 of 6 February 1962 (Form, content and other details concerning applications and notifications) (OJ No 35, 10.5.1962, p. 1118/62), as amended by:

- **368 R 1133**: Regulation (EEC) No 1133/68 of 26 July 1968 (OJ No L 189, 1.8.1968, p. 1),
- **375 R 1699**: Regulation (EEC) No 1699/75 of 2 July 1975 (OJ No L 172, 3.7.1975, p. 11),

- **1 79 H**: Act concerning the conditions of Accession and Adjustments to the Treaties—Accession to the European Communities of the Hellenic Republic (OJ No L 291, 19.11.1979, p. 94),
- **385 R 2526**: Regulation (EEC) No 2526/85 of 5 August 1985 (OJ No L 240, 7.9.1985, p. 1),
- **1 85 I**: Act concerning the conditions of Accession and Adjustments to the Treaties—Accession to the European Communities of the Kingdom of Spain and the Portuguese Republic (OJ No L 302, 15.11.1985, p. 166).

5. **363 R 0099**: Commission Regulation No 99/63 of 25 July 1963 on the hearings provided for in Article 19 (1) and (2) of Council Regulation (EEC) No 17/62 (OJ No 127, 20.8.1963, p. 2268/63).

Transport

6. **362 R 0141**: Council Regulation No 141/62 of 26 November 1962 exempting transport from the application of Council Regulation No 17 amended by Regulations Nos 165/65/EEC and 1002/67/EEC (OJ No 124, 28.11.1962, p. 2751/62).

7. **368 R 1017**: Article 6 and Articles 10 to 31 of Council Regulation (EEC) No 1017/68 of 19 July 1968 applying rules of competition to transport by rail, road and inland waterway (OJ No L 175, 23.7.1968, p. 1).

8. **369 R 1629**: Commission Regulation (EEC) No 1629/69 of 8 August 1969 on the form, content and other details of complaints pursuant to Article 10, applications pursuant to Article 12 and notifications pursuant to Article 14 (1) of Council Regulation (EEC) No 1017/68 of 19 July 1968 (OJ No L 209, 21.8.1969, p. 1).

9. **369 R 1630**: Commission Regulation (EEC) No 1630/69 of 8 August 1969 on the hearings provided for in Article 26 (1) and (2) of Council Regulation (EEC) No 1017/68 of 19 July 1968 (OJ No L 209, 21.8.1969, p. 11).

10. **374 R 2988**: Council Regulation (EEC) No 2988/74 of 26 November 1974 concerning limitation periods in proceedings and the enforcement of sanctions under the rules of the European Economic Community relating to transport and competition (OJ No L 319, 29.11.1974, p. 1).

11. **386 R 4056**: Section II of Council Regulation (EEC) No 4056/86 of 22 December 1986 laying down detailed rules for the application of Articles 85 and 86 of the Treaty to maritime transport (OJ No L 378, 31.12.1986, p. 4).

12. **388 R 4260**: Commission Regulation (EEC) No 4260/88 of 16 December 1988 on the communications, complaints and applications and the hearings provided for in Council Regulation (EEC) No 4056/86 laying down detailed rules for the application of Articles 85 and 86 of the Treaty to maritime transport (OJ No L 376, 31.12.1988, p. 1).

13. **387 R 3975**: Council Regulation (EEC) No 3975/87 of 14 December 1987 laying down the procedure for the application of the rules on competition to undertakings in the air transport sector (OJ No L 374, 31.12.1987, p. 1), as amended by:

- **391 R 1284**: Council Regulation (EEC) No 1284/91 of 14 May 1991 (OJ No L 122, 17.5.1991, p. 2).

14. **388 R 4261**: Commission Regulation (EEC) No 4261/88 of 16 December 1988 on the form, content and other details of complaints and of applications, and the hearings provided for in Council Regulation (EEC) No 3975/87 laying down the procedure for the application

of the rules of competition to undertakings in the air transport sector (OJ No L 376, 31.12.1988, p. 10).

2. In addition to the acts listed in Annexe XIV, the following acts reflect the powers and functions of the EC Commission for the application of the competition rules of the Treaty establishing the European Coal and Steel Community (ECSC):

1. Article (ECSC) 65 (2), subparagraphs 3 to 5, (3), (4), subparagraph 2, and (5).
2. Article (ECSC) 66 (2), subparagraphs 2 to 4, and (4) to (6).

3. **354 D 7026**: High Authority Decision No 26/54 of 6 May 1954 laying down in implementation of Article 66 (4) of the Treaty a regulation concerning information to be furnished (*Official Journal of the European Coal and Steel Community* No 9, 11.5.1954, p. 350/54).

4. **378 S 0715**: Commission Decision No 715/78/ECSC of 6 April 1978 concerning limitation periods in proceedings and the enforcement of sanctions under the Treaty establishing the European Coal and Steel Community (OJ No L 94, 8.4.1978, p. 22).

5. **384 S 0379**: Commission Decision No 379/84/ECSC of 15 February 1984 defining the powers of officials and agents of the Commission instructed to carry out the checks provided for in the ECSC Treaty and decisions taken in application thereof (OJ No L 46, 16.2.1984, p. 23).

Article 4

1. Agreements, decisions and concerted practices of the kind described in Article 53 (1) which come into existence after the entry into force of the Agreement and in respect of which the parties seek application of Article 53 (3) shall be notified to the competent surveillance authority pursuant to Article 56, Protocol 23 and the rules referred to in Articles 1 to 3 of this Protocol. Until they have been notified, no decision in application of Article 53(3) may be taken.

2. Paragraph 1 shall not apply to agreements, decisions and concerted practices where:

(a) the only parties thereto are undertakings from one EC Member State or from one EFTA State and the agreements, decisions or concerted practices do not relate either to imports or to exports between Contracting Parties;

(b) not more than two undertakings are party thereto, and the agreements only:

  (i) restrict the freedom of one party to the contract in determining the prices or conditions of business upon which the goods which he has obtained from the other party to the contract may be resold, or

  (ii) impose restrictions on the exercise of the rights of the assignee or user of industrial property rights—in particular patents, utility models, designs or trademarks—or of the person entitled under a contract to the assignment, or grant, of the right to use a method of manufacture or knowledge relating to the use and to the application of industrial processes;

(c) they have as their sole object:

  (i) the development or uniform application of standards or types, or

  (ii) joint research or development, or

  (iii) specialization in the manufacture of products including agreements necessary for achieving this:

    – where the products which are the subject of specialization do not, in a substantial part of the territory covered by the Agreement, represent more than 15 per cent of the volume of business done in identical products or those considered by consumers to be similar by reason of their characteristics, price and use, and

– where the total annual turnover of the participating undertakings does not exceed ECU 200 million.

These agreements, decisions and concerted practices may be notified to the competent surveillance authority pursuant to Article 56, Protocol 23 and the rules referred to in Articles 1 to 3 of this Protocol.

Article 5

1. Agreements, decisions and concerted practices of the kind described in Article 53 (1) which are in existence at the date of entry into force of the Agreement and in respect of which the parties seek application of Article 53 (3) shall be notified to the competent surveillance authority pursuant to the provisions in Article 56, Protocol 23 and the rules referred to in Articles 1 to 3 of this Protocol within six months of the date of entry into force of the Agreement.

2. Paragraph 1 shall not apply to agreements, decisions or concerted practices of the kind described in Article 53 (1) of the Agreement and falling under Article 4 (2) of this Protocol; these may be notified to the competent surveillance authority pursuant to Article 56, Protocol 23 and the rules referred to in Articles 1 to 3 of this Protocol.

Article 6

The competent surveillance authority shall specify in its decisions pursuant to Article 53 (3) the date from which the decisions shall take effect. That date may be earlier than the date of notification as regards agreements, decisions of associations of undertakings or concerted practices falling under Articles 4 (2) and 5 (2) of this Protocol, or those falling under Article 5 (1) of this Protocol which have been notified within the time-limit specified in Article 5 (1).

Article 7

1. Where agreements, decisions or concerted practices of the kind described in Article 53 (1) which are in existence at the date of entry into force of the Agreement and notified within the time limits specified in Article 5 (1) of this Protocol do not satisfy the requirements of Article 53 (3) and the undertakings or associations of undertakings concerned cease to give effect to them or modify them in such a manner that they no longer fall under the prohibition contained in Article 53 (1) or that they satisfy the requirements of Article 53 (3), the prohibition contained in Article 53 (1) shall apply only for a period fixed by the competent surveillance authority. A decision by the competent surveillance authority pursuant to the foregoing sentence shall not apply as against undertakings and associations of undertakings which did not expressly consent to the notification.

2. Paragraph 1 shall apply to agreements, decisions or concerted practices falling under Article 4 (2) of this Protocol which are in existence at the date of entry into force of the Agreement if they are notified within six months after that date.

Article 8

Applications and notifications submitted to the EC Commission prior to the date of entry into force of the Agreement shall be deemed to comply with the provisions on application and notification under the Agreement.

The competent surveillance authority pursuant to Article 56 of the Agreement and Article 10 of Protocol 23 may require a duly completed form as prescribed for the implementation of the Agreement to be submitted to it within such time as it shall appoint. In that event, applications and notifications shall be treated as properly made only if the forms are submitted within the prescribed period and in accordance with the provisions of the Agreement.

Article 9

Fines for infringement of Article 53 (1) shall not be imposed in respect of any act prior to notification of the agreements, decisions and concerted practices to which Articles 5 and 6 of this Protocol apply and which have been notified within the period specified therein.

Article 10

The Contracting Parties shall ensure that the measures affording the necessary assistance to officials of the EFTA Surveillance Authority and the EC Commission, in order to enable them to make their investigations as foreseen under the Agreement, are taken within six months of the entry into force of the Agreement.

Article 11

As regards agreements, decisions and concerted practices already in existence at the date of entry into force of the Agreement which fall under Article 53 (1), the prohibition in Article 53 (1) shall not apply where the agreements, decisions or practices are modified within six months from the date of entry into force of the Agreement so as to fulfil the conditions contained in the block exemptions provided for in Annexe XIV.

Article 12

As regards agreements, decisions of associations of undertakings and concerted practices already in existence at the date of entry into force of the Agreement which fall under Article 53 (1), the prohibition in Article 53 (1) shall not apply, from the date of entry into force of the Agreement, where the agreements, decisions or practices are modified within six months from the date of entry into force of the Agreement so as not to fall under the prohibition of Article 53 (1) any more.

Article 13

Agreements, decisions of associations of undertakings and concerted practices which benefit from an individual exemption granted under Article 85 (3) of the Treaty establishing the European Economic Community before the entry into force of the Agreement shall continue to be exempted as regards the provisions of the Agreement, until their date of expiry as provided for in the decisions granting these exemptions or until the EC Commission otherwise decides, whichever date is the earlier.

PROTOCOL 22
CONCERNING THE DEFINITION OF 'UNDERTAKING' AND 'TURNOVER' (ARTICLE 56)

Article 1

For the purposes of the attribution of individual cases pursuant to Article 56 of the Agreement, an 'undertaking' shall be any entity carrying out activities of a commercial or economic nature.

Article 2

'Turnover' within the meaning of Article 56 of the Agreement shall comprise the amounts derived by the undertakings concerned, in the territory covered by the Agreement, in the preceding financial year from the sale of products and the provision of services falling within the undertaking's ordinary scope of activities after deduction of sales rebates and of value added tax and other taxes directly related to turnover.

Article 3

In place of turnover, the following shall be used:

(a) for credit institutions and other financial institutions, their total assets multiplied by the ratio between loans and advances to credit institutions and customers in transactions with residents in the territory covered by the Agreement and the total sum of those loans and advances;

(b) for insurance undertakings, the value of gross premiums received from residents in the territory covered by the Agreement, which shall comprise all amounts received and receivable in respect of insurance contracts issued by or on behalf of the insurance undertakings, including also outgoing reinsurance premiums, and after deduction of taxes and parafiscal contributions or levies charged by reference to the amounts of individual premiums or the total value of premiums.

Article 4

1. In derogation from the definition of the turnover relevant for the application of Article 56 of the Agreement, as contained in Article 2 of this Protocol, the relevant turnover shall be constituted:

(a) as regards agreements, decisions of associations of undertakings and concerted practices related to distribution and supply arrangements between non-competing undertakings, of the amounts derived from the sale of goods or the provision of services which are the subject matter of the agreements, decisions or concerted practices, and from the other goods or services which are considered by users to be equivalent in view of their characteristics, price and intended use;

(b) as regards agreements, decisions of associations of undertakings and concerted practices related to arrangements on transfer of technology between non-competing undertakings, of the amounts derived from the sale of goods or the provision of services which result from the technology which is the subject matter of the agreements, decisions or concerted practices, and of the amounts derived from the sale of those goods or the provision of those services which that technology is designed to improve or replace.

2. However, where at the time of the coming into existence of arrangements as described in paragraph 1 (a) and (b) turnover as regards the sale of goods or the provision of services is not in evidence, the general provision as contained in Article 2 shall apply.

Article 5
1. Where individual cases concern products falling within the scope of application of Protocol 25, the relevant turnover for the attribution of those cases shall be the turnover achieved in these products.

2. Where individual cases concern products falling within the scope of application of Protocol 25 as well as products or services falling within the scope of application of Articles 53 and 54 of the Agreement, the relevant turnover is determined by taking into account all the products and services as provided for in Article 2.

PROTOCOL 23

CONCERNING THE CO-OPERATION BETWEEN THE SURVEILLANCE AUTHORITIES (ARTICLE 58)

General Principles

Article 1
The EFTA Surveillance Authority and the EC Commission shall exchange information and consult each other on general policy issues at the request of either of the surveillance authorities.

The EFTA Surveillance Authority and the EC Commission, in accordance with their internal rules, respecting Article 56 of the Agreement and Protocol 22 and the autonomy of both sides in their decisions, shall co-operate in the handling of individual cases falling under Article 56 (1) (b) and (c), (2), second sentence and (3), as provided for in the provisions below.

For the purposes of this Protocol, the term 'territory of a surveillance authority' shall mean for the EC Commission the territory of the EC Member States to which the Treaty establishing the European Economic Community or the Treaty establishing the European Coal and Steel Community, as the case may be, applies, upon the terms laid down in those Treaties, and for the EFTA Surveillance Authority the territories of the EFTA States to which the Agreement applies.

The Initial Phase of the Proceedings

Article 2
In cases falling under Article 56 (1) (b) and (c), (2), second sentence and (3) of the Agreement, the EFTA Surveillance Authority and the EC Commission shall without undue delay forward to each other notifications and complaints to the extent that it is not apparent that these have been addressed to both surveillance authorities. They shall also inform each other when opening *ex officio* procedures.

The surveillance authority which has received information as provided for in the first subparagraph may present its comments thereon within 40 working days of its receipt.

Article 3
The competent surveillance authority shall, in cases falling under Article 56 (1) (b) and (c), (2), second sentence and (3) of the Agreement, consult the other surveillance authority when:

- publishing its intention to give a negative clearance,
- publishing its intention to take a decision in application of Article 53 (3), or
- addressing to the undertakings or associations of undertakings concerned its statement of objections.

The other surveillance authority may deliver its comments within the time limits set out in the above-mentioned publication or statement of objections.

Observations received from the undertakings concerned or third parties shall be transmitted to the other surveillance authority.

Article 4
In cases falling under Article 56 (1) (b) and (c), (2), second sentence and (3) of the Agreement, the competent surveillance authority shall transmit to the other surveillance authority the administrative letters by which a file is closed or a complaint rejected.

Article 5
In cases falling under Article 56 (1) (b) and (c), (2), second sentence and (3) of the Agreement, the competent surveillance authority shall invite the other surveillance authority to be represented at hearings of the undertakings concerned. The invitation shall also extend to the States falling within the competence of the other surveillance authority.

Advisory Committees

Article 6
In cases falling under Article 56 (1) (b) and (c), (2), second sentence and (3) of the Agreement, the competent surveillance authority shall, in due time, inform the other surveillance authority of the date of the meeting of the Advisory Committee and transmit the relevant documentation.

All documents forwarded for that purpose from the other surveillance authority shall be presented to the Advisory Committee of the surveillance authority which is competent to decide on a case in accordance with Article 56 together with the material sent out by that surveillance authority.

Each surveillance authority and the States falling within its competence shall be entitled to be present in the Advisory Committees of the other surveillance authority and to express their views therein; they shall not have, however, the right to vote.

Request for Documents and the Right to Make Observations

Article 7
In cases falling under Article 56 (1) (b) and (c), (2), second sentence and (3) of the Agreement, the surveillance authority which is not competent to decide on a case in accordance with Article 56 may request at all stages of the proceedings copies of the most important documents lodged with the competent surveillance authority for the purpose of establishing the existence of infringements of Articles 53 and 54 or of obtaining a negative clearance or

exemption, and may furthermore, before a final decision is taken, make any observations it considers appropriate.

Administrative Assistance

Article 8

1. When sending a request for information to an undertaking or association of undertakings located within the territory of the other surveillance authority, the competent surveillance authority, as defined in Article 56 of the Agreement, shall at the same time forward a copy of the request to the other surveillance authority.

2. Where an undertaking or association of undertakings does not supply the information requested within the time limit fixed by the competent surveillance authority, or supplies incomplete information, the competent surveillance authority shall by decision require the information to be supplied. In the case of undertakings or associations of undertakings located within the territory of the other surveillance authority, the competent surveillance authority shall forward a copy of that decision to the other surveillance authority.

3. At the request of the competent surveillance authority, as defined in Article 56 of the Agreement, the other surveillance authority shall, in accordance with its internal rules, undertake investigations within its territory in cases where the competent surveillance authority so requesting considers it to be necessary.

4. The competent surveillance authority is entitled to be represented and take an active part in investigations carried out by the other surveillance authority in respect of paragraph 3.

5. All information obtained during such investigations on request shall be transmitted to the surveillance authority which requested the investigations immediately after their finalization.

6. Where the competent surveillance authority, in cases falling under Article 56 (1) (b) and (c), (2), second sentence and (3) of the Agreement, carries out investigations within its territory, it shall inform the other surveillance authority of the fact that such investigations have taken place and, on request, transmit to that authority the relevant results of the investigations.

Article 9

1. Information acquired as a result of the application of this Protocol shall be used only for the purpose of procedures under Articles 53 and 54 of the Agreement.

2. The EC Commission, the EFTA Surveillance Authority, the competent authorities of the EC Member States and the EFTA States, and their officials and other servants shall not disclose information acquired by them as a result of the application of this Protocol and of the kind covered by the obligation of professional secrecy.

3. Rules on professional secrecy and restricted use of information provided for in the Agreement or in the legislation of the Contracting Parties shall not prevent exchange of information as set out in this Protocol.

Article 10

1. Undertakings shall, in cases of notifications of agreements, address the notification to the competent surveillance authority in accordance with Article 56 of the Agreement. Complaints may be addressed to either surveillance authority.

2. Notifications or complaints addressed to the surveillance authority which, pursuant to

Article 56, is not competent to decide on a given case shall be transferred without delay to the competent surveillance authority.

3. If, in the preparation or initiation of *ex officio* proceedings, it becomes apparent that the other surveillance authority is competent to decide on a case in accordance with Article 56 of the Agreement, this case shall be transferred to the competent surveillance authority.

4. Once a case is transmitted to the other surveillance authority as provided for in paragraphs 2 and 3, a retransmission of the case may not take place. A transmission of a case may not take place after the publishing of the intention to give a negative clearance, the publishing of the intention to take a decision in application of Article 53 (3) of the Agreement, the addressing to undertakings or associations of undertakings concerned of the statement of objections or the sending of a letter informing the applicant that there are insufficient grounds for pursuing the complaint.

Article 11

The date of submission of an application or notification shall be the date on which it is received by the EC Commission or the EFTA Surveillance Authority, regardless of which of these is competent to decide on the case under Article 56 of the Agreement. Where, however, the application or notification is sent by registered post, it shall be deemed to have been received on the date shown on the postmark of the place of posting.

Languages

Article 12

Undertakings shall be entitled to address and be addressed by the EFTA Surveillance Authority and the EC Commission in an official language of an EFTA State or the European Community which they choose as regards notifications, applications and complaints. This shall also cover all instances of a proceeding, whether it be opened on notification, application or complaint or *ex officio* by the competent surveillance authority.

Protocol 24

On Co-operation in the Field of Control of Concentrations

General Principles

Article 1

1. The EFTA Surveillance Authority and the EC Commission shall exchange information and consult each other on general policy issues at the request of either of the surveillance authorities.

2. In cases falling under Article 57 (2) (a), the EC Commission and the EFTA Surveillance Authority shall cooperate in the handling of concentrations as provided for in the provisions set out below.

3. For the purposes of this Protocol, the term 'territory of a surveillance authority' shall mean for the EC Commission the territory of the EC Member States to which the Treaty establishing the European Economic Community or the Treaty establishing the European Coal and Steel Community, as the case may be, applies, upon the terms laid down in those

Treaties, and for the EFTA Surveillance Authority the territories of the EFTA States to which the Agreement applies.

Article 2

1. Co-operation shall take place, in accordance with the provisions set out in this Protocol, where:

(a) the combined turnover of the undertakings concerned in the territory of the EFTA States equals 25 per cent or more of their total turnover within the territory covered by the Agreement, or
(b) each of at least two of the undertakings concerned has a turnover exceeding ECU 250 million in the territory of the EFTA States, or
(c) the concentration is liable to create or strengthen a dominant position as a result of which effective competition would be significantly impeded in the territories of the EFTA States or a substantial part thereof.

2. Co-operation shall also take place where:

(a) the concentration threatens to create or strengthen a dominant position as a result of which effective competition would be significantly impeded on a market within an EFTA State which presents all the characteristics of a distinct market, be it a substantial part of the territory covered by this Agreement or not, or
(b) an EFTA State wishes to adopt measures to protect legitimate interests as set out in Article 7.

Initial Phase of the Proceedings

Article 3

1. The EC Commission shall transmit to the EFTA Surveillance Authority copies of notifications of the cases referred to in Article 2 (1) and (2) (a) within three working days and, as soon as possible, copies of the most important documents lodged with or issued by the EC Commission.

2. The EC Commission shall carry out the procedures set out for the implementation of Article 57 of the Agreement in close and constant liaison with the EFTA Surveillance Authority. The EFTA Surveillance Authority and EFTA States may express their views upon those procedures. For the purposes of Article 6 of this Protocol, the EC Commission shall obtain information from the competent authority of the EFTA State concerned and give it the opportunity to make known its views at every stage of the procedures up to the adoption of a decision pursuant to that Article. To that end, the EC Commission shall give it access to the file.

Hearings

Article 4

In cases referred to in Article 2 (1) and (2) (a), the EC Commission shall invite the EFTA Surveillance Authority to be represented at the hearings of the undertakings concerned. The EFTA States may likewise be represented at those hearings.

The EC Advisory Committee on Concentrations

Article 5

1. In cases referred to in Article 2 (1) and (2) (a), the EC Commission shall in due time inform the EFTA Surveillance Authority of the date of the meeting of the EC Advisory Committee on Concentrations and transmit the relevant documentation.

2. All documents forwarded for that purpose from the EFTA Surveillance Authority, including documents emanating from EFTA States, shall be presented to the EC Advisory Committee on Concentrations together with the other relevant documentation sent out by the EC Commission.

3. The EFTA Surveillance Authority and the EFTA States shall be entitled to be present in the EC Advisory Committee on Concentrations and to express their views therein; they shall not have, however, the right to vote.

Right of Individual States

Article 6

1. The EC Commission may, by means of a decision notified without delay to the undertakings concerned, to the competent authorities of the EC Member States and to the EFTA Surveillance Authority, refer a notified concentration to an EFTA State where a concentration threatens to create or strengthen a dominant position as a result of which effective competition would be significantly impeded on a market within that State, which presents all the characteristics of a distinct market, be it a substantial part of the territory covered by the Agreement or not.

2. In cases referred to in paragraph 1, any EFTA State may appeal to the European Court of Justice, on the same grounds and conditions as an EC Member State under Article 173 of the Treaty establishing the European Economic Community, and in particular request the application of interim measures, for the purpose of applying its national competition law.

Article 7

1. Notwithstanding the sole competence of the EC Commission to deal with concentrations of a Community dimension as set out in Council Regulation (EEC) No 4064/89 of 21 December 1989 on the control of concentrations between undertakings (OJ No L 395, 30.12.1989, p. 1, as corrected by OJ No L 257, 21.9.1990, p. 13), EFTA States may take appropriate measures to protect legitimate interests other than those taken into consideration according to the above Regulation and compatible with the general principles and other provisions as provided for, directly or indirectly, under the Agreement.

2. Public security, plurality of media and prudential rules shall be regarded as legitimate interests within the meaning of paragraph 1.

3. Any other public interest must be communicated to the EC Commission and shall be recognized by the EC Commission after an assessment of its compatibility with the general principles and other provisions as provided for, directly or indirectly, under the Agreement before the measures referred to above may be taken. The EC Commission shall inform the EFTA Surveillance Authority and the EFTA State concerned of its decision within one month of that communication.

Administrative Assistance

Article 8

1. In carrying out the duties assigned to it for the implementation of Article 57, the EC Commission may obtain all necessary information from the EFTA Surveillance Authority and EFTA States.

2. When sending a request for information to a person, an undertaking or an association of undertakings located within the territory of the EFTA Surveillance Authority, the EC Commission shall at the same time forward a copy of the request to the EFTA Surveillance Authority.

3. Where such persons, undertakings or associations of undertakings do not provide the information requested within the period fixed by the EC Commission, or provide incomplete information, the EC Commission shall by decision require the information to be provided and forward a copy of that decision to the EFTA Surveillance Authority.

4. At the request of the EC Commission, the EFTA Surveillance Authority shall undertake investigations within its territory.

5. The EC Commission is entitled to be represented and take an active part in investigations carried out pursuant to paragraph 4.

6. All information obtained during such investigations on request shall be transmitted to the EC Commission immediately after their finalization.

7. Where the EC Commission carries out investigations within the territory of the Community, it shall, as regards cases falling under Article 2 (1) and (2) (a), inform the EFTA Surveillance Authority of the fact that such investigations have taken place and on request transmit in an appropriate way the relevant results of the investigations.

Professional Secrecy

Article 9

1. Information acquired as a result of the application of this Protocol shall be used only for the purpose of procedures under Article 57 of the Agreement.

2. The EC Commission, the EFTA Surveillance Authority, the competent authorities of the EC Member States and of the EFTA States, and their officials and other servants shall not disclose information acquired by them as a result of the application of this Protocol and of the kind covered by the obligation of professional secrecy.

3. Rules on professional secrecy and restricted use of information provided for in the Agreement or the legislation of the Contracting Parties shall not prevent the exchange and use of information as set out in this Protocol.

Notifications

Article 10

1. Undertakings shall address their notifications to the competent surveillance authority in accordance with Article 57 (2) of the Agreement.

2. Notifications or complaints addressed to the authority which, pursuant to Article 57, is not competent to take decisions on a given case shall be transferred without delay to the competent surveillance authority.

Article 11
The date of submission of a notification shall be the date on which it is received by the competent surveillance authority.

The date of submission of a notification shall be the date on which it is received by the EC Commission or the EFTA Surveillance Authority, if the case is notified in accordance with the implementing rules under Article 57 of the Agreement, but falls under Article 53.

Languages

Article 12
1. Undertakings shall be entitled to address and be addressed by the EFTA Surveillance Authority and the EC Commission in an official language of an EFTA State or the Community which they choose as regards notifications. This shall also cover all instances of a proceeding.

2. If undertakings choose to address a surveillance authority in a language which is not one of the official languages of the States falling within the competence of that authority, or a working language of that authority, they shall simultaneously supplement all documentation with a translation into an official language of that authority.

3. As far as undertakings are concerned which are not parties to the notification, they shall likewise be entitled to be addressed by the EFTA Surveillance Authority and the EC Commission in an appropriate official language of an EFTA State or of the Community or in a working language of one of those authorities. If they choose to address a surveillance authority in a language which is not one of the official languages of the States falling within the competence of that authority, or a working language of that authority, paragraph 2 shall apply.

4. The language which is chosen for the translation shall determine the language in which the undertakings may be addressed by the competent authority.

Time Limits and Other Procedural Questions

Article 13
As regards time limits and other procedural provisions, the rules implementing Article 57 shall apply also for the purpose of the cooperation between the EC Commission and the EFTA Surveillance Authority and EFTA States, unless otherwise provided for in this Protocol.

Transition Rule

Article 14
Article 57 shall not apply to any concentration which was the subject of an agreement or announcement or where control was acquired before the date of entry into force of the Agreement. It shall not in any circumstances apply to a concentration in respect of which proceedings were initiated before that date by a national authority with responsibility for competition.

Protocol 25
On Competition Regarding Coal and Steel

Article 1

1. All agreements between undertakings, decisions by associations of undertakings and concerted practices in respect of particular products referred to in Protocol 14 which may affect trade between Contracting Parties tending directly or indirectly to prevent, restrict or distort normal competition within the territory covered by this Agreement shall be prohibited, and in particular those tending:

(a) to fix or determine prices,
(b) to restrict or control production, technical development or investment,
(c) to share markets, products, customers or sources of supply.

2. However, the competent surveillance authority, as provided for in Article 56 of the Agreement, shall authorize specialization agreements or joint-buying or joint-selling agreements in respect of the products referred to in paragraph 1, if it finds that:

(a) such specialization or such joint-buying or joint-selling will make for a substantial improvement in the production or distribution of those products;
(b) the agreement in question is essential in order to achieve these results and is not more restrictive than is necessary for that purpose, and
(c) the agreement is not liable to give the undertakings concerned the power to determine the prices, or to control or restrict the production or marketing, of a substantial part of the products in question within the territory covered by the Agreement, or to shield them against effective competition from other undertakings within the territory covered by the Agreement.

If the competent surveillance authority finds that certain agreements are strictly analogous in nature and effect to those referred to above, having particular regard to the fact that this paragraph applies to distributive undertakings, it shall authorize them also when satisfied that they meet the same requirements.

3. Any agreement or decision prohibited by paragraph 1 shall be automatically void and may not be relied upon before any court or tribunal in the EC Member States or the EFTA States.

Article 2

1. Any transaction shall require the prior authorization of the competent surveillance authority, as provided for in Article 56 of the Agreement, subject to the provisions of paragraph 3 of this Article, if it has in itself the direct or indirect effect of bringing about within the territory covered by the Agreement, as a result of action by any person or undertaking or group of persons or undertakings, a concentration between undertakings at least one of which is covered by Article 3, which may affect trade between Contracting Parties, whether the transaction concerns a single product or a number of different products, and whether it is effected by merger, acquisition of shares or parts of the undertaking or assets, loan, contract or any other means of control.

2. The competent surveillance authority, as provided for in Article 56 of the Agreement, shall grant the authorization referred to in paragraph 1 if it finds that the proposed transaction will not give to the persons or undertakings concerned the power, in respect of the product or products within its jurisdiction:

- to determine prices, to control or restrict production or distribution or to hinder effective competition in a substantial part of the market for those products, or
- to evade the rules of competition instituted under this Agreement, in particular by establishing an artificially privileged position involving a substantial advantage in access to supplies or markets.

3. Classes of transactions may, in view of the size of the assets or undertakings concerned, taken in conjunction with the kind of concentration to be effected, be exempted from the requirement of prior authorization.

4. If the competent surveillance authority, as provided for in Article 56 of the Agreement, finds that public or private undertakings which, in law or in fact, hold or acquire in the market for one of the products within its jurisdiction a dominant position shielding them against effective competition in a substantial part of the territory covered by this Agreement are using that position for purposes contrary to the objectives of this Agreement and if such abuse may affect trade between Contracting Parties, it shall make to them such recommendations as may be appropriate to prevent the position from being so used.

Article 3
For the purposes of Articles 1 and 2 as well as for the purposes of information required for their application and proceedings in connection with them, 'undertaking' means any undertaking engaged in production in the coal or the steel industry within the territory covered by the Agreement, and any undertaking or agency regularly engaged in distribution other than sale to domestic consumers or small craft industries.

Article 4
Annexe XIV to the Agreement contains specific provisions giving effect to the principles set out in Articles 1 and 2.

Article 5
The EFTA Surveillance Authority and the EC Commission shall ensure the application of the principles laid down in Articles 1 and 2 of this Protocol in accordance with the provisions giving effect to Articles 1 and 2 as contained in Protocol 21 and Annexe XIV to the Agreement.

Article 6
Individual cases referred to in Articles 1 and 2 of this Protocol shall be decided upon by the EC Commission or the EFTA Surveillance Authority in accordance with Article 56 of the Agreement.

Article 7
With a view to developing and maintaining a uniform surveillance throughout the European Economic Area in the field of competition and of promoting a homogeneous implementation, application and interpretation of the provisions of the Agreement to this end, the competent authorities shall cooperate in accordance with the provisions set out in Protocol 23.

Protocol 26

On the Powers and Functions of the EFTA Surveillance Authority in the Field of State Aid

The EFTA Surveillance Authority shall, in an agreement between the EFTA States, be entrusted with equivalent powers and similar functions to those of the EC Commission, at the time of the signature of the Agreement, for the application of the competition rules applicable to State aid of the Treaty establishing the European Economic Community, enabling the EFTA Surveillance Authority to give effect to the principles expressed in Articles 1 (2) (e), 49 and 61 to 63 of the Agreement. The EFTA Surveillance Authority shall also have such powers to give effect to the competition rules applicable to State aid relating to products falling under the Treaty establishing the European Coal and Steel Community as referred to in Protocol 14.

Protocol 27

On Co-operation in the Field of State Aid

In order to ensure a uniform implementation, application and interpretation of the rules on State aid throughout the territory of the Contracting Parties as well as to guarantee their harmonious development, the EC Commission and the EFTA Surveillance Authority shall observe the following rules:

(a) exchange of information and views on general policy issues such as the implementation, application and interpretation of the rules on State aid set out in the Agreement shall be held periodically or at the request of either surveillance authority;

(b) the EC Commission and the EFTA Surveillance Authority shall periodically prepare surveys on State aid in their respective States. These surveys shall be made available to the other surveillance authority;

(c) if the procedure referred to in the first and second subparagraphs of Article 93 (2) of the Treaty establishing the European Economic Community or the corresponding procedure set out in an agreement between the EFTA States establishing the EFTA Surveillance Authority is opened for State aid programmes and cases, the EC Commission or the EFTA Surveillance Authority shall give notice to the other surveillance authority as well as to the parties concerned to submit their comments;

(d) the surveillance authorities shall inform each other of all decisions as soon as they are taken;

(e) the opening of the procedure referred to in paragraph (c) and the decisions referred to in paragraph (d) shall be published by the competent surveillance authorities;

(f) notwithstanding the provisions of this Protocol, the EC Commission and the EFTA Surveillance Authority shall, at the request of the other surveillance authority, provide on a case-by-case basis information and exchange views on individual State aid programmes and cases;

(g) information obtained in accordance with paragraph (f) shall be treated as confidential.

Protocol 28
On Intellectual Property

Article 1
Substance of protection

1. For the purposes of this Protocol, the term 'intellectual property' shall include the protection of industrial and commercial property as covered by Article 13 of the Agreement.

2. Without prejudice to the provisions of this Protocol and of Annexe XVII, the Contracting Parties shall upon the entry into force of the Agreement adjust their legislation on intellectual property so as to make it compatible with the principles of free circulation of goods and services and with the level of protection of intellectual property attained in Community law, including the level of enforcement of those rights.

3. Subject to the procedural provisions of the Agreement and without prejudice to the provisions of this Protocol and of Annexe XVII, the EFTA States will adjust, upon request and after consultation between the Contracting Parties, their legislation on intellectual property in order to reach at least the level of protection of intellectual property prevailing in the Community upon signature of the Agreement.

Article 2
Exhaustion of rights

1. To the extent that exhaustion is dealt with in Community measures or jurisprudence, the Contracting Parties shall provide for such exhaustion of intellectual property rights as laid down in Community law. Without prejudice to future developments of case law, this provision shall be interpreted in accordance with the meaning established in the relevant rulings of the Court of Justice of the European Communities given prior to the signature of the Agreement.

2. As regards patent rights, this provision shall take effect at the latest one year after the entry into force of the Agreement.

Article 3
Community Patents

1. The Contracting Parties undertake to use their best endeavours to conclude within a period of three years after the entry into force of the Agreement relating to Community Patents (89/695/EEC) negotiations with a view to the participation of the EFTA States in that Agreement. However, for Iceland, this date will not be earlier than 1 January 1998.

2. The specific conditions for the participation of the EFTA States in the Agreement relating to Community Patents (89/695/EEC) shall be subject to future negotiations.

3. The Community undertakes, after the entry into force of the Agreement relating to Community Patents, to invite those EFTA States who so request to enter into negotiations, in accordance with Article 8 of the Agreement relating to Community Patents, provided they will have in addition respected the provisions of paragraphs 4 and 5.

4. The EFTA States shall comply in their law with the substantive provisions of the European Patent Convention of 5 October 1973.

5. As regards patentability of pharmaceutical and foodstuff products, Finland shall comply with the provisions of paragraph 4 by 1 January 1995. As regards patentability of pharmaceutical products, Iceland shall comply with the provisions of paragraph 4 by

1 January 1997. The Community shall however not address an invitation as mentioned in paragraph 3 to Finland and Iceland before these dates, respectively.

6. Notwithstanding Article 2, the holder, or his beneficiary, of a patent for a product mentioned in paragraph 5 filed in a Contracting Party at a time when a product patent could not be obtained in Finland or Iceland for that product may rely upon the rights granted by that patent in order to prevent the import and marketing of that product in the Contracting Parties where that product enjoys patent protection even if that product was put on the market in Finland or Iceland for the first time by him or with his consent.

This right may be invoked for the products referred to in paragraph 5 until the end of the second year after Finland or Iceland, respectively, has made these products patentable.

Article 4
Semiconductor products

1. The Contracting Parties shall have the right to take decisions on the extension of the legal protection of topographies of semiconductor products to persons from any third country or territory, which is not a Contracting Party to this Agreement, who do not benefit from the right to protection according to the provisions of this Agreement. They may also conclude agreements to this effect.

2. The Contracting Party concerned shall endeavour, where the right to protection for topographies of semiconductor products is extended to a non-Contracting Party, to ensure that the non-Contracting Party concerned will grant the right to protection to the other Contracting Parties to this Agreement under equivalent conditions to those granted to the Contracting Party concerned.

3. The extension of rights conferred by parallel or equivalent agreements or understandings or equivalent decisions between any of the Contracting Parties and third countries shall be recognized and respected by all of the Contracting Parties.

4. In respect of paragraphs 1 to 3, the general information, consultation and dispute settlement procedures contained in this Agreement shall apply.

5. In any case of different relations arising between any of the Contracting Parties and any third country, consultations shall take place without delay as set out in paragraph 4 concerning the implications of such a divergence for the continuation of the free circulation of goods under this Agreement. Whenever such an agreement, understanding or decision is adopted, despite continuing disagreement between the Community and any other Contracting Party concerned, Part VII of this Agreement shall apply.

Article 5
International conventions

1. The Contracting Parties shall undertake to obtain their adherence before 1 January 1995 to the following multilateral conventions on industrial, intellectual and commercial property:

(a) Paris Convention for the Protection of Industrial Property (Stockholm Act, 1967);
(b) Berne Convention for the Protection of Literary and Artistic Works (Paris Act, 1971);
(c) International Convention for the Protection of Performers, Producers of Phonograms and Broadcasting Organizations (Rome, 1961);
(d) Protocol relating to the Madrid Agreement concerning the international Registration of Marks (Madrid 1989);

(e) Nice Agreement concerning the International Classification of Goods and Services for the purpose of the Registration of Marks (Geneva 1977, amended 1979);
(f) Budapest Treaty on the International Recognition of the Deposit of Microorganisms for the purposes of Patent Procedure (1980);
(g) Patent Co-operation Treaty (1984).

2. For the adherence of Finland, Ireland and Norway to the Protocol relating to the Madrid Agreement the date mentioned in paragraph 1 shall be replaced by 1 January 1996 and, for Iceland, 1 January 1997, respectively.

3. Upon entry into force of this Protocol, the Contracting Parties shall comply in their internal legislation with the substantive provisions of the Conventions listed in paragraph 1 (a) to (c). However, Ireland shall comply in its internal legislation with the substantive provisions of the Berne Convention by 1 January 1995.

Article 6
Negotiations concerning the General Agreement on Tariffs and Trade
The Contracting Parties agree, without prejudice to the competence of the Community and its Member States in matters of intellectual property, to improve the regime established by the Agreement as regards intellectual property in light of the results of the Uruguay Round negotiations.

Article 7
Mutual information and consultation
The Contracting Parties undertake to keep each other informed in the context of work within the framework of international organizations and within the context of agreements dealing with intellectual property.

The Contracting Parties also undertake, in areas covered by a measure adopted in Community law, to engage upon request in prior consultation in the above-mentioned framework and contexts.

Article 8
Transitional provisions
The Contracting Parties agree to enter into negotiations in order to enable full participation of interested EFTA States in future measures concerning intellectual property which might be adopted in Community law.

Should such measures have been adopted before the entry into force of the Agreement, negotiations to participate in such measures shall begin at the earliest opportunity.

Article 9
Competence
The provisions of this Protocol shall be without prejudice to the competence of the Commmunity and of its Member States in matters of intellectual property.

[. . .]

PROTOCOL 35
ON THE IMPLEMENTATION OF EEA RULES

Whereas this Agreement aims at achieving a homogeneous European Economic Area, based on common rules, without requiring any Contracting Party to transfer legislative powers to any institution of the European Economic Area; and

Whereas this consequently will have to be achieved through national procedures;

Sole Article
For cases of possible conflicts between implemented EEA rules and other statutory provisions, the EFTA States undertake to introduce, if necessary, a statutory provision to the effect that EEA rules prevail in these cases.

[. . .]

ANNEXE III
PRODUCT LIABILITY

List provided for in Article 23 (c)

Introduction

When the acts referred to in this Annexe contain notions or refer to procedures which are specific to the Community legal order, such as:

- preambles,
- the addressees of the Community acts,
- references to territories or languages of the EC,
- references to rights and obligations of EC Member States, their public entities, undertakings or individuals in relation to each other, and
- references to information and notification procedures,

Protocol 1 on horizontal adaptations shall apply, unless otherwise provided for in this Annexe.

Act Referred to

385 L 0374: Council Directive 85/374/EEC of 25 July 1985 on the approximation of the laws, regulations and administrative provisions of the Member States concerning liability for defective products (OJ No L 210, 7.8.1985, p. 29).

The provisions of the Directive shall, for the purposes of the Agreement, be read with the following adaptations:

(a) as regards the liability of the importer as foreseen in Article 3 (2), the following shall apply:
  (i) without prejudice to the liability of the producer any person who imports into the EEA a product for sale, hire, leasing or any form of distribution in the course of his business shall be responsible as a producer;
  (ii) the same applies as concerns imports from an EFTA State into the Community or from the Community into an EFTA State or from an EFTA State into another EFTA State.

From the date of entry into force for any EC Member State or EFTA State of the Lugano Convention on jurisdiction and the enforcement of judgments in civil and commercial matters of 16 September 1988, the first sentence of this subparagraph shall no longer apply between those States which have ratified the Convention to the extent a national judgement in favour of the injured person is, by the fact of those ratifications, enforceable against the producer or the importer within the meaning of subparagraph (i);

(iii) Switzerland and Liechtenstein may waive importer's liability between themselves;

(b) as regards Article 14 the following shall apply:

the Directive shall not apply to injury or damage arising from nuclear accidents and covered by an international convention ratified by EFTA States and EC Member States.

For Switzerland and Liechtenstein in addition the Directive shall not apply if their national law provides equivalent protection to that afforded by international conventions within the meaning mentioned above.

[. . .]

Annexe XIV
Competition

List provided for in Article 60

Introduction

When the acts referred to in this Annexe contain notions or refer to procedures which are specific to the Community legal order, such as

- preambles;
- the addressees of the Community acts;
- references to territories or languages of the EC;
- references to rights and obligations of EC Member States, their public entities, undertakings or individuals in relation to each other; and
- references to information and notification procedures;

Protocol 1 on horizontal adaptations shall apply, unless otherwise provided for in this Annexe.

Sectoral Adaptations

Unless otherwise provided for, the provisions of this Annexe shall, for the purposes of the present Agreement, be read with the following adaptations:

I. the term 'Commission' shall read 'competent surveillance authority';

II. the term 'common market' shall read 'the territory covered by the EEA Agreement';

III. the term 'trade between Member States' shall read 'trade between Contracting Parties';

IV. the term 'the Commission and the authorities of the Member States' shall read 'the EC Commission, the EFTA Surveillance Authority, the authorities of the EC Member States and of the EFTA States';

V. References to Articles of the Treaty establishing the European Economic Community (EEC) or the Treaty establishing the European Coal and Steel Community (ECSC) shall be read as references to the EEA Agreement (EEA) as follows:

Article 85 (EEC)—Article 53 (EEA),
Article 86 (EEC)—Article 54 (EEA),
Article 90 (EEC)—Article 59 (EEA),
Article 66 (ECSC)—Article 2 of Protocol 25 to the EEA Agreement,
Article 80 (ECSC)—Article 3 of Protocol 25 to the EEA Agreement.

VI. the term 'this Regulation' shall read 'this Act';

VII. the term 'the competition rules of the Treaty' shall read 'the competition rules of the EEA Agreement';

VIII. the term 'High Authority' shall read 'competent surveillance authority'.

Without prejudice to the rules on control of concentrations, the term 'competent surveillance authority' as referred to in the rules below shall read 'the surveillance authority which is competent to decide on a case in accordance with Article 56 of the EEA Agreement'.

Acts Referred to

A. MERGER CONTROL

1. **389 R 4064:** Council Regulation (EEC) No 4064/89 of 21 December 1989 on the control of concentrations between undertakings (OJ No L 395, 30.12.1989, p. 1), as corrected by OJ No L 257, 21.9.1990, p. 13.

The provisions of Articles 1 to 5 of the Regulation shall, for the purposes of the Agreement, be read with the following adaptations:

(a) in Article 1 (1), the phrase ', or the corresponding provision envisaged in Protocol 21 to the EEA Agreement,' shall be inserted after the words 'Without prejudice to Article 22';
furthermore, the term 'Community dimension' shall be replaced by 'Community or EFTA dimension';

(b) in Article 1 (2), the term 'Community dimension' shall be replaced by 'Community or EFTA dimension respectively';
furthermore, the term 'Community-wide turnover' shall be replaced by 'Community-wide or EFTA-wide turnover';
in the last subparagraph, the term 'Member State' shall be replaced by 'State';

(c) Article 1 (3) shall not apply;

(d) in Article 2 (1), first subparagraph, the term 'common market' shall be replaced by 'functioning of the EEA Agreement';

(e) in Article 2 (2), at the end, the term 'common market' shall be replaced by 'functioning of the EEA Agreement';

(f) in Article 2 (3), at the end, the term 'common market' shall be replaced by 'functioning of the EEA Agreement';

(g) in Article 3 (5) (b), the term 'Member State' shall be replaced by 'EC Member State or an EFTA State';

(h) in Article 4 (1), the term 'Community dimension' shall be replaced by 'Community or EFTA dimension';
furthermore, in the first sentence, the phrase 'in accordance with Article 57 of the EEA Agreement' shall be inserted after the words '. . . shall be notified to the Commission';

(i) in Article 5 (1), the last subparagraph shall be replaced by the following:

'Turnover, in the Community or in an EC Member State, shall comprise products sold and services provided to undertakings or consumers, in the Community or in that EC Member State as the case may be. The same shall apply as regards turnover in the territory of the EFTA States as a whole or in an EFTA State.';

(j) in Article 5 (3) (a), second subparagraph, the term 'Community-wide turnover' shall be replaced by the words 'Community-wide or EFTA-wide turnover';
furthermore, the term 'Community residents' shall be replaced by 'Community or EFTA residents, respectively';

(k) in Article 5 (3) (a), third subparagraph, the term 'Member State' shall be replaced by 'EC Member State or EFTA State';

(l) in Article 5 (3) (b), the last phrase '. . ., gross premiums received from Community residents and from residents of one Member State respectively shall be taken into account.' shall be replaced by the following:

'. . . , gross premiums received from Community residents and from residents of one EC Member State respectively shall be taken into account. The same shall apply as regards gross premiums received from residents in the territory of the EFTA States as a whole and from residents in one EFTA State, respectively.'.

B. EXCLUSIVE DEALING AGREEMENTS

2. **383 R 1983**: Commission Regulation (EEC) No 1983/83 of 22 June 1983 on the application of Article 85 (3) of the Treaty to categories of exclusive distribution agreements (OJ No L 173, 30.6.1983, p. 1), as corrected by OJ No L 281, 13.10.1983, p. 24, and as amended by:

– **1 85 I**: Act concerning the conditions of Accession and Adjustments to the Treaties—Accession of the Kingdom of Spain and the Portuguese Republic (OJ No L 302, 15.11.1985, p. 166).

The provisions of the Regulation shall, for the purposes of the Agreement, be read with the following adaptations:

(a) in Article 5 (1), the term 'the Treaty' shall read 'the Treaty establishing the European Economic Community';

(b) in Article 6, introductory paragraph, the phrase 'pursuant to Article 7 of Regulation No 19/65/EEC' shall read 'either on its own initiative or at the request of the other surveillance authority or a State falling within its competence or of natural or legal persons claiming a legitimate interest';

(c) the following paragraph shall be added at the end of Article 6:

'The competent surveillance authority may in such cases issue a decision in accordance with Articles 6 and 8 of Regulation (EEC) No 17/62, or the corresponding provisions envisaged in Protocol 21 to the EEA Agreement, without any notification from the undertakings concerned being required.';

(d) Article 7 shall not apply;

(e) Article 10 shall read:

'This Act shall expire on 31 December 1997.'.

3. **383 R 1984**: Commission Regulation (EEC) No 1984/83 of 22 June 1983 on the application of Article 85 (3) of the Treaty to categories of exclusive purchasing agreements (OJ No L 173, 30.6.1983, p. 5), as corrected by OJ No L 281, 13.10.1983, p. 24, and as amended by:

– **1 85 I**: Act concerning the conditions of Accession and Adjustments to the Treaties—Accession of the Kingdom of Spain and the Portuguese Republic (OJ No L 302, 15.11.1985, p. 166).

The provisions of the Regulation shall, for the purposes of the Agreement, be read with the following adaptations:

(a) in Article 5 (1) the term 'the Treaty' shall read 'the Treaty establishing the European Economic Community';

(b) in Article 14, introductory paragraph, the phrase 'pursuant to Article 7 of Regulation No 19/65/EEC' shall read 'either on its own initiative or at the request of the other surveillance authority or a State falling within its competence or of natural or legal persons claiming a legitimate interest';

(c) the following paragraph shall be added at the end of Article 14:

'The competent surveillance authority may in such cases issue a decision in accordance with Articles 6 and 8 of Regulation (EEC) No 17/62, or the corresponding provisions envisaged in Protocol 21 to the EEA Agreement, without any notification from the undertakings concerned being required.';

(d) Article 15 shall not apply;

(e) Article 19 shall read:

'This Act shall expire on 31 December 1997.'.

4. **385 R 0123**: Commission Regulation (EEC) No 123/85 of 12 December 1984 on the application of Article 85 (3) of the Treaty to certain categories of motor vehicle distribution and servicing agreements (OJ No L 15, 18.1.1985, p. 16), as amended by:

– **1 85 I**: Act concerning the conditions of Accession and Adjustments to the Treaties—Accession to the European Communities of the Kingdom of Spain and the Portuguese Republic (OJ No L 302, 15.11.1985, p. 167).

The provisions of the Regulation shall, for the purposes of the Agreement, be read with the following adaptations:

(a) in Article 5 (1), subparagraph (2) (d), the term 'Member State' shall read 'EC Member State or EFTA State';

(b) Article 7 shall not apply;

(c) Article 8 shall not apply;

(d) Article 9 shall not apply;

(e) in Article 10, introductory paragraph, the phrase 'pursuant to Article 7 of Regulation No 19/65/EEC' shall read 'either on its own initiative or at the request of the other surveillance authority or a State falling within its competence or of natural or legal persons claiming a legitimate interest';

(f) in Article 10 (3), the term 'Member States' shall read 'Contracting Parties';

(g) the following paragraph shall be added at the end of Article 10:

'The competent surveillance authority may in such cases issue a decision in accordance with Articles 6 and 8 of Regulation (EEC) No 17/62, or the corresponding provisions envisaged in Protocol 21 to the EEA Agreement, without any notification from the undertakings concerned being required.';

(h) Article 14 shall read:

'This Act shall remain in force until 30 June 1995.'.

C. PATENT LICENSING AGREEMENTS

5. **384 R 2349**: Commission Regulation (EEC) No 2349/84 of 23 July 1984 on the application of Article 85 (3) of the Treaty to certain categories of patent licensing agreements (OJ No L 219, 16.8.1984, p. 15), as amended by:

– **1 85 I**: Act concerning the conditions of Accession and Adjustments to the Treaties—Accession of the Kingdom of Spain and the Portuguese Republic (OJ No L 302, 15.11.1985, p. 166).

The provisions of the Regulation shall, for the purposes of the Agreement, be read with the following adaptations:

(a) in Article 4 (1), the phrase 'on condition that the agreements in question are notified to the Commission in accordance with the provisions of Commission Regulation No 27, as last amended by Regulation (EEC) No 1699/75, and that the Commission does not oppose' shall read 'on condition that the agreements in question are notified to the EC Commission or the EFTA Surveillance Authority in accordance with the provisions of Commission Regulation No 27/62, as last amended by Regulation (EEC) No 2526/85, and the corresponding provisions envisaged in Protocol 21 to the EEA Agreement, and that the competent surveillance authority does not oppose';

(b) in Article 4 (2), the term 'the Commission' shall read 'the EC Commission or the EFTA Surveillance Authority';

(c) Article 4 (4) shall not apply;

(d) in Article 4 (5), the second sentence shall be replaced as follows:

'It shall oppose exemption if it receives a request to do so from a State falling within its competence within three months of the transmission to those States of the notification referred to in paragraph 1.';

(e) in Article 4 (6), the second sentence shall be replaced as follows:

'However, where the opposition was raised at the request of a State falling within its competence and this request is maintained, it may be withdrawn only after consultation of its Advisory Committee on Restrictive Practices and Dominant Positions.';

(f) the following shall be added to the end of Article 4 (9):

', or the corresponding provisions envisaged in Protocol 21 to the EEA Agreement.';

(g) Article 6 shall not apply;
(h) Article 7 shall not apply;
(i) Article 8 shall not apply;
(j) in Article 9, introductory paragraph, the phrase 'pursuant to Article 7 of Regulation No 19/65/EEC' shall read 'either on its own initiative or at the request of the other surveillance authority or a State falling within its competence or of natural or legal persons claiming a legitimate interest';
(k) the following paragraph shall be added at the end of Article 9:

'The competent surveillance authority may in such cases issue a decision in accordance with Articles 6 and 8 of Regulation (EEC) No 17/62, or the corresponding provisions envisaged in Protocol 21 to the EEA Agreement, without any notification from the undertakings concerned being required.';

(l) Article 14 shall read:

'This Act shall apply until 31 December 1994.'.

D. SPECIALIZATION AND RESEARCH AND DEVELOPMENT AGREEMENTS

6. **385 R 0417:** Commission Regulation (EEC) No 417/85 of 19 December 1984 on the application of Article 85 (3) of the Treaty to categories of specialization agreements (OJ No L 53, 22.2.1985, p. 1), as amended by:

- **1 85 I:** Act concerning the conditions of Accession and Adjustments to the Treaties—Accession of the Kingdom of Spain and the Portuguese Republic (OJ No L 302, 15.11.1985, p. 167).

The provisions of the Regulation shall, for the purposes of the Agreement, be read with the following adaptations:

(a) in Article 4 (1), the phrase 'on condition that the agreements in question are notified to the Commission in accordance with the provisions of Commission Regulation No 27 and that the Commission does not oppose' shall read 'on condition that the agreements in question are notified to the EC Commission or the EFTA Surveillance Authority in accordance with the provisions of Commission Regulation No 27/62, as last amended by Regulation (EEC) No 2526/85, and the corresponding provisions envisaged in Protocol 21 to the EEA Agreement, and that the competent surveillance authority does not oppose';
(b) in Article 4 (2) the term 'the Commission' shall read 'the EC Commission or the EFTA Surveillance Authority';
(c) Article 4 (4) shall not apply;
(d) in Article 4 (5), the second sentence shall be replaced as follows:

'It shall oppose exemption if it receives a request to do so from a State falling within its competence within three months of the forwarding to those States of the notification referred to in paragraph 1.';

(e) in Article 4 (6), the second sentence shall be replaced as follows:

'However, where the opposition was raised at the request of a State falling within its competence and this request is maintained, it may be withdrawn only after consultation of its Advisory Committee on Restrictive Practices and Dominant Positions.';

(f) the following shall be added to the end of Article 4 (9):

', or the corresponding provisions envisaged in Protocol 21 to the EEA Agreement.';

(g) in Article 8, introductory paragraph, the phrase 'pursuant to Article 7 of Regulation (EEC) No 2821/71' shall read 'either on its own initiative or at the request of the other surveillance authority or a State falling within its competence or of natural or legal persons claiming a legitimate interest';

(h) the following paragraph shall be added at the end of Article 8:

'The competent surveillance authority may in such cases issue a decision in accordance with Articles 6 and 8 of Regulation (EEC) No 17/62, or the corresponding provisions envisaged in Protocol 21 to the EEA Agreement, without any notification from the undertakings concerned being required.';

(i) Article 10 shall read:

'This Act shall apply until 31 December 1997.'.

7. **385 R 0418**: Commission Regulation (EEC) No 418/85 of 19 December 1984 on the application of Article 85 (3) of the Treaty to categories of research and development agreements (OJ No L 53, 22.2.1985, p. 5), as amended by:

– **1 85 I**: Act concerning the conditions of Accession and Adjustments to the Treaties—Accession of the Kingdom of Spain and the Portuguese Republic (OJ No L 302, 15.11.1985, p. 167).

The provisions of the Regulation shall, for the purposes of the Agreement, be read with the following adaptations:

(a) in Article 7 (1), the phrase 'on condition that the agreements in question are notified to the Commission in accordance with the provisions of Commission Regulation No 27 and that the Commission does not oppose' shall read 'on condition that the agreements in question are notified to the EC Commission or the EFTA Surveillance Authority in accordance with the provisions of Commission Regulation No 27/62, as last amended by Regulation (EEC) No 2526/85, and the corresponding provisions envisaged in Protocol 21 to the EEA Agreement, and that the competent surveillance authority does not oppose';

(b) in Article 7 (2), the term 'the Commission' shall read 'the EC Commission or the EFTA Surveillance Authority';

(c) Article 7 (4) shall not apply;

(d) in Article 7 (5), the second sentence shall be replaced as follows:

'It shall oppose exemption if it receives a request to do so from a State falling within its competence within three months of the forwarding to those States of the notification referred to in paragraph 1.';

(e) in Article 7 (6), the second sentence shall be replaced as follows:

'However, where the opposition was raised at the request of a State falling within its competence and this request is maintained, it may be withdrawn only after consultation of its Advisory Committee on Restrictive Practices and Dominant Positions.';

(f) the following shall be added to the end of Article 7 (9):

', or the corresponding provisions envisaged in Protocol 21 to the EEA Agreement.';

(g) in Article 10, introductory paragraph, the phrase 'pursuant to Article 7 of Regulation (EEC) No 2821/71' shall read 'either on its own initiative or at the request of the other surveillance authority or a State falling within its competence or of natural or legal persons claiming a legitimate interest';

(h) the following paragraph shall be added at the end of Article 10:

'The competent surveillance authority may in such cases issue a decision in accordance with Articles 6 and 8 of Regulation (EEC) No 17/62, or the corresponding provisions envisaged in Protocol 21 to the EEA Agreement, without any notification from the undertakings concerned being required.';

(i) Article 11 shall not apply;

(j) Article 13 shall read:

'This Act shall apply until 31 December 1997.'.

E. FRANCHISING AGREEMENTS

8. **388 R 4087**: Commission Regulation (EEC) No 4087/88 of 30 November 1988 on the application of Article 85 (3) of the Treaty to categories of franchise agreements (OJ No L 359, 28.12.1988, p. 46).

The provisions of the Regulation shall, for the purposes of the Agreement, be read with the following adaptations:

(a) in Article 6 (1), the phrase 'on condition that the agreements in question are notified to the Commission in accordance with the provisions of Commission Regulation No 27, and that the Commission does not oppose' shall read 'on condition that the agreements in question are notified to the EC Commission or the EFTA Surveillance Authority in accordance with the provisions of Commission Regulation No 27/62, as last amended by Regulation (EEC) No 2526/85, and the corresponding provisions envisaged in Protocol 21 to the EEA Agreement, and that the competent surveillance authority does not oppose';

(b) in Article 6 (2), the term 'the Commission' shall read 'the EC Commission or the EFTA Surveillance Authority';

(c) Article 6 (4) shall not apply;

(d) in Article 6 (5), the second sentence shall be replaced as follows:

'It shall oppose exemption if it receives a request to do so from a State falling within its competence within three months of the forwarding to those States of the notification referred to in paragraph 1.';

(e) in Article 6 (6), the second sentence shall be replaced as follows:

'However, where the opposition was raised at the request of a State falling within its competence and this request is maintained, it may be withdrawn only after consultation of its Advisory Committee on Restrictive Practices and Dominant Positions.';

(f) the following shall be added to the end of Article 6 (9):

', or the corresponding provisions envisaged in Protocol 21 to the EEA Agreement.';

(g) in Article 8, introductory paragraph, the phrase 'pursuant to Article 7 of Regulation No 19/65/EEC' shall read 'either on its own initiative or at the request of the other surveillance authority or a State falling within its competence or of natural or legal persons claiming a legitimate interest';

(h) the following paragraph shall be added at the end of Article 8:

'The competent surveillance authority may in such cases issue a decision in accordance with Articles 6 and 8 of Regulation No 17/62, or the corresponding provisions envisaged in Protocol 21 to the EEA Agreement, without any notification from the undertakings concerned being required.';

(i) in Article 8 (c), the term 'Member States' shall read 'EC Member States or EFTA States';

(j) Article 9 shall read:

'This Act shall remain in force until 31 December 1999.'.

F. KNOW-HOW LICENSING AGREEMENTS

9. **389 R 0556**: Commission Regulation (EEC) No 556/89 of 30 November 1988 on the application of Article 85 (3) of the Treaty to certain categories of know-how licensing agreements (OJ No L 61, 4.3.1989, p. 1).

The provisions of the Regulation shall, for the purposes of the Agreement, be read with the following adaptations:

(a) in Article 1 (2), the term 'EEC' shall read 'the territory covered by the EEA Agreement';

(b) Article 1(4) shall read:

'In so far as the obligations referred to in paragraph 1 (1) to (5) concern territories including EC Member States or EFTA States in which the same technology is protected by necessary patents, the exemption provided for in paragraph 1 shall extend for those States as long as the licensed product or process is protected in those States by such patents, where the duration of such protection exceeds the periods specified in paragraph 2.';

(c) in Article 1(7), points 6 and 8, the term 'Member States' shall read 'EC Member States or EFTA States';

(d) in Article 4 (1), the phrase 'on condition that the agreements in question are notified to the Commission in accordance with the provisions of Commission Regulation No 27 and that the Commission does not oppose' shall read 'on condition that the agreements in question are notified to the EC Commission or the EFTA Surveillance Authority in accordance with the provisions of Commission Regulation No 27/62, as last amended by Regulation (EEC) No 2526/85, and the corresponding provisions envisaged in Protocol 21 to the EEA Agreement, and that the competent surveillance authority does not oppose';

(e) in Article 4(3) the term 'the Commission' shall read 'the EC Commission or the EFTA Surveillance Authority';

(f) Article 4 (5) shall not apply;

(g) in Article 4 (6), the second sentence shall be replaced as follows:

'It shall oppose exemption if it receives a request to do so from a State falling within its competence within three months of the transmission to those States of the notification referred to in paragraph 1.';

(h) in Article 4 (7), the second sentence shall be replaced as follows:

'However, where the opposition was raised at the request of a State falling within its competence and this request is maintained, it may be withdrawn only after consultation of its Advisory Committee on Restrictive Practices and Dominant Positions.';

(i) the following shall be added to the end of Article 4 (10):

', or the corresponding provisions envisaged in Protocol 21 to the EEA Agreement.';

(j) in Article 7, introductory paragraph, the phrase 'pursuant to Article 7 of Regulation No 19/65/EEC' shall read 'either on its own initiative or at the request of the other surveillance authority or a State falling within its competence or of natural or legal persons claiming a legitimate interest';

(k) in Article 7, the following shall be added at the end of point (5) (a) and (b):

'The competent surveillance authority may in such cases issue a decision in accordance with Articles 6 and 8 of Regulation (EEC) No 17/62, or the corresponding provisions envisaged in Protocol 21 to the EEA Agreement, without any notification from the undertakings concerned being required;';

(l) Article 8 shall not apply;

(m) Article 9 shall not apply;

(n) Article 10 shall not apply;

(o) Article 12 shall read:

'This Act shall apply until 31 December 1999.'.

G. TRANSPORT

10. **368 R 1017**: Council Regulation (EEC) No 1017/68 of 19 July 1968 applying rules of competition to transport by rail, road and inland waterway (OJ No L 175, 23.7.1968, p. 1).

The provisions of Articles 1 to 5 and of Articles 7 to 9 of the Regulation shall, for the purposes of the Agreement, be read with the following adaptations:

(a) in Article 2, the introductory paragraph shall read as follows:

'Subject to the provisions of Articles 3 to 5, Article 6 of Regulation (EEC) No 1017/68 and to the provision corresponding to Article 6 as it is envisaged in Protocol 21 to the EEA Agreement, the following shall be prohibited as incompatible with the functioning of the EEA Agreement, no prior decision to that effect being required: all agreements between undertakings, decisions by associations of undertakings and concerted practices liable to affect trade between Contracting Parties which have as their object or effect the prevention, restriction or distortion of competition within the territory covered by the EEA Agreement, and in particular those which:';

(b) Article 3 (2) shall not apply;

(c) Article 6 shall not apply;

(d) in the first subparagraph of Article 8, the phrase 'incompatible with the common market' shall read 'incompatible with the functioning of the EEA Agreement';

(e) Article 9 (1) shall read:

'In the case of public undertakings and undertakings to which EC Member States or EFTA States grant special or exclusive rights, Contracting Parties shall ensure that there is neither enacted nor maintained in force any measure contrary to the provisions of the foregoing Articles.';

(f) in Article 9 (2), the term 'Community' shall read 'the Contracting Parties';

(g) Article 9 (3) shall read:

'The EC Commission and the EFTA Surveillance Authority shall see to it that the provisions of this Article are applied and shall, where necessary, address appropriate measures to States falling within their respective competence.'.

11. **386 R 4056**: Council Regulation (EEC) No 4056/86 of 22 December 1986 laying down detailed rules for the application of Articles 85 and 86 of the Treaty to maritime transport (OJ No L 378, 31.12.1986, p. 4).

The provisions of Section I of the Regulation shall, for the purposes of the Agreement, be read with the following adaptations:

(a) in Article 1 (2), the term 'Community ports' shall read 'ports in the territory covered by the EEA Agreement';

(b) Article 2 (2) shall not apply;

(c) in Article 7 (1), introductory paragraph, the term 'Section II' shall read 'Section II or the corresponding provisions envisaged in Protocol 21 to the EEA Agreement'; furthermore, in the second indent, the term 'Article 11 (4)' shall read 'Article 11 (4) or the corresponding provisions envisaged in Protocol 21 to the EEA Agreement';

(d) in Article 7 (2) (a), the term 'Section II' shall read 'Section II or the corresponding provisions envisaged in Protocol 21 to the EEA Agreement';

(e) the following subparagraphs shall be added to Article 7 (2) (c) (i):

'If any of the Contracting Parties intends to undertake consultations with a third country in accordance with this Regulation, it shall inform the EEA Joint Committee.

Whenever appropriate, the Contracting Party initiating the procedure may request the other Contracting Parties to co-operate in these procedures.

If one or more of the other Contracting Parties object to the intended action, a satisfactory solution will be sought within the EEA Joint Committee. If the Contracting Parties do not reach agreement, appropriate measures may be taken to remedy subsequent distortions of competition.';

(f) in Article 8 (2), the phrase 'at the request of a Member State' shall read 'at the request of a State falling within its competence';
furthermore, the term 'Article 10' shall read 'Article 10 or the corresponding provisions envisaged in Protocol 21 to the EEA Agreement';

(g) in Article 9 (1), the term 'Community trading and shipping interests' shall read 'the trading and shipping interests of the Contracting Parties';

(h) the following paragraph shall be added to Article 9:

'4. If any of the Contracting Parties intends to undertake consultations with a third country in accordance with this Regulation, it shall inform the EEA Joint Committee.

Whenever appropriate, the Contracting Party initiating the procedure may request the other Contracting Parties to co-operate in these procedures.

If one or more of the other Contracting Parties object to the intended action, a satisfactory solution will be sought within the EEA Joint Committee. If the Contracting Parties do not reach agreement, appropriate measures may be taken to remedy subsequent distortions of competition.'.

H. PUBLIC UNDERTAKINGS

12. **388 L 0301**: Commission Directive 88/301/EEC of 16 May 1988 on competition in the markets in telecommunications terminal equipment (OJ No L 131, 27.5.1988, p. 73).

The provisions of the Directive shall, for the purposes of the Agreement, be read with the following adaptations:

(a) in the second subparagraph of Article 2, the phrase 'notification of this Directive' shall be replaced by 'entry into force of the EEA Agreement';
(b) Article 10 shall not apply;
(c) in addition, the following shall apply:

as regards EFTA States, it is understood that the EFTA Surveillance Authority shall be the addressee of all the information, communications, reports and notifications which according to this Directive are, within the Community, addressed to the EC Commission.

As regards the different transition periods provided for in this act, a general transition period of six months as from the entry into force of the EEA Agreement shall apply.

13. **390 L 0388**: Commission Directive 90/388/EEC of 28 June 1990 on competition in the markets for telecommunications services (OJ No L 192, 24.7.1990, p. 10).

The provisions of the Directive shall, for the purposes of the Agreement, be read with the following adaptations:

(a) in Article 3, the fifth subparagraph shall be replaced by the following:

'Before they are implemented, the EC Commission or the EFTA Surveillance Authority shall, in their respective competence, verify the compatibility of these projects with the EEA Agreement.';

(b) in the second subparagraph of Article 6, the phrase 'harmonized Community rules adopted by the Council' shall be replaced by 'harmonized rules contained in the EEA Agreement';
(c) the first paragraph of Article 10 shall not apply;
(d) in addition, the following shall apply:

as regards EFTA States, it is understood that the EFTA Surveillance Authority shall be the addressee of all the information, communications, reports and notifications which according to this Directive are, within the Community, addressed to the EC Commission. Likewise, the EFTA Surveillance Authority shall be responsible, as regards EFTA States, for making the necessary reports or assessments.

As regards the different transition periods provided for in this act, a general transition period of six months as from the entry into force of the EEA Agreement shall apply.

I. COAL AND STEEL

14. **354 D 7024**: High Authority Decision No 24/54 of 6 May 1954 laying down in implementation of Article 66 (1) of the Treaty a regulation on what constitutes control of an undertaking (OJ of the ECSC No 9, 11.5.1954, p. 345/54).

The provisions of the Decision shall, for the purposes of the Agreement, be read with the following adaptation:

Article 4 shall not apply.

15. **367 D 7025**: High Authority Decision No 25/67 of 22 June 1967 laying down in implementation of Article 66 (3) of the Treaty a regulation concerning exemption from prior authorization (OJ No 154, 14.7.1967, p. 11), as amended by:

– **378 S 2495**: Commission Decision No 2495/78/ECSC of 20 October 1978 (OJ No L 300, 27.10.1978, p. 21).

The provisions of the Decision shall, for the purposes of the Agreement, be read with the following adaptations:

(a) in Article 1 (2), the phrase 'and within the EFTA States' shall be inserted after '... within the Community';
(b) in the heading of Article 2, the phrase 'the scope of the Treaty' shall read 'the scope of Protocol 25 to the EEA Agreement';
(c) in the heading of Article 3, the phrase 'the scope of the Treaty' shall read 'the scope of Protocol 25 to the EEA Agreement';
(d) Article 11 shall not apply.

Acts of which the EC Commission and the EFTA Surveillance Authority shall Take Due Account

In the application of Articles 53 to 60 of the Agreement and the provisions referred to in this Annex, the EC Commission and the EFTA Surveillance Authority shall take due account of the principles and rules contained in the following acts:

CONTROL OF CONCENTRATIONS

16. **C/203/90/p. 5**: Commission Notice regarding restrictions ancillary to concentrations (OJ No C 203, 14.8.1990, p. 5).

17. **C/203/90/p. 10**: Commission Notice regarding the concentrative and co-operative operations under Council Regulation (EEC) No 4064/89 of 21 December 1989 on the control of concentrations between undertakings (OJ No C 203, 14.8.1990, p. 10).

EXCLUSIVE DEALING AGREEMENTS

18. **C/101/84/p. 2**: Commission Notice concerning Commission Regulations (EEC) No 1983/83 and (EEC) No 1984/83 of 22 June 1983 on the application of Article 85 (3) of the Treaty to categories of exclusive distribution and exclusive purchasing agreements (OJ No C 101, 13.4.1984, p. 2).

19. **C/17/85/p. 4**: Commission Notice concerning Regulation (EEC) No 123/85 of 12

December 1984 on the application of Article 85 (3) of the Treaty to certain categories of motor vehicle distribution and servicing agreements (OJ No C 17, 18.1.1985, p. 4).

OTHER

20. **362 X 1224 (01)**: Commission Notice on exclusive dealing contracts with commercial agents (OJ No 139, 24.12.1962, p. 2921/62).

21. **C/75/68/p. 3**: Commission Notice concerning agreements, decisions and concerted practices in the field of co-operation between enterprises (OJ No C 75, 29.7.1968, p. 3) as corrected by OJ No C 84, 28.8.1968, p. 14.

22. **C/111/72/p. 13**: Commission Notice concerning imports into the Community of Japanese goods falling within the scope of the Rome Treaty (OJ No C 111, 21.10.1972, p. 13).

23. **C/1/79/p. 2**: Commission Notice of 18 December 1978 concerning its assessment of certain subcontracting agreements in relation to Article 85 (1) of the EEC Treaty (OJ No C 1, 3.1.1979, p. 2).

24. **C/231/86/p. 2**: Commission Notice on agreements of minor importance which do not fall under Article 85 (1) of the Treaty establishing the European Economic Community (OJ No C 231, 12.9.1986, p. 2).

25. **C/233/91/p. 2**: Guidelines on the application of EEC competition rules in the telecommunication sector (OJ No C 233, 6.9.1991, p. 2).

ANNEXE XV
STATE AID

List provided for in Article 63

Introduction

When the acts referred to in this Annexe contain notions or refer to procedures which are specific to the Community legal order, such as

- preambles;
- the addressees of the Community acts;
- references to territories or languages of the EC;
- references to rights and obligations of EC Member States, their public entities, undertakings or individuals in relation to each other; and
- references to information and notification procedures;

Protocol 1 on horizontal adaptations shall apply, unless otherwise provided for in this Annexe.

Acts Referred to

PUBLIC UNDERTAKINGS

1. **380 L 0723**: Commission Directive 80/723/EEC of 25 June 1980 on the transparency of financial relations between Member States and public undertakings (OJ No L 195, 29.7.1980, p. 35), as amended by:

– **385 L 0413**: Commission Directive 85/413/EEC of 24 July 1985 amending Directive 80/723/EEC on the transparency of financial relations between Member States and public undertakings (OJ No L 229, 28.8.1985, p. 20)

The provisions of this Directive shall, for the purposes of the present Agreement, be read with the following adaptations:

(a) The term 'Commission' shall read 'competent surveillance authority as defined in Article 62 of the EEA Agreement'.
(b) The term 'trade between Member States' shall read 'trade between Contracting Parties'.

Acts of which the EC Commission and the EFTA Surveillance Authority shall Take Due Account

In the application of Articles 61 to 63 of the Agreement and the provisions referred to in this Annexe, the EC Commission and the EFTA Surveillance Authority shall take due account of the principles and rules contained in the following acts:

SCRUTINY BY THE COMMISSION

Prior notification of State aid plans and other procedural rules

2. **C/252/80/p. 2**: The notification of State aids to the Commission pursuant to Article 93 (3) of the EEC Treaty; the failure of Member States to respect their obligations (OJ No C 252, 30.9.1980, p. 2)
3. Letter from the Commission to the Member States SG (81) 12740 of 2 October 1981
4. Letter from the Commission to the Member States SG (89) D/5521 of 27 April 1989
5. Letter from the Commission to the Member States SG (87) D/5540 of 30 April 1989: Procedure under Article 93 (2) of the EEC Treaty—Time limits
6. Letter from the Commission to the Member States SG (90) D/28091 of 11 October 1990: State aid—informing Member States about aid cases not objected by the Commission
7. Letter from the Commission to the Member States SG (91) D/4577 of 4 March 1991: Communication to the Member States concerning the procedure for the notification of aid plans and procedures applicable when aid is provided in breach of the rules of Article 93 (3) of the EEC Treaty

Evaluation of aid of minor importance

8. **C/40/90/p. 2**: Notification of an aid scheme of minor importance (OJ No C 40, 20.2.1990, p. 2)

Public authorities' holdings

9. Application of Articles 92 and 93 of the EEC Treaty to public authorities' holdings (Bulletin EC 9-1984)

Aid granted illegally

10. **C/318/83/p. 3**: Commission Communication on aids granted illegally (OJ No C 318, 24.11.1983, p. 3)

State guarantees

11. Letter from the Commission to the Member States SG (89) D/4328 of 5 April 1989
12. Letter from the Commission to the Member States SG (89) D/12772 of 12 October 1989

FRAMEWORKS ON SECTORAL AID SCHEMES

Textile and clothing industry

13. Commission Communication to the Member States on the Community framework on aid to the textile industry (SEC (71) 363 Final—July 1971)
14. Letter from the Commission to the Member States SG (77) D/1190 of 4 February 1977 and Annex (Doc. SEC (77) 317, 25.1.1977): Examination of the present situation with regard to aids to the textile and clothing industries

Synthetic fibres industry

15. **C/173/89/p. 5**: Commission Communication on aid to the EEC synthetic fibres industries (OJ No C 173, 8.7.1989, p. 5)

Motor vehicle industry

16. **C/123/89/p. 3**: Community framework on State aid to the motor vehicle industry (OJ No C 123, 18.5.1989, p. 3)
17. **C/81/91/p. 4**: Community framework on State aid to the motor vehicle industry (OJ No C 81, 26.3.1991, p. 4)

FRAMEWORKS ON GENERAL SYSTEMS OF REGIONAL AID

18. **471 Y 1104**: Council Resolution of 20 October 1971 on general systems of regional aid (OJ No C 111, 4.11.1971, p. 1)
19. **C/111/71/p. 7**: Commission Communication on Council Resolution of 20 October 1971 on general systems of regional aid (OJ No C 111, 4.11.1971, p. 7)
20. Commission Communication to the Council on general regional aid systems (COM (75) 77, final)
21. **C/31/79/p. 9**: Commission Communication of 21 December 1978 on regional aid systems (OJ No C 31, 3.2.1979, p. 9)
22. **C/212/88/p. 2**: Commission Communication on the method for the application of Article 92 (3) (a) and (c) to regional aid (OJ No C 212, 12.8.1988, p. 2)
23. **C/10/90/p. 8**: Commission Communication on the revision of the Communication of 21 December 1978 (OJ No C 10, 16.1.1990, p. 8)
24. **C/163/90/p. 5**: Commission Communication on the method of application of Article 92 (3) (c) to regional aid (OJ No C 163, 4.7.1990, p. 5)
25. **C/163/90/p. 6**: Commission Communication on the method of application of Article 92 (3) (a) to regional aid (OJ No C 163, 4.7.1990, p. 6)

HORIZONTAL FRAMEWORKS

Community framework on State aid in environmental matters

26. Letter from the Commission to the Member States S/74/30.807 of 7 November 1974
27. Letter from the Commission to the Member States SG (80) D/8287 of 7 July 1980
28. Commission Communication to the Member States (Annex to the letter of 7 July 1980)
29. Letter from the Commission to the Member States SG (87) D/3795 of 29 March 1987

Community framework on State aid to research and development

30. **C/83/86/p. 2**: Community framework for State aids for research and development (OJ No C 83, 11.4.1986, p. 2)
31. Letter from the Commission to the Member States SG (90) D/01620 of 5 February 1990

RULES APPLICABLE TO GENERAL AID SCHEMES

32. Letter from the Commission to the Member States SG (79) D/10478 of 14 September 1979
33. Control of aid for rescue and restructuring (Eighth Report on Competition Policy, point 228)

Rules applicable to cases of cumulation of aid for different purposes

34. **C/3/85/p. 2**: Commission Communication on the cumulation of aids for different purposes (OJ No C 3, 5.1.1985, p. 2)

AID TO EMPLOYMENT

35. Sixteenth Report on Competition Policy, point 253
36. Twentieth Report on Competition Policy, point 280

CONTROL OF AID TO THE STEEL INDUSTRY

37. **C/320/88/p. 3**: Framework for certain steel sectors not covered by the ECSC Treaty (OJ No C 320, 13.12.1988, p. 3)

Annexe XVI
Procurement

List provided for in Article 65 (1)

Introduction

When the acts referred to in this Annexe contain notions or refer to procedures which are specific to the Community legal order, such as

- preambles,

- the addressees of the Community acts,
- references to territories or languages of the EC,
- references to rights and obligations of EC Member States, their public entities, undertakings or individuals in relation to each other, and
- references to information and notification procedures,

Protocol 1 on horizontal adaptations shall apply, unless otherwise provided for in this Annexe.

Sectoral Adaptations

1. For the purposes of applying Directives 71/305/EEC, 89/440/EEC and 90/531/EEC referred to in this Annexe the following shall apply :

Until such time as they apply free movement of labour in accordance with Article 28 of the Agreement, the Contracting Parties shall ensure:

- effective free access for key employees of contractors of any Contracting Parties who have obtained public works contracts;
- non-discriminatory access to work-permits for contractors from any Contracting Parties who have obtained public works contracts.

2. When the acts referred to in this Annexe require the publication of notices or documents the following shall apply:

(a) the publication of notices and other documents as required by the acts referred to in this Annexe in the Official Journal of the European Communities and in the Tenders Electronic Daily shall be carried out by the Office for Official Publications of the European Communities;

(b) notices from the EFTA States shall be sent in at least one of the Community languages to the Office for Official Publications of the European Communities. They shall be published in the Community languages in the S-Series of the Official Journal of the European Communities and in the Tenders Electronic Daily. EC notices need not be translated into the languages of the EFTA States.

3. When applying Part VII, Chapter 3, of the Agreement to surveillance for the purposes of this Annexe, the competence for surveillance of alleged infringements lies with the EC Commission if the alleged infringement is committed by a contracting entity in the Community and with the EFTA Surveillance Authority if it is committed by a contracting entity in an EFTA State.

Acts Referred to

1. **371 L 0304**: Council Directive 71/304/EEC of 26 July 1971 concerning the abolition of restrictions on freedom to provide services in respect of public works contracts and on the award of public works contracts to contractors acting through agencies of branches (OJ No L 185, 16.8.1971, p. 1).

The provisions of the Directive shall, for the purposes of the present Agreement, be read with the following adaptations :

(a) the list of professional trade activities shall be replaced by Annexe II of Directive 89/440/EEC;

(b) with regard to Liechtenstein, the measures necessary to comply with this Directive shall enter into force by 1 January 1995;

with regard to Switzerland, the measures necessary to comply with this Directive shall enter into force by 1 January 1994;
during these transition periods the application of the Directive will be reciprocally suspended between these States and the other Contracting Parties.

2. **371 L 0305**: Council Directive 71/305/EEC of 26 July 1971 concerning the co-ordination of procedure for the award of public works contracts (OJ No L 185, 25.8.1971, p. 5), as amended by:

- 389 L 0440: Council Directive 89/440/EEC of 18 July 1989 (OJ No L 210, 21.7.1989, p. 1),
- 390 D 0380: Commission Decision 90/380/EEC of 13 July 1990 concerning the updating of Annexe I to Council Directive 89/440/EEC (OJ No L 187, 19.7.1990, p. 55).

The provisions of the Directive shall, for the purposes of the present Agreement, be read with the following adaptations:

(a) with regard to Liechtenstein, the measures necessary to comply with this Directive shall enter into force by 1 January 1995;
with regard to Switzerland, the measures necessary to comply with this Directive shall enter into force by 1 January 1994;
during these transition periods, the application of the Directive will be reciprocally suspended between these States and the other Contracting Parties;

(b) in Article 4 (a), the phrase 'in conformity with the EEC Treaty' shall read 'in conformity with the EEA Agreement';

(c) in Article 4 (a) (1) and 4 (a) (3), in so far as it is not introduced in Finland, Liechtenstein and Switzerland, VAT shall mean:

- 'Liikevaihtovero/omsättningsskatt' in Finland;
- 'Warenumsatzsteuer' in Liechtenstein;
- 'Warenumsatzsteuer/impôt sur le chiffre d'affaires/imposta sulla cifra d'affari' in Switzerland;

(d) in Article 4 (a) (2), the value of the thresholds in national currencies of the EFTA States shall be calculated so as to come into effect on 1 January 1993 and shall in principle be revised every two years with effect from 1 January 1995 and published in the Official Journal of the European Communities;

(e) Article 24 shall be supplemented as follows:

'– in Austria, the Firmenbuch, the Gewerberegister, the Mitgliederverzeichnisse der Landeskamern;
in Finland, the Kaupparekisteri, Handelsregistret;
in Iceland, the Firmaskrà;
in Liechtenstein, the Gewerberegister;
in Norway, the Foretaksregisteret;
in Sweden, the Aktiebolagsregistret, Handelsregistret;
in Switzerland, the Handelsregister, the Registre du Commerce, Registro di Commercio.';

(f) in Article 30 a (1), the date of 31 October 1993 shall be replaced by 31 October 1995;

(g) Annexe I is supplemented by Appendix 1 to this Annexe.

3. **377 L 0062**: Council Directive 77/62/EEC of 21 December 1976 co-ordinating

procedures for the award of public supply contracts (OJ No L 13, 15.1.1977, p. 1) as amended by Directive 80/767/EEC and Directive 88/295/EEC, as amended and supplemented by:

- 380 L 0767: Council Directive 80/767/EEC of 22 July 1980 adapting and supplementing in respect of certain contracting authorities Directive 77/62/EEC co-ordinating procedures for the award of public supply contracts (OJ No L 215, 18.8.1980, p. 1), as amended by Directive 88/295/EEC.
- 388 L 0295: Council Directive 88/295/EEC of 22 March 1988 amending Directive 77/62/EEC relating to the co-ordination of procedures on the award of public supply contracts and repealing certain provisions of Directive 80/767/EEC (OJ No L 127, 20.5.1988, p. 1).

The provisions of the Directive shall, for the purposes of the present Agreement, be read with the following adaptations:

(a) with regard to Liechtenstein, the measures necessary to comply with this Directive shall enter into force by 1 January 1995;
with regard to Switzerland, the measures necessary to comply with this Directive shall enter into force by 1 January 1994;
during these transition periods, the application of the Directive will be reciprocally suspended between these States and the other Contracting Parties;

(b) in Article 2 (a), the reference to 'Article 223 (1) (b) of the Treaty' shall be replaced by reference to 'Article 123 of the EEA Agreement';

(c) In Article 5 (1) (a), in so far as it is not introduced in Finland, Liechtenstein and Switzerland, VAT shall mean:
   - 'Liikevaihtovero/omsättningsskatt' in Finland,
   - 'Warenumsatzsteuer' in Liechtenstein,
   - 'Warenumsatzsteuer/impôt sur le chiffre d'affaires/imposta sulla cifra d'affari' in Switzerland;

(d) on the understanding that the threshold expressed in ECU shall only apply within the EEA, the following words shall be deleted in Article 5 (1) (c):
   - in the first sentence, the words 'and the threshold of the GATT Agreement expressed in ECU';
   - in the second sentence, the words 'and of the ECU expressed in SDR's';

(e) in Article 5 (1) (c), the value of the thresholds in the national currencies of the EFTA States shall be calculated so as to come into effect on 1 January 1993;

(f) in Article 9 (1), the date of 1 January 1989 shall be replaced by 1 January 1993;

(g) in Article 20 (4) the sentence 'within the time limit laid down in Article 30' shall read 'before 1 January 1993';

(h) Article 21 shall be supplemented as follows:
   - in Austria, the Firmenbuch, the Gewerberegister, the der Landeskamern,
   - in Finland, the Kaupparekisteri, Handelsregistret,
   - in Iceland, the Firmaskrà,
   - in Liechtenstein, the Gewerberegister,
   - in Norway, the Foretaksregisteret,

- in Sweden, the Aktiebolagsregistret, Handelsregistret,
- in Switzerland, the Handelsregister, the Registre du Commerce, Registro di Commercio;

(i) in Article 29 (1) (b), the date of 31 October 1991 shall be replaced by 31 October 1994;

(j) Annexe I to Directive 80/767/EEC shall be supplemented by Appendix 2 to this Annexe;

(k) Annexe I to Directive 88/295/EEC shall be supplemented by Appendix 3 to this Annexe.

4. **390 L 0531**: Council Directive 90/531/EEC of 17 September 1990 on the procurement procedures of entities operating in the water, energy, transport and telecommunications sectors (OJ No L 297, 29.10.1990, p. 1) .

The provisions of the Directive shall, for the purposes of the present Agreement, be read with the following adaptations :

(a) with regard to Liechtenstein, the measures necessary to comply with this Directive shall enter into force by 1 January 1995,
with regard to Switzerland, the measures necessary to comply with this Directive shall enter into force by 1 January 1994,
during these transition periods the application of the Directive will be reciprocally suspended between these States and the other Contracting Parties;

(b) with regard to Norway, the measures necessary to comply with this Directive shall enter into force on 1 January 1995 or before upon notification by Norway of having complied with this Directive. During this transition period the application of the Directive will be reciprocally suspended between Norway and the other Contracting Parties;

(c) in Article 3 (1) (e) the reference to 'Article 36 of the Treaty' shall be read as a reference to 'Article 13 of the EEA Agreement';

(d) in Article 11, point (1), the phrase 'in conformity with the Treaty' shall read 'in conformity with the EEA Agreement';

(e) in Article 12 (1) and 12 (6), in so far as it is not introduced in Finland, Liechtenstein and Switzerland VAT shall mean :

- 'Liikevaihtovero/omsättningsskatt' in Finland,
- 'Warenumsatzsteuer' in Liechtenstein,
- 'Warenumsatzsteuer/impôt sur le chiffre d'affaires/imposta sulla cifra d'affari' in Switzerland;

(f) in Article 27 (5) the reference to 'Article 93(3) of the Treaty' shall be replaced by a reference to 'Article 62 of the EEA Agreement';

(g) in Article 29, the term 'third countries' shall be understood as 'countries other than the Contracting Parties to the EEA Agreement';

(h) in Article 29 (1) the term 'Community' shall read 'Community, as regards Community entities, or the EFTA States, as regards their entities';

(i) in Article 29 (1) the term 'Community undertakings' shall read 'Community undertakings, as regards Community agreements, or EFTA States' undertakings, as regards EFTA States' agreements';

(j) in Article 29 (1) the words 'the Community or its Member States in respect of third countries' shall read 'either the Community or its Member States in respect of third countries or the EFTA States in respect of third countries';

(k) in Article 29 (5), the words 'by a Council decision' shall read 'by a decision in the context of the general decision-making procedure of the EEA Agreement';

(l) Article 29 (6) shall read as follows:

'6. In the context of the general institutional provisions of the EEA Agreement, annual reports shall be submitted on the progress made in multilateral or bilateral negotiations regarding access for Community and EFTA undertakings to the markets of third countries in the fields covered by this Directive, on any result which such negotiations may have achieved, and on the implementation in practice of all the agreements which have been concluded.

In the context of the general decision-making procedure of the EEA Agreement the provisions of this Article may be amended in the light of such developments.';

(m) in order to enable the contracting entities in the EEA to apply Article 29 (2) and (3), the Contracting Parties shall ensure that the suppliers established in their respective territories determine the origin of the products in their tenders for supply contracts in conformity with Regulation (EEC) No 802/68 of the Council of 27 June 1968 on the common definition of the concept of the origin of goods (OJ No L 148, 28.6.1968, p. 1);

(n) in order to obtain maximum convergence Article 29 will be applied in the EEA context on the understanding that:

- the operation of paragraph (3) is without prejudice to the existing degree of liberalization towards third countries,
- the Contracting Parties consult closely in their negotiations with third countries.

The application of this regime will be jointly reviewed during 1996;

(o) in Article 30, the values of the thresholds in national currencies of the EFTA States shall be calculated so as to come into effect on 1 January 1993. They shall in principle be revised every two years with effect from 1 January 1995;

(p) Annexes I to X are supplemented by Appendices 4 to 13 to this Annexe, respectively.

5. **389 L 0665**: Council Directive 89/665/EEC of 21 December 1989 on the co-ordination of the laws, regulations and administrative provisions relating to the application of review procedures to the award of public supply and public works contracts (OJ No L 395, 30.12.1989, p. 33).

The provisions of the Directive shall, for the purposes of the present Agreement, be read with the following adaptations:

(a) with regard to Liechtenstein, the measures necessary to comply with this Directive shall enter into force by 1 January 1995,
with regard to Switzerland, the measures necessary to comply with this Directive shall enter into force by 1 January 1994,
during these transition periods the application of the Directive will be reciprocally suspended between these States and the other Contracting Parties;

(b) in Article 2 (8), the reference to 'Article 177 of the EEC Treaty' shall be read as a reference to the 'criteria laid down by the Court of Justice in its interpretation of Article 177 of the EEC Treaty'.[1]

6. **371 R 1182:** Regulation (EEC/Euratom) No 1182 of 3 June 1971 determining the rules applicable to periods, dates and time limits (OJ No L 124, 8.6.1971, p. 1).[2]

The provisions of the Regulation shall, for the purposes of the present Agreement, be read with the following adaptations:

(a) with regard to Liechtenstein, the measures necessary to comply with this Regulation shall enter into force by 1 January 1995,
with regard to Switzerland, the measures necessary to comply with this Regulation shall enter into force by 1 January 1994,
during these transition periods the application of the Regulation will be reciprocally suspended between these States and the other Contracting Parties;

(b) the words 'Council and Commission acts' shall mean acts referred to in this Annexe.

Acts of which the Contracting Parties shall Take Note

In the application of the provisions of this Annexe, the Contracting Parties shall take note of the contents of the following acts:

7. Guide to the Community rules on open public procurement (OJ No C 358, 21.12.1987, p. 1).
8. Commission communication (COM (89) 400 of 27.7.1989) on regional and social aspects (OJ No C 311, 12.12.1989, p. 7).

Annexe XVII

Intellectual Property

List provided for in Article 65(2)

Introduction

When the acts referred to in this Annexe contain notions or refer to procedures which are specific to the Community legal order, such as:

- preambles,
- the addressees of the Community acts,
- references to territories or languages of the EC,
- references to rights and obligations of EC Member States, their public entities, undertakings or individuals in relation to each other, and
- references to information and notification procedures,

Protocol 1 on horizontal adaptations shall apply, unless otherwise provided for in this Annexe.

[1] Examples: Case 61/65 *Vaassen* v. *Beambtenfonds Mijnbedrijf* [1966] ECR 261, [1966] CMLR 508; Case 36/73 *Nederlandse Spoorwegen* v. *Minister van Verkeer en Waterstaat* [1973] ECR 1299, [1974] 2 CMLR 148; Case 246/80 *Broekmeulen* v. *Huisarts Registatie Commissie* [1981] ECR 2311, [1982] 1 CMLR 91.

[2] Art. 30 of Dir. 71/305/EEC and Art. 28 of Dir. 77/62/EEC refer to this Regulation, which needs therefore to be part of the *acquis*.

Acts Referred to

1. **387 L 0054:** Council Directive 87/54/EEC of 16 December 1986 on the legal protection of topographies of semiconductor products (OJ No L 24, 27.1.1987, p. 36).

The provisions of the Directive shall, for the purposes of the Agreement, be read with the following adaptations:

(a) in Article 1 (1) (c), the reference to 'Article 223 (1) (b) of the EEC Treaty' shall be replaced by reference to Article 123 of the EEA Agreement';
(b) Article 3 (6) to 3 (8) shall not apply;
(c) Article 5 (5) shall be replaced by the following:

'The exclusive rights to authorize or prohibit the acts specified in paragraph 1 (b) shall not apply to any such act committed after the topography or the semiconductor product has been put on the market in a Contracting Party by the person entitled to authorize its marketing or with his consent.'.

2. **390 D 0510:** First Council Decision 90/510/EEC of 9 October 1990 on the extension of the legal protection of topographies of semiconductor products to persons from certain countries and territories (OJ No L 285, 17.10.1990, p. 29).

The provisions of the Decision shall, for the purposes of the Agreement, be read with the following adaptations:

(a) in the Annexe, the references to Austria and Sweden shall be deleted;
(b) in addition, the following shall apply:

where a country or territory listed in the Annexe does not give the same protection as provided for in that Decision to persons from a Contracting Party, the Contracting Parties will use their best endeavours to ensure that such protection is given by the said country or territory to the said Contracting Party at the latest one year after the date of entry into force of this Agreement.

3. (a) **390 D 0511:** Second Council Decision 90/511/EEC of 9 October 1990 on the extension of the legal protection of topographies of semiconductor products to persons from certain countries and territories (OJ No L 285, 17.10.1990, p. 31).
(b) **390 D 0541:** Commission Decision 90/541/EEC of 26 October 1990 in accordance with Council Decision 90/511/EEC determining the countries to the companies or other legal persons of which legal protection of topographies of semiconductors is extended (OJ No L 307, 7.11.1990, p. 21).

In addition to these two Decisions, the following shall apply:

the EFTA States undertake to adopt for the purposes of this Agreement Council Decision 90/511/EEC and the decisions taken by the Commission in accordance with the said Council Decision, if their application is extended beyond 31 December 1992. Ensuing EC amendments or replacements shall be adopted by the EFTA States before the entry into force of the Agreement.

4. **389 L 0104:** First Council Directive 89/104/EEC of 21 December 1988 to approximate the laws of the Member States relating to trade marks (OJ No L 40, 11.2.1989, p. 1).

The provisions of the Directive shall, for the purposes of the Agreement, be read with the following adaptations:

(a) in Article 3 (2), the term 'trade mark law' shall be understood to be the trade mark law applicable in a Contracting Party;

(b) in Articles 4 (2) (a) (i), (2) (b) and (3), 9 and 14, the provisions concerning the Community Trade Mark shall not apply to EFTA States unless the Community Trade Mark extends to them;

(c) Article 7(1) shall be replaced by the following:

'The trade mark shall not entitle the proprietor to prohibit its use in relation to goods which have been put on the market in a Contracting Party under that trade mark by the proprietor or with his consent.'.

5. **391 L 0250:** Council Directive 91/250/EEC of 14 May 1991 on the legal protection of computer programs (OJ No L 122, 17.5.1991, p. 42).

The provisions of the Directive shall, for the purposes of the Agreement, be read with the following adaptation:

Article 4 (c) shall be replaced by the following:

'any form of distribution to the public, including the rental, of the original computer program or of copies thereof. The first sale in a Contracting Party of a copy of a programme by the rightholder or with his consent shall exhaust the distribution right within the territories of the Contracting Parties of that copy, with the exception of the right to control further rental of the program or a copy thereof.'.

[. . .]

Joint and Unilateral Declarations

Joint Declaration Concerning Rules on Competition

The Contracting Parties declare that the implementation of the EEA competition rules, in cases falling within the responsibility of the EC Commission, is based on the existing Community competences, supplemented by the provisions contained in the Agreement. In cases falling within the responsibility of the EFTA Surveillance Authority, the implementation of the EEA competition rules is based on the agreement establishing that authority as well as on the provisions contained in the EEA Agreement.

Joint Declaration on Article 61 (3) (b) of the Agreement

The Contracting Parties declare that in establishing whether a derogation can be granted under Article 61 (3) (b) the EC Commission shall take the interest of the EFTA States into account and the EFTA Surveillance Authority shall take the interest of the Community into account.

Joint Declaration on Article 61 (3) (c) of the Agreement

The Contracting Parties take note that even if eligibility of the regions has to be denied in the context of Article 61 (3) (a) and according to the criteria of the first stage of analysis under subparagraph (c) (see Commission Communication on the method for the application of Article 92 (3) (a) and (c) to regional aid, OJ No C 212, 12.8.1988, p. 2) examination according to other criteria, e.g. very low population density, is possible.

[. . .]

Joint Declaration on Shipbuilding

The Contracting Parties agree that, until the expiry of the 7th Shipbuilding Directive (i.e. at the end of 1993), they will refrain from the application of the general rules on State aid laid down in Article 61 of the Agreement to the sector of shipbuilding.

Article 62 (2) of the Agreement as well as the Protocols referring to State aid are applicable to the sector of shipbuilding.

[. . .]

Joint Declaration on the Agreed Interpretation of Article 4 (1) and (2) of Protocol 9 on Trade in Fish and Other Marine Products

1. While the EFTA States will not take over the *acquis communautaire* concerning the fishery policy, it is understood that, where reference is made to aid granted through State resources, any distortion of competition is to be assessed by the Contracting Parties in the context of Articles 92 and 93 of the EEC Treaty and in relation to relevant provisions of the *acquis communautaire* concerning the fishery policy and the content of the Joint Declaration regarding Article 61 (3) (c) of the Agreement.

2. While the EFTA States will not take over the *acquis communautaire* concerning the fishery policy, it is understood that, where reference is made to legislation relating to the organization of the market, any distortion of competition caused by such legislation is to be assessed in relation to the principles of the *acquis communautaire* concerning the common organization of the market.

Whenever an EFTA State maintains or introduces national provisions on market organization in the fisheries sector, such provisions shall be considered *a priori* to be compatible with the principles, referred to in the first subparagraph, if they contain at least the following elements:

(a) the legislation on producers' organizations reflects the principles of the *acquis communautaire* regarding:

- establishment on the producers' initiative;
- freedom to become and cease to be a member;
- absence of a dominant position, unless necessary in pursuance of objectives corresponding to those specified in Article 39 of the EEC Treaty;

(b) whenever the rules of producers' organizations are extended to non-members of producers' organizations, the provisions to be applied correspond to those laid down in Article 7 of Regulation (EEC) No 3687/91;

(c) whenever provisions in respect of interventions to support prices exist or are established, they correspond to those specified in Title III of Regulation (EEC) No 3687/91.

[. . .]

Declaration by the Governments of Finland, Iceland, Norway and Sweden on Alcohol Monopolies

Without prejudice to the obligations arising under the Agreement, Finland, Iceland, Norway and Sweden recall that their alcohol monopolies are based on important health and social policy considerations.

[. . .]

Declaration by the Government of Norway on the Direct Enforceability of Decisions by the EC Institutions Regarding Pecuniary Obligations Addressed to Enterprises Located in Norway

The attention of the Contracting Parties is drawn to the fact that the present constitution of Norway does not provide for direct enforceability of decisions by the EC institutions regarding pecuniary obligations addressed to enterprises located in Norway. Norway acknowledges that such decisions should continue to be addressed directly to these enterprises and that they should fulfil their obligations in accordance with the present practice. The said constitutional limitations to direct enforceability of decisions by the EC institutions regarding pecuniary obligations do not apply to subsidiaries and assets in the territory of the Community belonging to enterprises located in Norway.

If difficulties should arise, Norway is prepared to enter into consultations and work towards a mutually satisfactory solution.

Declaration by the European Community

The Commission will keep the situation referred to in Norway's unilateral declaration under constant review. It may at any time initiate consultations with Norway with a view to finding satisfactory solutions to such problems as may arise.

Declaration by the Government of Austria on the Enforcement on its Territory of Decisions by EC Institutions Regarding Pecuniary Obligations

Austria declares that its obligation to enforce on its territory decisions by EC institutions which impose pecuniary obligations shall only refer to such decisions which are fully covered by the provisions of the EEA Agreement.

Declaration by the European Community

The Community understands the Austrian declaration to mean that the enforcement of decisions imposing pecuniary obligations on undertakings will be ensured on Austrian territory to the extent that the decisions imposing such obligations are based—even if not exclusively—on provisions contained in the EEA Agreement.

The Commission may at any time initiate consultations with the Government of Austria with a view to finding satisfactory solutions to such problems as may arise.

Declaration by the European Community on Shipbuilding

It is the agreed policy of the European Community to progressively reduce the level of contract-related production aid paid to shipyards. The Commission is working to bring down the level of the ceiling as far as and as fast as is consistent with the 7th Directive (90/684/EEC).

The 7th Directive expires at the end of 1993. In deciding whether a new Directive is necessary, the Commission will also review the competitive situation in shipbuilding throughout the EEA in the light of progress made towards the reduction or elimination of contract-related production aid. When conducting this review the Commission will closely consult with the EFTA States, taking due account of the results of efforts in a wider international context and with a view to creating conditions which ensure that competition is not distorted.

[. . .]

Declaration by the European Community on the Rights for the EFTA States before the EC Court of Justice

1. In order to reinforce the legal homogeneity within the EEA through the opening of intervention possibilities for EFTA States and the EFTA Surveillance Authority before the EC Court of Justice, the Community will amend Articles 20 and 37 of the Statute of the Court of Justice and the Court of First Instance of the European Communities.

2. In addition, the Community will take the necessary measures to ensure that EFTA States, in so far as the implementation of Articles 2 (2) (b) and 6 of Protocol 24 to the EEA Agreement is concerned, will have the same rights as EC Member States under Article 9 (9) of Regulation (EEC) No 4064/89.

Declaration by the European Community on the Rights of Lawyers of the EFTA States under Community Law

The Community undertakes to amend the Statute of the Court of Justice and the Court of First Instance of the European Communities so as to ensure that agents appointed for each case, when representing an EFTA State or the EFTA Surveillance Authority, may be assisted by an adviser or by a lawyer entitled to practise before a court of an EFTA State. It also undertakes to ensure that lawyers entitled to practise before a court of an EFTA State may represent individuals and economic operators before the Court of Justice and the Court of First Instance of the European Communities.

Such agents, advisers and lawyers shall, when they appear before the Court of Justice and the Court of First Instance of the European Communities, enjoy the rights and immunities necessary to the independent exercise of their duties, under the conditions to be laid down in the rules of procedure of those Courts.

In addition, the Community will take the necessary measures in order to ensure lawyers of the EFTA States the same rights as to legal privilege under Community law as lawyers of EC Member States.

[. . .]

Agreed Minutes

of the negotiations for an Agreement between the European Economic Community, the European Coal and Steel Community and their Member States and the EFTA States on the European Economic Area

The Contracting Parties agreed that:

Ad Article 26 and Protocol 13

before the entry into force of the Agreement the Community shall, together with the interested EFTA States, examine whether the conditions are fulfilled in which Article 26 of the Agreement, irrespective of the provisions set forth in the first paragraph in Protocol 13, will apply between the Community and the EFTA States concerned in the fisheries sector;

Ad Article 56 (3)
the word 'appreciable' in Article 56 (3) of the Agreement is understood to have the meaning it has in the Commission Notice of 3 September 1986 on agreements of minor importance which do not fall under Article 85 (1) of the Treaty establishing the European Economic Community (OJ No C 231, 12.9.1986, p. 2);

[. . .]

Ad Article 123
they would not make improper use of provisions in Article 123 to prevent the disclosure of information in the field of competition;

[. . .]

2. AGREEMENT BETWEEN THE EFTA STATES ON THE ESTABLISHMENT OF A SURVEILLANCE AUTHORITY AND A COURT OF JUSTICE (ESA/COURT AGREEMENT)

THE REPUBLIC OF AUSTRIA, THE REPUBLIC OF FINLAND, THE REPUBLIC OF ICELAND, THE PRINCIPALITY OF LIECHTENSTEIN, THE KINGDOM OF NORWAY, THE KINGDOM OF SWEDEN AND THE SWISS CONFEDERATION,

HAVING REGARD to the EEA Agreement;

CONSIDERING that, in accordance with Article 108 (1) of the EEA Agreement, the EFTA States shall establish an independent surveillance authority (EFTA Surveillance Authority) as well as create procedures similar to those existing in the European Community including procedures for ensuring the fulfilment of the obligations under the EEA Agreement and for control of the legality of acts of the EFTA Surveillance Authority regarding competition;

FURTHER CONSIDERING that, in accordance with Article 108 (2) of the EEA Agreement, the EFTA States shall establish a court of justice of the EFTA States;

RECALLING the objective of the Contracting Parties to the EEA Agreement, in full deference to the independence of the courts, to arrive at and maintain a uniform interpretation and application of the EEA Agreement and those provisions of the Community legislation which are substantially reproduced in that Agreement and to arrive at an equal treatment of individuals and economic operators as regards the four freedoms and the conditions of competition;

REITERATING that the EFTA Surveillance Authority and the Commission of the European Communities shall co-operate, exchange information and consult each other on surveillance policy issues and individual cases;

CONSIDERING that the preambles to acts adopted in application of the Treaties establishing the

European Economic Community and the European Coal and Steel Community shall, in so far as those acts correspond to the provisions of Protocols 1 to 4 and to the provisions of the acts corresponding to those listed in Annexes I and II to this Agreement, be relevant to the extent necessary for the proper interpretation and application of the provisions of these Protocols and Annexes;

WHEREAS in the application of Protocols 1 to 4 to this Agreement due account shall be paid to the legal and administrative practices of the Commission of the European Communities prior to the entry into force of this Agreement;

HAVE DECIDED to conclude the following Agreement:

PART I

Article 1

For the purposes of this Agreement:

(a) the term 'EEA Agreement' means the main part of the EEA Agreement, its Protocols and Annexes as well as the acts referred to therein;

(b) the term 'EFTA State' means a Contracting Party which is a Member of the European Free Trade Association and is a Party to the EEA Agreement and to the present Agreement.

Article 2

The EFTA States shall take all appropriate measures, whether general or particular, to ensure fulfilment of the obligations arising out of this Agreement.

They shall abstain from any measure which could jeopardize the attainment of the objectives of this Agreement.

Article 3

1. Without prejudice to future developments of case law, the provisions of Protocols 1 to 4 and the provisions of the acts corresponding to those listed in Annexes I and II to this Agreement, in so far as they are identical in substance to corresponding rules of the Treaty establishing the European Economic Community and the Treaty establishing the European Coal and Steel Community and to acts adopted in application of these two Treaties, shall in their implementation and application be interpreted in conformity with the relevant rulings of the Court of Justice of the European Communities given prior to the date of signature of the EEA Agreement.

2. In the interpretation and application of the EEA Agreement and this Agreement, the EFTA Surveillance Authority and the EFTA Court shall pay due account to the principles laid down by the relevant rulings by the Court of Justice of the European Communities given after the date of signature of the EEA Agreement and which concern the interpretation of that Agreement or of such rules of the Treaty establishing the European Economic Community and the Treaty establishing the European Coal and Steel Community in so far as they are identical in substance to the provisions of the EEA Agreement or to the provisions of Protocols 1 to 4 and the provisions of the acts corresponding to those listed in Annexes I and II to the present Agreement.

PART II
THE EFTA SURVEILLANCE AUTHORITY

Article 4
An independent surveillance authority among the EFTA States, the EFTA Surveillance Authority, is hereby established.

Article 5
1. The EFTA Surveillance Authority shall, in accordance with the provisions of this Agreement and the provisions of the EEA Agreement and in order to ensure the proper functioning of the EEA Agreement:

(a) ensure the fulfilment by the EFTA States of their obligations under the EEA Agreement and this Agreement;
(b) ensure the application of the rules of the EEA Agreement on competition;
(c) monitor the application of the EEA Agreement by the other Contracting Parties to that Agreement.

2. To this end, the EFTA Surveillance Authority shall:

(a) take decisions and other measures in cases provided for in this Agreement and in the EEA Agreement;
(b) formulate recommendations, deliver opinions and issue notices or guidelines on matters dealt with in the EEA Agreement, if that Agreement or the present Agreement expressly so provides or if the EFTA Surveillance Authority considers it necessary;
(c) carry out co-operation, exchange of information and consultations with the Commission of the European Communities as provided for in this Agreement and the EEA Agreement;
(d) carry out the functions which, through the application of Protocol 1 to the EEA Agreement, follow from the acts referred to in the Annexes to that Agreement, as specified in Protocol 1 to the present Agreement.

Article 6
In accordance with the provisions of this Agreement and the EEA Agreement, the EFTA Surveillance Authority may, in carrying out the duties assigned to it, request all the necessary information from the Governments and competent authorities of the EFTA States and from undertakings and associations of undertakings.

Article 7
The EFTA Surveillance Authority shall consist of seven members, who shall be chosen on the grounds of their general competence and whose independence is beyond doubt.

Only nationals of EFTA States may be members of the EFTA Surveillance Authority.

Article 8
The members of the EFTA Surveillance Authority shall be completely independent in the performance of their duties. They shall neither seek nor take instructions from any Government or other body. They shall refrain from any action incompatible with their duties. Each EFTA State undertakes to respect this principle and not to seek to influence the members of the EFTA Surveillance Authority in the performance of their tasks.

The members of the EFTA Surveillance Authority shall not, during their term of office, engage in any other occupation, whether gainful or not.

When entering upon their duties they shall give a solemn undertaking that, both during and after their term of office, they will respect the obligations arising therefrom and in particular their duty to behave with integrity and discretion as regards the acceptance, after they have ceased to hold office, of certain appointments or benefits. In the event of any breach of these obligations, the EFTA Court may, on application by the EFTA Surveillance Authority, rule that the member concerned be, according to the circumstances, either compulsorily retired or deprived of his right to a pension or other benefits in its stead.

Article 9

The members of the EFTA Surveillance Authority shall be appointed by common accord of the Governments of the EFTA States.

Their term of office shall be four years. It shall be renewable.

Article 10

Apart from normal replacement, or death, the duties of a member of the EFTA Surveillance Authority shall end when he resigns or is compulsorily retired. The vacancy thus caused shall be filled for the remainder of the member's term of office.

Article 11

If a member of the EFTA Surveillance Authority no longer fulfils the conditions required for the performance of his duties or if he has been guilty of serious misconduct, the EFTA Court may, on application by the EFTA Surveillance Authority, compulsorily retire him.

Article 12

The President of the EFTA Surveillance Authority shall be appointed from among its members for a period of two years by common accord of the Governments of the EFTA States.

Article 13

The EFTA Surveillance Authority shall adopt its own rules of procedure.

Article 14

The EFTA Surveillance Authority shall appoint officials and other servants to enable it to function.

The EFTA Surveillance Authority may consult experts or decide to set up such committees and other bodies as it considers necessary to assist it in accomplishing its tasks.

In the performance of their duties, officials and other servants of the EFTA Surveillance Authority shall neither seek nor accept instructions from any Government or from any body external to the EFTA Surveillance Authority.

Members of the EFTA Surveillance Authority, officials and other servants thereof as well as members of committees shall be required, even after their duties have ceased, not to disclose information of the kind covered by the obligation of professional secrecy, in particular information about undertakings, their business relations or their cost components.

Article 15
The EFTA Surveillance Authority shall act by majority of its Members. In the event of an equal number of votes, the President shall have a casting vote.

The rules of procedure shall determine the quorum.

Article 16
Decisions of the EFTA Surveillance Authority shall state the reasons on which they are based.

Article 17
Save as otherwise provided in this Agreement or in the EEA Agreement, decisions of the EFTA Surveillance Authority shall be notified to those to whom they are addressed and shall take effect upon such notification.

Article 18
Decisions of the EFTA Surveillance Authority shall be published in accordance with the provisions of this Agreement and of the EEA Agreement.

Article 19
Decisions of the EFTA Surveillance Authority which impose a pecuniary obligation on persons other than States, shall be enforceable in accordance with Article 110 of the EEA Agreement.

Article 20
Individuals and economic operators shall be entitled to address and be addressed by the EFTA Surveillance Authority in any official language of the EFTA States and the European Communities as regards notifications, applications and complaints. This shall also cover all instances of a proceeding, whether it be opened on notification, application or complaint or ex officio by the EFTA Surveillance Authority.

Article 21
The EFTA Surveillance Authority shall annually publish a general report on its activities.

Part III

The EFTA States' Fulfilment of their Obligations under the EEA Agreement and the Present Agreement

Article 22
In order to ensure the proper application of the EEA Agreement, the EFTA Surveillance Authority shall monitor the application of the provisions of the EEA Agreement and of the present Agreement by the EFTA States.

Article 23
The EFTA Surveillance Authority shall, in accordance with Articles 22 and 37 of this Agreement and Articles 65 (1) and 109 of, and Annexe XVI to, the EEA Agreement as well as subject to the provisions contained in Protocol 2 to the present Agreement, ensure that the provisions of the EEA Agreement concerning procurement are applied by the EFTA States.

Article 24

The EFTA Surveillance Authority shall, in accordance with Articles 49, 61 to 64 and 109 of, and Protocols 14, 26, 27, and Annexes XIII, section I (iv), and XV to, the EEA Agreement, as well as subject to the provisions contained in Protocol 3 to the present Agreement, give effect to the provisions of the EEA Agreement concerning State aid as well as ensure that those provisions are applied by the EFTA States.

In application of Article 5 (2) (b), the EFTA Surveillance Authority shall, in particular, upon the entry into force of this Agreement, adopt acts corresponding to those listed in Annexe I.

Article 25

The EFTA Surveillance Authority shall, in accordance with Articles 53 to 60 and 109 of, and Protocols 21 to 25 and Annex XIV to, the EEA Agreement, as well as subject to the provisions contained in Protocol 4 to the present Agreement, give effect to the provisions of the EEA Agreement relating to the implementation of the competition rules applicable to undertakings as well as ensure that those provisions are applied.

In application of Article 5 (2) (b), the EFTA Surveillance Authority shall, in particular, upon the entry into force of this Agreement, adopt acts corresponding to those listed in Annexe II.

Article 26

Provisions governing the co-operation, exchange of information and consultation between the EFTA Surveillance Authority and the Commission of the European Communities concerning the application of the EEA Agreement are laid down in Article 109 as well as in Articles 58 and 62 (2) of, and Protocols 1, 23, 24, and 27 to, the EEA Agreement.

Part IV
The EFTA Court

Article 27

A court of justice of the EFTA States, hereinafter referred to as the EFTA Court, is hereby established. It shall function in accordance with the provisions of this Agreement and of the EEA Agreement.

Article 28

The EFTA Court shall consist of seven judges.

Article 29

The EFTA Court shall sit in plenary session. Decisions of the Court shall be valid only when an uneven number of its members is sitting in the deliberations. Decisions of the Court shall be valid if five members are sitting. At the request of the Court, the Governments of the EFTA States may, by common accord, allow it to establish chambers.

Article 30

The Judges shall be chosen from persons whose independence is beyond doubt and who possess the qualifications required for appointment to the highest judicial offices in their respective countries or who are jurisconsults of recognized competence. They shall be appointed by common accord of the Governments of the EFTA States for a term of six years.

Every three years there shall be a partial replacement of the Judges. Three and four Judges shall be replaced alternately. The three Judges to be replaced after the first three years shall be determined by lot.

Retiring Judges shall be eligible for reappointment.

The Judges shall elect the President of the EFTA Court from among their number for a term of three years. He may be re-elected.

Article 31

If the EFTA Surveillance Authority considers that an EFTA State has failed to fulfil an obligation under the EEA Agreement or of this Agreement, it shall, unless otherwise provided for in this Agreement, deliver a reasoned opinion on the matter after giving the State concerned the opportunity to submit its observations.

If the State concerned does not comply with the opinion within the period laid down by the EFTA Surveillance Authority, the latter may bring the matter before the EFTA Court.

Article 32

The EFTA Court shall have jurisdiction in actions concerning the settlement of disputes between two or more EFTA States regarding the interpretation or application of the EEA Agreement, the Agreement on a Standing Committee of the EFTA States or the present Agreement.

Article 33

The EFTA States concerned shall take the necessary measures to comply with the judgments of the EFTA Court.

Article 34

The EFTA Court shall have jurisdiction to give advisory opinions on the interpretation of the EEA Agreement.

Where such a question is raised before any court or tribunal in an EFTA State, that court or tribunal may, if it considers it necessary to enable it to give judgment, request the EFTA Court to give such an opinion.

An EFTA State may in its internal legislation limit the right to request such an advisory opinion to courts and tribunals against whose decisions there is no judicial remedy under national law.

Article 35

The EFTA Court shall have unlimited jurisdiction in regard to penalties imposed by the EFTA Surveillance Authority.

Article 36

The EFTA Court shall have jurisdiction in actions brought by an EFTA State against a decision of the EFTA Surveillance Authority on grounds of lack of competence, infringement of an essential procedural requirement, or infringement of this Agreement, of the EEA Agreement or of any rule of law relating to their application, or misuse of powers.

Any natural or legal person may, under the same conditions, institute proceedings before the EFTA Court against a decision of the EFTA Surveillance Authority addressed to that person or against a decision addressed to another person, if it is of direct and individual concern to the former.

The proceedings provided for in this Article shall be instituted within two months of the publication of the measure, or of its notification to the plaintiff, or, in the absence thereof, of the day on which it came to the knowledge of the latter, as the case may be.

If the action is well founded the decision of the EFTA Surveillance Authority shall be declared void.

Article 37

Should the EFTA Surveillance Authority, in infringement of this Agreement or the provisions of the EEA Agreement, fail to act, an EFTA State may bring an action before the EFTA Court to have the infringement established.

The action shall be admissible only if the EFTA Surveillance Authority has first been called upon to act. If, within two months of being so called upon, the EFTA Surveillance Authority has not defined its position, the action may be brought within a further period of two months.

Any natural or legal person may, under the conditions laid down in the preceding paragraph, complain to the EFTA Court that the EFTA Surveillance Authority has failed to address to that person any decision.

Article 38

If a decision of the EFTA Surveillance Authority has been declared void or if it has been established that the EFTA Surveillance Authority, in infringement of this Agreement or of the provisions of the EEA Agreement, has failed to act, the EFTA Surveillance Authority shall take the necessary measures to comply with the judgment.

This obligation shall not affect any obligation which may result from the application of Article 46, second paragraph.

Article 39

Save as otherwise provided for in Protocol 7 to this Agreement, the EFTA Court shall have jurisdiction in actions against the EFTA Surveillance Authority relating to compensation for damage provided for in Article 46, second paragraph.

Article 40

Actions brought before the EFTA Court shall not have suspensory effect. The EFTA Court may, however, if it considers that circumstances so require, order that application of the contested act be suspended.

Article 41

The EFTA Court may in any case before it prescribe any necessary interim measures.

PART V

GENERAL AND FINAL PROVISIONS

Article 42

The Protocols and Annexes to this Agreement shall form an integral part thereof.

Article 43
1. The Statute of the EFTA Court is laid down in Protocol 5 to this Agreement.
2. The EFTA Court shall adopt its rules of procedure to be approved by the Governments of the EFTA States by common accord.

Article 44
1. The legal capacity, privileges and immunities to be recognized and granted by the EFTA States in connection with the EFTA Surveillance Authority and the EFTA Court are laid down in Protocols 6 and 7 to this Agreement, respectively.
2. The EFTA Surveillance Authority and the EFTA Court, respectively, may conclude with the Government of the States in whose territory their seats are situated an agreement relating to the privileges and immunities to be recognized and granted in connection with it.

Article 45
The seat of the EFTA Surveillance Authority and the EFTA Court, respectively, shall be determined by common accord of the Governments of the EFTA States.

Article 46
The contractual liability of the EFTA Surveillance Authority shall be governed by the law applicable to the contract in question.

In the case of non-contractual liability, the EFTA Surveillance Authority shall, in accordance with the general principles of law, make good any damage caused by it, or by its servants, in the performance of its duties.

Article 47
The Governments of the EFTA States shall, on a proposal from the EFTA Surveillance Authority and after consulting a committee consisting of the members of Parliament of the EFTA States who are members of the EEA Joint Parliamentary Committee, each year before 1 January by common accord establish a budget for the coming year and the apportionment of those expenses between the EFTA States.

The EFTA Surveillance Authority shall be consulted before a decision modifying or amending its proposal for a budget is adopted.

Article 48
The Governments of the EFTA States shall, on a proposal from the EFTA Court, each year before 1 January by common accord establish a budget for the EFTA Court for the coming year and the apportionment of those expenses between them.

Article 49
The Governments of the EFTA States may, unless otherwise provided in this Agreement, on a proposal from or after hearing the EFTA Surveillance Authority, by common accord amend the main Agreement as well as Protocols 1 to 4 and 6 and 7. Such an amendment shall be submitted to the EFTA States for acceptance and shall enter into force provided it is approved by all EFTA States. Instruments of acceptance shall be deposited with the Government of Sweden which shall notify all other EFTA States.

Article 50

1. Any EFTA State which withdraws from the EEA Agreement shall *ipso facto* cease to be a Party to the present Agreement on the same day as that withdrawal takes effect.

2. Any EFTA State which accedes to the European Community shall *ipso facto* cease to be a Party to the present Agreement on the same day as that accession takes effect.

3. The Governments of the remaining EFTA States shall, by common accord, decide on the necessary amendments to be made to the present Agreement.

Article 51

Any EFTA State acceding to the EEA Agreement shall accede to the present Agreement on such terms and conditions as may be laid down by common accord by the EFTA States. The instrument of accession shall be deposited with the Government of Sweden which shall notify the other EFTA States.

Article 52

The EFTA States shall communicate to the EFTA Surveillance Authority the measures taken for the implementation of this Agreement.

Article 53

1. This Agreement, drawn up in a single copy and authentic in the English language, shall be ratified by the Contracting Parties in accordance with their respective constitutional requirements.

Before the entry into force of this Agreement, it shall also be drawn up and authenticated in Finnish, French, German, Icelandic, Italian, Norwegian and Swedish.

2. This Agreement shall be deposited with the Government of Sweden which shall transmit a certified copy to each EFTA State.

The instruments of ratification shall be deposited with the Government of Sweden which shall notify all other EFTA States.

3. This Agreement shall enter into force on 1 January 1993 provided that the EEA Agreement enters into force on that day and provided that the instruments of ratification of the present Agreement have been deposited by all EFTA States.

If the EEA Agreement does not enter into force on that day the present Agreement shall enter into force on the day the EEA Agreement enters into force or when all instruments of ratification of the present Agreement have been deposited by all EFTA States, whichever day is the later.

[. . .]

Protocol 2

On the Functions and Powers of the EFTA Surveillance Authority in the Field of Procurement

Article 1

1. Without prejudice to Article 31 of this Agreement, the EFTA Surveillance Authority may invoke the procedure for which the present Article provides when, prior to a contract being concluded, it considers that a clear and manifest infringement of the provisions of the EEA

Agreement in the field of procurement has been committed during a contract award procedure falling within the scope of the acts referred to in points 2 and 3 of Annex XVI to the EEA Agreement.

2. The EFTA Surveillance Authority shall notify the EFTA State and the contracting authority concerned of the reasons which have led it to conclude that a clear and manifest infringement has been committed and request its correction.

3. Within 21 days of receipt of the notification referred to in paragraph 2, the EFTA State concerned shall communicate to the EFTA Surveillance Authority:

(a) its confirmation that the infringement has been corrected; or
(b) a reasoned submission as to why no correction has been made; or
(c) a notice to the effect that the contract award procedure has been suspended either by the contracting authority on its own initiative or on the basis of the powers specified in Article 2 (1) (a) of the act referred to in point 5 Annex XVI to the EEA Agreement.

4. A reasoned submission in accordance with paragraph 3 (b) of this Article may rely among other matters on the fact that the alleged infringement is already the subject of judicial or other review proceedings or of a review as referred to in Article 2 (8) of the act referred to in point 5 of Annex XVI to the EEA Agreement. In such a case, the EFTA State shall inform the EFTA Surveillance Authority of the result of those proceedings as soon as it becomes known.

5. Where notice has been given that a contract award procedure has been suspended in accordance with paragraph 3 (c) of this Article, the EFTA State shall notify the EFTA Surveillance Authority when the suspension is lifted or another contract procedure relating in whole or in part to the same subject matter is begun. That notification shall confirm that the alleged infringement has been corrected or include a reasoned submission as to why no correction has been made.

Article 2

1. Not later than 1 January 1996, the EFTA Surveillance Authority shall, together with an advisory committee composed of representatives of the EFTA States, review the manner in which the provisions of this Protocol and the provisions of the act referred to in point 5 of Annex XVI of the EEA Agreement have been implemented and, if necessary, make proposals for amendments. The committee shall have as Chairman a representative of the EFTA Surveillance Authority. The committee shall be convened by its Chairman either on his own initiative or at the request of one of its members.

2. By 1 March each year the EFTA States shall communicate to the EFTA Surveillance Authority information on the operation of their national review procedures during the preceding calendar year. The nature of the information shall be determined by the EFTA Surveillance Authority in consultation with the advisory committee.

Protocol 3
On the Functions and Powers of the EFTA Surveillance Authority in the Field of State Aid

Article 1

1. The EFTA Surveillance Authority shall, in co-operation with the EFTA States, keep

under constant review all systems of aid existing in those States. It shall propose to the latter any appropriate measures required by the progressive development or by the functioning of the EEA Agreement.

2. If, after giving notice to the parties concerned to submit their comments, the EFTA Surveillance Authority finds that aid granted by an EFTA State or through EFTA State resources is not compatible with the functioning of the EEA Agreement having regard to Article 61 of the EEA Agreement, or that such aid is being misused, it shall decide that the EFTA State concerned shall abolish or alter such aid within a period of time to be determined by the Authority.

If the EFTA State concerned does not comply with this decision within the prescribed time, the EFTA Surveillance Authority or any other interested EFTA State may, in derogation from Articles 31 and 32 of this Agreement, refer the matter to the EFTA Court directly.

On application by an EFTA State, the EFTA States may, by common accord, decide that aid which that State is granting or intends to grant shall be considered to be compatible with the functioning of the EEA Agreement, in derogation from the provisions of Article 61 of the EEA Agreement, if such a decision is justified by exceptional circumstances. If, as regards the aid in question, the EFTA Surveillance Authority has already initiated the procedure provided for in the first subparagraph of this paragraph, the fact that the State concerned has made its application to the EFTA States shall have the effect of suspending that procedure until the EFTA States, by common accord, have made their attitude known.

If, however, the EFTA States have not made their attitude known within three months of the said application being made, the EFTA Surveillance Authority shall give its decision on the case.

3. The EFTA Surveillance Authority shall be informed, in sufficient time to enable it to submit its comments, of any plans to grant or alter aid. If it considers that any such plan is not compatible with the functioning of the EEA Agreement having regard to Article 61 of the EEA Agreement, it shall without delay initiate the procedure provided for in paragraph 2. The State concerned shall not put its proposed measures into effect until this procedure has resulted in a final decision.

Article 2

1. An advisory committee shall assist the EFTA Surveillance Authority in its examination of aid granted for transport by rail, road and inland waterway. The committee shall have as Chairman a representative of the EFTA Surveillance Authority and shall consist of representatives appointed by each EFTA State. Not less than ten days' notice of meetings of the committee shall be given and such notice shall include details of the agenda. This period may be reduced for urgent cases.

2. The committee may examine, and give an opinion on, all questions concerning the operation of the provisions of the EEA Agreement on the granting of aid in the transport sector.

3. The committee shall be kept informed of the nature and amount of aid granted to transport undertakings and, generally, of all relevant details concerning such aid, as soon as the latter is notified to the EFTA Surveillance Authority in accordance with the provisions laid down in Annexe XIII, section I (iv), to the EEA Agreement governing the granting of aid in the transport sector.

Protocol 4
On the Functions and Powers of the EFTA Surveillance Authority in the Field of Competition

Table of contents with references to the corresponding EC acts or provisions of the EEA Agreement

Part I General Rules

Chapter I Introduction

Article 1
This Protocol sets out provisions for the implementation of competition rules applicable to undertakings in the EEA Agreement, and in particular for the implementation of Protocols 21 to 25 to that Agreement.

Article 2
1. Chapters II to V, XIII and XIV apply to all sectors covered by the EEA Agreement unless otherwise provided.

2. Chapters II to IV shall not apply to agreements, decisions or concerted practices in the transport sector which have as their object or effect the fixing of transport rates and conditions, the limitation or control of the supply of transport or the sharing of transport markets; nor shall they apply to the abuse of a dominant position, within the meaning of Article 54 of the EEA Agreement, within the transport market. Such cases are covered by Chapters VI to XII.

3. Chapters II to V, XIII and XIV shall not apply to cases covered by Chapter XV, on the conditions set out therein.

Article 3
Chapter XVI sets out the transitional rules applicable for Chapters II to XV.

Article 4
The EFTA Surveillance Authority may, in accordance with Article 49 of this Agreement, submit to the Governments of the EFTA States proposals for amendments to this Protocol including its Appendices.

CHAPTER II GENERAL PROCEDURAL RULES IMPLEMENTING ARTICLES 53 AND 54 OF THE EEA AGREEMENT

Article 1
Basic provision
Without prejudice to Article 6 of this Chapter and Article 3 of Chapter XVI, agreements, decisions and concerted practices of the kind described in Article 53 (1) of the EEA Agreement and the abuse of a dominant position in the market, within the meaning of Article 54 of the EEA Agreement, shall be prohibited, no prior decision to that effect being required.

Article 2
Negative clearance
Upon application by the undertakings or associations of undertakings concerned, the EFTA Surveillance Authority may certify that, on the basis of the facts in its possession, there are no grounds under Article 53 (1) or Article 54 of the EEA Agreement for action on its part in respect of an agreement, decision or practice.

Article 3
Termination of infringements
1. Where the EFTA Surveillance Authority, upon application or upon its own initiative, finds that there is infringement of Article 53 or Article 54 of the EEA Agreement, it may by decision require the undertakings or associations of undertakings concerned to bring such infringement to an end.

2. Those entitled to make application are:

(a) EFTA States;
(b) natural or legal persons who claim a legitimate interest.

3. Without prejudice to the other provisions of this Protocol, the EFTA Surveillance Authority may, before taking a decision under paragraph 1, address to the undertakings or associations of undertakings concerned recommendations for termination of the infringement.

Article 4
Notification of new agreements, decisions and practices
1. Agreements, decisions and concerted practices of the kind described in Article 53 (1) of the EEA Agreement which come into existence after the entry into force of the EEA

Agreement and in respect of which the parties seek application of Article 53 (3) of the EEA Agreement shall be notified to the EFTA Surveillance Authority pursuant to Article 56 of the EEA Agreement, the rules referred to in Articles 1 to 3 of Protocol 21 and the rules referred to in Protocol 23 to the EEA Agreement, as well as in Chapters III, VI, VII, IX, X, XI, XII and XV. Until they have been notified, no decision in application of Article 53 (3) may be taken.

2. Paragraph 1 shall not apply to agreements, decisions and concerted practices where:

(a) the only parties thereto are undertakings from one EC Member State or from one EFTA State and the agreements, decisions or concerted practices do not relate either to imports or to exports between Contracting Parties to the EEA Agreement;

(b) not more than two undertakings are party thereto, and the agreements only:

  (i) restrict the freedom of one party to the contract in determining the prices or conditions of business upon which the goods which he has obtained from the other party to the contract may be resold; or

  (ii) impose restrictions on the exercise of the rights of the assignee or user of industrial property rights—in particular patents, utility models, designs or trademarks—or of the person entitled under a contract to the assignment, or grant, of the right to use a method of manufacture or knowledge relating to the use and to the application of industrial processes;

(c) they have as their sole object:

  (i) the development or uniform application of standards or types; or

  (ii) joint research or development; or

  (iii) specialization in the manufacture of products including agreements necessary for achieving this:

    – where the products which are the subject of specialization do not, in a substantial part of the territory covered by this Agreement, represent more than 15% of the volume of business done in identical products or those considered by consumers to be similar by reason of their characteristics, price and use; and

    – where the total annual turnover of the participating undertakings does not exceed 200 million ECU.

These agreements, decisions and concerted practices may be notified to the EFTA Surveillance Authority pursuant to Article 56 of the EEA Agreement, the rules referred to in Articles 1 to 3 of Protocol 21 and the rules referred to in Protocol 23 to the EEA Agreement, as well as in Chapters III, VI, VII, IX, X, XI, XII and XV.

Article 5
Notification of existing agreements, decisions and practices
(See Article 1 of Chapter XVI)

Article 6
Decisions pursuant to Article 53(3) of the EEA Agreement

1. Whenever the EFTA Surveillance Authority takes a decision pursuant to Article 53 (3) of the EEA Agreement, it shall specify therein the date from which the decision shall take effect. Such date shall not be earlier than the date of notification.

2. The second sentence of paragraph 1 shall not apply to agreements, decisions or

concerted practices falling within Article 4 (2) of this Chapter and Article 1 (2) of Chapter XVI, nor to those falling within Article 1 (1) of Chapter XVI which have been notified within the time-limit specified in Article 1 (1) of Chapter XVI.

Article 7
Special provisions for existing agreements, decisions and practices
(See Article 3 of Chapter XVI)

Article 8
Duration and revocation of decisions under Article 53 (3)
1. A decision in application of Article 53 (3) of the EEA Agreement shall be issued for a specified period and conditions and obligations may be attached thereto.

2. A decision may on application be renewed if the requirements of Article 53 (3) of the EEA Agreement continue to be satisfied.

3. The EFTA Surveillance Authority may revoke or amend its decision or prohibit specified acts by the parties:

(a) where there has been a change in any of the facts which were basic to the making of the decision;
(b) where the parties commit a breach of any obligation attached to the decision;
(c) where the decision is based on incorrect information or was induced by deceit;
(d) where the parties abuse the exemption from the provisions of Article 53 (1) of the EEA Agreement granted to them by the decision.

In cases to which subparagraphs (b), (c) or (d) apply, the decision may be revoked with retroactive effect.

Article 9
Powers
1. Subject to review of its decision by the EFTA Court in accordance with Article 108 (2) of the EEA Agreement and with the relevant provisions of this Agreement, the EFTA Surveillance Authority shall have sole power to declare Article 53 (1) inapplicable pursuant to Article 53 (3) of the EEA Agreement on the conditions set out in Article 56 of the EEA Agreement.

2. The EFTA Surveillance Authority shall have power to apply Article 53 (1) and Article 54 of the EEA Agreement; this power may be exercised notwithstanding that the time-limits specified in Articles 1 (1) and 3 (2) of Chapter XVI relating to notification have not expired.

3. As long as the EFTA Surveillance Authority has not initiated any procedure under Articles 2, 3 or 6, the authorities of the EFTA States shall remain competent to apply Article 53 (1) and Article 54; they shall remain competent in this respect notwithstanding that the time-limits specified in Articles 1 (1) and 3 (2) of Chapter XVI relating to notification have not expired.

Article 10
Liaison with the authorities of the EFTA States
1. The EFTA Surveillance Authority shall forthwith transmit to the competent authorities of the EFTA States a copy of the applications and notifications together with copies of the most important documents lodged with the EFTA Surveillance Authority for the purpose of

establishing the existence of infringements of Articles 53 or 54 of the EEA Agreement or of obtaining negative clearance or a decision in application of Article 53 (3).

The EFTA Surveillance Authority shall forthwith transmit to the competent authorities of the EFTA States a copy of notifications, complaints and information on opening of ex officio procedures received from the EC Commission pursuant to Articles 2 and 10 of Protocol 23 to the EEA Agreement.

The EFTA Surveillance Authority shall forthwith transmit to the competent authorities of the EFTA States a copy of documents received from the EC Commission pursuant to Article 7 of Protocol 23 to the EEA Agreement.

2. The EFTA Surveillance Authority shall carry out the procedure set out in the first subparagraph of paragraph 1 in close and constant liaison with the competent authorities of the EFTA States; such authorities shall have the right to express their views upon that procedure.

3. An Advisory Committee on Competition shall be consulted prior to the taking of any decision following upon a procedure under the first subparagraph of paragraph 1, and of any decision concerning the renewal, amendment or revocation of a decision pursuant to Article 53 (3) of the EEA Agreement.

The Advisory Committee shall be consulted prior to a proposal referred to in Article 22.

4. The Advisory Committee shall be composed of officials competent in the matter of restrictive practices and monopolies. Each EFTA State shall appoint an official to represent it who, if prevented from attending, may be replaced by another official.

The EC Commission and the EC Member States shall be entitled to be present in the Advisory Committee and to express their views therein. However, their representatives shall not have the right to vote.

5. The consultation shall take place at a joint meeting convened by the EFTA Surveillance Authority; such meeting shall be held not earlier than fourteen days after dispatch of the notice convening it. The notice shall, in respect of each case to be examined, be accompanied by a summary of the case together with an indication of the most important documents, and a preliminary draft decision.

In view of the participation provided for in the second subparagraph of paragraph 4, the EC Commission shall receive an invitation to the meeting and the relevant information as provided for in Article 6 of Protocol 23 to the EEA Agreement.

6. The Advisory Committee may deliver an opinion notwithstanding that some of its members or their alternates are not present. A report of the outcome of the consultative proceedings shall be annexed to the draft decision. It shall not be made public.

Article 11

Requests for information

1. In carrying out the duties assigned to it by Articles 55 and 58 of the EEA Agreement, by the provisions set out in Protocol 23 and in Annexe XIV to the EEA Agreement or by the provisions of this Chapter, the EFTA Surveillance Authority may obtain all necessary information from the Governments and competent authorities of the EFTA States and from undertakings and associations of undertakings.

2. When sending a request for information to an undertaking or association of undertakings, the EFTA Surveillance Authority shall at the same time forward a copy of the request to the competent authority of the EFTA State in whose territory the seat of the undertaking or association of undertakings is situated.

3. In its request the EFTA Surveillance Authority shall state the legal basis and the purpose of the request and also the penalties provided for in Article 15 (1) (b) for supplying incorrect information.

4. The owners of the undertakings or their representatives and, in the case of legal persons, companies or firms, or of associations having no legal personality, the persons authorized to represent them by law or by their constitution, shall supply the information requested.

5. Where an undertaking or association of undertakings does not supply the information requested within the time-limit fixed by the EFTA Surveillance Authority, or supplies incomplete information, the EFTA Surveillance Authority shall by decision require the information to be supplied. The decision shall specify what information is required, fix an appropriate time-limit within which it is to be supplied and indicate the penalties provided for in Article 15 (1) (b) and Article 16 (1) (c) and the right to have the decision reviewed by the EFTA Court in accordance with Article 108 (2) of the EEA Agreement and with the relevant provisions of this Agreement, in particular Article 35.

6. The EFTA Surveillance Authority shall at the same time forward a copy of its decision to the competent authority of the EFTA State in whose territory the seat of the undertaking or association of undertakings is situated.

Article 12

Inquiry into sectors of the economy

1. If in any sector of the economy the trend of trade, price movements, inflexibility of prices or other circumstances suggest that in the economic sector concerned competition is being restricted or distorted within the territory covered by the EEA Agreement, the EFTA Surveillance Authority may decide, in accordance with the provisions of Protocol 23 to the EEA Agreement, to conduct a general inquiry into that economic sector and in the course thereof may request undertakings in the sector concerned to supply the information necessary for giving effect to the principles formulated in Articles 53 and 54 of the EEA Agreement and for carrying out the duties entrusted to the EFTA Surveillance Authority.

2. The EFTA Surveillance Authority may in particular request every undertaking or association of undertakings in the economic sector concerned to communicate to it all agreements, decisions and concerted practices which are exempt from notification by virtue of Article 4 (2) of this Chapter and Article 1 (2) of Chapter XVI.

3. When making inquiries pursuant to paragraph 2, the EFTA Surveillance Authority shall also request undertakings or groups of undertakings whose size suggests that they occupy a dominant position within the territory covered by the EEA Agreement or a substantial part thereof to supply to the EFTA Surveillance Authority such particulars of the structure of the undertakings and of their behaviour as are requisite to an appraisal of their position in the light of Article 54 of the EEA Agreement.

4. Article 10 (3) to (6) and Articles 11, 13 and 14 shall apply correspondingly.

Article 13

Investigations by the authorities of the EFTA States

1. At the request of the EFTA Surveillance Authority, the competent authorities of the EFTA States shall undertake the investigations which the EFTA Surveillance Authority considers to be necessary under Article 14 (1), or which it has ordered by decision pursuant to Article 14 (3). The officials of the competent authorities of the EFTA States responsible for

conducting these investigations shall exercise their powers upon production of an authorization in writing issued by the competent authority of the EFTA State in whose territory the investigation is to be made. Such authorization shall specify the subject matter and purpose of the investigation.

2. If so requested by the EFTA Surveillance Authority or by the competent authority of the EFTA State in whose territory the investigation is to be made, the officials of the EFTA Surveillance Authority may assist the officials of such authority in carrying out their duties.

Article 14
Investigating powers of the EFTA Surveillance Authority

1. In carrying out the duties assigned to it by Articles 55 and 58 of the EEA Agreement, by the provisions set out in Protocol 23 and in Annexe XIV to the EEA Agreement or by the provisions of this Chapter, the EFTA Surveillance Authority may undertake all necessary investigations into undertakings and associations of undertakings in the territory of an EFTA State. To this end the officials authorized by the EFTA Surveillance Authority are empowered:

(a) to examine the books and other business records;
(b) to take copies of or extracts from the books and business records;
(c) to ask for oral explanations on the spot;
(d) to enter any premises, land and means of transport of undertakings.

2. The officials of the EFTA Surveillance Authority authorized for the purpose of these investigations shall exercise their powers upon production of an authorization in writing specifying the subject matter and purpose of the investigation and the penalties provided for in Article 15 (1) (c) in cases where production of the required books or other business records is incomplete. In good time before the investigation, the EFTA Surveillance Authority shall inform the competent authority of the EFTA State in whose territory the same is to be made of the investigation and of the identity of the authorized officials. The EFTA Surveillance Authority shall also provide such an authorization to representatives of the EC Commission who shall take part in the investigation in accordance with Article 8 (4) of Protocol 23 to the EEA Agreement.

3. Undertakings and associations of undertakings shall submit to investigations ordered by decision of the EFTA Surveillance Authority. The decision shall specify the subject matter and purpose of the investigation, appoint the date on which it is to begin and indicate the penalties provided for in Article 15 (1) (c) and Article 16 (1) (d) and the right to have the decision reviewed by the EFTA Court in accordance with Article 108 (2) of the EEA Agreement and with the relevant provisions of this Agreement, in particular Article 35.

4. The EFTA Surveillance Authority shall take decisions referred to in paragraph 3 after consultation with the competent authority of the EFTA State in whose territory the investigation is to be made.

5. Officials of the competent authority of the EFTA State in whose territory the investigation is to be made may, at the request of such authority or of the EFTA Surveillance Authority, assist the officials of the EFTA Surveillance Authority in carrying out their duties.

6. Where an undertaking opposes an investigation ordered pursuant to this Article, the EFTA State concerned shall afford the necessary assistance to the officials authorized by the EFTA Surveillance Authority to enable them to make their investigation.

7. EFTA States shall, after consultation with the EFTA Surveillance Authority, take the necessary measures to this end within six months of the entry into force of the EEA Agreement.

Article 15

Fines

1. The EFTA Surveillance Authority may by decision impose on undertakings or associations of undertakings fines of from 100 to 5 000 ECU where, intentionally or negligently:

(a) they supply incorrect or misleading information in an application pursuant to Article 2 or in a notification pursuant to Article 4 of this Chapter or Article 1 of Chapter XVI; or
(b) they supply incorrect information in response to a request made pursuant to Article 11 (3) or (5) or to Article 12, or do not supply information within the time-limit fixed by a decision taken under Article 11 (5); or
(c) they produce the required books or other business records in incomplete form during investigations under Article 13 or 14, or refuse to submit to an investigation ordered by decision issued in implementation of Article 14 (3).

2. The EFTA Surveillance Authority may by decision impose on undertakings or associations of undertakings fines of from 1 000 to 1 000 000 ECU, or a sum in excess thereof but not exceeding 10% of the turnover in the preceding business year of each of the undertakings participating in the infringement where, either intentionally or negligently:

(a) they infringe Article 53 (1) or Article 54 of the EEA Agreement; or
(b) they commit a breach of any obligation imposed pursuant to Article 8 (1).

In fixing the amount of the fine, regard shall be had both to the gravity and to the duration of the infringement.

3. Article 10 (3) to (6) shall apply.

4. Decisions taken pursuant to paragraphs 1 and 2 shall not be of a criminal law nature.

5. The fines provided for in paragraph 2 (a) shall not be imposed in respect of acts taking place:

(a) after notification to the EFTA Surveillance Authority and before its decision in application of Article 53 (3) of the EEA Agreement, provided they fall within the limits of the activity described in the notification;
(b) before notification and in the course of agreements, decisions or concerted practices in existence at the date of entry into force of the EEA Agreement, provided that notification was effected within the time-limits specified in Articles 1 (1) and 3 (2) of Chapter XVI.

6. Paragraph 5 shall not have effect where the EFTA Surveillance Authority has informed the undertakings concerned that after preliminary examination it is of the opinion that Article 53 (1) of the EEA Agreement applies and that application of Article 53 (3) is not justified.

Article 16

Periodic penalty payments

1. The EFTA Surveillance Authority may by decision impose on undertakings or

associations of undertakings periodic penalty payments of from 50 to 1 000 ECU per day, calculated from the date appointed by the decision, in order to compel them:

(a) to put an end to an infringement of Articles 53 or 54 of the EEA Agreement, in accordance with a decision taken pursuant to Article 3 of this Chapter;
(b) to refrain from any act prohibited under Article 8 (3);
(c) to supply complete and correct information which it has requested by decision taken pursuant to Article 11 (5);
(d) to submit to an investigation which it has ordered by decision taken pursuant to Article 14 (3).

2. Where the undertakings or associations of undertakings have satisfied the obligation which it was the purpose of the periodic penalty payment to enforce, the EFTA Surveillance Authority may fix the total amount of the periodic penalty payment at a lower figure than that which would arise under the original decision.

3. Article 10 (3) to (6) shall apply.

Article 17

Review by the EFTA Court

The EFTA Court, in accordance with Article 108 (2) of the EEA Agreement and with the relevant provisions of this Agreement, shall have unlimited jurisdiction within the meaning of Article 35 of this Agreement to review decisions whereby the EFTA Surveillance Authority has fixed a fine or periodic penalty payment; it may cancel, reduce or increase the fine or periodic penalty payment imposed.

Article 18

ECU

For the purposes of applying Articles 15 to 17, 'ECU' means the ECU as defined by the competent authorities of the European Communities.

Article 19

Hearing of the parties and of third persons

1. Before taking decisions as provided for in Articles 2, 3, 6, 8, 15 and 16 of this Chapter and in Article 3 of Chapter XVI, the EFTA Surveillance Authority shall give the undertakings or associations of undertakings concerned the opportunity of being heard on the matters to which the EFTA Surveillance Authority has taken objection.

2. If the EFTA Surveillance Authority or the competent authorities of the EFTA States consider it necessary, they may also hear other natural or legal persons. Applications to be heard on the part of such persons shall, where they show a sufficient interest, be granted.

3. Where the EFTA Surveillance Authority intends to give negative clearance pursuant to Article 2 or take a decision in application of Article 53 (3) of the EEA Agreement, it shall publish a summary of the relevant application or notification and invite all interested third parties to submit their observations within a time-limit which it shall fix being not less than one month. Publication shall have regard to the legitimate interest of undertakings in the protection of their business secrets.

Article 20

Professional secrecy

1. Without prejudice to Article 9 (3) of Protocol 23 to the EEA Agreement, information

acquired as a result of the application of Articles 11, 12, 13 and 14 of this Chapter or of Article 58 of the EEA Agreement and Protocol 23 thereto shall be used only for the purpose of the relevant request or investigation.

2. Without prejudice to the provisions of Articles 19 and 21, the EFTA Surveillance Authority and the competent authorities of the EFTA States, their officials and other servants shall not disclose information acquired by them as a result of the application of this Protocol or Article 58 of the EEA Agreement and Protocol 23 thereto and of the kind covered by the obligation of professional secrecy. This obligation shall also apply to the representatives of the EC Commission and of the EC Member States who participate in the Advisory Committee pursuant to Article 10 (4) and in the hearing pursuant to Article 8 (2) of Chapter IV.

3. The provisions of paragraphs 1 and 2 shall not prevent publication of general information or surveys which do not contain information relating to particular undertakings or associations of undertakings.

Article 21
Publication of decisions

1. The EFTA Surveillance Authority shall publish the decisions which it takes pursuant to Articles 2, 3, 6 and 8 of this Chapter and to Article 3 of Chapter XVI.

2. The publication shall state the names of the parties and the main content of the decision; it shall have regard to the legitimate interest of undertakings in the protection of their business secrets.

Article 22
Special provisions

The EFTA Surveillance Authority may submit to the attention of the EFTA States, for consultation within the Standing Committee in accordance with Article 2 of the Agreement on a Standing Committee of the EFTA States, proposals for exempting, in accordance with Article 53 (3) of the EEA Agreement, certain categories of agreement, decision and concerted practice from the prohibition set out in Article 53 (1) of that Agreement.

CHAPTER III FORM, CONTENT AND OTHER DETAILS CONCERNING APPLICATIONS AND NOTIFICATIONS

Article 1
Persons entitled to submit applications and notifications

1. Any undertaking which is party to agreements, decisions or practices of the kind described in Articles 53 and 54 of the EEA Agreement may submit an application under Article 2 of Chapter II or a notification under Article 4 of Chapter II and Article 1 of Chapter XVI. Where the application or notification is submitted by some, but not all, of the undertakings concerned, they shall give notice to the others.

2. Where applications and notifications under Articles 2, 3 (1), 3 (2) (b) and 4 of Chapter II and Article 1 of Chapter XVI are signed by representatives of undertakings, or associations of undertakings, or natural or legal persons such representatives shall produce written proof that they are authorized to act.

3. Where a joint application or notification is submitted a joint representative should be appointed.

Article 2

Submission of applications and notifications

1. Nine copies of each application and notification shall be submitted to the EFTA Surveillance Authority.

2. The supporting documents shall be either original or copies; copies must be certified as true copies of the original.

3. Applications and notifications shall be in an official language of an EFTA State or the European Community. Supporting documents shall be submitted in their original language. Where the original language is not an official language of an EFTA State or the European Community, a translation in one of these languages shall be attached.

Article 3

Effective date of submission of applications and registrations

The date of submission of an application or notification shall, without prejudice to Article 11 of Protocol 23 to the EEA Agreement, be the date on which it is received by the EFTA Surveillance Authority. Where, however, the application or notification is sent by registered post, it shall be deemed to have been received on the date shown on the postmark of the place of posting.

Article 4

Content of applications and notifications

1. Applications under Article 2 of Chapter II relating to the applicability of Article 53 (1) of the EEA Agreement and notifications under Article 4 of Chapter II or Article 1 (2) of Chapter XVI shall be submitted on forms issued for that purpose by the Governments of the EFTA States, by common accord, as shown in Appendix 1, or by the EC Commission.

2. Applications and notifications shall contain the information asked for in these forms.

3. Several participating undertakings may submit an application or notification on a single form.

4. Applications under Article 2 of Chapter II relating to the applicability of Article 54 of the EEA Agreement shall contain a full statement of the facts, specifying, in particular, the practice concerned and the position of the undertaking or undertakings within the territory covered by the EEA Agreement or a substantial part thereof in regard to products or services to which the practice relates. The forms issued for that purpose by the Governments of the EFTA States, by common accord, as shown in Appendix 1, or by the EC Commission may be used.

Article 5

Special provisions

The EFTA Surveillance Authority may submit to the Governments of the EFTA States, in accordance with the provisions of Article 49 of this Agreement, proposals for forms and complementary notes.

CHAPTER IV HEARINGS PROVIDED FOR IN ARTICLE 19 (1) AND (2) OF CHAPTER II

Article 1
Before consulting the Advisory Committee on Competition, the EFTA Surveillance Authority shall hold a hearing pursuant to Article 19 (1) of Chapter II.

Article 2
1. The EFTA Surveillance Authority shall inform undertakings and associations of undertakings in writing of the objections raised against them. The communication shall be addressed to each of them or to a joint agent appointed by them.

2. The EFTA Surveillance Authority may inform the parties by giving notice in the EEA Section of the Official Journal of the European Communities, if from the circumstances of the case this appears appropriate, in particular where notice is to be given to a number of undertakings but no joint agent has been appointed. The notice shall have regard to the legitimate interest of the undertakings in the protection of their business secrets.

3. A fine or a periodic penalty payment may be imposed on an undertaking or association of undertakings only if the objections were notified in the manner provided for in paragraph 1.

4. The EFTA Surveillance Authority shall, when giving notice of objections, fix a time-limit up to which the undertakings and associations of undertakings may inform the EFTA Surveillance Authority of their views.

Article 3
1. Undertakings and associations of undertakings shall, within the appointed time-limit, make known in writing their views concerning the objections raised against them.

2. They may in their written comments set out all matters relevant to their defence.

3. They may attach any relevant documents in proof of the facts set out. They may also propose that the EFTA Surveillance Authority hear persons who may corroborate those facts.

Article 4
The EFTA Surveillance Authority shall in its decisions deal only with those objections raised against undertakings and associations of undertakings in respect of which they have been afforded the opportunity of making known their views.

Article 5
If natural or legal persons showing a sufficient interest apply to be heard pursuant to Article 19 (2) of Chapter II, the EFTA Surveillance Authority shall afford them the opportunity of making known their views in writing within such time-limit as it shall fix.

Article 6
Where the EFTA Surveillance Authority, having received an application pursuant to Article 3 (2) of Chapter II, considers that on the basis of the information in its possession there are insufficient grounds for granting the application, it shall inform the applicants of its reasons and fix a time-limit for them to submit any further comments in writing.

Article 7
1. The EFTA Surveillance Authority shall afford to persons who have so requested in their

written comments the opportunity to put forward their arguments orally, if those persons show a sufficient interest or if the EFTA Surveillance Authority proposes to impose on them a fine or periodic penalty payment.

2. The EFTA Surveillance Authority may likewise afford to any other person the opportunity of orally expressing his views.

Article 8

1. The EFTA Surveillance Authority shall summon the persons to be heard to attend on such date as it shall appoint.

2. It shall forthwith transmit a copy of the summons to the competent authorities of the EFTA States, who may appoint an official to take part in the hearing. Likewise, the EFTA Surveillance Authority shall invite the EC Commission to be represented at the hearing. The invitation shall also extend to the EC Member States.

Article 9

1. Hearings shall be conducted by the persons appointed by the EFTA Surveillance Authority for that purpose.

2. Persons summoned to attend shall appear either in person or be represented by legal representatives or by representatives authorized by their constitution. Undertakings and associations of undertakings may moreover be represented by a duly authorized agent appointed from among their permanent staff.

Persons heard by the EFTA Surveillance Authority may be assisted by lawyers or advisers who are entitled to plead before the EFTA Court, or by other qualified persons.

3. Hearings shall not be public. Persons shall be heard separately or in the presence of other persons summoned to attend. In the latter case, regard shall be had to the legitimate interest of the undertakings in the protection of their business secrets.

4. The essential content of the statements made by each person heard shall be recorded in minutes which shall be read and approved by him.

Article 10

Without prejudice to Article 2 (2), information and summonses from the EFTA Surveillance Authority shall be sent to the addressees by registered letter with acknowledgement of receipt, or shall be delivered by hand against receipt.

Article 11

1. In fixing the time-limits provided for in Articles 2, 5 and 6, the EFTA Surveillance Authority shall have regard both to the time required for preparation of comments and to the urgency of the case. The time-limit shall be not less than two weeks; it may be extended.

2. Time-limits shall run from the day following receipt of a communication or delivery thereof by hand.

3. Written comments must reach the EFTA Surveillance Authority or be dispatched by registered letter before expiry of the time-limit. Where the time-limit would expire on a Sunday or public holiday, it shall be extended up to the end of the next following working day. For the purpose of calculating this extension, public holidays shall, in cases where the relevant date is the date of receipt of written comments, be those set out in Appendix 2 to this Protocol, and in cases where the relevant date is the date of dispatch, those appointed by law in the country of dispatch.

CHAPTER V LIMITATION PERIODS IN PROCEEDINGS AND THE ENFORCEMENT OF SANCTIONS UNDER THE RULES RELATING TO TRANSPORT AND COMPETITION AS CONTAINED IN CHAPTERS II TO IV AND VI TO XIV

Article 1
Limitation periods in proceedings

1. The power of the EFTA Surveillance Authority to impose fines or penalties for infringements of the rules of the EEA Agreement relating to transport or competition shall be subject to the following limitation periods:

(a) three years in the case of infringements of provisions concerning applications or notifications of undertakings or associations of undertakings, requests for information, or the carrying out of investigations;
(b) five years in the case of all other infringements.

2. Time shall begin to run upon the day on which the infringement is committed. However, in the case of continuing or repeated infringements, time shall begin to run upon the day on which the infringement ceases.

Article 2
Interruption of the limitation period in proceedings

1. Any action taken by the EFTA Surveillance Authority, by the EC Commission at the request of the EFTA Surveillance Authority pursuant to Article 8 of Protocol 23 to the EEA Agreement, or by any EFTA State, acting at the request of the EFTA Surveillance Authority, for the purpose of the preliminary investigation or proceedings in respect of an infringement shall interrupt the limitation period in proceedings. The limitation period shall be interrupted with effect from the date on which the action is notified to at least one undertaking or association of undertakings which have participated in the infringement.

Actions which interrupt the running of the period shall include in particular the following:

(a) written requests for information by the EFTA Surveillance Authority, or by the competent authority of an EFTA State acting at the request of the EFTA Surveillance Authority; or a decision by the EFTA Surveillance Authority requiring the requested information;
(b) written authorizations to carry out investigations issued to their officials by the EFTA Surveillance Authority or by the competent authority of any EFTA State at the request of the EFTA Surveillance Authority; or a decision by the EFTA Surveillance Authority ordering an investigation;
(c) the commencement of proceedings by the EFTA Surveillance Authority;
(d) notification of the EFTA Surveillance Authority's statement of objections.

2. The interruption of the limitation period shall apply for all the undertakings or associations of undertakings which have participated in the infringement.

3. Each interruption shall start time running afresh. However, the limitation period shall expire at the latest on the day on which a period equal to twice the limitation period has elapsed without the EFTA Surveillance Authority having imposed a fine or a penalty; that period shall be extended by the time during which limitation is suspended pursuant to Article 3.

Article 3

Suspension of the limitation period in proceedings

The limitation period in proceedings shall be suspended for as long as the decision of the EFTA Surveillance Authority is the subject of proceedings pending before the EFTA Court in accordance with Article 108 (2) of the EEA Agreement and with the relevant provisions of this Agreement.

Article 4

Limitation period for the enforcement of sanctions

1. The power of the EFTA Surveillance Authority to enforce decisions imposing fines, penalties, or periodic payments for infringements of the rules of the EEA Agreement relating to transport or competition shall be subject to a limitation period of five years.

2. Time shall begin to run upon the day on which the decision becomes final.

Article 5

Interruption of the limitation period for the enforcement of sanctions

1. The limitation period for the enforcement of sanctions shall be interrupted:

(a) by notification of a decision varying the original amount of the fine, penalty or periodic penalty payments or refusing an application for variation;

(b) by any action of the EFTA Surveillance Authority or of an EFTA State at the request of the EFTA Surveillance Authority, for the purpose of enforcing payments, of a fine, penalty or periodic penalty payment.

2. Each interruption shall start time running afresh.

Article 6

Suspension of the limitation period for the enforcement of sanctions

The limitation period for the enforcement of sanctions shall be suspended for so long as:

(a) time to pay is allowed; or

(b) enforcement of payment is suspended pursuant to a decision of the EFTA Court in accordance with Article 108 (2) of the EEA Agreement and with the relevant provisions of this Agreement.

[. . .]

Part V

Transitional and Other Rules

CHAPTER XVI TRANSITIONAL AND OTHER RULES

Section I Rules Applicable to Chapters II to XII and XV

Article 1

Notification of existing agreements, decisions and practices

1. Agreements, decisions and concerted practices of the kind described in Article 53 (1) of the EEA Agreement which are in existence at the date of entry into force of the EEA Agreement and in respect of which the parties seek application of Article 53 (3) of the EEA Agreement shall be notified to the EFTA Surveillance Authority pursuant to the provisions in Article 56 of the EEA Agreement, the rules referred to in Articles 1 to 3 of Protocol 21 and

Protocol 23 to the EEA Agreement, as well as Chapters III, VI, VII, IX, X, XI, XII and XV, within six months of the date of entry into force of the EEA Agreement.

2. Paragraph 1 shall not apply to agreements, decisions or concerted practices of the kind described in Article 53 (1) of the EEA Agreement and falling under Article 4 (2) of Chapter II; these may be notified to the EFTA Surveillance Authority pursuant to Article 56 of the EEA Agreement, the rules referred to in Articles 1 to 3 of Protocol 21 and Protocol 23 to the EEA Agreement, as well as Chapters III, VI, VII, IX, X, XI, XII and XV.

Article 2

Decisions pursuant to Article 53 (3) of the EEA Agreement

1. Whenever the EFTA Surveillance Authority takes a decision pursuant to Article 53 (3) of the EEA Agreement, it shall specify therein the date from which the decision shall take effect. Such date shall not be earlier than the date of notification.

2. The second sentence of paragraph 1 shall not apply to agreements, decisions or concerted practices falling within Article 4 (2) of Chapter II and Article 1 (2) of this Chapter, nor to those falling within Article 1 (1) which have been notified within the time-limit specified in Article 1 (1).

Article 3

Special provisions for existing agreements, decisions and practices

1. Where agreements, decisions or concerted practices of the kind described in Article 53 (1) of the EEA Agreement which are in existence at the date of entry into force of the EEA Agreement and notified within the time limits specified in Article 1 (1) of this Chapter do not satisfy the requirements of Article 53 (3) of the EEA Agreement and the undertakings or associations of undertakings concerned cease to give effect to them or modify them in such a manner that they no longer fall under the prohibition contained in Article 53 (1) or that they satisfy the requirements of Article 53 (3), the prohibition contained in Article 53 (1) shall apply only for a period fixed by the EFTA Surveillance Authority. A decision by the EFTA Surveillance Authority pursuant to the foregoing sentence shall not apply as against undertakings and associations of undertakings which did not expressly consent to the notification.

2. Paragraph 1 shall apply to agreements, decisions or concerted practices falling under Article 4 (2) of Chapter II which are in existence at the date of entry into force of the EEA Agreement if they are notified within six months after that date.

Article 4

Applications and notifications submitted to the EC Commission prior to the date of entry into force of the EEA Agreement shall be deemed to comply with the provisions on application and notification under that Agreement.

The EFTA Surveillance Authority pursuant to Article 56 of the EEA Agreement and Article 10 of Protocol 23 to the EEA Agreement may require a duly completed form as prescribed for the implementation of the EEA Agreement to be submitted to it within such time as it shall appoint. In that event, applications and notifications shall be treated as properly made only if the forms are submitted within the prescribed period and in accordance with the provisions of the EEA Agreement and of Chapters II, III, V, VII, X, XII and XV of this Protocol.

Article 5
Fines
Fines for infringement of Article 53 (1) of the EEA Agreement shall not be imposed in respect of any act prior to notification of the agreements, decisions and concerted practices to which Articles 1 and 2 of this Chapter apply and which have been notified within the period specified therein.

Article 6
The EFTA States shall ensure that the measures affording the necessary assistance to officials of the EFTA Surveillance Authority and the EC Commission, in order to enable them to make their investigations as foreseen under the Agreement, are taken within six months of the entry into force of the EEA Agreement.

Article 7
As regards agreements, decisions and concerted practices already in existence at the date of entry into force of the EEA Agreement which fall under Article 53 (1) of the EEA Agreement, the prohibition in Article 53 (1) shall not apply where the agreements, decisions or practices are modified within six months from the date of entry into force of the EEA Agreement so as to fulfil the conditions contained in the block exemptions provided for in Annexe XIV to the EEA Agreement.

Article 8
As regards agreements, decisions of associations of undertakings and concerted practices already in existence at the date of entry into force of the EEA Agreement which fall under Article 53 (1) of the EEA Agreement, the prohibition in Article 53 (1) shall not apply, from the date of entry into force of the Agreement, where the agreements, decisions or practices are modified within six months from the date of entry into force of the EEA Agreement so as not to fall under the prohibition of Article 53 (1) any more.

Article 9
Agreements, decisions of associations of undertakings and concerted practices which benefit from an individual exemption granted under Article 85 (3) of the Treaty establishing the European Economic Community before the entry into force of the EEA Agreement shall continue to be exempted as regards the provisions of the EEA Agreement, until their date of expiry as provided for in the decisions granting these exemptions or until the EC Commission otherwise decides, whichever date is the earlier.

Section II Rules Applicable to Chapters XIII and XIV

Article 10
The act as referred to in point 1 of Annexe XIV to the EEA Agreement (Regulation (EEC) No 4064/89) and Chapter XIII shall not apply to any concentration which was the subject of an agreement or announcement or where control was acquired within the meaning of Article 4 (1) of the said act before the entry into force of the EEA Agreement and they shall not in any circumstances apply to any concentration in respect of which proceedings were initiated before that date by an EFTA State's authority with responsibility for competition.

[. . .]

ANNEXE B

TABLE OF CORRESPONDENCE BETWEEN EEA AND EC PROVISIONS

This correspondence is given only for indicative purposes. In some instances the EEA text has merely been inspired from the EC text without necessarily the intention of being 'identical in substance' in the sense of Article 6 EEA.

MAIN PART OF THE AGREEMENT

EEA	EEC Treaty or rules	Subject-matter
1 (2) (*e*)	3 (*f*)	Non-distortion of competition
3	5	General loyalty principle
4	7 (1)	Non-discrimination
7	189 (2)–(3)	Legal effect of acts
10	12–13 and 16–17	Prohibition of customs duties
11	30	Prohibition of import restrictions
12	34 (1)	Prohibition of export restrictions
13	36	Non-economic reasons for restrictions
14	95 (1)–(2)	Prohibition of discriminatory internal taxation
15	96	Repayment of internal taxes
16	37 (1)	State monopolies
[. . .]		
53	85	Restrictive agreements
54	86	Abuse of dominant position
55	89	Application of competition rules
57 (1)	2 (3) Reg. 4064/89	Mergers
59	90	Public undertakings
61	92	State aid, basic principle
[. . .]		
110	192	Decisions imposing pecuniary obligations
121	233	Exception for more developed regional agreements
122	214	Professional secrecy
123	223–4	Security safeguard
124	221	National treatment for capital investment
125	222	Non-prejudice to property ownership system
128	237	New members
129	247–8	Authentification, ratification, entry into force

PROTOCOLS

EEA	EC	Subject-matter
Protocol 21 (on enforcement of competition rules)		
4	4 Reg. 17/62	Transition rule for new agreements
5	5 Reg. 17/62	Transition rule for existing agreements
6	6 Reg. 17/62	Date as from which exemption applies
7	7 Reg. 17/62	Transition rule for existing agreements
8	5 Reg. 27/62	Transition rule for already notified agreements
9	25 (3) Reg. 17/62	Immunity from fines
10	14 (6) Reg. 17/62	Assistance by national authorities in inspections
11	5 last sentence Reg. 65/65	Transition rule for existing agreements
Protocol 22 (defining 'undertaking' and 'turnover')		
2	5 (1) last sentence Reg. 4064/89	Definition of 'turnover' (general)
3	5 (3) Reg. 4064/89	Definition of 'turnover' (credit institutions and insurances undertakings)
Protocol 23 (on co-operation in Articles 53/54 EEA cases)		
9	20 Reg. 17/62	Professional secrecy
11	3 Reg. 27/62	Date of submission
Protocol 24 (on co-operation in merger cases)		
2 (1) (*b*)	1 (2) (*b*) Reg. 4064/89	Co-operation (turnover of 250 mio ECU)
2 (1) (*c*)	2 (3) Reg. 4064/89	Co-operation (creation or strengthening of a dominant position)
2 (2) (*a*)	9 (2) Reg. 4064/89	Co-operation (in case of distinct market in an EFTA State)
6 (1)	9 (1) and (2) Reg. 4064/89	Rights of EFTA States (distinct market referral)
6 (2)	9 (9) Reg. 4064/89	Rights of EFTA States (appeal to the ECJ)
7	21 (3) Reg. 4064/89	Rights of EFTA States (legitimate interests)
9	17 Reg. 4064/89	Professional secrecy
14	25 (2) Reg. 4064/89	Transition rule
Protocol 25 (on competition in coal and steel)		
1	65 (1), (2) (subp. 1 and 2), and (4) (subp. 1) ECSC Treaty	Restrictive agreements
2	66 (1), (2) (subp. 1), (3), and (7) (1st sentence) ECSC Treaty	Mergers and abuse of dominant position
3	80 ECSC Treaty	Definition of 'undertaking'

EEA	EC	Subject-matter
Protocol 28 (intellectual property)		
1 (2)	Para. 1 of Protocol 8 to Spanish Accession Act	Level of IPR protection
3 (6)	47 Spanish Accession Act	Transition rule for EEA-wide exhaustion of patents

ESA/COURT AGREEMENT

ESA/Court Agreement	EEC Treaty or rules	Subject-matter
7	157 (1)	Members of ESA
8	157 (2)	Obligations
9	158	Appointment
10	159	End of duties
11	160	Compulsory retirement
12	161 (1)	Appointment of the president
13	162 (2)	Adoption of procedure rules
14	214	Professional secrecy
15	163 (1)	Majority voting
16	190	Reasons for decisions
17	191 (2)	Notification of decisions
18	191 (1)	Publication of decisions
28	165 (1)	Number of judges
30	167	EFTA Court judges
31	169	Infringement action
33	171	Compliance with Court judgments (by States)
34	177	Preliminary advisory opinions (not rulings)
35	172	Unlimited jurisdiction as regards penalties
36	173	Action for annulment
37	175	Action for failure to act
38	176	Compliance with Court judgments (by ESA)
39	178	Actions for damages (non-contractual liability)
40	185	Suspensory effect
41	186	Interim measures
46	215	Contractual and non-contractual liability of ESA
Protocol 3 (State aid)		
1	93 EEC Treaty	Control of State aid by ESA
2	6 Reg. 1107/70	Advisory Committee on aid in inland transport

Protocol 4 (Competition)

The chapters of Protocol 4, except for the necessary vocabulary adaptations, reproduce word for word the procedural provisions contained in EC regulations and even reflect the same article numbers. The correspondence between the chapters of the Protocol and EC Regulations is indicated in the table of contents at the beginning of the Protocol.

ANNEXE C

EXAMPLE OF APPLICATION OF THE REFERENCE TECHNIQUE

The main principles laid down in Protocol 1 EEA on horizontal adaptations have been summarized in Chapter II, Section 4.2.1 of this book. The aim of the present annex is to give practical examples of the application of the Protocol on a piece of EC legislation contained in the EEA Agreement.

For illustrative purposes, this has been done by changing the actual text of the act, in such a way as to show how the act in question should be understood in the EEA context. The adaptations (or in some cases the omission of adaptations) have been put in square brackets, each with a footnote explaining the legal base for the adaptation. Wherever an article is applicable as such, the text has not been reproduced. The legal act chosen is a new approach directive, namely Council Directive 90/384/EEC on the harmonization of the laws of the Member States relating to non-automatic weighing instruments (*OJ* L 189 (20 July 1990), 1). It is contained in Annexe II, chapter IX, point 27 EEA. The annexes to the Directive are not reproduced.

This annexe is divided in two parts, containing:

- Council Directive 90/384/EEC on the harmonization of the Member States relating to non-automatic weighing instruments;
- The illustrative example of how to understand Directive 90/384/EEC in the EEA context.

COUNCIL DIRECTIVE OF 20 JUNE 1990 ON THE HARMONIZATION OF THE LAWS OF THE MEMBER STATES RELATING TO NON-AUTOMATIC WEIGHING INSTRUMENTS (90/384/EEC)

THE COUNCIL OF THE EUROPEAN COMMUNITIES,

Having regard to the Treaty establishing the European Economic Community, and in particular Article 100a thereof,

Having regard to the proposal from the Commission[1],

In co-operation with the European Parliament[2],

Having regard to the opinion of the Economic and Social Committee[3],

[1] OJ No C 55, 4.3.1989, p. 6, and OJ No C 297, 25.11.1989, p. 13.
[2] OJ No C 158, 26.6.1989, p. 221, and OJ No C 149, 18.6.1990.
[3] OJ No C 194, 31.7.1989, p. 1.

Whereas Member States have the responsibility of protecting the public against incorrect results of weighing operations by means of non-automatic weighing instruments when used for certain categories of applications;

Whereas, in each Member State, mandatory provisions fix in particular the necessary performance requirements of non-automatic weighing instruments by specifying metrological and technical requirements, together with inspection procedures before and after going into service; whereas these mandatory provisions do not necessarily lead to different levels of protection from one Member State to another but do, by their disparity, impede trade within the Community;

Whereas the national provisions ensuring such protection must be harmonized in order to guarantee the free movement of non-automatic weighing instruments while ensuring a justified level of protection in the Community;

Whereas Community legislation as it stands at present provides that, notwithstanding one of the fundamental rules of the Community, namely the free movement of goods, barriers to intra-Community movement resulting from disparities in national laws on the use of products have to be accepted in so far as the provisions of those national laws are recognized as necessary to ensure that the products concerned meet essential requirements; whereas the harmonization of laws in the present case must therefore be confined to those provisions needed to ensure that non-automatic weighing instruments satisfy the essential metrological and performance requirements; whereas, because they are essential, these requirements must replace the corresponding national provisions;

Whereas this Directive therefore contains only mandatory and essential requirements; whereas, to facilitate proof of conformity with the essential requirements, it is necessary to have harmonized standards at European level, in particular as to the metrological, design and construction characteristics, so that instruments complying with those harmonized standards may be assumed to conform to the essential requirements; whereas these standards, harmonized at European level, are drawn up by private bodies and must remain non-mandatory texts; whereas for that purpose the European Committee for Standardization (CEN) and the European Committee for Electrotechnical Standardization (Cenelec) are recognized as the competent bodies for the adoption of harmonized standards in accordance with the general guidelines for co-operation between the Commission and those two bodies signed on 13 November 1984; whereas, within the meaning of this Directive, a harmonized standard is a technical specification (European standard or harmonized document) adopted by one or both of those bodies upon a remit from the Commission in accordance with Council Directive 83/189/EEC of 28 March 1983 laying down a procedure for the provision of information in the field of technical standards and regulations[4], as amended by Directive 88/182/EEC[5], and the above-mentioned general guidelines;

Wheras assessment of conformity with the relevant metrological and technical provisions is necessary to provide effective protection for users and third parties; whereas, the existing conformity assessment procedures differ from one Member State to another; whereas, to avoid multiple assessments of conformity, which are in effect barriers to the free movement of the instruments, arrangements should be made for the mutual recognition of conformity assessment procedures by the Member States; whereas, to facilitate the mutual recognition

[4] OJ No L 109, 26.4.1983, p. 8.

[5] OJ No L 81, 26.3.1988, p. 75.

of conformity assessment procedures, harmonized Community procedures should be set up, together with harmonized criteria for the designation of the bodies responsible for carrying out tasks pertaining to the conformity assessment procedures;

Whereas it is therefore essential to ensure that such designated bodies ensure a high level of quality throughout the Community;

Whereas the presence on a non-automatic weighing instrument of the EC mark of conformity or of the sticker bearing the letter 'M' indicates that there is a presumption that it satisfies the provisions of this Directive and therefore makes it unnecessary to repeat the assessments of conformity already carried out;

Whereas the measures aimed at the gradual establishment of the internal market must be adopted by 31 December 1992; whereas the internal market consists of an area without internal frontiers within which the free movement of goods, persons, services and capital is guaranteed,

HAS ADOPTED THIS DIRECTIVE:

Chapter I

Scope, placing on the market, free movement

Article 1

1. A weighing instrument is defined as a measuring instrument serving to determine the mass of a body by using the action of gravity on that body. A weighing instrument may also serve to determine other mass-related magnitudes, quantities, parameters or characteristics.

A non-automatic weighing instrument is defined as a weighing instrument requiring the intervention of an operator during weighing.

This Directive applies to all non-automatic weighing instruments, hereinafter referred to as 'instruments'.

2. A distinction is made in this Directive between two categories of instrument use:

(a) 1. determination of mass for commercial transactions;
2. determination of mass for the calculation of a toll, tariff, tax, bonus, penalty, remuneration, indemnity or similar type of payment;
3. determination of mass for the application of laws or regulations; expert opinion given in court proceedings;
4. determination of mass in the practice of medicine for weighing patients for the purposes of monitoring diagnosis and medical treatment;
5. determination of mass for making up medicines on prescription in a pharmacy and determination of mass in analyses carried out in medical and pharmaceutical laboratories;
6. determination of price on the basis of mass for the purposes of direct sales to the public and the making-up of prepackages;

(b) all applications other than those listed in point 2 (a) of this Article.

Article 2

1. Member States shall take all steps to ensure that instruments may not be placed on the market unless they meet the requirements of this Directive which apply to them.

2. Member States shall take all steps to ensure that instruments may not be put into service for the uses referred to in Article 1 (2) (a) unless they meet the requirements of this Directive which apply to them.

Article 3

Instruments used for the applications listed in Article 1 (2) (a) must satisfy the essential requirements set out in Annexe I.

In cases where the instrument includes or is connected to devices which are not used for the applications listed in Article 1 (2) (a), such devices shall not be subject to the essential requirements.

Article 4

1. Member States shall not impede the placing on the market of instruments which meet the requirements of this Directive which apply to them.

2. Member States shall not impede the putting into service for the uses referred to in Article 1 (2) (a) of instruments which meet the requirements of this Directive which apply to them.

Article 5

1. Member States shall presume conformity with the essential requirements referred to in Article 3 in respect of instruments which comply with the relevant national standards implementing the harmonized standards that meet the essential requirements referred to in Article 3.

2. The Commission shall publish the references of the harmonized standards referred to in paragraph 1 in the *Official Journal of the European Communities.*

Member States shall publish the references of the national standards referred to in paragraph 1.

Article 6

Where a Member State or the Commission considers that the harmonized standards referred to in Article 5 (1) do not fully meet the essential requirements referred to in Article 3, the Commission or the Member State concerned shall bring the matter before the Standing Committee set up under Directive 83/189/EEC, hereinafter referred to as 'the Committee', giving its reasons for doing so. The Committee shall deliver an opinion without delay.

In the light of the Committee's opinion, the Commission shall inform the Member States whether or not it is necessary to withdraw those standards from the publications referred to in Article 5 (2).

Article 7

1. Where a Member State considers the instruments bearing the EC mark of conformity referred to in Annexe 2, sections 2, 3 and 4, do not meet the requirements of this Directive when properly installed and used for the purposes for which they are intended, it shall take all appropriate measures to withdraw those instruments from the market or to prohibit or restrict their being put into service and/or placed on the market.

The Member State concerned shall immediately inform the Commission of any such measure, indicating the reasons for its decision, and in particular whether non-compliance is due to:

(a) failure to meet the essential requirements referred to in Article 3, where instruments do not meet the standards referred to in Article 5 (1);
(b) incorrect application of the standards referred to in Article 5 (1);
(c) shortcomings in the standards referred to in Article 5 (1) themselves.

2. The Commission shall enter into consultation with the parties concerned as soon as possible.

After such consultation the Commission shall immediately inform the Member State, which took the action, of the result. Should it find that the measure is justified it shall immediately inform the other Member States.

If the decision is attributed to shortcomings in the standards, the Commission, after consulting the parties concerned, shall bring the matter before the Committee within two months if the Member State which has taken the measures intends to maintain them, and shall subsequently initiate the procedures referred to in Article 6.

3. Where an instrument which does not comply bears the EC mark of conformity, the competent Member State shall take appropriate action against whomsoever has affixed the mark and shall inform the Commission and the other Member States thereof.

4. The Commission shall ensure that the Member States are kept informed of the progress and outcome of this procedure.

Chapter II
Conformity assessment

Article 8

1. The conformity of instruments to the essential requirements set out in Annexe I may be certified by either of the following procedures as selected by the applicant:

(a) EC type examination as referred to in Annexe II.1, followed either by the EC declaration of type conformity (guarantee of production quality) as referred to in Annexe II.2, or by the EC verification as referred to in Annexe II.3.

However, EC type examination shall not be compulsory for instruments which do not use electronic devices and whose load-measuring devices does not use a spring to balance the load;

(b) EC unit verification as referred to in Annexe II.4.

2. The documents and correspondence relating to the procedures referred to in paragraph 1 shall be drafted in an official language of the Member State where the said procedures are to be carried out, or in a language accepted by the competent body.

3. Where the instruments are subject to other Community Directives concerning other aspects, the EC mark referred to in Article 10 shall indicate in these cases that the instruments also fulfil the requirements of the other Directives.

Article 9

1. Member States shall notify to the other Member States and the Commission the bodies which they have designated for carrying out tasks pertaining to the procedure referred to in Article 8, the specific tasks for which each body has been designated, and the identification codes of the designated bodies.

The Commission shall publish the list of these notified bodies, together with the tasks for which they have been designated, in the *Official Journal of the European Communities* and shall ensure that the list is kept up to date.

2. Member States shall apply the minimum criteria set out in Annexe V for the designation of bodies. Bodies which satisfy the criteria fixed by the relevant harmonized standards shall be presumed to satisfy the criteria set out in Annexe V.

3. A Member State which has designated a body shall cancel the designation if the body no longer meets the criteria for designation referred to in paragraph 2. It shall immediately inform the other Member States and the Commission thereof and withdraw the notification.

Chapter III

EC mark of conformity and inscriptions

Article 10

1. The EC mark of conformity and the required supplementary data as described in Annexe IV.1 shall be affixed in a clearly visible, easily legible and indelible form to instruments for which EC conformity has been established.

2. The inscriptions referred to in Annexe IV.2 shall be affixed in a clearly visible, easily legible and indelible form to all other instruments.

3. The affixing to instruments of marks which are likely to be confused with the EC mark of conformity shall be prohibited.

Article 11

Where it is established that the EC mark of conformity has been wrongly affixed to instruments:

- not conforming to the standards referred to in Article 5 (1), where the manufacturer has chosen to manufacture instruments that conform to those standards,
- not conforming to an approved type,
- conforming to an approved type which does not meet the essential requirements applicable to it,
- in respect of which the manufacturer has failed to fulfil his obligations under the EC declaration of type conformity (guarantee of production quality),

the competent notified body shall, where necessary, withdraw the EC type-approval and/or the approval of the quality system. Withdrawal of EC type-approval shall have the effect of prohibiting submission for EC verification and the EC declaration of type conformity (guarantee of production quality).

Article 12

Where an instrument which is used for any of the applications referred to in Article 1 (2) (a) includes or is connected to devices that have not been subject to conformity assessment as referred to in Article 8, each of these devices shall bear the symbol restricting its use as defined by Annexe IV.3. This symbol shall be affixed to the devices in a clearly visible and indelible form.

Chapter IV
Final provisions

Article 13
Member States shall take all steps to ensure that instruments bearing the EC mark attesting conformity with the requirements of this Directive continue to conform to those requirements.

Article 14
Any decision taken pursuant to this Directive and resulting in restrictions on the putting into service of an instrument shall state the exact grounds on which it is based. Such a decision shall be notified without delay to the party concerned, who shall at the same time be informed of the judicial remedies available to him under the laws in force in the Member State in question and of the time limits to which such remedies are subject.

Article 15
1. Member States shall, before 1 July 1992, adopt and publish the laws, regulations and administrative provisions necessary in order to comply with this Directive. They shall forthwith inform the Commission thereof.

2. Member States shall apply such provisions from 1 January 1993.

3. However, by way of derogation from paragraph 2, Member States shall permit during a period of 10 years from the date on which they apply the provisions referred to in paragraph 1 the placing on the market and/or putting into service of instruments which conform to the rules in force before that date.

4. Member States shall communicate to the Commission the texts of the provisions of national law which they adopt in the field covered by this Directive.

5. Directive 73/360/EEC shall be repealed as from 1 January 1993, except as regards the application of paragraph 3.

Article 16
This Directive is addressed to the Member States.

Done at Luxembourg, 20 June 1990.

For the Council
The President
D. J. O'MALLEY

COUNCIL DIRECTIVE OF 20 JUNE 1990 ON THE HARMONIZATION OF THE LAWS OF THE MEMBER STATES RELATING TO NON-AUTOMATIC WEIGHING INSTRUMENTS (90/384/EEC)[6]

The *preamble* is not adapted for the purposes of the EEA Agreement. It is relevant to the extent necessary for the proper interpretation and application, within the framework of the Agreement, of the provisions contained therein.[7]

Chapter I

Article 1
Applicable as such.

Article 2
'1. Member States [and EFTA States][8] shall take all steps to ensure that instruments may not be placed on the market unless they meet the requirements of this Directive which apply to them.

2. Member States [and EFTA States][9] shall take all steps to ensure that instruments may not be put into service for the uses referred to in Article 1 (2) (a) unless they meet the requirements of this Directive which apply to them.'

Article 3
Applicable as such.

Article 4
'1. Member States [and EFTA States][10] shall not impede the placing on the market of instruments which meet the requirements of this Directive which apply to them.

2. Member States [and EFTA States][11] shall not impede the putting into service for the uses referred to in Article 1 (2) (a) of instruments which meet the requirements of this Directive which apply to them.'

Article 5
'1. Member States [and EFTA States][12] shall presume conformity with the essential requirements referred to in Article 3 in respect of instruments which comply with the relevant national standards implementing the harmonized standards that meet the essential requirements referred to in Article 3.

2. The Commission shall publish the references of the harmonized standards referred to

[6] Annexe II, ch. IX, point 27 EEA.
[7] Protocol 1, para. 1 EEA (Introductory parts of the acts).
[8] Protocol 1, para. 7 EEA (Rights and obligations).
[9] Ibid.
[10] Ibid.
[11] Ibid.
[12] Ibid.

in paragraph 1 in the *Official Journal of the European Communities*. [The corresponding information regarding the EFTA States shall be published in a separate EEA section thereof].[13]

Member States [and EFTA States][14] shall publish the references of the national standards referred to in paragraph 1.'

Article 6

'Where a Member State [or an EFTA State][15] or the Commission [or the Standing Committee of the EFTA States][16] considers that the harmonized standards referred to in Article 5 (1) do not fully meet the essential requirements referred to in Article 3, the [Commission or the Member State concerned shall bring the matter before the Standing Committee set up under Directive 83/189/EEC, hereinafter referred to as "the Committee", giving its reasons for doing so. The Committee shall deliver an opinion without delay.][17]

In the light of the Committee's opinion, the Commission [and for the EFTA States, the Standing Committee of the EFTA States][18] shall inform the Member States whether or not it is necessary to withdraw those standards from the publication referred to in Article 5 (2).'

Article 7

'1. Where a Member State [or an EFTA State][19] considers that instruments bearing the EC mark of conformity referred to in Annex 2, sections 2, 3 and 4, do not meet the requirements of this Directive when properly installed and used for the purposes for which they are intended, it shall take all appropriate measures to withdraw those instruments from the market or to prohibit or restrict their being put into service and/or placed on the market.

The Member State [or EFTA State][20] concerned shall immediately inform the Commission [, and ESA and the Standing Committee of the EFTA States, respectively][21] of any such measure, indicating the reasons for its decision, and in particular whether non-compliance is due to:

[13] Protocol 1, para. 6 (*b*) EEA (Publication of information). It is not specified which entity on the EFTA side, ESA or the Standing Committee of the EFTA States, will be responsible for such a publication. See also Ch. IV, ss. 4.2.1 and 4.2.2.

[14] Protocol 1, para. 6 (*a*) EEA (Publication of information).

[15] See n. 8.

[16] Protocol 1, para. 4 (*d*) EEA (Exchange of information and notification procedures), and Protocol 1, Art. 1 (1) (*e*), first indent, SC Agreement.

[17] Protocol 1, para. 2 (Provisions on EC committees) and Art. 100 EEA. According to Art. 5 (1) SC Agreement, the Standing Committee may decide to set up subcommittees and other bodies to assist it in accomplishing its tasks. An exclusive EFTA forum, corresponding to that of the EC 83/189 Committee, could therefore be set up in the form of an EFTA committee.

[18] Protocol 1, para. 4 (*d*) EEA (Exchange of information and notification procedures). See nn. 13 and 17.

[19] See n. 8.

[20] Ibid.

[21] Protocol 1, para. 4 (*a*) EEA (Exchange of information and notification procedures). According to this, EFTA States have to send information to both ESA and the Standing Committee of the EFTA States. As the practicality of such a procedure was questionable, para. 4 (*a*) was slightly amended so as to make it more simple (e.g. that the information will have to be sent only to ESA, which then, in turn, will pass it on to the Standing Committee). Note also that the Commission and ESA are to exchange information thus received.

(a) failure to meet the essential requirements referred to in Article 3, where instruments do not meet the standards referred to in Article 5 (1);
(b) incorrect application of the standards referred to in Article 5 (1);
(c) shortcomings in the standards referred to in Article 5 (1) themselves.

2. The Commission [and ESA, respectively,][22] shall enter into consultations with the parties concerned as soon as possible.

After such consultations the Commission [and ESA, respectively] shall immediately inform the Member State [or EFTA State],[23] which took the action, of the result. Should it/they find that the measure is justified it/they shall immediately inform the other Member States [and EFTA States].

If the decision is attributed to shortcomings in the standards, the [Commission, after consulting the parties concerned, shall bring the matter before the Committee within two months if the Member State which has taken the measures intends to maintain them, and shall subsequently initiate the procedures referred to in Article 6].[24].

3. Where an instrument which does not comply bears the EC mark of conformity, the competent Member State [or EFTA State][25] shall take appropriate action against whomsoever has affixed the mark and shall inform the Commission [, and ESA and the Standing Committee of the EFTA States, respectively][26] and the other Member States [and EFTA States][27] thereof.

4. The Commission [and ESA][28] shall ensure that the Member States [and EFTA States][29] are kept informed of the progress and outcome of this procedure.'

Chapter II

Article 8 (1)
Applicable as such.

Article 8 (2) and (3)
'2. The documents and correspondence relating to the procedures referred to in paragraph 1 shall be drafted in an [official language of the Member State or EFTA State where the said procedure are to be carried out],[30] or in a language accepted by the competent body.

[22] Protocol 1, para. 4 (*d*) EEA (Exchange of information and notification procedures), and Art. 5 (2) (*d*) and Protocol 1, Art. 1 (1) (*a*) ESA/Court Agreement.

[23] Protocol 1, para. 4 (*d*) EEA, and Art. 5 (2) (*d*) and Protocol 1, Art. 1 (1) (*a*) ESA/Court Agreement. In case of safeguard measures, the co-operation obligation as expressed in Art. 109 EEA is of the utmost importance. It can be presumed that the Commission will be the responsible entity when a measure has been taken by a Community country, and that ESA will be the responsible entity when measures have been triggered by an EFTA country. On that issue, see Ch. IV s. 6.1.1.

[24] See nn. 16 and 17.

[25] See n. 8.

[26] See n. 21.

[27] Protocol 1, para. 4 (*b*) EEA (Exchange of information and notification procedures). Note however that no direct exchange of information is provided for between EC and EFTA States.

[28] See n. 22.

[29] See n. 8.

[30] Protocol 1, para. 10 EEA (Reference to languages).

3. Where the instruments are subject to other [Community Directives][31] concerning other aspects, the EC mark referred to in Article 10 shall indicate in these cases that the instruments also fulfil the requirements of the [other Directives].'[32]

Article 9
'1. Member States [and EFTA States][33] shall notify to the other Member States [and EFTA States][34] and the Commission [, and ESA and the Standing Committee of the EFTA States, respectively][35] the bodies which they have designated for carrying out tasks pertaining to the procedure referred to in Article 8, the specific tasks for which each body has been designated, and the identification codes of the designated bodies.

The Commission shall publish the list of these notified bodies, together with the tasks for which they have been designated, in the *Official Journal of the European Communities* and shall ensure that the list is kept up to date. [The corresponding information regarding the EFTA States shall be published in a separate EEA section thereof.][36]

2. Member States [and EFTA States][37] shall apply the minimum criteria set out in Annex V for the designation of bodies. Bodies which satisfy the criteria fixed by the relevant harmonized standards shall be presumed to satisfy the criteria set out in Annex V.

3. A Member State [or EFTA State][38] which has designated a body shall cancel the designation if the body no longer meets the criteria for designation referred to in paragraph 2. It shall immediately inform the other Member States [and EFTA States][39] and the Commission [, and ESA and the Standing Committee of the EFTA States, respectively][40] and withdraw the notification.'

Article 10
Applicable as such.

Article 11
Applicable as such.

Article 12
Applicable as such.

Article 13
'Member States [and EFTA States][41] shall take all steps to ensure that instruments bearing

[31] No specific adaptation foreseen. Those qualifying as 'intelligent readers' (cf. Ch. II n. 36) would, in this context, understand this reference to mean 'other Community directives forming part of the EEA Agreement'.

[32] See n. 31.

[33] See n. 8.

[34] See n. 27.

[35] See n. 21.

[36] Protocol 1, para. 6 (*b*) EEA (Publication of information). See n. 13. The updating of the list of notified bodies is a task for the Standing Committee of the EFTA States according to Protocol 1, Art. (1) (*c*) and (*e*), second indent, SC Agreement.

[37] See n. 8.

[38] Ibid.

[39] See n. 27.

[40] See n. 21.

[41] See n. 8.

the EC mark attesting conformity with the requirements of this Directive continue to conform to those requirements.'

Article 14
'Any decision taken pursuant to this Directive and resulting in restrictions on the putting into service of an instrument shall state the exact grounds on which it is based. Such a decision shall be notified without delay to the party concerned, who shall at the same time be informed of the judicial remedies available to him under the laws in force in the Member State [or EFTA States][42] in question and of the time limits to which such remedies are subject.'

Article 15 (1) and (2)
Not relevant for the purposes of the EEA Agreement. The time limits and dates for the EFTA States for bringing into force and implementing acts referred to follow from the date of entry into force of the Agreement, as well as from provisions on transitional arrangements.[43]

Article 15 (3)
3. 'However, by way of derogation from paragraph 2, Member States [and EFTA States][44] shall permit during a period of 10 years from the date on which they apply the provisions referred to in paragraph 1 the placing on the market and/or putting into service of instruments which conform to the rules in force before that date.'[45]

Article 15 (4)
4. 'Member States [and EFTA States][46] shall communicate to the Commission [, and ESA and the Standing Committee of the EFTA States, respectively][47] the texts of the provisions of national law which they adopt in the field covered by this Directive.'

Article 15 (5)
Applicable as such.[48]

Article 16
Not relevant for the purposes of the EEA Agreement.[49]

[42] See n. 3.

[43] Protocol 1, para. 11 EEA (Entry into force and implementations of acts), as amended by Art. 7 Protocol adjusting the Agreement on the European Economic Area.

[44] See n. 8.

[45] i.e. the ten-year transitional period put forward in the Directive would for the EFTA States be counted from the entry into force of the EEA Agreement.

[46] See n. 8.

[47] See n. 21.

[48] The Directive referred to (73/360/EEC) is part of the EEA Agreement, Annex II, ch. IX, point 8.

[49] Protocol 1, para. 12 EEA (Addressees of the Community acts).

ANNEXE D

ORGANIGRAMS AND ADDRESSES OF THE EFTA INSTITUTIONS

EFTA SURVEILLANCE AUTHORITY (ESA)

ESA COLLEGE

Knut ALMESTAD
President
General policies—Co-ordination—External relations—Administration
Legal Service—Executive Secretariat

Nic GRÖNVALL
Competition—Social policy
Consumer protection
Environment

Heinz ZOUREK
State aid—Monopolies
Public procurement
Free movement of persons
(incl. mutual recognition of diplomas, right of establishment, and social security)

Pekka SÄILÄ
Free movement of goods
(incl. technical barriers to trade, other trade matters, and veterinary and phytosanitary matters)

Björn FRIDFINNSSON
Capital movement and financial services
Transport
Telecommunications
New technology services

DIRECTORATES

Competition Anti-trust	Competition State Aid	Goods	Capital and Financial Services	Specific EEA Affairs	Legal Service	Administration	Executive Secretariat
L. GÖRANSON Director	J. PIHLATIE Director	H. SPINDLER Director	H. von HERTZEN Director	M. BERGER Director	H. BERGLIN Director	S. ARNEBERG Director	G. EK ULLAND Director
11 officers	4 officers	15 officers	5 officers	9 officers	5 officers	15 officers and employees	3 officers

EFTA SECRETARIAT

Georg REISCH
Secretary-General

Berndt Olof JOHANSSON
Deputy Secretary-General

Consultative Committee Secretariat
Parliamentary Committee Secretariat

Brussels Office	Trade Policy Affairs	Legal Affairs	Economic Affairs	Third Country Relations	Specific Integration Affairs	Press and Information	Council Secretariat	Administration
P. MANNES Director	H. TSCHÄNI Director	. . . Director	P. WIJKMAN Director	D. BERTRAND Head	J. LUGON Director	. . . Director	R. HALL Director	E. HOFF Director
C. QUERNER Standing Committee Secretary	C. ARVIUS Deputy Director (Brussels)	H. FRENNERED Deputy Director (Brussels)	J. LESKELÄ Deputy Director (Brussels)					J. ÖRTENGREN Deputy Director (Brussels)
officers: BRU: 6	officers: GE: 6 BRU: 10	officers: GE: 3 BRU: 8	officers: GE: 6 BRU: 6	officers: GE: 4	officers: BRU: 9	officers: GE: 4 BRU: 1	officers: GE: 4	officers and assistants: GE: 13 BRU: 6

Note: GE = Geneva; BRU = Brussels.

EFTA COURT

Judges

Leif SEVON (President)

Björn HAUG Kurt HERNDL Sven NORBERG Thor VILHJALMSSON

5 Legal Secretaries
+
5 Secretaries

Registry

K. HÖKBORG
+ 1 assistant registrar

Legal Editor	Legal research department
1	2
Administration	Library
5	2

ADDRESSES OF THE EFTA INSTITUTIONS

EFTA Surveillance Authority

1–3 rue Marie-Thérèse
B-1040 BRUSSELS

Tel.: (32.2) 226.68.11
Fax: (32.2) 226.68.00

EFTA Secretariat

Seat

9–11 rue de Varembé
CH-1211 GENEVA 20

Tel.: (41.22) 749.11.11
Fax: (41.22) 733.92.91
740.14.37

Brussels Office

74 rue de Trèves
B-1040 BRUSSELS

Tel.: (32.2) 286.17.11
Fax: (32.2) 286.17.50

EFTA Court

4 avenue des Morgines
CH-1213 PETIT-LANCY
Tel.: (41.22) 709.09.11
Fax: (41.22) 709.09.98

ANNEXE E

LIST OF HS CHAPTERS EXCLUDED FROM THE SCOPE OF THE EEA AGREEMENT (CHAPTERS 1–24)

SECTION I. LIVE ANIMALS; ANIMAL PRODUCTS

1. Live animals.
2. Meat and edible meat offal.
3. Fish and crustaceans, molluscs, and other aquatic invertebrates.
4. Dairy produce; birds' eggs; natural honey; edible products of animal origin not elsewhere specified or included.
5. Products of animal origin not elsewhere specified or included.

SECTION II. VEGETABLE PRODUCTS

6. Live trees and other plants; bulbs, roots, and the like; cut flowers and ornamental foliage.
7. Edible vegetables and certain roots and tubers.
8. Edible fruit and nuts; peel of citrus fruit or melons.
9. Coffee, tea, maté, and spices.
10. Cereals.
11. Products of the milling industry; malt; starches; inulin; wheat gluten.
12. Oil seeds and oleaginous fruits; miscellaneous grains, seeds, and fruit; industrial or medicinal plants; straw and fodder.
13. Lac; gums, resins, and other vegetable saps and extracts.
14. Vegetable plaiting materials; vegetable products not elsewhere specified or included.

SECTION III. ANIMAL OR VEGETABLE FATS AND OILS AND THEIR CLEAVAGE PRODUCTS; PREPARED EDIBLE FATS; ANIMAL OR VEGETABLE WAXES

15. Animal or vegetable fats and oils and their cleavage products; prepared edible fats; animal or vegetable waxes.

SECTION IV. PREPARED FOODSTUFFS; BEVERAGES, SPIRITS, AND VINEGAR; TOBACCO AND MANUFACTURED TOBACCO SUBSTITUTES

16. Preparations of meat, of fish, or of crustaceans, molluscs, or other aquatic invertebrates.
17. Sugars and sugar confectionery.
18. Cocoa and cocoa preparations.
19. Preparations of cereals, flour, starch, or milk; pastrycooks' products.
20. Preparations of vegetables, fruit, nuts, or other parts of plants.
21. Miscellaneous edible preparations.
22. Beverages, spirits, and vinegar.
23. Residues and waste from the food industries; prepared animal fodder.
24. Tobacco and manufactured tobacco substitutes.

ANNEXE F

ECJ CASES UNDER ARTICLES 30 TO 36 EEC WITH SHORT DESCRIPTIONS

(Listed according to case no.)

No.	Name/subject	Date and publication
7/68	*Commission* v. *Italy* Strict interpretation of Art. 36.	10 Dec. 1968 [1968] ECR 423
13/68	*Salgoil* Strict interpretation of Art. 36.	19 Dec. 1968 [1968] ECR 453
192/73	*Van Zuylen Frères* v. *Hag* Industrial and commercial property: trade marks (Art. 36). Prohibition of use of identical trade mark not justified.	3 July 1974 [1974] ECR 731
8/74	*Dassonville* Concept: 'All trading rules enacted by Member States which are capable of hindering, actually or potentially, intra-Community trade are to be considered as measures with an effect equivalent to quantitative restrictions.'	11 July 1974 [1974] ECR 837
12/74	*Sekt und Weinbrand* Industrial and commercial property. Indication of origin. Protection of a generic appellation (incl. Dir. 70/50).	20 Feb. 1975 [1975] ECR 181
15/74	*Centrafarm* v. *Sterling Drug* Industrial and commercial property. Extent and protection of patent rights (pharmaceuticals). Parallel imports. 'The exercise, by the patentee, of the right which he enjoys under the legislation of a Member State to prohibit the sale, in that State, of a product protected by the patent which has been marketed in another Member State by the patentee or with his consent is incompatible with the rules of the EEC Treaty.'	31 Oct. 1974 [1974] ECR 1147
16/74	*Centrafarm* v. *Winthrop* Industrial and commercial property. Extent and protection of trade mark rights (pharmaceuticals). Parallel imports. 'The exercise, by the owner of a trade mark, of the right which he enjoys under the legislation of Member State to prohibit the sale, in that State, of a product which has been marketed under the trade mark	31 Oct. 1974 [1974] ECR 1183

No.	Name/subject	Date and publication
	in another Member State by the trade mark owner or with his consent is incompatible with the rules of the EEC Treaty.'	
89/74	*Arnaud and Others*[a] National measures on control of wine.	30 Sept. 1975 [1975] ECR 1023
4/75	*Rewe-Zentral.* v. *Landwirtsch* Phytosanitary inspections at the frontier which plant products coming from another Member State are required to undergo constitute a breach of Art. 30. Can be justified under Art. 36, but may constitute arbitrary discrimination if domestic products are not subject to an equivalent examination.	8 July 1975 [1975] ECR 843
10–14/75	*Lahaille and Others* National controls when presumption of over-alcoholization of wine.	30 Sept. 1975 [1975] ECR 1053
18–19/75	See 89/74.	
51/75	*EMI Records* v. *CBS (UK)* Industrial property. Proprietor of a trade mark in all Member States. Similar products bearing the same mark and coming from a third country. Prevention (incl. Arts. 9, 10, 85, 86, 110).	15 June 1976 [1976] ECR 811
65/75	*Tasca* Price controls: maximum price applicable without distinction to domestic and imported products may have effect equivalent to quantitative restrictions when it is fixed at a level such that the sale of imported products becomes, if not impossible, more difficult than of domestic products.	26 Feb. 1976 [1976] ECR 291
86/75	*EMI Records* v. *CBS (DK)* Industrial property. Proprietor of a trade mark in all Member States. Similar products bearing the same mark and coming from a third country. Prevention (incl. Arts. 9, 10, 85, 86, 110).	15 June 1976 [1976] ECR 871
88–90/75	*SADAM* Maximum prices (cf. Case 65/75)	23 Feb. 1976 [1976] ECR 323
96/75	*EMI Records* v. *CBS (D)* Industrial property. Proprietor of a trade mark in all Member States. Similar products bearing the same mark and coming from a third country. Prevention (incl. Arts. 9, 10, 85, 86, 110).	15 June 1976 [1976] ECR 913

No.	Name/subject	Date and publication
104/75	*De Peijper* Pharmaceuticals. Parallel imports. 'National rules or practices which result in imports being channelled in such a way that only certain traders can effect these imports, whereas others are prevented from doing so, constitutes a measure having an effect equivalent to a quantitative restriction.	20 May 1976 [1976] ECR 613
119/75	*Terrapin* v. *Terranova* Industrial and commercial property. Products of an undertaking of a Member State bearing, by virtue of the legislation of that State, a name giving rise to confusion with the trade mark and name of an undertaking of another Member State (risk of confusion).	22 June 1976 [1976] ECR 1039
3, 4, 6/76	*Kramer* Biological resources of the sea. Measures involving a limitation of fishing activities with a view to conserving the resources of the sea do not constitute a measure under Art. 30 *et seq.* of the EEC Treaty.	14 July 1976 [1976] ECR 1279
35/76	*Simmenthal Spa* Veterinary and public health inspections.	15 Dec. 1976 [1976] ECR 1871
41/76	*Donckerwolcke* Concept: products in free circulation. Products originating in third countries (incl. Arts. 8, 9, 115).	15 Dec. 1976 [1976] ECR 1921
46/76	*Bauhuis* v. *Netherlands* Veterinary and public health inspections. Strict application of Art. 36 (incl. Arts. 9, 12, 13, 16, 95).	25 Jan. 1977 [1977] ECR 5
53/76	*Bouhelier* Lever escapement watches. 'The expression "quantitative restrictions on exports and any measures having equivalent effect" contained in Article 34 of the EEC Treaty must be understood as applying to rules adopted by a Member State which require in respect only of the export of certain goods either a licence or a standards certificate which is issued in place of such licence and may be refused if the quality does not conform to certain standards laid down by the body issuing the said certificate, even if such certificate does not give rise to the imposition of a charge.'	3 Feb. 1977 [1977] ECR 197
68/76	*Commission* v. *France* Agriculture (potatoes). Art. 34 (export). Mandatory submission of export declaration to a special body.	16 Mar. 1977 [1977] ECR 515

No.	Name/subject	Date and publication
74/76	*Iannelli* v. *Meroni* Direct effect of Art. 30; creating, 'at the end of the transitional period at the latest, for all persons subject to Community law, rights which national courts must protect' (incl. relation to Arts. 92, 93, 95).	22 Mar. 1977 [1977] ECR 557
89/76	*Commission* v. *the Netherlands* Phytosanitary inspections on exportation.	12 July 1977 [1977] ECR 1355
5/77	*Tedeschi* v. *Denkavit* Feeding stuff. Harmonizing directives providing for the necessary measures to ensure the protection of animal and human health; Art. 36 not applicable.	5 Oct. 1977 [1977] ECR 1555
13/77	*GB-INNO BM* v. *ATAB* Tobacco products. Price determined by the manufacturer or importer. Adherence imposed by a national rule.	16 Nov. 1977 [1977] ECR 2115
30/77	*Bouchereau* Notion of public policy.	27 Oct. 1977 [1977] ECR 1999
52/77	*Cayrol* v. *Rivoira* Commercial policy; fruit and vegetables. Requirements by the importing Member State regarding information (incl. country of origin) on customs declaration.	30 Nov. 1977 [1977] ECR 2261
82/77	*Van Tiggele* Fixed minimum price for gin. Indistinctly applicable measures. Applicable. Lower cost price of imported products not reflected in the selling price to consumers (incl. Art. 92).	24 Jan. 1978 [1978] ECR 25
102/77	*Hoffmann-La Roche* Industrial and commercial property. Repackaging of trade marked goods. Prevention of marketing by proprietor of trade mark right.	23 May 1978 [1978] ECR 1139
2/78	*Commission* v. *Belgium* Designations of origin. Examination of certificates of origin. Proportionality.	16 May 1979 [1979] ECR 1761
3/78	*American Home Products* Industrial and commercial property. Trade marks. Different marks for the same product in two different Member States (single proprietor).	10 Oct. 1978 [1978] ECR 1823
7/78	*Regina* v. *Thompson* Means of payment. Concept of 'goods'. Silver coins which are no longer legal tender.	23 Nov. 1978 [1978] ECR 2247

No.	Name/subject	Date and publication
13/78	*Eggers* v. *Bremen* Designations of quality for spirits. Designation of quality indicative neither of origin nor of source. Designation linked to the completion of the production process on national territory (incl. Dir. 70/50).	12 Oct. 1978 [1978] ECR 1935
119/78	*Distilleries Peureux* State monopolies of a commercial character. National provision prohibiting the distillation of raw materials coming from other Member States (incl. Arts. 9, 10, 37).	13 Mar. 1979 [1979] ECR 975
120/78	*Cassis de Dijon* Minimum alcohol content (beverage). Mandatory requirements: 'In the absence of common rules, obstacles to movement within the Community resulting from disparities between the national laws relating to the marketing of a product must be accepted in so far as those provisions may be recognized as being necessary in order to satisfy mandatory requirements relating in particular to the effectiveness of fiscal supervision, the protection of public health, the fairness of commercial transactions and the defence of the consumer.' State monopolies of a commercial character (incl. Art. 37). Principle of mutual recognition.	20 Feb. 1979 [1979] ECR 649
148/78	*Pubblico Ministero* v. *Ratti* Classification, packaging, and labelling of solvents. When Community directives provide for the harmonization of measures necessary to ensure the protection of the health of persons and animals and establish Community procedures to supervise compliance therewith, recourse to Art. 36 ceases to be justified.	5 Apr. 1979 [1979] ECR 1629
152/78	*Commission* v. *France* Advertising of alcoholic beverages. Indirect restrictions on marketing of imported products. Justifications; protection of human health (none); arbitrary discrimination (measures distinctly applied).	10 July 1980 [1980] ECR 2299
153/78	*Commission* v. *Germany* Meat preparations. Conditions relating to import of meat products. Protection of human health and life.	12 July 1979 [1979] ECR 2555
159/78	*Commission* v. *Italy* Frontier controls. Restrictions on the representation of owners of goods for the purpose of customs declarations.	25 Oct. 1979 [1979] ECR 3247

No.	Name/subject	Date and publication
179/78	*Rivoira* Concept: 'free circulation'. Product originating in non-member countries.	28 Mar. 1979 [1979] ECR 1147
251/78	*Denkavit Futtermittel* Veterinary and public health inspections (double-check). Need for co-operation between authorities of the Member States. Existence of harmonizing directives, inapplicability of Art. 36.	8 Nov. 1979 [1979] ECR 3369
5/79	*Buys* Agricultural price freeze. Indistinctly applicable price freeze rules may be prohibited when prices are fixed at such a level that the sale of imported products becomes either impossible or more difficult than that of domestic products. That is in particular the case of national price freeze rules which, by preventing increases in the prices of imported products from being passed on in selling prices, freeze prices at such a low level that, having regard to the general situation of imported products compared to that of domestic products, dealers wishing to import can do so only at a loss or, in the light of the level of the frozen prices of national products, are induced to give preference to the latter.	18 Oct. 1979 [1979] ECR 3203
15/79	*Horsemeat* (Art. 34; export.) Prohibition of manufacture of meat products based on horsemeat.	8 Nov. 1979 [1979] ECR 3409
16–20/79	*Joseph Danis* Agricultural price freeze. National rules which impose on all producers and importers the obligation to give at least two months' notice of any price increases and which empower the authorities in the Member State concerned to delay beyond reasonable limits the passing on of increases in the prices of imported products.	6 Nov. 1979 [1979] ECR 3327
34/79	*Regina* v. *Henn & Darby* Pornographic articles. Justification on grounds of public morality.	14 Dec. 1979 [1979] ECR 3795
94/79	*Vriend* National marketing system for material for plant propagation. Compulsory affiliation to a body approving such material.	26 Feb. 1980 [1980] ECR 327
788/79	*Gilli & Andres* Prohibition on importing and marketing products containing acetic acid not derived from the acetic fermentation of wine. Protection of public health.	26 June 1980 [1980] ECR 2071

No.	Name/subject	Date and publication
27/80	*Fietje* Mandatory description of alcoholic beverage.	16 Dec. 1980 [1980] ECR 3839
32/80	*Kortmann* Pharmaceutical products. Parallel imports (Art. 36 does not prevent national authorities from checking whether the products are identical to those which have already been registered) (incl. Arts. 9, 12, 13).	28 Jan. 1981 [1981] ECR 251
53/80	*Nisine (Kaasfabriek Eyssen)* Foodstuffs—additives. Protection of health. Arbitrary discrimination (incl. Dir. 64/54).	5 Feb. 1981 [1981] ECR 409
55, 57/80	*Musik-Vertrieb membran* v. *GEMA* Industrial and commercial property. Copyright: sound recordings marketed in a Member State with the consent of the owner of the copyright. Importation into another Member State (Art. 36). Differences between royalties. Additional fees.	20 Jan. 1981 [1981] ECR 147
58/80	*Dansk supermarked* Copyright, trade marks. Exhaustion of rights. Fairness of commercial transactions.	22 Jan. 1981 [1981] ECR 181
113/80	*Ireland: Imported Jewellery* Indication of origin or the word 'Foreign'. Justifications: consumer protection, fair trading (none).	17 June 1981 [1981] ECR 1625
130/80	*Kelderman* Foodstuffs—bread. Disparities between national laws relating to the marketing of bread. Power of the national administration to grant exemptions. Protection of health, fair trading, and consumer protection.	19 Feb. 1981 [1981] ECR 527
132/80	*United Foods & Van den Abeele* Public health inspection of fish. Detailed implementing rules exceeding requirements of controls. Double-checks.	7 Apr. 1981 [1981] ECR 995
155/80	*Oebel* Prohibition on night work in bakeries. Also Art. 34 (export).	14 July 1981 [1981] ECR 1993
187/80	*Merck* v. *Stephar and Exler* Industrial and commercial property. Patents—pharmaceutical products. Product protected in one Member State marketed by the proprietor of the patent in another Member State where the product is not patentable. Objection by proprietor to importation of product into the Member State where protection exists.	14 July 1981 [1981] ECR 2063

No.	Name/subject	Date and publication
193/80	*Vinegar (II)* National legislation restricting the designation 'vinegar' to wine vinegar alone. Defence of the consumer.	9 Dec. 1981 [1981] ECR 3019
206, 207 209, 210/80	*Orlandi* Advance payment in foreign currency for imports rendered subject to the lodging of security.	9 June 1982 [1982] ECR 2147
270/80	*Polydor* v. *Harlequin Records* Gramophone records—copyright. Free Trade Agreement (Portugal–EC). The similarity between the terms used in Arts. 30 and 36 EEC and 14 (2) and 23 FTA is not a sufficient reason for transposing to the FTA the case-law of the Court (FTAs do not have the same purpose as the EEC Treaty).	9 Feb. 1982 [1982] ECR 329
272/80	*Biologische Producten* Plant protection products. Approval for imported products which have already been approved in another Member State. 'The authorities of the importing State are however not entitled unnecessarily to require technical or chemical analyses or tests when the same analyses or tests have already been carried out in another Member State and their results are available to those authorities or may at their request be placed at their disposal. A Member State operating an approvals procedure must ensure that no unnecessary control expenses are incurred.'	17 Dec. 1981 [1981] ECR 3277
1/81	*Pfizer* v. *Eurim-Pharm* Industrial and commercial property. Trade marks: trade mark lawfully affixed to a product in a Member State. Repackaging by a third party and importation into another Member State.	3 Dec. 1981 [1981] ECR 2913
6/81	*Industrie Dienstenv Beele* Imported product almost identical to another product already marketed in the same Member State (restraining precise imitation). Fairness of commercial transactions.	2 Mar. 1982 [1982] ECR 707
75/81	*Blesgen* Restriction on the marketing of spirits (consumption in places open to the public).	31 Mar. 1982 [1982] ECR 1211
95/81	*Commission* v. *Italy* Advance payment in foreign currency for imports rendered subject to the lodging of security. Strict interpretation of Art. 36.	9 June 1982 [1982] ECR 2187

No.	Name/subject	Date and publication
124/81	*Commission* v. *UK* Milk sterilized by the UHT process. Protection of health of humans and animals. System of import licences. Requirement to have imported UHT milk heat-treated a second time and repacked. Proportionality.	8 Feb. 1983 [1983] ECR 203
144/81	*Keurkoop* v. *Nancy Kean* Industrial and commercial property design (Art. 36). Exclusive right acquired by virtue of the first filing of the design.	14 Sept. 1982 [1982] ECR 2853
220/81	*Robertson* Prohibition on the sale of silver-plated articles not bearing a lawful hallmark. Application to similar articles imported from other Member States.	22 June 1982 [1982] ECR 2349
141–3/81	*Holdijk* Protection of animals: national minimum standards for enclosures for fattening calves.	1 Apr. 1982 [1982] ECR 1299
247/81	*Commission* v. *Germany* Pharmaceutical products. Placing on the market reserved to undertakings having their headquarters in the national territory. Justification: protection of human health (none).	28 Feb. 1984 [1984] ECR 1111
249/81	*Commission* v. *Ireland* Publicity campaign to promote domestic products (the 'buy Irish campaign'). The fact that Arts. 92 and 93 may be applicable does not exclude application of Art. 30. Such a campaign cannot escape from the Art. 30 prohibition solely because it is not based on decisions which are binding upon undertakings.	24 Nov. 1982 [1982] ECR 4005
261/81	*Rau (Margarine)* Requirement of a particular form of packaging. Non-essential condition for protecting and informing the consumer.	10 Nov. 1982 [1982] ECR 3961
286/81	*Oosthoeks Uitgeversmaatschappij* QRs on export (concept). Prohibition of a free-gift scheme introduced for sales promotion purposes.	15 Dec. 1982 [1982] ECR 4575
314–16/18	*Waterkeyn* (joined cases)[b] Advertising of alcoholic beverages (Arts. 169 and 171). Duty to ensure that the Court's judgment is complied with.	14 Dec. 1982 [1982] ECR 4337
2–4/82	*Delhaize Frères Le Lion* Public health inspection. Occasional inspections are permissible, provided that the number is not increased to such an extent as to constitute a disguised restriction	6 Oct. 1983 [1983] ECR 2973

No.	Name/subject	Date and publication
	on trade between Member States (also Dirs. 64/433 and 71/118).	
29/82	*Van Luipen* QR on exports. Compulsory membership of fruit and vegetable exporters in a quality-control authority (incl. common organization of the market in fruit and vegetables).	3 Feb. 1983 [1983] ECR 151
40/82	*Commission* v. *UK* Protection of animal health. Import licensing system.	31 Jan. 1984 [1984] ECR 283
42/82	*Commission* v. *France* Oenological and health checks on wine imported from another Member State. Random analyses. Substantial periods of suspension of imports.	22 Mar. 1983 [1983] ECR 1013
59/82	*Schutzverband (Vermouth)* Alcoholic content (measures distinctly applied; discrimination).	20 Apr. 1983 [1983] ECR 1217
74/82	*Commission* v. *Ireland* Protection of animal health. Import licensing system.	31 Jan. 1984 [1984] ECR 317
78/82	*Commission* v. *Italy* Price controls (mainly dealing with Art. 37; adjustment of the national monopoly in manufactured tobacco).	7 June 1983 [1983] 1955
83/82	See 314–16/81.	
90/82	*Commission* v. *France* Restriction on the freedom to import tobacco from another Member State: fixing of the retail selling price of manufactured tobacco by national authorities within the framework of the national monopoly of retail sales (incl. Art. 37).	21 June 1983 [1983] ECR 2011
94/82	*De Kikvorsch* Marketing of beers. Prohibition of the marketing of beer whose acidity exceeds a maximum level. Prohibition of statement of strength of original wort of the beer on prepackaging or label thereof. Extension of prohibition to beer lawfully produced and marketed in the exporting Member State. Defence of the consumer.	17 Mar. 1983 [1983] ECR 947
155/82	*Commission* v. *Belgium* Phyto-pharmaceutical products. Legislation restricting the granting of approval of pesticides and phyto-pharmaceutical products to persons established on its territory.	2 Mar. 1983 [1983] ECR 531
172/82	*Inter-Huiles* QRs on export. Collection and disposal of waste oils by approved undertakings. National legislation prohibiting	10 Mar. 1983 [1983] ECR 555

No.	Name/subject	Date and publication
	exports to authorized undertakings of other Member States (incl. Art. 90).	
174/82	*Sandoz* Foodstuffs—addition of vitamins. Prior authorization for marketing. Protection of health.	14 July 1983 [1983] ECR 2445
177, 178/82	*Van den Haar & Kaveka de Meern* Fixed price for tobacco products by the manufacturer or importer (incl. relation to Art. 85).	5 Apr. 1984 [1984] ECR 1797
181/82	*Roussel* Prices (price control) for imported medicines: differentiation between domestic and imported products.	29 Nov. 1983 [1983] ECR 3849
202/82	*Commission* v. *France* Pasta products. 'Although Article 30 of the Treaty obliges Member States . . . to take active steps to ensure the free movement of goods legally produced and marketed in other Member States, in particular by accepting certificates issued by the competent authorities in other Member States, that obligation does not go so far as to require them to carry out inspections according to the legislation of the other Member States.'	21 Feb. 1984 [1984] ECR 933
222/82	*Apple and Pear Development Council* National measures for development of the production and sale of domestic apples and pears.	13 Dec. 1983 [1983] ECR 4083
227/82	*Van Bennekom* Concept of 'Medicinal products'. Protection of health. Relation to harmonization: 'It is only when Community directives in pursuance of Article 100 of the Treaty, make provision for the full harmonization of all the measures needed to ensure the protection of human and animal life and institute Community procedures to monitor compliance therewith that recourse to Article 36 ceases to be justified.'	30 Nov. 1983 [1983] ECR 3883
237/82	*Jongeneel Kaas* v. *Netherlands* Foodstuffs (national rules in the cheese sector). Rules to improve the quality of domestic production. QRs on exports; standards of quality for cheese production and compulsory use of stamps, marks, or inspection documents.	7 Feb. 1984 [1984] ECR 483
238/82	*Duphar* Medicinal products. Health insurance reimbursement schemes. Measures promoting financial stability.	7 Feb. 1984 [1984] ECR 523
295/82	*Rhône Alpes Huiles* QRs on exports. Right of a holder or an approved	9 Feb. 1984 [1984] ECR 575

No.	Name/subject	Date and publication
	collector in a Member States to deliver waste oils to an authorized disposal undertaking in another Member State.	
15/83	*Denkavit Nederland* Agriculture. Art. 34: prohibition applies not only to national measures but also to measures adopted by the Community institutions.	17 May 1984 [1984] ECR 2171
16/83	*Prantl* Industrial and commercial property. Designation and presentation of wine.	13 Mar. 1984 [1984] ECR 1299
37/83	*Rewe-Zentrale* v. *L.w.s.k.Reinl* Harmonization of phytosanitary inspections. 'Although it is true that Articles 30 to 36 of the Treaty apply primarily to unilateral measures adopted by the Member States, nevertheless the Community institutions themselves must also have due regard to freedom of trade within the Community.'	29 Feb. 1984 [1984] ECR 1229
50/83	*Commission* v. *Italy* Motor vehicles. Non-admission of certain imported used buses (vehicle registration rules). Vehicle roadworthiness tests.	27 Mar. 1984 [1984] ECR 1633
51/83	*Commission* v. *Italy* Foodstuffs. Products lawfully manufactured and marketed in other Member States. Protection of consumers (incl. Dir. 74/329).	11 July 1984 [1984] ECR 2793
72/83	*Campus Oil Ltd.* Supply of petroleum products. Obligation to purchase from a national refinery. Art. 36; unnecessary or disproportionate measures. Public security.	10 July 1984 [1984] ECR 2727
94/83	*Heijn* Prohibition of pesticides for apples. Protection of public health.	19 Sept. 1984 [1984] ECR 3263
97/83	*Melkunie* Microbiological requirements applying to milk products. Protection of human health.	6 June 1984 [1984] ECR 2367
173/83	*Commission* v. *France* Waste oils—export (Art. 34).	7 Feb. 1985 [1985] ECR 491
177/83	*Kohl* v. *Ringelhan & Rennett* Lawful use of a distinctive company symbol in a Member State. Prohibition of its use in another Member State (legislation on unfair competition). Interpretation of 'public policy' in Art. 36. Considerations of consumer protection.	6 Nov. 1984 [1984] ECR 3651

No.	Name/subject	Date and publication
207/83	*Commission* v. *UK* Legislation requiring an indication of origin on certain products. Justification: consumer protection (none).	25 Apr. 1985 [1985] ECR 1201
229/83	*Fixed Prices for Books* The following is contrary to Art. 30: '(*a*) provisions whereby the importer responsible for complying with the statutory requirement to deposit one copy of each imported book with the authorities, that is to say the principal distributor, is responsible for fixing the retail price, and (*b*) provisions requiring the retail price fixed by the publisher to be applied to books published in the Member State concerned and reimported following exportation to another Member State, unless it is established that those books were exported for the sole purpose of reimportation in order to circumvent the legislation in question.'	10 Jan. 1985 [1985] ECR 2515
231/83	*Cullet* v. *Leclerc* National rules on fuel prices.	29 Jan. 1985 [1985] ECR 305
240/83	*Défense des brûleurs d'huiles usagées* Disposal of waste oils.	7 Feb. 1985 [1985] ECR 5
251/83	*Haug-Adrion* QR on export. Motor vehicles insurance rates. Vehicles bearing custom registration plates.	13 Dec. 1984 [1984] ECR 4277
269/83	*Commission* v. *France* Preferential postal tariff reserved for domestic publications.	14 Mar. 1985 [1985] ECR 837
281/83	*Commission* v. *Italy* Arts. 169 and 171 (following up the *Vinegar* case). Compliance with the judgment in full.	15 Oct. 1985 [1985] ECR 3397
288/83	*Commission* v. *Ireland* Commercial policy—potato imports. Scope—products originating in the Community and imported products put into free circulation.	11 June 1985 [1985] ECR 1761
299/83	*Leclerc and Others* v. *Libraires de Loire* Fixed price for books.	11 July 1985 [1985] ECR 2515
11/84	*Gratiot* National rules on fuel prices.	25 Sept. 1985 [1985] ECR 2907
18/84	*Commission* v. *France* National provisions by which a Member State deprives newspaper publishers of certain tax advantages in respect of publications which they print in other Member States are contrary to Art. 30.	7 May 1985 [1985] ECR 1339

No.	Name/subject	Date and publication
19/84	*Pharmon* v. *Hoechst* Industrial and commercial property—patents. Extent of protection; exhaustion of patent rights where a compulsory licence has been granted in respect of a parallel patent.	9 July 1985 [1985] ECR 2281
21/84	*Commission* v. *France* Refusal of approval for postal franking machines.	9 May 1985 [1985] ECR 1355
28/84	*Commission* v. *Germany* Compound feedingstuffs. Protection of public health. Harmonizing directives.	3 Oct. 1985 [1985] ECR 3097
34/84	*Leclerc* National rules on fuel prices.	25 Sept. 1985 [1985] ECR 2915
35/84	*Commission* v. *Italy* Health checks on imports of curds. Detention of lorries at the frontier, excessive duration of the admission procedure. Isolated cases justified on grounds of the protection of health.	18 Feb. 1986 [1986] ECR 545
60, 61/84	*Cinéthèque* Distribution of video films (prohibition for a limited period).	11 July 1985 [1985] ECR 2605
79, 80/84	*Chabaud & Rémy* National rules on fuel prices.	25 Sept. 1985 [1985] ECR 2953
95/84	*Boriello* v. *Darras & Tostain* Fixed prices for books. Promotion of culture.	10 July 1986 [1986] ECR 2253
103/84	*Commission* v. *Italy* Concept of Art. 30 (measures do not fall outside the scope merely because the hindrance to imports is slight). The fact that measures might be regarded as aid (Art. 92) is not a sufficient reason to exempt them from the prohibition of Art. 30. Art. 36 to be interpreted strictly. Question of financial aid linked to the purchase of vehicles of national manufacture.	5 June 1986 [1986] ECR 1759
114, 115/84	*Piszko* v. *Leclerc* National rules on fuel prices.	25 Sept. 1985 [1985] ECR 2961
149/84	*Binet* National rules on fuel prices.	25 Sept. 1985 [1985] ECR 2969

No.	Name/subject	Date and publication
176/84	*Commission* v. *Greece* Food additives. Taxation of beer on the basis of the quantities of a particular raw material used. Prohibition of the import where the beer is manufactured without that raw material. Justification: effectiveness of fiscal supervision (none). Prohibition of the importation of beer not corresponding to consumers' expectations as regards its composition. Protection of public health.	12 Mar. 1987 [1987] ECR 1193
178/84	*German Beer (Purity)* Legislation restricting a generic designation to products manufactured in accordance with national rules. Protection of public health and defence of the consumer.	12 Mar. 1987 [1987] ECR 1227
182/84	*Miro (Jenever)* Appellation of spirituous beverages; minimum alcohol content. Fair trading.	26 Nov. 1985 [1985] ECR 3731
188/84	*Woodworking Machines* Type approval; imported products to comply with technical standards and undergo a type-approval procedure.	28 Jan. 1986 [1986] ECR 419
192/84	*Commission* v. *Greece* Granting of credit terms favouring the purchase of domestic products.	11 Dec. 1985 [1985] ECR 3967
201/84	*Gontier* National rules on fuel prices.	25 Sept. 1985 [1985] ECR 2977
202/84	*Girault* National rules on fuel prices.	25 Sept. 1985 [1985] ECR 2985
215/84	*Héricotte* National rules on fuel prices.	25 Sept. 1985 [1985] ECR 2993
216/84	*Commission* v. *France* Foodstuffs: Member States may not rely on the requirement of consumer protection in order to prohibit the importation and sale of substitutes for a food product on the ground that there is a danger of confusion. Consumer information may be ensured by an adequate system of descriptions and labelling. Likewise, a Member State may not rely on the requirements of the protection of public health on the ground that the nutritional value of the substitute is lower than that of the product it serves to replace.	23 Feb. 1988 [1988] ECR 793

No.	Name/subject	Date and publication
247/84	*Motte* Directive introducing partial harmonization. Rules on the use of a colouring additive for a specific type of foodstuff.	10 Dec. 1985 [1985] ECR 3887
271–4/84	See 6, 7/85.	
304/84	*Müller & Kampmeyer* Use of emulsifying agent in foodstuffs authorized in one Member State but not in another.	6 May 1986 [1986] ECR 1511
6, 7/85	*Chiron* (joined cases)[c] National rules on fuel prices.	6 Feb. 1986 [1986] ECR 529
50/85	*Schloh* Motor vehicles. Registration of imported vehicles; requirement of a roadworthiness test despite possession of a certificate of conformity. Justification: protection of human health and life. Fees collected.	12 June 1986 [1986] ECR 1855
54/85	*Mirepoix* Prohibition of the use of a pesticide.	13 Mar. 1986 [1986] ECR 1067
80, 159/85	*Nederlandse Bakkerij* v. *Edah* Bread prices. National legislation prescribing a minimum retail price for bread. Reverse discrimination: difference of treatment favouring imported bread (incl. discrimination, Art. 7).	13 Nov. 1986 [1986] ECR 3359
87, 88/85	*Legia & Gyselinx* Medicinal products. Restrictions on the supply of pharmacies by an importer established in another Member State. Justifications: protection of public health (none) (incl. Dir. 65/65, 75/319).	27 May 1986 [1986] ECR 1707
121/85	*Conegate* Public morality; prohibition on the importation of goods considered to be indecent or obscene. Prohibition on the manufacture and marketing of the same goods on the national territory.	11 Mar. 1986 [1986] ECR 1007
124/85	*Commission* v. *Greece* Fresh meat. Conceptual questions. Potential effect on imports enough. Proportionality criteria; recourse to less restrictive measures.	16 Dec. 1986 [1986] ECR 3935
154/85	*Commission* v. *Italy* Parallel imports of vehicles. Increase in the number of administrative requirements. Public policy.	17 June 1987 [1987] ECR 2717
154/85 R	*Commission* v. *Italy* Order of the President of the Court. See 154/85.	7 June 1985 [1985] ECR 1753

No.	Name/subject	Date and publication
159/85	See 80/85.	
179/85	*Pétillant de raisin* Marketing of beverages in the presentation in which they are usually manufactured and marketed in their country.	4 Dec. 1986 [1986] ECR 3879
261/85	*Commission* v. *UK* Foodstuffs. National rules on the production and marketing of pasteurized milk products. Total prohibition of imports. Protection of human health. Disproportionate.	4 Feb. 1988 [1988] ECR 547
263/85	*Commission* v. *Italy* Relation to Art. 92 EEC: that a measure qualifies as aid in the meaning of Art. 92 does not exclude the application of Art. 30.	16 May 1991 [1991] ECR 2457
311/85	*Vlaamse Reisbureaus* v. *Sociale Dienst* Travel agent: statutory prohibition on the grant of rebates. Art. 30 not applicable.	1 Oct. 1987 [1987] ECR 3801
355/85	*Driancourt* v. *Cognet* Fixed prices for books (see 168/86). Reverse discrimination.	23 Oct. 1986 [1986] ECR 3231
402/85	*Basset* v. *SACEM* Industrial and commercial property. 'Articles 30 and 36 of the EEC Treaty . . . do not preclude the application of national legislation allowing a national copyright-management society to charge a royalty called a "supplementary mechanical reproduction fee", in addition to a performance royalty, on the public performance of sound recordings, even where such a supplementary fee is not provided for in the Member State where those sound recordings were lawfully placed on the market.'	9 Apr. 1987 [1987] ECR 1747
406/85	*Gofette & Gilliard* Registration of imported vehicles. Checking (approval) procedure for imported, already approved, vehicles permissible only if not entailing unreasonable cost or delay. Presentation of satisfactory documents issued in the exporting Member State should suffice.	11 June 1987 [1987] ECR 2525
407/85	*Pasta Products I* National provisions prohibiting sale of pasta made from common wheat (see also 90/86).	14 July 1988 [1988] ECR 4233
434/85	*Allen & Hanburys* v. *Generics* Industrial and commercial property. Patent rights; grant of licences subject to conditions impeding imports (distinctly applicable).	3 Mar. 1988 [1988] ECR 1245

No.	Name/subject	Date and publication
76/86	*Commission* v. *Germany* Foodstuffs. Prohibition on the marketing of milk substitutes. Justification: consumer protection, fair trading (none).	11 May 1989 [1989] ECR 1021
90/86	*Pasta Products II* (See 407/85).	14 July 1988 [1988] ECR 4285
98/86	*Mathot* Foodstuffs-labelling. Reverse discrimination; difference of treatment in favour of imported products.	18 Feb. 1987 [1987] ECR 809
118/86	*Nertsvoederfabriek Nederland* Obligation of producers of poultry offal to deliver it to approved rendering plants (incl. common organization of the market).	6 Oct. 1987 [1987] ECR 3883
158/86	*Warner Brothers* Industrial and commercial property. Arts. 30 and 36 EEC Treaty do not prohibit the application of national legislation which gives an author the right to make the hiring-out of video-cassettes subject to his permission, when the video-cassettes in question have already been put into circulation with his consent in another Member State whose legislation enables the author to control the initial sale, without giving him the right to prohibit hiring-out.	17 May 1988 [1988] ECR 2605
160/86	*Verbrugge* Fixed price for books, see 168/86.	9 Apr. 1987 [1987] ECR 1783
168/86	*Rousseau* Fixed price for books. National legislation on the price of books. Difference of treatment in favour of reimported books (incl. discrimination on grounds of nationality, Art. 7).	25 Feb. 1987 [1987] ECR 995
188/86	*Lefèvre* Beef and veal—price rules. National rules regulating the retail prices of beef and veal (incl. competition rules and the common organization of the market).	2 July 1987 [1987] ECR 2963
241/86	*Bodin and Minguet & Thomas* Motor vehicles. Differences in national rules on the maximum permitted height of vehicles and trailers (incl. Dir. 85/3).	11 June 1987 [1987] ECR 2573
252/86	*Bergandi* Automatic games machines. Scope of Art. 30; measures covered by Art. 95.	3 Mar. 1988 [1988] ECR 1343

No.	Name/subject	Date and publication
270/86	*Bizon's Club* v. *SACEM* (see Case 402/85).	12 Dec. 1990 [1990] ECR 4607
272/86	*Commission* v. *Greece* Restrictions on trade in olive oil (main issue: Arts. 5, 155, 164, 169).	22 Sept. 1988 [1988] ECR 4875
286/86	*Deserbais* National legislation protecting the trade name for a type of cheese.	22 Sept. 1988 [1988] ECR 4907
302/86	*Danish Bottle Case* Mandatory system of returnable containers for beer and soft drinks. Protection of the environment.	20 Sept. 1988 [1988] ECR 4607
317/86	*Lambert and Others* (joined cases)[d] Automatic games machines. Scope of Art. 30; measures covered by Art. 95.	15 Mar. 1989 [1989] ECR 787
29/87	*Dansk Denkavit Aps* Additives in feedingstuffs: identification and purity. Nature (degree) of harmonization (Dir. 70/524). Importation of feedingstuffs containing additives subject to prior authorization. Levies charged to cover cost of control (compatibility with the Directive and Arts. 9 and 95).	14 June 1988 [1988] ECR 2965
35/87	*Thetford* Industrial and commercial property: patents. National legislation recognizing the principle of the relative novelty of an invention. Question of compatibility with Art. 36.	30 June 1988 [1988] ECR 3585
45/87 R	*Commission* v. *Ireland* Order of the President of the Court. Public procurement (works). Community tender procedure (interim measures). Technical specifications on pipes.	13 Mar. 1987 [1987] ECR 1369
45/87	*Commission* v. *Ireland* Public procurement (works). Technical specification requiring the materials used to comply with a national standard (incl. Dir. 71/305).	22 Sept. 1988 [1988] ECR 4929
48–9/87	See 317/86.	
53/87	*Maxicar* Industrial and commercial property: design and models (car bodywork components). Exercise of rights by the manufacturer who is the proprietor thereof.	5 Oct. 1988 [1988] ECR 6039
56/87	*Commission* v. *Italy* National rules governing the prices of pharmaceutical products. Rules favouring national pharmaceutical products over imported products.	9 June 1988 [1988] ECR 2919

No.	Name/subject	Date and publication
169/87	*Commission* v. *France* Price control. Fixing of selling prices of manufactured tobacco.	13 July 1988 [1988] ECR 4093
190/87	*Moormann* Systematic health inspection on the importation of fresh poultry meat. Justification: protection of public health. Existence of a harmonizing directive (71/118).	20 Sept. 1988 [1988] ECR 4689
215/87	*Schumacher* Medicinal products. Rules restricting the import by private individuals of medicinal preparations authorized and available without prescription in the Member State of importation, but purchased in a pharmacy in another Member State. Justification: protection of public health (none).	7 Mar. 1989 [1989] ECR 617
254/87	*Librairies de Normandie* v. *Leclerc* Fixed price for books.	14 July 1988 [1988] ECR 4457
266, 267/87	*Royal Pharmaceutical Society (UK)* Pharmaceutical products. Parallel imports (trade marks). Concept: measures adopted by a professional body for pharmacy. Rules prohibiting pharmacists from substituting a therapeutically equivalent medicinal product for that prescribed by the doctor. Justification: protection of public health.	18 May 1989 [1989] ECR 1295
274/87	*Commission* v. *Germany* Foodstuffs. Ban on (1) the importation and marketing of meat products containing ingredients other than meat, (2) the importation of a foodstuff imposed on the ground that its nutritional value is lower than that of a foodstuff already on the market (indistinctly applicable). Justifications: consumer protection, fair trading (none).	2 Feb. 1989 [1989] ECR 229
285/87	See 317/86.	
298/87	*Smanor* Prohibition of the name 'deep-frozen yoghurt'.	14 July 1988 [1988] ECR 4489
382/87	*Buet & Others* Ban on canvassing at private homes for sales of educational material. Justification: protection of consumers.	16 May 1989 [1989] ECR 1235
363–7/87	See 317/86.	
395/87	*Tournier* Copyright. Sound recordings marketed in a Member State with the consent of the author. Importation into another Member State. Charging of copyright royalties.	13 July 1989 [1989] ECR 2521

No.	Name/subject	Date and publication
18/88	*GB-INNO-BM* Requirement of approval by a public undertaking of telephones intended to be connected to the network. No possibility for appeal. Consumer protection.	13 Dec. 1991 [1991] ECR 5941
21/88	*Du Pont de Nemours Italiana* Public procurement (supply). Reservation of 30% of public supply contracts to undertakings located in a particular region.	20 Mar. 1990 [1990] ECR 889
25/88	*Bouchara* Provisions requiring the person responsible for placing a product on the market for the first time to verify its conformity with the rules regarding the health and safety of persons, fair trading, and consumer protection. Proportionality of the obligation imposed on importers. Account to be taken of certificates issued by the authorities of the Member State of production.	11 May 1989 [1989] ECR 1105
52/88	*Commission* v. *Belgium* Foodstuffs. Prohibition of the importation of meat-based products containing more than a given quantity of edible gelatine. Justifications: fairness of commercial transactions, consumer protection.	11 May 1989 [1989] ECR 1137
65/88	See 317/86.	
67/88	*Commission* v. *Italy* Foodstuffs. Rules prescribing the addition of colour-reactive sesame oil for the marketing of certain imported edible fats (indistinctly applicable). Justifications: fairness of commercial transactions, protection of consumers (none).	27 Nov. 1990 [1990] ECR 4285
69/88	*Krantz* Power of the tax authorities to seize goods sold with reservation of title.	7 Mar. 1990 [1990] ECR 583
78–80/88	See 317/86.	
125/88	*Nijman* Prohibition on the marketing and use of unapproved plant protection products. Protection of public health (incl. Arts. 13 (1) and 20 of FTA EEC–Sweden).	7 Nov. 1989 [1989] ECR 3533
145/88	*Torfaen Borough Council* Prohibition of Sunday trading.	23 Nov. 1989 [1989] ECR 3851
186/88	*Commission* v. *Germany* Requirement to make a prior declaration for the purpose of ensuring that a veterinarian is involved in the completion of the administrative formalities upon the	28 Nov. 1989 [1989] ECR 3997

No.	Name/subject	Date and publication
	importation of fresh poultry meat (incl. Dirs. 71/118, 83/643).	
202/88	*France* v. *Commission* Telecom final equipment; exclusive importation and marketing right granted by Member State. Obligation, in order to ensure equal opportunities between economic agents, to entrust the drawing up of technical specifications and type approval of equipment to an independent body.	19 Mar. 1991 [1991] ECR 1223
212/88	*Levy* Common commercial policy. National requirement of an import licence for a product originating in a non-member country, although already in free circulation within the Community, is prohibited, except where the Member State has been authorized by the Commission under Art. 115.	26 Oct. 1989 [1989] ECR 3511
249/88	*Commission* v. *Belgium* Pharmaceutical products—pricing rules. Legislation giving preference to national pharmaceutical products to the detriment of imported products.	19 Mar. 1991 [1991] ECR 1275
302/88	*Hennen Olie* Art. 34 (export). Non-reimbursement of a charge connected with the stockpiling of petroleum products in the event of exportation.	12 Dec. 1990 [1990] ECR 4625
306/88	*Rochdale Borough Council** Sunday trading: the prohibition in Art. 30 does not apply to national legislation prohibiting Sunday trading.	16 Dec. 1992 [1992] ECR 6457
347/88	*Commission* v. *Greece* State monopoly. Rules requiring companies engaged in the distribution of petroleum products to obtain a proportion of their supplies from public-sector refineries. System of marketing quotas (also Art. 37).	13 Dec. 1990 [1990] ECR 4747
351/88	*Laboratori Bruneau* v. *Unità sanitaria* Public procurement. Reservation of a proportion of a public supply contract to undertakings located in a particular region of the national territory.	11 June 1991 [1991] ECR 3641
362/88	*GB-INNO-BM* Cross-frontier advertising. Prohibition against referring, in advertisements for a special purchase offer, to the duration of the offer or the price previously charged. Application hereof to advertising lawfully distributed in another Member State. Justifications: consumer protection (not justifiable).	7 Mar. 1990 [1990] ECR 667

No.	Name/subject	Date and publication
369/88	*Delattre* Concept of medicinal product. Monopoly of pharmacists. (Dir. 65/65.) Justifications: protection of public health or of consumers.	21 Mar. 1991 [1991] ECR 1487
10/89	*Hag II* Trade marks; proprietor of trade mark can oppose importation of products marketed by other undertaking under its own trade mark; common origin of two marks prior to expropriation not relevant.	17 Oct. 1990 [1990] ECR 3711
23/89	*Quietlynn Ltd. & Richards* National legislation prohibiting the sale of lawful sex articles from unlicensed sex establishments not contrary to Art. 30.	11 July 1990 [1990] ECR 3059
60/89	*Monteil & Samanni* Concept of medicinal product (cf. Case 369/88).	21 Mar. 1991 [1991] ECR 1547
T-69/89	*Radio Telefis Eirann* Copyright on weekly TV guides. Competition; intellectual property rights.	10 July 1991 [1991] ECR II-485
T-70/89	*BBC* v. *Commission* See T-69/89.	10 July 1991 [1991] ECR II-535
T-76/89	*ITP* v. *Commission* See T-69/89.	10 July 1991 [1991] ECR II-575
95/89	*Commission* v. *Italy** Food additives to cheese. Protection of health.	16 July 1992 [1992] ECR 4545
111/89	*Bakken Hillegom* Fees for plant health inspections. (Arts. 12, 16; 'charges having equivalent effect') Art. 36 cannot be interpreted as permitting the imposition of charges.	2 May 1990 [1990] ECR 1735
128/89	*Commission* v. *Italy* Plant health checks on grapefruit. Member States' power to adopt health protection measures under the harmonizing directives may not under any circumstances exceed the limits laid down by Art. 36.	12 July 1990 [1990] ECR 3239
177/89	*Commission* v. *Italy* Foodstuffs (marketing). Subjecting the marketing of food extracts imported from other Member States to restrictive conditions, incl. previous authorization.	19 June 1990 [1990] ECR 2429
196/89	*Nespoli & Crippa* Foodstuffs—cheese. National rules on cheese requiring compliance with a minimum fat content.	11 Oct. 1990 [1990] ECR 3647

No.	Name/subject	Date and publication
205/89	*Commission* v. *Greece* Provisions subjecting imports of pasteurized butter to the requirement of a health certificate. Justification: protection of public health (none).	19 Mar. 1991 [1991] ECR 1361
210/89	*Commission* v. *Italy* Foodstuffs—marketing of cheese. Rules on the minimum fat content hindering the importation/marketing under the name 'cheese' of cheeses originating in other Member States. Justifications: consumer protection, fair trading (none).	11 Oct. 1990 [1991] ECR 3697
235/89	*Commission* v. *Italy* Compulsory patent licences.	18 Feb. 1992 [1992] ECR 777
238/89	*Pall* Trade marks—misleading advertising. National rules permitting an objection to the marketing of (R)-marked products if the affixed trade mark has not been registered in that Member State. Justifications: consumer protection, fair trading.	13 Dec. 1990 [1990] ECR 4827
241/89	*SARPP* Foodstuffs (label, advertising). National rules prohibiting any statement alluding to sugar in the advertising of artificial sweeteners (incl. Dir. 79/112).	12 Dec. 1990 [1990] ECR 4695
243/89	*Storebaelt** Public procurement; award of works contract. Invitation to tender on the basis of a condition requiring the use to the greatest possible extent of Danish materials.	22 June 1993 Not yet pub.
260/89	*ERT* v. *DEP and Others* Grant of television monopoly coupled with exclusive rights in respect of certain materials and products.	18 June 1991 [1991] ECR 2925
269/89	*Bonfait* Meat products. National rules restricting the use of the description 'prepared meat product' to products which comply with certain requirements concerning composition.	13 Nov. 1990 [1990] ECR 4169
270/89	*Cholay* Industrial and commercial property. National legislation permitting the charging, on the public use of imported sound recordings, in addition to the performance royalty of a supplement reproduction royalty not provided for in the legislation of the Member State of origin.	12 Dec. 1990 [1990] ECR 4607
287/89	*Commission* v. *Belgium* Retail price system for manufactured tobacco; minimum selling prices for manufactured tobacco imposed by	7 May 1991 [1991] ECR 2233

No.	Name/subject	Date and publication
	means of tax measures without consideration of the cost prices of importers are contrary to Art. 30.	
293/89	*Commission* v. *Greece** Food additives to cheese. Protection of health.	16 July 1992 [1992] ECR 4577
312/89	*Conforama & Others* National legislation prohibiting the employment of workers in retail shops on Sundays.	28 Feb. 1991 [1991] ECR 997
332/89	*Marchandise & Others* National legislation prohibiting the employment of workers in retail shops on Sundays after 12 noon (incl. Arts. 3 (*f*), 5, 59–66, and 85).	28 Feb. 1991 [1991] ECR 1027
339/89	*Alsthom* v. *Sulzer* Art. 34 (export). Product liability. National rules concerning a vendor's liability for defective products which are stricter than those in force in the other Member States.	24 Jan. 1991 [1991] ECR 107
347/89	*Eurim-Pharm* Proprietary medicinal products. Packaging not in accordance with national law. Protection of health (incl. Dirs. 65/65, 73/319).	16 Apr. 1991 [1991] ECR 1747
350/89	*Sheptonhurst* National legislation prohibiting the sale of sex articles from unlicensed sex establishment not contrary to Art. 30 (cf. Case 23/89).	7 May 1991 [1991] ECR 2387
369/89	*Peeters* Foodstuffs: labelling and presentation. Language: national law cannot require the exclusive use of a specific language for the labelling of foodstuffs, without allowing for the possibility of using another language easily understood by purchasers or of ensuring that the purchaser is informed by other measures.	18 June 1991 [1991] ECR 2971
1, 176/90	*Aragonesa* Legislation of an autonomous community of a Member State prohibiting in its territory certain forms of advertisement of beverages having a high alcohol content.	25 July 1991 [1991] ECR 4151
2/90	*Free movement of waste** Waste, recyclable or not, is to be treated as a product for which the free movement pursuant to Art. 30 could not, in principle, be restricted. Measures distinctly applied; still not discriminatory. Environment protection.	9 July 1992 [1992] ECR 4431

No.	Name/subject	Date and publication
30/90	*Commission* v. *UK* Compulsory patent licences (see 235/89).	18 Feb. 1992 [1992] ECR 829
39/90	*Denkavit Futtermittel* Requirement to indicate the ingredients used in compound feedingstuffs in descending order of their proportion. Justification: protection of health, consumer protection, fair trading.	20 June 1991 [1991] ECR 3069
42/90	*Bellon* Foodstuffs (preservatives). Justification: protection of public health (incl. Dir. 64/54).	13 Dec. 1990 [1991] ECR 4863
47/90	*Delhaize & Le Lion* v. *Promal. & Bodegas** Art. 34 (export). Export of wine in bulk. Designation of origin.	9 June 1992 [1992] ECR 3669
62/90	*Commission* v. *Germany* Prohibition of importation, from another Member State, of medical products by an individual for personal needs constitutes a breach of Arts. 30 *et seq*. Protection of public health and human life.	8 Apr. 1992 [1992] ECR I-2601
176/90	See 1/90.	
191/90	*Generics** Patents. Licences of right.	27 Oct. 1992 [1992] ECR 5335
239/90	*Boscher* Motor vehicles. Sale by public auction of imported second-hand cars. Requirement of entry of the owner in the local trade register. Justifications: consumer protection, public policy.	30 Apr. 1991 [1991] ECR 2023
290/90	*Commission* v. *Germany** Concept of medicinal product; cosmetics (eye-wash solutions).	20 May 1992 [1992] ECR 3317
304/90	*Reading Borough Council** Sunday trading, see 306/88.	16 Dec. 1992 [1992] ECR 6493
344/90	*Commission* v. *France** Food additives. Protection of health.	16 July 1992 [1992] ECR 4719
375/90	*Commission* v. *Greece** Foodstuffs. National legislation fixing micro-biological requirements. Absence of harmonizing measures on Community level.	27 Apr. 1993 [1993] ECR 2055
3/91	*Export./LOR & Confis. du Tech** Intellectual and commercial property. Import prohibition due to a bilateral agreement between	10 Nov. 1992 [1992] ECR 5529

No.	Name/subject	Date and publication
	Member States relating to the protection of designation of origin.	
13, 113/91	*Debus** Foodstuffs—beer. National legislation relating to additives. Protection of health.	4 June 1992 [1992] ECR 3617
126/91	*Yves Rocher** National rules concerning commercial advertising. Art. 30 must be regarded as rendering inapplicable legislation of Member State A which prohibits an undertaking established in that State and engaged in the mail order sale by catalogue or prospectus of goods imported from Member State B from advertising by means of prices when a new price is contrasted in an eye-catching manner with a higher price indicated in an earlier catalogue or sales prospectus.	18 May 1993 [1993] ECR 2361
137/91	*Commission* v. *Greece** Arts. 5 and 30.	24 June 1992 [1992] ECR 4023
169/91	*City of Stoke-on-Trent etc.** Sunday trading, see 306/88.	16 Dec. 1992 [1992] ECR 6635
207/91	*Eurim-Pharm* v. *Bundesgesundheitsamt** FTA Austria–EEC; Arts. 13 and 20. Parallel imports of medicinal products. Protection of public health and human life.	1 July 1993 [1993] ECR 3723
219/91	*Ter Voort** Concept of 'medicinal product'.	28 Oct. 1992 [1992] ECR 5502
228/91	*Commission* v. *Italy** Health inspections; requirement by the State of destination of a health inspection of goods which have already been inspected in the State of origin and which are accompanied by a health certificate. FTA EEC–Norway.	25 May 1993 [1993] ECR 2701
235/91	*Commission* v. *Ireland** Import licences for meat.	17 Nov. 1992 (1992) ECR 5917
267, 268/91	*Keck & Mithouard** Prohibition of resale at a loss. Definition 'measures having equivalent effect' (towards a more narrow definition?).	24 Nov. 1993 Not yet pub.
271/92	*Prothèses Oculaires** National legislation prohibiting the sale of contact lenses by non-holders of an optician's certificate or equivalent qualification. Protection of public health.	25 May 1993 [1993] ECR 2899

No.	Name/subject	Date and publication
373/92	*Commission* v. *Belgium** Medicinal products; an obligation in the Member State of importation to duplicate tests already carried out in the Member State of origin constitutes a breach of Arts. 30 and 36.	8 June 1993 [1993] ECR 3107

Notes: The list should provide the reader with a quick guide to Arts. 30 to 36 EEC cases. It does not, however, aim at being totally comprehensive. In the light of the EEA Agreement, not all aspects of all cases might be considered relevant (see Art. 6 EEA).

* Judgment given after the date of signature of the EEA Agreement (2 May 1992). Cases from the Court of First Instance are marked by 'T' before the case number, and by 'II-' before the ECR number.

[a] Joined Cases 89/74, 18 and 19/75.

[b] Joined Cases 314–16/81 and 83/82.

[c] Joined Cases 271–4/84 and 6 and 7/85.

[d] Joined Cases 317/86, 48, 49, 285 and 363–7/87, 65 and 78–80/88.

ANNEXE G

INTERNATIONAL CONVENTIONS IN THE FIELDS OF INDUSTRIAL PROPERTY AND COPYRIGHT

I. INDUSTRIAL PROPERTY

The 12 agreements concluded within the framework of the Paris Union and administered by WIPO are the following:

Name of the convention	Contracting States	Characteristics
Madrid Agreement of 14 Apr. 1891[a] for the Repression of False or Deceptive Indications of Source on Goods	31 States (among which F, D, IRL, I, FL, P, E, S, CH, and UK)	Measures against importation (seizure, prohibition, or other action) of goods falsely or deceptively indicating a contracting State as place of origin
Nairobi Treaty of 26 Sept. 1981 on the Protection of the Olympic Symbol	33 States (among which GR and I)	Protection of the Olympic symbol against commercial use without authorization and sharing of fees between Olympic Committees
'PCT' Patent Co-operation Treaty of 19 June 1970[b]	59 States (among which A, B, DK, FIN, F, D, GR, IRL, I, FL, L, NL, N, P, E, S, CH, and UK)	Facilitation of patent registration—international search—longer priority period
Budapest Treaty of 28 Apr. 1977[c] on the International Recognition of the Deposit of Micro-organisms for the Purposes of Patent Procedure	26 States (among which A, B, DK, FIN, F, D, GR, I, FL, NL, N, E, S, CH, and UK)	Recognition of a single deposit in any agreed international depository authority as valid for patent procedure purposes

Name of the convention	Contracting States	Characteristics
Madrid Agreement of 14 Apr. 1891[d] concerning the International Registration of Marks	36 States (among which A, B, F, D, I, FL, L, NL, P, E, and CH)	Facilitation of trade mark registration through single international registration with WIPO, after a first national registration—presumption of agreement by designated States if no opposition within one year
Protocol of 27 June 1989 relating to the Madrid Agreement concerning the International Registration of Marks (not yet in force)	27 signatory States (among which A, B, DK, FIN, F, D, GR, IRL, I, FL, L, NL, P, E, S, CH, and UK) and one ratification by E	Facilitation of trade mark registration through single international registration with WIPO, after first national registration or application—presumption of agreement by designated States if no opposition within 18 months—links with the Community trade mark system)
Lisbon Agreement of 31 Oct. 1958[e] for the protection of Appellations of Origin and their International Registration	17 States (among which F, I, and P)	Protection and registration of appellations of origin—recognition in all contracting States one year after communication of registration, except for those States which opposed within the year
Hague Agreement of 6 Nov. 1925[f] concerning the International Deposit of Industrial Designs	22 States (among which B, F, D, I, FL, L, NL, E, and CH)	International deposit with WIPO of an industrial design—presumption of agreement by designated States if no opposition within 6 months from publication by WIPO—renewability every five years

Name of the convention	Contracting States	Characteristics
Strasbourg Agreement of 24 Mar. 1971[g] concerning the International Patent Classification	27 States (among which A, B, DK, FIN, F, D, IRL, I, L, NL, N, P, E, S, CH, and UK)	Division of technologies into 8 main sections and about 64,000 subdivisions, each having a symbol (combination of numerals and letters) which is then indicated on the patent documents issued by patent offices—facilitation of search for 'prior art'—used in practice in about 70 countries
Nice Agreement of 15 June 1957[h] concerning the International Classification of Goods and Services for the Purposes of the Registration of Marks	37 States (among which A, B, DK, FIN, F, D, IRL, I, FL, L, NL, N, P, E, S, CH, and UK)	Classification consisting of a list of classes (34 for goods and 8 for services) and an alphabetical list of goods and services comprising about 11,000 items
Locarno Agreement of 8 Oct. 1968[i] establishing an International Classification for Industrial Designs	20 States (among which A, DK, FIN, F, D, IRL, I, NL, N, E, S, and CH)	Classification consisting of 32 classes and 223 subclasses and an alphabetical list of goods
Vienna Agreement of 12 June 1973 establishing an International Classification of the Figurative Elements of Marks	5 States (among which F, L, NL, and S)	Classification consisting of 29 categories, 144 divisions, and 1,569 sections
In addition, the two following agreements have been concluded:		
'IPIC' Treaty of 26 May 1989 on Intellectual Property in Respect of Integrated Circuits (known as 'Washington Treaty')	8 signatory States and one ratification	8 years' protection of topographies of integrated circuits—national treatment—minimum level of protection (right of reproduction, importation, sale, or other commercial distribution)—conditions for compulsory licence—protection dependent either on commercial exploitation or on registration—dispute settlement mechanism

Name of the convention	Contracting States	Characteristics
International Convention for the Protection of New Varieties of Plants of 2 Dec. 1961[j]	24 States (among which B, DK, FIN, F, D, IRL, I, NL, N, E, S, CH, and UK)	Creates a new Union called the International Union for the Protection of New Varieties of Plants ('UPOV') situated in the same building as WIPO—establishes a system of protection for breeders of new plant varieties—national treatment—right of priority—common substantive rules (such as protection through special title or through a patent, protection of the largest possible number of botanical genera and species, exclusive rights production, offering for sale and marketing, protection for at least 15 years, independence between protection rights)

Note: A: Austria; B: Belgium; CH: Switzerland; D: Germany; DK: Denmark; E: Spain; F: France; FIN: Finland; FL: Liechtenstein; GR: Greece; I: Italy; IRL: Ireland; IS: Iceland; L: Luxembourg; N: Norway; NL: the Netherlands; P: Portugal; S: Sweden; UK: United Kingdom.

[a] Last revised in Stockholm in 1967.

[b] Last modified in 1984.

[c] Last amended in 1980.

[d] Last revised in Stockholm in 1967.

[e] Last revised in Stockholm in 1967.

[f] Last revised in 1960 and completed by the Monaco Act of 1961 and the Stockholm Act of 1967.

[g] Last amended in 1979.

[h] Last revised in Geneva in 1977.

[i] Last amended in 1979.

[j] Last revised in 1978. Information status 13 Sept. 1993.

Source: WIPO: General Information (Geneva, 1993); Doc. 423 (*e*) (status of membership on 1 May 1993); Doc. AB/XXIV/g (of 25 Aug. 1993).

II. COPYRIGHT

Name of the convention	Contracting States	Characteristics
Berne Convention of 9 Sept. 1886[a] for the Protection of Literary and Artistic Works	100 States (among which A, B, DK, FIN, F, D, GR, IS, IRL, I, FL, L, NL, N, P, E, S, CH, and UK)	National treatment—automatic protection—independence of the protection—states minimum standards of protection (works and rights protected and duration)
Rome Convention of 26 Oct. 1961 for the protection of Performers, Producers of Phonograms and Broadcasting Organisations	43 States (among which A, DK, FIN, F, D, GR, IRL, I, L, NL, N, E, S, CH, and UK)	Secures protection in performances of performers (right to broadcast, communicate to the public, fix, and reproduce such fixation), phonograms of producers (reproduction right), and broadcasts of broadcasting organizations (right to fix, reproduce such fixations, and communicate to the public)
Geneva Convention of 29 Oct. 1971 for the protection of Producers of Phonograms against Unauthorized Duplication of their Phonograms	48 States (among which A, DK, FIN, F, D, I, L, NL, N, E, S, CH, and UK)	Obligation to protect phonogram producers against the making of unauthorized duplicates and their importation when this is made for distribution to the public
Brussels Convention of 21 May 1974 relating to the Distribution of Programme-Carrying Signals Transmitted by Satellite	15 States (among which A, D, GR, and I)	Obligation to take measures to prevent unauthorized distribution on or from its territory on a programme-carrying signal transmitted by satellite
Film Register Treaty (Treaty on the International Registration of Audiovisual Works) of 18 Apr. 1989	8 States (among which A and F)	Establishes an international register of audio-visual works—registration is considered as true until the contrary is proved (rebuttable presumption)

Name of the convention	Contracting States	Characteristics
Universal Copyright Convention of 6 Sept. 1952[b] (administered by UNESCO)	91 States to the original Convention (among which all EC and EFTA States) and 56 States to the revised version (among which A, D, DK, E, FIN, F, I, N, NL, P, CH, S, and UK)	National treatment—states a minimum level of protection (adequate and effective protection)—simplifies the formalities of protection regarding those countries which do not have automatic protection: for being protected in these countries, it is enough that the published work mentions the symbol ©, the name of the right owner, and the year of the first publication.

Note: A: Austria; B: Belgium; CH: Switzerland; D: Germany; DK: Denmark; E: Spain; F: France; FIN: Finland; FL: Liechtenstein; GR: Greece; I: Italy; IRL: Ireland; IS: Iceland; L: Luxembourg; N: Norway; NL: the Netherlands; P: Portugal; S: Sweden; UK: United Kingdom.

[a] Last completed in Paris in 1971.

[b] Last revised in Paris in 1971. Information status 1 Oct. 1993.

Sources: WIPO: General Information (Geneva, 1993); Doc. 423 (*e*) (status of membership on 1 May 1993); Doc. AB/XXIV/9 (of 25 Aug. 1993); UNESCO.

ANNEXE H

EXCERPTS OF RELEVANT CASES IN THE FIELD OF INTELLECTUAL PROPERTY

1. MEANING OF THE WORDS 'INDUSTRIAL AND COMMERCIAL PROPERTY' IN ARTICLE 36 EEC

Joined Cases 55 and 57/80 *GEMA* [1981] ECR 147 (grounds 9 and 12)
'The latter expression ["industrial and commercial property" in Article 36 EEC] includes the protection conferred by copyright, especially when exploited commercially in the form of licences capable of affecting distribution in the various Member States of goods incorporating the protected literary or artistic work.'

'It is true that copyright comprises moral rights . . . However, it also comprises other rights, notably the right to exploit commercially the marketing of the protected work, particularly in the form of licences granted in return for payment of royalties. It is this economic aspect of copyright which is the subject of the question . . . and . . . in the application of Article 36 of the Treaty, there is no reason to make a distinction between copyright and other industrial and commercial property rights.'

2. ARTICLE 222 EEC: EXISTENCE/EXERCISE OF IPRS

Joint Cases 56 and 58/64 *Consten and Grundig* [1966] ECR 299
'Article 222 confines itself to stating that the "Treaty shall in no way prejudice the rules in Member States governing the system of property ownership". The injunction . . . [contained in the contested Commission Decision] to refrain from using rights under national trade-mark law in order to set an obstacle in the way of parallel imports does not affect the grant of those rights but only limits their exercise to the extent necessary to give effect to the prohibition under Article 85 (1).'

Case 78/70 *Deutsche Grammophon* [1971] ECR 487 (ground 11)
'[A]lthough the Treaty does not affect the existence of rights recognized by the legislation of a Member State with regard to industrial and commercial property, the exercise of such rights may nevertheless fall within the prohibitions laid down by the Treaty.'

Case 262/81 *Coditel II* [1982] ECR 3381 (ground 13)
'The distinction, implicit in Article 36, between the existence of a right conferred by the legislation of a Member State in regard to the protection of artistic and intellectual property, which cannot be affected by the provisions of the Treaty, and the exercise of such right, which might constitute a disguised restriction on trade between Member States, also applies where that right is exercised in the context of the movement of services.'

3. APPLICATION OF ARTICLES 85 AND 86 EEC TO IPRS: CONDITIONS AND LIMITS

(A) In general

Joint Cases 56 and 58/64 *Consten and Grundig* [1966] ECR 299
'Such a body of rules [the Community rules on competition], by reason of its nature described above and its function, does not allow the improper use of rights under any national trade-mark in order to frustrate the Community's law on cartels.'

Case 24/67 *Parke Davis* [1968] ECR 55 (operative part, para. 2)
'The exercise of such rights [IPRs] cannot of itself fall either under Article 85 (1), in the absence of any agreement, decision or concerted practice prohibited by this provision, or under Article 86, in the absence of any abuse of dominant position.'

(B) Article 85 EEC

(i) Agreement or a concerted practice

Case 24/67 *Parke Davis* [1968] ECR 55
'A patent taken by itself and independently of any agreement of which it may be the subject, is unrelated to any of these categories [enumerated in Article 85 (1)], but is the expression of a legal status granted by a State to products meeting certain criteria, and thus exhibits none of the elements of contract or concerted practice required by Article 85 (1). Nevertheless it is possible that the provisions of this article may apply if the use of one or more patents, in concert between undertakings, should lead to the creation of a situation which may come within the concepts of agreements between undertakings, decisions of associations of undertakings or concerted practices within the meaning of Article 85 (1).'

Case 78/70 *Deutsche Grammophon* [1971] ECR 487 (ground 6)
'The exercise of the exclusive right referred to in the question [copyright] might fall itself under the prohibition set out by this provision [Article 85 (1)] each time it manifests itself as the subject, the means or the result of an agreement which, by preventing imports from other Member States of products lawfully distributed there, has as its effect the partitioning of the market.'

(ii) 'Delimitation' or settlement agreements

Commission press release on informal settlement in case *Persil* of 22 February 1978 reproduced in [1978] 1 CMLR 395 (para. 9)
'An agreement as to the appearance of trade marks aiming to ensure that there can be no confusion in the consumer's mind about the difference between the relevant goods, with the result that they can then be traded in freely throughout the Community without either party having to give up the use of his well-established trade mark for certain products, is to be

attributed to the preservation of the existence of the trade mark and is accordingly outside the prohibition in Article 85 (1).'

Commission Decision 78/193/EEC *Penneys* of 23 December 1977, OJ L 60/19 (para. II (4) (*b*))

'[T]he assignment . . . has not as object or effect to prevent, restrict or distort competition within the common market. It could be otherwise, in particular, if such an assignment or waiver were the means of a market sharing agreement.'

'In general the enterprises involved in a situation such as this must seek the least restrictive solution possible, such as incorporating distinguishing marks, shapes or colours to differentiate the products of the two enterprises which bear identical or confusingly similar marks. A contractual obligation for the parties to assign or waive their trademark and trade name rights which would make it necessary for them to re-establish goodwill under other names may, under certain circumstances, have restrictive effects.'

Commission Decision 82/897/EEC *Toltec/Dorcet* of 15 December 1982, OJ L 379/19 (para. II (3) (A) (*e*) and II (4))

'However, the greater the difference in the products or the less likely the risk of confusion, the more the agreement must take account of the overriding goal of common market unity. Of all the possible solutions to the conflict, the parties therefore have to adopt that which least restricts the use of both marks throughout the whole of the common market. This includes agreements to reproduce the disputed mark only in a certain way (colour, form of lettering, inclusion of trade name, etc.) or possibly to use it for certain products only.'

'[I]t is problematical, if not impossible on economic grounds, to replace an established mark by another mark, because of the consequent loss of the advertising impact of the established mark and other practical difficulties.'

(c) Article 86

(i) Dominant position

Case 24/67 *Parke Davis* [1968] ECR 55

'For this prohibition [Article 86] to apply it is thus necessary that three elements shall be present together: the existence of a dominant position, the abuse of this position and the possibility that trade between Member States may be affected thereby. Although a patent confers on its holder a special protection at national level, it does not follow that the exercise of the rights thus conferred implies the presence together of all three elements in question. It could only do so if the use of the patent were to degenerate into an abuse of the abovementioned protection.'

Case 40/70 *Sirena* [1971] ECR 69 (ground 16)

'[T]he proprietor of a trade-mark does not enjoy a "dominant position" within the meaning of Article 86 merely because he is in a position to prevent third parties from putting into circulation, on the territory of a Member State, products bearing the same trade-mark.'

Case 78/70 *Deutsche Grammophon* [1971] ECR 487 (ground 16)

'A manufacturer of sound recordings who holds a right related to copyright does not occupy a dominant position within the meaning of Article 86 of the Treaty merely by exercising his exclusive right to distribute the protected articles.'

(ii) Abuse

Case 78/70 *Deutsche Grammophon* [1971] ECR 487 (ground 19)
'For it to fall within Article 86 a dominant position must further be abused. The difference between the controlled price and the price of the product reimported from another Member State does not necessarily suffice to disclose such an abuse; it may however, if unjustified by any objective criteria and if it is particularly marked, be a determining factor in such abuse.'

Case 238/87 *Volvo* [1988] ECR 6211 (ground 9)
'[T]he exercise of an exclusive right by the proprietor of a registered design in respect of car body panels may be prohibited by Article 86 if it involves . . . certain abusive conduct such as refusal to supply spare parts to independent repairers, the fixing of prices for spare parts at an unfair level or a decision no longer to produce spare parts for a particular model even though many cars of that model are still in circulation, provided that such conduct is liable to affect trade between Member States.'

4. SPECIFIC SUBJECT-MATTER OF THE DIFFERENT IPRS

(A) Patent

Case 15/74 *Sterling Drug* [1974] ECR 1147 (ground 9)
'In relation to patents, the specific subject matter of the industrial property is the guarantee that the patentee, to reward the creative effort of the inventor, has the exclusive right to use an invention with a view to manufacturing industrial products and putting them into circulation for the first time, either directly or by the grant of licences to third parties, as well as the right to oppose infringements.'

Case 187/80 *Merck* v. *Stephar* [1981] ECR 2063 (ground 9)
'[I]n accordance with the definition of the specific purpose of the patent . . . the substance of a patent right lies essentially in according the inventor an exclusive right of first placing the product on the market.'

(B) Trade mark

Case 16/74 *Winthrop* [1974] ECR 1183 (ground 8)
'In relation to trade marks, the specific subject-matter of the industrial property is the guarantee that the owner of the trade mark has the exclusive right to use that trade mark, for the purpose of putting products protected by the trade mark into circulation for the first time, and is therefore intended to protect him against competitors wishing to take advantage of the status and reputation of the trade mark by selling products illegally bearing that trade mark.'

Case 102/77 *Hoffmann-La Roche* [1978] ECR 1139 (ground 7)
'[T]he essential function of the trade-mark . . . is to guarantee the identity of the origin of the trade-marked product to the consumer or ultimate user, by enabling him without any possibility of confusion to distinguish that product from products which have another origin. This guarantee of origin means that the consumer or ultimate user can be certain that a trade-marked product which is sold to him has not been subject at a previous stage of marketing to interference by a third person, without the authorization of the proprietor of the trade-mark, such as to affect the original condition of the product. The right attributed to the proprietor of preventing any use of the trade-mark which is likely to impair the guarantee of origin so understood is therefore part of the specific subject-matter of the trade-mark right.'

Case 3/78 *American Home Products* [1978] ECR 1823 (grounds 13–17)
'13. This guarantee of origin means that only the proprietor may confer an identity upon the product by affixing the mark.

14. The guarantee of origin would in fact be jeopardized if it were permissible for a third party to affix the mark to the products, even to an original product.

15. It is thus in accordance with the essential function of the mark that national legislation, even where the manufacturer or distributor is the proprietor of two different marks for the same product, prevent an unauthorized third party from usurping the right to affix one or other mark to any part whatsoever of the production or change the marks affixed by the proprietor to different parts of the production.

16. The guarantee of the origin of the product requires that the exclusive right of the proprietor should be protected in the same manner where the different parts of the production, bearing different marks, come from two different Member States.

17. The right granted to the proprietor to prohibit any unauthorized affixing of his mark to his product accordingly comes within the specific subject-matter of the trade-mark.'

(c) Copyright

Performing rights in a cinematographic film

Case 62/79 *Coditel I* [1980] ECR 831 (ground 14)
'[T]he right of a copyright owner and his assigns to require fees for any showing of a film is part of the essential function of copyright in this type of literary and artistic work.'

(d) Other IPRs

(i) Design

Case 238/87 *Volvo* [1988] ECR 6211 (ground 8)
'[T]he right of the proprietor of a protected design to prevent third parties from manufacturing and selling or importing, without its consent, products incorporating the design constitutes the very subject-matter of his exclusive right.'

(ii) Designation of origin

Case 12/74 *Commission* v. *Germany* [1975] ECR 181 (ground 7)
'To the extent to which these appellations are protected by law they must satisfy the objectives of such protection, in particular the need to ensure not only that the interests of the producers concerned are safeguarded against unfair competition, but also that consumers are protected against information which may mislead them.

These appellations only fulfil their specific purpose if the product which they describe does in fact possess qualities and characteristics which are due to the fact that it originated in a specific geographical area . . . the geographical area of origin of a product must . . . confer on it a specific quality and specific characteristics of such a nature as to distinguish it from all other products.'

5. EC-WIDE EXHAUSTION PRINCIPLE

(A) Patent

Case 15/74 *Sterling Drug* [1974] ECR 1147 (ground 15)
'[T]he exercise, by a patentee, of the right which he enjoys under the legislation of a Member State to prohibit the sale, in that State, of a product protected by the patent which has been marketed in another Member State by the patentee or with his consent is incompatible with the rules of the EEC Treaty concerning the free movement of goods within the Common Market.'

Case 19/84 *Pharmon* [1985] ECR 2281 (grounds 25 and 27)
'[W]here the competent authorities . . . grant a third party a compulsory licence . . . , the patentee cannot be deemed to have consented to the operation of that third party. Such a measure deprives the patent proprietor from his right to determine freely the conditions under which he markets his product.'

'. . . It is therefore necessary to allow the patent proprietor to prevent the importation and marketing of products manufactured under a compulsory licence in order to protect the substance of his exclusive rights under his patent.'

Case 187/80 *Merck* v. *Stephar* [1981] ECR 2063 (ground 11)
'It is for the proprietor of the patent to decide . . . under what conditions he will market his product, including the possibility of marketing it in a Member State where the law does not provide patent protection for the product in question. If he decides to do so he must then accept the consequences of his choice as regards the free movement of the product.'

(B) Trade mark

Case 192/73 *Hag I* [1974] ECR 731 (ground 15)
'[T]o prohibit the marketing in a Member State of a product legally bearing a trade mark in another Member State, for the sole reason that an identical trade mark having the same origin exists in the first state is incompatible with the provisions for free movement of goods within the Common Market.'

Case C-10/89 *Hag II* [1990] ECR 3711 (ground 19)
'[I]n a situation . . . in which the mark originally had one sole proprietor and the single ownership was broken as a result of expropriation, each of the trade mark proprietors must be able to oppose the importation and marketing, in a Member State in which the trade mark belongs to him, of goods originating from the other proprietor, in so far as they are similar products bearing an identical mark or one which is liable to lead to confusion.'

Case 119/75 *Terrapin* v. *Terranova* [1976] ECR 1039 (ground 8)
'[I]t is compatible with the provisions of the EEC Treaty relating to free movement of goods for an undertaking established in a Member State, by virtue of a right to a trade-mark and a right to a commercial name . . . to prevent the importation of products of an undertaking established in another Member State and bearing by virtue of the legislation of that State a name giving rise to confusion with the trade-mark and commercial name of the first undertaking, provided that there are no agreements restricting competition and no legal or economic ties between the undertakings and that their respective rights have arisen independently of one another.'

(c) Design

Case 144/81 *Nancy Kean Gifts* [1982] ECR 2853 (ground 29)
'The proprietor of a right to a design . . . may oppose the importation of products from another Member State which are identical in appearance to the design which has been filed, provided that the products in question have not been put into circulation in the other Member State by, or with the consent of, the proprietor of the right or a person legally or economically dependent on him.'

(d) Copyright: neighbouring rights

Cases 55 and 57/80 *GEMA* [1981] ECR 147 (ground 18)
'[N]o provision of national legislation may permit an undertaking which is responsible for the management of copyrights and has a monopoly on the territory of a Member State by virtue of that management to charge a levy on products imported from another Member State where they were put into circulation by or with the consent of the right owner and thereby cause the Common Market to be partitioned.'

Case 62/79 *Coditel I* [1980] ECR 881 (ground 12 and operative part)
'12. A cinematographic film belongs to the category of literary and artistic works made available to the public by performances which may be indefinitely repeated. In this respect the problems involved . . . are not the same as those which arise in connection with literary and artistic works the placing of which at the disposal of the public is inseparable from the circulation of the material form of the works, as it is the case of books or records.

(operative part) The provisions of the Treaty relating to the freedom to provide services do not preclude an assignee of the performing rights in a cinematographic film in a Member State from relying upon his right to prohibit the exhibition of that film in that State, without his authority, by means of cable diffusion if the film so exhibited is picked up and transmitted after being broadcast in another Member State by a third party with the consent of the original owner of the right.'

ANNEXE I

PROVISIONS CONCERNING EXHAUSTION IN THE DIFFERENT EXISTING OR DRAFT EC LEGISLATION

COMMUNITY PATENTS[1]

As regards Community patents

'The rights conferred by a Community patent shall not extend to acts concerning a product covered by that patent which are done within the territories of the Contracting States after that product has been put on the market in one of these States by the proprietor of the patent or with his express consent, unless there are grounds which, under Community law, would justify the extension to such acts of the rights conferred by the patent.'

As regards national patents

'1. The rights conferred by a national patent in a Contracting State shall not extend to acts concerning a product covered by that patent which are done within the territory of that Contracting State after that product has been put on the market in any Contracting State by the proprietor of the patent or with his express consent, unless there are grounds which, under Community law, would justify the extension to such acts of the rights conferred by the patent.

2. Paragraph 1 shall also apply with regard to a product put on the market by the proprietor of a national patent, granted for the same invention in another Contracting State, who has economic connections with the proprietor of the patent referred to in paragraph 1. For the purpose of this paragraph, two persons shall be deemed to have economic connections where one of them is in a position to exert a decisive influence on the other, directly or indirectly, with regard to the exploitation of a patent, or where a third party is in a position to exercise such an influence on both persons.

3. The preceding paragraph shall not apply in the case of a product put on the market under a compulsory licence.'

BIOTECHNOLOGICAL INVENTIONS[2]

'The protection referred to in Article 10 shall not extend to biological material derived from biological material that has been marketed by the patent holder or with his consent if the

[1] Arts. 28 and 76 of Council Agreement 89/695/EEC of 15 Dec. 1989 relating to Community patents (*OJ* L 401 (30 Dec. 1989), 1) (not yet in force).

[2] Art. 11 of amended Commission proposal for a Council Directive on the legal protection of biotechnological inventions (COM (92) 589 final, 16 Dec. 1992).

multiplication or propagation results from the application for which the material was marketed.'

COMMUNITY PLANT VARIETY RIGHTS[3]

'1. The rights conferred by a Community plant variety right shall not extend to acts involving individuals of the variety that were disposed of to others in any part of the Community by the holder or with his consent. This shall also be applicable in respect of other material that was disposed of to others pursuant to the first sentence or that was obtained from individuals as referred to in the first sentence.

2. Paragraph 1 shall not apply where the individuals have been or are being used as propagating material for the production of further individuals without having been intended for that purpose when they were disposed of.'

TRADE MARKS

Harmonization Directive[4]

'1. The trade mark shall not entitle the proprietor to prohibit its use in relation to goods which have been put on the market in the Community under that trade mark by the proprietor or with his consent.

2. Paragraph 1 shall not apply where there exist legitimate reasons for the proprietor to oppose further commercialization of the goods, especially where the condition of the goods is changed or impaired after they have been put on the market.'

Community trade mark[5]

'1. A Community trade mark shall not entitle the proprietor to prohibit its use in relation to goods which have been put on the market in the Community under that trade mark by the proprietor or with his consent.

2. Paragraph 1 shall not apply where there exist legitimate reasons for the proprietor to oppose further commercialization of the goods, especially where the condition of the goods is changed or impaired after they have been put on the market.'

[3] Art. 15 of Commission proposal for a Council regulation on Community plant variety rights (COM (90) 347 final) (*OJ* C 244 (28 Sept. 1990), 1), not changed in the amended proposal of 29 March 1993 (COM (93) 104 final).

[4] Art. 7 of First Council Dir. 89/104/EEC of 21 Dec. 1988 to approximate the laws of the Member States relating to trade marks (*OJ* L 40 (11 Feb. 1989), 1).

[5] Art. 13 of Council Regulation on the Community trade mark (*OJ* L 11 (14 Jan. 1984), 1). In this regard, it is interesting to note that the original Commission proposal was almost totally codifying the Court case-law on exhaustion of trade marks with provisions on goods put on the market outside the EC (*EMI* v. *CBS*) and on repackaging (*Hoffmann-La Roche* and *American Home Products*).

DESIGNS

Proposed Harmonization Directive[6]

'The rights conferred by a design right upon registration shall not extend to acts relating to a product in which a design included within the scope of protection of the design right is incorporated or to which it is applied, when the product has been put on the market in the Community by the holder of the design or with his consent.'

Community Design

'The rights conferred by a Community Design shall not extent to acts relating to a product in which a design included within the scope of protection of the Community Design is incorporated or to which it is applied, when the product has been put on the market in the Community by the holder of the design or with his consent.'

RENTAL AND LENDING RIGHTS AND NEIGHBOURING RIGHTS[7]

Rental and lending rights

'4. The rights referred to in paragraph 1[8] shall not be exhausted by any sale or other act of distribution of originals and copies of works and other subject matter as set out in Article 2 (1).'[9]

Distribution right

'2. The distribution right shall not be exhausted within the Community in respect of an object as referred to in paragraph 1,[10] except where the first sale in the Community of that object is made by the rightholder or with his consent.

3. The distribution right shall be without prejudice to the specific provisions of Chapter I, in particular Article 1 (4).'

[6] Respectively, Art. 15 of the Commission proposal for a Directive on the legal protection of designs (COM (93) 244 final–COD 464, of 3 Dec. 1993) and Art. 24 of the Commission proposal for a Regulation on the Community Design (COM (93) 342 final–COD 463, of 3 Dec. 1993).

[7] Arts. 1 (4) and 9 (2) and (3) of Council Dir. 92/100/EEC of 19 Nov. 1992 on rental right and lending right and on certain rights related to copyright in the field of intellectual property (*OJ* L 346 (27 Nov. 1992), 61).

[8] Rental and lending rights of originals and copies of copyright works.

[9] Which tells who is the right owner and what is the subject-matter of his right.

[10] Performances, phonograms, films, and broadcasts. Only the distribution right is exhausted (not the other rights such as fixation, reproduction or broadcasting, and communication to the public).

COMPUTER PROGRAMS[11]

'The first sale in the Community of a copy of a program by the rightholder or with his consent shall exhaust the distribution right within the Community of that copy, with the exception of the right to control further rental of the program or a copy thereof.'

DATABASES[12]

'[T]he first sale in the Community of a copy of the database by the rightholder or with his consent shall exhaust the distribution right within the Community of that copy, with the exception of the right to control further rental of the database or a copy thereof.'

TOPOGRAPHIES OF SEMICONDUCTOR PRODUCTS[13]

'The exclusive rights to authorize or prohibit the acts specified in paragraph 1 (b)[14] shall not apply to any such act committed after the topography or the semiconductor product has been put on the market in a Member State by the person entitled to authorize its marketing or with his consent.'

[11] Art. 4 (*c*) of Council Dir. 91/250/EEC of 14 May 1991 on the legal protection of computer programs (*OJ* L 122 (17 May 1991), 42).

[12] Art. 6 (*d*) of amended Commission proposal for a Council directive on the legal protection of databases (COM (93) 464 final).

[13] Art. 5 (5) of Council Dir. 87/54/EEC of 16 Dec. 1986 on the legal protection of topographies of semiconductor products (*OJ* L 24 (21 Jan. 1987), 36).

[14] Para. 1 (*b*) reads: 'The exclusive rights . . . shall include the rights to authorize or prohibit . . .: (b) commercial exploitation or the importation for that purpose of a topography or of a semiconductor product manufactured by using the topography.'

ANNEXE J

INTERNATIONAL EXHAUSTION IN EC AND EFTA COUNTRIES

The description below is only a rough indication of the tendency in the different countries, without entering into details on the different nuances. Furthermore, the information regarding trade mark in the EC Member States is based on a study made by Prof. A. von Mülendahl and F.-K. Beier, from the Max-Planck Institute, for the EC Commission in 1979.[1] As regards semiconductor topographies, very few EC Member States had a national legislation before the Semiconductor Directive (87/54/EEC) was made. Finally, concerning patents: like the EFTA countries, EC Member States all practised national exhaustion before turning to EC-wide exhaustion due to the ECJ case-law.

TRADE MARKS

There are some variations in the different national laws or jurisprudence as to the conditions under which international exhaustion applies. Regarding the notion of 'right holder', the exhaustion rule may apply either only when the right holders are identical in both the importing and exporting countries or also where the right holders are different but have contractual or economic links. Regarding the notion of 'marketed', this may concern only retail trade or also include wholesale.

EC Member States

Benelux[2]	International exhaustion (same right owner)	*Grundig* (1956)[3] (same right owner); *Email-Diamant* (1949)[4] (same right owner)
Denmark	International exhaustion	Danish trade mark law is worded the same as the Swedish law (see below under Sweden)

[1] Doc. III/D/1424/79, III, G, No 46.

[2] There has apparently been no definite case-law on international exhaustion from Benelux courts since the entry into force of the uniform Benelux Law on trade marks in 1970, but only from the Dutch and Belgian courts based on their previous respective national laws. Before the entry into force of this uniform law, the Dutch courts allowed parallel imports both in instances where the right owners were the same (*Grundig* (1956)) and where there was a parent–subsidiary relation (*Grundig* (1965), *Graetz* (1962), etc.). The Belgian courts did not however allow parallel imports in case of different ownership of the trade mark (*St Nicholas* (1953)).

[3] Dutch case by Hoge Raad, 14 Dec. 1956, GRUR 1957, 259.

[4] Belgian case by Cour de Cassation, 23 May 1945, Ing.-Cons. 1949, 31.

France	(No jurisprudence on a parallel import case in the trade mark law context)	
Germany	International exhaustion (same right owner or linked owners (economically: parent/subsidiary or legally: licence))	*Maja* (1964)[5] (same right owner); *Cinzano* (1973)[6] (parent/subsidiary)
Italy	International exhaustion (only if same right owner and no exclusive licence granted for Italy)	*Palmolive* (1956)[7]; *Colgate* (1957).[8]
Ireland	International exhaustion (same right owner)	Irish trade mark law is worded the same as the UK law (see below under UK)
UK	International exhaustion (same right owner, even if exclusive licence granted, or linked right owners (parent/subsidiary))	*Champagne Heidsieck* (1926)[9] (same right owner); *Revlon* (1979)[10] (parent/subsidiary); s. 4 (3) (*a*) of the UK Trade Mark Act 1938.

EFTA States

Austria	International exhaustion (same right owner and linked right owners)	*Agfa* (1970)[11] (same owner)
Finland	International exhaustion (same right owner and linked right owners (agent of the producer))	*Felicia* (1968).[12]
Iceland	International exhaustion	No case-law but legislation worded the same as in other Nordic countries (see below under Sweden)
Liechtenstein	If no risk of consumer deception, case-law results in almost the same situation as if there were international exhaustion	Liechtenstein legislation is identical (with minor exceptions) to Swiss law (see below under Switzerland)

[5] BGHZ 41, 44; see in GRUR Int. 1964, 202.
[6] BGHZ 60, 185; see in GRUR Int. 1973, 502.
[7] Cass., 20 Oct. 1956, Riv. Dir. Ind. 1957, ii. 358.
[8] Cass., 5 Apr. 1957, Foro Pad. 1959, i. 35: see also in GRUR-Ber. 2103/58.
[9] *Champagne Heidsieck & Cie.* v. *Buxton* (1930) 47 RPC 28 (Ch. 1929).
[10] *Revlon Inc. and Others* v. *Cripps and Lee Limited and Others* 22 Nov. 1979, by the Court of Appeal (Civil Division).
[11] GRUR Int. 1971, 90.
[12] NIR 1969, 96—Supreme Court Decision of 31 Jan. 1968.

Norway	International exhaustion	No Supreme Court cases but cases in lower courts apply international exhaustion
Sweden	International exhaustion (same right owner and linked right owners (representative, agent, company belonging to a group))	*Polycolor* (1967)[13]
Switzerland	If no risk of consumer deception, case-law results in almost the same situation as if there were international exhaustion	*Saba* (1958)[14]; *Philips* (1960)[15] (the trade mark law does not expressly address the issue of exhaustion)

COPYRIGHT

EC MEMBER STATES

In the field of copyright, international exhaustion is applied by most of the EC Member States. However, due to differences in the national laws regarding the scope of protection, international exhaustion is usually applied only in the narrower instances where the right owner is identical in both the importing and exporting countries and where there are related right owners (e.g. parent/subsidiary).

Denmark	International exhaustion of the distribution right	Arts. 23 and 25 of the Danish Copyright Law
Italy	International exhaustion only concerning imported copies which have originally been produced domestically, have been exported, and are reimported	Art. 17 of the Italian Copyright Law
The Netherlands	International exhaustion of the distribution right[16]	Art. 12 of the Dutch Copyright Law
France and Belgium	Any distribution and import which is not desired by the author can be prevented by means of the 'right of determination' interpreted broadly (provided that there is a clear notice of this right on the copies)	

[13] NJA 1967, 458 (NIR 1968 S. 404).

[14] TF, 17 Oct. 1958, ATF 84 IV 119; see in GRUR Int. 1959, 241.

[15] TF, 4 Oct. 1960, ATF 86 II 270; see in GRUR Int. 1961, 294.

[16] Certain legal scholars are of the opinion that the distribution right is not exhausted in the case of divided rights (i.e. publishing rights divided between related right holders).

Germany	International exhaustion for copies marketed abroad by the right owner himself	
UK and Ireland	International exhaustion for copies published by the same right owner	

EFTA States

Austria	EFTA-EC exhaustion for sound recording and national exhaustion in other cases	Art. 16 (3) of the Austrian Copyright Law
Finland	International exhaustion, including the author's distribution right for cinematographic works	Arts. 23 and 25 of the Copyright Act, as amended (amendment entered into force on 1 June 1993).
Iceland	International exhaustion. The international exhaustion of musical and cinematographic works does not allow copies of those works to be rented to the public without the consent of the creator. Written music may not be rented or lent without the consent of the creator	Arts. 24 and 25 of the Copyright Act
Liechtenstein	International exhaustion	
Norway	International exhaustion. The international exhaustion of musical and cinematographic works does not allow copies of those works to be rented to the public without the consent of the creator	Arts. 21 and 23 of the Copyright Law
Sweden	International exhaustion concerning putting on the market of copies of copyright protected work with the exception of cinematographic works	Arts. 23 and 25 of the Copyright Act
Switzerland	Copies of the work, once marketed by the right owner or with his consent, may be further marketed or otherwise distributed (looks like international exhaustion	Art. 12 of the Copyright Law of 9 Oct. 1992 (entered into force 1 July 1993)

	but leaves it to the courts to decide what is the reference territory for the exhaustion, national, regional, or international)	

SEMICONDUCTOR TOPOGRAPHIES

Austria	The question of exhaustion is left to the competence of the courts; no case-law yet	
Finland	Possible exhaustion of the importation right but the extent of such exhaustion will be decided in a government decree (it is expected that this decree will provide for EEA-wide exhaustion)	Finnish Act on the right to the layout design of integrated circuits (entered into force on 1 July 1991)
Iceland	International exhaustion	Art. 3.2 (4) of Law 78/1993 of 7 May 1993, entered into force on 18 May 1993
Norway	International exhaustion. When a copy of a circuit design has been commercially exploited with the consent of the right holder, that copy may be commercially exploited and imported by others	Art. 3 of the 1990 Law on the Protection of Circuit Designs of Integrated Circuits
Sweden	International exhaustion. Copies of a layout design or products which contain a layout design and which have been distributed to the public with the consent of the right holder may be further distributed to the public	Art. 3 of the Law on the Protection of Semiconductor Designs
Switzerland	Copies of a topography sold by the producer or with his consent may be sold or otherwise distributed further (looks like international exhaustion but leaves it to the courts to decide what is the reference territory for the exhaustion, national, regional, or international)	Art. 6 of the Law on Topographies of Semiconductors

PATENTS

EFTA States

The information below has to be read in connection with Protocol 28 to the EEA Agreement which obliges those EFTA States parties to the EEA (i.e. not Switzerland) to pass from national exhaustion to EEA-wide exhaustion (with the limitations provided for in Article 3 (6) of Protocol 28 concerning Finland and Iceland).

Austria	National exhaustion. Once a product made by use of the patent has been put on the market in Austria by the right holder or with his consent, the right holder can no longer control the use third persons make of this product[17]	Art. 22 of the Austrian Patent Law
Finland	National exhaustion. The holder of a patent can prevent imports of protected products or products which have been produced abroad according to the patented method	Art. 3 of the Finnish Patent Law
Iceland	National exhaustion. There is a conditional clause providing for EEA-wide exhaustion once the EEA has entered into force	A new Patent Law entered into force on 1 Jan. 1992 with wording along the lines of that contained in laws of the Nordic countries
Liechtenstein	Liechtenstein forms a Patent Union with Switzerland, administered by the Swiss authorities	
Norway	National exhaustion. The holder of a patent can prevent imports of protected products or products which have been produced abroad according to the patented method	Art. 3 of the Norwegian Patent Law
Sweden[18]	National exhaustion. The holder of a patent can prevent imports of protected products or products which have been produced abroad according to the patented method	Art. 3 of the Swedish Patent Act

[17] In 1973 the Austrian Supreme Court held that the Austrian patent holder cannot rely on his right to block imports to Austria made by his German licensee, these imports being considered as having been marketed not abroad, but in Austria.

[18] As regards designs, Sweden also applies national exhaustion (Art. 5 of the Design Protection Act). The same goes for plant breeders' rights (Art. 4 of the Plant Breeder's Protection Act). Iceland (on 21 May 1993, entry into force 31 May 1994) and Austria (on 7 June 1990, entry into force 1 Jan. 1991) have also adopted design protection laws, but the question of exhaustion is not addressed.

Switzerland	National exhaustion. The case-law and the doctrine assume that to market a patented product abroad does not exhaust the patent right in Switzerland. However, there is no decision from the Supreme Court answering clearly the question of exhaustion of patent right. A decision of 1982 from the Cantonal Court of Zurich applies the principle of national exhaustion in the field of patents

TABLE OF LEGISLATION

EC TREATIES AND SECONDARY LEGISLATION

EEC Treaty (version before being amended by the European Union Treaty)

Directives

EEA AGREEMENT (ARTICLES, PROTOCOLS, ANNEXES)

EFTA CONVENTIONS AND AGREEMENTS

OTHER

TABLE OF CASES

Numerical

TABLE OF CASES

Alphabetical

Opinions of the ECJ

Decisions of the EC Commission

Other

BIBLIOGRAPHY

GENERAL

Boulouis, J., *Droit institutionnel des Communautés Européennes* (2nd edn., Paris, 1990).

—— 'Les Avis de la Cour de Justice des Communautés sur la compatibilité avec le Traité CEE du projet d'accord créant l'Espace Économique Européen', *Revue trimestrielle de droit européen* (1992), 457–63.

Bourgeois, J. H. J., 'L'Espace Économique Européen', *Revue du Marché Unique Européen*, 2 (1992), 11–24.

Burtscher, W., 'Der Europäische Wirtschaftsraum (EWR) und die Beziehungen der EG zu den EFTA-Staaten', *Handbuch der europäisches Integration* (1991), 499–526.

—— *Das Abkommen über den Europäischen Wirtschaftsraum (EWR)* (Vienna, 1992).

Frennered, H., 'The Protocols adjusting the EEA Agreement and the EFTA Agreements', *European Business Law Review* (1993), 167–69.

Green, N., Hartley, T. C., and Usher, J. A., *The Legal Foundations of the Single European Market* (Oxford, 1991).

Hartley, T. C., *The Foundations of European Community Law* (2nd edn., Oxford, 1988).

Jacot-Guillarmod, O., *Accord EEE: Commentaire et réflexions—EWR Abkommen: Erste Analysen—EEA Agreement: Comments and Reflections* (Zurich, 1992).

Kapteyn, P. J. G., and VerLoren van Themaat, P., *Introduction to the Law of the European Communities* (2nd edn., Deventer, 1990).

Krafft, M.-C., 'Le Système institutionnel de l'EEE', *European Journal of International Law* (1992), 285.

Lasok, D., and Bridge, J. W., *Law & Institutions of the European Communities* (5th edn., London, 1991).

Louis, J.-V., Vandersanden, G., Waelbroeck, D., and Waelbroeck M., *Commentaire Mégret 10: La Cour de Justice—les actes des institutions* (2nd edn., Brussels, 1993).

Norberg, S., 'The Agreement on a European Economic Area', *Common Market Law Review*, 29 (1992), 1171–98.

—— Hökborg, K., Johansson, M., Eliasson, D., and Dedichen, L., *EEA Law: A Commentary on the EEA Agreement* (Stockholm, 1993).

Prate, A., *Quelle Europe?* (Paris, 1991).

Reymond, C., 'Institutions, decision-making procedure and settlement of disputes in the European Economic Area', *Common Market Law Review*, 30 (1993), 449–80.

Schermers, H. G., and Waelbroeck, D. F., *Judicial Protection in the European Community* (5th edn., Deventer, 1992).

Sevón, L., 'The EEA judicial system and the Supreme Courts of the EFTA States', *European Journal of International Law* (1992), 329.

Steiner, J., *Textbook on EEC Law* (3rd edn., London, 1992).

Van Gerven, W., 'The genesis of EEA law and the principles of primacy and direct effect', *Fordham International Law Journal*, 16 (1993), 955–89.

Wyatt, D., and Dashwood, A., *European Community Law* (3rd edn., London, 1993).

FREE MOVEMENT OF GOODS IN GENERAL

COCKBORNE, J.-E. DE, DEFALQUE, L., DURAND, C.-F., PRAHL, H., and VANDERSANDEN, G., *Commentaire Mégret 1 : préambule—principes—libre circulation des marchandises* (2nd edn., Brussels, 1992).

MATTERA, A., *Le Marché Unique Européen* (2nd edn., Paris, 1990).

OLIVER, P., *Free Movement of Goods in the EEC* (2nd edn., London, 1988).

CUSTOMS MATTERS

LASOK, D., *The Customs Law of the European Economic Community* (2nd edn., Deventer, 1990).

NASSIET, J.-R., *La Réglementation douanière européenne* (Paris, 1988).

TECHNICAL BARRIERS TO TRADE

DEBOYSER, P., 'Le Marché Unique des produits pharmaceutiques', *Revue du Marché Unique Européen*, 3 (1991), 101–76.

EVANS, A., and FALK, P., *Law and Integration: Sweden and the European Community* (Stockholm, 1991).

GEDDES, A., 'Free movement of pharmaceuticals within the Community: the remaining barriers', *European Law Review* (1991), 295–306.

GORMLEY, L., 'Recent case law on the free movement of goods: some hot potatoes', *Common Market Law Review*, 27 (1990), 825–57.

MATTERA, A., 'L'Article 30 du Traité CEE, la jurisprudence "Cassis de Dijon" et le principe de la reconnaissance mutuelle', *Revue du Marché Unique Européen*, 4 (1992), 13–71.

STEINER, J., 'Drawing the line: uses and abuses of Article 30 EEC', *Common Market Law Review*, 29 (1992), 749–74.

SWEDAC (Swedish Board for Technical Accreditation), *Marknadskontroll: en EG-anpassning till följd av EES-avtalet* (including summary in English), Doc. 93: 7 (Stockholm, 1993).

Utrikesdepartementet (Ministry for Foreign Affairs, Sweden), *Romfördragets Artikel 30: Om EG-rättens s.k. Cassis de Dijon-princip: En studie rörande handelshinder i Västeuropa)*, Ds 1990: 76 and Ds 1991: 46 (remissyttranden).

THIARD, A., and PFAU, W., *Research & Development and Standardization: A Guide: Commission of the European Communities, EFTA* (Luxembourg, 1992).

WALLIN C.-H., *Market Control in Finland* (Helsinki, 1992).

INTELLECTUAL PROPERTY

ABBEY, M., 'Exhaustion of IP rights under the EEA Agreement does not apply to third country goods', *European Competition Law Review*, 6 (1992), 231–3.

Butterworths European Information Service, *Compendium of EC Intellectual Property Law* (London, 1990).

GROVES, P., MARTINO, T., MISKIN, C., and RICHARDS, J., *Intellectual Property and the Internal Market of the European Community* (London, 1993).

PRÄNDL, F., 'Exhaustion of IP rights in the EEA applies to third-country goods placed on the EEA market', *European Competition Law Review*, 2 (1993), 43–5.

REINBOTHE J., and VON LEWINSKI, S., *The EC Directive on Rental and Lending Rights and on Piracy* (London, 1993).

TROLLER, A., *Précis de droit de la propriété immatérielle* (Basle, 1978).

YUSUF, A. A., and MONCAYO VON HASE, A., 'Intellectual property protection and international trade: exhaustion or rights revisited', *World Competition*, 16 (1992–3), 115–31.

PRODUCT LIABILITY

DUTOIT, B., *La Convention de Lugano et l'EEE: EEA Agreement—Comments and reflexions*, Collection de droit européen, 9 (Zurich, 1992).

GEDDES, A., *Product and Service Liability in the EEC* (London, 1992).

KELLY, P., and ATTRE, R., *European Product Liability* (London, 1992).

SMITH, D. G., 'The European Community Directive on Product Liability: a comparative study of its implementation in the UK, France and West Germany', *Legal Issues of European Integration* (1990/2) (Deventer), 101–42.

Swiss Institute of Comparative Law, *Lugano Convention: Convention on Jurisdiction and the Enforcement of Judgments in Civil and Commercial Matters Done at Lugano on 16 September 1988*, 13 (Texts and Explanatory Reports) and 14 (*Travaux préparatoires*) (Zurich, 1991).

PUBLIC PROCUREMENT

ARROWSMITH, S., *Remedies for Enforcing the Public Procurement Rules* (Earlsgate, 1993).

FLAMME, M.-A., and FLAMME, P., 'La Réglementation communautaire en matière de marchés publics: le point sur le contentieux', *Revue du Marché Unique Européen*, 3 (1993), 13–58.

LEE, P., *Public Procurement*, Current EC Legal Developments Series (London, 1992).

MARGUE, T.-L., 'Ouverture des marchés publics dans la Communauté', *Revue du Marché Unique Européen*, 2, 3, and 4 (1991), 143–79, 177–221, and 111–73.

MATTERA, A., 'Les Marchés publics: dernier rempart du protectionnisme des États', *Revue du Marché Unique Européen*, 3 (1993), 5–12.

MENSI, M., 'L'Ouverture à la concurrence des marchés publics de services', *Revue du Marché Unique Européen*, 3 (1993), 59–86.

SEYTRE, D., *Public Procurement in the EC: The Rules of Competition with Effect from 1993* (Brussels, 1991; with update of Feb. 1993).

TREPTE, P.-A., *Public Procurement in the EC* (Bicester, 1993).

WINTER, J., 'Public Procurement in the EEC', *Common Market Law Review*, 28 (1991), 741–82.

COMPETITION

BELLAMY, C., and CHILD, G., *Common Market Law of Competition* (4th edn., London 1993).

BOS, P., STUYCK, J., and WYTINCK, P., *Concentration Control in the European Economic Community* (London, 1992).

Commission of the European Communities, *Brochure Concerning the Competition Rules Applicable to Undertakings as Contained in the EEA Agreement and their Implementation by the EEC Commission and the EFTA Surveillance Authority* (Luxembourg, 1992).

Cook, J., and Kerse, C., *EEC Merger Control: Regulation 4064/89* (London, 1991).

Davies, J., and Lavoie, C., 'EEC merger control: a half-term report before the 1993 review?', *World Competition*, 16 (1992–3), 26–36.

Ham, A. D., 'International cooperation in the anti-trust field and in particular the Agreement between the United States of America and the Commission of the European Communities', *Common Market Law Review*, 30 (1993), 571–97.

Hawk, B. E., *United States, Common Market and International Antitrust: A Comparative Guide*, 2 vols. (2nd edn., New York, 1987).

Jacob-Siebert, T., 'Competition rules in the EEC and Switzerland: a comparison of law and practice', *European Competition Law Review*, 6 [1990], 255–63.

—— 'Wettbewerbspolitik im europäischen Wirtschftsraum (EWR): das Zwei-Pfeiler-System', *Wirtschaft und Wettbewerb*, 5 (1992), 387–400.

—— 'EEA and Eastern European agreements with the European Community', in 'International antitrust law & policy', ch. 18, *19th Annual Proceeding of the Fordham Corporate Law Institute (22–23 Oct. 1992)* (1992), 403–36.

Kerse, C. S., *EEC Antitrust Procedure* (2nd edn., London, 1988).

Pappalardo, A., 'Concentrations entre entreprises et droit communautaire', *Revue du Marché Unique Européen*, 2 (1991), 11–45.

Renold, M.-A., *Les Conflits de lois en droit antitrust: contribution à l'étude de l'application international du droit économique*, Études suisses de droit international, 69 (Zurich, 1991).

Rodriguez Galindo, B., 'L'Application des règles de concurrence du traité CEE: les pouvoirs d'enquête de la Commission', *Revue du Marché Unique Européen*, 2 (1991), 75–99.

Rouam, C., 'L'Espace Économique Européen: un horizon nouveau pour la politique de concurrence?', *Revue du Marché Commun* (1992), 53–7.

Stragier, J., 'The competition rules of the EEA Agreement and their implementation', *European Competition Law Review*, 1 (1993), 30–8.

Van Bael, I., and Bellis, J.-F., *Competition Law of the EEC* (2nd edn., Oxford, 1990).

Van Gerven, W., 'EC jurisdiction in antitrust matters: the *Wood Pulp* judgement', in '1992 and the EEC/U.S. competition and trade law', ch. 21, *16th Annual Proceeding of the Fordham Corporate Law Institute (26–27 Oct. 1989)*, 451–83.

Vermulst, E. A., 'A European practitioner's view of the GATT system: should competition law violations distorting international trade be subject to GATT panels?', *World Competition*, 16 (1992–3), 5–25.

STATE MONOPOLIES AND PUBLIC UNDERTAKINGS

Marenco, G., 'Legal monopolies in the case-law of the Court of Justice of the European Communities', in 'EC and U.S. competition law and policy', ch. 11, *18th Annual Proceeding of the Fordham Corporate Law Institute (24–25 Oct. 1991)* (1991), 197–222.

Wainwright, R., 'Public undertakings under Article 90', in '1992 and the EEC/U.S. competition and trade law', ch. 13, *16th Annual Proceeding of the Fordham Corporate Law Institute (26–27 Oct. 1989)*, 239–70.

EEA GLOSSARY

JOINT INSTITUTIONS

EEA Council

The highest common EC–EFTA body responsible for giving political impetus in the implementation of the EEA Agreement as well as laying down general guidelines for the work of the EEA Joint Committee. It consists of members of the EC Council, EC Commission, and one member of the government of each EFTA State (ministerial level).

EEA Joint Committee

Responsible for the day-to-day management of the EEA Agreement. It shall ensure the effective implementation and operation of the Agreement: introduction of new legislation, a forum for exchange of views and information, as well as dispute settlement (level of high officials).

EEA Parliamentary Committee

Forum for dialogue and debate. It is composed of 33 representatives from the European Parliament and 33 from the parliaments of the EFTA States.

EEA Consultative Committee

Forum for co-operation between social and economic partners. It is composed of members of the Economic and Social Committee of the Community and members of the EFTA Consultative Committee.

EFTA INSTITUTIONS FOR EEA MATTERS

EFTA Surveillance Authority

Independent organ entrusted with powers and functions equivalent to those of the Commission: surveillance of the EFTA States' fulfilment of the obligations under the Agreement and application of competition rules. It consists of a college of five members and some 100 staff members, based in Brussels.

EFTA Court

Court entrusted with similar powers to the ECJ. It can decide on infringement actions, actions for annulment and failure to act, disputes between EFTA States under the EEA, as well as give advisory opinions on the interpretation of the Agreement. It consists of five judges and some 30 staff members, based in Geneva.

Standing Committee (of the EFTA States)

Committee of the EFTA States with the task of preparing, on the EFTA side, the decisions to be taken in the EEA Council and the EEA Joint Committee (co-ordinating EFTA opinions).

It has various administrative and management tasks under the Agreement and it is served by a Secretariat of more than 100 staff members, mainly based in Brussels.

JARGON

Acquis Communautaire

The body of Community legislation in force.

Two pillar approach/system

The institutional structure chosen in the EEA Agreement, meaning that the EFTA countries have established their own institutions (EFTA Surveillance Authority, EFTA Court, etc.) and the EC uses its existing ones (Commission, ECJ, etc.). Each side takes care of its own internal matters.

Reference technique

The legislative technique used for integrating the EEA-relevant Community secondary legislation into the EEA Agreement by listing the acts in the annexes to the Agreement with a reference to their title and publication data in the *EC Official Journal*.

Adaptations

Key to understanding, in the EEA context, the EC secondary legislation listed in the annexes. Adaptations are made on three levels: horizontal (through Protocol 1 EEA, applicable to all acts listed in the annexes); sectoral (applicable for a specific annexe or chapter of an annexe); specific (applicable for a specific act).

Binding and non-binding acts

The acts in the annexes have been divided into two categories. The first category, binding acts, is the regulations, directives, and decisions, all listed under the heading 'Acts referred to'. The second category, non-binding acts, comprises acts such as recommendations, notices, communications, guidelines, resolutions, etc., which have been listed under the heading 'Acts of which the Contracting Parties shall take note'.

Adjusting Protocol

The Protocol negotiated as a result of the Swiss failure to ratify the EEA Agreement. It deletes all references to Switzerland and adjusts certain time limits.

Cut-off date

This is 31 July 1991, which was chosen for closing the EEA Annexes. It means that the original Agreement only contains acts adopted in the EC before that date.

Additional package

The package of EC acts adopted between the cut-off date (31 July 1991) and the entry into force of the EEA Agreement to be integrated in the Agreement by a decision of the EEA Joint Committee.

Pipeline acquis

EC legislation under preparation (also called planned or pending *acquis*.

Decision-shaping

Preparatory stages of the EC legislative process involving the EFTA countries.

Decision-making

The procedure whereby a new EC legal act is integrated in the EEA Agreement.

SUBJECT INDEX

Note: The method of alphabetization used is word-by-word. References in bold indicate material contained in the Annexes to the text.